ADVANCED
MACROECONOMICS

McGRAW-HILL ADVANCED SERIES IN ECONOMICS

Consulting Editor
N. Gregory Mankiw

Economic Growth
  by Robert J. Barro and Xavier Sala-i-Martin

Advanced Macroeconomics
  by David Romer

ABOUT THE AUTHOR

David Romer is professor of economics at the University of California, Berkeley. He received his A.B. from Princeton University, where he was valedictorian, and his Ph.D. from M.I.T. He has been on the faculty at Princeton and has been a visiting faculty member at M.I.T. and Stanford. He is also a Research Associate of the National Bureau of Economic Research and serves on the editorial boards of several economics journals. His main research interests are monetary policy, the foundations of price stickiness, empirical evidence on economic growth, and asset-price volatility. He is married to Christina Romer, who is also an economist, and has two children, Katherine and Paul.

To Christy

CONTENTS IN BRIEF

CONTENTS

Chapter 5   TRADITIONAL KEYNESIAN THEORIES
OF FLUCTUATIONS   195

Chapter 6   MICROECONOMIC FOUNDATIONS
OF INCOMPLETE NOMINAL
ADJUSTMENT   241

EMPIRICAL APPLICATIONS

ACKNOWLEDGMENTS

This book owes a great deal to many people. The book is an outgrowth of courses I have taught at Princeton, M.I.T., Stanford, and especially Berkeley. I want to thank the many students in these courses for their feedback, their patience, and their encouragement.

Four people provided detailed, thoughtful, and constructive comments on almost every aspect of the book: Laurence Ball, A. Andrew John, N. Gregory Mankiw, and Christina Romer. Each of them significantly improved the book, and I am deeply grateful to them for their efforts.

In addition, Susanto Basu, Matthew Cushing, Charles Engel, Mark Gertler, Mary Gregory, A. Stephen Holland, Gregory Linden, Maurice Obtsfeld, and Robert Rasche made valuable comments and suggestions concerning some or all of the book. Jeffrey Rohaly not only prepared the superb *Solutions Manual* to accompany the book, but also read the page proofs with great care and made many corrections. Teresa Cyrus helped with the preparation of some of the tables and figures. Finally, the editorial staff at McGraw-Hill and the production staff at Publication Services, Inc., especially Leon Jeter, Victoria Richardson, Scott Schriefer, Scott Stratford, and Lucille Sutton, did an excellent job of turning the manuscript into a finished product. I thank all of these people for their help.

INTRODUCTION

Macroeconomics is the study of the economy as a whole. It is therefore concerned with some of the most important questions in economics. Why are some countries rich and others poor? Why do countries grow? What are the sources of recessions and booms? Why is there unemployment, and what determines its extent? What are the sources of inflation? How do government policies affect output, unemployment, and inflation? These and related questions are the subject of macroeconomics.

This book is an introduction to the study of macroeconomics at an advanced level. It presents the major theories concerning the central questions of macroeconomics. Its goal is to provide both an overview of the field for students who will not continue in macroeconomics and a starting point for students who will go on to more advanced courses and research in macroeconomics and monetary economics.

The book takes a broad view of the subject matter of macroeconomics; it views it as the study not just of aggregate fluctuations but of other features of the economy as a whole. A substantial portion of the book is devoted to economic growth, and separate chapters are devoted to theories of the natural rate of unemployment and to theories of inflation. Within each part, the major issues and competing theories are presented and discussed. Throughout, the presentation is motivated by substantive questions about the world. Models and techniques are used extensively, but they are treated as tools for gaining insight into important issues, not as ends in themselves.

The first three chapters are concerned with growth. The analysis focuses on two fundamental questions: Why are some economies so much richer than others, and what accounts for the huge increases in real incomes over time? Chapter 1 is devoted to the Solow growth model, which is the basic reference point for almost all analyses of growth. The Solow model takes technological progress as given and investigates the effects of the division of output between consumption and investment on capital accumulation and growth. The chapter presents and analyzes the model and assesses its ability to answer the central questions concerning growth.

Chapter 2 relaxes the Solow model's assumption that the saving rate is exogenous and fixed. It covers both a model where the set of households in the economy is fixed (the Ramsey model) and one where there is turnover (the Diamond model).

Chapter 3 presents the new growth theory. The first part of the chapter explores the sources of the accumulation of knowledge, the allocation of resources to knowledge accumulation, and the effects of that accumulation on growth. The second part investigates the accumulation of human as well as physical capital.

Chapters 4 through 6 are devoted to short-run fluctuations—the year-to-year and quarter-to-quarter ups and downs of employment, unemployment, and output. Chapter 4 investigates models of fluctuations where there are no imperfections, externalities, or missing markets, and where the economy is subject only to real disturbances. This presentation of real-business-cycle theory considers both a baseline model whose mechanics are fairly transparent and a more sophisticated model that incorporates additional important features of fluctuations.

Chapters 5 and 6 then turn to Keynesian models of fluctuations. These models are based on sluggish adjustment of nominal wages and prices, and emphasize monetary as well as real disturbances. Chapter 5 takes the existence of sluggish adjustment as given. It first reviews the closed-economy and open-economy versions of the traditional *IS-LM* model. It then investigates the implications of alternative assumptions about price and wage rigidity, market structure, and inflationary expectations for the cyclical behavior of real wages, productivity, and markups, and for the relationship between output and inflation.

Chapter 6 examines the fundamental assumption of Keynesian models that nominal wages and prices do not adjust immediately to disturbances. The chapter covers the Lucas imperfect-information model, models of staggered adjustment of prices or wages, and new Keynesian theories of small frictions in price-setting. The chapter concludes with a brief discussion of theories of fluctuations based on coordination failures and real non-Walrasian features of the economy.

The analysis in the first six chapters suggests that the behavior of consumption and investment is central to both growth and fluctuations. Chapters 7 and 8 therefore investigate the determinants of consumption and investment in more detail. In each case, the analysis begins with a baseline model and then considers alternative views. For consumption, the baseline is the life-cycle/permanent-income hypothesis; for investment, it is q theory.

The final two chapters are devoted to inflation and unemployment. Chapter 9 begins by explaining the central role of money growth in causing inflation and by investigating the effects of money growth on inflation, interest rates, and the real money stock. The remainder of the chapter considers two sets of theories of the sources of high money growth: theories emphasizing output-inflation tradeoffs (particularly theories based on the dynamic inconsistency of low-inflation monetary policy), and theories emphasizing governments' need for revenue from money creation.

The main subject of Chapter 10 is the determinants of an economy's natural rate of unemployment. The chapter also investigates the impact of fluctuations in labor demand on real wages and employment. The main theories considered are efficiency-wage theories, contracting and insider/outsider theories, and search and matching models.[1]

Macroeconomics is both a theoretical and an empirical subject. Because of this, the presentation of the theories is supplemented with examples of relevant empirical work. Even more so than with the theoretical sections, the purpose of the empirical material is not to provide a survey of the literature; nor is it to teach econometric techniques. Instead, the goal is to illustrate some of the ways that macroeconomic theories can be applied and tested. The presentation of this material is for the most part fairly intuitive and presumes no more knowledge of econometrics than a general familiarity with regressions. In a few places where it can be done naturally, the empirical material includes discussions of the ideas underlying more advanced econometric techniques.

Each chapter concludes with an extensive set of problems. The problems range from relatively straightforward variations on the ideas in the text to extensions that tackle important new issues. The problems thus serve both as a way for readers to strengthen their understanding of the material and as a compact way of presenting significant extensions of the ideas in the text.[2]

The fact that the book is an *advanced* introduction to macroeconomics has two main consequences. The first is that the book uses a series of formal models to present and analyze the theories. Models identify particular features of reality and study their consequences in isolation. They thereby allow us to see clearly how different elements of the economy interact and what their implications are. As a result, they provide a rigorous way of investigating whether a proposed theory can answer a particular question and whether it generates additional predictions.

The book contains literally dozens of models. The main reason for this multiplicity is that we are interested in many issues. The features of the economy that are crucial to one issue are often unimportant to others. Money, for example, is almost surely central to inflation and is probably not central to long-run growth. Incorporating money into models of growth would only obscure the analysis. Thus instead of trying to build a single

---

[1] The chapters are largely independent. The growth and fluctuations sections are almost entirely self-contained (although Chapter 4 builds moderately on Part A of Chapter 2). There is also considerable independence among the chapters in each section. New growth theory (Chapter 3) can be covered either before or after the Ramsey and Diamond models (Chapter 2), and Keynesian models (Chapters 5 and 6) can be covered either before or after real-business-cycle theory (Chapter 4). Finally, the last four chapters are largely self-contained (although Chapter 7 relies moderately on Chapter 2, Chapter 9 relies moderately on Chapter 5, and Chapter 10 relies moderately on Chapter 6).

[2] A solutions manual prepared by Jeffrey Rohaly is available for use with the book.

model to analyze all of the issues we are interested in, the book develops a series of models.

An additional reason for the multiplicity of models is that there is considerable disagreement about the answers to many of the questions we will be examining. When there is disagreement, the book presents the leading views and discusses their strengths and weaknesses. Because different theories emphasize different features of the economy, again it is more enlightening to investigate distinct models than to build one model incorporating all of the features emphasized by the different views.

The second consequence of the book's advanced level is that it presumes some background in mathematics and economics. Mathematics provides compact ways of expressing ideas and powerful tools for analyzing them. The models are therefore mainly presented and analyzed mathematically. The key mathematical requirements are a thorough understanding of single-variable calculus and an introductory knowledge of multivariable calculus. Tools such as functions, logarithms, derivatives and partial derivatives, maximization subject to constraint, and Taylor-series approximations are used relatively freely. Knowledge of the basic ideas of probability—random variables, means, variances, covariances, and independence—is also assumed.

No mathematical background beyond this level is needed. More advanced tools (such as simple differential equations, the calculus of variations, and dynamic programming) are used sparingly, and they are explained as they are used. Indeed, since mathematical techniques are essential to further study and research in macroeconomics, models are sometimes analyzed in more detail than is otherwise needed in order to illustrate the use of a particular method.

In terms of economics, the book assumes an understanding of microeconomics through the intermediate level. Familiarity with such ideas as profit-maximization and utility-maximization, supply and demand, equilibrium, efficiency, and the welfare properties of competitive equilibria is presumed. Little background in macroeconomics itself is absolutely necessary. Readers with no prior exposure to macroeconomics, however, are likely to find some of the concepts and terminology difficult, and to find that the pace is rapid (most notably in Chapter 5). These readers may wish to review an intermediate macroeconomics text before beginning the book, or to study such a book in conjunction with this one.

The book was designed for first-year graduate courses in macroeconomics. But it can be used in more advanced graduate courses, and (either on its own or in conjunction with an intermediate text) for students with strong backgrounds in mathematics and economics in professional schools and advanced undergraduate programs. It can also provide a tour of the field for economists and others working in areas outside macroeconomics.

Chapter 1
THE SOLOW GROWTH MODEL

1.1 Theories of Economic Growth

Standards of living differ among parts of the world by amounts that almost defy comprehension. Although precise comparisons are difficult, the best available estimates suggest that average real incomes in such countries as the United States, Germany, and Japan exceed those in such countries as Bangladesh and Zaire by a factor of twenty or more. There are also large differences in countries' growth records. Some countries, such as South Korea, Turkey, and Israel, appear to be making the transition to membership in the group of relatively wealthy industrialized economies. Others, including many in South America and sub-Saharan Africa, have difficulty simply in obtaining positive growth rates of real income per person. Finally, we see vast differences in standards of living over time: the world is much richer today than it was three hundred years ago, or even fifty years ago.

The implications of these differences in standards of living for human welfare are enormous. The real income differences across countries are associated with large differences in nutrition, literacy, infant mortality, life expectancy, and other direct measures of well-being. And the welfare consequences of long-run growth swamp any possible effects of the short-run fluctuations that macroeconomics traditionally focuses on. During an average recession in the United States, for example, real income per person falls by a few percent relative to its usual path. In contrast, the *productivity slowdown*—the fact that average annual productivity growth since the 1970s has been about 1 percentage point below its previous level—has reduced real income per person in the United States by about 20 percent relative to what it otherwise would have been. Other examples are even more startling. If real income per person in India continues to grow at its postwar average rate of 1.3 percent per year, it will take about two hundred years for Indian real incomes to reach the current U.S. level. If India achieves 3 percent growth, the process will take less than one hundred years. And if it achieves Japan's average growth rate, 5.5 percent, the time will be reduced to only fifty years. To quote Robert Lucas (1988), "Once one starts to think about [economic growth], it is hard to think about anything else."

The first three chapters of this book are therefore devoted to economic growth. We will investigate several models of growth. Although we will examine the models' mechanics in considerable detail, our ultimate goal is to learn what insights they offer concerning worldwide growth and income differences across countries.

This chapter focuses on the model that economists have traditionally used to study these issues, the Solow growth model.[1] The Solow model is the starting point for almost all analyses of growth. Even models that depart fundamentally from Solow's are often best understood through comparison with the Solow model. Thus understanding the model is essential to understanding theories of growth.

The principal conclusion of the Solow model is that the accumulation of physical capital cannot account for either the vast growth over time in output per person or the vast geographic differences in output per person. Specifically, suppose that the mechanism through which capital accumulation affects output is through the conventional channel that capital makes a direct contribution to production, for which it is paid its marginal product. Then the Solow model implies that the differences in real incomes that we are trying to understand are far too large to be accounted for by differences in capital inputs. The model treats other potential sources of differences in real incomes as either exogenous and thus not explained by the model (in the case of technological progress, for example), or absent altogether (in the case of positive externalities from capital, for example). Thus to address the central questions of growth theory we must move beyond the Solow model.

Chapters 2 and 3 therefore extend and modify the Solow model. Chapter 2 investigates the determinants of saving and investment. The Solow model has no optimization in it; it simply takes the saving rate as exogenous and constant. Chapter 2 presents two models that make saving endogenous and potentially time-varying. In the first, saving and consumption decisions are made by infinitely-lived households; in the second, they are made by households with finite horizons.

Relaxing the Solow model's assumption of a constant saving rate has three advantages. First, and most important for studying growth, it demonstrates that the Solow model's conclusions about the central questions of growth theory do not hinge on its assumption of a fixed saving rate. Second, it allows us to consider welfare issues. A model that directly specifies relations among aggregate variables does not provide a way to judge whether some outcomes are better or worse than others: without individuals in the model, we cannot say whether different outcomes make individuals better or worse off. The infinite-horizon and finite-horizon models are built up from the behavior of individuals, and can therefore be used to discuss welfare issues. Third, infinite- and finite-horizon models are used to study

---

[1]The Solow model—sometimes known as the Solow–Swan model—was developed by Robert Solow (Solow, 1956) and T. W. Swan (Swan, 1956).

many issues in economics other than economic growth; thus they are valuable tools.

Chapter 3 investigates more fundamental departures from the Solow model. Its models, in contrast to Chapter 2's, provide different answers than the Solow model does to the central questions of growth theory. The models depart from the Solow model in two basic ways. First, they make technological progress endogenous. We will investigate various models where growth occurs as the result of conscious decisions on the part of economic actors to invest in the accumulation of knowledge. We will also consider the determinants of the decisions to invest in knowledge accumulation.

Second, the models examine the possibility that the role of capital is considerably larger than is suggested by considering physical capital's share in income. This can occur if the capital relevant for growth is not just physical capital but also human capital. It can also occur if there are positive externalities from capital accumulation, so that what capital earns in the market understates its contribution to production. We will see that models based on endogenous technological progress and on a larger role of capital provide candidate explanations of both worldwide growth and cross-country income differences.

We now turn to the Solow model.

1.2   Assumptions

Inputs and Output

The Solow model focuses on four variables: output (Y), capital (K), labor (L), and "knowledge" or the "effectiveness of labor" (A). At any time, the economy has some amounts of capital, labor, and knowledge, and these are combined to produce output. The production function takes the form

$$Y(t) = F(K(t), A(t)L(t)), \tag{1.1}$$

where t denotes time.

Two features of the production function should be noted. First, time does not enter the production function directly, but only through K, L, and A. That is, output changes over time only if the inputs into production change. In particular, the amount of output obtained from given quantities of capital and labor rises over time—there is technological progress—only if the amount of knowledge increases.

Second, A and L enter multiplicatively. AL is referred to as *effective labor,* and technological progress that enters in this fashion is known as *labor-augmenting* or *Harrod-neutral.*[2] This way of specifying how A enters,

---

[2]If knowledge enters in the form $Y = F(AK, L)$, technological progress is *capital-augmenting.* If it enters in the form $Y = AF(K, L)$, technological progress is *Hicks-neutral.*

together with the other assumptions of the model, will imply that the ratio of capital to output, K/Y, eventually settles down. In practice, capital-output ratios do not show any clear upward or downward trend over extended periods. In addition, building the model so that the ratio is eventually constant makes the analysis much simpler. Assuming that A multiplies L is therefore very convenient.

The central assumptions of the Solow model concern the properties of the production function and the evolution of the three inputs into production (capital, labor, and knowledge) over time. We discuss each in turn.

Assumptions Concerning the Production Function

The model's critical assumption concerning the production function is that it has constant returns to scale in its two arguments, capital and effective labor. That is, doubling the quantities of capital and effective labor (for example, by doubling K and L with A held fixed) doubles the amount produced. More generally, multiplying both arguments by any nonnegative constant c causes output to change by the same factor:

$$F(cK, cAL) = cF(K, AL) \qquad \text{for all } c \geq 0. \tag{1.2}$$

The assumption of constant returns can be thought of as combining two assumptions. The first is that the economy is big enough that the gains from specialization have been exhausted. In a very small economy, there are probably enough possibilities for further specialization that doubling the amounts of capital and labor more than doubles output. The Solow model assumes, however, that the economy is sufficiently large that, if capital and labor double, the new inputs are used in essentially the same way as the existing inputs, and thus that output doubles.

The second assumption is that inputs other than capital, labor, and knowledge are relatively unimportant. In particular, the model neglects land and other natural resources. If natural resources are important, doubling capital and labor could less than double output. In practice, however, the availability of natural resources does not appear to be a major constraint on growth. Assuming constant returns to capital and labor alone therefore appears to be a reasonable approximation.[3]

The assumption of constant returns allows us to work with the production function in *intensive form*. Setting $c = 1/AL$ in equation (1.2) yields

$$F\left(\frac{K}{AL}, 1\right) = \frac{1}{AL}F(K, AL). \tag{1.3}$$

---

[3] *Growth accounting*, which is described in Section 1.7, can be used to formalize the argument that natural resources are not very important to growth. Problem 1.10 investigates a simple model where natural resources cause there to be diminishing returns to capital and labor. Finally, Chapter 3 examines the implications of increasing returns.

K/AL is the amount of capital per unit of effective labor, and $F(K, AL)/AL$ is Y/AL, output per unit of effective labor. Define $k = K/AL$, $y = Y/AL$, and $f(k) = F(k, 1)$. Then we can rewrite (1.3) as

$$y = f(k). \tag{1.4}$$

That is, we can write output per unit of effective labor as a function of capital per unit of effective labor.

To see the intuition behind (1.4), think of dividing the economy into AL small economies, each with 1 unit of effective labor and K/AL units of capital. Since the production function has constant returns, each of these small economies produces $1/AL$ as much as is produced in the large, undivided economy. Thus the amount of output per unit of effective labor depends only on the quantity of capital per unit of effective labor, and not on the overall size of the economy. This is what is expressed mathematically in equation (1.4). If we wish to find the total amount of output, as opposed to the amount per unit of effective labor, we can multiply by the quantity of effective labor: $Y = ALf(k)$.

The intensive-form production function, $f(k)$, is assumed to satisfy $f(0) = 0, f'(k) > 0, f''(k) < 0.$[4] It is straightforward to show that $f'(k)$ is the marginal product of capital: since $F(K, AL) = ALf(K/AL)$, $\partial F(K/AL)/\partial K = ALf'(K/AL)(1/AL) = f'(k)$. Thus these assumptions imply that the marginal product of capital is positive, but that it declines as capital (per unit of effective labor) rises. In addition, $f(\cdot)$ is assumed to satisfy the *Inada conditions* (Inada, 1964): $\lim_{k \to 0} f'(k) = \infty, \lim_{k \to \infty} f'(k) = 0$. These conditions (which are stronger than is needed for the model's central results) state that the marginal product of capital is very large when the capital stock is sufficiently small and that it becomes very small as the capital stock becomes large; their role is to ensure that the path of the economy does not diverge. A production function satisfying $f'(\cdot) > 0, f''(\cdot) < 0$, and the Inada conditions is shown in Figure 1.1.

A specific example of a production function is the Cobb–Douglas:

$$F(K, AL) = K^{\alpha}(AL)^{1-\alpha}, \qquad 0 < \alpha < 1. \tag{1.5}$$

This production function is easy to use, and it appears to be a good first approximation to actual production functions. As a result, it is very useful.

It is easy to check that the Cobb–Douglas function has constant returns. Multiplying both inputs by c gives us

$$F(cK, cAL) = (cK)^{\alpha}(cAL)^{1-\alpha}$$

$$= c^{\alpha}c^{1-\alpha}K^{\alpha}(AL)^{1-\alpha} \tag{1.6}$$

$$= cF(K, AL).$$

---

[4] $f'(\cdot)$ denotes the first derivative of $f(\cdot)$, and $f''(\cdot)$ the second derivative.

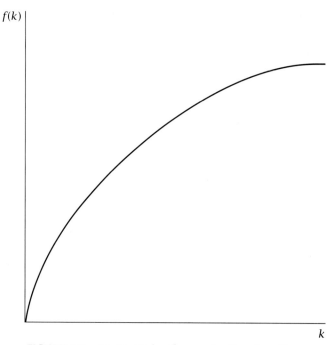

FIGURE 1.1   An example of a production function

To find the intensive form of the production function, divide both inputs by AL; this yields

$$f(k) \equiv F\left(\frac{K}{AL}, 1\right)$$

$$= \left(\frac{K}{AL}\right)^{\alpha} \tag{1.7}$$

$$= k^{\alpha}.$$

Equation (1.7) implies $f'(k) = \alpha k^{\alpha-1}$. It is straightforward to check that this expression is positive, that it approaches infinity as k approaches zero, and that it approaches zero as k approaches infinity. Finally, $f''(k) = -(1-\alpha)\alpha k^{\alpha-2}$, which is negative.[5]

---

[5]Note that with Cobb–Douglas production, labor-augmenting, capital-augmenting, and Hicks-neutral technological progress (see n. 2) are all essentially the same. For example, to rewrite (1.5) so that technological progress is Hicks-neutral, simply define $\tilde{A} = A^{1-\alpha}$; then $Y = \tilde{A}(K^{\alpha}L^{1-\alpha})$.

The Evolution of the Inputs into Production

The remaining assumptions of the model concern how the stocks of labor, knowledge, and capital change over time. The model is set in continuous time; that is, the variables of the model are defined at every point in time.[6]

The initial levels of capital, labor, and knowledge are taken as given. Labor and knowledge grow at constant rates:

$$\dot{L}(t) = nL(t), \tag{1.8}$$

$$\dot{A}(t) = gA(t), \tag{1.9}$$

where n and g are exogenous parameters and where a dot over a variable denotes a derivative with respect to time (that is, $\dot{X}(t)$ is shorthand for $dX(t)/dt$). Equations (1.8) and (1.9) imply that L and A grow exponentially. That is, if $L(0)$ and $A(0)$ denote their values at time 0, (1.8) and (1.9) imply $L(t) = L(0)e^{nt}, A(t) = A(0)e^{gt}$.[7]

Output is divided between consumption and investment. The fraction of output devoted to investment, s, is exogenous and constant. One unit of output devoted to investment yields one unit of new capital. In addition, existing capital depreciates at rate δ. Thus:

$$\dot{K}(t) = sY(t) - \delta K(t). \tag{1.10}$$

Although no restrictions are placed on n, g, and δ individually, their sum is assumed to be positive. This completes the description of the model.

Since this is the first model (of many!) we will encounter, a general comment about modeling is called for. The Solow model is grossly simplified in a host of ways. To give just a few examples, there is only a single good; government is absent; fluctuations in employment are ignored; production is described by an aggregate production function with just three inputs; and the rates of saving, depreciation, population growth, and technological progress are constant. It is natural to think of these features of the model as defects: the model omits many obvious features of the world, and surely some of those features are important to growth. But the purpose of a model is not to be realistic. After all, we already possess a model that is completely realistic—the world itself. The problem with that "model" is that it is too complicated to understand. A model's purpose is to provide

---

[6]The alternative is discrete time, where the variables are defined only at specific dates (usually $t = 0, 1, 2, \ldots$). The choice between continuous and discrete time is usually based on convenience. For example, the Solow model has essentially the same implications in discrete as in continuous time, but is easier to analyze in continuous time.

[7]To verify this, note that $L(t) = L(0)e^{nt}$ implies that $\dot{L}(t) = L(0)e^{nt}n = nL(t)$ and that the initial value of L is $L(0)e^{0}$, or $L(0)$ (and similarly for A).

insights about particular features of the world. If a simplifying assumption causes a model to give incorrect answers *to the questions it is being used to address,* then that lack of realism may be a defect. (Even then, the simplification—by showing clearly the consequences of those features of the world in an idealized setting—may be a useful reference point.) If the simplification does not cause the model to provide incorrect answers to the questions it is being used to address, however, then the lack of realism is a virtue: by isolating the effect of interest more clearly, the simplification makes it easier to understand.

1.3   The Dynamics of the Model

We want to determine the behavior of the economy we have just described. The evolution of two of the three inputs into production, labor and knowledge, is exogenous. Thus to characterize the behavior of the economy we must analyze the behavior of the third input, capital.

The Dynamics of *k*

Because the economy may be growing over time, it turns out to be convenient to focus on the capital stock per unit of effective labor, k, rather than the unadjusted capital stock, K. Since $k = K/AL$, we can use the chain rule to find[8]

$$\dot{k}(t) = \frac{\dot{K}(t)}{A(t)L(t)} - \frac{K(t)}{[A(t)L(t)]^2}[A(t)\dot{L}(t) + L(t)\dot{A}(t)]$$

$$= \frac{\dot{K}(t)}{A(t)L(t)} - \frac{K(t)}{A(t)L(t)}\frac{\dot{L}(t)}{L(t)} - \frac{K(t)}{A(t)L(t)}\frac{\dot{A}(t)}{A(t)}.$$

(1.11)

K/AL is simply k. From (1.8) and (1.9), $\dot{L}/L$ and $\dot{A}/A$ are n and g. $\dot{K}$ is given by (1.10). Substituting these facts into (1.11) yields

$$\dot{k}(t) = \frac{sY(t) - \delta K(t)}{A(t)L(t)} - k(t)n - k(t)g$$

$$= s\frac{Y(t)}{A(t)L(t)} - \delta k(t) - nk(t) - gk(t).$$

(1.12)

---

[8]That is, since k is a function of K, L, and A, each of which are functions of t, then

$$\dot{k} = \frac{\partial k}{\partial K}\dot{K} + \frac{\partial k}{\partial L}\dot{L} + \frac{\partial k}{\partial A}\dot{A}.$$

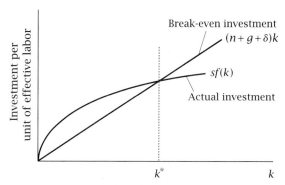

FIGURE 1.2 Actual and break-even investment

Finally, using the fact that Y/AL is given by $f(k)$, we have

$$\dot{k}(t) = sf(k(t)) - (n + g + \delta)k(t). \tag{1.13}$$

Equation (1.13) is the key equation of the Solow model. It states that the rate of change of the capital stock per unit of effective labor is the difference between two terms. The first, $sf(k)$, is actual investment per unit of effective labor: output per unit of effective labor is $f(k)$, and the fraction of that output that is invested is s. The second term, $(n + g + \delta)k$, is *break-even investment,* the amount of investment that must be done just to keep k at its existing level. There are two reasons that some investment is needed to prevent k from falling. First, existing capital is depreciating; this capital must be replaced to keep the capital stock from falling. This is the δk term in (1.13). Second, the quantity of effective labor is growing. Thus doing enough investment to keep the capital stock (K) constant is not enough to keep the capital stock per unit of effective labor (k) constant. Instead, since the quantity of effective labor is growing at rate $n + g$, the capital stock must grow at rate $n + g$ to hold k steady. This is the $(n + g)k$ term in (1.13).[9]

When actual investment per unit of effective labor exceeds the investment needed to break even, k is rising. When actual investment falls short of break-even investment, k is falling. And when the two are equal, k is constant.

Figure 1.2 plots the two terms of the expression for $\dot{k}$ as functions of k. Break-even investment, $(n + g + \delta)k$, is proportional to k. Actual investment, $sf(k)$, is a constant times output per unit of effective labor.

Since $f(0) = 0$, actual investment and break-even investment are equal at $k = 0$. The Inada conditions imply that at $k = 0$, $f'(k)$ is large, and thus that

---

[9]The *growth rate* of a variable, X, refers its proportional rate of change, $\dot{X}/X$. It is easy to verify that the growth rate of the product of two variables, $X_1 X_2$, is the sum of their growth rates, $\dot{X}_1/X_1 + \dot{X}_2/X_2$. Similarly, the growth rate of the ratio of two variables, X_1/X_2, is the difference of their growth rates, $\dot{X}_1/X_1 - \dot{X}_2/X_2$. Thus, the growth rate of $k = K/AL$ is $\dot{K}/K - (\dot{A}/A + \dot{L}/L)$. It follows that keeping k constant requires $\dot{K}/K = n + g$.

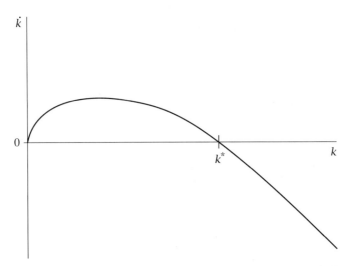

FIGURE 1.3   The phase diagram for k in the Solow model

the $sf(k)$ line is steeper than the $(n + g + \delta)k$ line. Thus, for small values of k, actual investment is larger than break-even investment. The Inada conditions also imply that $f'(k)$ falls toward zero as k becomes large. At some point, the slope of the actual investment line falls below the slope of the break-even investment line. With the $sf(k)$ line flatter than the $(n + g + \delta)k$ line, the two must eventually cross. Finally, the fact that $f''(k) < 0$ implies that the two lines intersect only once for $k > 0$. We let k^* denote the value of k where actual investment and break-even investment are equal.

Figure 1.3 summarizes this information in the form of a *phase diagram,* which shows $\dot{k}$ as a function of k. If k is initially less than k^*, actual investment exceeds break-even investment, and so $\dot{k}$ is positive—that is, k is rising. If k exceeds k^*, $\dot{k}$ is negative. Finally, if k equals k^*, $\dot{k}$ is zero. Thus, regardless of where k starts, it converges to k^*.[10]

The Balanced Growth Path

Since k converges to k^*, it is natural to ask how the variables of the model behave when k equals k^*. By assumption, labor and knowledge are growing at rates n and g, respectively. The capital stock, K, equals ALk; since k is constant at k^*, K is growing at rate $n + g$ (that is, $\dot{K}/K$ equals $n + g$). With both capital and effective labor growing at rate $n + g$, the assumption of constant returns implies that output, Y, is also growing at that rate. Finally, capital per worker, K/L, and output per worker, Y/L, are growing at rate g.

Thus the Solow model implies that, regardless of its starting point, the economy converges to a *balanced growth path*—a situation where each

---

[10]If k is initially zero, it remains there. We ignore this possibility in what follows.

variable of the model is growing at a constant rate. On the balanced growth path, the growth rate of output per worker is determined solely by the rate of technological progress.

The balanced growth path of the Solow model fits several of the major stylized facts about growth described by Kaldor (1961). In most of the major industrialized countries over the past century, it is a reasonable first approximation to say that the growth rates of labor, capital, and output are each roughly constant. The growth rates of output and capital are about equal (so that the capital-output ratio is approximately constant) and are larger than the growth rate of labor (so that output per worker and capital per worker are rising). The balanced growth path of the Solow model has these properties.

1.4   The Impact of a Change in the Saving Rate

The parameter of the Solow model that policy is most likely to affect is the saving rate. The division of the government's purchases between consumption and investment goods, the division of its revenues between taxes and borrowing, and its tax treatments of saving and investment are all likely to affect the fraction of output that is invested. Thus it is natural to investigate the effects of a change in the saving rate.

For concreteness, we will consider a Solow economy that is on a balanced growth path, and suppose that there is a permanent increase in s. In addition to demonstrating the model's implications concerning the role of saving, this experiment will illustrate the model's properties when the economy is not on a balanced growth path.

The Impact on Output

The increase in s shifts the actual investment line upward, and so k^* rises. This is shown in Figure 1.4. k does not immediately jump to the new value of k^*, however. Initially, k is equal to the old value of k^*. At this level, actual investment now exceeds break-even investment—more resources are being devoted to investment than are needed to hold k constant—and so $\dot{k}$ is positive. Thus k begins to rise. It continues to rise until it reaches the new value of k^*, at which point it remains constant.

The behavior of output per worker, Y/L, is something we are likely to be particularly interested in. Y/L equals $Af(k)$. When k is constant, Y/L grows at rate g, the growth rate of A. When k is increasing, Y/L grows both because A is increasing and because k is increasing. Thus its growth rate exceeds g. When k reaches the new value of k^*, however, again only the growth of A contributes to the growth of Y/L, and so the growth rate of Y/L returns to g. Thus a *permanent* increase in the saving rate produces a

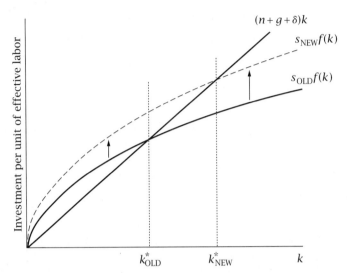

FIGURE 1.4   The effects of an increase in the saving rate on investment

temporary increase in the growth rate of output per worker: k is rising for a time, but eventually it increases to the point where the additional saving is devoted entirely to maintaining the higher level of k.

These results are summarized in Figure 1.5. t_0 denotes the time of the increase in the saving rate. By assumption, s jumps at time t_0 and remains constant thereafter. k rises gradually from the old value of k^* to the new value. The *growth rate* of output per worker, which is initially g, jumps upward at t_0 and then gradually returns to its initial level. Thus output per worker begins to rise above the path it was on and gradually settles into a higher path parallel to the first.[11]

In sum, a change in the saving rate has a *level effect* but not a *growth effect:* it changes the economy's balanced growth path, and thus the level of output per worker at any point in time, but it does not affect the growth rate of output per worker on the balanced growth path. Indeed, in the Solow model only changes in the rate of technological progress have growth effects; all other changes have only level effects.

The Impact on Consumption

If we were to introduce households into the model, their welfare would depend not on output but on consumption: investment is simply an input into production in the future. Thus for many purposes we are likely to be more interested in the behavior of consumption than in the behavior of output.

---

[11]The reason that Figure 1.5 shows the log of output per worker rather than its level is that when a variable is growing at a constant rate, a graph of the log of the variable as a function of time is a straight line. That is, the growth rate of a variable is the derivative with respect to time of the log of the variable: $d \ln(X)/dt = (1/X)\, dX/dt = \dot{X}/X$.

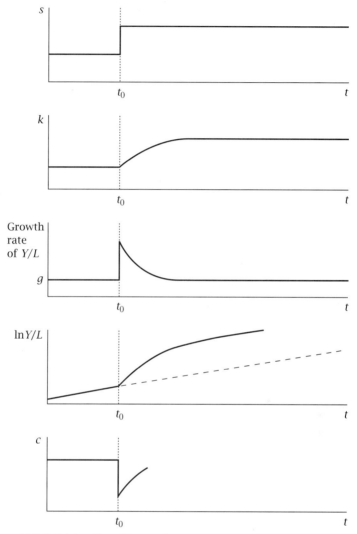

FIGURE 1.5   The effects of an increase in the saving rate

Consumption per unit of effective labor equals output per unit of effective labor, $f(k)$, times the fraction of that output that is consumed, $1 - s$. Thus, since s changes discontinuously at t_0 and k does not, initially consumption per unit of effective labor jumps downward. Consumption then rises gradually as k rises and s remains at its higher level. This is shown in the last panel of Figure 1.5.

Whether consumption eventually exceeds its level before the rise in s is not immediately clear. Let c^* denote consumption per unit of effective labor on the balanced growth path. c^* equals output per unit of effective labor, $f(k^*)$, minus investment per unit of effective labor, $sf(k^*)$. On the balanced growth path, actual investment equals break-even investment, $(n + g + \delta)k^*$. Thus,

$$c^* = f(k^*) - (n + g + \delta)k^*. \tag{1.14}$$

k^* is determined by s and the other parameters of the model, n, g, and δ; we can therefore write $k^* = k^*(s, n, g, \delta)$. Thus (1.14) implies

$$\frac{\partial c^*}{\partial s} = [f'(k^*(s, n, g, \delta)) - (n + g + \delta)]\frac{\partial k^*(s, n, g, \delta)}{\partial s}. \tag{1.15}$$

We know that the increase in s raises k^*. Thus whether the increase raises or lowers consumption in the long run depends on whether $f'(k^*)$— the marginal product of capital—is more or less than $n + g + \delta$. Intuitively, when k rises, investment (per unit of effective labor) must rise by $n + g + \delta$ times the change in k for the increase to be sustained. If $f'(k^*)$ is less than $n + g + \delta$, then the additional output from the increased capital is not enough to maintain the capital stock at its higher level. In this case, consumption must fall to maintain the higher capital stock. If $f'(k^*)$ exceeds $n + g + \delta$, on the other hand, there is more than enough additional output to maintain k at its higher level, and so consumption rises.

$f'(k^*)$ can be either smaller or larger than $n + g + \delta$. This is shown in Figure 1.6. The figure shows not only $(n + g + \delta)k$ and $sf(k)$, but also $f(k)$. On the balanced growth path, consumption equals output less break-even investment; thus c is the distance between $f(k)$ and $(n + g + \delta)k$. In the top panel, $f'(k^*)$ is less than $n + g + \delta$, and so an increase in the saving rate lowers consumption even when the economy has reached the new balanced growth path. In the middle panel, the reverse holds, and so an increase in s raises consumption in the long run.

Finally, in the bottom panel, $f'(k^*)$ just equals $n + g + \delta$—that is, the $f(k)$ and $(n + g + \delta)k$ lines are parallel at $k = k^*$. In this case, a marginal change in s has no effect on consumption in the long run, and consumption is at its maximum possible level among balanced growth paths. This value of k^* is known as the *golden-rule* level of the capital stock. We will discuss the golden-rule capital stock further in Chapter 2. Among the questions we will address are whether the golden-rule capital stock is in fact desirable and whether there are situations in which a decentralized economy with endogenous saving converges to that capital stock. Of course, in the Solow model, where saving is exogenous, there is no more reason to expect the capital stock on the balanced growth path to equal the golden-rule level than there is to expect it to equal any other possible value.

1.5   Quantitative Implications

We are often interested not just in a model's qualitative implications, but in its quantitative predictions. If, for example, the impact of a moderate

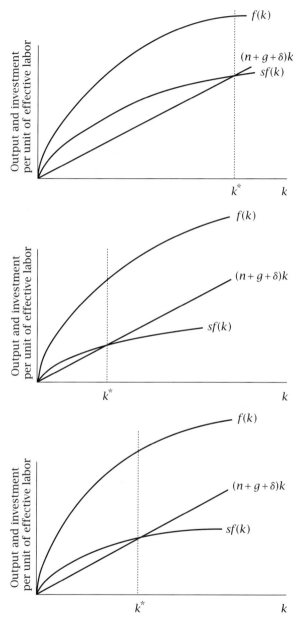

FIGURE 1.6 Output, investment, and consumption on the balanced growth path

increase in saving on growth remains large after several centuries, the result that the impact is temporary is of limited interest.

For most models, including this one, obtaining exact quantitative results requires specifying functional forms and values of the parameters; it often also requires analyzing the model numerically. But in many cases, it is possible to learn a great deal by considering approximations around the long-run equilibrium. That is the approach we take here.

The Effect on Output in the Long Run

The long-run effect of a rise in saving on output is given by

$$\frac{\partial y^*}{\partial s} = f'(k^*)\frac{\partial k^*(s, n, g, \delta)}{\partial s}, \tag{1.16}$$

where $y^* = f(k^*)$ is the level of output per unit of effective labor on the balanced growth path. Thus to find $\partial y^*/\partial s$, we need to find $\partial k^*/\partial s$. To do this, note that k^* is defined by the condition that $\dot{k} = 0$; thus k^* satisfies

$$sf(k^*(s, n, g, \delta)) = (n + g + \delta)k^*(s, n, g, \delta). \tag{1.17}$$

Equation (1.17) holds for all values of s (and of n, g, and δ). Thus the derivatives of the two sides with respect to s are equal:[12]

$$sf'(k^*)\frac{\partial k^*}{\partial s} + f(k^*) = (n + g + \delta)\frac{\partial k^*}{\partial s}, \tag{1.18}$$

where the arguments of k^* are omitted for simplicity. This can be rearranged to obtain[13]

$$\frac{\partial k^*}{\partial s} = \frac{f(k^*)}{(n + g + \delta) - sf'(k^*)}. \tag{1.19}$$

Substituting (1.19) into (1.16) yields

$$\frac{\partial y^*}{\partial s} = \frac{f'(k^*)f(k^*)}{(n + g + \delta) - sf'(k^*)}. \tag{1.20}$$

Two changes help in interpreting this expression. The first is to convert it to an elasticity by multiplying both sides by s/y^*. The second is to use the fact that $sf(k^*) = (n + g + \delta)k^*$ to substitute for s. Making these changes gives us

---

[12]This technique is known as *implicit differentiation*. Even though (1.17) does not explicitly give k^* as a function of s, n, g, and δ, it still determines how k^* depends on those variables. We can therefore differentiate the equation with respect to s and solve for $\partial k^*/\partial s$.

[13]We saw in the previous section that an increase in s raises k^*. To check that this is also implied by equation (1.19), note that $n + g + \delta$ is the slope of the break-even investment line and that $sf'(k^*)$ is the slope of the actual investment line at k^*. Since the break-even investment line is steeper than the actual investment line at k^* (see Figure 1.2), it follows that the denominator of (1.19) is positive and thus that $\partial k^*/\partial s > 0$.

$$\frac{s}{y^*} \frac{\partial y^*}{\partial s} = \frac{s}{f(k^*)} \frac{f'(k^*)f(k^*)}{(n + g + \delta) - sf'(k^*)}$$

$$= \frac{(n + g + \delta)k^*f'(k^*)}{f(k^*)[(n + g + \delta) - (n + g + \delta)k^*f'(k^*)/f(k^*)]} \quad (1.21)$$

$$= \frac{k^*f'(k^*)/f(k^*)}{1 - [k^*f'(k^*)/f(k^*)]}.$$

$k^*f'(k^*)/f(k^*)$ is the elasticity of output with respect to capital at $k = k^*$. Denoting this by $\alpha_K(k^*)$, we have

$$\frac{s}{y^*} \frac{\partial y^*}{\partial s} = \frac{\alpha_K(k^*)}{1 - \alpha_K(k^*)}. \quad (1.22)$$

If markets are competitive and there are no externalities, capital earns its marginal product. In this case, the total amount received by capital (per unit of effective labor) on the balanced growth path is $k^*f'(k^*)$. Thus if capital earns its marginal product, the share of total income that goes to capital on the balanced growth path is $k^*f'(k^*)/f(k^*)$, or $\alpha_K(k^*)$.

In most countries, the share of income paid to capital is about one-third. If we use this as an estimate of $\alpha_K(k^*)$, it follows that the elasticity of output with respect to the saving rate in the long run is about one-half. Thus, for example, a 10 percent increase in the saving rate (from 20% of output to 22%, for instance) raises output per worker in the long run by about 5 percent relative to the path it would have followed. Even a 50 percent increase in s raises y^* only by about 22 percent. Thus significant changes in saving have only moderate effects on the level of output on the balanced growth path.

Intuitively, a small value of $\alpha_K(k^*)$ makes the impact of saving on output low for two reasons. First, it implies that the actual investment curve, $sf(k)$, bends fairly sharply; as a result, an upward shift of the curve moves its intersection with the break-even investment line relatively little. Thus the impact of a change in s on k^* is small. Second, a low value of $\alpha_K(k^*)$ means that the impact of a change in k^* on y^* is small.

The Speed of Convergence

In practice, we are interested not only in the eventual effects of some change (such as a change in the saving rate), but also in how rapidly those effects occur. Again, we can use approximations around the long-run equilibrium to address this issue.

For simplicity, we focus on the behavior of k rather than y. Our goal is thus to determine how rapidly k approaches k^*. We know that $\dot{k}$ is de- termined by k (see [1.13]); thus we can write $\dot{k} = \dot{k}(k)$. When k equals k^*,

$\dot{k}$ is zero. A first-order Taylor-series approximation of $\dot{k}(k)$ around $k = k^*$ therefore yields

$$\dot{k} \simeq \left(\left. \frac{\partial \dot{k}(k)}{\partial k} \right|_{k=k^*} \right) (k - k^*). \tag{1.23}$$

That is, $\dot{k}$ is approximately equal to the product of the difference between k and k^* and the derivative of $\dot{k}$ with respect to k at $k = k^*$.

Differentiating expression (1.13) for $\dot{k}$ with respect to k and evaluating the resulting expression at $k = k^*$ yields

$$\left. \frac{\partial \dot{k}(k)}{\partial k} \right|_{k=k^*} = sf'(k^*) - (n + g + \delta)$$

$$= \frac{(n + g + \delta)k^* f'(k^*)}{f(k^*)} - (n + g + \delta) \tag{1.24}$$

$$= [\alpha_K(k^*) - 1](n + g + \delta),$$

where the second line again uses the fact that $sf(k^*) = (n + g + \delta)k^*$ to substitute for s, and where the last line uses the definition of α_K. Substituting (1.24) into (1.23) yields

$$\dot{k}(t) \simeq -[1 - \alpha_K(k^*)](n + g + \delta)[k(t) - k^*]. \tag{1.25}$$

Equation (1.25) implies that, in the vicinity of the balanced growth path, capital per unit of effective labor converges toward k^* at a speed proportional to its distance from k^*. That is, defining $x(t) = k(t) - k^*$ and $\lambda = (1 - \alpha_K)(n + g + \delta)$, (1.25) implies $\dot{x}(t) \simeq -\lambda x(t)$: the growth rate of x is constant and equals $-\lambda$. The path of x is therefore given by $x(t) \simeq x(0)e^{-\lambda t}$, where $x(0)$ is the initial value of x. In terms of k, this means

$$k(t) - k^* \simeq e^{-(1-\alpha_K)(n+g+\delta)t}(k(0) - k^*). \tag{1.26}$$

One can show that y approaches y^* at the same rate that k approaches k^*; that is, $y(t) - y^* \simeq e^{-\lambda t}[y(0) - y^*]$.

We can calibrate (1.26) to see how quickly actual economies are likely to approach their balanced growth paths. $n + g + \delta$ is typically about 6% per year (this would arise, for example, with 1 to 2% population growth, 1 to 2% growth in output per worker, and 3 to 4% depreciation). If capital's share is roughly one-third, $(1 - \alpha_K)(n + g + \delta)$ is thus roughly 4%. k and y therefore move 4% of the remaining distance toward k^* and y^* each year, and take approximately eighteen years to get halfway to their balanced-growth-path values.[14] Thus in our example of a 10% increase in the saving rate, output is

---

[14]The time it takes for a variable (in this case, $y-y^*$) with a constant negative growth rate to fall in half is approximately equal to 70 divided by its growth rate in percent (similarly,

0.04(5%) = 0.2% above its previous path after 1 year; is 0.5(5%) = 2.5% above after 18 years; and asymptotically approaches 5% above the previous path. Thus not only is the overall impact of a substantial change in the saving rate modest, but it does not occur very quickly.[15]

1.6   The Solow Model and the Central Questions of Growth Theory

The Solow model identifies two possible sources of variation—either over time or across parts of the world—in output per worker: differences in capital per worker (K/L) and differences in the effectiveness of labor (A). We have seen, however, that only growth in the effectiveness of labor can lead to permanent growth in output per worker, and that for reasonable cases the impact of changes in capital per worker on output per worker is modest. As a result, only differences in the effectiveness of labor have any reasonable hope of accounting for the vast differences in wealth across time and space. Specifically, the central conclusion of the Solow model is that if the returns that capital commands in the market are a rough guide to its contributions to output, then variations in the accumulation of physical capital do not account for a significant part of either worldwide economic growth or cross-country income differences.

There are two problems with trying to account for large differences in incomes on the basis of differences in capital. First, the required differences in capital are far too large. Consider, for example, a tenfold difference in output per worker. Output per worker in the United States today, for instance, is on the order of ten times larger than it was a hundred years ago, and than it is in India today. Recall that α_K is the elasticity of output with respect to the capital stock. Thus accounting for a tenfold difference in output per worker on the basis of differences in capital requires a difference of a factor of $10^{1/\alpha_K}$ in capital per worker. For $\alpha_K = \frac{1}{3}$, this is a factor of a thousand. Even if capital's share is one-half, which is well above what data on capital income suggest, one still needs a difference of a factor of a hundred.

There is no evidence of such differences in capital stocks. One of the stylized facts about growth mentioned in Section 1.3 is that capital-output

---

the doubling time of a variable with positive growth is 70 divided by the growth rate). Thus in this case the *half-life* is roughly 70/(4%/year), or about eighteen years. More exactly, the half-life, t^*, is the solution to $e^{-\lambda t^*} = 0.5$, where λ is the rate of decrease. Taking logs of both sides, $t^* = -\ln(0.5)/\lambda \simeq 0.69/\lambda$.

[15]These results are derived from a Taylor-series approximation around the balanced growth path. Thus, formally, we can rely on them only in an arbitrarily small neighborhood around the balanced growth path. The question of whether Taylor-series approximations provide good guides for finite changes does not have a general answer. For the Solow model with conventional production functions, and for moderate changes in parameter values (such as those we have been considering), the Taylor-series approximations are generally quite reliable.

ratios are roughly constant over time. Thus the U.S. capital stock per worker
is roughly ten times larger than it was a hundred years ago, not a hundred or a thousand times larger. Similarly, although capital-output ratios
vary somewhat across countries, the variation is not great. For example, the
capital-output ratio appears to be two to three times larger in the United
States than in India; thus capital per worker is "only" about twenty to thirty
times larger in the United States. In sum, differences in capital per worker
are far smaller than those needed to account for the differences in output
per worker that we are trying to understand.[16]

The second difficulty is that attributing differences in output to differences in capital without differences in the effectiveness of labor implies
immense variation in the rate of return on capital (Lucas, 1990a). If markets
are competitive, the rate of return on capital equals its marginal product,
$f'(k)$, minus depreciation, δ. Suppose that the production function is Cobb–
Douglas (see equation [1.5]), which in intensive form is $f(k) = k^\alpha$. With this
production function, the elasticity of output with respect to capital is simply
α. The marginal product of capital is

$$f'(k) = \alpha k^{\alpha-1}$$
$$= \alpha y^{(\alpha-1)/\alpha}. \tag{1.27}$$

Equation (1.27) implies that the elasticity of the marginal product of capital
with respect to output is $-(1-\alpha)/\alpha$. If $\alpha = \frac{1}{3}$, a tenfold difference in output
per worker arising from differences in capital per worker thus implies a
hundredfold difference in the marginal product of capital. And since the
return to capital is $f'(k) - \delta$, the difference in rates of return is even larger.

Again, there is no evidence of such differences in rates of return. Direct measurement of returns on financial assets, for example, suggests only
moderate variation over time and across countries. More tellingly, we can
learn much about cross-country differences simply by examining where the
holders of capital want to invest. If rates of return were larger by a factor
of ten or a hundred in poor countries than in rich countries, there would be
immense incentives to invest in poor countries. Such differences in rates of
return would swamp such considerations as capital-market imperfections,
government tax policies, fear of expropriation, and so on, and we would observe immense flows of capital from rich to poor countries. We do not see
such flows.[17]

---

[16]One can make the same point in terms of the rates of saving, population growth, and
so on that determine capital per worker. For example, the elasticity of y^* with respect to s
is $\alpha_K/(1-\alpha_K)$ (see [1.22]). Thus accounting for a difference of a factor of ten in output per
worker on the basis of differences in s would require a difference of a factor of a hundred
in s if $\alpha_K = \frac{1}{3}$ and a difference of a factor of ten if $\alpha_K = \frac{1}{2}$. Variations in actual saving rates
are much smaller than this.

[17]One can try to avoid this conclusion by considering production functions where capital's marginal product falls less rapidly as k rises than it does in the Cobb–Douglas case. This

Thus differences in physical capital per worker cannot account for the differences in output per worker that we observe, at least if capital's contribution to output is roughly reflected by its private returns.

The other potential source of variation in output per worker in the Solow model is the effectiveness of labor. Attributing differences in standards of living to differences in the effectiveness of labor does not require huge differences in capital or in rates of return. Along a balanced growth path, for example, capital is growing at the same rate as output; and the marginal product of capital, $f'(k)$, is constant.

The Solow model's treatment of the effectiveness of labor is highly incomplete, however. Most obviously, the growth of the effectiveness of labor is exogenous: the model takes as given the behavior of the variable that it identifies as the driving force of growth. Thus it is only a small exaggeration to say that we have been modeling growth by assuming it.

More fundamentally, the model does not identify what the "effectiveness of labor" is; it is just a catchall for factors other than labor and capital that affect output. To proceed, we must take a stand concerning what we mean by the effectiveness of labor and what causes it to vary. One natural possibility is that the effectiveness of labor corresponds to abstract knowledge. To understand worldwide growth it would then be necessary to analyze the determinants of the stock of knowledge over time. To understand cross-country differences in real incomes, one would have to explain why firms in some countries have access to more knowledge than firms in other countries, and why that greater knowledge is not rapidly transferred to poorer countries.

There are other possible interpretations of A: the education and skills of the labor force, the strength of property rights, the quality of infrastructure, cultural attitudes toward entrepreneurship and work, and so on. Or A may reflect a combination of forces. For any proposed view of what A represents, one would again have to address the questions of how it affects output, how it evolves over time, and why it differs across parts of the world.

The other possible way to proceed is to consider the possibility that capital is more important than the Solow model implies. If capital encompasses more than just physical capital, or if physical capital has positive externalities, then the private return on physical capital is not an accurate guide to capital's importance in production. In this case, the calculations we have done may be misleading, and it may be possible to resuscitate the view that differences in capital are central to differences in incomes.

These possibilities for addressing the fundamental questions of growth theory are the subject of Chapter 3.

---

approach would encounter two major difficulties. First, since the marginal product of capital would be similar in rich and poor countries, capital's share would be much larger in rich countries. Second, and similarly, real wages would be only slightly larger in rich than in poor countries. These implications appear grossly inconsistent with the facts.

1.7   Empirical Applications

Growth Accounting

In the Solow model, long-run growth of output per worker depends only on technological progress. But short-run growth can result from either technological progress or capital accumulation. Thus the model implies that determining the sources of short-run growth is an empirical issue. *Growth accounting*, which was pioneered by Abramovitz (1956) and Solow (1957), provides a way of tackling this subject.

To see how growth accounting works, consider again the production function $Y(t) = F(K(t), A(t)L(t))$. This implies

$$\dot{Y}(t) = \frac{\partial Y(t)}{\partial K(t)}\dot{K}(t) + \frac{\partial Y(t)}{\partial L(t)}\dot{L}(t) + \frac{\partial Y(t)}{\partial A(t)}\dot{A}(t). \tag{1.28}$$

$\partial Y / \partial L$ and $\partial Y / \partial A$ denote $[\partial Y / \partial (AL)]A$ and $[\partial Y / \partial (AL)]L$, respectively. Dividing both sides by $Y(t)$ and rewriting the terms on the right-hand side yields

$$\frac{\dot{Y}(t)}{Y(t)} = \frac{K(t)}{Y(t)}\frac{\partial Y(t)}{\partial K(t)}\frac{\dot{K}(t)}{K(t)} + \frac{L(t)}{Y(t)}\frac{\partial Y(t)}{\partial L(t)}\frac{\dot{L}(t)}{L(t)} + \frac{A(t)}{Y(t)}\frac{\partial Y(t)}{\partial A(t)}\frac{\dot{A}(t)}{A(t)}$$

$$\equiv \alpha_K(t)\frac{\dot{K}(t)}{K(t)} + \alpha_L(t)\frac{\dot{L}(t)}{L(t)} + R(t). \tag{1.29}$$

Here $\alpha_L(t)$ is the elasticity of output with respect to labor at time t, $\alpha_K(t)$ is again its elasticity with respect to capital, and $R(t) \equiv [A(t)/Y(t)][\partial Y(t)/\partial A(t)][\dot{A}(t)/A(t)]$. Subtracting $\dot{L}(t)/L(t)$ from both sides and using the fact that $\alpha_L(t) + \alpha_K(t) = 1$ (see Problem 1.7, at the end of this chapter) gives us an expression for the growth rate of output per worker:

$$\frac{\dot{Y}(t)}{Y(t)} - \frac{\dot{L}(t)}{L(t)} = \alpha_K(t)\left[\frac{\dot{K}(t)}{K(t)} - \frac{\dot{L}(t)}{L(t)}\right] + R(t). \tag{1.30}$$

The growth rates of Y, K, and L are straightforward to measure. And we know that if capital earns its marginal product, α_K can be measured using data on the share of income that goes to capital. $R(t)$ can then be measured as the residual in (1.30). Thus (1.30) provides a way of decomposing the growth of output per worker into the contribution of growth of capital per worker and a remaining term, the *Solow residual*. The Solow residual is sometimes interpreted as a measure of the contribution of technological progress. As the derivation shows, however, it reflects all sources of growth other than the contribution of capital accumulation via its private return.

This basic framework can be extended in many ways (see, for example, Denison, 1967). The most common extensions are to consider different types of capital and labor and to adjust for changes in the quality of inputs. But more complicated adjustments are also possible. For example, if there is evidence of imperfect competition, one can try to adjust the data on income shares to obtain a better estimate of the elasticity of output with respect to the different inputs.

Growth accounting has been applied to many issues. For example, Young (1994) uses detailed growth accounting to argue that the unusually rapid growth of Hong Kong, Singapore, South Korea, and Taiwan over the past three decades is almost entirely due to rising investment, increasing labor-force participation, and improving labor quality (in terms of education), and not to rapid technological progress and other forces affecting the Solow residual.[18]

To give another example, growth accounting has been used extensively to study the productivity slowdown—the reduced growth rate of output per worker-hour in the United States and other industrialized countries that began in the early 1970s (see, for example, Denison, 1985; Baily and Gordon, 1988; Griliches, 1988; and Jorgenson, 1988). Some candidate explanations that have been proposed on the basis of this research include slower growth in workers' skills, the disruptions caused by the oil-price increases of the 1970s, a slowdown in the rate of inventive activity, and the effects of government regulations.

Convergence

An issue that has attracted considerable attention in empirical work on growth is whether poor countries tend to grow faster than rich countries. There are at least three reasons that one might expect such convergence. First, the Solow model predicts countries converge to their balanced growth paths. Thus to the extent that differences in output per worker arise from countries being at different points relative to their balanced growth paths, one would expect the poorer countries to catch up to the richer. Second, the Solow model implies that the rate of return on capital is lower in countries with more capital per worker. Thus there are incentives for capital to flow from rich to poor countries; this will also tend to cause convergence. And third, if there are lags in the diffusion of knowledge, income differences can arise because some countries are not yet employing the best available technologies. These differences might tend to shrink as poorer countries gain access to state-of-the-art methods.

Baumol (1986) examines convergence from 1870 to 1979 among the 16 industrialized countries for which Maddison (1982) provides data. Baumol regresses output growth over this period on a constant and initial income; that is, he estimates

$$\ln[(Y/N)_{i,1979}] - \ln[(Y/N)_{i,1870}] = a + b \ln[(Y/N)_{i,1870}] + \varepsilon_i. \quad (1.31)$$

---

[18]Other authors examining the same issue, however, argue for a larger role for the residual. See, for example, Page (1994).

Here $\ln(Y/N)$ is log income per person, ε is an error term, and i indexes countries.[19] If there is convergence, b will be negative: countries with higher initial incomes have lower growth. A value for b of -1 corresponds to perfect convergence: higher initial income on average lowers subsequent growth one-for-one, and so output per person in 1979 is uncorrelated with its value in 1870. A value for b of 0, on the other hand, implies that growth is uncorrelated with initial income and thus that there is no convergence.

The results are

$$\ln[(Y/N)_{i,1979}] - \ln[(Y/N)_{i,1870}] = 8.457 - \underset{(0.094)}{0.995} \ln[(Y/N)_{i,1870}],$$

$$R^2 = 0.87, \quad \text{s.e.e.} = 0.15,$$

(1.32)

where the number in parentheses, 0.094, is the standard error of the regression coefficient. Figure 1.7 shows the scatterplot corresponding to this regression.

The regression suggests almost perfect convergence. The estimate of b is almost exactly equal to -1, and it is estimated fairly precisely; the two-standard-error confidence interval is $(0.81, 1.18)$. In this sample, per capita income today is essentially unrelated to per capita income a hundred years ago.

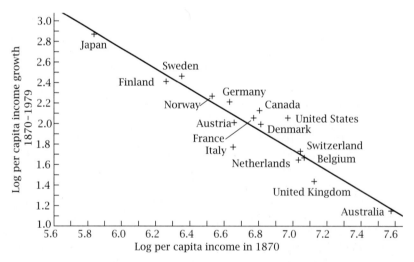

FIGURE 1.7   Initial income and subsequent growth in Baumol's sample (from De Long, 1988; used with permission)

---

[19]Baumol considers output per worker rather than output per person. This choice has little effect on the results.

De Long (1988) demonstrates, however, that Baumol's finding is largely spurious. There are two problems. The first is *sample selection*. Since historical data are constructed retrospectively, the countries that have long data series are generally those that are the most industrialized today. Thus countries that were not rich a hundred years ago are typically in the sample only if they grew rapidly over the next hundred years. Countries that were rich a hundred years ago, in contrast, are generally included even if their subsequent growth was only moderate. Because of this, we are likely to see poorer countries growing faster than richer ones in the sample of countries we consider even if there is no tendency for this to occur on average.

The natural way to eliminate this bias is to use a rule for choosing the sample that is not based on the variable we are trying to explain, which is growth over the period 1870–1979. Lack of data makes it impossible to include the entire world. De Long therefore considers the richest countries as of 1870; specifically, his sample consists of all countries at least as rich as the second poorest country in Baumol's sample in 1870, Finland. This causes him to add seven countries to Baumol's list (Argentina, Chile, East Germany, Ireland, New Zealand, Portugal, and Spain), and to drop one (Japan).[20]

Figure 1.8 shows the scatterplot for the unbiased sample. The inclusion of the new countries weakens the case for convergence considerably. The

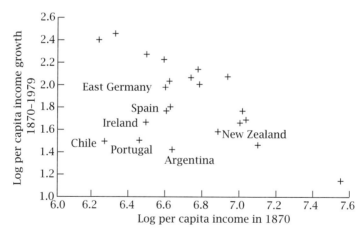

FIGURE 1.8 Initial income and subsequent growth in the expanded sample (from De Long, 1988; used with permission)

---

[20]Since a large fraction of the world was richer than Japan in 1870, it is not possible to consider all countries at least as rich as Japan. In addition, one has to deal with the fact that countries' borders are not fixed. De Long chooses to use 1979 borders. Thus his 1870 income estimates are estimates of average incomes in 1870 in the geographic regions defined by 1979 borders.

regression now produces an estimate of b of -0.566, with a standard error of 0.144. Thus accounting for the selection bias in Baumol's procedure eliminates about half of the convergence that he finds.

The second problem that De Long identifies is *measurement error*. Estimates of real income per capita in 1870 are imprecise. Measurement error again creates bias toward finding convergence. When 1870 income is overstated, growth over the period 1870–1979 is understated by an equal amount; when 1870 income is understated, the reverse occurs. Thus measured growth tends to be lower in countries with higher measured initial income even if there is no relation between actual growth and actual initial income.

De Long therefore considers the following model:

$$\ln[(Y/N)_{i,1979}] - \ln[(Y/N)_{i,1870}]^* = a + b\ln[(Y/N)_{i,1870}]^* + \varepsilon_i, \quad (1.33)$$

$$\ln[(Y/N)_{i,1870}] = \ln[(Y/N)_{i,1870}]^* + u_i, \quad (1.34)$$

where $\ln[(Y/N)_{1870}]^*$ is the true value of log income per capita in 1870 and $\ln[(Y/N)_{1870}]$ is the measured value. ε and u are assumed to be uncorrelated with each other and with $\ln[(Y/N)_{1870}]^*$.

Unfortunately, it is not possible to estimate this model using only data on $\ln[(Y/N)_{1870}]$ and $\ln[(Y/N)_{1979}]$. The problem is that there are different hypotheses that make identical predictions about the data. For example, suppose we find that measured growth is negatively related to measured initial income. This is exactly what one would expect either if measurement error is unimportant and there is true convergence or if measurement error is important and there is no true convergence. Technically, the model is *not identified*.

De Long argues, however, that we have at least a rough idea of how good the 1870 data are, and thus have a sense of what is a reasonable value for the standard deviation of the measurement error. $\sigma_u = 0.01$, for example, implies that we have measured initial income to within an average of 1 percent; this is implausibly low. Similarly, $\sigma_u = 0.50$—an average error of 50 percent—seems implausibly high. De Long shows that if we fix a value of σ_u, we can estimate the remaining parameters.

Even moderate measurement error has a substantial impact on the results. For the unbiased sample, the estimate of b reaches 0 (no tendency toward convergence) for $\sigma_u \simeq 0.15$, and is 1 (tremendous divergence) for $\sigma_u \simeq 0.20$. Thus plausible amounts of measurement error eliminate most or all of the remainder of Baumol's estimate of convergence.

It is also possible to investigate convergence for different samples of countries and different time periods. Figure 1.9 is a *convergence scatterplot* analogous to Figures 1.7 and 1.8 for virtually the entire non-Communist world for the period 1960–1985. As the figure shows, there is little evidence of convergence. We return to the issue of convergence at the end of Chapter 3.

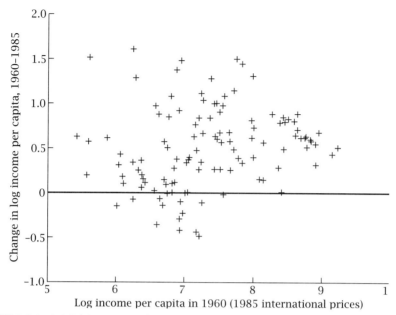

FIGURE 1.9   Initial income and subsequent growth in the postwar period (data from Summers and Heston, 1991)

Saving and Investment

Consider a world where every country is described by the Solow model and where all countries have the same amount of capital per unit of effective labor. Now suppose that the saving rate in one country rises. If all of the additional saving were invested domestically, the marginal product of capital in that country would fall. There would therefore be incentives for residents of the country to invest abroad. Indeed, in the absence of any impediments to capital flows, the investment resulting from the increased saving would be spread uniformly over the whole world; the fact that the rise in saving occurred in one country would have no special effect on investment there. Thus there would be no reason to expect countries with high saving to also have high investment.

Feldstein and Horioka (1980) examine the association between saving and investment rates. They find that, contrary to this simple view, saving and investment rates are strongly correlated. Specifically, Feldstein and Horioka run a cross-country regression for 21 industrialized countries of the average share of investment in GDP during the period 1960–1974 on a constant and the average share of saving in GDP over the same period. The results are

$$(I/Y)_i = \underset{(0.018)}{0.035} + \underset{(0.074)}{0.887}(S/Y)_i, \qquad R^2 = 0.91, \qquad (1.35)$$

where again the numbers in parentheses are standard errors. Thus, rather than there being no relation between saving and investment, there is an almost one-to-one relation.

There are various possible explanations for Feldstein and Horioka's finding (see Obstfeld, 1986, for a discussion). One possibility, suggested by Feldstein and Horioka, is that significant barriers to capital mobility exist. In this case, differences in saving and investment across countries would be associated with rate of return differences.

Another possibility is that there are underlying variables that affect both saving and investment. For example, high tax rates can reduce both saving and investment (Barro, Mankiw, and Sala-i-Martin, 1995). Similarly, countries whose citizens have low discount rates, and thus high saving rates, may provide favorable investment climates in ways other than the high saving; for example, they may limit workers' ability to form strong unions.

Finally, the strong association between saving and investment can arise from government policies that offset forces that would otherwise make saving and investment differ. Governments may be averse to large gaps between saving and investment—after all, a large gap must be associated with a large trade deficit (if investment exceeds saving) or a large trade surplus (if saving exceeds investment). If economic forces would otherwise give rise to a large imbalance between saving and investment, the government may choose to adjust its own saving behavior or its tax treatment of saving or investment to bring them into rough balance.

In sum, the strong relationship between saving and investment differs dramatically from the predictions of a natural baseline model. Whether this difference reflects major departures from the baseline (such as large barriers to capital mobility) or something less fundamental (such as underlying forces affecting both saving and investment) is not known.

Investment, Population Growth, and Output

According to the Solow model, saving and population growth affect output per worker through their impact on capital per worker. A country that saves more of its output has more capital per worker, and hence more output per worker; a country with higher population growth devotes more of its saving to maintaining its capital-labor ratio, and so has less capital and output per worker.

The model makes not just qualitative but quantitative predictions about the impact of saving and population growth on output. We saw in Section 1.5 that the elasticity of output on the balanced growth path with respect to s is $\alpha/(1 - \alpha)$, where α is capital's share. Similarly, one can show that its elasticity with respect to $n + g + \delta$ is $-\alpha/(1 - \alpha)$ (see Problem 1.5). Thus,[21]

---

[21] One can also derive (1.36) by assuming that the production function is Cobb–Douglas; in this case, no approximations are needed (see Problem 1.2).

$$\ln y^* \simeq a + \frac{\alpha}{1 - \alpha} \ln s - \frac{\alpha}{1 - \alpha} \ln(n + g + \delta). \qquad (1.36)$$

Mankiw, D. Romer, and Weil (1992) estimate equation (1.36) empirically using cross-country data. Their basic specification is

$$\ln y_i = a + b[\ln s_i - \ln(n_i + g + \delta)] + \varepsilon_i, \qquad (1.37)$$

where i indexes countries. Finding empirical counterparts for y, s, and n is fairly straightforward. Mankiw, Romer, and Weil measure y as real GDP per person of working age in 1985, s as the average share of real private and government investment in real GDP over the period 1960–1985, and n as the average growth rate of the population of working age over the same period.[22] Finally, $g + \delta$ is set to 0.05 for all countries.

The results for the broadest set of countries considered by Mankiw, Romer, and Weil are:

$$\begin{aligned} \ln y_i = \ \ &6.87 \ + \ \ 1.48[\ln s_i - \ln(n_i + 0.05)], \\ &(0.12) \ \ \ \ (0.12) \end{aligned} \qquad (1.38)$$

$$\overline{R}^2 = 0.59, \qquad \text{s.e.e.} = 0.69.$$

Saving and population growth enter in the directions predicted by the model and are highly statistically significant, and the regression accounts for a large portion of cross-country differences in income. In this sense, the model is a success.

There is one major difficulty, however: the estimated effect of saving and population growth is far larger than the model predicts. The estimate of $\hat{b} = 1.48$ implies $\hat{\alpha} = 0.60$ (with a standard error of 0.02).[23] Thus the relationship between saving and population growth and real income is far stronger than the model predicts for reasonable values of the capital share, and the data are grossly inconsistent with the hypothesis that α is in the vicinity of one-third. Thus, Mankiw, Romer, and Weil's results confirm the conclusion that the Solow model cannot account for important features of cross-country income differences.

---

[22] The data are from the Summers and Heston (1988) cross-country data set. See Summers and Heston (1991) for a more recent version.

[23] Finding estimates and standard errors for parameters that are nonlinear functions of regression coefficients is straightforward. In the case of (1.36)–(1.38), solving $b = \alpha/(1 - \alpha)$ for α yields $\alpha = b/(1 + b)$. The estimate of $\hat{\alpha} = 0.60$ is thus obtained by computing $\hat{\alpha} = \hat{b}/(1 + \hat{b}) = 1.48/(1 + 1.48)$. In addition, a first-order Taylor-series approximation of $\alpha = b/(1 + b)$ around $b = \hat{b}$ yields $\alpha \simeq [\hat{b}/(1 + \hat{b})] + [1/(1 + \hat{b})^2](b - \hat{b})$. Thus the difference between the true α and $\hat{\alpha}$ is approximately $1/(1 + \hat{b})^2$, or 0.16, times the difference between the true b and $\hat{b}$. The standard error of α is therefore approximately 0.16 times the standard error of b, or $0.16(0.12) = 0.02$. (Because of the nonlinearity and the use of approximations, the formal econometric justification for these procedures relies on asymptotic theory. See, for example, Greene, 1993, Section 10.3.3; or Judge et al., 1985, Section 5.3.4.)

Problems

1.1. Consider a Solow economy that is on its balanced growth path. Assume for simplicity that there is no technological progress. Now suppose that the rate of population growth falls.

    (a) What happens to the balanced-growth-path values of capital per worker, output per worker, and consumption per worker? Sketch the paths of these variables as the economy moves to its new balanced growth path.

    (b) Describe the effect of the fall in population growth on the path of output (that is, total output, not output per worker).

1.2. Suppose that the production function is Cobb–Douglas.

    (a) Find expressions for k^*, y^*, and c^* as functions of the parameters of the model, s, n, δ, g, and α.

    (b) What is the golden-rule value of k?

    (c) What saving rate is needed to yield the golden-rule capital stock?

1.3. Consider the constant elasticity of substitution (CES) production function, $Y = [K^{(\sigma-1)/\sigma} + (AL)^{(\sigma-1)/\sigma}]^{\sigma/(\sigma-1)}$, where $0 < \sigma < \infty$ and $\sigma \neq 1$. (σ is the elasticity of substitution between capital and effective labor. In the special case of $\sigma \rightarrow 1$, the CES function reduces to the Cobb–Douglas.)

    (a) Show that this production function exhibits constant returns to scale.

    (b) Find the intensive form of the production function.

    (c) Under what conditions does the intensive form satisfy $f'(\bullet) > 0, f''(\bullet) < 0$?

    (d) Under what conditions does the intensive form satisfy the Inada conditions?

1.4. Consider an economy with technological progress but without population growth that is on its balanced growth path. Now suppose there is a one-time jump in the number of workers.

    (a) At the time of the jump, does output per unit of effective labor rise, fall, or stay the same? Why?

    (b) After the initial change (if any) in output per unit of effective labor when the new workers appear, is there any further change in output per unit of effective labor? If so, does it rise or fall? Why?

    (c) Once the economy has again reached a balanced growth path, is output per unit of effective labor higher, lower, or the same as it was before the new workers appeared? Why?

1.5. Find the elasticity of output per unit of effective labor on the balanced growth path, y^*, with respect to the rate of population growth, n. If $\alpha_K(k^*) = \frac{1}{3}$, $g = 2\%$, and $\delta = 3\%$, by about how much does a fall in n from 2% to 1% raise y^*?

1.6. Suppose that, despite the political obstacles, the United States permanently reduces its budget deficit from 3% of GDP to zero. Suppose that initially $s = 0.15$ and that investment rises by the full amount of the fall in the deficit. Assume that capital's share is $\frac{1}{3}$.

(*a*) By about how much does output eventually rise relative to what it would have been without the deficit reduction?

(*b*) By about how much does consumption rise relative to what it would have been without the deficit reduction?

(*c*) What is the immediate effect of the deficit reduction on consumption? About how long does it take for consumption to return to what it would have been without the deficit reduction?

1.7. Factor payments in the Solow model. Assume that both labor and capital are paid their marginal products. Let w denote $\partial F(K, AL)/\partial L$ and r denote $\partial F(K, AL)/\partial K$.

(*a*) Show that the marginal product of labor, w, is $A[f(k) - kf'(k)]$.

(*b*) Show that if both capital and labor are paid their marginal products, constant returns to scale implies that the total amount paid to the factors of production equals total output. That is, show that under constant returns, $wL + rK = F(K, AL)$.

(*c*) Two additional stylized facts about growth listed by Kaldor (1961) are that the return to capital (r) is approximately constant and that the shares of output going to capital and labor are each roughly constant. Does a Solow economy on a balanced growth path exhibit these properties? What are the growth rates of w and r on a balanced growth path?

(*d*) Suppose the economy begins with a level of k less than k^*. As k moves toward k^*, is w growing at a rate greater than, less than, or equal to its growth rate on the balanced growth path? What about r?

1.8. Suppose that, as in Problem 1.7, capital and labor are paid their marginal products. In addition, suppose that all capital income is saved and all labor income is consumed. Thus $\dot{K} = [\partial F(K, AL)/\partial K]K - \delta K$.

(*a*) Show that this economy converges to a balanced growth path.

(*b*) Is k on the balanced growth path greater than, less than, or equal to the golden-rule level of k? What is the intuition for this result?

1.9. The Harrod–Domar model. (See Harrod, 1939, and Domar, 1946.) Suppose the production function is Leontief, $Y(t) = \min[c_K K(t), c_L e^{gt} L(t)]$, where c_K, c_L, and g are all positive. As in the Solow model, $\dot{L}(t) = nL(t)$ and $\dot{K}(t) = sY(t) - \delta K(t)$. Finally, assume $c_K K(0) = c_L L(0)$.

(*a*) Under what condition does $c_K K(t) = c_L e^{gt} L(t)$ for all t? If c_K, c_L, g, s, δ, and n are determined by separate considerations, is there any reason to expect that this condition holds?

(*b*) If $c_L e^{gt} L(t)$ is growing faster than $c_K K(t)$ (and if the excess labor is assumed to be unemployed), what happens to the unemployment rate over time?

(*c*) If $c_K K(t)$ is growing faster than $c_L e^{gt} L(t)$ (and if the excess capital is assumed to be unused), what happens to the fraction of the capital stock that is used over time?

1.10. Natural resources in the Solow model. At least since Malthus, some have argued that the fact that some factors of production (notably land and natural resources) are available in finite supply must eventually bring growth to a halt. This problem asks you to address this idea in the context of the Solow model.

Let the production function be $Y = K^\alpha (AL)^\beta R^{1-\alpha-\beta}$, where R is the amount of land. Assume $\alpha > 0$, $\beta > 0$, and $\alpha + \beta < 1$. The factors of production evolve according to $\dot{K} = sY - \delta K$, $\dot{A} = gA$, $\dot{L} = nL$, and $\dot{R} = 0$.

(a) Does this economy have a unique and stable balanced growth path? That is, does the economy converge to a situation in which each of Y, K, L, A, and R are growing at constant (but not necessarily equal) rates? If so, what are those growth rates? If not, why not?

(b) In light of your answer, does the fact that the stock of land is constant imply that permanent growth is not possible? Explain intuitively.

1.11. Embodied technological progress. (This follows Solow, 1960, and Sato, 1966.) One view of technological progress is that the productivity of capital goods built at t depends on the state of technology at t and is unaffected by subsequent technological progress. This is known as *embodied technological progress* (technological progress must be "embodied" in new capital before it can raise output). This problem asks you to investigate its effects.

(a) As a preliminary, let us modify the basic Solow model to make technological progress capital-augmenting rather than labor-augmenting. So that a balanced growth path exists, assume that the production function is Cobb–Douglas: $Y(t) = [A(t)K(t)]^\alpha L(t)^{1-\alpha}$. Assume that A grows at rate μ: $\dot{A}(t) = \mu A(t)$.

Show that the economy converges to a balanced growth path, and find the growth rates of Y and K on the balanced growth path. (Hint: show that we can write $Y/(A^\phi L)$ as a function of $K/(A^\phi L)$, where $\phi = \alpha/(1-\alpha)$. Then analyze the dynamics of $K/(A^\phi L)$.)

(b) Now consider embodied technological progress. Specifically, let the production function be $Y(t) = J(t)^\alpha L(t)^{1-\alpha}$, where $J(t)$ is the effective capital stock. The dynamics of $J(t)$ are given by $\dot{J}(t) = sA(t)Y(t) - \delta J(t)$. The presence of the $A(t)$ term in this expression means that the productivity of investment at t depends on the technology at t.

Show that the economy converges to a balanced growth path. What are the growth rates of Y and J on the balanced growth path? (Hint: let $\bar{J}(t) = J(t)/A(t)$. Then use the same approach as in (a), focusing on $\bar{J}/(A^\phi L)$ instead of $K/(A^\phi L)$.)

(c) What is the elasticity of output on the balanced growth path with respect to s?

(d) In the vicinity of the balanced growth path, how rapidly does the economy converge to the balanced growth path?

(e) Compare your results for (c) and (d) with the corresponding results in the text for the basic Solow model.

1.12. Consider a Solow economy on its balanced growth path. Suppose the growth-accounting techniques described in Section 1.7 are applied to this economy.

(a) What fraction of growth in output per worker does growth accounting attribute to growth in capital per worker? What fraction does it attribute to technological progress?

(b) How can you reconcile your results in (a) with the fact that the Solow model implies that the growth rate of output per worker on the balanced growth path is determined solely by the rate of technological progress?

1.13. (a) In the model of convergence and measurement error in equations (1.33)-(1.34), suppose the true value of b is -1. Does a regression of $\ln(Y/N)_{1979} - \ln(Y/N)_{1870}$ on a constant and $\ln(Y/N)_{1870}$ yield a biased estimate of b? Explain.

(b) Suppose there is measurement error in measured 1979 income per capita but not in 1870 income per capita. Does a regression of $\ln(Y/N)_{1979} - \ln(Y/N)_{1870}$ on a constant and $\ln(Y/N)_{1870}$ yield a biased estimate of b? Explain.

Chapter 2
BEHIND THE SOLOW MODEL: INFINITE-HORIZON AND OVERLAPPING-GENERATIONS MODELS

This chapter investigates two models that resemble the Solow model but in which the dynamics of economic aggregates are determined by decisions at the microeconomic level. Both models continue to treat the growth rates of labor and knowledge as exogenous. But the models derive the evolution of the capital stock from the interaction of maximizing households and firms in competitive markets. As a result, the saving rate is no longer exogenous, and it need not be constant.

The first model is conceptually the simplest. Competitive firms rent capital and hire labor to produce and sell output, and a fixed number of infinitely-lived households supply labor, hold capital, consume, and save. This model, which was developed by Ramsey (1928), Cass (1965), and Koopmans (1965), avoids all market imperfections and all issues raised by heterogeneous households and links among generations. It therefore provides a natural benchmark case.

The second model is the overlapping-generations model developed by Diamond (1965). The key difference between the Diamond model and the Ramsey–Cass–Koopmans model is that the Diamond model assumes that there is continual entry of new households into the economy. As we will see, this seemingly small change has important consequences.

Part A   The Ramsey-Cass-Koopmans Model

2.1   Assumptions

Firms

There is a large number of identical firms. Each has access to the production function $Y = F(K, AL)$, which satisfies the same assumptions as in Chapter 1. The firms hire workers and rent capital in competitive factor markets, and sell their output in a competitive output market. Firms take A as given; as in the Solow model, A grows exogenously at rate g. The firms maximize profits. They are owned by the households, so any profits they earn accrue to the households.

Households

There is also a large number of identical households. The size of each household grows at rate n. Each member of the household supplies one unit of labor at every point in time. In addition, the household rents whatever capital it owns to firms. It has initial capital holdings of $K(0)/H$, where $K(0)$ is the initial amount of capital in the economy and H is the number of households. For simplicity, in this chapter we assume that there is no depreciation. The household divides its income (from the labor and capital it supplies and, potentially, from the profits it receives from firms) at each point in time between consumption and saving so as to maximize lifetime utility.

The household's utility function takes the form

$$U = \int_{t=0}^{\infty} e^{-\rho t} u(C(t)) \frac{L(t)}{H} \, dt. \tag{2.1}$$

$C(t)$ is the consumption of each member of the household at time t. $u(\cdot)$ is the *instantaneous utility function,* which gives each member's utility at a given date. $L(t)$ is the total population of the economy; $L(t)/H$ is therefore the number of members of the household. Thus $u(C(t))L(t)/H$ is the household's total instantaneous utility at t. Finally, ρ is the discount rate; the greater is ρ, the less the household values future consumption relative to current consumption.[1]

---

[1]One could also write utility as $\int_{t=0}^{\infty} e^{-\rho' t} u(C(t)) dt$, where $\rho' \equiv \rho - n$. Since $L(t) = L(0)e^{nt}$, this expression equals the expression in equation (2.1) divided by $L(0)/H$, and thus has the same implications for behavior.

The instantaneous utility function takes the form

$$u(C(t)) = \frac{C(t)^{1-\theta}}{1-\theta}, \qquad \theta > 0, \quad \rho - n - (1-\theta)g > 0. \tag{2.2}$$

This utility function is known as constant-relative-risk-aversion (or CRRA) utility. The reason for the name is that the coefficient of relative risk aversion (which is defined as $-Cu''(C)/u'(C)$) for this utility function is θ, and thus is independent of C.

Since there is no uncertainty in this model, the household's attitude toward risk is not directly relevant. But θ also determines the household's willingness to shift consumption between different periods: the smaller is θ, the more slowly marginal utility falls as consumption rises, and so the more willing the household is to allow its consumption to vary over time. If θ is close to zero, for example, utility is almost linear in C, and so the household is willing to accept large swings in its consumption to take advantage of small differences between its discount rate and the rate of return it gets on its saving. Specifically, one can show that the elasticity of substitution between consumption at any two points in time is $1/\theta$.[2]

Three additional features of the instantaneous utility function are worth mentioning. First, $C^{1-\theta}$ is increasing in C if $\theta < 1$ but decreasing if $\theta > 1$; dividing $C^{1-\theta}$ by $1-\theta$ thus ensures that the marginal utility of consumption is positive regardless of the value of θ. Second, in the special case of $\theta \to 1$, the instantaneous utility function simplifies to $\ln C$; this is often a useful case to consider.[3] And third, the assumption that $\rho - n - (1-\theta)g > 0$ ensures that lifetime utility does not diverge: if this condition does not hold, the household can attain infinite lifetime utility, and its maximization problem does not have a well-defined solution.[4]

2.2   The Behavior of Households and Firms

Firms

Firms' behavior is relatively simple. At each point in time they employ the stocks of labor and capital, pay them their marginal products, and sell the

---

[2] See Problem 2.2.

[3] To see this, first subtract $1/(1-\theta)$ from the utility function; since this simply changes utility by a constant, it does not affect behavior. Then take the limit as θ approaches 1; this requires using l'Hôpital's rule. The result is $\ln C$.

[4] Phelps (1966a) discusses how growth models can be analyzed when households can obtain infinite utility.

resulting output. Because the production function has constant returns and the economy is competitive, firms earn zero profits.

As described in Chapter 1, the marginal product of capital, $\partial F(K, AL)/\partial K$, is $f'(k)$, where $f(\cdot)$ is the intensive form of the production function. Because markets are competitive, capital earns its marginal product. And because there is no depreciation, the real rate of return on capital equals its earnings per unit time. Thus the real interest rate at time t is

$$r(t) = f'(k(t)). \tag{2.3}$$

The marginal product of effective labor is $\partial F(K, AL)/\partial AL$. In terms of $f(\cdot)$, this is $f(k) - kf'(k)$.[5] Thus the real wage per unit of effective labor is

$$w(t) = f(k(t)) - k(t)f'(k(t)). \tag{2.4}$$

Since the marginal product of labor (as opposed to effective labor) is $A\,\partial F(K, AL)/\partial AL$, a worker's labor income at time t is $A(t)w(t)$.

Households' Maximization Problem

The representative household takes the paths of r and w as given. Its budget constraint is that the present value of its lifetime consumption cannot exceed its initial wealth plus the present value of its lifetime labor income. To write the budget constraint formally, we need to account for the fact that r may vary over time. To do this, define $R(t)$ as $\int_{\tau=0}^{t} r(\tau)d\tau$. One unit of the output good invested at time 0 yields $e^{R(t)}$ units of the good at t; equivalently, the value of one unit of output at time t in terms of output at time 0 is $e^{-R(t)}$. For example, if r is constant at some level $\bar{r}$, $R(t)$ is simply $\bar{r}t$ and the present value of one unit of output at t is $e^{-\bar{r}t}$. More generally, $e^{R(t)}$ shows the effects of continuously compounding interest over the period $[0, t]$.

Since the household has $L(t)/H$ members, its labor income at t is $A(t)w(t)L(t)/H$, and its consumption expenditures are $C(t)L(t)/H$. The household's budget constraint is therefore

$$\int_{t=0}^{\infty} e^{-R(t)}C(t)\frac{L(t)}{H}\,dt \le \frac{K(0)}{H} + \int_{t=0}^{\infty} e^{-R(t)}A(t)w(t)\frac{L(t)}{H}\,dt. \tag{2.5}$$

As in the Solow model, it is easier to work with variables normalized by the quantity of effective labor. To do this, we need to express the budget constraint in terms of consumption and labor income per unit of effective labor. Define $c(t)$ to be consumption per unit of effective labor. The

---

[5] See Problem 1.7, in Chapter 1.

household's total consumption at t, $C(t)L(t)/H$, equals consumption per unit of effective labor, $c(t)$, times the household's quantity of effective labor, $A(t)L(t)/H$. Similarly, its initial capital holdings are $k(0)$, capital per unit of effective labor at time zero, times $A(0)L(0)/H$. Thus we can rewrite (2.5) as

$$\int_{t=0}^{\infty} e^{-R(t)} c(t) \frac{A(t)L(t)}{H} \, dt \leq k(0) \frac{A(0)L(0)}{H} + \int_{t=0}^{\infty} e^{-R(t)} w(t) \frac{A(t)L(t)}{H} \, dt. \quad (2.6)$$

$A(t)L(t)$ equals $A(0)L(0)e^{(n+g)t}$. Substituting this fact into (2.6) and dividing both sides by $A(0)L(0)/H$ yields

$$\int_{t=0}^{\infty} e^{-R(t)} c(t) e^{(n+g)t} \, dt \leq k(0) + \int_{t=0}^{\infty} e^{-R(t)} w(t) e^{(n+g)t} \, dt. \quad (2.7)$$

In many cases, it is difficult to find the integrals in (2.7). Fortunately, we can express the budget constraint in terms of the limiting behavior of the household's capital holdings; even when it is not possible to compute the integrals in (2.7), it is often possible to describe the limiting behavior of the economy. To see how the budget constraint can be rewritten in this way, first bring all of the terms of (2.6) over to the same side and combine the two integrals; this gives us

$$\frac{K(0)}{H} + \int_{t=0}^{\infty} e^{-R(t)} [w(t) - c(t)] A(t) \frac{L(t)}{H} \, dt \geq 0, \quad (2.8)$$

where we have used the fact that $k(0)A(0)L(0) = K(0)$. We can write the integral from $t = 0$ to $t = \infty$ as a limit. Thus (2.8) is equivalent to

$$\lim_{s \to \infty} \left[\frac{K(0)}{H} + \int_{t=0}^{s} e^{-R(t)} [w(t) - c(t)] A(t) \frac{L(t)}{H} \, dt \right] \geq 0. \quad (2.9)$$

Now note that the household's capital holdings at time s are

$$\frac{K(s)}{H} = e^{R(s)} \frac{K(0)}{H} + \int_{t=0}^{s} e^{R(s)-R(t)} [w(t) - c(t)] \frac{A(t)L(t)}{H} \, dt. \quad (2.10)$$

To understand (2.10), note that $e^{R(s)} K(0)/H$ is the contribution of the household's initial wealth to its wealth at s. The household's saving at t is $[w(t) - c(t)]A(t)L(t)/H$ (which may be negative); $e^{R(s)-R(t)}$ shows how the value of that saving changes from t to s.

The expression in (2.10) is $e^{R(s)}$ times the expression in brackets in (2.9). Thus we can write the budget constraint simply as

$$\lim_{s \to \infty} e^{-R(s)} \frac{K(s)}{H} \geq 0. \quad (2.11)$$

Expressed in this form, the budget constraint states that the present value of the household's asset holdings cannot be negative in the limit. Since $K(s)$ is proportional to $k(s)e^{(n+g)s}$, we can also write this as

$$\lim_{s \to \infty} e^{-R(s)}e^{(n+g)s}k(s) \geq 0. \tag{2.12}$$

Finally, we can also rewrite the household's objective function, (2.1)-(2.2), in terms of consumption per unit of effective labor. $C(t)$, consumption per worker, equals $A(t)c(t)$. Thus,

$$\frac{C(t)^{1-\theta}}{1-\theta} = \frac{[A(t)c(t)]^{1-\theta}}{1-\theta}$$

$$= \frac{[A(0)e^{gt}]^{1-\theta}c(t)^{1-\theta}}{1-\theta} \tag{2.13}$$

$$= A(0)^{1-\theta}e^{(1-\theta)gt}\frac{c(t)^{1-\theta}}{1-\theta}.$$

Substituting (2.13) and the fact that $L(t) = L(0)e^{nt}$ into the household's objective function yields

$$U = \int_{t=0}^{\infty} e^{-\rho t}\frac{C(t)^{1-\theta}}{1-\theta}\frac{L(t)}{H}dt.$$

$$= \int_{t=0}^{\infty} e^{-\rho t}\left[A(0)^{1-\theta}e^{(1-\theta)gt}\frac{c(t)^{1-\theta}}{1-\theta}\right]\frac{L(0)e^{nt}}{H}dt$$

$$\tag{2.14}$$

$$= A(0)^{1-\theta}\frac{L(0)}{H}\int_{t=0}^{\infty} e^{-\rho t}e^{(1-\theta)gt}e^{nt}\frac{c(t)^{1-\theta}}{1-\theta}dt$$

$$\equiv B\int_{t=0}^{\infty} e^{-\beta t}\frac{c(t)^{1-\theta}}{1-\theta}dt, \qquad B \equiv A(0)^{1-\theta}\frac{L(0)}{H}, \qquad \beta \equiv \rho - n - (1-\theta)g.$$

From (2.2), β is assumed to be positive.

Household Behavior

The household's problem is to choose the path of $c(t)$ to maximize lifetime utility subject to the budget constraint. Although this involves choosing c at each instant of time (rather than choosing a finite set of variables, as in standard maximization problems), conventional maximization techniques can be used. Since the marginal utility of consumption is always positive, the household satisfies its budget constraint with equality. We can therefore use the objective function, (2.14), and the budget constraint, (2.7), to set up the Lagrangian:[6]

$$\mathcal{L} = B \int_{t=0}^{\infty} e^{-\beta t} \frac{c(t)^{1-\theta}}{1-\theta} \, dt$$
$$+ \lambda \left[k(0) + \int_{t=0}^{\infty} e^{-R(t)} e^{(n+g)t} w(t) dt - \int_{t=0}^{\infty} e^{-R(t)} e^{(n+g)t} c(t) dt \right]. \tag{2.15}$$

The household chooses c at each point in time; that is, it chooses infinitely many $c(t)$'s. The first-order condition for an individual $c(t)$ is[7]

$$B e^{-\beta t} c(t)^{-\theta} = \lambda e^{-R(t)} e^{(n+g)t}. \tag{2.16}$$

The household's behavior is characterized by (2.16) and the budget constraint, (2.7).

To see what (2.16) implies for the behavior of consumption, first take logs of both sides:

$$\ln B - \beta t - \theta \ln c(t) = \ln \lambda - R(t) + (n+g)t. \tag{2.17}$$

Now note that since the two sides of (2.17) are equal for every t, the derivatives of the two sides with respect to t must be the same. This condition is

$$-\beta - \theta \frac{\dot{c}(t)}{c(t)} = -r(t) + (n+g), \tag{2.18}$$

where we have used the definition of $R(t)$ as $\int_{\tau=0}^{t} r(\tau) d\tau$ to find $dR(t)/dt$. Solving (2.18) for $\dot{c}(t)/c(t)$ yields

$$\frac{\dot{c}(t)}{c(t)} = \frac{r(t) - n - g - \beta}{\theta}$$
$$= \frac{r(t) - \rho - \theta g}{\theta}, \tag{2.19}$$

where the second line uses the definition of β as $\rho - n - (1-\theta)g$.

To interpret (2.19), note that since $C(t)$ (consumption per worker, rather than consumption per unit of effective labor) equals $c(t)A(t)$, the growth

---

[6]For an introduction to maximization subject to equality constraints, see Dixit (1990, Chapter 2), Simon and Blume (1994, Chapters 18–19), or Chiang (1984, Chapter 12). For the case of inequality constraints, see Dixit (Chapter 3), Simon and Blume (Chapter 18), Chiang (Chapter 21), or Kreps (1990, Appendix 1).

[7]This step is slightly informal; the difficulty is that the terms in (2.16) are of order dt in (2.15); that is, they make an infinitesimal contribution to the Lagrangian. There are various ways of addressing this issue more formally than simply "canceling" the dt's (which is what we do in [2.16]). For example, we can model the household as choosing consumption over the finite intervals $[0, \Delta t), [\Delta t, 2\Delta t), [2\Delta t, 3\Delta t), \ldots$, with its consumption required to be constant within each interval, and then take the limit as Δt approaches zero. This also yields (2.16). Another possibility is to use the *calculus of variations* (see n. 11, below).

rate of C equals the growth rate of c plus the growth rate of A. That is, (2.19) implies that consumption per worker is growing at rate $[r(t) - \rho]/\theta$. Thus, (2.19) states that consumption per worker is rising if the real return exceeds the rate at which the household discounts future consumption, and is falling if the reverse holds. The smaller is θ—the less marginal utility changes as consumption changes—the larger are the changes in consumption in response to differences between the real interest rate and the discount rate.

Equation (2.19) is known as the *Euler equation* for this maximization problem. A more intuitive way of deriving (2.19) is to think of the household's consumption at two consecutive moments in time. Specifically, imagine the household reducing c at some date t by a small (formally, infinitesimal) amount Δc, investing this additional saving for a short (again, infinitesimal) period of time Δt, and then consuming the proceeds at time $t + \Delta t$; assume that when it does this, the household leaves consumption and capital holdings at all times other than t and $t + \Delta t$ unchanged. If the household is optimizing, the marginal impact of this change on lifetime utility must be zero. From (2.14), the marginal utility of $c(t)$ is $Be^{-\beta t}c(t)^{-\theta}$. Thus the change has a utility cost of $Be^{-\beta t}c(t)^{-\theta}\Delta c$. Since the instantaneous rate of return is $r(t)$, c at time $t + \Delta t$ can be increased by $e^{[r(t)-n-g]\Delta t}\Delta c$. Similarly, since c is growing at rate $\dot{c}(t)/c(t)$, we can write $c(t + \Delta t)$ as $c(t)e^{[\dot{c}(t)/c(t)]\Delta t}$; thus the marginal utility of $c(t + \Delta t)$ is $Be^{-\beta(t+\Delta t)}c(t + \Delta t)^{-\theta} = Be^{-\beta(t+\Delta t)}[c(t)e^{[\dot{c}(t)/c(t)]\Delta t}]^{-\theta}$. Thus for the path of consumption to be utility-maximizing, it must satisfy

$$Be^{-\beta t}c(t)^{-\theta}\,\Delta c = Be^{-\beta(t+\Delta t)}[c(t)e^{[\dot{c}(t)/c(t)]\Delta t}]^{-\theta}e^{[r(t)-n-g]\Delta t}\,\Delta c. \quad (2.20)$$

Dividing by $Be^{-\beta t}c(t)^{-\theta}\,\Delta c$ and taking logs yields:

$$-\beta\,\Delta t - \theta\frac{\dot{c}(t)}{c(t)}\,\Delta t + [r(t) - n - g]\Delta t = 0. \quad (2.21)$$

Finally, dividing by Δt and rearranging yields the Euler equation in (2.19).

Intuitively, the Euler equation describes how c must behave over time given $c(0)$: if c does not evolve according to (2.19), the household can rearrange its consumption in a way that raises lifetime utility without changing the present value of its lifetime spending. The choice of $c(0)$ is then determined by the requirement that the present value of lifetime consumption over the resulting path equals initial wealth plus the present value of future earnings. When $c(0)$ is chosen too low, consumption spending along the path satisfying (2.19) does not exhaust lifetime wealth, and so a higher path is possible; when $c(0)$ is set too high, consumption spending more than uses up lifetime wealth, and so the path is not feasible.[8]

---

[8]Formally, (2.19) implies $c(t) = c(0)e^{[R(t)-(\rho+\theta g)t]/\theta}$, which implies $e^{-R(t)}e^{(n+g)t}c(t) = c(0)e^{[(1-\theta)R(t)+(\theta n-\rho)t]/\theta}$. $c(0)$ is thus determined by the fact that $c(0)\int_{t=0}^{\infty}e^{[(1-\theta)R(t)+(\theta n-\rho)t]/\theta}\,dt$ must equal the right-hand side of the budget constraint, (2.7).

2.3   The Dynamics of the Economy

The most convenient way to describe the behavior of the economy is in terms of the evolution of c and k.

The Dynamics of c

Since all households are the same, equation (2.19) describes the evolution of c not just for a single household but for the economy as a whole. Since $r(t) = f'(k(t))$, we can rewrite (2.19) as

$$\frac{\dot{c}(t)}{c(t)} = \frac{f'(k(t)) - \rho - \theta g}{\theta}. \tag{2.22}$$

Thus $\dot{c}$ is zero when $f'(k)$ equals $\rho + \theta g$. Let k^* denote this level of k. When k exceeds k^*, $f'(k)$ is less than $\rho + \theta g$, and so $\dot{c}$ is negative; when k is less than k^*, $\dot{c}$ is positive.

This information is summarized in Figure 2.1. The arrows show the direction of motion of c. Thus c is rising if $k < k^*$ and falling if $k > k^*$. The $\dot{c} = 0$ line at $k = k^*$ indicates that c is constant for this value of k.

The Dynamics of k

As in the Solow model, $\dot{k}$ equals actual investment minus break-even investment. Since we are assuming that there is no depreciation, break-even

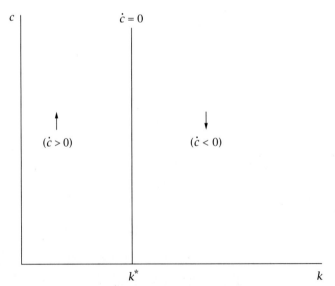

FIGURE 2.1   The dynamics of c

investment is $(n + g)k$. Actual investment is output minus consumption, $f(k) - c$. Thus:

$$\dot{k}(t) = f(k(t)) - c(t) - (n + g)k(t). \tag{2.23}$$

For a given k, the level of c that implies $\dot{k} = 0$ is given by $f(k) - (n + g)k$; in terms of Figure 1.6 (Chapter 1), $\dot{k}$ is zero when consumption equals the difference between the actual output and break-even investment lines. This value of c is increasing in k until $f'(k) = n + g$ (the golden-rule level of k) and then decreasing. When c exceeds the level that yields $\dot{k} = 0$, k is falling; when c is less than this level, k is rising. For k sufficiently large, break-even investment exceeds total output, and so $\dot{k}$ is negative for all positive values of c. This information is summarized in Figure 2.2; the arrows show the direction of motion of k.

The Phase Diagram

Figure 2.3 combines the information in Figures 2.1 and 2.2. The arrows now show the directions of motion of both c and k. To the left of the $\dot{c} = 0$ locus and above the $\dot{k} = 0$ locus, for example, $\dot{c}$ is positive and $\dot{k}$ negative. Thus c is rising and k falling, and so the arrows point up and to the left. The arrows in the other sections of the diagram are based on similar reasoning. On the $\dot{c} = 0$ and $\dot{k} = 0$ curves, only one of c and k is changing. On the $\dot{c} = 0$ line above the $\dot{k} = 0$ locus, for example, c is constant and k is falling; thus the

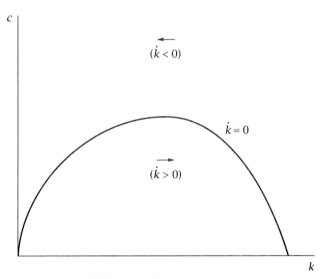

FIGURE 2.2   The dynamics of k

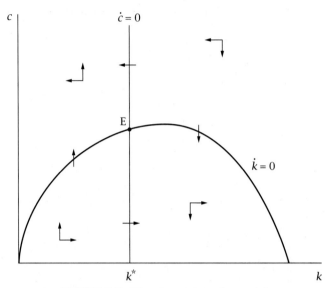

FIGURE 2.3   The dynamics of c and k

arrow points to the left. Finally, at Point E both $\dot{c}$ and $\dot{k}$ are zero; thus there is no movement from this point.[9]

Figure 2.3 is drawn with k^* (the level of k that implies $\dot{c} = 0$) less than the golden-rule level of k (the value of k associated with the peak of the $\dot{k} = 0$ locus). To see that this must be the case, recall that k^* is defined by $f'(k^*) = \rho + \theta g$, and that the golden-rule k is defined by $f'(k_{GR}) = n + g$. Since $f''(k)$ is negative, k^* is less than k_{GR} if and only if $\rho + \theta g$ is greater than $n + g$. This is equivalent to $\rho - n - (1 - \theta)g > 0$, which we have assumed to hold so that lifetime utility does not diverge (see [2.2]). Thus k^* is to the left of the peak of the $\dot{k} = 0$ curve.

The Initial Value of c

Figure 2.3 shows how c and k must evolve over time to satisfy households' intertemporal optimization condition (equation [2.22]) and the equation relating the change in k to output and consumption (equation [2.23]) *given initial values of* c *and* k. The initial value of k is given; but the initial value of c must be determined.

---

[9]There are two other points where c and k are constant. The first is the origin: if the economy starts with no capital and no consumption, it remains there. The second is the point where the $\dot{k} = 0$ curve crosses the horizontal axis. Here all of output is being used to hold k constant, so $c = 0$ and $f(k) = (n + g)k$. Since having consumption change from zero to any positive amount violates households' intertemporal optimization condition, (2.22), if the economy is at this point it must remain there to satisfy (2.22) and (2.23). As we will see shortly, however, the economy is never at this point.

This issue is addressed in Figure 2.4. For concreteness, $k(0)$ is assumed to be less than k^*. The figure shows the trajectory of c and k for various assumptions concerning the initial level of c. If $c(0)$ is above the $\dot{k} = 0$ curve, at a point like A, $\dot{c}$ is positive and $\dot{k}$ negative; thus the economy moves continually up and to the left in the diagram. If $c(0)$ is such that $\dot{k}$ is initially zero (Point B), the economy begins by moving directly up in (k,c) space; thereafter $\dot{c}$ is positive and $\dot{k}$ negative, and so the economy again moves up and to the left. If the economy begins slightly below the $\dot{k} = 0$ locus (Point C), $\dot{k}$ is initially positive but small (since $\dot{k}$ is a continuous function of c), and $\dot{c}$ is again positive. Thus in this case the economy initially moves up and slightly to the right; when it crosses the $\dot{k} = 0$ locus, however, $\dot{k}$ becomes negative and once again the economy is on a path of rising c and falling k.

Point D shows a case of very low initial consumption. Here $\dot{c}$ and $\dot{k}$ are both initially positive. From (2.22), $\dot{c}$ is proportional to c; when c is small, $\dot{c}$ is therefore small. Thus c remains low, and so the economy eventually crosses the $\dot{c} = 0$ line. At this point, $\dot{c}$ becomes negative, and $\dot{k}$ remains positive. Thus the economy moves down and to the right.

$\dot{c}$ and $\dot{k}$ are continuous functions of c and k. Thus there must be some critical point between Points C and D—Point F in the diagram—such that at that level of initial c, the economy converges to the stable point, Point E. For any level of consumption above this critical level, the $\dot{k}$ curve is crossed before the $\dot{c} = 0$ line is reached, and so the economy ends up on a path of perpetually rising consumption and falling capital. And if consumption is less than the critical level, the $\dot{c} = 0$ locus is reached first, and so the

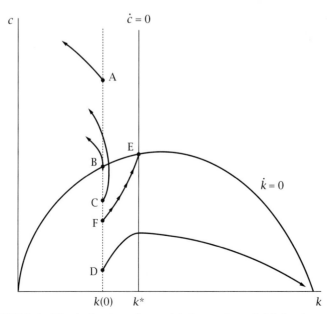

FIGURE 2.4   The behavior of c and k for various initial values of c

economy embarks on a path of falling consumption and rising capital. But if consumption is just equal to the critical level, the economy converges to the point where both c and k are constant.

All of these various trajectories satisfy equations (2.22) and (2.23). But we have not yet imposed the requirement that households satisfy their budget constraint, nor have we imposed the requirement that the economy's capital stock cannot be negative. These conditions determine which of the trajectories in fact describes the behavior of the economy.

If the economy starts at some point above F, k must eventually become negative for (2.22) and (2.23) to continue to be satisfied. Since this is not possible, we can rule out such paths.

To rule out paths starting below F, we use the budget constraint expressed in terms of the limiting behavior of capital holdings, equation (2.12). If the economy starts at a point like D, k eventually exceeds the golden-rule capital stock. After that time, the real interest rate, $f'(k)$, is less than $n+g$, so $e^{-R(s)}e^{(n+g)s}$ is rising. Since k is also rising, $e^{-R(s)}e^{(n+g)s}k(s)$ diverges. Thus $\lim_{s\to\infty} e^{-R(s)}e^{(n+g)s}k(s)$ is infinity; from the derivation of (2.12), we know that this is equivalent to the statement that the present value of households' lifetime income is infinitely larger than the present value of their lifetime consumption. Thus households can attain higher utility, and so such a path cannot be an equilibrium.

Finally, if the economy begins at Point F, k converges to k^*, and so r converges to $f'(k^*) = \rho + \theta g$. Thus eventually $e^{-R(s)}e^{(n+g)s}$ is falling at rate $\rho - n - (1 - \theta)g = \beta > 0$, and so $\lim_{s\to\infty} e^{-R(s)}e^{(n+g)s}k(s)$ is zero. Thus the path beginning at F, and only that path, is possible.

The Saddle Path

Although all of this discussion has been in terms of a single value of k, the idea is general. For any positive initial level of k, there is a unique initial level of c that is consistent with households' intertemporal optimization, the dynamics of the capital stock, households' budget constraint, and the requirement that k cannot be negative. The function giving this initial c as a function of k is known as the *saddle path*; it is shown in Figure 2.5. For any starting value for k, the initial c must be the value on the saddle path. The economy then moves along the saddle path to Point E.

2.4   Welfare

A natural question is whether the equilibrium of this economy represents a desirable outcome. The answer to this question is simple. The *First Welfare theorem*, from microeconomics, tells us that, if markets are competitive and complete and there are no externalities (and if the number of agents is finite), the decentralized equilibrium is Pareto-efficient—that is, it is im-

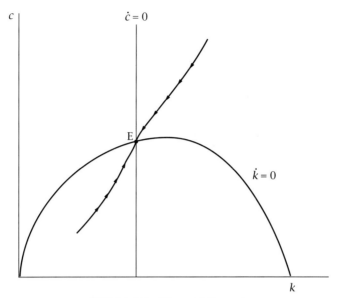

FIGURE 2.5   The saddle path

possible to make anyone better off without making someone else worse off. Since the conditions of the First Welfare theorem hold in our model, the equilibrium must be Pareto-efficient. And since all households have the same utility, this means that the decentralized equilibrium produces the highest possible utility among allocations that treat all households in the same way.

To see this more clearly, consider the problem facing a social planner who can dictate the division of output between consumption and investment at each date and who wants to maximize the lifetime utility of a representative household. This problem is identical to that of an individual household except that, rather than taking the paths of w and r as given, the planner takes into account the fact that these are determined by the path of k, which is in turn determined by (2.23).

The intuitive argument involving consumption at consecutive moments used to derive (2.19) or (2.22) applies to the social planner as well: reducing c by Δc at time t and investing the proceeds allows the planner to increase c at time $t + \Delta t$ by $e^{f'(k(t))\Delta t}e^{-(n+g)\Delta t}\Delta c$.[10] Thus $c(t)$ along the path chosen by the planner must satisfy (2.22). And since equation (2.23) giving the

---

[10]Note that this change does affect r and w over the (brief) interval from t to $t+\Delta t$. r falls by $f''(k)$ times the change in k, while w rises by $-f''(k)k$ times the change in k. But the effect of these changes on total income (per unit of effective labor), which is given by the change in w plus k times the change in r, is zero. That is, since capital is paid its marginal product, total payments to labor and to previously existing capital remain equal to the previous level of output (again per unit of effective labor). This is just a specific instance of the general result that the *pecuniary externalities*—externalities operating through prices—balance in the aggregate under competition.

evolution of k reflects technology, not preferences, the social planner must obey it as well. Finally, as with the household's optimization problem, paths that require that the capital stock becomes negative can be ruled out on the grounds that this is not feasible, and paths that cause consumption to approach zero can be ruled out on the grounds that they do not maximize households' utility.

In short, the solution to the social planner's problem is for the initial value of c to be given by the value on the saddle path, and for c and k to then move along the saddle path. That is, the competitive equilibrium maximizes the welfare of the representative household.[11]

2.5   The Balanced Growth Path

Properties of the Balanced Growth Path

The behavior of the economy once it has converged to Point E is identical to that of the Solow economy on the balanced growth path. Capital, output, and consumption per unit of effective labor are constant. Since y and c are constant, the saving rate, $(y - c)/y$, is also constant. The total capital stock, total output, and total consumption grow at rate $n + g$. And capital per worker, output per worker, and consumption per worker grow at rate g.

Thus the central implications of the Solow model concerning the driving forces of economic growth do not hinge on its assumption of a constant saving rate. Even when saving is endogenous, growth in the effectiveness of labor remains the only possible source of persistent growth in output per worker. And since the production function is the same as in the Solow model, one can repeat the calculations of Chapter 1 demonstrating that significant differences in output per worker can arise from differences in capital per worker only if the differences in capital per worker, and in rates of return to capital, are enormous.

The Balanced Growth Path and the Golden-Rule Level of Capital

The only notable difference between the balanced growth paths of the Solow and Ramsey-Cass-Koopmans models is that a balanced growth path with a capital stock above the golden-rule level is not possible in the Ramsey-Cass-Koopmans model. In the Solow model, a sufficiently high saving rate causes the economy to reach a balanced growth path with the property that there

---

[11]A formal solution to the planner's problem involves the use of the calculus of variations. For a formal statement and solution of the problem, see Blanchard and Fischer (1989, pp. 38–43). For an introduction to the calculus of variations, see Section 8.2, Kamien and Schwartz (1991), or Dixit (1990, Chapter 10).

are feasible alternatives that involve higher consumption at every moment. In the Ramsey–Cass–Koopmans model, in contrast, saving is derived from the behavior of households whose utility depends on their consumption, and there are no externalities. As a result, it cannot be an equilibrium for the economy to follow a path where higher consumption can be attained in every period; if the economy were on such a path, households would reduce their saving and take advantage of this opportunity.

This can be seen in the phase diagram. Consider again Figure 2.5. If the initial capital stock exceeds the golden-rule level (that is, if $k(0)$ is greater than the k associated with the peak of the $\dot{c} = 0$ locus), initial consumption is above the level needed to keep k constant; thus $\dot{k}$ is negative. k gradually approaches k^*, which is below the golden-rule level.

Finally, the fact that k^* is less than the golden-rule capital stock implies that the economy does not converge to the balanced growth path that yields the maximum sustainable level of c. The intuition for this result is clearest in the case of g equal to zero, so that there is no long-run growth of consumption and output per worker. In this case, k^* is defined by $f'(k^*) = \rho$ (see [2.22]) and k_{GR} is defined by $f'(k_{GR}) = n$, and our assumption that $\rho - n - (1 - \theta)g > 0$ simplifies to $\rho > n$. Since k^* is less than k_{GR}, an increase in saving starting at $k = k^*$ would cause consumption per worker to eventually rise above its previous level and remain there (see Figure 1.5). But, because households value present consumption more than future consumption, the benefit of the eventual permanent increase in consumption is bounded. At some point—specifically, when k exceeds k^*—the tradeoff between the temporary short-term sacrifice and the permanent long-term gain is sufficiently unfavorable that accepting it reduces rather than raises lifetime utility. Thus k converges to a value below the golden-rule level. Because k^* is the optimal level of k for the economy to converge to, it is known as the *modified golden-rule* capital stock.

2.6 The Effects of a Fall in the Discount Rate

Consider a Ramsey–Cass–Koopmans economy that is on its balanced growth path, and suppose that there is a fall in ρ, the discount rate. Since ρ is the parameter governing households' preferences between current and future consumption, this change is the closest analogue in this model to a rise in the saving rate in the Solow model.

Qualitative Effects

Since the evolution of k is determined by technology rather than preferences, ρ enters the equation for $\dot{c}$ but not the one for $\dot{k}$. Thus only the $\dot{c} = 0$

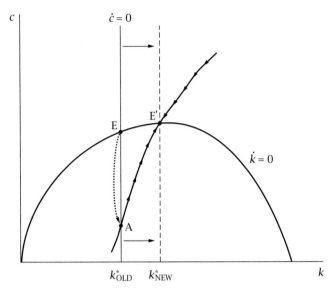

FIGURE 2.6   The effects of a fall in the discount rate

locus is affected. Recall equation (2.22): $\dot{c}(t)/c(t) = [f'(k(t))-\rho-\theta g]/\theta$. Thus a fall in ρ means that, for a given k, $\dot{c}/c$ is lower than before. Since $f''(k)$ is negative, the k needed for $\dot{c}$ to equal zero therefore rises. Thus the $\dot{c} = 0$ line shifts to the right. This is shown in Figure 2.6.

At the time of the change in ρ, the value of k—the *stock* of capital per unit of effective labor—is given by the history of the economy, and it cannot change discontinuously. In particular, k at the time of the change equals the k^* on the old balanced growth path. In contrast, c—the *rate* at which households are consuming—can jump at the time of the shock.

Given our analysis of the dynamics of the economy, it is clear what occurs: at the instant of the change, c jumps down so that the economy is on the new saddle path (Point A in Figure 2.6).[12] Thereafter, c and k rise gradually to their new balanced-growth-path values; these are higher than their values on the original balanced growth path.

Thus the effects of a fall in the discount rate are similar to the effects of a rise in the saving rate in the Solow model with a capital stock below the golden-rule level. In both cases, k rises gradually to a new higher level, and in both c initially falls but then rises to a level above the one it started at. Thus, just as with a permanent rise in the saving rate in the Solow model, the permanent fall in the discount rate produces temporary increases in the growth rates of capital per worker and output per worker. The only

---

[12]We are assuming that the change is unexpected. Thus the discontinuous change in c does not imply that households are not optimizing. Their original behavior is optimal given their beliefs (which includes the belief that ρ will not change); the fall in c is the optimal response to the new information that ρ is lower. (See Section 2.7 and Problems 2.9 and 2.10 for examples of how to analyze anticipated changes.)

difference between the two experiments is that, in the case of the fall in ρ, in general the fraction of output that is saved is not constant during the adjustment process.

The Rate of Adjustment and the Slope of the Saddle Path

Equations (2.22) and (2.23) describe $\dot{c}(t)$ and $\dot{k}(t)$ as functions of $k(t)$ and $c(t)$. A fruitful way to analyze their quantitative implications for the dynamics of the economy is to replace these nonlinear equations with linear approximations around the balanced growth path. Thus we begin by taking first-order Taylor approximations to (2.22) and (2.23) around $k = k^*$, $c = c^*$. That is, we write

$$\dot{c} \simeq \frac{\partial \dot{c}}{\partial k}[k - k^*] + \frac{\partial \dot{c}}{\partial c}[c - c^*], \qquad (2.24)$$

$$\dot{k} \simeq \frac{\partial \dot{k}}{\partial k}[k - k^*] + \frac{\partial \dot{k}}{\partial c}[c - c^*], \qquad (2.25)$$

where $\partial \dot{c}/\partial k$, $\partial \dot{c}/\partial c$, $\partial \dot{k}/\partial k$, and $\partial \dot{k}/\partial c$ are all evaluated at $k = k^*$, $c = c^*$. Our strategy will be to treat (2.24) and (2.25) as exact and analyze the dynamics of the resulting system.[13]

Since c^* is a constant, $\dot{c}$ equals $c \div c^*$ (that is, $dc(t)/dt$ equals $d[c(t) - c^*]/dt$). Similarly, $\dot{k}$ equals $k \div k^*$. We can therefore rewrite (2.24) and (2.25) as

$$c \div c^* \simeq \frac{\partial \dot{c}}{\partial k}[k - k^*] + \frac{\partial \dot{c}}{\partial c}[c - c^*], \qquad (2.26)$$

$$k \div k^* \simeq \frac{\partial \dot{k}}{\partial K}[k - k^*] + \frac{\partial \dot{k}}{\partial c}[c - c^*]. \qquad (2.27)$$

(Again, the derivatives are all evaluated at $k = k^*$, $c = c^*$.) Using (2.22) and (2.23) to compute these derivatives yields

$$c \div c^* \simeq \frac{f''(k^*)c^*}{\theta}[k - k^*], \qquad (2.28)$$

$$k \div k^* \simeq [f'(k^*) - (n + g)][k - k^*] - [c - c^*]$$

$$= [(\rho + \theta g) - (n + g)][k - k^*] - [c - c^*] \qquad (2.29)$$

$$= \beta[k - k^*] - [c - c^*],$$

---

[13]For a more formal introduction to the analysis of systems of differential equations (such as [2.24]-[2.25]), see Simon and Blume (1994, Chapter 25).

where the second line of (2.29) uses the fact that (2.22) implies that $f'(k^*) = \rho + \theta g$ and the third line uses the definition of β as $\rho - n - (1 - \theta)g$. Dividing both sides of (2.28) by $c - c^*$ and both sides of (2.29) by $k - k^*$ yields expressions for the growth rates of $c - c^*$ and $k - k^*$:

$$\frac{c \overset{\cdot}{-} c^*}{c - c^*} \simeq \frac{f''(k^*)c^*}{\theta} \frac{k - k^*}{c - c^*}, \tag{2.30}$$

$$\frac{k \overset{\cdot}{-} k^*}{k - k^*} \simeq \beta - \frac{c - c^*}{k - k^*}. \tag{2.31}$$

Equations (2.30) and (2.31) imply that the growth rates of $c - c^*$ and $k - k^*$ depend only on the ratio of $c - c^*$ to $k - k^*$. Given this, consider what happens if the values of c and k are such that $c - c^*$ and $k - k^*$ are falling at the same rate (that is, if they imply $(c \overset{\cdot}{-} c^*)/(c - c^*) = (k \overset{\cdot}{-} k^*)/(k - k^*)$). This implies that the ratio of $c - c^*$ to $k - k^*$ is not changing, and thus that their growth rates are also not changing. Thus $c - c^*$ and $k - k^*$ continue to fall at equal rates. In terms of the diagram, from a point where $c - c^*$ and $k - k^*$ are falling at equal rates, the economy moves along a straight line to (k^*, c^*), with the distance from (k^*, c^*) falling at a constant rate.

Let μ denote $(c \overset{\cdot}{-} c^*)/(c - c^*)$. Equation (2.30) implies

$$\frac{c - c^*}{k - k^*} = \frac{f''(k^*)c^*}{\theta} \frac{1}{\mu}. \tag{2.32}$$

From (2.31), the condition that $(k \overset{\cdot}{-} k^*)/(k - k^*)$ equal $(c \overset{\cdot}{-} c^*)/(c - c^*)$ is thus

$$\mu = \beta - \frac{f''(k^*)c^*}{\theta} \frac{1}{\mu}, \tag{2.33}$$

or

$$\mu^2 - \beta\mu + \frac{f''(k^*)c^*}{\theta} = 0. \tag{2.34}$$

This is a quadratic equation in μ. The solutions are

$$\mu = \frac{\beta \pm [\beta^2 - 4f''(k^*)c^*/\theta]^{1/2}}{2}. \tag{2.35}$$

Let μ_1 and μ_2 denote these two values of μ.

If μ is positive, then $c(t) - c^*$ and $k(t) - k^*$ are growing; that is, instead of moving along a straight line toward (k^*, c^*), the economy is moving on a straight line away from (k^*, c^*). Thus if the economy is to converge to (k^*, c^*), μ must be negative. Inspection of (2.35) shows that only one of the μ_i's, namely $\{\beta - [\beta^2 - 4f''(k^*)c^*/\theta]^{1/2}\}/2$, is negative. Let μ_1 denote this value of μ. Equation (2.32) (with $\mu = \mu_1$) then tells us how $c - c^*$ must be related to $k - k^*$ for both to be falling at rate μ_1.

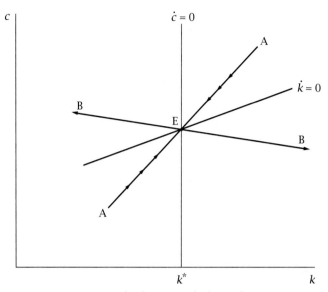

FIGURE 2.7   The linearized phase diagram

Figure 2.7 shows the line along which the economy converges smoothly to (k^*,c^*) (the saddle path AA in the figure). It also shows the line along which the economy moves directly away from (k^*,c^*) (the line BB). If the initial values of $c(0)$ and $k(0)$ lay along this line, (2.30) and (2.31) would imply that $c - c^*$ and $k - k^*$ would grow steadily at rate μ_2.[14] Since $f''(\bullet)$ is negative, (2.32) implies that the relation between $c - c^*$ and $k - k^*$ has the opposite sign from μ. Thus the saddle path AA is positively sloped, and the BB line is negatively sloped.

Thus if we linearize the equations for $\dot{c}$ and $\dot{k}$, we can characterize the dynamics of the economy in terms of the model's parameters. At time 0, c must jump to $c^* + [f''(k^*)c^*/(\theta\mu_1)](k - k^*)$. Thereafter, c and k converge to their balanced-growth-path values at rate μ_1; that is, $k(t) = k^* + e^{\mu_1 t}[k(0) - k^*]$ and $c(t) = c^* + e^{\mu_1 t}[c(0) - c^*]$.[15]

---

[14] Of course, it is not possible for the initial value of (k,c) to lie along the BB line. As we saw in Section 2.3, if it did, either k would eventually become negative or households would accumulate infinite wealth.

[15] This analysis can be used to characterize the path of k and c that would be implied by (2.28) and (2.29) if the initial value of (k, c) were on neither the AA nor BB lines. (Again, this could not in fact occur in equilibrium; see n. 14.) Consider a point $(k - k^*, c - c^*)$ that can be written as a sum of a point on AA and a point on BB. That is, suppose we can find a k_a and a k_b such that

$$(k(0) - k^*, c(0) - c^*) = \left(k_a - k^*, \frac{f''(k^*)c^*}{\theta\mu_1}(k_a - k^*)\right) + \left(k_b - k^*, \frac{f''(k^*)c^*}{\theta\mu_2}(k_b - k^*)\right)$$

$$\equiv (k_a - k^*, c_a - c^*) + (k_b - k^*, c_b - c^*).$$

(continued)

The Speed of Adjustment

To understand the implications of (2.35) for the speed of convergence to the balanced growth path, consider our usual example of Cobb–Douglas production, $f(k) = k^\alpha$. This implies $f''(k^*) = \alpha(\alpha-1)k^{*\alpha-2} = [(\alpha-1)/\alpha]r^{*2}/f(k^*)$, where $r^* = \alpha k^{*\alpha-1}$ is the real interest rate on the balanced growth path. Thus in this case we can write the expression for μ_1 as

$$\mu_1 = \frac{1}{2}\left\{\beta - \left[\beta^2 + \frac{4}{\theta}\frac{1-\alpha}{\alpha}r^{*2}(1-s^*)\right]^{1/2}\right\}, \tag{2.36}$$

where $s^* = 1 - [c^*/f(k^*)]$ is the saving rate on the balanced growth path.

On the balanced growth path, saving is $(n+g)k^*$; thus $s^* = (n+g)k^*/k^{*\alpha} = \alpha(n+g)/r^*$. Finally, (2.19) implies $r^* = \rho+\theta g$. Substituting these facts into (2.36) yields

$$\mu_1 = \frac{1}{2}\left\{\beta - \left[\beta^2 + \frac{4}{\theta}\frac{1-\alpha}{\alpha}(\rho+\theta g)(\rho + \theta g - \alpha(n+g))\right]^{1/2}\right\}. \tag{2.37}$$

Equation (2.37) expresses the rate of adjustment in terms of the underlying parameters of the model.

To get a feel for the magnitudes involved, suppose $\alpha = 1/3$, $\rho = 4\%$, $n = 2\%$, $g = 1\%$, and $\theta = 1$. Using the facts above, these parameter values imply $r^* = 5\%$ and $s^* = 20\%$; in addition, the definition of β as $\rho - n - (1-\theta)g$ implies $\beta = 2\%$. Equation (2.36) or (2.37) then implies $\mu_1 \simeq -5.4\%$. Thus adjustment is quite rapid in this case; for comparison, the Solow model with the same values of α, n, and g (and as here, no depreciation) implies an adjustment speed of 2% per year (see equation [1.26]). The reason for the difference is that in this example, the saving rate is greater than s^* when k is less than k^*

The first point on the right-hand side is on AA and the second is on BB (see [2.32]). Because $(k(0) - k^*, c(0) - c^*)$ is the sum of $(k_a - k^*, c_a - c^*)$ and $(k_b - k^*, c_b - c^*)$, and because (2.28) and (2.29) are linear, the economy's dynamics starting at $(k(0) - k^*, c(0) - c^*)$ are the sum of what they would be starting at $(k_a - k^*, c_a - c^*)$ and what they would be starting at $(k_b - k^*, c_b - c^*)$. Thus,

$$k(t) - k^* = e^{\mu_1 t}(k_a - k^*) + e^{\mu_2 t}(k_b - k^*),$$

and similarly for $c(t) - c^*$. Because μ_1 is negative and μ_2 positive, the first term goes to zero and the second term diverges. Thus asymptotically $k(t) - k^*$ and $c(t) - c^*$ grow at rate μ_2, and the economy approaches the BB line. The only way to avoid this outcome is for $k_b - k^*$ to be zero (which implies that $c_b - c^*$ is also zero)—that is, for the economy to begin on the saddle path AA.

Finally, note that we can write any point in $(k - k^*, c - c^*)$ space as a sum of a point on AA and a point on BB: the first equation above can be written as two linearly independent equations, one for $k(0) - k^*$ and one for $c(0) - c^*$, in two unknowns, $k_a - k^*$ and $k_b - k^*$. Thus this approach can be used to characterize the dynamics implied by (2.28) and (2.29) for any assumed initial values of k and c.

and less than s^* when k is greater than k^*; in the Solow model, in contrast, s is constant by assumption.

2.7 The Effects of Government Purchases

Thus far, we have left government out of our model. Yet modern economies devote their resources not just to investment and private consumption but also to public uses. In the United States, for example, about 20 percent of total output is purchased by the government; in many other countries the figure is considerably higher. It is thus natural to extend our model to include a government sector.

Adding Government to the Model

Assume that the government buys output at rate $G(t)$ per unit of effective labor per unit time. Government purchases are assumed not to affect utility from private consumption; this can occur either if the government devotes the goods to some activity that does not affect utility at all, or if utility equals the sum of utility from private consumption and utility from government-provided goods. Similarly, the purchases are assumed not to affect future output; that is, they are devoted to public consumption rather than public investment. The purchases are financed by lump-sum taxes of amount $G(t)$ per unit of effective labor per unit time; thus the government always runs a balanced budget. The next section discusses deficit finance.

Investment is now the difference between output and the sum of private consumption and government purchases. Thus the equation of motion for k, (2.23), becomes

$$\dot{k}(t) = f(k(t)) - c(t) - G(t) - (n + g)k(t). \tag{2.38}$$

A higher value of G shifts the $\dot{k} = 0$ locus down: the more goods that are purchased by the government, the fewer that can be purchased privately if k is to be held constant.

By assumption, households' preferences ([2.1]–[2.2] or [2.14]) are unchanged. Since the Euler equation ([2.19] or [2.22]) is derived from households' preferences without imposing their lifetime budget constraint, this condition continues to hold as before. The taxes that finance the government's purchases affect households' budget constraint, however. Specifically, (2.7) becomes

$$\int_{t=0}^{\infty} e^{-R(t)} c(t) e^{(n+g)t} \, dt \leq k(0) + \int_{t=0}^{\infty} e^{-R(t)} [w(t) - G(t)] e^{(n+g)t} \, dt. \tag{2.39}$$

Reasoning parallel to that used before shows that this implies the same expression as before for the limiting behavior of k (equation [2.12]).

The Effects of Permanent and Temporary Changes in Government Purchases

To see the implications of the model, suppose that the economy is on a balanced growth path with $G(t)$ constant at some level G_L, and that there is an unexpected, permanent increase in G to G_H. From (2.38), the $\dot{k} = 0$ locus shifts down by the amount of the increase in G. Since government purchases do not affect the Euler equation, the $\dot{c} = 0$ locus is unaffected. This is shown in Figure 2.8.

We know that in response to such a change, c must jump so that the economy is on its new saddle path. If not, then as before, either capital would become negative at some point or households would accumulate infinite wealth. In this case, the adjustment takes a simple form: c falls by the amount of the increase in G, and the economy is immediately on its new balanced growth path. Intuitively, the permanent increases in government purchases and taxes reduce households' lifetime wealth. Thus consumption falls immediately, and the capital stock and the real interest rate are unaffected.

A more interesting case is provided by an unanticipated increase in G that is expected to be temporary; for simplicity, assume that the terminal date is known with certainty. In this case, c does not fall by the full amount of the increase in G, $G_H - G_L$. To see this, note that if it did, consumption would jump up discontinuously at the time that government purchases re-

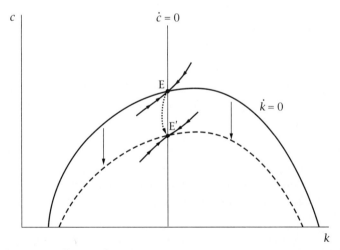

FIGURE 2.8   The effects of a permanent increase in government purchases

turned to G_L; thus marginal utility would fall discontinuously. But since the return of G to G_L is anticipated, the discontinuity in marginal utility would also be anticipated, which cannot be optimal for households.

During the period of time that government purchases are high, $\dot{k}$ is determined by the capital-accumulation equation, (2.38), with $G = G_H$; after G returns to G_L, it is governed by (2.38) with $G = G_L$. The Euler equation, (2.22), determines the dynamics of c throughout, and c cannot change discontinuously at the time that G returns to G_L. These facts determine what happens at the time of the increase in G: c must jump to the value such that the dynamics implied by (2.38) with $G = G_H$ (and by [2.22]) bring the economy to the old saddle path at the time that G returns to its initial level. Thereafter, the economy moves along that saddle path to the old balanced growth path.[16]

This is depicted in Figure 2.9. Panel (a) shows a case where the increase in G is relatively long-lasting. In this case c falls by most of the amount of the increase in G. As the time of the return of G to G_L approaches, however, households increase their consumption and decrease their capital holdings in anticipation of the fall in G.

Since $r = f'(k)$, we can deduce the behavior of r from the behavior of k. Thus r rises gradually during the period that government spending is high and then slowly returns to its initial level. This is shown in Panel (b); t_0 denotes the time of the increase in G, and t_1 the time of its return to its initial value.

Finally, Panel (c) shows the case of a short-lived rise in G. Here households change their consumption relatively little, choosing instead to pay for most of the temporarily higher taxes out of their savings. Because government purchases are high for only a short period, the effects on the capital stock and the real interest rate are small.

Empirical Application: Wars and Real Interest Rates

This analysis suggests that temporarily high government purchases cause real interest rates to rise, whereas permanently high purchases do not. Intuitively, when the government's purchases are high only temporarily, households expect their consumption to be greater in the future than it is in the present. To make them willing to accept this, the real interest rate must be high. When the government's purchases are permanently high, on the other hand, households' current consumption is low, and they expect it to remain low. Thus in this case, no movement in real interest rates is needed for households to accept their current low consumption.

---

[16]As in the example in the previous section, because the initial change in G is unexpected, the discontinuities in consumption and marginal utility at that point do not mean that households are not behaving optimally. See n. 12.

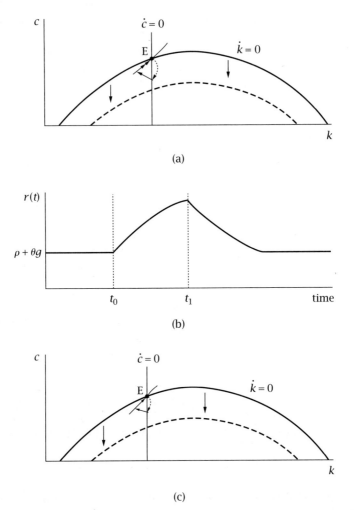

FIGURE 2.9   The effects of a temporary increase in government purchases

A natural example of a period of temporarily high government purchases is a war. Thus our analysis predicts that real interest rates are high during wars. Barro (1987) tests this prediction by examining military spending and interest rates in the United Kingdom from 1729 to 1918. The most signif-icant complication he faces is that, instead of having data on short-term real interest rates, he has data only on long-term nominal interest rates. Long-term interest rates should be, loosely speaking, a weighted average of expected short-term interest rates.[17] Thus, since our analysis implies that temporary increases in government purchases raise the short-term rate over an extended period, it also implies that they raise the long-term rate. Simi-

---

[17]See Section 9.3.

FIGURE 2.10 Temporary military spending and the long-term interest rate in the United Kingdom (from Barro, 1987; used with permission)

larly, since the analysis implies that permanent increases never change the short-term rate, it predicts that they do not affect the long-term rate. In addition, the real interest rate equals the nominal rate minus expected inflation; thus the nominal rate should be corrected for changes in expected inflation. Barro does not find any evidence, however, of systematic changes in expected inflation in his sample period; thus the data are at least consistent with the view that movements in nominal rates represent changes in real rates.

Figure 2.10 plots British military spending as a share of GNP (relative to the mean of this series for the full sample) and the long-term interest rate. The spikes in the military spending series correspond to wars; for example, the spike around 1760 reflects the Seven Years' War, and the spike around 1780 corresponds to the American Revolution. The figure suggests that the interest rate is indeed higher during periods of temporarily high government purchases.

To test this formally, Barro estimates a process for the military purchases series and uses it to construct estimates of the temporary component of military spending. Not surprisingly in light of the figure, the estimated temporary component differs little from the raw series.[18] Barro then regresses the long-term interest rate on this estimate of temporary military

---

[18]Since there is little permanent variation in military spending, the data cannot be used to investigate the effects of permanent changes in government purchases on interest rates.

spending. Because the residuals are serially corrected, he includes a first-order serial correlation correction. The results are

$$R_t = \underset{(0.27)}{3.54} + \underset{(0.7)}{2.6}\, \tilde{G}_t, \qquad \lambda = \underset{(0.03)}{0.91}$$

$$R^2 = 0.89, \qquad \text{s.e.e.} = 0.248, \qquad \text{D.W.} = 2.1. \tag{2.40}$$

R_t is the long-term nominal interest rate, $\tilde{G}_t$ is the estimated value of temporary military spending as a fraction of GNP, λ is the first-order autoregressive parameter of the residual, and the numbers in parentheses are standard errors. Thus there is a statistically significant link between temporary military spending and interest rates. The results are even stronger when World War I is excluded: stopping the sample period in 1914 raises the coefficient on $\tilde{G}_t$ to 6.1 (and the standard error to 1.3). Barro argues that the comparatively small rise in the interest rate given the tremendous rise in military spending in World War I may have occurred because the government imposed price controls and used a variety of nonmarket means of allocating resources. If this is right, the results for the shorter sample may provide a better estimate of the impact of government purchases on interest rates in a market economy.

Thus the evidence from the United Kingdom supports the predictions of the theory. The success of the theory is not universal, however. In particular, for the United States real interest rates appear to have been, if anything, generally lower during wars than in other periods (Barro, 1993, pp. 321–322). The reasons for this anomalous behavior are not well understood. Thus the theory does not provide a full account of how real interest rates respond to changes in government purchases.

2.8 Bond and Tax Finance

So far we have assumed that government spending is financed entirely with current taxes. But in fact governments rely not only on taxes but also on bonds as a means of finance. This section therefore examines the choice between tax and bond finance.

The Government's Budget Constraint

The government's budget constraint is that the present value of its purchases must be less than or equal to its initial wealth plus the present value of its tax revenues. Let $G(t)$ and $T(t)$ denote government purchases and taxes per unit of effective labor at time t; thus total purchases at t are $G(t)e^{(n+g)t}A(0)L(0)$, and total taxes are $T(t)e^{(n+g)t}A(0)L(0)$. In addition, let

$b(t)$ denote the outstanding stock of government debt per unit of effective labor at t.

We assume that the government satisfies its budget constraint with equality. If it did not, its wealth would be growing forever relative to the economy, which does not seem realistic.[19] With this assumption, the government's budget constraint is

$$\int_{t=0}^{\infty} e^{-R(t)}[G(t)e^{(n+g)t}A(0)L(0)]dt$$

$$= -b(0)A(0)L(0) + \int_{t=0}^{\infty} e^{-R(t)}[T(t)e^{(n+g)t}A(0)L(0)]dt. \tag{2.41}$$

Note that because $b(0)$ represents debt rather than wealth, it enters negatively into the budget constraint. Dividing both sides of (2.41) by $A(0)L(0)$ yields

$$\int_{t=0}^{\infty} e^{-R(t)}G(t)e^{(n+g)t} dt = -b(0) + \int_{t=0}^{\infty} e^{-R(t)}T(t)e^{(n+g)t} dt. \tag{2.42}$$

Just as the household's budget constraint, when it is satisfied with equality, implies $\lim_{s\to\infty} e^{-R(s)}e^{(n+g)s}k(s) = 0$ (see equation [2.12]), one can show that (2.42) implies

$$\lim_{s\to\infty} e^{-R(s)}e^{(n+g)s}b(s) = 0. \tag{2.43}$$

This condition states that the value of the government's outstanding debt, in units of time-zero output, must approach zero. We know that on the balanced growth path, r is equal to $\rho + \theta g$, which is greater than $n + g$; thus eventually $e^{-R(s)}e^{(n+g)s}$ is falling. Equation (2.43) therefore permits the government to follow policies that cause debt per unit of effective labor, $b(s)$, to converge to some positive level. But it rules out policies that cause $b(s)$ to grow forever at too rapid a rate.

Implications for the Economy

When there are taxes, the household's budget constraint is that the present value of consumption must be less than or equal to initial wealth plus the present value of lifetime after-tax labor income; the initial wealth now includes both capital and bond holdings. Stated in terms of quantities per unit of effective labor (analogously to equation [2.7] for the case without taxes),

---

[19]Moreover, if the government attempts such a policy, an equilibrium may not exist if its debt is denominated in real terms. See, for example, Aiyagari and Gertler (1985) and Woodford (1994).

this condition is

$$\int_{t=0}^{\infty} e^{-R(t)} c(t) e^{(n+g)t}\, dt$$

(2.44)

$$\le k(0) + b(0) + \int_{t=0}^{\infty} e^{-R(t)} [w(t) - T(t)] e^{(n+g)t}\, dt.$$

The integral on the right-hand side of (2.44) equals the present value of labor income minus the present value of taxes. The government budget constraint, (2.42), implies that the present value of taxes equals initial debt, $b(0)$, plus the present value of government spending, $\int_{t=0}^{\infty} e^{-R(t)} G(t) e^{(n+g)t}\, dt$. Thus we can rewrite (2.44) as

$$\int_{t=0}^{\infty} e^{-R(t)} c(t) e^{(n+g)t}\, dt$$

(2.45)

$$\le k(0) + \int_{t=0}^{\infty} e^{-R(t)} w(t) e^{(n+g)t}\, dt - \int_{t=0}^{\infty} e^{-R(t)} G(t) e^{(n+g)t}\, dt.$$

Equation (2.45) shows that we can express households' budget constraint in terms of the present value of government purchases without reference to the division of the financing of those purchases at any point in time between taxes and bonds. In addition, neither government purchases nor taxes enter households' preferences (see equation [2.14]), and it is only purchases that affect the dynamics of the capital stock (see equation [2.38]).

Thus we have a key result: only the path of government purchases, and not the path of the taxes that finance those purchases, affects the economy. For example, the impact of the temporary increase in government purchases considered in the previous section is the same if those purchases are financed by bond issues paid off by taxes levied at some point in the future rather than by current taxes.

2.9   The Ricardian Equivalence Debate

Overview

The result of the irrelevance of the government's financing decisions is the famous *Ricardian equivalence* between debt and taxes.[20] The logic of the result is simple. To see it clearly, think of the government giving some amount B of bonds to each household at some date t_1 and planning to re-

---

[20]The name comes from the fact that this idea appears to have first been proposed (though ultimately rejected) by David Ricardo; see Buchanan (1976).

tire this debt at a later date t_2; this requires that each household be taxed amount $e^{R(t_2)-R(t_1)}B$ at t_2. Such a policy has two effects on the representative household. First, the household has acquired an asset—the bond—that has present value as of t_1 of B. Second, it has acquired a liability—the future tax obligation—that also has present value as of t_1 of B. Thus the bond does not represent "net wealth" to the household, and it therefore does not affect the household's consumption behavior. In effect, the household simply saves the bond and the interest that the bond is accumulating until t_2, at which point it uses the bond and the interest to pay the taxes the government is levying to retire the bond. This conclusion follows solely from the household's and the government's budget constraints, and not from any other features of the model.

Traditional economic models, and many informal discussions, assume that a shift from tax to bond finance increases consumption. Traditional analyses of consumption, for example, often model consumption as depending only on current disposable income, $Y - T$. The Ricardian and traditional views of consumption have very different implications for important policy issues. For example, the United States has run large budget deficits since the early 1980s. The traditional view implies that these deficits are increasing consumption, and thus reducing capital accumulation and growth. But the Ricardian view implies that they are having no effect on consumption or capital accumulation. To give another example, governments often cut taxes during recessions to increase consumption spending. But if Ricardian equivalence holds, these efforts are futile. Thus it is important to determine which view is closer to the truth.

There are of course many reasons that Ricardian equivalence may not hold exactly. The relevant question, however, is not whether it is exactly correct, but whether there are large departures from it.

The Entry of New Households into the Economy

One obvious reason that Ricardian equivalence is likely not to be exactly correct is that there is turnover in the population. When new individuals are entering the economy, some of the future tax burden associated with a bond issue is borne by individuals who are not alive when the bond is issued. Because of this, the bond represents net wealth to the individuals who are living at the time of the bond issue, and it thus affects their behavior. This possibility is illustrated by the Diamond overlapping-generations model developed in the second half of this chapter.

There are two difficulties with this objection to Ricardian equivalence. First, a series of individuals with finite lifetimes may behave as if they are a single household. In particular, if individuals care about the welfare of their descendants and if that concern is sufficiently strong that they make positive bequests, the government's financing decisions may again be irrelevant.

Again this result follows from the logic of budget constraints. Consider the example of a bond issue today repaid by a tax levied several generations in the future. It is possible for the consumption of all of the generations involved to remain unchanged. All that is needed is for each generation, beginning with the one alive at the time of the bond issue, to increase its bequest by the size of the bond issue plus the accumulated interest; the generation living at the time of the tax increase can then use those funds to pay the tax levied to retire the bond.

Thus individuals can keep their consumption paths unchanged in response to the bond issue. But this leaves the question of whether they do. The bond issue does provide each generation involved (other than the last) with some possibilities it did not have before. Because government spending is assumed unchanged, the bond issue is associated with a cut in current taxes. The bond issue therefore increases the lifetime resources available to the individuals then alive. *But the fact that the individuals are already planning to leave positive bequests means that they are at an interior optimum in choosing between their own consumption and that of their descendants;* thus they do not change their behavior. Only if the requirement that bequests cannot be negative is a binding constraint—that is, only if bequests are zero—does the bond issue affect consumption. Since we have assumed that this is not the case, the individuals do not change their consumption; instead they pass the bond and the accumulated interest on to the next generation. Those individuals, for the same reason, do the same, and the process continues until the generation that has to retire the debt uses its additional inheritance to do so.

The result that intergenerational links might cause a series of individuals with finite lifetimes to behave as if they are a household with an infinite horizon is due to Barro (1974). It was this insight that started the debate on Ricardian equivalence, and it has led to a large literature on the reasons for bequests and transfers among generations, their extent, and their implications for Ricardian equivalence and many other issues.[21]

The second difficulty with the argument that finite lifetimes cause Ricardian equivalence to fail is more prosaic: as a practical matter, lifetimes are long enough that if the only reason that governments' financing decisions matter is because lifetimes are finite, Ricardian equivalence remains a good approximation (Poterba and Summers, 1987). There are two reasons for this. First, for realistic cases, large parts of the present value of the taxes associated with bond issues are levied during the lifetimes of the individuals alive at the time of the issue. For example, Poterba and Summers calculate that most of the burden of retiring the United States's World War II debt was borne by people who were already of working age at the time of the war;

---

[21] For a few examples, see Bernheim, Shleifer, and Summers (1985); Bernheim and Bagwell (1988); Bernheim (1991); and Altonji, Hayashi, and Kotlikoff (1992). See Bernheim (1987a) for a survey.

and they find that similar results hold for other wartime debt issues. Second, the fact that lifetimes are long means that an increase in wealth has only a modest impact on current consumption. For example, if individuals spread out the spending of an unexpected wealth increase equally over the remainder of their lives, an individual with 30 years left to live increases consumption spending in response to a one-dollar increase in wealth only by about three cents.[22]

Thus it appears that if Ricardian equivalence fails in a quantitatively important way, it must be for some reason other than an absence of intergenerational links. Three possibilities have received the most attention: liquidity constraints, non-lump-sum taxes, and rule-of-thumb consumption behavior.

Liquidity Constraints

The first possibility is that households may face limits on their ability to borrow—that is, they may face *liquidity constraints*. When the government issues a bond to a household to be repaid by higher taxes on that household at some later date, it is in effect borrowing on the household's behalf. If, as we have been assuming, the household already had the option of borrowing at the same interest rate as the government, the policy has no effect on its opportunities and thus no effect on its behavior. But if it cannot borrow and lend freely at the government's interest rate, the bond issue may matter. In particular, suppose the household faces a higher interest rate for borrowing than the government does. If the household would borrow at the government interest rate and increase its current consumption if that were possible, it will respond to the government's borrowing on its behalf by increasing its consumption (see, for example, Tobin, 1980, and Hubbard and Judd, 1986).

Again, there are two difficulties with this potential source of failure of Ricardian equivalence. First, empirically, although surely households do not face the same terms for borrowing as the government does, the evidence is not clear concerning how much these constraints matter for aggregate consumption.[23]

Second, liquidity constraints are not exogenously given. Instead—as a huge literature on credit markets emphasizes—they reflect calculations by potential lenders of borrowers' likelihood of repaying their loans. When the government issues bonds today to be repaid by future taxes, households' future liabilities are increased. If lenders do not change the amounts and terms on which they are willing to lend, the chances that their loans will

---

[22]This of course is not exactly what an optimizing individual would do; see, for example, Problem 2.4.

[23]Some examples of studies of liquidity constraints are Hall and Mishkin (1982); Zeldes (1989); Runkle (1991); Flavin (1992); and Shea (1995).

be repaid therefore fall. Rational lenders therefore respond to the bond issue by reducing the amounts they lend. This mitigates the impact of the bond issue on current consumption. In fact, there are natural cases in which the amount that households can borrow falls one-for-one with government bond issues, so that Ricardian equivalence holds even in the presence of liquidity constraints (Hayashi, 1985; Yotsuzuka, 1987). Thus, determining the implications of liquidity constraints for Ricardian equivalence requires not only investigating the extent of those constraints, but also understanding their sources and how they are affected by bond issues.

Non-Lump-Sum Taxes

The second potentially important reason for failure of Ricardian equivalence is that taxes are not lump-sum; instead, they are a function of income. Consider our standard example of a bond issue today to be paid off by a tax increase in the future. Even when taxes are a function of income, this policy has no effect on the *expected* present value of the household's lifetime after-tax income. But, since the tax liability is large if future income is high and low if future income is low, the policy reduces the household's uncertainty about its lifetime resources. Under plausible conditions, the household responds to this change by increasing its current consumption, and the response may be quantitatively important (Barsky, Mankiw, and Zeldes, 1986; see also Problem 2.12 and Section 7.6).

   In addition, the fact that taxes are not lump-sum may interact with liquidity constraints. When a borrower fails to repay a loan, it is usually because his or her income has turned out to be low. But, if taxes are a function of income, this is precisely the case when the borrower's share of the tax liability associated with a bond issue is small. Thus a bond issue is likely to have a much smaller effect on the borrower's probability of repaying a loan when taxes are a function of income than when they are lump-sum. As a result, bond issues may have relatively little impact on the amounts that households can borrow. Thus non-lump-sum taxes and liquidity constraints together may cause large departures from Ricardian equivalence (Bernheim, 1987b).[24]

---

[24]The fact that taxes are not lump-sum may also affect Ricardian equivalence through its impact on government policy. A bond issue accompanied by a tax cut increases the revenue that the government must raise in the future, and therefore implies that future tax rates must be higher. Since non-lump-sum taxes involve distortions and since those distortions are greater at higher tax rates, this means that the marginal cost of obtaining revenue has increased. As a result, the optimal response by the government to a bond-financed tax cut generally involves a mix of higher taxes and lower government spending. The lower government spending increases households' lifetime resources, and therefore increases current consumption. (Bohn, 1992.)

Rule-of-Thumb Consumption Behavior

The third major reason that Ricardian equivalence may fail significantly is that individuals may not optimize fully over long horizons. The assumption of full rationality is a powerful modeling device, and it provides a good first approximation to how individuals respond to many changes. At the same time, it does not provide a perfect description of how people behave. There are well-documented cases in which individuals appear to depart consistently and systematically from the predictions of standard models of utility maximization, and in which those departures are quantitatively important (see, for example, Tversky and Kahneman, 1974, and Loewenstein and Thaler, 1989). This may be the case with choices between consumption and saving. The calculations involved are complex, the time periods are long, and there is a great deal of uncertainty that is difficult to quantify. So instead of attempting to be completely optimizing, individuals may follow "rules of thumb" in choosing their consumption that put a great deal of weight on current after-tax income. Both the macroeconomic and the microeconomic evidence offer some support for the view that individuals do in fact follow such rules of thumb.[25] If people do follow such rules, they increase their current consumption in response to a bond-financed tax cut even if their lifetime budget constraints are not affected. Thus rule-of-thumb consumption behavior provides an additional possible reason that Ricardian equivalence may fail.

Conclusion

What, in the end, should one make of the Ricardian equivalence debate? Economists take a wide range of positions on the issue. At one extreme is the view that Ricardian equivalence is a theoretical abstraction so unrelated to reality that it is of little interest. At the other extreme is the position that despite the many reasons for it not to hold exactly, it is nonetheless a good first approximation. A reasonable middle ground is that Ricardian equivalence is a useful theoretical baseline but not a useful empirical one. It is valuable as a theoretical baseline because it is so simple and logical. Specifically, any candidate explanation of why governments' choices between bonds and taxes affect consumption must spell out precisely how the assumptions underlying Ricardian equivalence fail and why those failures matter. Other models are more difficult to use as building blocks for more detailed analyses. For example, models of liquidity constraints are generally so complex

---

[25]See, for example, Campbell and Mankiw (1989a); Carroll and Summers (1991); and Shefrin and Thaler (1988). Of course, these findings could reflect features of individuals' optimization that are not yet fully understood.

to begin with that they are difficult to develop further. And models based on rule-of-thumb behavior involve sufficiently unconventional assumptions that it is often hard to know how they should be extended.

At the same time, it is likely that departures from Ricardian equivalence are quantitatively important. At the very least, the data do not clearly reject the importance of any of the potential sources of failure of Ricardian equivalence we have discussed. Thus despite its logical appeal, there does not appear to be a strong case for using Ricardian equivalence to gauge the likely effects of governments' financing decisions in practice.

Part B   The Diamond Model

2.10   Assumptions

We now turn to the Diamond overlapping-generations model. The central difference between the Diamond model and the Ramsey–Cass–Koopmans model is that there is turnover in the population: rather than there being a fixed number of infinitely-lived households, new individuals are continually being born, and old individuals are continually dying.

With turnover, it turns out to be simpler to assume that time is discrete rather than continuous; that is, the variables of the model are defined for $t = 0, 1, 2, \dots$ rather than for all values of $t \geq 0$. To further simplify the analysis, the model assumes that each individual lives for only two periods. It is the general assumption of turnover in the population, however, and not the specific assumptions of discrete time and two-period lifetimes, that is crucial to the model's results.[26]

L_t individuals are born in period t. As before, population grows at rate n; thus $L_t = (1 + n)L_{t-1}$. Since individuals live for two periods, at time t there are L_t individuals in the first period of their lives and $L_{t-1} = L_t/(1 + n)$ individuals in their second periods. Each individual supplies one unit of labor when he or she is young and divides the resulting labor income between first-period consumption and saving; in the second period, the individual simply consumes the saving and any interest he or she earns.

Let C_{1t} and C_{2t} denote the consumption in period t of young and old individuals. Thus the utility of an individual born at t, denoted U_t, depends

---

[26]See Problem 2.14 for a discrete-time version of the Solow model. Blanchard (1985) develops a tractable continuous-time model in which the extent of the departure from the infinite-horizon benchmark is governed by a continuous parameter. Weil (1989a) considers a variant of Blanchard's model where new households enter the economy but existing households do not leave. He shows that the arrival of new households is sufficient to generate most of the main results of the Diamond and Blanchard models. Finally, Auerbach and Kotlikoff (1987) use simulations to investigate a much more realistic overlapping-generations model.

on C_{1t} and C_{2t+1}. We again assume constant-relative-risk-aversion utility:

$$U_t = \frac{C_{1t}^{1-\theta}}{1-\theta} + \frac{1}{1+\rho}\frac{C_{2t+1}^{1-\theta}}{1-\theta}, \qquad \theta > 0, \quad \rho > -1. \tag{2.46}$$

As before, this functional form is needed for balanced growth. Because lifetimes are finite, we no longer have to assume $\rho > n + (1-\theta)g$ to ensure that lifetime utility does not diverge. If $\rho > 0$, individuals place greater weight on first-period than second-period consumption; if $\rho < 0$, the situation is reversed. The assumption $\rho > -1$ ensures that the weight on second-period consumption is positive.

Production is described by the same assumptions as before. There are many firms, each with the production function $Y_t = F(K_t, A_t L_t)$. $F(\bullet)$ again has constant returns to scale and satisfies the Inada conditions, and A again grows at exogenous rate g (so $A_t = [1 + g]A_{t-1}$). Markets are competitive; thus labor and capital earn their marginal products, and firms earn zero profits. As in the first part of the chapter, there is no depreciation. The real interest rate and the wage per unit of effective labor are therefore given as before by $r_t = f'(k_t)$ and $w_t = f(k_t) - k_t f'(k_t)$. Finally, there is some initial capital stock K_0 that is owned equally by all old individuals.

Thus, in period 0 the capital owned by the old and the labor supplied by the young are combined to produce output. Capital and labor are paid their marginal products. The old consume both their capital income and their existing wealth; they then die and exit the model. The young divide their labor income, $w_t A_t$, between consumption and saving. They carry their saving forward to the next period; thus the capital stock in period $t + 1$, K_{t+1}, equals the number of young individuals in period t, L_t, times each of these individuals' saving, $w_t A_t - C_{1t}$. This capital is combined with the labor supplied by the next generation of young individuals, and the process continues.

2.11 Household Behavior

The second-period consumption of an individual born at t is

$$C_{2t+1} = (1 + r_{t+1})(w_t A_t - C_{1t}). \tag{2.47}$$

Dividing both sides of this expression by $1 + r_{t+1}$ and bringing C_{1t} over to the left-hand side yields the budget constraint:

$$C_{1t} + \frac{1}{1 + r_{t+1}}C_{2t+1} = A_t w_t. \tag{2.48}$$

This condition states that the present value of lifetime consumption equals initial wealth (which is zero) plus the present value of lifetime labor income (which is $A_t w_t$).

The individual maximizes utility, (2.46), subject to the budget constraint, (2.48). The Lagrangian is

$$\mathcal{L} = \frac{C_{1t}^{1-\theta}}{1-\theta} + \frac{1}{1+\rho}\frac{C_{2t}^{1-\theta}}{1-\theta} + \lambda\left[A_t w_t - \left(C_{1t} + \frac{1}{1+r_{t+1}}C_{2t+1}\right)\right]. \quad (2.49)$$

The first-order conditions are

$$C_{1t}^{-\theta} = \lambda, \quad (2.50)$$

$$\frac{1}{1+\rho}C_{2t+1}^{-\theta} = \frac{1}{1+r_{t+1}}\lambda. \quad (2.51)$$

Substituting the first equation into the second yields

$$\frac{1}{1+\rho}C_{2t+1}^{-\theta} = \frac{1}{1+r_{t+1}}C_{1t}^{-\theta}, \quad (2.52)$$

or

$$\frac{C_{2t+1}}{C_{1t}} = \left[\frac{1+r_{t+1}}{1+\rho}\right]^{1/\theta}. \quad (2.53)$$

This expression is analogous to the Euler equation, (2.19), in our analysis of the infinite-horizon model. It implies that whether an individual's consumption is increasing or decreasing over time depends on whether the real rate of return is greater than or less than the discount rate. θ again determines how much individuals' consumption varies in response to differences between r and ρ. If (2.53) fails, the individual can rearrange consumption over his or her lifetime to raise total utility without changing the present value of the consumption stream.[27]

We can use (2.53) and the budget constraint, (2.48), to express C_{1t} in terms of labor income and the real interest rate. Specifically, multiplying both sides of (2.53) by C_{1t} and substituting into the budget constraint gives

$$C_{1t} + \frac{(1+r_{t+1})^{(1-\theta)/\theta}}{(1+\rho)^{1/\theta}}C_{1t} = A_t w_t. \quad (2.54)$$

This implies

---

[27] One can also derive (2.53) along the lines of the intuitive derivation of the Euler equation in (2.20)–(2.21). Specifically, imagine the individual decreasing C_{1t} by a small amount ΔC and then using the resulting additional saving and capital income to raise C_{2t} by $(1+r_{t+1})\Delta C$. This change has a utility cost of $C_{1t}^{-\theta}\Delta C$ and a utility benefit of $(1/(1+\rho))C_{2t}^{-\theta}(1+r_{t+1})\Delta C$. Equating the cost and benefit and rearranging yields (2.53).

$$C_{1t} = \frac{(1 + \rho)^{1/\theta}}{(1 + \rho)^{1/\theta} + (1 + r_{t+1})^{(1-\theta)/\theta}} A_t w_t. \tag{2.55}$$

Equation (2.55) shows that the interest rate determines the fraction of income the individual consumes in the first period. Letting $s(r)$ denote the fraction of income saved, (2.55) implies

$$s(r) = \frac{(1 + r)^{(1-\theta)/\theta}}{(1 + \rho)^{1/\theta} + (1 + r)^{(1-\theta)/\theta}}. \tag{2.56}$$

We can therefore rewrite (2.55) as

$$C_{1t} = [1 - s(r_{t+1})]A_t w_t. \tag{2.57}$$

Equation (2.56) implies that young individuals' saving is increasing in r if and only if $(1 + r)^{(1-\theta)/\theta}$ is increasing in r. The derivative of $(1 + r)^{(1-\theta)/\theta}$ with respect to r is $[(1 - \theta)/\theta](1 + r)^{(1-2\theta)/\theta}$. Thus s is increasing in r if θ is less than 1, and decreasing if θ is greater than 1. Intuitively, a rise in r has both an income and a substitution effect. The fact that the tradeoff between consumption in the two periods has become more favorable for second-period consumption tends to increase saving (the substitution effect), but the fact that a given amount of saving yields more second-period consumption tends to decrease saving (the income effect). When individuals are very willing to substitute consumption between the two periods to take advantage of rate-of-return incentives (that is, when θ is low), the substitution effect dominates. When individuals have strong preferences for similar levels of consumption in the two periods (that is, when θ is high), the income effect dominates. And in the special case of $\theta = 1$ (logarithmic utility), the two effects balance, and young individuals' saving rate is independent of r.

2.12   The Dynamics of the Economy

The Equation of Motion of k

As in the infinite-horizon model, we can aggregate individuals' behavior to characterize the dynamics of the economy. As described above, the capital stock in period $t + 1$ is the amount saved by young individuals in period t. Thus,

$$K_{t+1} = s(r_{t+1})L_t A_t w_t. \tag{2.58}$$

Note that because saving in period t depends on labor income in that period and on the return on capital that savers expect in the next period, it is w in period t and r in period $t + 1$ that enter the expression for the capital stock in period $t + 1$.

Dividing both sides of (2.58) by $L_{t+1}A_{t+1}$ gives us an expression for $K_{t+1}/A_{t+1}L_{t+1}$, capital per unit of effective labor:

$$k_{t+1} = \frac{1}{(1 + n)(1 + g)}s(r_{t+1})w_t. \tag{2.59}$$

We can then substitute for r_{t+1} and w_t to obtain

$$k_{t+1} = \frac{1}{(1 + n)(1 + g)}s(f'(k_{t+1}))[f(k_t) - k_t f'(k_t)]. \tag{2.60}$$

The Evolution of k

Equation (2.60) implicitly defines k_{t+1} as a function of k_t. (It defines k_{t+1} only implicitly because k_{t+1} appears on the right-hand side as well as the left-hand side.) It therefore determines how k evolves over time given its initial value. A value of k_t such that $k_{t+1} = k_t$ satisfies (2.60) is an equilibrium value of k: once k reaches that value, it remains there. We therefore want to know whether there is an equilibrium value (or values) of k, and whether k converges to such a value if it does not begin at one.

To answer these questions, we need to describe how k_{t+1} depends on k_t. Unfortunately, we can say relatively little about this for the general case. We therefore begin by considering the case of logarithmic utility and Cobb–Douglas production. With these assumptions, (2.60) takes a particularly simple form. We then briefly discuss what occurs when these assumptions are relaxed.

Logarithmic Utility and Cobb–Douglas Production

When θ is 1, the fraction of labor income saved is $1/(2 + \rho)$ (see equation [2.56]). And when production is Cobb–Douglas, $f(k)$ is k^α and w is $(1 - \alpha)k^\alpha$. Equation (2.60) therefore becomes

$$k_{t+1} = \frac{1}{(1 + n)(1 + g)}\frac{1}{2 + \rho}(1 - \alpha)k_t^\alpha \equiv Dk_t^\alpha. \tag{2.61}$$

Figure 2.11 shows k_{t+1} as a function of k_t. A point where the k_{t+1} function intersects the 45-degree line is a point where k_{t+1} equals k_t. In the special case we are considering, k_{t+1} equals k_t at $k_t = 0$; it rises above k_t when k_t is small; and it then crosses the 45-degree line and remains below. There is thus a unique equilibrium level of k (aside from $k = 0$), which is denoted k^*.

k^* is globally stable: wherever k starts (other than at 0), it converges to k^*. Suppose, for example, that the initial value of k, k_0, is greater than k^*. Because k_{t+1} is less than k_t when k_t exceeds k^*, k_1 is less than k_0. And

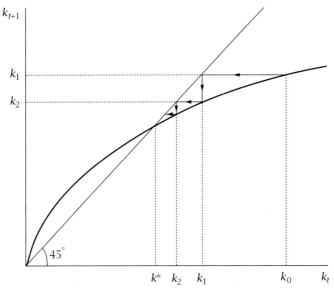

FIGURE 2.11   The dynamics of k

because k_0 exceeds k^* and k_{t+1} is increasing in k_t, k_1 is larger than k^*. Thus k_1 is between k^* and k_0: k moves part way toward k^*. This process is repeated each period, and so k converges smoothly to k^*. A similar analysis applies when k_0 is less than k^*.

These dynamics are shown by the arrows in Figure 2.11. Given k_0, the height of the k_{t+1} function shows k_1 on the vertical axis. To find k_2, we first need to find k_1 on the horizontal axis; to do this, we move across to the 45-degree line. The height of the k_{t+1} function at this point then shows k_2, and so on.

The properties of the economy once it has converged to its balanced growth path are the same as those of the Solow and Ramsey economies on their balanced growth paths: the saving rate is constant, output per worker is growing at rate g, the capital-output ratio is constant, and so on.

To see how the economy responds to shocks, consider our usual example of a fall in the discount rate, ρ, when the economy is initially on its balanced growth path. The fall in the discount rate causes the young to save a greater fraction of their labor income. Thus the k_{t+1} function shifts up. This is depicted in Figure 2.12. The upward shift of the k_{t+1} function increases k^*, the value of k on the balanced growth path. As the figure shows, k rises monotonically from the old value of k^* to the new one.

Thus the effects of a fall in the discount rate in the Diamond model in the case we are considering are similar to its effects in the Ramsey-Cass–Koopmans model, and to the effects of a rise in the saving rate in the Solow model. The change shifts the paths over time of output and capital per worker permanently up, but it leads only to temporary increases in the growth rates of these variables.

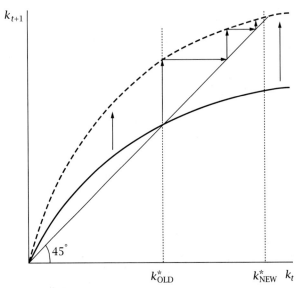

FIGURE 2.12   The effects of a fall in the discount rate

The Speed of Convergence

To analyze formally how the economy converges to its balanced growth path, once again we linearize the equation of motion around k^*. Equation (2.61), $k_{t+1} = Dk_t^\alpha$, implies

$$\left.\frac{dk_{t+1}}{dk_t}\right|_{k_t=k^*} = D\alpha k^{*(\alpha-1)}. \tag{2.62}$$

Equation (2.61) also implies that k^*, the value of k_t such that $k_{t+1} = k_t$, is given by

$$k^* = D^{1/(1-\alpha)}. \tag{2.63}$$

Substituting (2.63) into (2.62) shows that dk_{t+1}/dk_t evaluated at $k_t = k^*$ is simply α. Replacing (2.61) by its first-order Taylor approximation around $k = k^*$ therefore gives us

$$k_{t+1} \simeq k^* + \alpha(k_t - k^*). \tag{2.64}$$

Since we can write this as $k_{t+1} - k^* \simeq \alpha(k_t - k^*)$, (2.64) implies

$$k_t - k^* \simeq \alpha^t(k_0 - k^*). \tag{2.65}$$

k_t therefore converges smoothly to k^*.[28] If α is one-third, for example, k

---

[28]The properties of a system of form $x_{t+1} - x^* = \lambda(x_t - x^*)$ are determined by λ. If λ is between 0 and 1 (which is what happens in this model), the system converges smoothly. If λ is between -1 and 0, there are damped oscillations toward x^*: x alternates between

moves two-thirds of the way toward k^* each period. (Note, however, that each period in the model corresponds to half of a person's lifetime.)

Expression (2.65) differs from the corresponding expression in the Solow model (and in a discrete-time version of the Solow model—see Problem 2.14). The reason is that although the saving of the young is a constant fraction of their income and their income is a constant fraction of total income, the dissaving of the old is not a constant fraction of total income. The dissaving of the old as a fraction of output is $K_t/F(K_t, A_t L_t)$, or $k_t/f(k_t)$. The fact that there are diminishing returns to capital implies that this ratio is increasing in k. Since this term enters negatively into saving, it follows that total saving as a fraction of output is a decreasing function of k. Thus total saving as a fraction of output is above its balanced-growth-path value when $k < k^*$ and is less when $k > k^*$. As a result, convergence is more rapid than in the Solow model.

The General Case

Let us now consider what occurs when the assumptions of logarithmic utility and Cobb–Douglas production are relaxed. It turns out that, despite the simplicity of the model, a wide range of behaviors of the economy are possible. Rather than attempting a comprehensive analysis, we simply discuss some of the more interesting cases.[29]

To understand the possibilities intuitively, it is helpful to rewrite the equation of motion, (2.60), as

$$k_{t+1} = \frac{1}{(1+n)(1+g)} s(f'(k_{t+1})) \frac{[f(k_t) - k_t f'(k_t)]}{f(k_t)} f(k_t). \qquad (2.66)$$

Equation (2.66) expresses capital per unit of effective labor in period $t+1$ as the product of four terms. From right to left, those four terms are the following: output per unit of effective labor at t, the fraction of that output that is paid to labor, the fraction of that labor income that is saved, and the ratio of the amount of effective labor in period t to the amount in period $t+1$.

Figure 2.13 shows some possible forms for the relation between k_{t+1} and k_t other than the well-behaved case shown in Figure 2.11. Panel (a) shows a case with multiple k^*'s. In the case shown, k_1^* and k_3^* are stable: if k starts slightly away from one of these points, it converges to that level. k_2^* is unstable (as is $k = 0$). If k starts slightly below k_2^*, k_{t+1} is less than k_t each period, and k converges to k_1^*. If k begins slightly above k_2^*, it converges to k_3^*.

To understand the possibility of multiple k^*'s, note that since output per unit of capital is lower when k is higher (capital has a diminishing marginal

---

being greater than and less than x^*, but each period it gets closer. If λ is greater than 1, the system explodes. Finally, if λ is less than -1, there are explosive oscillations.

[29]Galor and Ryder (1989) analyze some of these issues in more detail.

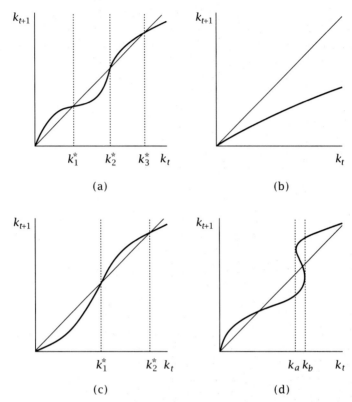

FIGURE 2.13   Various possibilities for the relationship between k_t and k_{t+1}

product), for there to be two k^*'s the saving of the young as a fraction of total output must be higher at the higher k^*. When the fraction of output going to labor and the fraction of labor income saved are constant, the saving of the young is a constant fraction of total output, and so multiple k^*'s are not possible. This is what occurs with Cobb-Douglas production and logarithmic utility. But if labor's share is greater at higher levels of k (which occurs if $f(\cdot)$ is more sharply curved than in the Cobb-Douglas case) or if workers save a greater fraction of their income when the rate of return is lower (which occurs if $\theta > 1$), or both, there may be more than one level of k at which saving reproduces the existing capital stock.

Panel (b) shows a case in which k_{t+1} is always less than k_t, and in which k therefore converges to zero regardless of its initial value. What is needed for this to occur is for either labor's share or the fraction of labor income saved (or both) to approach zero as k approaches zero.

Panel (c) shows a case in which k converges to zero if its initial value is sufficiently low but to a strictly positive level if its initial value is sufficiently high. Specifically, if $k_0 < k_1^*$, k approaches zero; if $k_0 > k_1^*$, k converges to k_2^*.

Finally, Panel (d) shows a case in which k_{t+1} is not uniquely determined by k_t: when k_t is between k_a and k_b, there are three possible values of k_{t+1}. This can happen if saving is a decreasing function of the interest rate. When saving is decreasing in r, saving is high if individuals expect a high value of k_{t+1} and therefore expect r to be low, and is low when individuals expect a low value of k_{t+1}. If saving is sufficiently responsive to r, and if r is sufficiently responsive to k, there can be more than one value of k_{t+1} that is consistent with a given k_t. Thus the path of the economy is indeterminate: equation (2.60) (or [2.66]) does not fully determine how k evolves over time given its initial value. This raises the possibility that *self-fulfilling prophecies* and *sunspots* can affect the behavior of the economy and that the economy can exhibit fluctuations even though there are no exogenous disturbances. Depending on precisely what is assumed, various dynamics are possible.[30]

Thus assuming that there are overlapping generations rather than infinitely-lived households has potentially important implications for the dynamics of the economy: for example, sustained growth may not be possible, or it may depend on initial conditions.

At the same time, the model does no better than the Solow and Ramsey models at answering our basic questions about growth. Because of the Inada conditions, k_{t+1} must be less than k_t for k_t sufficiently large. Specifically, since the saving of the young cannot exceed the economy's total output, k_{t+1} must be less than or equal to $f(k_t)/[(1 + n)(1 + g)]$. And because the marginal product of capital approaches zero as k becomes large, this must eventually be less than k_t. The fact that k_{t+1} is eventually less than k_t implies that unbounded growth of k is not possible. Thus, once again, growth in the effectiveness of labor is the only potential source of long-run growth in output per worker. Because of the possibility of multiple k^*'s, the model does imply that otherwise identical economies can converge to different balanced growth paths simply because of differences in their initial conditions. But, as in the Solow and Ramsey models, we can account for quantitatively large differences in output per worker in this way only by positing immense differences in capital per worker and in rates of return.

2.13   The Possibility of Dynamic Inefficiency

The one major difference between the balanced growth paths of the Diamond and Ramsey–Cass–Koopmans models involves welfare. We saw that the equilibrium of the Ramsey–Cass–Koopmans model maximizes the welfare of the representative household. In the Diamond model, individuals born at different times attain different levels of utility, and so the appropriate

---

[30]These issues are briefly discussed further in Section 6.14.

way to evaluate social welfare is not clear. If we specify welfare as some weighted sum of the utilities of different generations, there is no reason to expect the decentralized equilibrium to maximize welfare, since the weights we assign to the different generations are arbitrary.

A minimal criterion for efficiency, however, is that the equilibrium be Pareto-efficient. It turns out that the equilibrium of the Diamond model need not satisfy even this standard. In particular, the capital stock on the balanced growth path of the Diamond model may exceed the golden-rule level, so that a permanent increase in consumption is possible.

To see this possibility as simply as possible, assume that utility is logarithmic, production is Cobb–Douglas, and g is zero. Equation (2.63) (together with the definition of D in [2.61]) implies that in this case the value of k on the balanced growth path is

$$k^* = \left[\frac{1}{1+n} \frac{1}{2+\rho}(1-\alpha) \right]^{1/(1-\alpha)}. \tag{2.67}$$

Thus the marginal product of capital on the balanced growth path, $\alpha k^{*\alpha-1}$, is

$$f'(k^*) = \frac{\alpha}{1-\alpha}(1+n)(2+\rho). \tag{2.68}$$

The golden-rule capital stock is defined by $f'(k_{GR}) = n$. $f'(k^*)$ can be either more or less than $f'(k_{GR})$. In particular, for α sufficiently small, $f'(k^*)$ is less than $f'(k_{GR})$—the capital stock on the balanced growth path exceeds the golden-rule level.

To see why it is inefficient for k^* to exceed k_{GR}, imagine introducing a social planner into a Diamond economy that is on its balanced growth path with $k^* > k_{GR}$. If the planner does nothing to alter k, the amount of output per worker available each period for consumption is output, $f(k^*)$, minus the new investment needed to maintain k at k^*, nk^*. This is shown by the crosses in Figure 2.14. Suppose instead, however, that in some period, period t_0, the planner allocates more resources to consumption and fewer to saving than usual, so that capital per worker the next period is k_{GR}, and that thereafter he or she maintains k at k_{GR}. Under this plan, the resources per worker available for consumption in period t_0 are $f(k^*)+(k^*-k_{GR})-nk_{GR}$. In each subsequent period, the output per worker available for consumption is $f(k_{GR}) - nk_{GR}$. Since k_{GR} maximizes $f(k) - nk$, $f(k_{GR}) - nk_{GR}$ exceeds $f(k^*) - nk^*$. And since k^* is greater than k_{GR}, $f(k^*) + (k^* - k_{GR}) - nk_{GR}$ is even larger than $f(k_{GR}) - nk_{GR}$. The path of total consumption under this policy is shown by the circles in Figure 2.14. As the figure shows, this policy makes more resources available for consumption in every period than the policy of maintaining k at k^*. Given this, it must be possible for the planner to allocate consumption between the young and the old each period to make every generation better off.

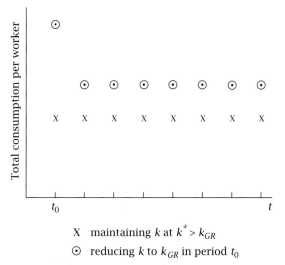

FIGURE 2.14   **How reducing k to the golden-rule level affects the path of consumption per worker**

Thus the equilibrium of the Diamond model can be Pareto-inefficient. This may seem puzzling: given that markets are competitive and there are no externalities, how can the usual result that equilibria are Pareto-efficient fail? The reason is that the standard result assumes not only competition and an absence of externalities, but also a finite number of agents. Specifically, the possibility of inefficiency in the Diamond model stems from the fact that the infinity of generations gives the planner a means of providing for the consumption of the old that is not available to the market. If individuals in the market economy want to consume in old age, their only choice is to hold capital, even if its rate of return is low. The planner, however, need not have the consumption of the old determined by the capital stock and its rate of return. Instead, he or she can divide the resources available for consumption between the young and old in any manner. The planner can take, for example, one unit of labor income from each young person and transfer it to the old; since there are $1 + n$ young people for each old person, this increases the consumption of each old person by $1 + n$ units. The planner can prevent this change from making anyone worse off by requiring the next generation of young to do the same thing in the following period, and then continuing this process every period. If the marginal product of capital is less than n—that is, if the capital stock exceeds the golden-rule level—this way of transferring resources between youth and old age is more efficient than saving, and so the planner can improve on the decentralized allocation.

Because this type of inefficiency differs from conventional sources of inefficiency, and because it stems from the intertemporal structure of the economy, it is known as *dynamic inefficiency*.[31]

---

[31]Problem 2.19 investigates the sources of dynamic inefficiency further.

Empirical Application: Are Modern Economies Dynamically Efficient?

The Diamond model shows that it is possible for a decentralized economy to accumulate capital beyond the golden-rule level, and thus to produce an allocation that is Pareto-inefficient. Given that capital accumulation in actual economies is not dictated by social planners, this raises the issue of whether actual economies might be dynamically inefficient. If they were, there would be important implications for public policy: the great concern about low rates of saving would be entirely misplaced, and there would be an easy way of increasing both present and future consumption.

At first glance, dynamic inefficiency appears to be a possibility for the United States and other major economies. A balanced growth path is dynamically inefficient if the real rate of return, $f'(k^*) - \delta$, is less than the growth rate of the economy. A straightforward measure of the real rate of return is the real interest rate on short-term government debt. In the United States over the past fifty years, this interest rate has averaged only a few tenths of a percent; this is much less than the average growth rate of the economy, which is about 3 percent. Similar findings hold for other major industrialized countries. Thus the real interest rate is less than the golden-rule level, which suggests that these economies have overaccumulated capital.

There is a problem with this argument, however. In a world of certainty, all interest rates must be equal; thus there is no ambiguity in what is meant by "the" rate of return. But if there is uncertainty, different assets can have different expected returns. Suppose, for example, we assess dynamic efficiency by examining the marginal product of capital net of depreciation instead of the return on a fairly safe asset. If capital earns its marginal product, the net marginal product can be estimated as the ratio of overall capital income minus total depreciation to the value of the capital stock. For the United States, this ratio is about 10 percent, which is much more than the economy's growth rate. Thus, using this approach we would conclude that the U.S. economy is dynamically efficient. Our simple theoretical model, in which the marginal product of capital and the safe interest rate are the same, provides no guidance concerning which of these contradictory conclusions is correct.

Abel, Mankiw, Summers, and Zeckhauser (1989) tackle the issue of how to assess dynamic efficiency in a world of uncertainty. Their principal theoretical result is that under uncertainty, the condition for dynamic efficiency is that net capital income exceed investment. For the balanced growth path of an economy with certainty, this condition is the same as the usual comparison of the real interest rate with the economy's growth rate. In this case, net capital income is the real interest rate times the stock of capital, and investment is the growth rate of the economy times the stock of capital. Thus capital income exceeds investment if and only if the real interest rate exceeds the economy's growth rate. But Abel et al. show that under uncertainty these two conditions are not equivalent, and that it is the comparison of capital income and investment that provides the correct way of judging whether there is dynamic efficiency. Intuitively, a capital sector that is on net making resources available by producing more output than it is using for new investment is contributing to consumption, whereas one that is using more in resources than it is producing is not.

Abel et al.'s principal empirical result is that the condition for dynamic efficiency seems to be satisfied in practice. They measure capital income as national income minus employees' compensation and the part of the income of the self-employed that appears to represent labor income;[32] investment is taken directly from the national income accounts. They find that capital income consistently exceeds investment in the United States and in the six other major industrialized countries they consider. Even in Japan, where investment is remarkably high, the profit rate is so great that the returns to capital comfortably exceed investment. Thus, although decentralized economies can produce dynamically inefficient outcomes in principle, they do not appear to in practice.

2.14   Government in the Diamond Model

As in the infinite-horizon model, a natural question to ask of the Diamond model is what occurs if we introduce a government that makes purchases, levies taxes, and issues debt. For simplicity, we focus on the case of logarithmic utility and Cobb–Douglas production.

The Effects of Government Purchases

Let G_t denote the government's purchases of goods per unit of effective labor in period t. Assume for the moment that it finances those purchases by lump-sum taxes on the young.

When the government finances its purchases entirely with taxes, workers' after-tax income in period t is $(1 - \alpha)k_t^\alpha - G_t$ rather than $(1 - \alpha)k_t^\alpha$. The equation of motion for k, equation (2.61), therefore becomes

$$k_{t+1} = \frac{1}{(1 + n)(1 + g)} \frac{1}{2 + \rho} [(1 - \alpha)k_t^\alpha - G_t]. \tag{2.69}$$

A higher G_t therefore reduces k_{t+1} for a given k_t.

---

[32]They argue that adjusting these figures to account for land income and monopoly rents does not change the basic results.

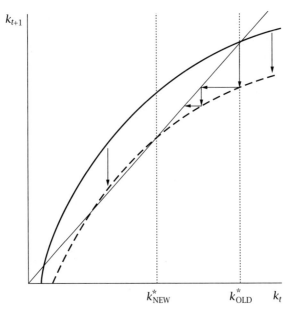

FIGURE 2.15   The effects of a permanent increase in government purchases

To see the effects of government purchases, suppose that the economy is on a balanced growth path with G constant, and that G increases permanently. From (2.69), this shifts the k_{t+1} function down; this is shown in Figure 2.15. The downward shift of the k_{t+1} function reduces k^*. Thus—in contrast to what occurs in the infinite-horizon model—higher government purchases lead to a lower capital stock and a higher equilibrium real interest rate. Intuitively, since individuals live for two periods, they reduce their first-period consumption less than one-for-one with the increase in G. But since taxes are levied only in the first period of life, this means that their saving falls. As usual, the economy moves smoothly from the initial balanced growth path to the new one.

As a second example, consider a temporary increase in government purchases from G_L to G_H, again with the economy initially on its balanced growth path. The dynamics of k are thus described by (2.69) with $G = G_H$ during the period that government purchases are high and by (2.69) with $G = G_L$ before and after. That is, the fact that individuals know that government purchases will return to G_L does not affect the behavior of the economy during the time that purchases are high. The saving of the young— and hence next period's capital stock—is determined by their after-tax labor income, which is determined by the current capital stock and by the government's current purchases. Thus during the time that government purchases are high, k gradually falls and r gradually increases. Once G returns to G_L, k rises gradually back to its initial level.[33]

---

[33]The result that future values of G do not affect the current behavior of the economy

Tax Versus Bond Finance

The possibility of the government using debt as well as taxes to finance its purchases requires that we change equation (2.69). First, some of the saving of the young takes the form of bonds instead of capital; thus the left-hand side of (2.69) becomes $k_{t+1} + b_{t+1}$, where b is the stock of bonds per unit of effective labor. (Paralleling our timing convention with capital, b_{t+1} refers to bonds purchased in period t. Thus to increase b_{t+1} by 1 unit, the government must issue $(1 + n)(1 + g)$ bonds per unit of effective labor in t.) Second, taxes and purchases need not be equal; thus T_t replaces G_t on the right-hand side of (2.69).[34] Moving the b_{t+1} term over to the right-hand side, we therefore have

$$k_{t+1} = \frac{1}{(1 + n)(1 + g)} \frac{1}{2 + \rho}[(1 - \alpha)k_t^\alpha - T_t] - b_{t+1}. \qquad (2.70)$$

Equation (2.70) shows that taxes and bonds have different effects on capital accumulation. When the government cuts taxes and issues bonds, the taxes to repay those bonds are levied on future generations. Thus the individuals currently alive are better off, and they therefore increase their consumption. Thus a switch from tax to bond finance reduces the capital stock.

Since bonds represent net wealth in this economy, the government can use them to provide individuals with a way other than holding capital to transfer resources between youth and old age. Because of this, the government can use bonds to prevent the economy from accumulating too much capital.[35] Consider an economy where the balanced growth path in the absence of a government involves $k^* > k_{GR}$. If the capital stock in some period, period t, equals its golden-rule level, the labor income of the young is $(1 - \alpha)k_{GR}^\alpha$, and they save fraction $1/(2 + \rho)$ of this. Thus $k_{t+1} + b_{t+1}$ equals

$$\frac{1}{(1 + n)(1 + g)} \frac{1}{2 + \rho}(1 - \alpha)k_{GR}^\alpha \equiv a_{GR}. \qquad (2.71)$$

Thus for the economy to be on a balanced growth path with the capital stock at the golden-rule level, b must equal the difference between the total amount the young wish to save when $k = k_{GR}$, a_{GR}, and the amount of that saving that must take the form of capital, k_{GR}. By issuing quantity $a_{GR} - k_{GR}$

---

does not depend on the assumption of logarithmic utility. Without logarithmic utility, the saving of the current period's young depends on the rate of return as well as on after-tax labor income. But the rate of return is determined by the next period's capital-labor ratio, which is not affected by government purchases in that period.

[34]Of course, T and G are related. The government's expenditures per unit of effective labor in period t are G_t for purchases and $[1 + f'(k_t)]b_t$ to retire the existing debt. The government's receipts are T_t from taxes and $(1 + n)(1 + g)b_{t+1}$ from issuing new debt. Since expenditures and receipts must be equal, T_t equals $G_t + [1 + f'(k_t)]b_t - (1 + n)(1 + g)b_{t+1}$.

[35]The government can also do this through a social security program. See Problem 2.16.

of bonds, the government can thus cause the balanced-growth-path value of k to equal its golden-rule value.[36]

Problems

2.1. Consider N firms each with the constant returns to scale production function $Y = F(K, AL)$, or (using the intensive form) $Y = ALf(k)$. Assume $f'(\cdot) > 0, f''(\cdot) < 0$. Assume that all firms can hire labor at wage wA and rent capital at cost r, and that all firms have the same value of A.

(a) Consider the problem of a firm trying to produce Y units of output at minimum cost. Show that the cost-minimizing level of k is uniquely defined and is independent of Y, and that all firms therefore choose the same value of k.

(b) Show that the total output of the N cost-minimizing firms equals the output that a single firm with the same production function has if it uses all of the labor and capital used by the N firms.

2.2. **The elasticity of substitution with constant-relative-risk-aversion utility.** Consider an individual who lives for two periods and whose utility is given by equation (2.46). Let P_1 and P_2 denote the prices of consumption in the two periods, and let W denote the value of the individual's lifetime income; thus the budget constraint is $P_1 C_1 + P_2 C_2 = W$.

(a) What are the individual's utility-maximizing choices of C_1 and C_2 given P_1, P_2, and W?

(b) The elasticity of substitution between consumption in the two periods is $-[(P_1/P_2)/(C_1/C_2)][\partial(C_1/C_2)/\partial(P_1/P_2)]$, or $-\partial \ln(C_1/C_2)/\partial \ln(P_1/P_2)$. Show that with the utility function (2.46), the elasticity of substitution between C_1 and C_2 is $1/\theta$.

2.3. Assume that the instantaneous utility function $u(C)$ in equation (2.1) is $\ln C$. Consider the problem of a household maximizing (2.1) subject to (2.5). Find an expression for C at each time as a function of initial wealth plus the present value of labor income, the path of $r(t)$, and the parameters of the utility function.

---

[36]This policy involves no costs to the government, and no taxes, on the balanced growth path. When $k = k_{GR}$, $1+f'(k) = (1+n)(1+g)$ (see Problem 2.14). Thus the amount the government needs, per unit of effective labor, to pay off its existing debt in period t is $(1+n)(1+g)b_t$. But the amount of new debt it issues in t is b_{t+1} per unit of period-$t + 1$ effective labor; this is $(1+n)(1+g)b_{t+1}$ per unit of period-t effective labor. When b is constant, these two quantities are equal, and so the new debt issues are just enough to pay off the outstanding debt.

Finally, if the economy begins with $k > k_{GR}$, the government needs to levy taxes to move k to its golden-rule level. Specifically, suppose $k_0 > k_{GR}$. If the government levies lump-sum taxes per unit of effective labor of amount $(1 - \alpha)k_0^\alpha - (1 - \alpha)k_{GR}^\alpha$ in period 0, the saving of the young per unit of period-1 effective labor is $[1/(1 + n)(1 + g)][1/(2 + \rho)](1 - \alpha)k_{GR}^\alpha = a_{GR}$. With $b_1 = a_{GR} - k_{GR}$, this ensures that $k_1 = k_{GR}$. The government can use the revenue from the taxes and the initial bond issue to increase the consumption of the period-0 old.

2.4. Consider a household with utility given by (2.1)-(2.2). Assume that the real interest rate is constant, and let W denote the household's initial wealth plus the present value of its lifetime labor income (the right-hand side of [2.5]). Find the utility-maximizing path of C given r, W, and the parameters of the utility function.

2.5. The productivity slowdown and saving. Consider a Ramsey–Cass–Koopmans economy that is on its balanced growth path, and suppose there is a permanent fall in g.

(a) How, if at all, does this affect the $\dot{k} = 0$ curve?

(b) How, if at all, does this affect the $\dot{c} = 0$ curve?

(c) What happens to c at the time of the change?

(d) Find an expression for the impact of a marginal change in g on the fraction of output that is saved on the balanced growth path. Can one tell whether this expression is positive or negative?

(e) For the case where the production function is Cobb–Douglas, $f(k) = k^{\alpha}$, rewrite your answer to part (d) in terms of ρ, n, g, θ, and α. (Hint: use the fact that $f'(k^*) = \rho + \theta g$.)

2.6. Describe how each of the following affect the $\dot{c} = 0$ and $\dot{k} = 0$ curves in Figure 2.5, and thus how they affect the balanced-growth-path values of c and k:

(a) A rise in θ.

(b) A downward shift of the production function.

(c) A change in the rate of depreciation from the value of zero assumed in the text to some positive level.

2.7. Derive an expression analogous to (2.37) for the case of a positive depreciation rate.

2.8. Capital taxation in the Ramsey–Cass–Koopmans model. Consider a Ramsey–Cass–Koopmans economy that is on its balanced growth path. Suppose that at some time, which we will call time 0, the government switches to a policy of taxing investment income at rate τ. Thus the real interest rate that households face is now given by $r(t) = (1 - \tau)f'(k(t))$. Assume that the government returns the revenue it collects from this tax through lump-sum transfers. Finally, assume that this change in tax policy is unanticipated.

(a) How does the tax affect the $\dot{c} = 0$ locus? The $\dot{k} = 0$ locus?

(b) How does the economy respond to the adoption of the tax at time 0? What are the dynamics after time 0?

(c) How do the values of c and k on the new balanced growth path compare with their values on the old balanced growth path?

(d) (This is based on Barro, Mankiw, and Sala-i-Martin, 1995.) Suppose there are many economies like this one. Workers' preferences are the same in each country, but the tax rates on investment income may vary across countries. Assume that each country is on its balanced growth path.

(i) Show that the saving rate on the balanced growth path, $(y^* - c^*)/y^*$, is decreasing in τ.

(ii) Do citizens in low-τ, high-k^*, high-saving countries have any incentive to invest in low-saving countries? Why or why not?

(e) Does your answer to part (c) imply that a policy of *subsidizing* investment (that is, making $\tau < 0$), and raising the revenue for this subsidy through lump-sum taxes, increases welfare? Why or why not?

(f) How, if at all, do the answers to parts (a) and (b) change if the government does not rebate the revenue from the tax but instead uses it to make government purchases?

2.9. Using the phase diagram to analyze the impact of an anticipated change. Consider the policy described in Problem 2.8, but suppose that instead of announcing and implementing the tax at time 0, the government announces at time 0 that at some later time, time t_1, investment income will begin to be taxed at rate τ.

(a) Draw the phase diagram showing the dynamics of c and k after time t_1.

(b) Can c change discontinuously at time t_1? Why or why not?

(c) Draw the phase diagram showing the dynamics of c and k before t_1.

(d) In light of your answers to parts (a), (b), and (c), what must c do at time 0?

(e) Summarize your results by sketching the paths of c and k as functions of time.

2.10. Using the phase diagram to analyze the impact of unanticipated and anticipated temporary changes. Analyze the following two variations on Problem 2.9:

(a) At time 0, the government announces that it will tax investment income at rate τ from time 0 until some later date t_1; thereafter investment income will again be untaxed.

(b) At time 0, the government announces that from time t_1 to some later time t_2, it will tax investment income at rate τ; before t_1 and after t_2, investment income will not be taxed.

2.11. The analysis of government policies in the Ramsey–Cass–Koopmans model in the text assumes that government purchases do not affect utility from private consumption. The opposite extreme is that government purchases and private consumption are perfect substitutes. Specifically, suppose that the utility function (2.14) is modified to be

$$U = B \int_{t=0}^{\infty} e^{-\beta t} \frac{[c(t) + G(t)]^{1-\theta}}{1 - \theta} dt.$$

If the economy is initially on its balanced growth path and if households' preferences are given by U, what are the effects of a temporary increase in government purchases on the paths of consumption, capital, and the interest rate?

2.12. Precautionary saving, non-lump-sum taxation, and Ricardian equivalence.
(This follows Leland, 1968, and Barsky, Mankiw, and Zeldes, 1986.) Consider
an individual who lives for two periods. The individual has no initial wealth
and earns labor incomes of amounts Y_1 and Y_2 in the two periods. Y_1 is
known, but Y_2 is random; assume for simplicity that $E[Y_2] = Y_1$. The government taxes income at rate τ_1 in period 1 and τ_2 in period 2. The individual can
borrow and lend at a fixed interest rate, which for simplicity is assumed to be
zero. Thus second-period consumption is $C_2 = [(1-\tau_1)Y_1 - C_1] + (1-\tau_2)Y_2$. The
individual chooses C_1 to maximize expected lifetime utility, $U(C_1) + E[U(C_2)]$.

(a) Find the first-order condition for C_1.

(b) Show that $E[C_2] = C_1$ if Y_2 is not random or if utility is quadratic. (Hint:
if utility is quadratic, $U'(C_2)$ is a linear function of C_2, so $E[U'(C_2)] =
U'(E[C_2])$.

(c) Show that if $U'''(\bullet) > 0$ and Y_2 is random, $E[C_2] > C_1$. (Such saving due to
uncertainty is known as *precautionary* saving. See Section 7.6.)

(d) Suppose that the government marginally lowers τ_1 and raises τ_2 by the
same amount, so that its expected total revenue, $\tau_1 Y_1 + \tau_2 E[Y_2]$, is unchanged. Implicitly differentiate the first-order condition in part (a) to
find an expression for how C_1 responds to this change.

(e) Show that C_1 is unaffected by this change if Y_2 is not random or if utility
is quadratic.

(f) Show that C_1 increases in response to this change if $U'''(\bullet) > 0$ and Y_2 is
random.

(g) If the utility function is constant-relative-risk-aversion, what is the sign
of $U'''(\bullet)$?

2.13. Consider the Diamond model with logarithmic utility and Cobb–Douglas production. Describe how each of the following affects k_{t+1} as a function of k_t.

(a) A rise in n.

(b) A downward shift of the production function (that is, $f(k)$ takes the form
Bk^α, and B falls).

(c) A rise in α.

2.14. A discrete-time version of the Solow model. Suppose $Y_t = F(K_t, A_t L_t)$, with
$F(\bullet)$ having constant returns to scale and the intensive form of the production
function satisfying the Inada conditions. Suppose also that $A_{t+1} = (1 + g)A_t$,
$L_{t+1} = (1 + n)L_t$, and $K_{t+1} = K_t + sY_t - \delta K_t$.

(a) Find an expression for k_{t+1} as a function of k_t.

(b) Sketch k_{t+1} as a function of k_t. Does the economy have a balanced growth
path? If the initial level of k differs from the value on the balanced growth
path, does the economy converge to the balanced growth path?

(c) Find an expression for consumption per unit of effective labor on the
balanced growth path as a function of the balanced-growth-path value
of k. What is the marginal product of capital, $f'(k)$, when k maximizes
consumption per unit of effective labor on the balanced growth path?

(d) Assume that the production function is Cobb–Douglas.

(i) What is k_{t+1} as a function of k_t?

(ii) What is k^*, the value of k on the balanced growth path?

(iii) Along the lines of equations (2.62)–(2.64), in the text, linearize the expression in subpart (i) around $k_t = k^*$, and find the rate of convergence of k to k^*.

2.15. **Depreciation in the Diamond model and microeconomic foundations for the Solow model.** Suppose that in the Diamond model capital depreciates at rate δ, so that $r_t = f'(k_t) - \delta$.

(a) How, if at all, does this change in the model affect equation (2.60) giving k_{t+1} as a function of k_t?

(b) In the special case of logarithmic utility, Cobb–Douglas production, and $\delta = 1$, what is the equation for k_{t+1} as a function of k_t? Compare this with the analogous expression for the discrete-time version of the Solow model with $\delta = 1$ from part (a) of Problem 2.14.

2.16. **Social security in the Diamond model.** Consider a Diamond economy where g is zero, production is Cobb–Douglas, and utility is logarithmic.

(a) **Pay-as-you-go social security.** Suppose the government taxes each young individual amount T and uses the proceeds to pay benefits to old individuals; thus each old person receives $(1 + n)T$.

(i) How, if at all, does this change affect equation (2.61) giving k_{t+1} as a function of k_t?

(ii) How, if at all, does this change affect the balanced-growth-path value of k?

(iii) If the economy is initially on a balanced growth path that is dynamically efficient, how does a marginal increase in T affect the welfare of current and future generations? What happens if the initial balanced growth path is dynamically inefficient?

(b) **Fully funded social security.** Suppose the government taxes each young person amount T and uses the proceeds to purchase capital. Individuals born at t therefore receive $(1 + r_{t+1})T$ when they are old.

(i) How, if at all, does this change affect equation (2.61) giving k_{t+1} as a function of k_t?

(ii) How, if at all, does this change affect the balanced-growth-path value of k?

2.17. **The basic overlapping-generations model.** (This follows Samuelson, 1958, and Allais, 1947.) Suppose, as in the Diamond model, that N_t 2-period-lived individuals are born in period t and that $N_t = (1 + n)N_{t-1}$. For simplicity, let utility be logarithmic with no discounting: $U_t = \ln(C_{1t}) + \ln(C_{2t+1})$.

The production side of the economy is simpler than in the Diamond model. Each individual born at time t is endowed with A units of the economy's single good. The good can either be consumed or stored. Each unit stored yields $x > 0$ units of the good in the following period.[37]

---

[37] Note that this is the same as the Diamond economy with $g = 0$, $F(K_t, AL_t) = AL_t + xK_t$,

Finally, assume that in the initial period, period 0, in addition to the N_0 young individuals each endowed with A units of the good, there are $[1/(1 + n)]N_0$ individuals who are alive only in period 0. Each of these "old" individuals is endowed with some amount Z of the good; their utility is simply their consumption in the initial period, C_{20}.

(a) Describe the decentralized equilibrium of this economy. (Hint: given the overlapping-generations structure, will the members of any generation engage in transactions with members of another generation?)

(b) Consider paths where the fraction of agents' endowments that is stored, f_t, is constant over time. What is total consumption (that is, consumption of all the young plus consumption of all the old) per person on such a path as a function of f? If $x < 1 + n$, what value of f satisfying $0 \leq f \leq 1$ maximizes consumption per person? Is the decentralized equilibrium Pareto-efficient in this case? If not, how can a social planner raise welfare?

2.18. **Stationary monetary equilibria in the Samuelson overlapping-generations model.** (Again this follows Samuelson, 1958.) Consider the setup described in Problem 2.17. Assume that $x < 1 + n$. Suppose that the old individuals in period 0, in addition to being endowed with Z units of the good, are each endowed with M units of a storable, divisible commodity, which we will call money. Money is not a source of utility.

(a) Consider an individual born at t. Suppose the price of the good in units of money is P_t in t and P_{t+1} in $t + 1$. Thus the individual can sell units of endowment for P_t units of money and then use that money to buy P_t/P_{t+1} units of the next generation's endowment the following period. What is the individual's behavior as a function of P_t/P_{t+1}?

(b) Show that there is an equilibrium with $P_{t+1} = P_t/(1 + n)$ for all $t \geq 0$ and no storage, and thus that the presence of "money" allows the economy to reach the golden-rule level of storage.

(c) Show that there are also equilibria with $P_{t+1} = P_t/x$ for all $t \geq 0$.

(d) Finally, explain why $P_t = \infty$ for all t (that is, money is worthless) is also an equilibrium. Explain why this is the *only* equilibrium if the economy ends at some date, as in Problem 2.19(b), below. (Hint: reason backward from the last period.)

2.19. **The source of dynamic inefficiency.** There are two ways in which the Diamond and Samuelson models differ from textbook models. First, markets are incomplete: because individuals cannot trade with individuals who have not been born, some possible transactions are ruled out. Second, because time goes on forever, there is an infinite number of agents. This problem asks you to investigate which of these is the source of the possibility of dynamic inefficiency. For simplicity, it focuses on the Samuelson overlapping-generations model (see the previous two problems), again with log utility and no discounting. To simplify further, it assumes $n = 0$ and $0 < x < 1$. The basic issues, however, are general.

---

and $\delta = 1$. With this production function, since individuals supply 1 unit of labor when they are young, an individual born in t obtains A units of the good. And each unit saved yields $1 + r = 1 + \partial F(K, AL)/\partial K - \delta = 1 + x - 1 = x$ units of second-period consumption.

(a) **Incomplete markets.** Suppose we eliminate incomplete markets from the model by allowing all agents to trade in a competitive market "before" the beginning of time. That is, a Walrasian auctioneer calls out prices $Q_0, Q_1, Q_2, \ldots$ for the good at each date. Individuals can then make sales and purchases at these prices given their endowments and their ability to store. The budget constraint of an individual born at t is thus $Q_t C_{1t} + Q_{t+1} C_{2t+1} = Q_t(A - S_t) + Q_{t+1} x S_t$, where S_t (which must satisfy $0 \le S_t \le A$) is the amount the individual stores.

   (i) Suppose the auctioneer announces $Q_{t+1} = Q_t/x$ for all $t > 0$. Show that in this case individuals are indifferent concerning how much to store, that there is a set of storage decisions such that markets clear at every date, and that this equilibrium is the same as the equilibrium described in part (a) of Problem 2.17.

   (ii) Suppose the auctioneer announces prices that fail to satisfy $Q_{t+1} = Q_t/x$ at some date. Show that at the first date that does not satisfy this condition the market for the good cannot clear, and thus that the proposed price path cannot be an equilibrium.

(b) **Infinite duration.** Suppose that the economy ends at some date T. That is, suppose the individuals born at T live only one period (and hence seek to maximize C_{1T}), and that thereafter no individuals are born. Show that the decentralized equilibrium is Pareto-efficient.

(c) In light of these answers, is it incomplete markets or infinite duration that is the source of dynamic inefficiency?

2.20. **Explosive paths in the Samuelson overlapping-generations model** (See Black, 1974; Brock, 1975; and Calvo, 1978a.) Consider the setup described in Problem 2.18. Assume that x is zero, and assume that utility is constant-relative-risk-aversion with $\theta < 1$ rather than logarithmic. Finally, assume for simplicity that $n = 0$.

(a) What is the behavior of an individual born at t as a function of P_t/P_{t+1}? Show that the amount of his or her endowment that the individual sells for money is an increasing function of P_t/P_{t+1} and approaches zero as this ratio approaches zero.

(b) Suppose $P_0/P_1 < 1$. How much of the good are the individuals born in period 0 planning to buy in period 1 from the individuals born then? What must P_1/P_2 be for the individuals born in period 1 to want to supply this amount?

(c) Iterating this reasoning forward, what is the qualitative behavior of P_t/P_{t+1} over time? Does this represent an equilibrium path for the economy?

(d) Can there be an equilibrium path with $P_0/P_1 > 1$?

Chapter 3
BEYOND THE SOLOW MODEL: NEW GROWTH THEORY

The models we have seen so far do not provide satisfying answers to our central questions about economic growth. The models' principal result is a negative one: if capital's earnings reflect its contribution to output and if its share in total income is modest, then capital accumulation cannot account for a large part of either long-run growth or cross-country income differences. And the only determinant of income in the models other than capital is a mystery variable, the "effectiveness of labor" (*A*), whose exact meaning is not specified and whose behavior is taken as exogenous.

This chapter therefore investigates the fundamental questions of growth theory more deeply. It considers two broad views. The first view is that the driving force of growth is the accumulation of knowledge. This view agrees with the Solow model and the models of Chapter 2 that capital accumulation is not central to growth. But it differs from these models in explicitly interpreting the effectiveness of labor as knowledge and in formally modeling its evolution over time. This view is the subject of Part A of the chapter. We will analyze the dynamics of the economy when knowledge accumulation is modeled explicitly and consider various views concerning how knowledge is produced and what determines the allocation of resources to knowledge production.

The second view is that, contrary to the Solow model and the models of Chapter 2, capital is central to growth. Specifically, we will consider models that take a broader view of capital than we have considered so far—most importantly, extending it to include human capital. These models imply that physical capital's income share may not be a good guide to the overall importance of capital. We will see that, as a result, it is possible for capital accumulation alone to have large effects on real incomes. These models are the subject of Part B of the chapter.

Part A   Research and Development Models

3.1   Framework and Assumptions

Overview

The view of growth that is most in keeping with the models we have seen is that the effectiveness of labor represents knowledge or technology. Certainly it is plausible that technological progress is the reason that more output can be produced today from a given quantity of capital and labor than could be produced a century or two ago. The natural extension of Chapters 1 and 2 is thus to model the growth of *A* rather than to take it as given.

To do this, we need to introduce an explicit *research and development* (or *R&D*) sector, and then model the production of new technologies. We also need to model the allocation of resources between conventional goods production and R&D.

In our formal modeling, we will take a fairly mechanical view of the production of new technologies. Specifically, we will assume a largely conventional production function in which labor, capital, and technology are combined to produce improvements in technology in a deterministic way. Of course, this is not a complete description of technological progress. But it is reasonable to think that, all else equal, devoting more resources to research yields more discoveries; this is what the production function captures. Since we are interested in growth over extended periods, modeling the randomness in technological progress would give little additional insight. And if we want to analyze the consequences of changes in other determinants of the success of R&D, we can introduce a shift parameter in the knowledge production function and examine the effects of changes in that parameter. The model provides no insight, however, concerning what those other determinants of the success of research activity are.

We make two other major simplifications. First, both the R&D and goods production functions are assumed to be generalized Cobb–Douglas functions. Second, in the spirit of the Solow model, the model takes the fraction of output saved and the fractions of the labor force and the capital stock used in the R&D sector as exogenous and constant. These assumptions do not change the model's main implications.

Specifics

The specific model we consider is a simplified version of the models of R&D and growth developed by P. Romer (1990), Grossman and Helpman

(1991a), and Aghion and Howitt (1992).[1] The model, like the others we have studied, involves four variables: labor (L), capital (K), technology (A), and output (Y). The model is set in continuous time. There are two sectors, a goods-producing sector where output is produced and an R&D sector where additions to the stock of knowledge are made. Fraction a_L of the labor force is used in the R&D sector and fraction $1 - a_L$ in the goods-producing sector; similarly, fraction a_K of the capital stock is used in R&D and the rest in goods production. Both sectors use the full stock of knowledge, A: because the use of an idea or a piece of knowledge in one place does not prevent it from being used elsewhere, we do not have to consider the division of the stock of knowledge between the two sectors.

The quantity of output produced at time t is thus

$$Y(t) = [(1 - a_K)K(t)]^\alpha [A(t)(1 - a_L)L(t)]^{1-\alpha}, \qquad 0 < \alpha < 1. \qquad (3.1)$$

Aside from the $1 - a_K$ and $1 - a_L$ terms and the restriction to the Cobb–Douglas functional form, this production function is identical to those of our earlier models. Note that equation (3.1) implies constant returns to capital and labor: with a given technology, doubling the inputs doubles the amount that can be produced.

The production of new ideas depends on the quantities of capital and labor engaged in research and on the level of technology:

$$\dot{A}(t) = G(a_K K(t), a_L L(t), A(t)). \qquad (3.2)$$

Under the assumption of generalized Cobb-Douglas production, this becomes

$$\dot{A}(t) = B[a_K K(t)]^\beta [a_L L(t)]^\gamma A(t)^\theta, \qquad B > 0, \quad \beta \geq 0, \quad \gamma \geq 0, \qquad (3.3)$$

where B is a shift parameter.

Notice that the production function for knowledge is not assumed to have constant returns to scale to capital and labor.[2] The standard argument that there must be at least constant returns is a replication one: if the inputs double, the new inputs can do exactly what the old ones were doing, thereby doubling the amount produced. But in the case of knowledge production, exactly replicating what the existing inputs were doing would cause the same set of discoveries to be made twice, thereby leaving $\dot{A}$ unchanged. Thus it is possible that there are diminishing returns in R&D. At the same time, interactions among researchers, fixed setup costs, and so on may be important enough in R&D that doubling capital and labor more than doubles output. We therefore also allow for the possibility of increasing returns.

---

[1] See also Uzawa (1965); Shell (1966, 1967); and Phelps (1966b).

[2] The fact that the function does not necessarily have constant returns is the reason for referring to it as a generalized Cobb–Douglas function.

In addition, there does not appear to be any strong basis for restricting how increases in the stock of knowledge affect the production of new knowledge; thus no restriction is placed on θ in (3.3). If $\theta = 1$, $\dot{A}$ is proportional to A; the effect is stronger if $\theta > 1$ and is weaker if $\theta < 1$.

As in the Solow model, the saving rate is exogenous and constant. In addition, depreciation is set to zero for simplicity. Thus,

$$\dot{K}(t) = sY(t). \tag{3.4}$$

Finally, we continue to treat population growth as exogenous:

$$\dot{L}(t) = nL(t), \quad n \geq 0. \tag{3.5}$$

This completes the description of the model.[3]

Because the model has two stock variables whose behavior is endogenous, K and A, it is more complicated to analyze than the Solow model. We therefore begin by considering the model without capital; that is, we set α and β to zero. This case shows most of the model's central messages. We then turn to the general case.

3.2   The Model without Capital

The Dynamics of Knowledge Accumulation

When there is no capital in the model, the production function for output (equation [3.1]) becomes

$$Y(t) = A(t)(1 - a_L)L(t). \tag{3.6}$$

Similarly, the production function for new knowledge (equation [3.3]) is now

$$\dot{A}(t) = B[a_L L(t)]^\gamma A(t)^\theta. \tag{3.7}$$

Population growth continues to be described by equation (3.5).

Equation (3.6) implies that output per worker is proportional to A, and thus that the growth rate of output per worker equals the growth rate of A. We therefore focus on the dynamics of A, which are given by (3.7). The growth rate of A, denoted g_A, is

$$g_A(t) \equiv \frac{\dot{A}(t)}{A(t)} \tag{3.8}$$

$$= Ba_L^\gamma L(t)^\gamma A(t)^{\theta-1}.$$

---

[3]The model contains the Solow model with Cobb–Douglas production as a special case: if β, γ, a_K, and a_L are all equal to zero and θ is 1, the production function for knowledge becomes $\dot{A} = BA$ (which implies that A grows at a constant rate), and the other equations of the model simplify to the corresponding equations of the Solow model.

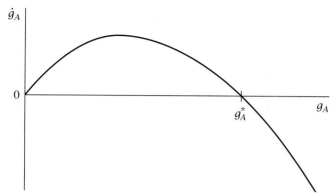

FIGURE 3.1   The dynamics of the growth rate of knowledge when $\theta < 1$

Since B and a_L are constant, whether g_A is rising, falling, or constant depends on the behavior of $L^{\gamma} A^{\theta-1}$. In particular, (3.8) implies that the *growth rate* of g_A is γ times the growth rate of L plus $\theta - 1$ times the growth rate of A. Thus,[4]

$$\dot{g}_A(t) = [\gamma n + (\theta - 1)g_A(t)]g_A(t). \qquad (3.9)$$

The initial values of L and A and the parameters of the model determine the initial value of g_A (by [3.8]). Equation (3.9) then determines the subsequent behavior of g_A.

The production function for knowledge, (3.7), implies that g_A is always positive. Thus g_A is rising if $\gamma n + (\theta - 1)g_A$ is positive, falling if this quantity is negative, and constant if it is zero. g_A is therefore constant when

$$g_A = \frac{\gamma n}{1 - \theta} \qquad (3.10)$$

$$\equiv g_A^*.$$

To describe further how the growth rate of A behaves (and thus to characterize the behavior of output per worker), we must distinguish among the cases $\theta < 1$, $\theta > 1$, and $\theta = 1$. We discuss each in turn.

Case 1: $\theta < 1$

Equation (3.9) implies that, when θ is less than 1, g_A is falling if it exceeds g_A^* and is rising if it is less than g_A^*. Thus, regardless of the initial conditions, g_A converges to g_A^*. The phase diagram is shown in Figure 3.1. Once g_A reaches g_A^*, both A and Y/L grow steadily at this rate; thus the economy is on a balanced growth path.

---

[4]To derive (3.9) formally, differentiate (3.8) with respect to time to find $\dot{g}_A$, and then use the definition of g_A.

This model is our first example of a model of *endogenous growth*. In this model, in contrast to the Solow, Ramsey, and Diamond models, the long-run growth rate of output per worker is determined within the model rather than by an exogenous rate of technological progress.

The model implies that the long-run growth rate of output per worker, g_A^*, is an increasing function of the rate of population growth, n. Indeed, positive population growth is necessary for sustained growth of output per worker. This may seem troubling; for example, the growth rate of output per worker is not on average higher in countries with faster population growth.

If we think of the model as one of *worldwide* economic growth, however, this result is reasonable. A natural interpretation of the model is that A represents knowledge that can be used anywhere in the world. With this interpretation, the model does not imply that countries with greater population growth enjoy greater income growth, but only that higher worldwide population growth raises worldwide income growth. And it is plausible that, at least up to the point where resource limitations (which are omitted from the model) become important, higher population is beneficial to the growth of worldwide knowledge: the larger the population is, the more people there are to make new discoveries. What the result about the necessity of positive population growth to sustained growth of output per worker is telling us is that, if adding to the stock of knowledge becomes more difficult as the stock of knowledge rises (that is, if $\theta < 1$), growth would taper off in the absence of population growth. We discuss this issue further (and even consider some relevant empirical evidence) in Section 3.7.

Equation (3.10) also implies that although the rate of population growth affects long-run growth, the fraction of the labor force engaged in R&D (a_L) does not. This too may seem surprising: since growth is driven by technological progress and technological progress is endogenous, it is natural to expect an increase in the fraction of the economy's resources devoted to technological progress to increase long-run growth. The reason that this does not occur is that, because θ is less than 1, the increase in a_L has a level effect but not a growth effect on the path of A. Equation (3.8) implies that the increase in a_L causes an immediate increase in g_A. But as the phase diagram shows, because of the limited contribution of the additional knowledge to the production of new knowledge, this increase in the growth rate of knowledge is not sustained. Thus, paralleling the impact of a rise in the saving rate on the path of output in the Solow model, the increase in a_L results in a rise in g_A followed by a gradual return to its initial level; the level of A therefore moves gradually to a parallel path higher than its initial one. This is shown in Figure 3.2.[5]

---

[5] See Problem 3.1 for an analysis of how the change in a_L affects the path of output.

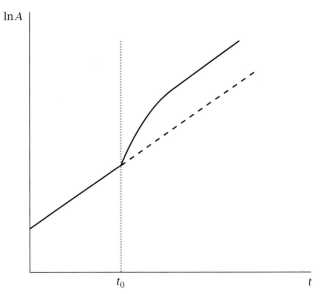

FIGURE 3.2 **The impact of a rise in the fraction of the labor force engaged in R&D when $\theta < 1$**

Case 2: $\theta > 1$

The second case to consider is θ greater than 1. In this case, (3.9) implies that $\dot{g}_A$ is increasing in g_A; and since g_A is necessarily positive, it also implies that $\dot{g}_A$ must be positive. The phase diagram is shown in Figure 3.3.

The implications of this case for long-run growth are very different from those of the previous case. As the phase diagram shows, the economy now exhibits ever-increasing growth rather than converging to a balanced

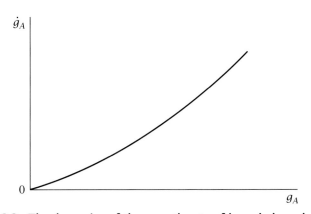

FIGURE 3.3 **The dynamics of the growth rate of knowledge when $\theta > 1$**

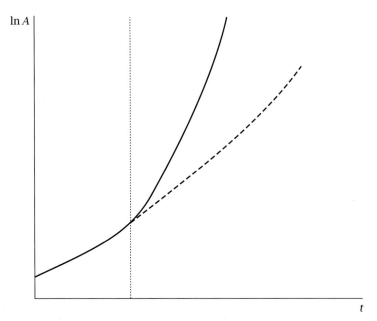

FIGURE 3.4   The impact of a rise in the fraction of the labor force engaged in R&D when $\theta > 1$

growth path. Intuitively, here knowledge is so useful in the production of new knowledge that each marginal increase in its level results in so much more new knowledge that the growth rate of knowledge rises rather than falls. Thus once the accumulation of knowledge begins—which it necessarily does in the model—the economy embarks on a path of ever-increasing growth.

The impact of an increase in the fraction of the labor force engaged in R&D is now dramatic. From Equation (3.8), an increase in a_L causes an immediate increase in g_A, as before. But $\dot{g}_A$ is an increasing function of g_A; thus $\dot{g}_A$ rises as well. And the more rapidly g_A rises, the more rapidly its growth rate rises. Thus the increase in a_L leads to an ever-widening gap between the new path of A and the path it otherwise would have followed. This is depicted in Figure 3.4.

Case 3: $\theta = 1$

When θ is exactly equal to 1, the expressions for g_A and $\dot{g}_A$ simplify to

$$g_A(t) = Ba_L^\gamma L(t)^\gamma, \qquad (3.11)$$

$$\dot{g}_A(t) = \gamma n g_A(t). \qquad (3.12)$$

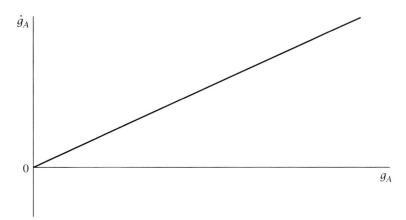

$\dot{g}_A$

0

g_A

FIGURE 3.5   The dynamics of the growth rate of knowledge when $\theta = 1$ and $n > 0$

If population growth is positive, g_A is growing over time; in this case the dynamics of the model are similar to those when $\theta > 1$. Figure 3.5 shows the phase diagram for this case.[6]

If population growth is zero (or if γ is zero), g_A is constant regardless of its initial situation. In this case, knowledge is just useful enough in producing new knowledge that the level of A has no impact on its growth rate. Thus there is no adjustment toward a balanced growth path: no matter where it begins, the economy immediately exhibits steady growth. As equations (3.6) and (3.11) show, the growth rates of knowledge, output, and output per worker are all equal to $Ba_L^\gamma L^\gamma$ in this case. Thus in this case a_L affects the long-run growth rate of the economy.

Since the output good in this economy has no use other than in consumption, it is natural to think of it as being entirely consumed. Thus $1 - a_L$ is the fraction of society's resources devoted to producing goods for current consumption, and a_L is the fraction devoted to producing a good (namely knowledge) that is useful for producing output in the future. Thus one can think of a_L as a measure of saving in this economy.

---

[6]One slightly awkward feature of using the generalized Cobb-Douglas production function is that, in the cases of $\theta > 1$ and of $\theta = 1$ and $n > 0$, it implies not merely that growth is increasing, but that it rises so fast that output reaches infinity in a finite amount of time. Consider, for example, the case of $\theta > 1$ with $n = 0$. One can check that $A(t) = c_1/(c_2-t)^{1/(\theta-1)}$, with $c_1 = 1/[(\theta-1)Ba_L^\gamma L^\gamma]^{1/(\theta-1)}$ and c_2 chosen so that $A(0)$ equals the initial value of A, satisfies (3.7). Thus A explodes at time c_2. Since output cannot reach infinity in a finite time, this implies that the generalized Cobb-Douglas production function must break down at some point. But it does not mean that the function cannot provide a good description over the relevant range. Indeed, Section 3.7 presents evidence that a model similar to this one provides a good approximation to historical data over thousands of years.

With this interpretation, this case of the model provides a simple example of a model where the saving rate affects long-run growth. Models of this form are known as *linear growth models;* for reasons that will become clear in Section 3.4, they are also known as $Y = AK$ *models.* Because of their simplicity, linear growth models have received a great deal of attention in work on endogenous growth.

The Importance of Returns to Scale to Produced Factors

The reason that these three cases have such different implications is that whether θ is less than, greater than, or equal to 1 determines whether there are decreasing, increasing, or constant returns to scale to *produced* factors of production. The growth of labor is exogenous, and we have eliminated capital from the model; thus knowledge is the only produced factor. There are constant returns to knowledge in goods production. Thus whether there are on the whole increasing, decreasing, or constant returns to knowledge in this economy is determined by the returns to scale to knowledge in knowledge production—that is, by θ.

To see why the returns to the produced input are critical to the behavior of the economy, suppose that the economy is on some path, and suppose there is an exogenous increase in A of 1 percent. If θ is exactly equal to 1, $\dot{A}$ grows by 1 percent as well: knowledge is just productive enough in the production of new knowledge that the increase in A is self-sustaining. Thus the jump in A has no effect on its growth rate. If θ exceeds 1, the 1 percent increase in A causes more than a 1 percent increase in $\dot{A}$. Thus in this case the increase in A raises the growth rate of A. Finally, if θ is less than 1, the 1 percent increase in A results in an increase of less than 1 percent in $\dot{A}$, and so the growth rate of knowledge falls.

3.3   The General Case

We now want to reintroduce capital into the model and determine how this modifies the earlier analysis. Thus the model is now described by equations (3.1) and (3.3)–(3.5) rather than by (3.5)–(3.7).

The Dynamics of Knowledge and Capital

As mentioned above, when the model includes capital, there are two endogenous stock variables, A and K. Paralleling our analysis of the simple model, here we focus on the dynamics of the growth rates of A and K. Substituting the production function, (3.1), into the expression for capital accumulation, (3.4), yields

$$\dot{K}(t) = s(1 - a_K)^{\alpha}(1 - a_L)^{1-\alpha}K(t)^{\alpha}A(t)^{1-\alpha}L(t)^{1-\alpha}. \tag{3.13}$$

Dividing both sides by $K(t)$ and defining $c_K = s(1 - a_K)^{\alpha}(1 - a_L)^{1-\alpha}$ gives us

$$g_K(t) \equiv \frac{\dot{K}(t)}{K(t)}$$

$$= c_K \left[\frac{A(t)L(t)}{K(t)} \right]^{1-\alpha}. \tag{3.14}$$

Thus whether g_K is rising, falling, or holding steady depends on the behavior of AL/K. The growth rate of this ratio is $g_A + n - g_K$. Thus g_K is rising if $g_A + n - g_K$ is positive, falling if this expression is negative, and constant if it is zero. This information is summarized in Figure 3.6. In (g_A, g_K) space, the locus of points where g_K is constant has an intercept of n and a slope of one. Above the locus, g_K is falling; below the locus, it is rising.

Similarly, dividing both sides of equation (3.3) by $A(t)$ yields an expression for the growth rate of A:

$$g_A(t) = c_A K(t)^{\beta} L(t)^{\gamma} A(t)^{\theta - 1}, \tag{3.15}$$

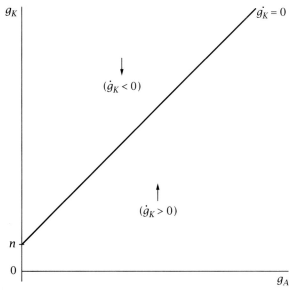

FIGURE 3.6 The dynamics of the growth rate of capital in the general version of the model

where $c_A \equiv B a_K^\beta a_L^\gamma$. Aside from the presence of the K^β term, this is essentially the same as equation (3.8) in the simple version of the model. Equation (3.15) implies that the behavior of g_A depends on $\beta g_K + \gamma n + (\theta - 1)g_A$: g_A is rising if this expression is positive, falling if it is negative, and constant if it is zero. This is shown in Figure 3.7. The set of points where g_A is constant has an intercept of $-\gamma n/\beta$ and a slope of $(1 - \theta)/\beta$ (the figure is drawn for the case of $\theta < 1$, so this slope is shown as positive). Above this locus, g_A is rising; and below the locus, it is falling.

The production function for output (equation [3.1]) exhibits constant returns to scale in the two produced factors of production, capital and knowledge. Thus whether there are on net increasing, decreasing, or constant returns to scale to the produced factors depends on their returns to scale in the production function for knowledge, equation (3.3). As that equation shows, the degree of returns to scale to K and A in knowledge production is $\beta + \theta$: increasing both K and A by a factor of X increases $\dot{A}$ by a factor of $X^{\beta+\theta}$. Thus the key determinant of the economy's behavior is now not how θ compares with 1, but how $\beta + \theta$ compares with 1. As before, we discuss each of the three possibilities.

Case 1: $\beta + \theta < 1$

If $\beta + \theta$ is less than 1, $(1 - \theta)/\beta$ is greater than 1. Thus the locus of points where $\dot{g}_A = 0$ is steeper than the locus where $\dot{g}_K = 0$. This case is shown in

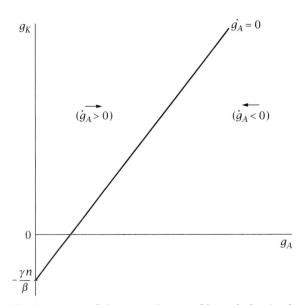

FIGURE 3.7   The dynamics of the growth rate of knowledge in the general version of the model

Figure 3.8. The initial values of g_A and g_K are determined by the parameters of the model and by the initial values of A, K, and L. Their dynamics are then as shown in the figure.

The figure shows that regardless of where g_A and g_K begin, they converge to Point E in the diagram. Both $\dot{g}_A$ and $\dot{g}_K$ are zero at this point. Thus the values of g_A and g_K at Point E, which we denote g_A^* and g_K^*, must satisfy

$$g_A^* + n - g_K^* = 0 \tag{3.16}$$

and

$$\beta g_K^* + \gamma n + (\theta - 1)g_A^* = 0. \tag{3.17}$$

Rewriting (3.16) as $g_K^* = g_A^* + n$ and substituting into (3.17) yields

$$\beta g_A^* + (\beta + \gamma)n + (\theta - 1)g_A^* = 0, \tag{3.18}$$

or

$$g_A^* = \frac{\beta + \gamma}{1 - (\theta + \beta)} n. \tag{3.19}$$

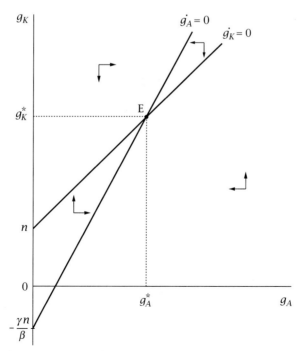

FIGURE 3.8 The dynamics of the growth rates of capital and knowledge when $\beta + \theta < 1$

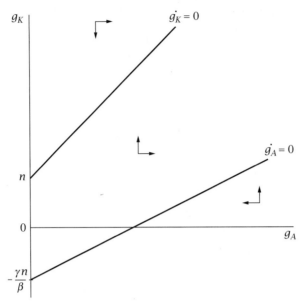

FIGURE 3.9   The dynamics of the growth rates of capital and knowledge when $\beta + \theta > 1$

From above, g_K^* is simply $g_A^* + n$. Equation (3.1) then implies that when A and K are growing at these rates, output is growing at rate g_K^*. Output per worker is therefore growing at rate g_A^*.

This case is similar to the case when θ is less than 1 in the version of the model without capital. Here, as in that case, the long-run growth rate of the economy is endogenous, and again long-run growth is an increasing function of population growth and is zero if population growth is zero. The fractions of the labor force and the capital stock engaged in R&D, a_L and a_K, do not affect long-run growth; nor does the saving rate, s. The reason that these parameters do not affect long-run growth is essentially the same as the reason that a_L does not affect long-run growth in the simple version of the model.[7]

Case 2: $\beta + \theta > 1$

In this case, the loci where g_A and g_K are constant diverge, as shown in Figure 3.9. As the phase diagram shows, regardless of where the economy starts, it eventually enters the region between the two loci. Once this occurs, the growth rates of both A and K, and hence the growth rate of output, increase continually. One can show that increases in s and n cause output per worker to rise above its previous trajectory by an ever-increasing amount.

---

[7]See Problem 3.5 for a more detailed analysis of the impact of a change in the saving rate in this model.

The effects of changes in a_L and a_K are more complicated, however, since they involve shifts of resources between the two sectors. Thus this case is analogous to the case when θ exceeds 1 in the simple model.

Case 3: $\beta + \theta = 1$

The final possibility is that $\beta + \theta$ equals 1. In this case, $(1 - \theta)/\beta$ equals 1, and thus the $\dot{g}_A = 0$ and $\dot{g}_K = 0$ loci have the same slope. If n is positive, the $\dot{g}_K = 0$ line lies above the $\dot{g}_A = 0$ line, and the dynamics of the economy are similar to those when $\beta + \theta > 1$; this case is shown in Panel (a) of Figure 3.10.

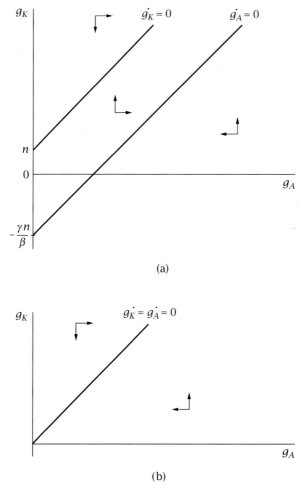

(a)

(b)

FIGURE 3.10 The dynamics of the growth rates of capital and knowledge when $\beta + \theta = 1$

If n is zero, on the other hand, the two loci lie directly on top of one another, as shown in Panel (b) of the figure. The figure shows that, regardless of where the economy begins, it converges to a balanced growth path. As in the case of $\theta = 1$ and $n = 0$ in the model without capital, the phase diagram does not tell us what balanced growth path the economy converges to. One can show, however, that the economy has a unique balanced growth path, and that the economy's growth rate on that path is a complicated function of the parameters. Increases in the saving rate and in the size of the population increase this long-run growth rate; the intuition is essentially the same as the intuition for why increases in a_L and L increase long-run growth when there is no capital. And, as in Case 2, increases in a_L and a_K have ambiguous effects on long-run growth. Unfortunately, the derivation of the long-run growth rate is tedious and not particularly insightful. Thus we will not work through the details.[8]

A specific example of a model of knowledge accumulation and growth whose macroeconomic side fits into this framework is P. Romer's model of "endogenous technological change" (Romer, 1990; the microeconomic side of Romer's model, which may be of more importance, is discussed in Section 3.4). As here, population growth is zero, and there are constant returns to scale to the produced inputs in both sectors. In addition, R&D uses labor and the existing stock of knowledge, but not physical capital. Thus in our notation, the production function for new knowledge is

$$\dot{A}(t) = Ba_L LA(t). \tag{3.20}$$

Since all physical capital is used to produce goods, goods production is

$$Y(t) = K(t)^\alpha [(1 - a_L)LA(t)]^{1-\alpha}. \tag{3.21}$$

Our usual assumption of a constant saving rate (so $\dot{K}(t) = sY(t)$) completes the model.[9] This is the case we have been considering with $\beta = 0$, $\theta = 1$, and $\gamma = 1$. To see the implications of this version of the model, note that (3.20) implies that A grows steadily at rate $Ba_L L$. This means the model is identical to the Solow model with $n = \delta = 0$ and with the rate of technological progress equal to $Ba_L L$. Thus (since there is no population growth), the growth rates of output and capital on the balanced growth path are $Ba_L L$. This model provides a simple example of a situation where long-run growth is endogenous (and depends on parameters other than population growth), but is not affected by the saving rate.

---

[8]See Problem 3.6.

[9]At the aggregate level, Romer's model differs in two minor respects from this. First, a_L and s are built up from microeconomic relationships, and are thus endogenous and potentially time-varying; in equilibrium they are constant, however. Second, his model distinguishes between skilled and unskilled labor; unskilled labor is used only in goods production. The stocks of both types of labor are exogenous and constant, however.

3.4   The Nature of Knowledge and the Determinants of the Allocation of Resources to R&D

Overview

Virtually all of the previous discussion takes the saving rate, s, and the fractions of inputs devoted to R&D, a_L and a_K, as given. The models of Chapter 2 (and of Chapter 7 as well) show the ingredients that are needed to make s endogenous. This leaves the question of what determines a_L and a_K. This section is devoted to that issue.

So far we have simply described the "A" variable produced by R&D as knowledge. But knowledge comes in many forms. It is useful to think of there being a continuum of types of knowledge, ranging from the highly abstract to the highly applied. At one extreme is basic scientific knowledge with broad applicability, such as the Pythagorean theorem, the germ theory of disease, and the theory of quantum mechanics. At the other extreme is knowledge about specific goods, such as how to start a particular lawn mower on a cold morning. In between is a wide range of ideas relevant to various classes of products, from the design of the transistor or the invention of the record player to an improved layout for the kitchen of a fast-food restaurant or a recipe for a better-tasting soft drink.

Many of these different types of knowledge play important roles in economic growth. Imagine, for example, that a hundred years ago there had been a halt to basic scientific progress, or to the invention of applied technologies useful in broad classes of goods, or to the invention of new products, or to improvements in the design and use of products after their invention. These changes would have had different effects on growth, and those effects would have occurred with different lags, but it seems likely that all of them would have led to substantial reductions in growth.

There is no reason to expect the determinants of the accumulation of these different types of knowledge to be the same: the forces underlying, for example, the advancement of basic mathematics are different from those behind improvements in the design of fast-food restaurants. There is thus no reason to expect a unified theory of the growth of knowledge. Rather, we should expect to find various factors underlying the accumulation of knowledge.

At the same time, as Romer (1990) emphasizes, all types of knowledge share one essential feature: they are *nonrival*. That is, the use of an item of knowledge, whether it is the Pythagorean theorem or a soft-drink recipe, in one application makes its use by someone else no more difficult. Conventional private economic goods, in contrast, are *rival:* the use of, say, an item of clothing by one individual precludes its simultaneous use by someone else.

An immediate implication of this fundamental property of knowledge is that the production and allocation of knowledge cannot be completely governed by competitive market forces. The marginal cost of supplying an item of knowledge to an additional user, once the knowledge has been discovered, is zero. Thus the rental price of knowledge in a competitive market is zero. But then the creation of knowledge could not be motivated by the desire for private economic gain. It follows that either knowledge is sold at above its marginal cost or its development is not motivated by market forces. Thus some departure from a competitive model is needed.

Romer emphasizes that, although all knowledge is nonrival, it is heterogeneous along a second dimension: *excludability*. A good is excludable if it is possible to prevent others from using it. Thus conventional private goods are excludable: the owner of a piece of clothing can prevent others from using it.

In the case of knowledge, excludability depends on both the nature of the knowledge itself and on economic institutions governing property rights. Patent laws, for example, give inventors rights over the use of their designs and discoveries. Under a different set of laws, inventors' ability to prevent the use of their discoveries by others might be smaller. To give another example, copyright laws give an author who finds a better organization for a textbook little ability to prevent other authors from adopting that organization. Thus the excludability of the superior organization is limited. (Because, however, the copyright laws prevent other authors from simply copying the entire textbook, adoption of the improved organization requires some effort; as a result there is some degree of excludability, and thus some potential to earn a return from the superior organization.) But it would be possible to alter the law to give authors stronger rights concerning the use of similar organizations by others.

In some cases, excludability is more dependent on the nature of the knowledge and less dependent on the legal system. The recipe for Coca-Cola is sufficiently complex that it can be kept secret without copyright or patent protection. The technology for recording television programs onto videocassette is sufficiently simple that the makers of the programs were unable to prevent viewers from recording the programs (and the "knowledge" they contained) even before courts ruled that such recording for personal use is legal.

The degree of excludability is likely to have a strong influence on how the development and allocation of knowledge depart from perfect competition. If a type of knowledge is entirely nonexcludable, there can be no private gain in its development; thus R&D in these areas must come from elsewhere. But when knowledge is excludable, the producers of new knowledge can license the right to use the knowledge at positive prices, and hence hope to earn positive returns on their R&D efforts.

With these broad remarks, we can now turn to a discussion of some of the major forces governing the allocation of resources to the development of knowledge. Four forces have received the most attention: support for basic scientific research, private incentives for R&D and innovation, alternative opportunities for talented individuals, and learning-by-doing.

Support for Basic Scientific Research

Basic scientific knowledge has traditionally been made available relatively freely; the same is true of the results of research undertaken in such institutions as modern universities and medieval monasteries. Thus this research is not motivated by the desire to earn private returns in the market. Instead it is supported by governments, charities, and wealthy individuals and is pursued by individuals motivated by this support, by desire for fame, and perhaps even by love of knowledge.

The economics of this type of knowledge are relatively straightforward. Since it is given away at zero cost and since it is useful in production, it has a positive externality. Thus its production should be subsidized.[10] If one added, for example, the infinitely-lived households of the Ramsey model to a model of growth based on this view of knowledge accumulation, one could compute the optimal research subsidy. Phelps (1966b), Nordhaus (1967), and Shell (1966, 1967) provide examples of this type of analysis.

Private Incentives for R&D and Innovation

Many innovations, ranging from the introductions of entirely new products to small improvements in existing goods, receive little or no external support and are motivated almost entirely by the desire for private gain. The modeling of these private R&D activities and their implications for economic growth has been the subject of considerable recent research; important examples include Romer (1990), Grossman and Helpman (1991a), and Aghion and Howitt (1992).

As suggested above, for R&D to result from economic incentives, the knowledge created by this R&D must be at least somewhat excludable. Thus the developer of a new idea has some degree of market power. Typically, the developer is modeled as having exclusive control over the use of the idea and as licensing its use to the producers of final goods. The fee that the innovator can charge for the use of the idea is limited by the usefulness of the idea in production, or by the possibility that others, motivated by the prospect of high returns, will devote resources to learning the idea. The quantities of the factors of production engaged in R&D are modeled in turn as resulting from factor movements that equate the private factor payments in R&D with the factor payments in the production of final goods.

---

[10]This implication makes academics sympathetic to this view of knowledge.

The Romer, Grossman–Helpman, and Aghion–Howitt models provide examples of complete models that formalize these notions. At the macroeconomic level, the models are similar to the third case in the previous section ($\theta + \beta = 1$ and $n = 0$), since that model is tractable and since it implies that the quantity of resources engaged in R&D may affect long-run growth. The models' microeconomic structures, however, are much richer.

Since economies like these are not perfectly competitive, their equilibria are not in general optimal. In particular, the decentralized equilibria may have inefficient divisions of resources between R&D and conventional goods production. Three externalities from R&D have been identified: the *consumer-surplus* effect, the *business-stealing* effect, and the *R&D* effect.

The consumer-surplus effect is that the individuals or firms licensing ideas from innovators obtain some surplus, since innovators cannot engage in perfect price discrimination. Thus this is a positive externality from R&D.

The business-stealing effect is that the introduction of a superior technology typically makes existing technologies less attractive, and therefore harms the owners of those technologies. This externality is negative.[11]

Finally, the R&D effect is that innovators are generally assumed not to control the use of their knowledge in the production of additional knowledge. In terms of the model of the previous section, innovators are assumed to earn returns on the use of their knowledge in goods production (equation [3.1]) but not in knowledge production (equation [3.3]). This assumption matches the institutional fact that a description of a new technology must be made available after a patent is granted, so that the knowledge can be used by other inventors. Thus the development of new knowledge has a positive externality on others engaged in R&D.

The net effect of these three externalities is ambiguous. It is possible to construct examples where the business-stealing externality outweighs both the consumer-surplus and R&D externalities. In this case the incentives to capture the profits being earned by other innovators cause too many resources to be devoted to R&D. The result is that the economy's equilibrium growth rate may be inefficiently high (Aghion and Howitt, 1992). It is generally believed, however, that the normal situation is for the overall externality from R&D to be positive. In the model developed by Romer (1990), for example, the consumer-surplus and business-stealing effects just balance, so on net only the positive R&D effect remains. In this case the equilibrium level of R&D is inefficiently low, and R&D subsidies can increase welfare.

There can be additional externalities as well. For example, if innovators have only incomplete control over the use of their ideas in goods production

---

[11]Both the consumer-surplus and business-stealing effects are pecuniary externalities: they operate through markets rather than outside them. As described in Chapter 2, such externalities do not cause inefficiency in a competitive market. For example, the fact that an individual's love of carrots drives up the price of carrots harms other carrot buyers, but benefits carrot producers. In the competitive case, these harms and benefits balance, and so the competitive equilibrium is Pareto-efficient. But when there are departures from perfect competition, pecuniary externalities can cause inefficiency.

(that is, if there is only partial excludability), there is an additional reason that the private return to R&D is below the social return. On the other hand, the fact that the first individual to create an invention is awarded exclusive rights to the invention can create excessive incentives for some kinds of R&D; for example, the private returns to activities that cause one inventor to complete an invention just ahead of a competitor can exceed the social returns.[12]

Alternative Opportunities for Talented Individuals

Baumol (1990) and Murphy, Shleifer, and Vishny (1991) observe that major innovations and advances in knowledge are often the result of the work of extremely talented individuals. They also observe that highly talented individuals typically have choices other than just pursuing innovations and producing goods. These observations suggest that the economic incentives and social forces influencing the activities of highly talented individuals may be important to the accumulation of knowledge.

Baumol takes a historical view of this issue. He argues that, in various places and times, military conquest, political and religious leadership, tax collection, criminal activity, philosophical contemplation, financial dealings, and manipulation of the legal system have been attractive to the most talented members of society. He also argues that these activities often have negligible (or even negative) social returns. That is, his argument is that these activities are often forms of *rent-seeking*—attempts to capture existing wealth rather than to create new wealth. Finally, he argues that there has been a strong link between how societies direct the energies of their most able members and whether societies flourish over the long term.

Murphy, Shleifer, and Vishny provide a general discussion of the forces that influence talented individuals' decisions whether to pursue activities that are socially productive. They emphasize three factors in particular. The first is the size of the relevant market: the larger is the market from which a talented individual can reap returns, the greater are the incentives to enter a given activity. Thus, for example, low transportation costs and an absence of barriers to trade encourage entrepreneurship; poorly defined property rights that make much of an economy's wealth vulnerable to expropriation encourage rent-seeking. The second factor is the degree of diminishing returns. Activities whose scale is limited by the entrepreneur's time (such as performing surgeries, for example) do not offer the same potential returns as activities whose returns are limited only by the scale of the market (such as creating inventions, for instance). Thus, for example, well-functioning capital markets that permit firms to expand rapidly tend to promote entrepreneurship over rent-seeking. The final factor

---

[12]See Reinganum (1989) for an introduction to some of the issues raised by such *patent races.*

is the ability to keep the returns from one's activities. Thus, clear property rights tend to encourage entrepreneurship, whereas legally sanctioned rent-seeking (through government or religion, for example) tends to encourage socially unproductive activities.

Learning-by-Doing

The final determinant of knowledge accumulation is somewhat different in character. The central idea is that, as individuals produce goods, they inevitably think of ways of improving the production process. For example, Arrow (1962) cites the empirical regularity that after a new airplane design is introduced, the time required to build the frame of the marginal aircraft is inversely proportional to the cube root of the number of aircraft of that model that have already been produced; this improvement in productivity occurs without any evident innovations in the production process. Thus the accumulation of knowledge occurs in part not as a result of deliberate efforts, but as a side effect of conventional economic activity. This type of knowledge accumulation is known as *learning-by-doing*.

When learning-by-doing is the source of technological progress, the rate of knowledge accumulation depends not on the fraction of the economy's resources engaged in R&D, but on how much new knowledge is generated by conventional economic activity. Analyzing learning-by-doing therefore requires some slight changes to our model. All inputs are now engaged in goods production; thus the production function becomes

$$Y(t) = K(t)^\alpha [A(t)L(t)]^{1-\alpha}. \tag{3.22}$$

The simplest case of learning-by-doing is when learning occurs as a side effect of the production of new capital. With this formulation, since the increase in knowledge is a function of the increase in capital, the stock of knowledge is a function of the stock of capital. Thus there is only one stock variable whose behavior is endogenous.[13] Making our usual choice of a power function, we have

$$A(t) = BK(t)^\phi, \qquad B > 0, \quad \phi > 0. \tag{3.23}$$

Equations (3.22)–(3.23), together with (3.4)–(3.5) describing the accumulation of capital and labor, characterize the economy.

To analyze the properties of this economy, begin by substituting (3.23) into (3.22); this yields

$$Y(t) = K(t)^\alpha B^{1-\alpha} K(t)^{\phi(1-\alpha)} L(t)^{1-\alpha}. \tag{3.24}$$

---

[13] See Problem 3.7 for the case in which knowledge accumulation occurs as a side effect of goods production rather than of capital accumulation.

Since $\dot{K}(t) = sY(t)$, the dynamics of K are given by

$$\dot{K}(t) = sB^{1-\alpha}K(t)^{\alpha}K(t)^{\phi(1-\alpha)}L(t)^{1-\alpha}. \tag{3.25}$$

In our model of knowledge accumulation without capital in Section 3.2, the dynamics of A are given by $\dot{A}(t) = B[a_L L(t)]^{\gamma}A(t)^{\theta}$ (equation [3.7]). Comparing equation (3.25) of the learning-by-doing model with this equation shows that the structures of the two models are similar. In the model of Section 3.2, there is a single productive input, knowledge. Here, we can think of there also being only one productive input, capital. As equations (3.7) and (3.25) show, the dynamics of the two models are essentially the same. Thus we can use the results of our analysis of the earlier model to analyze this one. There, the key determinant of the economy's dynamics is how θ compares with 1. Here, by analogy, it is how $\alpha + \phi(1 - \alpha)$ compares with 1, which is equivalent to how ϕ compares with 1.

If ϕ is less than 1, the long-run growth rate of the economy is a function of the rate of population growth, n. If ϕ is greater than 1, there is explosive growth. And if ϕ equals 1, there is explosive growth if n is positive and steady growth if n equals 0.

Once again, a case that has received particular attention is $\phi = 1$ and $n = 0$. In this case, the production function (equation [3.24]) becomes

$$Y(t) = bK(t), \qquad b \equiv B^{1-\alpha}L^{1-\alpha}. \tag{3.26}$$

Capital accumulation is therefore given by

$$\dot{K}(t) = sbK(t). \tag{3.27}$$

As in the similar cases we have already considered, the dynamics of this economy are straightforward. Equation (3.27) immediately implies that K grows steadily at rate sb. And since output is proportional to K, it also grows at this rate. Thus we have another example of a model in which long-run growth is endogenous and depends on the saving rate. Here it occurs because the contribution of capital is larger than its conventional contribution: increased capital not only raises output through its direct contribution to production (the K^{α} term in [3.24]), but also by indirectly contributing to the development of new ideas and thereby making all other capital more productive (the $K^{\phi(1-\alpha)}$ term in [3.24]). Because the production function in these models is often written using the symbol "A" rather than the "b" used in (3.26), these models are often referred to as "$Y = AK$" models.[14]

---

[14]The model in P. Romer (1986) that launched the new growth theory fits fairly well into this category. There are two main differences. First, the role played by physical capital here is played by knowledge in Romer's model: privately controlled knowledge both contributes directly to production at a particular firm and adds to aggregate knowledge, which contributes to production at all firms. Second, knowledge accumulation occurs through a separate production function rather than through foregone output; there are increasing returns to knowledge in goods production and (asymptotically) constant returns in knowledge accumulation. As a result, the economy converges to a constant growth rate.

3.5   Endogenous Saving in Models of Knowledge Accumulation: An Example[15]

The analysis in the previous sections, following the spirit of the Solow model, takes the saving rate as given. But again we sometimes want to model saving behavior as arising from the choices of optimizing individuals or households, particularly if we are interested in welfare issues.

Making saving endogenous in models like the ones we have been considering is often difficult. Here we consider only the simplest case: a single produced input, constant returns to that input, and no population growth. That is, we consider the case of $\theta = 1$ and $n = 0$ in the model with knowledge but without physical capital, or the case of $\phi = 1$ and $n = 0$ in the learning-by-doing model. For concreteness, the discussion is phrased in terms of the learning-by-doing model.[16]

Assume that the division of output between consumption and saving is determined by the choices of infinitely-lived households like those of the Ramsey model of Chapter 2. Since there is no population growth, we can assume that each household has exactly one member. Thus the utility function of the representative household is

$$U = \int_{t=0}^{\infty} e^{-\rho t} \frac{c(t)^{1-\sigma}}{1-\sigma} \, dt, \qquad \rho > 0, \quad \sigma > 0, \tag{3.28}$$

where c is the household's consumption, ρ is its discount rate, and σ is its coefficient of relative risk aversion. (Except for the use of σ rather than θ and the fact that the size of the household is normalized to 1, this is identical to equations [2.1]–[2.2].) Capital and labor are paid their private marginal products. Households take their initial wealth and the paths of interest rates and wages as given, and choose the path of consumption to maximize U.

When $\phi = 1$, the aggregate production function, (3.24), is $Y = B^{1-\alpha} K^{\alpha} K^{1-\alpha} L^{1-\alpha}$. Recall that the K^{α} term is capital's direct contribution to output, and that the $K^{1-\alpha}$ term is its indirect contribution through the accumulation of ideas. Thus the production function for a single firm, firm i, is

$$Y_i(t) = B^{1-\alpha} K_i(t)^{\alpha} K(t)^{1-\alpha} L_i(t)^{1-\alpha}, \tag{3.29}$$

---

[15]Readers who have not read Chapter 2 may wish to skip this section.

[16]Making saving endogenous in the cases either of multiple produced inputs or nonconstant returns is considerably more complex. Mulligan and Sala-i-Martin (1993) analyze the case of two produced inputs and no population growth, with constant returns to the two inputs. Romer (1986) is an example of a model with a single produced input, nonconstant returns, and endogenous saving.

where K_i and L_i are the amounts of capital and labor employed by the firm and K is the aggregate capital stock, which the firm takes as given. Thus the private marginal product of capital—the contribution of an additional unit of capital employed by firm i to the firm's output—is $\alpha B^{1-\alpha} K_i^{-(1-\alpha)} K^{1-\alpha} L_i^{1-\alpha}$. The firm hires capital up to the point where the private marginal product of capital equals the real interest rate.

In equilibrium, the capital-labor ratio is equated across firms. Thus K_i/L_i must equal the aggregate capital-labor ratio, which is K/L. Substituting this fact into the expression for the private marginal product of capital gives us

$$r(t) = \alpha B^{1-\alpha} K(t)^{-(1-\alpha)} K(t)^{1-\alpha} L^{1-\alpha}$$

$$= \alpha b \tag{3.30}$$

$$\equiv \bar{r},$$

where the second line uses the definition of b as $B^{1-\alpha} L^{1-\alpha}$. Thus with constant returns to capital and no population growth, the real interest rate is constant.

Similarly, the wage is given by the private marginal product of labor:

$$w(t) = (1-\alpha)B^{1-\alpha} K_i(t)^{\alpha} K(t)^{1-\alpha} L_i(t)^{-\alpha}$$

$$= (1-\alpha)B^{1-\alpha} K(t) L^{-\alpha}, \tag{3.31}$$

$$= (1-\alpha)bK(t)/L,$$

where the second line again uses the fact that, in equilibrium, each firm's capital-labor ratio equals the aggregate ratio, K/L. Thus the real wage is proportional to the capital stock.

From Chapter 2, we know that the consumption path of a household whose utility is given by (3.28) satisfies

$$\frac{\dot{c}(t)}{c(t)} = \frac{r(t) - \rho}{\sigma} \tag{3.32}$$

(see equation [2.19]). Since r is constant and equal to $\bar{r}$, consumption grows steadily at rate $(\bar{r} - \rho)/\sigma$. Let $\bar{g}$ denote this growth rate, and assume that it is less than $\bar{r}$.

The fact that consumption grows at rate $\bar{g}$ suggests that the capital stock and output also grow at this rate: if they did not, the saving rate would be continually rising or continually falling. To see if this is indeed the case, we need to check whether assuming a growth rate of the capital stock of $\bar{g}$ causes households to choose a level of consumption that actually causes capital to grow at this rate. That is, our procedure is to guess that K and Y grow at the same rate as consumption, and then to verify that this is an equilibrium.

If the capital stock grows at rate $\bar{g}$, the wage at time t is $(1-\alpha)bK(0)e^{\bar{g}t}/L$ (see [3.31]). Since the interest rate is constant at $\bar{r}$, this implies that the representative household's initial wealth plus the present value of its lifetime labor income is $K(0)/L + (1-\alpha)bK(0)/[(\bar{r}-\bar{g})L]$. And since consumption grows at rate $\bar{g}$, the present value of lifetime consumption is $c(0)/(\bar{r}-\bar{g})$. Equating the present value of lifetime consumption with lifetime wealth and solving for $c(0)$ yields

$$c(0) = (\bar{r} - \bar{g}) \left[\frac{K(0)}{L} + \frac{(1-\alpha)b}{L} \frac{K(0)}{\bar{r}-\bar{g}} \right]$$

$$= [(1-\alpha)b + \bar{r} - \bar{g}]\frac{K(0)}{L} \tag{3.33}$$

$$= (b - \bar{g})\frac{K(0)}{L},$$

where the last line uses the fact that $\bar{r} = \alpha b$.

We can now verify that this consumption behavior causes the capital stock to grow at rate $\bar{g}$. Since c and K are both growing at rate $\bar{g}$ and since there are L households, (3.33) implies that total consumption, $c(t)L$, is given by

$$C(t) = (b - \bar{g})K(t). \tag{3.34}$$

Substituting (3.34) and the production function, $Y = bK$, into the equation of motion for K, $\dot{K} = Y - C$, yields

$$\dot{K}(t) = bK(t) - (b - \bar{g})K(t)$$

$$= \bar{g}K(t). \tag{3.35}$$

Thus consumption, capital, and output all grow at a constant rate.[17]

This analysis implies that if the economy is subjected to some kind of shock (a change in ρ, for example), the ratio of consumption to the capital stock jumps immediately to its new balanced-growth-path value, and consumption, capital, and output all immediately begin growing at a constant rate. Thus there are no transitional dynamics to reach the balanced growth path. Intuitively, the fact that production is linear means that there is nothing special about any particular level of the capital stock or of the

---

[17]In addition, one can show that this is the only equilibrium. To see this, suppose $C(0)$ exceeds $(b-\bar{g})K(0)$. Then consumption must be higher at every point in time than under (3.34) (since C must grow at rate $\bar{g}$), and capital must therefore be lower. This implies that the present value of lifetime consumption is higher than before and that the present value of lifetime labor income is lower. But this means that households are violating their budget constraint, and thus that this path is not possible. A similar argument shows that if $C(0)$ is less than $(b-\bar{g})K(0)$, the present value of lifetime consumption is less than lifetime wealth.

capital-labor ratio. For example, if a war suddenly halves the capital stock, households respond simply by halving their consumption at every date.

The growth rate of the economy, $\overline{g}$, is $(\alpha b - \rho)/\sigma$. Since $\dot{K}(t)/K(t) = s(t)b$, where $s(t)$ is the fraction of output that is saved, the fact that $\dot{K}(t)/K(t)$ is constant and equal to $(\alpha b - \rho)/\sigma$ implies that $s(t)$ is constant and equal to $(\alpha b - \rho)/\sigma b$. Thus, for example, a lower value of households' discount rate, ρ, raises the saving rate and thereby increases long-run growth. A higher value of α also increases saving and growth: the higher the private marginal product of capital (αb) is relative to the social marginal product (b), the more households save, and thus the higher growth is. One implication is that unless α equals 1, the growth rate produced by the decentralized equilibrium is less than the socially optimal growth rate: a social planner would account for the full marginal product of capital rather than just the private marginal product, and would thus choose a saving rate of $(b - \rho)/\sigma b$, and hence a growth rate of $(b - \rho)/\sigma$.

3.6 Models of Knowledge Accumulation and the Central Questions of Growth Theory

Our analysis of economic growth is motivated by two issues: the growth over time in standards of living, and their disparities across different parts of the world. It is therefore natural to ask what the models of R&D and knowledge accumulation have to say about these issues.

With regard to worldwide growth, it seems plausible that the forces that the models focus on are important. At an informal level, the growth of knowledge appears to be the central reason that output and standards of living are so much higher today than in previous centuries. And as described in Chapter 1, formal growth-accounting studies attribute large portions of the increases in output per worker over extended periods to the unexplained residual component, which may reflect technological progress.

It would of course be desirable to refine the ideas we have been considering by improving our understanding of what types of knowledge are most important for growth, their quantitative importance, and the forces determining how knowledge is accumulated. But it seems likely that the kinds of forces we have been considering are important. Thus, the general directions of research suggested by these models seem promising for understanding worldwide growth.

With regard to cross-country differences in real incomes, the relevance of the models is less clear. There are two difficulties. The first is quantitative. As Problem 3.11 asks you to demonstrate, if one believes that economies are described by something like the Solow model but do not all have access to the same technology, the lags in the diffusion of knowledge from rich to poor countries that are needed to account for observed differences in incomes are extremely long—on the order of a century or more. It is hard to believe that the reason that some countries are so poor is that they do not have access to the improvements in technology that have occurred over the past century.

The second difficulty is conceptual. As emphasized in Section 3.5, technology is nonrival: its use by one firm does not prevent its use by others. This naturally raises the question of why poor countries do not have access to the same technology as rich countries. If the relevant knowledge is publicly available, poor countries can become rich by having their workers or managers read the appropriate literature. And if the relevant knowledge is proprietary knowledge produced by private R&D, poor countries can become rich by instituting a credible program for respecting foreign firms' property rights. With such a program, the firms in developed countries with proprietary knowledge would open factories in poor countries, hire their inexpensive labor, and produce output using the proprietary technology. The result would be that the marginal product of labor in poor countries, and hence wages, would rapidly rise to the level of developed countries.

Although lack of confidence on the part of foreign firms in the security of their property rights is surely an important problem in many poor countries, it is difficult to believe that this alone is the cause of the countries' poverty. There are numerous examples of poor regions or countries, ranging from European colonies over the past few centuries to many countries today, where foreign investors can establish plants and use their know-how with a high degree of confidence that the political environment will be relatively stable, their plants will not be nationalized, and their profits will not be taxed at exorbitant rates. Yet we do not see incomes in those areas jumping to the levels of industrialized countries.

One may reasonably object to this argument on the grounds that the difficulty that such countries face is not lack of access to advanced technologies, but lack of ability to use that technology. But this objection implies that the main source of differences in standards of living is not different levels of knowledge or technology, but differences in whatever factors allow richer countries to take better advantage of advanced technology. Understanding differences in incomes therefore requires understanding the reasons for the differences in these factors. This task is taken up in Part B of the chapter.

3.7 Empirical Application: Population Growth and Technological Change since 1 Million B.C.

The discussion in the previous section may seem to imply that models of endogenous knowledge accumulation are almost untestable. The models' predictions concern worldwide growth; thus cross-country differences cannot be used to test them. In addition, since many factors, such as wars and business cycles, affect short-term growth substantially, short-run time-series data are also of little value. Thus we are left only with long-run data for the world as a whole, which one might expect to be insufficient to provide strong tests between alternative views.

Kremer (1993) demonstrates, however, that the hypothesis that growth arises from endogenous knowledge accumulation can be tested despite these difficulties. He first notes that essentially all models of the endogenous growth of knowledge predict that technological progress is an increasing function of population size. The reasoning is simple: the larger the population, the more people there are to make discoveries, and thus the more rapidly knowledge accumulates.[18]

Kremer then argues that over almost all of human history, technological progress has led mainly to increases in population rather than increases in output per person. Population grew by several orders of magnitude between prehistoric times and the Industrial Revolution. But since incomes on the eve of the Industrial Revolution were not far above subsistence levels, it is not possible that output per person rose by anything close to the same amount. Only in the past few centuries, Kremer argues, has the impact of technological progress fallen to any substantial degree on output per person. Putting these observations together, Kremer concludes that models of endogenous technological progress predict that over most of human history, the rate of population growth should have been rising.[19]

Kremer's formal model is a straightforward variation on the models we have been considering. The simplest version consists of three equations. First, output depends on technology, labor, and land:

$$Y(t) = R^{\alpha}[A(t)L(t)]^{1-\alpha}, \tag{3.36}$$

where R denotes the fixed stock of land. (Capital is neglected for simplicity, and land is included to keep population finite.) Second, the growth rate of knowledge is proportional to population:

$$\frac{\dot{A}(t)}{A(t)} = BL(t). \tag{3.37}$$

And third, population adjusts so that output per person equals the subsistence level, denoted $\bar{y}$:

$$\frac{Y(t)}{L(t)} = \bar{y}. \tag{3.38}$$

---

[18]This effect can be seen clearly in the models we have been considering in the case of constant returns to produced inputs and no population growth.

[19]See Jones (1994) for tests of endogenous growth models that focus on recent history.

Aside from this Malthusian assumption about the determination of population, this model is similar to the model of Section 3.2 with $\gamma = \theta = 1$.[20]

To solve the model, begin by noting that (3.38) implies $Y(t) = \bar{y}L(t)$. Substituting this into (3.36) yields

$$\bar{y}L(t) = R^{\alpha}[A(t)L(t)]^{1-\alpha}, \tag{3.39}$$

or

$$L(t) = \left(\frac{1}{\bar{y}}\right)^{1/\alpha} A(t)^{(1-\alpha)/\alpha} R. \tag{3.40}$$

This equation states that the population that can be supported is decreasing in the subsistence level of output, increasing in technology, and proportional to the amount of land.

Since $\bar{y}$ and R are constant, (3.40) implies that the growth rate of L is $(1 - \alpha)/\alpha$ times the growth rate of A. Expression (3.37) for the growth rate of A therefore implies

$$\frac{\dot{L}(t)}{L(t)} = \frac{1 - \alpha}{\alpha} BL(t). \tag{3.41}$$

Thus, in this simple form, the model implies not just that the growth rate of population is rising over time, but that it is proportional to the level of population.[21]

Kremer tests this prediction by using population estimates extending back to 1 million B.C. that have been constructed by archaeologists and anthropologists. Figure 3.11 shows the resulting scatterplot of population growth against population. Each observation shows the level of population at the beginning of some period and the average annual growth rate of population over that period. The length of the periods considered falls gradually from many thousand years early in the sample to 10 years at the end. Because the periods considered for the early part of the sample are so long, even substantial errors in the early population estimates would have little impact on the estimated growth rates.

The figure shows a strongly positive, and approximately linear, relationship between population growth and the level of population. A regression of growth on a constant and population (in billions) yields

$$n_t = -0.0023 \quad + \; 0.524 \; L_t, \qquad R^2 = 0.92, \quad D.W. = 1.10, \tag{3.42}$$
$$\quad\;\; (0.0355) \quad\;\; (0.026)$$

---

[20]For other recent growth models that treat population growth as endogenous, see Barro and Becker (1988, 1989) and Becker, Murphy, and Tamura (1990).

[21]Kremer considers numerous variations on this model. Many of the simplifying assumptions prove not to be essential to the main results.

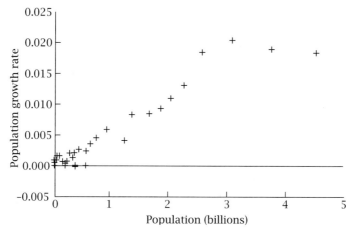

FIGURE 3.11   The level and growth rate of population, 1 million B.C. to 1990 (from Kremer, 1993; used with permission)

where n is population growth and L is population, and where the numbers in parentheses are standard errors. Thus there is an overwhelmingly statistically significant association between the level of population and its growth rate.[22]

The argument that technological progress is a worldwide phenomenon fails if there are regions that are completely cut off from one another. Kremer uses this observation to propose a second test of theories of endogenous knowledge accumulation. From the disappearance of the intercontinental land bridges at the end of the last ice age to the voyages of the European explorers, Eurasia-Africa, the Americas, Australia, and Tasmania were almost completely isolated from one another. The model implies that at the time of the separation, the populations of each region had the same technology; thus the initial populations should have been approximately proportional to the land areas of the regions (see equation [3.40]). The model predicts that during the period that the regions were separated, technological progress was faster in the regions with larger populations. The theory thus predicts that, when contact between the regions was reestablished around 1500, population density was highest in the largest regions. Intuitively, inventions that would allow a given area to support more people, such as the domestication of animals and the development of agriculture, were much more likely in Eurasia-Africa, with its population of millions, than in Tasmania, with its population of a few thousand.

The data confirm this prediction. The land areas of the four regions are 84 million square kilometers for Eurasia-Africa, 38 million for the Americas,

---

[22]The relationship appears to break down somewhat for the last two observations in the figure, which correspond to the period after 1970. For this period it is plausible that the Malthusian model of population (equation [3.38]) is no longer a good first approximation.

8 million for Australia, and 0.1 million for Tasmania. Population estimates for the four regions in 1500 imply densities of approximately 4.9 people per square kilometer for Eurasia-Africa, 0.4 for the Americas, and 0.03 for both Australia and Tasmania.[23]

Part B   Human Capital

3.8   Introduction

The discussion in Section 3.6 suggests that theories based on knowledge accumulation are unlikely to explain cross-country differences in incomes. This part of the chapter therefore investigates another strand of the new growth theory: models that emphasize the accumulation of human capital.

Although the acquisition of human capital by a worker involves learning, there is a clear conceptual distinction between human capital and abstract knowledge. Human capital consists of the abilities, skills, and knowledge of particular workers. Thus, like conventional economic goods, human capital is rival and excludable. If, for example, an engineer's full effort is being devoted to one activity, that precludes the use of his or her skills in another. In contrast, if an algorithm is being used in one activity, that in no way makes its use in another more difficult or less productive.

The models of this section therefore resemble the Solow model (and the Ramsey and Diamond models) in assuming constant returns to scale. Thus they do not provide candidate explanations for worldwide economic growth. (An exception occurs in Section 3.10, where the case of increasing returns is discussed briefly.) But the models differ from the Solow model in implying that moderate changes in the resources devoted to physical and human capital accumulation may lead to large changes in output per worker. As a result, they have the potential to account for large differences across countries in incomes.

To see why introducing human capital has the potential to greatly increase our ability to account for cross-country differences, recall that in models with only physical capital, the effect of a change in the saving rate on output depends on capital's share. In the Solow model, the long-run elasticity of output with respect to the saving rate is $\alpha/(1-\alpha)$, where α is capital's share (see equation [1.22]). If capital's share is moderate, this elasticity is not large. In terms of our familiar Solow-model diagram, a moderate value of capital's share means that $sf(k)$ is relatively curved, and thus that an in-

---

[23]Kremer argues that, since Australia is largely desert, these figures understate Australia's effective population density. He also argues that direct evidence suggests that Australia was more technologically advanced than Tasmania. Finally, he notes that there was in fact a fifth separate region, Flinders Island, a 680-square-kilometer island between Tasmania and Australia. Humans died out entirely on Flinders Island around 3000 B.C.

crease in s does not have a large impact on k^*. This is shown in Panel (a) of Figure 3.12. In addition, the moderate value of capital's share means that $f(k^*)$ is not very responsive to k^*. The end result is that output is not greatly affected by changes in the saving rate.

If capital's share is close to 1, on the other hand, $sf(k)$ is nearly linear; thus a small increase in s causes a large increase in k^*. This is shown in Panel (b) of the figure. The increase in capital's share also increases the effect of k^* on $f(k^*)$. Thus in this case the long-run elasticity of output with respect to the saving rate is large. And in the extreme case where capital's share is 1 (such as in the linear growth models discussed in the first part of the chapter), a change in s has a permanent effect on the growth rate of output; thus its effect on the level of output grows without bound.

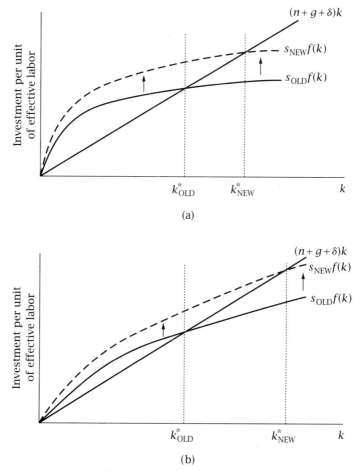

FIGURE 3.12 How capital's share affects the impact of a change in the saving rate in the Solow model

Some of workers' earnings reflect acquired skills rather than their inherent abilities. Thus recognizing the existence of human capital implies that we must raise our estimate of the share of income that is paid to capital of all kinds. In addition, the accumulation of human capital is broadly similar to the accumulation of physical capital: devoting more resources to the accumulation of either type of capital increases the amount of output that can be produced in the future. Thus, as the analysis that follows shows, adding human capital to our models increases the output effects of changes in the resources devoted to capital accumulation, just as raising physical capital's share in the Solow model increases the output effects of changes in the saving rate. It is this fact that makes the models able to account for large cross-country differences in incomes.

3.9   A Model of Human Capital and Growth

We now turn to a simple model of physical and human capital accumulation and growth.[24] Aside from the inclusion of human capital, the model resembles the Solow model with Cobb–Douglas production.

Assumptions

Output is given by

$$Y(t) = K(t)^\alpha H(t)^\beta [A(t)L(t)]^{1-\alpha-\beta}, \qquad \alpha > 0, \quad \beta > 0, \quad \alpha + \beta < 1, \quad (3.43)$$

where H is the stock of human capital. L continues to denote the number of workers; thus a skilled worker supplies both 1 unit of L and some amount of H.[25] Note that (3.43) implies that there are constant returns to K, H, and L together.

We make our usual assumptions about the dynamics of K and L:

$$\dot{K}(t) = s_K Y(t), \qquad\qquad\qquad (3.44)$$

$$\dot{L}(t) = nL(t), \qquad\qquad\qquad (3.45)$$

where we now use s_K to denote the fraction of output devoted to physi-

---

[24]The model follows Mankiw, D. Romer, and Weil (1992). For other models of human capital and growth, see Lucas (1988); Azariadis and Drazen (1990); Becker, Murphy, and Tamura (1990); Rebelo (1991); Kremer and Thomson (1994); and Problem 3.15.

[25]A way of writing (3.43) that may be more intuitive is $Y = K^\alpha (H/AL)^\beta (AL)^{1-\alpha}$. This formulation expresses output in terms of capital, labor, and human capital per worker.

cal capital accumulation, and where we again assume no depreciation for simplicity. In addition, because our goal here is not to explain worldwide growth, the model follows the Solow model and assumes constant and exogenous technological progress:

$$\dot{A}(t) = gA(t). \tag{3.46}$$

Finally, for simplicity, human capital accumulation is modeled in the same way as physical capital accumulation:

$$\dot{H}(t) = s_H Y(t), \tag{3.47}$$

where s_H is the fraction of resources devoted to human capital accumulation.[26]

This model can be generalized in several ways without affecting its central messages. The Cobb–Douglas function can be replaced by a general production function $Y = F(K, H, AL)$ that exhibits constant returns to scale and that, in intensive form, satisfies a two-variable analogue of the Inada conditions. The assumption of exogenous technological progress can be replaced by a model of endogenous growth of knowledge along the lines of the models in Part A of this chapter. And the assumption that the technology for producing new human capital is the same as the technology for producing output can be relaxed. None of these changes affect the model's central messages about cross-country differences in incomes.

The Dynamics of the Economy

The analysis of the dynamics of this economy parallels the analysis of the Solow model. The main difference is that, instead of just considering the dynamics of physical capital, we now consider the dynamics of both physical and human capital. Specifically, define $k = K/AL$, $h = H/AL$, and $y = Y/AL$. These definitions and (3.43) imply

$$y(t) = k(t)^\alpha h(t)^\beta. \tag{3.48}$$

Consider k first. The definition of k and the equations of motion for K, L, and A imply

---

[26]It is more appealing to interpret (3.47) as saying not that some output is "saved" in the form of human capital, but that the technology for producing new human capital combines physical capital, human capital, and raw labor in the same way as the technology for producing goods. That is, suppose that $\dot{H} = K_E^\alpha H_E^\beta [AL_E]^{1-\alpha-\beta}$, where K_E, H_E, and L_E denote the quantities of physical capital, human capital, and raw labor devoted to education; and suppose that $K_E = s_H K$, $H_E = s_H H$, and $L_E = s_H L$. Then it immediately follows that $\dot{H} = s_H [K^\alpha H^\beta (AL)^{1-\alpha-\beta}]$.

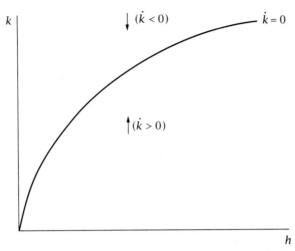

FIGURE 3.13   The dynamics of physical capital per unit of effective labor

$$\dot{k}(t) = \frac{\dot{K}(t)}{A(t)L(t)} - \frac{K(t)}{[A(t)L(t)]^2}[A(t)\dot{L}(t) + L(t)\dot{A}(t)]$$

$$= \frac{s_K Y(t)}{A(t)L(t)} - \frac{K(t)}{A(t)L(t)}\left[\frac{\dot{L}(t)}{L(t)} + \frac{\dot{A}(t)}{A(t)}\right] \tag{3.49}$$

$$= s_K y(t) - (n+g)k(t)$$

$$= s_K k(t)^\alpha h(t)^\beta - (n+g)k(t).$$

Thus $\dot{k}$ is zero when $s_K k^\alpha h^\beta = (n+g)k$. This condition is equivalent to $k^{1-\alpha} = [s_K/(n+g)]h^\beta$, or $k = [s_K/(n+g)]^{1/(1-\alpha)}h^{\beta/(1-\alpha)}$. The combinations of h and k satisfying this condition are shown in Figure 3.13; since $\beta < 1-\alpha$, the second derivative of k with respect to h along this locus is negative. In addition, (3.49) implies that $\dot{k}$ is increasing in h. Thus to the right of the $\dot{k} = 0$ locus $\dot{k}$ is positive, and to the left it is negative.

Now consider h. Reasoning parallel to that used to derive (3.49) yields

$$\dot{h}(t) = s_H k(t)^\alpha h(t)^\beta - (n+g)h(t). \tag{3.50}$$

$\dot{h}$ is zero when $s_H k^\alpha h^\beta = (n+g)h$, or $k = [(n+g)/s_H]^{1/\alpha}h^{(1-\beta)/\alpha}$. This set of points is shown in Figure 3.14; since $1 - \beta > \alpha$, its second derivative is positive. $\dot{h}$ is positive above this locus and negative below.

The initial values of K, H, A, and L determine the initial levels of k and h, which then evolve according to (3.49) and (3.50). Figure 3.15 shows the dynamics of k and h together. Point E is globally stable: whatever the economy's initial position, it converges to Point E. Once it reaches E, it remains there.[27]

---

[27]As in Chapter 1, we ignore the possibility of beginning without capital. If the initial value of k or h is zero, the economy converges to $k = h = 0$.

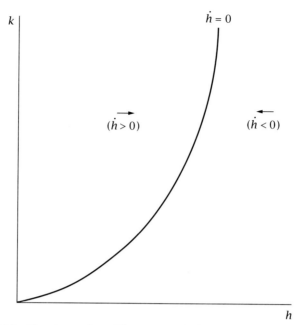

FIGURE 3.14   The dynamics of human capital per unit of effective labor

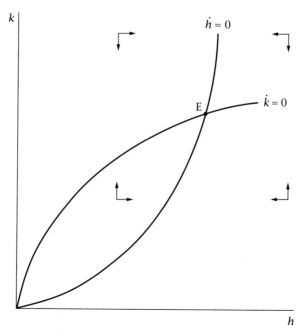

FIGURE 3.15   The dynamics of k and h

3.10   Implications

Qualitative Implications

When the economy reaches Point E, it is on a balanced growth path. On the balanced growth path, k, h, and y are constant; total physical capital, human capital, and output (K, H, and Y) are growing at rate $n + g$; and physical capital per worker, human capital per worker, and output per worker (K/L, H/L, and Y/L) are growing at rate g. Thus, as in the Solow model, the long-run growth rate of output per worker is determined by the exogenous rate of technological progress.

To see how changes in saving affect the economy, suppose that initially it is on a balanced growth path, and that s_K increases. Equations (3.49) and (3.50) imply that this change affects the $\dot{k} = 0$ locus but not the $\dot{h} = 0$ locus. The $\dot{k} = 0$ locus shifts up; this is shown in Figure 3.16. The old balanced growth path, Point E, is on the $\dot{h} = 0$ locus but is below the new $\dot{k} = 0$ locus. Thus initially h is constant and k is rising, and so the economy moves upward in (h, k) space. This moves the economy above the $\dot{h} = 0$ locus, and so h also begins to rise. Thereafter k and h both increase, and the economy moves up and to the right in (h, k) space until it reaches the new balanced growth path, Point E'.

We can write output per worker, Y/L, as $A(Y/AL)$, or $Ak^{\alpha}h^{\beta}$. During the transition between the two balanced growth paths, output per worker is

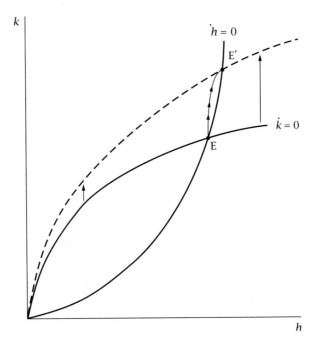

FIGURE 3.16   The effects of an increase in the saving rate

rising both for the usual reason that A is rising and because k and h are rising. Thus output per worker is growing at a rate greater than g. When the economy reaches the new balanced growth path, k and h are again constant, and so the growth rate of output per worker returns to g. Thus the permanent increase in the saving rate leads to a temporary increase in the economy's growth rate. In short, the model's qualitative implications are almost identical to the Solow model's.

Quantitative Implications

The model does not, however, share the Solow model's implications concerning the magnitude of the effects of changes in saving rates and population growth. To see this, it is helpful to solve for the level of y on the balanced growth path, y^*.[28] Let k^* and h^* denote the values of k and h on the balanced growth path. Since $\dot{k} = \dot{h} = 0$ on the balanced growth path, (3.49) and (3.50) imply

$$s_K k^{*\alpha} h^{*\beta} = (n + g)k^*, \tag{3.51}$$

$$s_H k^{*\alpha} h^{*\beta} = (n + g)h^*. \tag{3.52}$$

Taking logs of these two equations:

$$\ln s_K + \alpha \ln k^* + \beta \ln h^* = \ln(n + g) + \ln k^*, \tag{3.53}$$

$$\ln s_H + \alpha \ln k^* + \beta \ln h^* = \ln(n + g) + \ln h^*. \tag{3.54}$$

We can solve these two linear equations for $\ln k^*$ and $\ln h^*$; this yields

$$\ln k^* = \frac{1 - \beta}{1 - \alpha - \beta} \ln s_K + \frac{\beta}{1 - \alpha - \beta} \ln s_H - \frac{1}{1 - \alpha - \beta} \ln(n + g), \tag{3.55}$$

$$\ln h^* = \frac{\alpha}{1 - \alpha - \beta} \ln s_K + \frac{1 - \alpha}{1 - \alpha - \beta} \ln s_H - \frac{1}{1 - \alpha - \beta} \ln(n + g). \tag{3.56}$$

Finally, the production function (3.43) implies $\ln y^* = \alpha \ln k^* + \beta \ln h^*$. Substituting (3.55) and (3.56) into this expression and combining terms yields:

$$\ln y^* = \frac{\alpha}{1 - \alpha - \beta} \ln s_K + \frac{\beta}{1 - \alpha - \beta} \ln s_H - \frac{\alpha + \beta}{1 - \alpha - \beta} \ln(n + g). \tag{3.57}$$

The analogous expression for the Solow model is the same as (3.57) with β

---

[28] An alternative approach, paralleling the analysis in Section 1.5, is to assume a general production function in place of (3.43) and then consider approximations around the balanced growth path. This yields essentially the same results.

set to zero (see Problem 1.2):

$$\ln y^*_{\text{Solow}} = \frac{\alpha}{1 - \alpha} \ln s_K - \frac{\alpha}{1 - \alpha} \ln(n + g). \tag{3.58}$$

To assess the model's quantitative implications, we need a rough estimate of β, human capital's share. There are various ways to obtain such a figure. For concreteness, consider the United States. Kendrick's (1976) estimates of the value of the human capital stock are slightly larger than estimates of the value of the physical capital stock; this suggests that β is slightly more than $\frac{1}{3}$. The wage earned by unskilled workers, as approximated by the minimum wage, is typically between $\frac{1}{3}$ and $\frac{1}{2}$ of the average wage. This suggests that between $\frac{1}{2}$ and $\frac{2}{3}$ of the total payments to labor represent returns to human capital, or that $\frac{1}{2}(1 - \alpha) < \beta < \frac{2}{3}(1 - \alpha)$. This implies a value of β between $\frac{1}{3}$ and $\frac{4}{9}$. In the era before comprehensive coverage of minimum-wage laws, unskilled immigrants to the United States earned roughly $\frac{1}{4}$ of the average wage. This suggests $\beta \simeq \frac{1}{2}$.[29]

To see the importance of human capital, suppose that β is 0.4 and α is 0.35. Equation (3.57) implies that with these parameter values, output has elasticities of 1.4 with respect to s_K, 1.6 with respect to s_H, and -3 with respect to $n + g$. In the model without human capital, in contrast, a value for α of 0.35 implies that output's elasticity with respect to s_K is 0.54 and its elasticity with respect to $n + g$ is -0.54.

Because of the large elasticities of output with respect to its underlying determinants, the model has the potential to account for large cross-country income differences. Consider, for example, two countries with the same production function and technology, and continue to assume $\alpha = 0.35$ and $\beta = 0.4$. Suppose that s_K and s_H are twice as large in the second country as in the first, and that $n + g$ is 20 percent smaller; differences of these magnitudes do not appear uncommon in practice. Equation (3.57) implies that these differences lead to a difference in log output per worker on the balanced growth path of

---

[29]There is a sense in which essentially all of the payments to labor must reflect return to human capital: the marginal product of a person with no child-rearing or education would be virtually zero. There are two possible responses to this observation. One, suggested by Mankiw, Romer, and Weil (1992), is to argue that there is some minimum level of human capital—the ability to talk, to read and write, and so on—that most individuals obtain more or less automatically. This component of human capital accumulation would not be well described by equation (3.47), but instead would simply grow with population. This component could therefore be included in L. The second response, which is developed in Problem 3.15, is to accept the argument that raw labor is not directly useful in producing output, but to argue that it is useful in producing human capital: raw labor (that is, children and students) is an important input into child-rearing and education.

$$\ln y_2^* - \ln y_1^* = \frac{\alpha}{1 - \alpha - \beta}(\ln s_{K2} - \ln s_{K1}) + \frac{\beta}{1 - \alpha - \beta}(\ln s_{H2} - \ln s_{H1})$$

$$- \frac{\alpha + \beta}{1 - \alpha - \beta}[\ln(n_2 + g) - \ln(n_1 + g)] \tag{3.59}$$

$$= 1.4(\ln 2) + 1.6(\ln 2) - (3\ln 0.8) \simeq 2.75.$$

Since $e^{2.75} \simeq 15.6$, output per worker is almost 16 times larger in the second country. Thus differences in saving rates and population growth that are not extraordinary give rise to differences in incomes comparable to the vast gaps we are trying to understand.

The Solow model, as we saw in Chapter 1, cannot do this. For the same parameter values (except with β set to zero), (3.58) implies that the gap in log incomes is

$$\ln y_2^* - \ln y_1^* = \frac{\alpha}{1 - \alpha}(\ln s_{K2} - \ln s_{K1}) - \frac{\alpha}{1 - \alpha}[\ln(n_2 + g) - \ln(n_1 + g)] \tag{3.60}$$

$$= \frac{0.35}{0.65}(\ln 2 - \ln 0.8) \simeq 0.49.$$

Since $e^{0.49} \simeq 1.6$, the Solow model implies only a 60 percent difference in incomes.

Finally, because the model assumes diminishing marginal products of physical and human capital, it implies that rates of return are lower in rich than in poor countries. Thus the model does not answer the question of why capital does not flow to poor countries. At the same time, because the marginal products are only slowly diminishing, large differences in incomes are not associated with vast differences in rates of return. One can show that the marginal products of physical and human capital on the balanced growth path are

$$MPK^* = \alpha(n + g)/s_K, \tag{3.61}$$

$$MPH^* = \beta(n + g)/s_H \tag{3.62}$$

(see Problem 3.16). Since the variation in population growth and saving rates needed to account for large income differences is limited, large income differences imply only moderate differences in rates of return.

In the example above, for instance, $s_{K2} = 2s_{K1}$, $s_{H2} = 2s_{H1}$, and $n_2 + g = 0.8(n_1 + g)$; thus (3.61) and (3.62) imply $MPK_2^* = 0.4MPK_1^*$ and $MPH_2^* = 0.4MPH_1^*$. Although these differences are substantial, it is not out of the question that tax policies, the possibility of expropriation, capital-market imperfections, and so on could cause capital not to flow to poorer countries in the face of such differentials. And if β is larger, the differences in saving and population growth, and hence the differences in rates of return, needed to account for large income differences are even smaller. In the Solow model with a conventional value of capital's share, in contrast, we know from Chapter 1 that large income differences require vast differences in saving rates and rates of population growth, and thus that they imply vast differences in rates of return.

The Case of Increasing Returns

All of the analysis in this part of the chapter has assumed diminishing returns to physical and human capital together. But it is possible that there are constant or increasing returns to capital. There are several reasons that this might occur. First, as in the learning-by-doing model of Section 3.4, learning can occur as a by-product of capital accumulation. Second, there can be some other source of *external economies of scale*.[30] For example, the presence of other firms producing similar products can foster the development of a skilled labor force and of specialized support firms, and can therefore make production at a given firm more efficient. And third, there can be *internal economies of scale:* methods of production that are highly efficient at high levels of output may be impractical at low levels.

Relaxing the assumption of diminishing returns to physical and human capital together would have important implications for the analysis. As in the models of Part A of this chapter, growth rates would become endogenous and potentially ever-increasing. Changes in the resources devoted to capital accumulation could lead not just to large differences in the level of output per worker, but to permanent differences in growth rates. A simple example of such a model arises in the model we have been considering in the special case of $\alpha + \beta = 1$. This model, which is similar to the linear growth models of Part A, is analyzed in Problem 3.17. More elaborate models of constant or increasing returns to capital include P. Romer (1986); Lucas (1988); Rebelo (1991); and Murphy, Shleifer, and Vishny (1989a, 1989b).

Increasing returns to capital provide a candidate explanation other than knowledge accumulation of worldwide economic growth. But, as with the endogenous growth models of Part A of this chapter, there is reason to be skeptical of the importance of increasing returns for cross-country income differences. The key issue is the area over which the increasing returns occur. Clearly they must occur at least at the scale of entire economies if they are to be the driving force of economy-wide growth. And there is no reason for them to be limited by political boundaries: surely firms in Luxembourg can take advantage of increasing returns as well as firms in Germany can.

---

[30]External economies of scale occur when a doubling of inputs by a single firm only doubles its output, but a doubling of inputs by all firms together more than doubles their output. Internal economies of scale occur when a doubling of inputs by a single firm more than doubles its output.

If outputs are approximately linear in capital with little or no role for raw labor, then only by accident would total output (not output per worker) be higher in areas with larger populations. If there are constant or increasing returns to capital and a role for labor, there must be increasing returns to capital and labor together. But then, unless the increasing returns are worldwide, it is puzzling why output per unit of input is not much lower in such places as New Zealand and Hawaii, which are far removed from the rest of the world, than in such places as Western Europe and the Eastern United States. A final possibility is that the increasing returns are potentially worldwide but that economies differ in their ability to tap into those increasing returns. But then (just as with the argument that economies differ in their success in using worldwide knowledge) the source of cross-country income differences is not increasing returns, but whatever determines the differences in this success. Thus it appears to be difficult to use increasing returns to capital to account for income differences across parts of the world.

3.11 Empirical Application: Physical and Human Capital Accumulation and Cross-Country Differences in Incomes

The previous section shows that, when we allow for human capital, variations in population growth and capital accumulation have the potential to account for large cross-country differences in incomes. Mankiw, Romer, and Weil (1992) address the question of whether those variations in fact account for the differences.[31]

As described in Section 1.7, Mankiw, Romer, and Weil find that the estimated impact of saving and population growth on income is far larger than predicted by the Solow model with a capital share in the vicinity of one-third. Since the model with human capital predicts much larger impacts of saving and population growth on output than the Solow model does, this finding is encouraging for the human-capital model.

Mankiw, Romer, and Weil's strategy is to estimate equation (3.57), $\ln y^* = [\alpha/(1-\alpha-\beta)]\ln s_K + [\beta/(1-\alpha-\beta)]\ln s_H - [(\alpha+\beta)/(1-\alpha-\beta)]\ln(n+g)$. Their measures of y, s_K, and n are discussed in Chapter 1. As before, g is set to 0.05 for all countries.[32] They measure s_H as the average

---

[31]There is a large empirical literature on cross-country income differences. Among the factors that have been identified as potentially important to income are political stability (Barro, 1991), equipment investment (De Long and Summers, 1991, 1992), the financial system (King and Levine, 1993a, 1993b; Jappelli and Pagano, 1994), microeconomic distortions (Easterly, 1993), corruption (Mauro, 1993), and inflation (Fischer, 1991, 1993).

[32]When depreciation is included in the model, $g + \delta$ appears in place of g in (3.57). The value of 0.05 is thus intended as an estimate of $g + \delta$ rather than of g.

fraction of the population of working age that is in secondary school over the years 1960–1985. This is clearly an imperfect measure of the fraction of a country's resources devoted to human capital accumulation. Because s_H enters (3.57) logarithmically, if the true s_H is proportional to this measure, only the constant term of the regression will be affected. Nonetheless, measurement error in s_H is a concern.

Rewriting (3.57) slightly, the equation that Mankiw, Romer, and Weil estimate is

$$\ln y_i = a + b[\ln s_{Ki} - \ln(n_i + 0.05)] + c[\ln s_{Hi} - \ln(n_i + 0.05)] + \varepsilon_i, \quad (3.63)$$

where i indexes countries. The results for the broadest sample of countries are

$$\ln y_i = \underset{(0.14)}{7.86} + \underset{(0.12)}{0.73} \,[\ln s_{Ki} - \ln(n_i + 0.05)]$$

$$+ \underset{(0.07)}{0.67} \,[\ln s_{Hi} - \ln(n_i + 0.05)], \qquad\qquad (3.64)$$

$$N = 98, \qquad \overline{R}^2 = 0.78, \qquad \text{s.e.e.} = 0.51,$$

where the numbers in parentheses are standard errors. The values of α and β implied by these estimates of b and c (again with standard errors in parentheses) are $\alpha = 0.31\,(0.04)$ and $\beta = 0.28\,(0.03)$. In addition, when $\ln(n_i + 0.05)$ is entered separately, its coefficient is approximately equal to minus the sum of the coefficients on $\ln s_{Ki}$ and $\ln s_{Hi}$, as the model predicts, and this restriction is not rejected statistically. Thus the model fits the data remarkably well: the implied shares of physical and human capital are reasonable, and the regression accounts for almost 80 percent of cross-country variation in output per worker.

A natural concern is that the saving rates, particularly s_H, are endogenous: it may be that in countries that are wealthy for reasons not captured by the model, a larger fraction of the population is in school. But, as Mankiw, Romer, and Weil observe, this would cause upward bias in the estimate of β; the fact that the estimated β is if anything somewhat below direct estimates of human capital's share is therefore inconsistent with this possible explanation of the results.

Mankiw, Romer and Weil then turn to the issue of convergence, which we discussed in Chapter 1. They begin by noting that the model implies that countries with different levels of s_K, s_H, and n have different levels of output per worker on their balanced growth paths; thus there is a component of cross-country income differences that persists over time. But differences that arise because countries are initially at different points in relation to their balanced growth paths gradually disappear as the countries converge to those balanced growth paths. The model therefore predicts convergence controlling for the determinants of income on the balanced growth path, or *conditional convergence*.[33]

Specifically, one can show that the model implies that, in the vicinity of the balanced growth path, y converges to y^* at rate $(1 - \alpha - \beta)(n + g) \equiv \lambda$:[34]

$$\frac{d \ln y(t)}{dt} \simeq -\lambda[\ln y(t) - \ln y^*]. \tag{3.65}$$

Equation (3.65) implies that $\ln y$ approaches $\ln y^*$ exponentially:

$$\ln y(t) - \ln y^* \simeq e^{-\lambda t}[\ln y(0) - \ln y^*], \tag{3.66}$$

where $y(0)$ is the value of y at some initial date. (By differentiating [3.66], it is straightforward to check that it implies that $y(t)$ obeys [3.65].) If α and β are each $\frac{1}{3}$ and $n + g$ is 6 percent, λ is 2 percent; this implies that a country moves halfway to its balanced growth path in 35 years.

Adding $\ln y^* - \ln y(0)$ to both sides of (3.66) yields an expression for the growth of income:

$$\ln y(t) - \ln y(0) \simeq -(1 - e^{-\lambda t})[\ln y(0) - \ln y^*]. \tag{3.67}$$

Note that (3.67) implies conditional convergence: countries with initial incomes that are low *relative to their balanced growth paths* have higher growth. Finally, using equation (3.57) to substitute for $\ln y^*$ yields:

$$\ln y(t) - \ln y(0) \simeq (1 - e^{-\lambda t}) \ln y^* - (1 - e^{-\lambda t}) \ln y(0)$$

$$= (1 - e^{-\lambda t}) \frac{\alpha}{1 - \alpha - \beta} [\ln s_K - \ln(n + g)]$$

$$+ (1 - e^{-\lambda t}) \frac{\beta}{1 - \alpha - \beta} [\ln s_H - \ln(n + g)]$$

$$- (1 - e^{-\lambda t}) \ln y(0). \tag{3.68}$$

Mankiw, Romer, and Weil estimate this equation, using the same data as before. The results are

$$\ln y_i(t) - \ln y_i(0) = \underset{(0.48)}{2.46} + \underset{(0.082)}{0.500} [\ln s_{Ki} - \ln(n_i + g)]$$

$$+ \underset{(0.060)}{0.238} [\ln s_{Hi} - \ln(n_i + g)] - \underset{(0.061)}{0.299} \ln y_i(0), \tag{3.69}$$

$$N = 98, \qquad \overline{R}^2 = 0.46, \qquad \text{s.e.e.} = 0.33.$$

---

[33] Barro and Sala-i-Martin (1991, 1992) also investigate conditional convergence empirically.

[34] See Problem 3.19.

The implied values of the parameters are $\alpha = 0.48\,(0.07)$, $\beta = 0.23\,(0.05)$, and $\lambda = 0.0142\,(0.0019)$. The estimates are broadly in line with the predictions of the model: countries converge toward their balanced growth paths at about the rate that the model predicts, and the estimated capital shares are broadly similar to what direct evidence suggests.

Overall, the evidence suggests that a model that maintains the assumption of diminishing returns to capital but that adopts a broader definition of capital than traditional physical capital, and therefore implies a total capital share closer to 1 than to $\frac{1}{3}$, provides a good first approximation to the cross-country data.

Problems

3.1. Consider the model of Section 3.2 with $\theta < 1$.

(a) On the balanced growth path, $\dot{A} = g_A^* A(t)$, where g_A^* is the balanced-growth-path value of g_A. Use this fact and equation (3.7) to derive an expression for $A(t)$ on the balanced growth path in terms of B, a_L, γ, θ, and $L(t)$.

(b) Use your answer to part (a) and the production function, (3.6), to obtain an expression for $Y(t)$ on the balanced growth path. Find the value of a_L that maximizes output on the balanced growth path.

3.2. Consider two economies (indexed by $i = 1, 2$) described by $Y_i(t) = K_i(t)^\theta$ and $\dot{K}_i(t) = s_i Y_i(t)$, where $\theta > 1$. Suppose that the two economies have the same initial value of K, but that $s_1 > s_2$. Show that Y_1/Y_2 is continually rising.

3.3. Lags in a model of growth with an explicit knowledge-production sector. Assume that final-goods production is given by $Y(t) = A(t)(1 - a_L)L$, where a_L is the fraction of the population engaged in knowledge production and L is population. a_L and L are exogenous and constant.

Suppose that knowledge becomes useful in generating new knowledge only with a lag, so that $\dot{A}(t) = Ba_L LJ(t)$, where J is the stock of knowledge useful in generating new knowledge. $J(t)$ is given by $\int_{\tau=0}^{\infty}(1 - e^{-\nu\tau})\dot{A}(t - \tau)d\tau$, where $\nu > 0$. A simple way to check if there is a balanced growth path is to guess that it is possible for A to follow $A(t) = Ce^{gt}$, and look for candidate values of g.

(a) Show that the equation for $J(t)$ and the guess that $A(t) = Ce^{gt}$ imply $J(t) = [\nu/(\nu + g)]A(t)$.

(b) Is there any positive value of g such that, with $J(t)$ given by the expression in part (a) and $\dot{A}(t)$ given by $Ba_L LJ(t)$, $A(t)$ in fact follows $A(t) = Ce^{gt}$? How does that value of g depend on ν? What is its value as ν approaches infinity? Explain intuitively how it is possible for a temporary delay in the availability of knowledge to permanently reduce the growth rate of the economy.

3.4. Consider the economy analyzed in Section 3.3. Assume that $\theta + \beta < 1$ and $n > 0$, and that the economy is on its balanced growth path. Describe how each of the following changes affects the $\dot{g}_A = 0$ and $\dot{g}_K = 0$ lines and the position of the economy in (g_A, g_K) space at the moment of the change:

(a) An increase in n.

(b) An increase in a_K.

(c) An increase in θ.

3.5. Consider the economy described in Section 3.3, and assume $\beta + \theta < 1$ and $n > 0$. Suppose the economy is initially on its balanced growth path, and that there is a permanent increase in s.

(a) How, if at all, does the change affect the $\dot{g}_A = 0$ and $\dot{g}_K = 0$ loci? How, if at all, does it affect the location of the economy in (g_A, g_K) space at the time of the change?

(b) What are the dynamics of g_A and g_K after the increase in s? Sketch the path of log output per worker.

(c) Intuitively, how does the effect of the increase in s compare with its effect in the Solow model?

3.6. Consider the model of Section 3.3 with $\beta + \theta = 1$ and $n = 0$.

(a) Using (3.14) and (3.15), find the value that A/K must have for g_K and g_A to be equal.

(b) Using your result in part (a), find the growth rate of A and K when $g_K = g_A$.

(c) How does an increase in s affect the long-run growth rate of the economy?

(d) What value of a_K maximizes the long-run growth rate of the economy? Intuitively, why is this value not increasing in β, the importance of capital in the R&D sector?

3.7. Learning-by-doing. Suppose that output is given by equation (3.22), $Y(t) = K(t)^\alpha [A(t)L(t)]^{1-\alpha}$, that L is constant and equal to 1, that $\dot{K}(t) = sY(t)$, and that knowledge accumulation occurs as a side effect of goods production: $\dot{A}(t) = BY(t)$.

(a) Find expressions for $g_A(t)$ and $g_K(t)$ in terms of $A(t)$, $K(t)$, and the parameters.

(b) Sketch the $\dot{g}_A = 0$ and $\dot{g}_K = 0$ lines in (g_A, g_K) space.

(c) Does the economy converge to a balanced growth path? If so, what are the growth rates of K, A, and Y on the balanced growth path?

(d) How does an increase in s affect long-run growth?

3.8. Suppose that output at firm i is given by $Y_i = K_i^\alpha L_i^{1-\alpha} [K^\phi L^{-\phi}]$, where K_i and L_i are the amounts of capital and labor used by the firm, K and L are the aggregate amounts of capital and labor, and $\alpha > 0$, $\phi > 0$, and $0 < \alpha + \phi < 1$. Assume that factors are paid their private marginal products; thus $r = \partial Y_i / \partial K_i$. Assume that the dynamics of K and L are given by $\dot{K} = sY$ and $\dot{L} = nL$, and that K_i/L_i is the same for all firms.

(a) What is r as a function of K/L?

(b) What is K/L on the balanced growth path? What is r on the balanced growth path?

(c) "If an increase in domestic saving raises domestic investment, positive externalities from capital would mitigate the decline in the private marginal product of capital. Thus the combination of positive externalities from capital and moderate barriers to capital mobility may be the source of Feldstein and Horioka's findings about saving and investment described in Chapter 1." Does your analysis in parts (a) and (b) support this claim? Explain intuitively.

3.9. (This follows Rebelo, 1991.) Assume that there are two factors of production, capital and land. Capital is used in both sectors, whereas land is used only in producing consumption goods. Specifically, the production functions are $C(t) = K_C(t)^\alpha R^{1-\alpha}$ and $\dot{K}(t) = BK_K(t)$, where K_C and K_K are the amounts of capital used in the two sectors (so $K_C(t) + K_K(t) = K(t)$) and R is the amount of land, and $0 < \alpha < 1$ and $B > 0$. Factors are paid their marginal products, and capital can move freely between the two sectors. R is normalized to 1 for simplicity.

(a) Let $P_K(t)$ denote the price of capital goods relative to consumption goods at time t. Use the fact that the earnings of capital in units of consumption goods in the two sectors must be equal to derive a condition relating $P_K(t)$, $K_C(t)$, and the parameters α and B. If K_C is growing at rate $g_K(t)$, at what rate must P_K be growing (or falling)? Let $g_P(t)$ denote this growth rate.

(b) The real interest rate in terms of consumption is $B + g_P(t)$.[35] Thus, assuming that households have our standard utility function, (3.28), the growth rate of consumption must be $(B + g_P - \rho)/\sigma \equiv g_C$. Assume $\rho < B$.

  (i) Use your results in part (a) to express $g_C(t)$ in terms of $g_K(t)$ rather than $g_P(t)$.

  (ii) Given the production function for consumption goods, at what rate must K_C be growing for C to be growing at rate $g_C(t)$?

  (iii) Combine your answers to (i) and (ii) to solve for $g_K(t)$ and $g_C(t)$ in terms of the underlying parameters.

(c) Suppose that investment income is taxed at rate τ, so that the real interest rate households face is $(1 - \tau)(B + g_P)$. How, if at all, does τ affect the equilibrium growth rate of consumption?

3.10. (This follows Krugman, 1979; see also Grossman and Helpman, 1991b.) Suppose the world consists of two regions, the "North" and the "South." Output and capital accumulation in region i ($i = N, S$) are given by $Y_i(t) = K_i(t)^\alpha [A_i(t)(1 - a_{Li})L_i]^{1-\alpha}$, $\dot{K}_i(t) = s_i Y_i(t)$. New technologies are developed in the North. Specifically, $\dot{A}_N(t) = Ba_{LN}L_N A_N(t)$. Improvements in Southern technology, on the other hand, are made by learning from Northern technology: $\dot{A}_S(t) = \mu a_{LS}L_S[A_N(t) - A_S(t)]$ if $A_N(t) > A_S(t)$; otherwise $\dot{A}_S(t) = 0$. a_{LN}

---

[35]To see this, note that capital in the investment sector produces new capital at rate B and changes in value relative to the consumption good at rate g_P. (Because the return to capital is the same in the two sectors, the same must be true of capital in the consumption sector.)

is the fraction of the Northern labor force engaged in R&D, and a_{LS} is the fraction of the Southern labor force engaged in learning Northern technology; the rest of the notation is standard. Note that L_N and L_S are assumed constant.

(a) What is the long-run growth rate of Northern output per worker?

(b) Define $Z(t) = A_S(t)/A_N(t)$. Find an expression for $\dot{Z}$ as a function of Z and the parameters of the model. Is Z stable? If so, what value does it converge to? What is the long-run growth rate of Southern output per worker?

(c) Assume $a_{LN} = a_{LS}$ and $s_N = s_S$. What is the ratio of output per worker in the South to output per worker in the North when both economies have converged to their balanced growth paths?

3.11. Delays in the transmission of knowledge to poor countries.

(a) Assume that the world consists of two regions, the North and the South. The North is described by $Y_N(t) = A_N(t)(1 - a_L)L_N$ and $\dot{A}_N(t) = a_L L_N A_N(t)$. The South does not do R&D but simply uses the technology developed in the North; however, the technology used in the South lags the North's by τ years. Thus $Y_S(t) = A_S(t)L_S$ and $A_S(t) = A_N(t - \tau)$. If the growth rate of output per worker in the North is 3 percent per year, and if a_L is close to 0, what must τ be for output per worker in the North to exceed that in the South by a factor of 10?

(b) Suppose instead that both the North and the South are described by the Solow model: $y_i(t) = f(k_i(t))$, where $y_i(t) \equiv Y_i(t)/A_i(t)L_i(t)$ and $k_i(t) \equiv K_i(t)/A_i(t)L_i(t)$ ($i = N, S$). As in the Solow model, assume $\dot{K}_i(t) = sY_i(t) - \delta K_i(t)$ and $\dot{L}_i(t) = nL_i(t)$; the two countries are assumed to have the same saving rates and rates of population growth. Finally, $\dot{A}_N(t) = gA_N(t)$ and $A_S(t) = A_N(t - \tau)$.

(i) Show that the value of k on the balanced growth path, k^*, is the same for the two countries.

(ii) Does introducing capital change the answer to part (a)? Explain. (Continue to assume $g = 3\%$.)

3.12. Consider an economy described by the model of Part B of this chapter that is on its balanced growth path. Suppose there is a permanent increase in the rate of population growth. How does this affect output per worker over time?

3.13. Consider the model of Part B of the chapter.

(a) What is consumption per unit of effective labor on the balanced growth path?

(b) What values of s_K and s_H maximize this value?

3.14. Suppose that, despite the political obstacles, the United States permanently reduces its budget deficit from 3 percent of GDP to zero. Suppose that the economy is described by the model of Part B of the chapter, and that $\alpha = 0.35$ and $\beta = 0.4$. Suppose that initially $s_K = s_H = 0.15$, and that s_K rises by the full amount of the fall in the deficit.

(*a*) By how much does output eventually rise relative to what it would have been without the deficit reduction?

(*b*) By how much does consumption rise relative to what it would have been without the deficit reduction?

(*c*) What is the immediate effect of the deficit reduction on consumption? About how long does it take for consumption to return to what it would have been without the deficit reduction?

(*d*) Compare your results with the results of Problem 1.6.

3.15. Consider the following variant of our model with physical and human capital:

$$Y(t) = [(1 - a_K)K(t)]^\alpha [(1 - a_H)H(t)]^{1-\alpha}, \quad 0 < \alpha < 1, \quad 0 < a_K < 1, \quad 0 < a_H < 1,$$

$$\dot{K}(t) = sY(t) - \delta_K K(t),$$

$$\dot{H}(t) = B[a_K K(t)]^\gamma [a_H H(t)]^\phi [A(t)L(t)]^{1-\gamma-\phi} - \delta_H H(t), \quad \gamma > 0, \quad \phi > 0, \quad \gamma + \phi < 1,$$

$$\dot{L}(t) = nL(t),$$

$$\dot{A}(t) = gA(t),$$

where a_K and a_H are the fractions of the stocks of physical and human capital used in the education sector.

This model assumes that human capital is produced in its own sector with its own production function. Bodies (*L*) are useful only as something to be educated, not as an input into the production of final goods. Similarly, knowledge (*A*) is useful only as something that can be conveyed to students, not as a direct input into goods production.

(*a*) Define $k = K/AL$ and $h = H/AL$. Derive equations for $\dot{k}$ and $\dot{h}$.

(*b*) Find an equation describing the set of combinations of h and k such that $\dot{k} = 0$. Sketch in (h, k) space. Do the same for $\dot{h} = 0$.

(*c*) Does this economy have a balanced growth path? If so, is it unique? Is it stable? What are the growth rates of output per person, physical capital per person, and human capital per person on the balanced growth path?

(*d*) Suppose the economy is initially on a balanced growth path, and that there is a permanent increase in *s*. How does this change affect the path of output per person over time?

3.16. Use the production function, (3.43), and equations (3.55) and (3.56) to derive the expressions in equations (3.61) and (3.62) for the marginal products of physical and human capital on the balanced growth path of the model of Part B of this chapter.

3.17. Constant returns to physical and human capital together. Suppose the production function is $Y(t) = K(t)^\alpha H(t)^{1-\alpha}$ ($0 < \alpha < 1$), and that *K* and *H* evolve according to $\dot{K}(t) = s_K Y(t)$, $\dot{H}(t) = s_H Y(t)$.

(*a*) Show that regardless of the initial levels of *K* and *H* (as long as both are positive), the ratio K/H converges to some balanced-growth-path level, $(K/H)^*$.

(b) Once K/H has converged to $(K/H)^*$, what are the growth rates of K, H, and Y?

(c) How, if at all, does the growth rate of Y on the balanced growth path depend on s_K and s_H?

(d) Suppose K/H starts off at a level that is smaller than $(K/H)^*$. Is the initial growth rate of Y greater than, less than, or equal to its growth rate on the balanced growth path?

3.18. Increasing returns in a model with human capital. (This follows Lucas, 1988.) Suppose that $Y(t) = K(t)^\alpha [(1 - a_H)H(t)]^\beta$, $\dot{H}(t) = Ba_H H(t)$, and $\dot{K}(t) = sY(t)$, and assume $\alpha + \beta > 1$.[36]

(a) What is the growth rate of H?

(b) Does the economy converge to a balanced growth path? If so, what are the growth rates of K and Y on the balanced growth path?

3.19. The speed of convergence in the model of Part B of this chapter.

(a) Use the production function, (3.48), and the equations of motion for k and h, (3.49) and (3.50), to find an expression for $d[\ln y(t)]/dt$.

(b) Take a first-order Taylor approximation of the expression in part (a) in $\ln k$ and $\ln h$ around $\ln k = \ln k^*$, $\ln h = \ln h^*$.

(c) Using the expressions for $\ln k^*$ and $\ln h^*$ in equations (3.55) and (3.56), show that the expression you obtained in part (b) can be simplified to yield (3.65) in the text.

---

[36]Lucas's model differs from this formulation by letting a_H and s be endogenous and potentially time-varying, and by assuming that the social and private returns to human capital differ.

Chapter 4
REAL-BUSINESS-CYCLE THEORY

4.1 Introduction: Some Facts about Economic Fluctuations

Modern economies undergo significant short-run variations in aggregate output and employment. At some times, output and employment are falling and unemployment is rising; at others, output and employment are rising rapidly and unemployment is falling. Consider, for example, the United States in the early 1980s. Between the third quarter of 1981 and the third quarter of 1982, real GDP fell by 2.8%, the fraction of the adult population employed fell by 1.3 percentage points, and the unemployment rate rose from 7.3% to 9.9%. Then over the next two years, real GDP grew by 11.0%, the fraction of the adult population employed rose by 1.9 percentage points, and the unemployment rate fell back to 7.3%.

Understanding the causes of aggregate fluctuations is a central goal of macroeconomics. This chapter and the two that follow present the leading theories concerning the sources and nature of macroeconomic fluctuations. Before turning to the theories, this section presents a brief overview of some major facts about short-run fluctuations. For concreteness, and because of the central role of the U.S. experience in shaping macroeconomic thought, the focus is on the United States.

A first important fact about fluctuations is that they do not exhibit any simple regular or cyclical pattern. Figure 4.1 plots seasonally adjusted real GDP quarterly since 1947, and Table 4.1 summarizes the behavior of real GDP in the nine postwar recessions.[1] The figure and table show that output declines vary considerably in size and spacing. The falls in real GDP range from 0.8% in 1960 to 4.1% in 1973–1975; the times between the end of one recession and the beginning of the next range from

---

[1] The formal dating of recessions for the United States is not based solely on the behavior of real GDP. Instead, recessions are identified judgmentally by the National Bureau of Economic Research (NBER) on the basis of various indicators. For that reason, the dates of the official NBER peaks and troughs differ slightly from the dates shown in Table 4.1. Burns and Mitchell (1944) and Moore and Zarnowitz (1986) describe the modern NBER methodology. C. Romer (1994) describes the NBER methodology for the pre-World War II era.

FIGURE 4.1   U.S. real GDP, 1947–1994 (data from Citibase)

five quarters in 1980–1981 to nine years in 1960–1969 and in 1982–1991. The patterns of the output declines also vary greatly. In the 1980 recession, the full decline of 2.6% took place in a single quarter; in the 1990–1991 recession, the decline of 1.6% took place gradually over three quarters; and in the 1973–1975 recession, output fell irregularly by a total of 1.9% over four quarters and then dropped 2.2% in the final quarter of the recession.

Because output movements are not regular, modern macroeconomics has generally turned away from attempts to interpret fluctuations as combinations of deterministic cycles of different lengths; efforts to discern regular Kitchin (3-year), Juglar (10-year), Kuznets (20-year), and Kondratiev (50-year) cycles have been largely abandoned as unproductive.[2] Instead,

TABLE 4.1   Recessions in the United States since World War II

Year and quarter of peak in real GDP	Number of quarters until trough in real GDP	Change in real GDP, peak to trough
1948:4	4	−1.1%
1953:2	4	−2.2
1957:3	2	−3.3
1960:1	3	−0.8
1969:3	3	−0.9
1973:4	5	−4.1
1980:1	1	−2.6
1981:3	4	−2.8
1990:2	3	−1.6

Source: Citibase.

---

[2]There is an important exception to the claim that fluctuations are irregular: there are large seasonal fluctuations that are similar in many ways to conventional business-cycle fluctuations. See Barsky and Miron (1989).

TABLE 4.2   Behavior of the components of output in recessions

Component of GDP	Average share in GDP	Average share in fall in GDP in recessions relative to normal growth
Consumption		
Durables	6.9%	8.7%
Nondurables	24.8	14.3
Services	31.3	7.2
Investment		
Residential	5.1	14.7
Fixed nonresidential	10.1	21.1
Inventories	0.6	30.7
Net Exports	−0.6	−6.1
Government purchases	21.8	9.4

Source: Citibase.

the prevailing view is that the economy is perturbed by disturbances of various types and sizes at more or less random intervals, and that those disturbances then propagate through the economy. Where the major macro-economic schools of thought differ is in their hypotheses concerning these shocks and propagation mechanisms.

A second important fact is that fluctuations are distributed very un-evenly over the components of output. Table 4.2 shows both the average shares of each of the components in total output and their average shares in the declines in output (relative to its normal growth) in recessions. As the table shows, even though inventory investment on average accounts for only a trivial fraction of GDP, its fluctuations account for almost one-third of the shortfall in growth relative to normal in recessions: inventory accu-mulation is on average large and positive at peaks, and large and negative at troughs. Residential investment (that is, housing) and nonresidential fixed investment (that is, business investment other than inventories) also ac-count for disproportionate shares of output fluctuations; the same is true, to a lesser extent, of consumer purchases of durable goods. Finally, con-sumer purchases of nondurables and services, government purchases, and net exports are relatively stable.[3] Although there is some variation across recessions, the general pattern shown in Table 4.2 holds in most. And the same components that decline disproportionately when aggregate output is falling also rise disproportionately when output is growing at above-normal rates.

A third set of facts involves asymmetries in output movements. There are no large asymmetries between rises and falls in output; that is, output growth is distributed roughly symmetrically around its mean. There does,

---

[3]The entries for net exports indicate that they are on average negative over the postwar period, and that they typically grow—that is, become less negative—during recessions.

however, appear to be asymmetry of a second type: output seems to be characterized by relatively long periods when it is slightly above its usual path, interrupted by brief periods when it is relatively far below.[4]

A fourth set of facts concerns the nature of output fluctuations before the postwar era. In a series of papers, C. Romer (1986a, 1986b, 1989, 1994) demonstrates that there are important biases in traditional estimates of major macroeconomic time series for the period before World War II. She shows that once those biases are accounted for, aggregate fluctuations do not appear dramatically different before the Great Depression than after World War II. Output movements in the era before the depression appear slightly larger, and slightly less persistent; but there has been no sharp change in the character of fluctuations. Since such features of the economy as the sectoral composition of output and role of government were very different in the two eras, this suggests either that the character of fluctuations is determined by forces that have changed much less over time, or that there have been a set of changes to the economy that have had roughly offsetting effects on overall fluctuations.[5]

A corollary of these findings about output movements before the Great Depression is that the collapse in the depression and the rebound of the 1930s and World War II dwarf any fluctuations before or since. Real GDP in the United States fell by 30% between 1929 and 1933, with estimated unemployment reaching 25% in 1933. Over the next 11 years, real GDP rose at an average annual rate of 10%; as a result, unemployment in 1944 was 1.2%. Finally, real GDP declined by 23% between 1944 and 1947, and unemployment rose to 3.9%. In contrast, Romer's (1989) estimates imply that the largest decline in real GNP in the period 1869–1929 was a fall of 4.2% from 1907 to 1908. And as described above, the largest postwar decline has been 4.1% in 1973–1975. Likewise, the tremendous output gains of 1933–1944, and the remarkable unemployment rates of both the early 1930s and the mid-1940s, are unparalleled in the historical record.[6]

Finally, Table 4.3 summarizes the behavior of some important macroeconomic variables during recessions. Not surprisingly, employment falls and unemployment rises during recessions. The table shows that, in addition, the length of the average workweek falls. The declines in employment and hours are generally small relative to the falls in output. Thus productivity —output per worker-hour—generally declines during recessions. The conjunction of the declines in productivity and hours implies that movements

---

[4]More precisely, periods of extremely low growth quickly followed by extremely high growth are much more common than periods exhibiting the reverse pattern. See, for example, De Long and Summers (1986a); Sichel (1993); Beaudry and Koop (1993); and McQueen and Thorley (1993).

[5]See Balke and Gordon (1989) and Sheffrin (1988) for further discussion of pre-Depression versus post-World War II fluctuations.

[6]For two recent discussions of the status of our understanding of the Great Depression, see C. Romer (1993) and Bernanke's (1993) review of Eichengreen (1992).

TABLE 4.3   Behavior of some important macroeconomic variables in recessions

Variable	Average change in recessions	Number of recessions in which variable falls
Real GDP*	−4.7%	9/9
Employment*	−2.2%	9/9
Unemployment rate (percentage points)	+2.1	0/9
Average weekly hours, production workers, manufacturing	−0.9%	9/9
Output per hour, nonfarm business*	−1.4%	8/9
Inflation (GDP deflator; percentage points)	−0.9	5/8†
Real compensation per hour, nonfarm business*	−0.5%	7/9
Interest rate on 3-month Treasury bills (percentage points)	−1.9	9/9
Real money stock (M-2/GDP deflator)*‡	−1.4%	5/6

*Change in recessions is computed relative to the variable's average growth over the full postwar period, 1947–1992.

†Inflation was zero at both the peak and the trough of the 1948–49 recession.

‡Available only beginning in 1959.

Source: Citibase.

in the unemployment rate are generally smaller than the movements in output. The relationship between movements in output and the unemployment rate is known as *Okun's law*. As originally formulated by Okun (1962), the "law" stated that a shortfall in GDP of 3% relative to normal growth produces a 1 percentage point rise in the unemployment rate; a more accurate description of the current relationship is 2 to 1.

The remaining lines of Table 4.3 summarize the behavior of various price and financial variables. Inflation generally (but not always) falls.[7] The real wage, at least as measured in aggregate data, tends to fall slightly in recessions. And nominal interest rates and the real money stock both generally decline.

4.2   Theories of Fluctuations

It is natural to begin by asking whether aggregate fluctuations can be understood using a *Walrasian* model—that is, a competitive model without any externalities, asymmetric information, missing markets, or other imperfections. If they can, then the analysis of fluctuations may not require any fundamental departure from conventional microeconomic analysis.

---

[7]Other ways of summarizing the cyclical behavior of inflation and the price level give different results. Because of this, the cyclical behavior of inflation and the price level, and the implications of that behavior, are controversial. See Kydland and Prescott (1990); Cooley and Ohanian (1991); Backus and Kehoe (1992); Ball and Mankiw (1994); and Rotemberg (1994).

As emphasized in Chapter 2, the Ramsey model is the natural Walrasian baseline model of the aggregate economy: the model excludes not only market imperfections, but also all issues raised by heterogeneity among households. This chapter is therefore devoted to extending a variant of the Ramsey model to incorporate aggregate fluctuations.[8] This requires modifying the model in two ways. First, there must be a source of disturbances: without shocks, the Ramsey model converges to a balanced growth path and then grows smoothly. The initial extensions of the Ramsey model to include fluctuations emphasized shocks to the economy's technology—that is, changes in the production function from period to period.[9] More recently, work in this area has also emphasized changes in government purchases.[10] Both types of shocks represent real—as opposed to monetary, or nominal—disturbances: technology shocks change the amount that is produced from a given quantity of inputs, and government-purchases shocks change the quantity of goods available to the private economy for a given level of production. For this reason, the models are known as *real-business-cycle* (or *RBC*) models.

The second change that is needed to the Ramsey model is to allow for variations in employment. In all the models we have seen, labor supply is exogenous and either constant or growing smoothly. Real-business-cycle theory focuses on the question of whether a Walrasian model provides a good description of the main features of observed fluctuations. Models in this literature therefore allow for changes in employment by making households' utility depend not just on their consumption but also on the amount they work; employment is then determined by the intersection of labor supply and labor demand.

As discussed in the final section of this chapter, there is considerable debate about whether fluctuations can in fact be understood using Walrasian models. In particular, a large number of macroeconomists believe that the technology shocks and the propagation mechanisms of real-business-cycle models are of little relevance to actual fluctuations, and that nominal disturbances and a failure of nominal prices and wages to adjust fully to those disturbances are central to fluctuations.

Chapters 5 and 6 are therefore devoted to *Keynesian* theories of fluctuations. To keep the analysis tractable, and to do justice to how macroeconomics is actually done, Chapters 5 and 6 do not pursue the strategy of adding incomplete nominal adjustment to a Ramsey-style model. Instead, to focus on the consequences and causes of incomplete nominal adjustment, they investigate price stickiness in models that are dramatically simplified on the real side. Chapter 5 takes nominal stickiness as given and investigates

---

[8]King, Plosser, and Rebelo (1988, Section 3) and King and Rebelo (1986) investigate the consequences of using an endogenous growth model rather than the Ramsey model as the starting point for analyzing fluctuations.

[9]The seminal papers include Kydland and Prescott (1982); Long and Plosser (1983); Prescott (1986); and Black (1982).

[10]See Aiyagari, Christiano, and Eichenbaum (1992); Baxter and King (1993); and Christiano and Eichenbaum (1992a).

its effects. Chapter 6 tackles the questions of why nominal prices might not respond fully to disturbances.

One conclusion of Chapter 6 is that significant nominal stickiness is much more likely to arise if there are departures from a Walrasian model in addition to some type of direct impediment to instantaneous nominal adjustment: imperfections in the goods, credit, and labor markets may greatly magnify the consequences of barriers to nominal flexibility. Thus modern Keynesian theories differ from real-business-cycle models not only by including barriers to complete nominal adjustment, but also in their analysis of how the economy would operate in the absence of those barriers.

This division of theories of fluctuations into ones focusing on real shocks impinging on a Walrasian economy and ones focusing on nominal disturbances affecting an economy with significant imperfections omits the possibility of *real non-Walrasian* theories. That is, it may be that nominal shocks and nominal stickiness are not important to fluctuations, but that there are other departures from the Walrasian baseline that are central to fluctuations. There are a host of possible non-Walrasian features of the economy—such as imperfect competition, externalities, asymmetric information, departures from rationality, and failures of markets to clear—and thus a host of possible real non-Walrasian theories of fluctuations. Thus we will not attempt to discuss them comprehensively. Instead, we will consider them briefly at the end of Chapter 6.

4.3   A Baseline Real-Business-Cycle Model

We now turn to a specific real-business-cycle model. The assumptions and functional forms are similar to those used in most such models (see, for example, Prescott, 1986; Christiano and Eichenbaum, 1992a; Baxter and King, 1993; and Campbell, 1994). The model is a discrete-time variation of the Ramsey model of Chapter 2. Because our goal is to describe the quantitative behavior of the economy, we will assume specific functional forms for the production and utility functions.

The economy consists of a large number of identical, price-taking firms and a large number of identical, price-taking households. As in the Ramsey model, households are infinitely-lived. The inputs to production are again capital (K), labor (L), and "technology" (A). The production function is Cobb–Douglas; thus output in period t is

$$Y_t = K_t^\alpha (A_t L_t)^{1-\alpha}, \qquad 0 < \alpha < 1. \tag{4.1}$$

Output is divided among consumption (C), investment (I), and government purchases (G). Fraction δ of capital depreciates each period. Thus the capital stock in period $t + 1$ is

$$K_{t+1} = K_t + I_t - \delta K_t$$

$$= K_t + Y_t - C_t - G_t - \delta K_t. \tag{4.2}$$

The government's purchases are financed by lump-sum taxes.[11] Because households are infinitely-lived and there are no capital-market imperfections, the precise timing of the tax levies does not affect household behavior—that is, Ricardian equivalence holds.

Labor and capital are paid their marginal products. Thus the real wage and the real interest rate in period t are

$$w_t = (1 - \alpha)K_t^\alpha (A_t L_t)^{-\alpha} A_t$$

$$= (1 - \alpha)\left(\frac{K_t}{A_t L_t}\right)^\alpha A_t, \tag{4.3}$$

$$r_t = \alpha\left(\frac{A_t L_t}{K_t}\right)^{1-\alpha} - \delta. \tag{4.4}$$

The representative household maximizes the expected value of

$$U = \sum_{t=0}^{\infty} e^{-\rho t} u(c_t, 1 - \ell_t)\frac{N_t}{H}. \tag{4.5}$$

$u(\bullet)$ is the instantaneous utility function of the representative member of the household, and ρ is the discount rate.[12] N_t is population and H is the number of households; thus N_t/H is the number of members of the household. Population grows exogenously at rate n:

$$\ln N_t = \overline{N} + nt, \qquad n < \rho. \tag{4.6}$$

Thus the level of N_t is given by $N_t = e^{\overline{N}+nt}$.

The instantaneous utility function, $u(\bullet)$, has two arguments. The first is consumption per member of the household, c. The second is leisure per member, which is the difference between the time endowment per member (normalized to 1 for simplicity) and the amount each member works, ℓ. Since all households are the same, $c = C/N$ and $\ell = L/N$. For simplicity, $u(\bullet)$ is log-linear in the two arguments:

$$u_t = \ln c_t + b\ln(1 - \ell_t), \qquad b > 0. \tag{4.7}$$

The final assumptions of the model concern the behavior of the two driving variables, technology and government purchases. Consider technology

---

[11] Section 4.9 briefly discusses real-business-cycle models with distortionary taxes.

[12] The usual way to express discounting in a discrete-time model is as $1/(1 + \rho)^t$ rather than as $e^{-\rho t}$. But because of the log-linear structure of this model, the exponential formulation is more natural here. There is no important difference between the two approaches, however; specifically, if we define $\rho' = e^\rho - 1$, then $e^{-\rho t} = 1/(1 + \rho')^t$.

first. To capture trend growth, the model assumes that in the absence of any shocks, $\ln A_t$ would be $\overline{A} + gt$, where g is the rate of technological progress. But technology is also subject to random disturbances. Thus,

$$\ln A_t = \overline{A} + gt + \tilde{A}_t, \tag{4.8}$$

where $\tilde{A}$ reflects the effects of the shocks. $\tilde{A}$ is assumed to follow a *first-order autoregressive process*. That is,

$$\tilde{A}_t = \rho_A \tilde{A}_{t-1} + \varepsilon_{A,t}, \qquad -1 < \rho_A < 1, \tag{4.9}$$

where the $\varepsilon_{A,t}$'s are *white-noise* disturbances—a series of mean-zero shocks that are uncorrelated with one another. Equation (4.9) states that the random component of $\ln A_t$, $\tilde{A}_t$, equals fraction ρ_A of its previous period's value plus a random term. If ρ_A is positive, this means that the effects of a shock to technology disappear gradually over time.

We make similar assumptions about government purchases. The trend growth rate of per capita government purchases equals the trend growth rate of technology; if this were not the case, over time government purchases would become arbitrarily large or arbitrarily small relative to the economy. Thus,

$$\ln G_t = \overline{G} + (n + g)t + \tilde{G}_t, \tag{4.10}$$

$$\tilde{G}_t = \rho_G \tilde{G}_{t-1} + \varepsilon_{G,t}, \qquad -1 < \rho_G < 1, \tag{4.11}$$

where the ε_G's are white-noise disturbances that are uncorrelated with the ε_A's. This completes the description of the model.

4.4   Household Behavior

The two most important differences between this model and the Ramsey model are the inclusion of leisure in the utility function and the introduction of randomness in technology and government purchases. Before analyzing the model's general properties, this section therefore discusses these features' implications for households' behavior.

Intertemporal Substitution in Labor Supply

To see what the utility function implies for labor supply, consider first the case where the household lives only for one period and has no initial wealth. In addition, assume for simplicity that the household has only one member. In this case, the household's objective function is simply $\ln c + b \ln(1 - \ell)$, and its budget constraint is simply $c = w\ell$.

The Lagrangian for the household's maximization problem is

$$\mathcal{L} = \ln c + b\ln(1 - \ell) + \lambda(w\ell - c). \tag{4.12}$$

The first-order conditions for c and ℓ, respectively, are

$$\frac{1}{c} - \lambda = 0, \tag{4.13}$$

$$-\frac{b}{1 - \ell} + \lambda w = 0. \tag{4.14}$$

Since the budget constraint requires $c = w\ell$, (4.13) implies $\lambda = 1/w\ell$. Substituting this into (4.14) yields

$$-\frac{b}{1 - \ell} + \frac{1}{\ell} = 0. \tag{4.15}$$

The wage does not enter (4.15). Thus labor supply (the value of ℓ that satisfies [4.15]) is independent of the wage. Intuitively, because utility is logarithmic in consumption and the household has no initial wealth, the income and substitution effects of a change in the wage offset each other.

The fact that the level of the wage does not affect labor supply in the static case does not mean that variations in the wage do not affect labor supply when the household's horizon is more than one period. This can be seen most easily when the household lives for two periods. Continue to assume that it has no initial wealth and that it has only one member; in addition, assume that there is no uncertainty about the interest rate or the second-period wage.

The household's lifetime budget constraint is now

$$c_1 + \frac{1}{1 + r}c_2 = w_1\ell_1 + \frac{1}{1 + r}w_2\ell_2, \tag{4.16}$$

where r is the real interest rate. The Lagrangian is

$$\mathcal{L} = \ln c_1 + b\ln(1 - \ell_1) + e^{-\rho}[\ln c_2 + b\ln(1 - \ell_2)]$$

$$+\lambda\left[w_1\ell_1 + \frac{1}{1 + r}w_2\ell_2 - c_1 - \frac{1}{1 + r}c_2\right]. \tag{4.17}$$

The household's choice variables are c_1, c_2, ℓ_1, and ℓ_2. Only the first-order conditions for ℓ_1 and ℓ_2 are needed, however, to show the effect of the relative wage in the two periods on relative labor supply. These first-order conditions are

$$\frac{b}{1 - \ell_1} = \lambda w_1, \tag{4.18}$$

$$\frac{e^{-\rho}b}{1-\ell_2} = \frac{1}{1+r}\lambda w_2.$$

(4.19)

To see the implications of (4.18)–(4.19), divide both sides of (4.18) by w_1 and both sides of (4.19) by $w_2/(1+r)$, and equate the two resulting expressions for λ. This yields

$$\frac{e^{-\rho}b}{1-\ell_2}\frac{1+r}{w_2} = \frac{b}{1-\ell_1}\frac{1}{w_1},$$

(4.20)

or

$$\frac{1-\ell_1}{1-\ell_2} = \frac{1}{e^{-\rho}(1+r)}\frac{w_2}{w_1}.$$

(4.21)

Equation (4.21) implies that relative labor supply in the two periods responds to the relative wage. If, for example, w_1 rises relative to w_2, the household decreases first-period leisure relative to second-period leisure; that is, it increases first-period labor supply relative to second-period supply. Because of the logarithmic functional form, the elasticity of substitution between leisure in the two periods is 1.

Equation (4.21) also implies that a rise in the interest rate raises first-period labor supply relative to second-period supply. Intuitively, a rise in r increases the attractiveness of working today and saving relative to working tomorrow. As we will see, this effect of the interest rate on labor supply is crucial to employment fluctuations in real-business-cycle models. These responses of labor supply to the relative wage and the interest rate are known as *intertemporal substitution* in labor supply (Lucas and Rapping, 1969).

Household Optimization under Uncertainty

The second way that the household's optimization problem differs from its problem in the Ramsey model is that it faces uncertainty about rates of return and future wages. Because of this uncertainty, the household does not choose deterministic paths for consumption and labor supply. Instead, its choices of c and ℓ at any date potentially depend on all of the shocks to technology and government purchases up to that date. This makes a complete description of the household's behavior quite complicated. Fortunately, we can describe key features of its behavior without fully solving its optimization problem. Recall that in the Ramsey model, we were able to derive an equation relating present consumption to the interest rate and consumption a short time later (the Euler equation) before imposing the budget constraint and determining the level of consumption. With uncertainty, the analogous equation relates consumption in the current period to *expectations* concern-

ing interest rates and consumption in the next period. We will derive this
equation using the informal approach we used in equations (2.20)–(2.21) to
derive the Euler equation.[13]

Consider the household in period t. Suppose it reduces current consumption per member by a small amount Δc and then uses the resulting
greater wealth to increase consumption per member in the next period
above what it otherwise would have been. If the household is behaving optimally, a marginal change of this type must leave expected utility unchanged.

Equations (4.5) and (4.7) imply that the marginal utility of consumption per member in period t is $e^{-\rho t}(N_t/H)(1/c_t)$. Thus the utility cost of
this change is $e^{-\rho t}(N_t/H)(\Delta c/c_t)$. Since the household has e^n times as many
members in period $t+1$ as in period t, the increase in consumption per member in period $t+1$ is $e^{-n}(1+r_{t+1})\Delta c$. The marginal utility of period-$t+1$ consumption per member is $e^{-\rho(t+1)}(N_{t+1}/H)(1/c_{t+1})$. Thus the expected utility
benefit as of period t is $E_t[e^{-\rho(t+1)}(N_{t+1}/H)e^{-n}(1+r_{t+1})/c_{t+1}]\Delta c$, where E_t
denotes expectations conditional on what the household knows in period
t (that is, given the history of the economy up through period t). Equating
the costs and expected benefits implies

$$e^{-\rho t}\frac{N_t}{H}\frac{\Delta c}{c_t} = E_t\left[e^{-\rho(t+1)}\frac{N_{t+1}}{H}e^{-n}\frac{1}{c_{t+1}}(1+r_{t+1})\right]\Delta c. \qquad (4.22)$$

Since $e^{-\rho(t+1)}(N_{t+1}/H)e^{-n}$ is not uncertain and since $N_{t+1} = N_t e^n$, this simplifies to

$$\frac{1}{c_t} = e^{-\rho}E_t[\frac{1}{c_{t+1}}(1+r_{t+1})]. \qquad (4.23)$$

This is the analogue of equation (2.19) in the Ramsey model.

Note that the expression on the right-hand side of (4.23) is *not* the same
as $e^{-\rho}E_t[1/c_{t+1}]E_t[1+r_{t+1}]$. That is, the tradeoff between present and future consumption depends not just on the expectations of future marginal
utility and the rate of return, but also on their interaction. Specifically, the
expectation of the product of two variables equals the product of their expectations plus their covariance. Thus (4.23) implies

$$\frac{1}{c_t} = e^{-\rho}\left(E_t[\frac{1}{c_{t+1}}]E_t[1+r_{t+1}] + \text{Cov}(\frac{1}{c_{t+1}}, 1+r_{t+1})\right), \qquad (4.24)$$

where $\text{Cov}(1/c_{t+1}, 1+r_{t+1})$ denotes the covariance of $1/c_{t+1}$ and $1+r_{t+1}$.
Suppose, for example, that when r_{t+1} is high, c_{t+1} is also high. In this
case, $\text{Cov}(1/c_{t+1}, 1+r_{t+1})$ is negative—that is, the return to saving is high in

---

[13]The household's problem can be analyzed more formally using *dynamic programming*
(see Section 10.4, below; Dixit, 1990, Chapter 11; or Kreps, 1990, Appendix 2). This also yields
(4.23), below.

the times when the marginal utility of consumption is low. This makes saving less attractive than it is if $1/c_{t+1}$ and r_{t+1} are uncorrelated, and thus tends to raise current consumption.

Chapter 7 discusses the impact of uncertainty on optimal consumption further.

The Tradeoff between Consumption and Labor Supply

The household chooses not only consumption at each date, but also labor supply. Thus a second first-order condition for the household's optimization problem relates its current consumption and labor supply. Specifically, imagine the household increasing its labor supply per member in period t by a small amount $\Delta\ell$ and using the resulting income to increase its consumption in that period. Again if the household is behaving optimally, a marginal change of this type must leave expected utility unchanged.

From equations (4.5) and (4.7), the marginal disutility of working in period t is $e^{-\rho t}(N_t/H)[b/(1 - \ell_t)]$. Thus the change has a utility cost of $e^{-\rho t}(N_t/H)[b/(1 - \ell_t)]\Delta\ell$. And since the change raises consumption by $w_t\Delta\ell$, it has a utility benefit of $e^{-\rho t}(N_t/H)(1/c_t)w_t\Delta\ell$. Equating the cost and benefit gives us

$$e^{-\rho t}\frac{N_t}{H}\frac{b}{1 - \ell_t}\Delta\ell = e^{-\rho t}\frac{N_t}{H}\frac{1}{c_t}w_t\Delta\ell, \qquad (4.25)$$

or

$$\frac{c_t}{1 - \ell_t} = \frac{w_t}{b}. \qquad (4.26)$$

Equation (4.26) relates current leisure and consumption given the wage. Because it involves current variables, which are known, uncertainty does not enter. Equations (4.23) and (4.26) are the key equations describing households' behavior.

4.5   A Special Case of the Model

Simplifying Assumptions

The model of Section 4.3 cannot be solved analytically. The basic problem, as Campbell (1994) emphasizes, is that it contains a mixture of ingredients that are linear—such as depreciation and the division of output into consumption, investment, and government purchases—and ones that are log-linear—such as the production function and preferences. In this section, we therefore investigate a simplified version of the model.

Specifically, we make two changes to the model: we eliminate government and we assume 100% depreciation each period.[14] Thus equations (4.10) and (4.11) are dropped from the model, and equations (4.2) and (4.4) become

$$K_{t+1} = Y_t - C_t, \tag{4.27}$$

$$1 + r_t = \alpha \left(\frac{A_t L_t}{K_t} \right)^{1-\alpha}. \tag{4.28}$$

The elimination of government can be justified on the grounds that doing so allows us to isolate the effects of technology shocks. The grounds for the assumption of complete depreciation, on the other hand, are only that it allows the model to be solved.

Solving the Model

Because markets are competitive, externalities are absent, and individuals are infinitely-lived, the model's equilibrium must correspond to the Pareto optimum. Because of this, we can find the equilibrium either by ignoring markets and finding the social optimum directly, or by solving for the competitive equilibrium. We will take the second approach, on the grounds that it is easier to apply to variations of the model where Pareto optimality fails. Finding the social optimum is sometimes easier, however; as a result, many real-business-cycle models are solved that way.[15]

The solution to the model focuses on two variables, labor supply per person, ℓ, and the fraction of output that is saved, s. The basic strategy is to rewrite the equations of the model in log-linear form, substituting $(1-s)Y$ for C whenever it appears. We will then determine how ℓ and s must depend on the current technology and on the capital stock inherited from the previous period to satisfy the equilibrium conditions. We will focus on the two conditions for household optimization, (4.23) and (4.26); the remaining equations follow mechanically from accounting and from competition.

We will find that s is independent of technology and the capital stock. Intuitively, the combination of logarithmic utility, Cobb–Douglas production, and 100% depreciation causes movements in both technology and capital to have offsetting income and substitution effects on saving. It is the fact that s is constant that allows the model to be solved analytically.

---

[14]With these changes, the model corresponds to a one-sector version of Long and Plosser's (1983) real-business-cycle model. McCallum (1989) investigates this model. In addition, except for the assumption of $\delta = 1$, the model corresponds to the basic case considered by Prescott (1986). It is straightforward to assume that a constant fraction of output is purchased by the government instead of eliminating government altogether.

[15]See Problem 4.11 for the solution using the social-optimum approach.

Consider (4.23) first; this condition is $1/c_t = e^{-\rho}E_t[(1 + r_{t+1})/c_{t+1}]$. Since $c_t = (1 - s_t)Y_t/N_t$, rewriting (4.23) along the lines just suggested gives us

$$-\ln\left[(1 - s_t)\frac{Y_t}{N_t}\right] = -\rho + \ln E_t\left[\frac{1 + r_{t+1}}{(1 - s_{t+1})\dfrac{Y_{t+1}}{N_{t+1}}}\right]. \tag{4.29}$$

Since the production function is Cobb-Douglas and depreciation is 100%, $1 + r_{t+1} = \alpha Y_{t+1}/K_{t+1}$. In addition, 100% depreciation implies that $K_{t+1} = Y_t - C_t = s_t Y_t$. Substituting these facts into (4.29) yields

$$-\ln(1 - s_t) - \ln Y_t + \ln N_t$$

$$= -\rho + \ln E_t\left[\frac{\alpha Y_{t+1}}{K_{t+1}(1 - s_{t+1})\dfrac{Y_{t+1}}{N_{t+1}}}\right] \tag{4.30}$$

$$= -\rho + \ln E_t\left[\frac{\alpha N_{t+1}}{s_t(1 - s_{t+1})Y_t}\right]$$

$$= -\rho + \ln \alpha + \ln N_t + n - \ln s_t - \ln Y_t + \ln E_t\left[\frac{1}{1 - s_{t+1}}\right],$$

where the final line uses the facts that α, N_{t+1}, s_t, and Y_t are known at date t and that N is growing at rate n. Equation (4.30) simplifies to

$$\ln s_t - \ln(1 - s_t) = -\rho + n + \ln \alpha + \ln E_t\left[\frac{1}{1 - s_{t+1}}\right]. \tag{4.31}$$

A and K—technology and capital—do not enter (4.31). Thus there is a constant value of s that satisfies this condition. To see this, note that if s is constant at some value $\hat{s}$, s_{t+1} is not uncertain, and so $E_t[1/(1 - s_{t+1})]$ is simply $1/(1 - \hat{s})$. Thus (4.31) becomes

$$\ln \hat{s} = \ln \alpha + n - \rho, \tag{4.32}$$

or

$$\hat{s} = \alpha e^{n-\rho}. \tag{4.33}$$

Thus the saving rate is constant.

Now consider (4.26), which states $c_t/(1 - \ell_t) = w_t/b$. Since $c_t = C_t/N_t = (1 - \hat{s})Y_t/N_t$, we can rewrite this condition as

$$\ln[(1 - \hat{s})Y_t/N_t] - \ln(1 - \ell_t) = \ln w_t - \ln b. \tag{4.34}$$

Since the production function is Cobb-Douglas, $w_t = (1 - \alpha)Y_t/(\ell_t N_t)$. Substituting this fact into (4.34) yields

$$\ln(1 - \hat{s}) + \ln Y_t - \ln N_t - \ln(1 - \ell_t)$$
$$= \ln(1 - \alpha) + \ln Y_t - \ln \ell_t - \ln N_t - \ln b.$$

(4.35)

Canceling terms and rearranging gives us

$$\ln \ell_t - \ln(1 - \ell_t) = \ln(1 - \alpha) - \ln(1 - \hat{s}) - \ln b.$$

(4.36)

Finally, straightforward algebra yields

$$\ell_t = \frac{1 - \alpha}{(1 - \alpha) + b(1 - \hat{s})}$$

(4.37)

$$\equiv \hat{\ell}.$$

Thus labor supply is also constant. The reason this occurs despite households' willingness to substitute their labor supply intertemporally is that movements in either technology or capital have offsetting impacts on the relative-wage and interest-rate effects on labor supply. An improvement in technology, for example, raises current wages relative to expected future wages, and thus acts to raise labor supply. But, by raising the amount saved, it also lowers the expected interest rate, which acts to reduce labor supply. In the specific case we are considering, these two effects exactly balance.

The remaining equations of the model do not involve optimization; they follow from technology, accounting, and competition. Thus we have found a solution to the model with s and ℓ constant.

As described above, any competitive equilibrium of this model is also a solution to the problem of maximizing the expected utility of the representative household. Standard results about optimization imply that this problem has a unique solution (see Stokey, Lucas, and Prescott, 1989, for example). Thus the equilibrium we have found must be the only one.

Discussion

This model provides an example of an economy where real shocks drive output movements. Because there are no market failures, the movements are the optimal responses to the shocks. Thus, contrary to the conventional wisdom about macroeconomic fluctuations, here fluctuations do not reflect any market failures, and government interventions to mitigate them can only reduce welfare. In short, the implication of real-business-cycle models, in their strongest form, is that observed aggregate output movements simply represent the time-varying Pareto optimum.

The specific form of the output fluctuations implied by the model is determined by the dynamics of technology and the behavior of the capital stock.[16] In particular, the production function, $Y_t = K_t^\alpha (A_t L_t)^{1-\alpha}$, implies

---

[16]The discussion that follows is based on McCallum (1989).

$$\ln Y_t = \alpha \ln K_t + (1 - \alpha)(\ln A_t + \ln L_t). \tag{4.38}$$

We know that $K_t = \hat{s} Y_{t-1}$ and $L_t = \hat{\ell} N_t$; thus

$$\ln Y_t = \alpha \ln \hat{s} + \alpha \ln Y_{t-1} + (1 - \alpha)(\ln A_t + \ln \hat{\ell} + \ln N_t)$$

$$= \alpha \ln \hat{s} + \alpha \ln Y_{t-1} + (1 - \alpha)(\overline{A} + gt) \tag{4.39}$$

$$+ (1 - \alpha)\tilde{A}_t + (1 - \alpha)(\ln \hat{\ell} + \overline{N} + nt),$$

where the last line uses the facts that $\ln A_t = \overline{A} + gt + \tilde{A}_t$ and $\ln N_t = \overline{N} + nt$ (see [4.6] and [4.8]).

The two components of the right-hand side of (4.39) that do not follow deterministic paths are $\alpha \ln Y_{t-1}$ and $(1 - \alpha)\tilde{A}_t$. It must therefore be possible to rewrite (4.39) in the form

$$\tilde{Y}_t = \alpha \tilde{Y}_{t-1} + (1 - \alpha)\tilde{A}_t, \tag{4.40}$$

where $\tilde{Y}_t$ is the difference between $\ln Y_t$ and the value it would take if $\ln A_t$ equaled $\overline{A} + gt$ each period (see Problem 4.14 for details).

To see what (4.40) implies concerning the dynamics of output, note that since it holds each period, it implies $\tilde{Y}_{t-1} = \alpha \tilde{Y}_{t-2} + (1 - \alpha)\tilde{A}_{t-1}$, or

$$\tilde{A}_{t-1} = \frac{1}{1 - \alpha}\left(\tilde{Y}_{t-1} - \alpha \tilde{Y}_{t-2}\right). \tag{4.41}$$

Recall that (4.9) states that $\tilde{A}_t = \rho_A \tilde{A}_{t-1} + \varepsilon_{A,t}$. Substituting this fact and (4.41) into (4.40), we obtain

$$\tilde{Y}_t = \alpha \tilde{Y}_{t-1} + (1 - \alpha)(\rho_A \tilde{A}_{t-1} + \varepsilon_{A,t})$$

$$= \alpha \tilde{Y}_{t-1} + \rho_A(\tilde{Y}_{t-1} - \alpha \tilde{Y}_{t-2}) + (1 - \alpha)\varepsilon_{A,t} \tag{4.42}$$

$$= (\alpha + \rho_A)\tilde{Y}_{t-1} - \alpha\rho_A \tilde{Y}_{t-2} + (1 - \alpha)\varepsilon_{A,t}.$$

Thus, departures of log output from its normal path follow a *second-order autoregressive process*—that is, $\tilde{Y}$ can be written as a linear combination of its two previous values plus a white-noise disturbance.[17]

---

[17]Readers who are familiar with the use of *lag operators* can derive (4.42) using that approach. In lag-operator notation, $\tilde{Y}_{t-1}$ is $L\tilde{Y}_t$, where L maps variables to their previous period's value. Thus (4.40) can be written as $\tilde{Y}_t = \alpha L\tilde{Y}_t + (1 - \alpha)\tilde{A}_t$, or $(1 - \alpha L)\tilde{Y}_t = (1 - \alpha)\tilde{A}_t$. Similarly, we can rewrite (4.9) as $(1 - \rho_A L)\tilde{A}_t = \varepsilon_{A,t}$, or $\tilde{A}_t = (1 - \rho_A L)^{-1}\varepsilon_{A,t}$. Thus we have $(1 - \alpha L)\tilde{Y}_t = (1 - \alpha)(1 - \rho_A L)^{-1}\varepsilon_{A,t}$. "Multiplying" through by $1 - \rho_A L$ yields $(1 - \alpha L)(1 - \rho_A L)\tilde{Y}_t = (1 - \alpha)\varepsilon_{A,t}$, or $[1 - (\alpha + \rho_A)L + \alpha\rho_A L^2]\tilde{Y}_t = (1 - \alpha)\varepsilon_{A,t}$. This is equivalent to $\tilde{Y}_t = (\alpha + \rho_A)L\tilde{Y}_t - \alpha\rho_A L^2 \tilde{Y}_t + (1 - \alpha)\varepsilon_{A,t}$, which corresponds to (4.42). (See Section 6.8 for a discussion of lag operators and of the legitimacy of manipulating them in these kinds of ways.)

The combination of a positive coefficient on the first lag of $\tilde{Y}_t$ and a negative coefficient on the second lag can cause output to have a "hump-shaped" response to disturbances. Suppose, for example, that $\alpha = \frac{1}{3}$ and $\rho_A = 0.9$. Consider a one-time shock of $1/(1-\alpha)$ to ε_A. Using (4.42) iteratively shows that the shock raises log output relative to the path it would have otherwise followed by 1 in the period of the shock ($1 - \alpha$ times the shock), 1.23 in the next period ($\alpha + \rho_A$ times 1), 1.22 in the following period ($\alpha + \rho_A$ times 1.23, minus α times ρ_A times 1), then 1.14, 1.03, 0.94, 0.84, 0.76, 0.68, ... in subsequent periods.

Because α is not large, the dynamics of output are determined largely by the persistence of the technology shocks, ρ_A. If $\rho_A = 0$, for example, (4.42) simplifies to $\tilde{Y}_t = \alpha \tilde{Y}_{t-1} + (1 - \alpha)\varepsilon_{A,t}$. If $\alpha = \frac{1}{3}$, this implies that almost nine-tenths of the initial effect of a shock disappears after only two periods. Even if $\rho_A = \frac{1}{2}$, two-thirds of the initial effect is gone after three periods. Thus the model does not have any mechanism that translates transitory technology disturbances into significant long-lasting output movements. We will see that the same is true of the more general version of the model.

Nonetheless, these results show that this model yields interesting output dynamics. Indeed, if actual U.S. log output is detrended linearly, it follows a process similar to the hump-shaped one described above (Blanchard, 1981).[18]

In other ways, however, this special case of the model does not do a good job of matching major features of fluctuations. Most obviously, the saving rate is constant—so that consumption and investment are equally volatile—and labor input does not vary. In practice, as we saw in Section 4.1, investment varies much more than consumption, and employment and hours are strongly procyclical—that is, they move in the same direction as aggregate output. In addition, the model predicts that the real wage is highly procyclical. Because of the Cobb–Douglas production function, the real wage is $(1-\alpha)Y/L$; since L does not respond to technology shocks, this means that the real wage rises one-for-one with Y. In actual fluctuations, in contrast, the real wage appears to be at most only moderately procyclical.

Thus the model must be modified if it is to capture many of the major features of observed output movements. The next section shows that introducing depreciation of less than 100% and shocks to government purchases improves the model's predictions concerning movements in employment, saving, and the real wage.

To see intuitively how lower depreciation improves the fit of the model, consider the extreme case of no depreciation and no growth, so that investment is zero in the absence of shocks. In this situation, a positive technology shock, by raising the marginal product of capital in the next period, makes it optimal for households to undertake some investment. Thus the saving

---

[18]This result is sensitive to the detrending, however.

rate rises. The fact that saving is temporarily high means that expected consumption growth is higher than it would be with a constant saving rate; from consumer's intertemporal optimization condition, (4.23), this requires the interest rate to be higher. But we know that a higher interest rate increases current labor supply. Thus introducing incomplete depreciation causes investment and employment to respond more to shocks.

The reason that introducing shocks to government purchases improves the fit of the model is straightforward: it breaks the tight link between output and the real wage. Since an increase in government purchases increases households' lifetime tax liability, it reduces their lifetime wealth. This causes them to consume less leisure—that is, to work more. When labor supply rises without any change in technology, the real wage falls; thus output and the real wage move in opposite directions. With output fluctuations coming from changes in L instead of changes in A, real wages move in the opposite direction from output. It follows that with shocks to both government purchases and technology, the model can generate an overall pattern of real wage movements that is not strongly procyclical or countercyclical.

4.6   Solving the Model in the General Case

Overview

As discussed above, the full model of Section 4.3 cannot be solved analytically. This is true of almost all real-business-cycle models. Papers in this area generally address this difficulty by solving the models numerically. That is, once a model is presented, parameter values are chosen, and the model's quantitative implications for the variances and correlations of various macroeconomic variables are discussed.

As Campbell (1994) emphasizes, this procedure provides little guidance concerning the sources of the models' implications. He argues that one should instead take first-order Taylor approximations of the equations of the models in the logs of the relevant variables around the models' balanced growth paths in the absence of shocks, and then investigate the properties of these approximate models.[19] He also argues that one should focus on how the variables of a model respond to shocks instead of merely describing the model's implications for variances and correlations.

This section applies Campbell's method to the model of Section 4.3. Unfortunately, even though taking a log-linear approximation to the model allows it to be solved analytically, the analysis remains cumbersome. For that reason, we will only describe the broad features of the derivation and results without going through the specifics in detail.

---

[19]Kimball (1991) employs a similar approach.

Log-Linearizing the Model around the Balanced Growth Path[20]

In any period, the state of the economy is described by the capital stock inherited from the previous period and by the current values of technology and government purchases. The two variables that are endogenous each period are consumption and employment.

If we log-linearize the model around the nonstochastic balanced growth path, the rules for consumption and employment must take the form

$$\tilde{C}_t \simeq a_{CK}\tilde{K}_t + a_{CA}\tilde{A}_t + a_{CG}\tilde{G}_t, \tag{4.43}$$

$$\tilde{L}_t \simeq a_{LK}\tilde{K}_t + a_{LA}\tilde{A}_t + a_{LG}\tilde{G}_t, \tag{4.44}$$

where the a's will be functions of the underlying parameters of the model. As before, a tilde (˜) over a variable denotes the difference between the log of that variable and the log of its balanced-growth-path value. Thus, for example, $\tilde{A}_t$ denotes $\ln A_t - (\bar{A} + gt)$. Equations (4.43) and (4.44) state that log consumption and log employment are linear functions of the logs of K, A, and G, and that consumption and employment are equal to their balanced-growth-path values when K, A, and G are all equal to theirs. Since we are building a version of the model that is log-linear around the balanced growth path by construction, we know that these conditions must hold. To solve the model, we must determine the values of the a's.

As with the simple version of the model, we will focus on the two conditions for household optimization, (4.23) and (4.26). For a set of a's to be a solution to the model, they must imply that households are satisfying these conditions. It turns out that the restrictions that this requirement puts on the a's fully determine them, and thus tell us the solution to the model.

This solution method is known as the *method of undetermined coefficients*. The idea is to use theory (or, in some cases, educated guesswork) to find the general functional form of the solution, and then to determine what values the coefficients in the functional form must take to satisfy the equations of the model. This method is useful in many situations.

The Intratemporal First-Order Condition

To see how the method works in this case, begin by considering households' first-order condition for the tradeoff between current consumption and labor supply, $c_t/(1 - \ell_t) = w_t/b$ (equation [4.26]). Using equation (4.3) to substitute for the wage and taking logs, we can write this condition as

$$\ln c_t - \ln(1 - \ell_t) = \ln\left(\frac{1 - \alpha}{b}\right) + (1 - \alpha)\ln A_t + \alpha \ln K_t - \alpha \ln L_t. \tag{4.45}$$

---

[20]See Problem 4.10 for the balanced growth path of the model in the absence of shocks.

We want to find a first-order Taylor-series approximation to this expression in the logs of the variables of the model around the balanced growth path the economy would follow if there were no shocks. Approximating the right-hand side is straightforward: the difference between the actual value of the right-hand side and its balanced-growth-path value is $(1-\alpha)\tilde{A}_t + \alpha\tilde{K}_t - \alpha\tilde{L}_t$. To approximate the left-hand side, note that since population growth is not affected by the shocks, $\tilde{C}_t = \tilde{c}_t$: log total consumption differs from its balanced-growth-path value only to the extent that log consumption per worker differs from its balanced-growth-path value. Similarly, $\tilde{\ell}_t = \tilde{L}_t$. The derivative of the left-hand side of (4.45) with respect to $\ln c_t$ is simply 1. The derivative with respect to $\ln \ell_t$ at $\ell_t = \ell^*$ is $\ell^*/(1-\ell^*)$, where ℓ^* is the value of ℓ on the balanced growth path. Thus, log-linearizing (4.45) around the balanced growth path yields

$$\tilde{C}_t + \frac{\ell^*}{1-\ell^*}\tilde{L}_t = (1-\alpha)\tilde{A}_t + \alpha\tilde{K}_t - \alpha\tilde{L}_t. \tag{4.46}$$

We can now use the fact that $\tilde{C}_t$ and $\tilde{L}_t$ are linear functions of $\tilde{K}_t, \tilde{A}_t$, and $\tilde{G}_t$. Substituting (4.43) and (4.44) into (4.46) yields

$$a_{CK}\tilde{K}_t + a_{CA}\tilde{A}_t + a_{CG}\tilde{G}_t + \left(\frac{\ell^*}{1-\ell^*} + \alpha\right)(a_{LK}\tilde{K}_t + a_{LA}\tilde{A}_t + a_{LG}\tilde{G}_t)$$
$$= \alpha\tilde{K}_t + (1-\alpha)\tilde{A}_t. \tag{4.47}$$

Equation (4.47) must hold for all values of $\tilde{K}, \tilde{A}$, and $\tilde{G}$. If it does not, then for some combinations of $\tilde{K}, \tilde{A}$, and $\tilde{G}$, households can raise their utility by changing their current consumption and labor supply. Thus the coefficients on $\tilde{K}$ on the two sides of (4.47) must be equal, and similarly for the coefficients on $\tilde{A}$ and on $\tilde{G}$. Thus the a's must satisfy:

$$a_{CK} + \left(\frac{\ell^*}{1-\ell^*} + \alpha\right)a_{LK} = \alpha, \tag{4.48}$$

$$a_{CA} + \left(\frac{\ell^*}{1-\ell^*} + \alpha\right)a_{LA} = 1 - \alpha, \tag{4.49}$$

$$a_{CG} + \left(\frac{\ell^*}{1-\ell^*} + \alpha\right)a_{LG} = 0. \tag{4.50}$$

To understand these conditions, consider first (4.50), which relates the responses of consumption and employment to movements in government purchases. Government purchases do not directly enter (4.45); that is, they do not affect the wage for a given level of labor supply. If households increase their labor supply in response to an increase in government purchases, the wage falls and the marginal disutility of working rises. Thus, they will do this only if the marginal utility of consumption is higher—that is, if consumption is lower. Thus if labor supply and consumption respond to changes in government purchases, they must move in opposite directions. Equation (4.50) tells us not only this qualitative result, but also how the movements in labor supply and consumption must be related.

Now consider an increase in A (equation [4.49]). An improvement in technology raises the wage for a given level of labor supply. Thus if neither labor supply nor consumption respond, households can raise their utility by working more and increasing their current consumption. Thus households must increase either labor supply or consumption (or both); this is what is captured in (4.49).

Finally, the restrictions that (4.45) puts on the responses of labor supply and consumption to movements in capital are similar to the restrictions it puts on their responses to movements in technology. The only difference is that the elasticity of the wage with respect to capital, given L, is α rather than $1 - \alpha$. This is what is shown in (4.48).

The Intertemporal First-Order Condition

The analysis of the first-order condition relating current consumption and next period's consumption, $1/c_t = e^{-\rho}E_t[(1 + r_{t+1})/c_{t+1}]$ (equation [4.23]), is more complicated. The basic idea is the following. Begin by defining $\tilde{Z}_{t+1}$ as the difference between the log of $(1 + r_{t+1})/c_{t+1}$ and the log of its balanced-growth-path value. Now note that since (4.43) holds at each date, it implies

$$\tilde{C}_{t+1} \simeq a_{CK}\tilde{K}_{t+1} + a_{CA}\tilde{A}_{t+1} + a_{CG}\tilde{G}_{t+1}. \tag{4.51}$$

We can then use this expression for $\tilde{C}_{t+1}$ and equation (4.4) for r_{t+1} to express $\tilde{Z}_{t+1}$ in terms of $\tilde{K}_{t+1}, \tilde{A}_{t+1}$, and $\tilde{G}_{t+1}$.[21] Since $\tilde{K}_{t+1}$ is an endogenous variable, we need to eliminate it from this expression. Specifically, we can log-linearize the equation of motion for capital, (4.2), to write $\tilde{K}_{t+1}$ in terms of $\tilde{K}_t, \tilde{A}_t, \tilde{G}_t, \tilde{L}_t$, and $\tilde{C}_t$; we can then use (4.43) and (4.44) to substitute for $\tilde{L}_t$ and $\tilde{C}_t$. This yields an expression of the form

$$\tilde{K}_{t+1} \simeq b_{KK}\tilde{K}_t + b_{KA}\tilde{A}_t + b_{KG}\tilde{G}_t, \tag{4.52}$$

where the b's are complicated functions of the parameters of the model and of the a's.[22]

Substituting (4.52) into the expression for $\tilde{Z}_{t+1}$ in terms of $\tilde{K}_{t+1}, \tilde{A}_{t+1}$, and $\tilde{G}_{t+1}$ then gives us an expression for $\tilde{Z}_{t+1}$ in terms of $\tilde{A}_{t+1}, \tilde{G}_{t+1}, \tilde{K}_t, \tilde{A}_t$, and $\tilde{G}_t$. The final step is to use this to find $E_t[\tilde{Z}_{t+1}]$ in terms of $\tilde{K}_t, \tilde{A}_t$, and $\tilde{G}_t$.[23] Substituting this into (4.23) gives us three additional restrictions on

---

[21]Equation (4.44) for $\tilde{L}$ is used to substitute for $\tilde{L}_{t+1}$ in the expression for r_{t+1}.

[22]See Problem 4.15.

[23]There is one complication here. As emphasized in Section 4.4, (4.23) involves not just the expectations of next-period values, but their entire distribution. That is, what is appro-

the a's; this is enough to determine the a's in terms of the underlying parameters.

Unfortunately, the model is sufficiently complicated that solving for the a's is tedious, and the resulting expressions for the a's in terms of the underlying parameters of the model are complicated. Even if we wrote down those expressions, the effects of the parameters of the model on the a's, and hence on the economy's response to shocks, would not be transparent.

Thus, despite the comparative simplicity of the model and our use of approximations, we must still resort to numerical methods to describe the model's properties. What we will do is choose a set of baseline parameter values and discuss their implications for the a's in (4.43)–(4.44) and the b's in (4.52). Once we have determined the values of the a's and b's, equations (4.43), (4.44), and (4.52) specify (approximately) how consumption, employment, and capital respond to shocks to technology and government purchases. The remaining equations of the model can then be used to describe the responses of the model's other variables—output, investment, the wage, and the interest rate. For example, we can substitute equation (4.44) for $\tilde{L}$ into the log-linearized version of the production function to find the model's implications for output:

$$\tilde{Y}_t = \alpha\tilde{K}_t + (1 - \alpha)(\tilde{L}_t + \tilde{A}_t)$$

$$= \alpha\tilde{K}_t + (1 - \alpha)(a_{LK}\tilde{K}_t + a_{LA}\tilde{A}_t + a_{LG}\tilde{G}_t + \tilde{A}_t) \tag{4.53}$$

$$= [\alpha + (1 - \alpha)a_{LK}]\tilde{K}_t + (1 - \alpha)(1 + a_{LA})\tilde{A}_t + a_{LG}\tilde{G}_t.$$

4.7   Implications

Following Campbell, assume that each period corresponds to a quarter, and take for baseline parameter values $\alpha = \frac{1}{3}$, $g = 0.5\%$, $n = 0.25\%$, $\delta = 2.5\%$, $\rho_A = 0.95$, $\rho_G = 0.95$, and $\overline{G}$, ρ, and b such that $(G/Y)^* = 0.2$, $r^* = 1.5\%$, and $\ell^* = \frac{1}{3}$.[24]

---

priate in the log-linearized version of (4.23) is not $E_t[\tilde{Z}_{t+1}]$, but $\ln E_t[e^{\tilde{Z}_{t+1}}]$. Campbell (1994) addresses this difficulty by assuming that $\tilde{Z}$ is normally distributed with constant variance; that is, $e^{\tilde{Z}}$ has a *lognormal* distribution. Standard results about this distribution then imply that $\ln E_t[e^{\tilde{Z}_{t+1}}]$ equals $E_t[\tilde{Z}_{t+1}]$ plus a constant (see, for example, Mood, Graybill, and Boes [1974] or any other statistics textbook). Thus we can express the log of the right-hand side of (4.23) in terms of $E_t[\tilde{Z}_{t+1}]$ and constants. Finally, Campbell notes that given the log-linear structure of the model, if the underlying shocks—the ε_A's and ε_G's in (4.9) and (4.11)—are normally distributed with constant variance, his assumption about the distribution of $\tilde{Z}_{t+1}$ is correct.

[24]See Problem 4.10 for the implications of these parameter values for the balanced growth path.

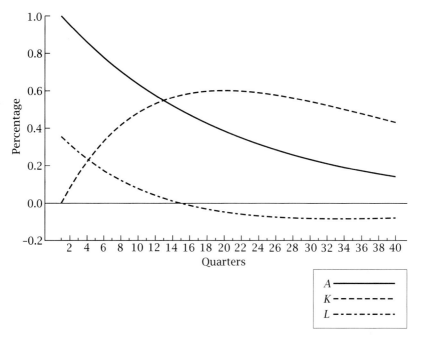

FIGURE 4.2 The effects of a 1% technology shock on the paths of technology, capital, and labor

The Effects of Technology Shocks

One can show that these parameter values imply $a_{LA} \simeq 0.35$, $a_{LK} \simeq -0.31$, $a_{CA} \simeq 0.38$, $a_{CK} \simeq 0.59$, $b_{KA} \simeq 0.08$, and $b_{KK} \simeq 0.95$. These values can be used to trace out the effects of a change in technology. Consider, for example, a positive 1% technology shock. In the period of the shock, capital (which is inherited from the previous period) is unchanged, labor supply rises by 0.35%, and consumption rises by 0.38%. Since the production function is $K^{1/3}(AL)^{2/3}$, output increases by 0.90%. In the next period, technology is 0.95% above normal (since $\rho_A = 0.95$), capital is higher by 0.08% (since $b_{KA} \simeq 0.08$), labor supply is higher by 0.31% (0.35 times 0.95, minus 0.31 times 0.08), and consumption is higher by 0.41% (0.38 times 0.95, plus 0.59 times 0.08); the effects on A, K, and L imply that output is 0.86% above normal. And so on.

Figures 4.2 and 4.3 show the shock's effects on the major quantity variables of the model. By assumption, the effects on the level of technology die away slowly. Capital accumulates gradually and then slowly returns to normal; the peak effect is an increase of 0.60% after 20 quarters. Labor supply jumps by 0.35% in the period of the shock and then declines relatively rapidly, falling below normal after 15 quarters. It reaches a low of −0.09% after 33 quarters, and then slowly comes back to normal. The net result of

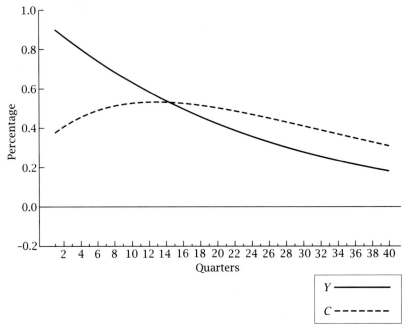

FIGURE 4.3 The effects of a 1% technology shock on the paths of output and consumption

the movements in A, K, and L is that output increases in the period of the shock and then gradually returns to normal. Consumption responds less, and more slowly, than output; thus investment is more volatile than consumption.

Figure 4.4 shows the percentage movement in the wage and the change in percentage points in the interest rate at an annual rate. The wage rises and then returns very slowly to normal. Because the changes in the wage (after the unexpected jump at the time of the shock) are small, wage movements contribute little to the variations in labor supply. The annual interest rate increases by about one-seventh of a percentage point in the period of the shock and then returns to normal fairly quickly. Because the capital stock moves more slowly than labor supply, the interest rate dips below normal after 14 quarters. These movements in the interest rate are the main source of the movements in labor supply.

To understand the movements in the interest rate and consumption, consider for simplicity the case where labor supply is inelastic, and recall that $r = \alpha(AL/K)^{1-\alpha} - \delta$. The immediate effect of the increase in A is to raise r. Since the increase in A dies out only slowly, r must remain high unless K increases rapidly. But since depreciation is low, a rapid rise in K would require a large increase in the fraction of output that is invested. But

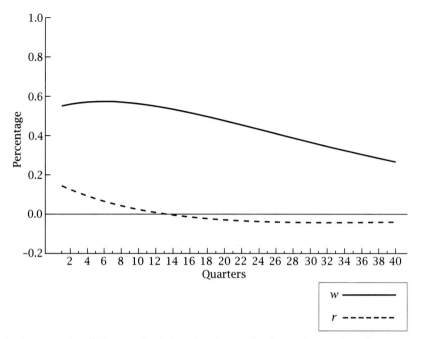

FIGURE 4.4 **The effects of a 1% technology shock on the paths of the wage and the interest rate**

if the saving rate were to rise by so much that r returned immediately to its usual level, this would mean that consumption was expected to grow rapidly even though r equaled its normal value; this would violate households' intertemporal first-order condition, (4.23). Thus, instead, households raise the fraction of their income that they save, but not by enough to return r immediately to its usual level. And since the increase in A is persistent, the increase in the saving rate is also persistent. As technology returns to normal, the slow adjustment of the capital stock eventually causes A/K to fall below its initial value, and thus causes r to fall below its usual value. When this occurs, the saving rate falls below its balanced-growth-path level.

When we allow for variations in labor supply, some of the adjustments of the capital stock occur through changes in labor supply rather than the saving rate: households build up the capital stock during the early phase partly by increasing labor supply, and bring it back to normal in the later phase partly by decreasing labor supply.

The parameter that the results are most sensitive to is ρ_A. When technology shocks are less persistent, the wealth effect of a shock is smaller (because its impact is shorter-lived), and its intertemporal-substitution effect is larger. As a result, a_{CA} is increasing in ρ_A, and a_{LA} and b_{KA} are decreasing; a_{CK}, a_{LK}, and b_{KK} are unaffected. If ρ_A declines from the baseline value of 0.95 to 0.5, for example, a_{CA} falls from 0.38 to 0.11, a_{LA} rises from 0.35 to 0.66, and b_{KA} rises from 0.08 to 0.12. The result is sharper, shorter output fluctuations. In this case, a 1% technology shock raises output by 1.11% in the period of the shock, but only by 0.30% two periods later. If $\rho_A = 1$, a_{CA} rises to 0.63, a_{LA} falls to 0.05, and b_{KA} falls to 0.04. The result is that employment fluctuations are small and output fluctuations are much more gradual. For example, a 1% shock causes output to increase by 0.70% immediately (only slightly larger than the direct effect of 0.67%), and then to rise very gradually to 1% above its initial level.

In addition, suppose we generalize the way that leisure enters the instantaneous utility function, (4.7), to allow the intertemporal elasticity of substitution in labor supply to take on values other than 1.[25] With this change, this elasticity also has important effects on the economy's response to shocks: the larger the elasticity, the more responsive labor supply is to technology and capital. If the elasticity rises from 1 to 2, for example, a_{LA} increases from 0.35 to 0.48, and a_{LK} increases from −0.31 to −0.41 (in addition, a_{CA}, a_{CK}, b_{KA}, and b_{KK} all change moderately). As a result, fluctuations are larger when the intertemporal elasticity of substitution is higher.[26]

The Effects of Changes in Government Purchases

Our baseline parameter values imply $a_{CG} \simeq -0.13$, $a_{LG} \simeq 0.15$, and $b_{KG} \simeq -0.004$; a_{CK}, a_{LK}, and b_{KK} are as before. Intuitively, an increase in government purchases causes consumption to fall and labor supply to rise because of its negative wealth effects. And because the rise in government purchases is not permanent, agents also respond by decreasing their capital holdings.

Since the elasticity of output with respect to L is two-thirds, the value of a_{LG} of 0.15 means that output rises by about 0.1% in response to a 1% government-purchases shock. Since output on the balanced growth path is five times government purchases, this means that Y rises by about one-half as much as G. And since one can show that consumption on the balanced growth path is about two-and-one-half times government purchases, the value of a_{CG} of −0.13 means that C falls by about one-third as much as G increases. The remaining one-sixth of the adjustment takes the form of lower investment.

Figures 4.5–4.7 trace out the effects of a positive 1% government-purchases shock. The capital stock is only slightly affected; the maximum impact is a decline of 0.03% after 20 quarters. Employment increases and then gradually returns to normal; in contrast to what occurs with tech-

---

[25]See Campbell (1994) and Problem 4.4.

[26]In addition, Kimball (1991) shows that if we relax the assumption of a Cobb–Douglas production function, the elasticity of substitution between capital and labor has important effects on the economy's response to shocks.

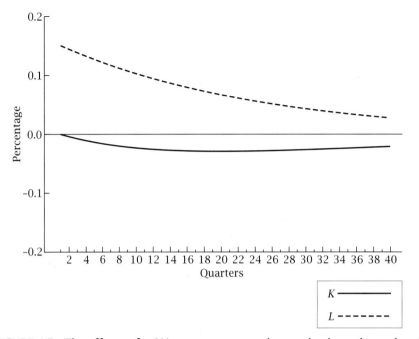

FIGURE 4.5   The effects of a 1% government-purchases shock on the paths of capital and labor

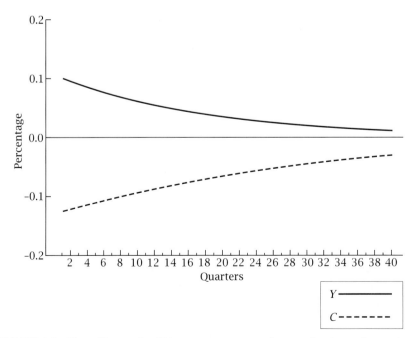

FIGURE 4.6   The effects of a 1% government-purchases shock on the paths of output and consumption

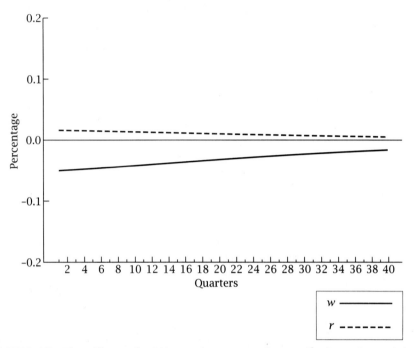

FIGURE 4.7   The effects of a 1% government-purchases shock on the paths of the wage and the interest rate

nology shocks, there is no overshooting. Because technology is unchanged and the capital stock moves little, the movements in output are small and track the changes in employment fairly closely. Consumption declines at the time of the shock and then gradually returns to normal. The increase in employment and the fall in the capital stock cause the wage to fall and the interest rate to rise. The anticipated wage movements after the period of the shock are small and positive; thus, as before, the source of the increases in labor supply are the increases in the interest rate.

As with technology, the persistence of movements in government purchases has important effects on how the economy responds to shocks. If ρ_G falls to 0.5, for example, a_{CG} falls from -0.13 to -0.03, a_{LG} falls from 0.15 to 0.03, and b_{KG} increases from -0.004 to -0.020: because movements in purchases are much shorter-lived, much more of the response takes the form of reductions in capital holdings. These values imply that output rises by about one-tenth of the increase in government purchases, that consumption falls by about one-tenth of the increase, and that investment falls by about four-fifths of the increase. In response to a 1% shock, for example, output increases by just 0.02% in the period of the shock and then falls below normal, with a low of -0.004% after seven quarters.

4.8 Empirical Application: The Persistence of Output Fluctuations

Introduction

Real-business-cycle models emphasize shifts in technology as a central source of output fluctuations. The specific model analyzed in this chapter assumes that technology fluctuates around a deterministic trend; as a result, the effects of a given technological shock eventually approach zero. But this assumption is made purely for convenience. It seems plausible that changes in technology have a significant permanent component. For example, an innovation today may have little impact on the likelihood of additional innovations in the future, and thus on the expected behavior of the *growth* of technology in the future. In this case, the innovation raises the expected path of the *level* of technology permanently. Thus real-business-cycle models are quite consistent with a large permanent component of output fluctuations. In traditional Keynesian models, in contrast, output movements are largely the result of monetary and other aggregate demand disturbances coupled with sluggish adjustment of nominal prices or wages. Since the models assume that prices and wages adjust eventually, under natural assumptions they imply that changes in aggregate demand have no long-run effects. For this reason, natural baseline versions of these models predict that output fluctuates around a deterministic trend path. These considerations have sparked a considerable literature on the persistence of output movements.

Nelson and Plosser's Test

The persistence of fluctuations was first addressed by Nelson and Plosser (1982), who consider the question of whether fluctuations have a permanent component (see also McCulloch, 1975). The idea behind their test is conceptually simple, though it turns out to involve some econometric complications. If output movements are fluctuations around a deterministic trend, then output growth will tend to be less than normal when output is above its trend and more than normal when it is below its trend. That is, consider a regression of form

$$\Delta \ln y_t = a + b\{\ln y_{t-1} - [\alpha + \beta(t-1)]\} + \varepsilon_t, \qquad (4.54)$$

where $\ln y$ is log real GDP, $\alpha + \beta t$ is its trend path, and ε_t is a mean-zero disturbance uncorrelated with $\ln y_{t-1} - [\alpha + \beta(t-1)]$. (The regression can also include other variables that may affect output growth.) The term $\ln y_{t-1} - [\alpha + \beta(t-1)]$ is the difference between log output and the trend in period

$t - 1$. Thus if output tends to revert toward the trend, b is negative; if it does not, b is zero.

We can rewrite (4.54) as

$$\Delta \ln y_t = \alpha' + \beta' t + b \ln y_{t-1} + \varepsilon_t, \tag{4.55}$$

where $\alpha' \equiv a - b\alpha + b\beta$ and $\beta' \equiv -b\beta$. Thus to test for trend-reversion versus permanent shocks, we need only estimate (4.55) and test whether $b = 0$. Note that with this formulation, the null hypothesis is that output does not revert toward a trend. Formally, the null hypothesis is that output is *nonstationary* or has a *unit root*; the alternative is that it is *trend-stationary*.[27]

There is, however, an important econometric complication in carrying out this test: under the null hypothesis, ordinary least squares (OLS) estimates of b are biased toward negative values. To see why, consider the case of $\beta = 0$; thus (4.55) becomes

$$\Delta \ln y_t = \alpha' + b \ln y_{t-1} + \varepsilon_t. \tag{4.56}$$

Assume for simplicity that the ε's are independent, identically distributed, mean-zero disturbances. The $\ln y_{t-1}$'s are combinations of the ε's. Specifically, under the null hypothesis of $b = 0$, $\ln y_{t-1}$ is $\ln y_0 + (t - 1)\alpha' + \varepsilon_1 + \varepsilon_2 + \cdots + \varepsilon_{t-1}$. Since the ε's are not correlated with one another, ε_t is uncorrelated with $\ln y_{t-1}$. It might therefore appear that OLS is unbiased. But the requirement for OLS to be unbiased is not just that the disturbance term is uncorrelated with the *contemporaneous* value of the right-hand-side variable, but that it is uncorrelated with the right-hand-side variable *at all leads and lags*. The fact that the past ε's enter positively into $\ln y_{t-1}$ means that $\ln y_{t-1}$ is positively correlated with *past* values of the error term. One can show that this causes the estimates of b from OLS to be biased toward negative values.[28] That is, even when the null hypothesis that output has no tendency to revert toward a trend is true, OLS tends to suggest that output is trend-reverting.

This econometric complication is an example of a more general difficulty: the behavior of statistical estimators when variables are highly per-

---

[27] The term *trend-stationary* means that the difference between actual output and a deterministic trend is not explosive. The term *unit root* arises from the lag-operator methodology (see n. 17, above, and Section 6.8). If output has a permanent component, it must be differenced to produce a stationary series. In lag-operator notation, $\ln y_{t-1}$ is written as $L \ln y_t$, and thus $\Delta \ln y_t$ is written as $(1 - L) \ln y_t$. The polynomial $1 - L$ is equal to zero for $L = 1$; that is, it has a "unit root." For comparison, consider, for example, the stationary process $\ln y_t = \rho \ln y_{t-1} + \varepsilon_t, |\rho| < 1$. In lag-operator notation, this is $(1 - \rho L) \ln y_t = \varepsilon_t$. The polynomial $1 - \rho L$ is equal to zero for $L = 1/\rho$, which is greater than 1 in absolute value. More generally, stationary processes have roots *outside the unit circle*.

[28] For a simple case, see Problem 4.16.

sistent is often complex and unintuitive. Care needs to be taken in such situations, and conventional econometric tests often cannot be used.[29]

Because of the negative bias in estimates of b under the null hypothesis, one cannot use conventional t-tests of the significance of the OLS estimates of b from (4.55) or (4.56) to test whether output is trend-stationary. Nelson and Plosser therefore employ a *Dickey–Fuller unit-root test* (Dickey and Fuller, 1979). Dickey and Fuller use a Monte Carlo experiment to determine the distribution of the t-statistic on b from OLS estimates of equations like (4.55) and (4.56) when the true value of b is zero. That is, they use a random-number generator to choose ε's; they then generate a time series for $\ln y$ using (4.55) or (4.56) with b set to zero; and then they estimate (4.55) or (4.56) by OLS and find the t-statistic on b. They repeat this procedure many times. The resulting distribution of the t-statistic, instead of being symmetric around zero, is considerably skewed toward negative values. For example, Nelson and Plosser report that for the case of 100 observations with true parameter values of $\alpha' = 1$ and $b = 0$, the average value of the t-statistic on b is -2.22. The t-statistic is greater in absolute value than the standard 5% critical value of -1.96 65% of the time, and it is greater than -3.45 5% of the time. Thus an investigator who is unaware of the econometric complications and therefore uses standard critical values is more likely than not to reject the hypothesis of nonstationarity at the 5% level even if it is true. In a Dickey–Fuller test, however, one compares the t-statistic on b not with the standard t-distribution, but with the distribution produced by the Monte Carlo experiment. Thus, for example, a t-statistic greater than -3.45 in absolute value is needed to reject the null hypothesis of $b = 0$ at the 5% level.

With this lengthy econometric preface, we can now describe Nelson and Plosser's results. They estimate equations slightly more complex than (4.55) for U.S. real GNP, real GNP per capita, industrial production, and employment; they find that the OLS estimates of b are between -0.1 and -0.2, with t-statistics ranging from -2.5 to -3.0. All of these are comfortably less than the correct 5% critical value of -3.45. Based on this and other evidence, Nelson and Plosser conclude that one cannot reject the null hypothesis that fluctuations have a permanent component.

Campbell and Mankiw's Test

An obvious limitation of simply testing for the existence of a permanent component of fluctuations is that it cannot tell us anything about how big such a permanent component might be. The literature since Nelson and

---

[29]See Stock and Watson (1988) and Campbell and Perron (1991) for introductions to the issues arising in time-series econometrics when series are highly persistent.

Plosser has therefore focused on determining the extent of persistence in output movements. Campbell and Mankiw (1987) propose a natural measure of persistence. They consider several specific processes for the change in log output. To take one example, they consider the third-order autoregressive (or AR-3) case:

$$\Delta \ln y_t = a + b_1 \Delta \ln y_{t-1} + b_2 \Delta \ln y_{t-2} + b_3 \Delta \ln y_{t-3} + \varepsilon_t. \quad (4.57)$$

Campbell and Mankiw estimate (4.57) and compute the implied response of the level of $\ln y$ to a one-unit shock to ε.[30] Their measure of persistence is the value that this forecast converges to. Intuitively, this measure is the answer to the question: If output is 1 percent higher this period than expected, by what percent should I change my forecast of output in the distant future? If output is trend-stationary, the answer to this question is zero. If output is a random walk (so $\Delta \ln y_t$ is simply $a + \varepsilon_t$), the answer is 1 percent.

Campbell and Mankiw's results are surprising: this measure of persistence generally *exceeds* 1. That is, shocks to output are generally followed by further output movements in the same direction. For the AR-3 case considered in (4.57), the estimated persistence measure is 1.57. Campbell and Mankiw consider a variety of other processes for the change in log output; for most of them (though not all), the persistence measure takes on similar values.

Discussion

There are two major problems with the general idea of investigating the persistence of fluctuations, one statistical and one theoretical. The statistical problem is that it is difficult to learn about long-term characteristics of output movements from data from limited time spans. The existence of a permanent component to fluctuations and the asymptotic response of output to an innovation concern characteristics of the data at infinite horizons. As a result, no finite amount of data can shed *any* light on these issues. Suppose, for example, output movements are highly persistent in some sample. Although this is consistent with the presence of a permanent component to fluctuations, it is equally consistent with the view that output reverts extremely slowly to a deterministic trend. Alternatively, suppose we observe that output returns rapidly to some trend over a sample. Such a finding is completely consistent not only with trend stationarity, but also with the view that a small portion of output movements are not just perma-

---

[30]If ε is perturbed by 1 in a single period, (4.57) implies that $\Delta \ln y$ is changed by 1 in that period, b_1 in the next period, $b_1^2 + b_2$ in the following period, and so on. $\ln y$ is therefore changed by 1 in the period of the shock, $1 + b_1$ in the next period, $1 + b_1 + b_1^2 + b_2$ in the following period, and so on.

nent, but explosive—so that the correct reaction to an output innovation is to drastically revise one's forecast of output in the distant future.[31]

Thus at the very least, the appropriate questions are whether output fluctuations have a large, highly persistent component, and how output forecasts at moderately long horizons should be affected by output innovations, and not questions about characteristics of the data at infinite horizons. Clearly, similar modifications are needed in any other situation where researchers claim to be providing evidence about the properties of series at infinite horizons.

Even if we shift the focus from infinite to moderately long horizons, the data are unlikely to be highly informative. Consider, for example, Campbell and Mankiw's procedure for the AR-3 case described above. Campbell and Mankiw are using the relationship between current output growth and its three most recent lagged values to make inferences about output's long-run behavior. This is risky. Suppose, for example, that output growth is actually AR-20 instead of AR-3, and that the coefficients on the 17 additional lagged values of $\Delta \ln y$ are all small, but all negative. In a sample of plausible size, it is difficult to distinguish this case from the AR-3 case. But the long-run effects of an output shock may be much smaller.

This difficulty arises from the brevity of the sample, not from the specifics of Campbell and Mankiw's procedure. The basic problem is that samples of plausible length contain few independent, long subsamples. As a result, no procedure is likely to provide decisive evidence about the long-term effects of shocks. Various approaches to studying persistence have been employed. The point estimates generally suggest considerable persistence (though probably somewhat less than Campbell and Mankiw found). At horizons of more than about five years, however, the estimates are not very precise. Thus the data are also consistent with the view that the effects of output shocks die out gradually at moderate horizons.[32]

The theoretical difficulty with this literature is that there is only a weak case that the persistence of output movements, even if it could be measured precisely, provides much information about the driving forces of economic fluctuations. Since technology may have an important trend-reverting component, and since real-business-cycle models allow for shocks coming from sources other than technology, these models are consistent with low as well as high persistence. And Keynesian models do not require that persistence be low. To begin with, although they attribute the bulk of short-run fluctuations to aggregate demand disturbances, they do not assume that the processes that drive long-run growth follow a deterministic trend; thus they allow at least one part of output movements to be highly persistent. More

---

[31] See Blough (1992a, 1992b) and Campbell and Perron (1991).

[32] See, for example, Cochrane (1988, 1994); Christiano and Eichenbaum (1990); Perron (1989); Watson (1986); and Beaudry and Koop (1993). Campbell and Mankiw (1989b) and Cogley (1990) present evidence for countries other than the United States.

importantly, the part of fluctuations that is due to aggregate demand movements may also be quite persistent. A shift by the Federal Reserve to a policy of extended gradual disinflation, for example, may reduce output over a long period if nominal prices and wages adjust only gradually. And if technological progress results in part from learning-by-doing (see Section 3.4), output changes caused by aggregate demand movements affect technology.

Thus in the end, the main contribution of the literature on persistence is to sound some warnings about time-series econometrics: mechanically removing trends or otherwise ignoring the potential complications caused by persistent movements can cause statistical procedures to yield highly misleading results.

4.9   Additional Empirical Applications

Calibrating a Real-Business-Cycle Model

How should we judge how well a real-business-cycle model fits the data? The standard approach is *calibration* (Kydland and Prescott, 1982). The basic idea of calibration is to choose parameter values on the basis of microeconomic evidence, and then to compare the model's predictions concerning the variances and covariances of various series with those in the data.

Calibration has two potential advantages over estimating models econometrically. First, because parameter values are selected on the basis of microeconomic evidence, a large body of information beyond that usually employed can be brought to bear, and the models can therefore be held to a higher standard. Second, the economic importance of a statistical rejection, or lack of rejection, of a model is often hard to interpret. A model that fits the data well along every dimension except one unimportant one may be overwhelmingly rejected statistically. Or a model may fail to be rejected simply because the data are consistent with a wide range of possibilities.[33]

To see how calibration works in practice, consider the baseline real-business-cycle model of Prescott (1986) and Hansen (1985). This model differs from the model we have been considering in two ways. First, government is absent. Second, the trend component of technology is not assumed to follow a simple linear path; instead, a smooth but nonlinear trend is removed from the data before the model's predictions and actual fluctuations are compared.[34]

We consider the parameter values proposed by Hansen and Wright (1992), which are similar to those suggested by Prescott and by Hansen.

---

[33]See Altug (1989) and Christiano and Eichenbaum (1992a) for examples of traditional econometric estimation of real-business-cycle models.

[34]The detrending procedure that is used is known as the *Hodrick–Prescott filter* (Hodrick and Prescott, 1980). As the discussion of permanent shocks and detrending in the previous section suggests, this procedure may not be innocuous (Cogley and Nason, 1995).

TABLE 4.4   A calibrated real-business-cycle model vs. actual data

	U.S. data	Baseline real-business-cycle model
σ_Y	1.92	1.30
σ_C / σ_Y	0.45	0.31
σ_I / σ_Y	2.78	3.15
σ_L / σ_Y	0.96	0.49
Corr($L, Y/L$)	-0.14	0.93

Source: Hansen and Wright (1992).

Based on data on factor shares, the capital-output ratio, and the investment-output ratio, Hansen and Wright set $\alpha = 0.36$, $\delta = 2.5\%$ per quarter, and $\rho = 1\%$ per quarter. Based on the average division of discretionary time between work and nonwork activities, they set b to 2. They choose the parameters of the process for technology on the basis of the empirical behavior of the Solow residual, $\ln R_t \equiv \ln Y_t - [\alpha \ln K_t + (1 - \alpha) \ln L_t]$. As described in Chapter 1, the Solow residual is a measure of all influences on output growth other than the contributions of capital and labor through their private marginal products. Under the assumptions of real-business-cycle theory, the only such other influence on output is technology, and so the Solow residual is a measure of technological change. Based on the behavior of the Solow residual, Hansen and Wright set $\rho_A = 0.95$ and the standard deviation of the quarterly ε_A's to 1.1%.[35]

The model's implications for some key features of fluctuations are shown in Table 4.4. The figures in the first column are from actual U.S. data; those in the second column are from the model. All of the numbers are based on the deviation-from-trend components of the variables, with the trends found using the nonlinear procedure employed by Prescott and Hansen.

The first line of the table reports the standard deviation of output. The model produces output fluctuations that are only moderately smaller than those observed in practice. This finding is the basis for Prescott's (1986) famous conclusion that aggregate fluctuations are not just consistent with a competitive, neoclassical model, but are in fact predicted by such a model. The second and third lines of the table show that both in the United States and in the model, consumption is considerably less volatile than output, and investment is considerably more volatile.

---

[35]In addition, Prescott argues that, under the assumption that technology multiplies an expression of form $F(K, L)$, the absence of a strong trend in capital's share suggests that $F(\bullet)$ is approximately Cobb–Douglas. Similarly, he argues on the basis of the lack of a trend in leisure per person and of studies of substitution between consumption in different periods that (4.7) provides a good approximation to the instantaneous utility function. Thus the choices of functional forms are not arbitrary.

The final two lines of the table show that the baseline model is less successful in its predictions about the contributions of variations in labor input and in output per unit of labor input to aggregate fluctuations. In the U.S. economy, labor input is nearly as volatile as output; in the model it is much less so. And in the United States, labor input and productivity are essentially uncorrelated; in the model they move together closely.

Thus a simple calibration exercise can be used to identify a model's major successes and failures. In doing so, it suggests ways in which the model might be modified to improve its fit with the data. For example, additional sources of shocks would be likely to increase output fluctuations and to reduce the correlation between movements in labor input and in productivity. Indeed, Hansen and Wright show that, for their suggested parameter values, adding government-purchases shocks along the lines of the model of this chapter lowers the correlation of L and Y/L from 0.93 to 0.49; the change has little effect on the magnitude of output fluctuations, however.

Productivity Movements in the Great Depression

Technological shocks are one of the key ingredients of real-business-cycle models. The main piece of macroeconomic evidence for the presence of substantial technological shocks is the considerable short-term variation in the Solow residual. For example, as described above, Prescott and Hansen and Wright estimate the magnitude of technology shocks from the behavior of the Solow residual.

The alternative to the view that variations in the Solow residual largely reflect shifts in technology is that output fluctuations arising from other sources affect the measured Solow residual. If there are increasing returns to scale, for example, an increase in output occurring for reasons other than technological change will cause a Solow residual computed under the assumption of constant returns to rise. Similarly, if firms use their labor and capital more intensively when output is high, a Solow residual calculated assuming constant utilization will rise when output increases.

If we can identify a source of output movements other than changes in technology, we can test between these two views of the source of short-run variation in the Solow residual. The real-business-cycle view predicts that the Solow residual will not move systematically in the face of output fluctuations that do not result from technology shocks. The alternative view—that the variation is caused by output movements and that technology shocks have little to do with short-run output fluctuations—predicts that the Solow residual will move just as much with aggregate output when the output movements are known not to be due to technology shocks as it does at other times.

Bernanke and Parkinson (1991) carry out a simple test along these lines. Given that output per person fell sharply in the Great Depression, and given that substantial technological regress is unlikely, the output movements in the Great Depression were probably not due to technology shocks. Bernanke and Parkinson therefore propose to compare how the measured Solow residual moves with output in the Great Depression with how it moves with output in the postwar period. If technology shocks are a central source of fluctuations in the postwar period but not in the depression, the Solow residual and output will move together only in the postwar period.

Because of a lack of reliable data on capital, Bernanke and Parkinson do not follow precisely this procedure. Instead of looking at the relation between movements in the Solow residual and in output, they look at the relation between movements in output and in labor input. Their basic regression is

$$\Delta \ln y_{it} = a + b_i \Delta \ln L_{it} + \varepsilon_{it}, \tag{4.58}$$

where $\Delta \ln y$ is the change in log output, $\Delta \ln L$ is the change in the log of the number of person-hours, and i indexes industries and t indexes time.

If the capital stock exhibits little short-run variation (which is true in the postwar period), then the Solow residual is approximately equal to the percentage change in output minus the product of labor's share and the percentage change in person-hours (see equation [1.29]). Since the real-business-cycle view is that output movements not arising from technology shocks do not affect the Solow residual, it therefore predicts that the estimated b_i's for the depression sample will roughly equal labor's share (which averages about 0.5 for the industries considered by Bernanke and Parkinson). For a period like the postwar sample, where the real-business-cycle view is that the fluctuations in labor input arise largely from technology shocks, the estimated b_i's should be higher. The alternative view predicts that the estimated b_i's will be roughly the same in the two periods.

Bernanke and Parkinson estimate (4.58) using quarterly data for each of ten industries for two sample periods, 1929–1939 and 1955–1988. Table 4.5 summarizes their results. In the depression sample, the estimated b_i's exceed 1 for eight of the ten industries, with an average value of 1.07. The average for the postwar sample is 0.96. Eight of the ten b_i's are actually larger in the depression than in the postwar period. Thus it appears that supporters of real-business-cycle theory must argue either that the depression was caused by large negative technological shocks, or that for some reason the Solow residual is a poor measure of technological change in the depression but not in other periods.

4.10   Extensions and Limitations

Extensions

This chapter focuses on a specific real-business-cycle model. Research in this area, however, has considered many variations and extensions of this basic model. Here we discuss a few of the most important.

TABLE 4.5   Bernanke and Parkinson's results

Industry	Estimate of b	
	1929–1939	1955–1988
Steel	1.51	1.66
	(0.17)	(0.10)
Lumber	1.07	0.86
	(0.05)	(0.05)
Autos	1.21	1.05
	(0.15)	(0.06)
Petroleum	0.42	−0.04
	(0.07)	(0.03)
Textiles	1.09	1.03
	(0.17)	(0.13)
Leather	0.58	0.83
	(0.08)	(0.03)
Rubber	1.21	0.98
	(0.07)	(0.06)
Pulp	1.11	1.04
	(0.10)	(0.38)
Stone, clay, and glass	1.11	0.94
	(0.07)	(0.10)
Nonferrous metals	1.38	1.23
	(0.03)	(0.07)

Standard errors are in parentheses.

Source: Bernanke and Parkinson (1991).

One variation of the model that has attracted considerable attention is the *indivisible-labor* version. Changes in labor input come not just from continuous changes in hours, but also from movements into and out of employment. To investigate the implications of this fact, Rogerson (1988) and Hansen (1985) consider the extreme case where ℓ for each individual has only two possible values, zero (which corresponds to not being employed) and some positive value, ℓ_0 (which corresponds to being employed). Rogerson and Hansen justify this assumption by arguing that there are fixed costs of working.

This change in the model greatly increases the responsiveness of labor input to shocks; this in turn increases both the size of output fluctuations and the share of changes in labor input in those fluctuations. From the results of the calibration exercise described in the previous section, we know that these changes improve the fit of the model.

To see why assuming all-or-nothing employment increases fluctuations in labor input, assume that once the number of workers employed is determined, individuals are divided between employment and unemployment randomly. The number of workers employed in period t, E_t, must satisfy $E_t \ell_0 = L_t$; thus the probability that any given individual is employed in period t is $(L_t/\ell_0)/N_t$. Each individual's expected utility from leisure in period t is therefore

$$\frac{L_t/\ell_0}{N_t} b \ln(1 - \ell_0) + \frac{N_t - (L_t/\ell_0)}{N_t} b \ln 1. \tag{4.59}$$

This expression is *linear* in L_t: individuals are not averse to employment fluctuations. In contrast, when all individuals work the same amount, utility from leisure in period t is $b \ln[1 - (L_t/N_t)]$. This expression has a negative second derivative with respect to L_t: there is increasing marginal disutility of working. As a result, L_t varies less in response to a given amount of variation in wages in the conventional version of the model than in the indivisible-labor version. Hansen and Wright (1992) report that introducing indivisible labor into the Prescott model discussed in the previous section raises the standard deviation of output from 1.30% to 1.73% (versus 1.92% in the data), and the ratio of the standard deviation of total hours to the standard deviation of output from 0.49 to 0.76 (versus 0.96 in the data).[36]

A second major extension is to include distortionary taxes (see Greenwood and Huffman, 1991; Baxter and King, 1993; Campbell, 1994; Braun, 1994; and McGrattan, 1994). A particularly appealing case is proportional output taxation, so $T_t = \tau_t Y_t$, where τ_t is the tax rate in period t. Output taxation corresponds to equal tax rates on capital and labor, which is a reasonable first approximation for many countries. With output taxation, a change in $1 - \tau$ is, from the point of view of private agents, just like a change in technology, $A^{1-\alpha}$: it changes the amount of output they obtain from a given amount of capital and labor. Thus for a given process for $1 - \tau$, after-tax output behaves just as total output does in a model without taxation in which $A^{1-\alpha}$ follows that same process. This makes the analysis of distortionary taxation straightforward (Campbell, 1994).

Since tax revenues are used to finance government purchases, it is natural to analyze the effects of distortionary taxation and government purchases together. Doing this can change our earlier analysis of the effects of government purchases significantly. Baxter and King (1993) show, for example, that in response to a temporary increase in government purchases financed by a temporary increase in distortionary taxation, the tax-induced incentives for intertemporal substitution typically outweigh the interest-rate effects, so that aggregate output falls rather than rises.

---

[36]Because the instantaneous utility function, (4.7), is separable between consumption and leisure, expected utility is maximized when employed and unemployed workers have the same consumption. Thus the indivisible-labor model implies that the unemployed are better off than the employed. See Problem 10.6 and Rogerson and Wright (1988).

Another important extension of real models of fluctuations is the inclusion of multiple sectors and sector-specific shocks. Long and Plosser (1983) develop a multisector model similar to the model of Section 4.5 and investigate its implications for the transmission of shocks among sectors. Lilien (1982), building on the theoretical work of Lucas and Prescott (1974), proposes a distinct mechanism through which sectoral technology or relative-demand shocks can cause employment fluctuations. The basic idea is that if the reallocation of labor across sectors is time-consuming, employment falls more rapidly in the sectors suffering negative shocks than it rises in the sectors facing favorable shocks. As a result, sector-specific shocks cause temporary increases in unemployment. Lilien found that a simple measure of the size of sector-specific disturbances appeared to account for a large fraction of the variation in aggregate employment. Subsequent research, however, has shown that Lilien's original measure is flawed and that his results are almost surely too strong. This work has not reached any firm conclusions concerning the contribution of sectoral shocks to fluctuations or to average unemployment, however.[37]

These are only a few of a large number of extensions of real-business-cycle models. At this point, these models are an active and rapidly evolving subject of research.[38]

Objections

The real-business-cycle approach to analyzing economic fluctuations is controversial. Four objections have received particular attention.[39]

The first criticism concerns the technology shocks. Real-business-cycle models posit technology shocks with a standard deviation of about 1 percent each quarter. It seems likely that such large technological innovations would often be readily apparent. Yet it is usually difficult to identify specific innovations associated with the large quarter-to-quarter swings in the Solow residual.

---

[37]See Abraham and Katz (1986); Murphy and Topel (1987a); Lougani, Rush, and Tave (1990); Davis and Haltiwanger (1990); and Brainard and Cutler (1993).

[38]Some of the other factors that have been incorporated into the models include: lags in the investment process, or *time-to-build* (Kydland and Prescott, 1992); non-time-separable utility (so that instantaneous utility at t does not depend just on c_t and ℓ_t) (Kydland and Prescott, 1982); home production (Benhabib, Rogerson, and Wright, 1991); roles for government-provided goods and capital in utility and production (for example, Christiano and Eichenbaum, 1992a, and Baxter and King, 1993); multiple countries (for example, Baxter and Crucini, 1993); embodied technological change and variable capital utilization (Greenwood, Hercowitz, and Huffman, 1988); and *labor hoarding* (Burnside, Eichenbaum, and Rebelo, 1993).

[39]Most of these objections are raised by Summers (1986a) and Mankiw (1989).

More importantly, there is significant evidence that short-run variations in the Solow residual reflect more than changes in the pace of technological innovation. As described above, Bernanke and Parkinson find that the Solow residual moves just as much with output in the Great Depression as it does in the postwar period, even though it seems unlikely that the depression was caused by technological regress. This is just one example of a broader pattern. Mankiw (1989) shows that the Solow residual behaves similarly in the World War II boom—which was also probably not due to technology shocks—as it does during other periods. Hall (1988a) demonstrates that movements in the Solow residual are correlated with the political party of the President, changes in military purchases, and oil-price movements; yet none of these variables seem likely to affect technology significantly in the short run.[40] If true technology shocks are considerably smaller than the variation in the Solow residual suggests, real-business-cycle models' ability to account for fluctuations is much smaller than the calibration exercise of the previous section implies.

The second criticism of these models concerns not their shocks but one of their central propagation mechanisms, intertemporal substitution in labor supply. Variations in the incentives to work in different periods drive employment fluctuations in the models. Thus a significant willingness to substitute labor supply between periods is needed for important employment fluctuations in the models. Microeconomic studies, however, have had little success in detecting significant intertemporal elasticities of substitution in labor supply. The results of Ball (1990) are typical (see also Altonji, 1986, and Card, 1991). Ball divides the workers in a panel data set into those who say that their labor-supply decisions are constrained by the availability of jobs or hours and those who say they are unconstrained. He then investigates the predictions of a model where fluctuations in work are driven by intertemporal optimization for each of the two groups. The results are consistent with what the workers report: the model is rejected for the ones who say they are constrained, and not rejected for the ones who say they are unconstrained. More tellingly, for the workers who say they are unconstrained, the estimated labor-supply elasticities in response to transitory wage changes are small. Thus Ball's results suggest that fluctuations in overall labor supply are driven primarily by forces other than intertemporal substitution.

The third criticism concerns real-business-cycle models' omission of monetary disturbances. A central feature of the models is that fluctuations are due to real rather than monetary shocks. Yet, as described at the beginning of the chapter, Keynesian macroeconomists argue that monetary disturbances are central to understanding aggregate fluctuations.

---

[40]As Hall explains, oil-price movements should not affect productivity once oil's role in production is accounted for.

If monetary shocks have important real effects, this would mean more than just that real-business-cycle models omit one source of output movements. As described in the next two chapters, the leading candidate explanations of real effects of monetary changes rest on incomplete adjustment of nominal prices or wages. But, as we will see there, incomplete nominal adjustment implies a new channel through which other disturbances, such as changes in government purchases, have real effects. We will also see that incomplete nominal adjustment is most likely to arise when labor, credit, and goods markets depart significantly from the competitive assumptions of real-business-cycle theory. Thus if there is substantial monetary nonneutrality, many of the central features of the real-business-cycle approach might need to be abandoned or greatly modified.[41]

The final criticism of the approach concerns its empirical philosophy rather than the specifics of its models. As described in Section 4.9, the empirical fit of real-business-cycle models is evaluated mainly through calibration exercises. Although calibration has some advantages, it has disadvantages as well. First, as our discussion of extensions of the basic model suggests, there are now many potential ingredients for real-business-cycle models, and a large number of potential ways of combining them. Moreover, not all of the functional forms and parameter values of these ingredients are pinned down by microeconomic evidence. Thus the models have some flexibility in matching characteristics of the data. How much flexibility they have is, at this point, not known. Thus we do not know how informative it is that there are real-business-cycle models that can match important moments of the data relatively well. Nor, because the models are generally not tested against alternatives, do we know whether there are other, perhaps completely different, models that can match the moments just as well.

Second, given the state of economic knowledge, it is not clear that matching the major moments of the data should be viewed as a desirable feature of a model.[42] Even the most complicated real-business-cycle models are grossly simplified descriptions of reality. They generally omit such considerations as heterogeneity in goods, capital, and labor; adjustment costs; and departures from simple functional forms. And, as later chapters describe, consumption and investment behavior and the characteristics of financial, labor, and goods markets may depart significantly from the simple assumptions made in real-business-cycle models. It would be remarkable if none of these potential complications (or any others) have quantitatively important effects on the properties of fluctuations. But given this, it is hard to see how the fact that real-business-cycle models do or do not match aggregate data is informative about their overall usefulness.

---

[41] Section 5.6 discusses some of the empirical evidence concerning the effects of monetary shocks.

[42] The argument that follows is due to Matthew Shapiro.

These potential problems with calibration suggest that focusing on the components of a model individually may be a better strategy than trying to evaluate its overall fit with macroeconomic data. That is, the most useful way to evaluate real-business-cycle models may be to examine the evidence concerning their assumptions of significant technological shocks, substantial short-run elasticities of labor supply, consumption and labor-supply decisions driven by intertemporal optimization, and so on. If the evidence supports these assumptions, then we should investigate their implications for aggregate fluctuations even if a model based on them alone does not match important features of the data. And if the evidence fails to support the assumptions, the issue of whether a model constructed from them matches the data does not appear particularly important.[43]

Convergence?

It is natural to conclude that real-business-cycle models probably provide the explanation of some but not all of observed macroeconomic fluctuations. In this view, the appropriate next step is to attempt to integrate real-business-cycle models with other views of fluctuations. Similarly, it is natural to say that both calibration and traditional econometric tests are useful ways of evaluating models, and that we should therefore employ both.

Cho and Cooley (1990) and King (1991) take the first steps toward integrating real-business-cycle and Keynesian models of fluctuations. These papers introduce rigid nominal prices or wages and monetary disturbances into real-business-cycle models and analyze the resulting models' successes and failures in matching major features of fluctuations. The papers conclude that the models' performance is mixed. But they may represent a first step toward a synthesis of real-business-cycle and Keynesian models.

It is possible, however, that attempting to integrate the competing theories is a recipe for obscuring rather than uncovering the truth. To take one extreme, if quarter-to-quarter technology shocks are small, if there is little intertemporal substitution in labor supply, and if markets are highly non-Walrasian—all of which are possible—then real-business-cycle models are essentially irrelevant to actual fluctuations. In this case, by insisting

---

[43]There are other important objections to real-business-cycle theory. For example, Barro and King (1984) and Mankiw, Rotemberg, and Summers (1985) observe that times of high consumption are typically also times of low leisure. But households' first-order condition relating current labor supply and consumption (equation [4.26]) implies that this can occur only if the real wage is high. Thus, even when there are sources of shocks other than technology, the models appear to require a highly procyclical real wage. To give another example, Rotemberg and Woodford (1994) argue that the size and characteristics of predictable movements in output differ sharply from the predictions of real-business-cycle models.

on incorporating real-business-cycle ingredients into our models, we would only be making it more difficult to identify the forces that actually drive economic fluctuations. At the other extreme, if the assumptions of, say, the Prescott model are approximately correct—which is also possible—then that model provides a parsimonious representation of the central features of most actual fluctuations. By insisting on complexity we would again be missing the essence of fluctuations. Similar comments apply to the issue of calibration versus traditional statistical procedures: if one approach is more informative than the other, pursuing both is costly.

It is of course possible that actual fluctuations are complicated and involve important elements of both real-business-cycle and Keynesian theories. Thus we cannot rule out the real-business-cycle view, the Keynesian view, or intermediate views of the sources and nature of aggregate fluctuations. As a result, macroeconomists have little choice but to make tentative judgments, based on the currently available models and evidence, about what lines of inquiry are most promising. And they must remain open to the possibility that those judgments will need to be revised.

Problems

4.1. Redo the calculations reported in Table 4.1 for any country other than the United States.

4.2. Redo the calculations reported in Table 4.3 for the following:[44]

(*a*) Employees' compensation as a share of national income.

(*b*) The labor force participation rate.

(*c*) The federal government budget deficit as a share of GDP.

(*d*) The Standard and Poor 500 composite stock price index.

(*e*) The difference in yields between Moody's BAA and AAA bonds.

(*f*) The difference in yields between 10-year and 3-month U.S. Treasury securities.

(*g*) The weighted average exchange rate of the U.S. dollar against the currencies of other G-10 countries.

4.3. Let $\ln A_0$ denote the value of A in period 0, and let the behavior of $\ln A$ be given by equations (4.8)–(4.9).

(*a*) Express $\ln A_1$, $\ln A_2$, and $\ln A_3$ in terms of $\ln A_0, \varepsilon_{A1}, \varepsilon_{A2}, \varepsilon_{A3}, \overline{A}$, and g.

(*b*) In light of the fact that the expectations of the ε_A's are zero, what are the expectations of $\ln A_1, \ln A_2$, and $\ln A_3$ given $\ln A_0, \overline{A}$, and g?

---

[44]Annual values for all of these series are published in the *Economic Report of the President*. Quarterly values are available from the Citibase data bank.

4.4. Suppose the period-t utility function, u_t, is $u_t = \ln c_t + b(1 - \ell_t)^{1-\gamma}/(1 - \gamma)$, $b > 0$, $\gamma > 0$, rather than by (4.7).

(a) Consider the one-period problem analogous to that investigated in (4.12)–(4.15). How, if at all, does labor supply depend on the wage?

(b) Consider the two-period problem analogous to that investigated in (4.16)–(4.21). How does the relative demand for leisure in the two periods depend on the relative wage? How does it depend on the interest rate? Explain intuitively why γ affects the responsiveness of labor supply to wages and the interest rate.

4.5. Consider the problem investigated in (4.16)–(4.21).

(a) Show that an increase in both w_1 and w_2 that leaves w_1/w_2 unchanged does not affect ℓ_1 or ℓ_2.

(b) Now assume that the household has initial wealth of amount $Z > 0$.

(i) Does (4.23) continue to hold? Why or why not?

(ii) Does the result in (a) continue to hold? Why or why not?

4.6. Suppose an individual lives for two periods and has utility $\ln C_1 + \ln C_2$.

(a) Suppose the individual has labor income of Y_1 in the first period of life and zero in the second period. Second-period consumption is thus $(1 + r)(Y_1 - C_1)$; r, the rate of return, is potentially random.

(i) Find the first-order condition for the individual's choice of C_1.

(ii) Suppose r changes from being certain to being uncertain, without any change in $E[r]$. How, if at all, does C_1 respond to this change?

(b) Suppose the individual has labor income of zero in the first period and Y_2 in the second. Second-period consumption is thus $Y_2 - (1 + r)C_1$. Y_2 is certain; again, r may be random.

(i) Find the first-order condition for the individual's choice of C_1.

(ii) Suppose r changes from being certain to being uncertain, without any change in $E[r]$. How, if at all, does C_1 respond to this change?

4.7. (a) Use an argument analogous to that used to derive equation (4.23) to show that household optimization requires $b/(1 - \ell_t) = e^{-\rho}E_t[w_t(1 + r_{t+1})b/[w_{t+1}(1 - \ell_{t+1})]]$.

(b) Show that this condition is implied by (4.23) and (4.26). (Note that [4.26] must hold in every period.)

4.8. A simplified real-business-cycle model with additive technology shocks. (This follows Blanchard and Fischer, 1989, pp. 329–331.) Consider an economy consisting of a constant population of infinitely-lived individuals. The representative individual maximizes the expected value of $\sum_{t=0}^{\infty} u(C_t)/(1+\rho)^t$, $\rho > 0$. The instantaneous utility function, $u(C_t)$, is $u(C_t) = C_t - \theta C_t^2$, $\theta > 0$. Assume that C is always in the range where $u'(C)$ is positive.

Output is linear in capital, plus an additive disturbance: $Y_t = AK_t + e_t$. There is no depreciation; thus $K_{t+1} = K_t + Y_t - C_t$, and the interest rate is A.

Assume $A = \rho$. Finally, the disturbance follows a first-order autoregressive process: $e_t = \phi e_{t-1} + \varepsilon_t$, where $-1 < \phi < 1$ and where the ε_t's are mean-zero, i.i.d. shocks.

(a) Find the first-order condition (Euler equation) relating C_t and expectations of C_{t+1}.

(b) Guess that consumption takes the form $C_t = \alpha + \beta K_t + \gamma e_t$. Given this guess, what is K_{t+1} as a function of K_t and e_t?

(c) What values must the parameters α, β, and γ have for the first-order condition in part (a) to be satisfied for all values of K_t and e_t?

(d) What are the effects of a one-time shock to ε on the paths of Y, K, and C?

4.9. A simplified real-business-cycle model with taste shocks. (This follows Blanchard and Fischer, 1989, p. 361.) Consider the setup in Problem 4.8. Assume, however, that the technological disturbances (the e's) are absent, and that the instantaneous utility function is $u(C_t) = C_t - \theta(C_t + v_t)^2$. The v's are mean-zero, i.i.d. shocks.

(a) Find the first-order condition (Euler equation) relating C_t and expectations of C_{t+1}.

(b) Guess that consumption takes the form $C_t = \alpha + \beta K_t + \gamma v_t$. Given this guess, what is K_{t+1} as a function of K_t and v_t?

(c) What values must the parameters α, β, and γ have for the first-order condition in (a) to be satisfied for all values of K_t and v_t?

(d) What are the effects of a one-time shock to v on the paths of Y, K, and C?

4.10. The balanced growth path of the model of Section 4.3. Consider the model of Section 4.3 without any shocks. Let y^*, k^*, c^*, and G^* denote the values of $Y/AL, K/AL, C/AL$, and G/AL on the balanced growth path; w^* the value of w/A; ℓ^* the value of L/N; and r^* the value of r.

(a) Use equations (4.1)–(4.4), (4.23), and (4.26) and the fact that y^*, k^*, c^*, w^*, ℓ^*, and r^* are constant on the balanced growth path to find six equations in these six variables. (Hint: the fact that c in (4.23) is consumption per person, C/N, and c^* is the balanced-growth-path value of consumption per unit of effective labor, C/AL, implies that $c = c^*\ell^*A$ on the balanced growth path.)

(b) Consider the parameter values assumed in Section 4.7. What are the implied shares of consumption and investment in output on the balanced growth path? What is the implied ratio of capital to annual output on the balanced growth path?

4.11. Solving a real-business-cycle model by finding the social optimum.[45] Consider the model of Section 4.5. Assume for simplicity that $n = g = \overline{A} = \overline{N} = 0$. Let $V(K_t, A_t)$, the *value function*, be the expected present value from the cur-

---

[45] This problem uses dynamic programming and the method of undetermined coefficients. These two methods are explained in Section 10.4 and Section 4.6, respectively.

rent period forward of lifetime utility of the representative individual as a function of the capital stock and technology.

(a) Explain intuitively why $V(\bullet)$ must satisfy

$$V(K_t, A_t) = \max_{C_t, \ell_t}\{[\ln C_t + b\ln(1 - \ell_t)] + e^{-\rho}E_t[V(K_{t+1}, A_{t+1})]\}.$$

This condition is known as the *Bellman equation*.

Given the log-linear structure of the model, let us guess that $V(\bullet)$ takes the form $V(K_t, A_t) = \beta_0 + \beta_K \ln K_t + \beta_A \ln A_t$, where the values of the β's are to be determined. Substituting this conjectured form and the facts that $K_{t+1} = Y_t - C_t$ and $E_t[\ln A_{t+1}] = \rho_A \ln A_t$ into the Bellman equation yields

$$V(K_t, A_t) = \max_{C_t, \ell_t}\{[\ln C_t + b\ln(1 - \ell_t)] + e^{-\rho}[\beta_0 + \beta_K \ln(Y_t - C_t) + \beta_A\rho_A \ln A_t]\}.$$

(b) Find the first-order condition for C_t. Show that it implies that C_t/Y_t does not depend on K_t or A_t.

(c) Find the first-order condition for ℓ_t. Use this condition and the result in part (b) to show that ℓ_t does not depend on K_t or A_t.

(d) Substitute the production function and the results in parts (b) and (c) for the optimal C_t and ℓ_t into the equation above for $V(\bullet)$, and show that the resulting expression has the form $V(K_t, A_t) = \beta_0' + \beta_K' \ln K_t + \beta_A' \ln A_t$.

(e) What must β_K and β_A be so that $\beta_K' = \beta_K$ and $\beta_A' = \beta_A$?[46]

(f) What are the implied values of C/Y and ℓ? Are they the same as those found in Section 4.5 for the case of $n = g = 0$?

4.12. Suppose the behavior of technology is described by some process other than (4.8)–(4.9). Do $s_t = \hat{s}$ and $\ell_t = \hat{\ell}$ for all t continue to solve the model of Section 4.5? Why or why not?

4.13. Consider the model of Section 4.5. Suppose, however, that the instantaneous utility function, u_t, is given by $u_t = \ln c_t + b(1 - \ell_t)^{1-\gamma}/(1 - \gamma), b > 0, \gamma > 0$, rather than by (4.7) (see Problem 4.4).

(a) Find the first-order condition analogous to equation (4.26) that relates current leisure and consumption given the wage.

(b) With this change in the model, is the saving rate (s) still constant?

(c) Is leisure per person $(1 - \ell)$ still constant?

4.14. (a) If the $\tilde{A}_t$'s are uniformly zero and if $\ln Y_t$ evolves according to (4.39), what path does $\ln Y_t$ settle down to? (Hint: note that we can rewrite (4.39) as $\ln Y_t - (n + g)t = Q + \alpha[\ln Y_{t-1} - (n + g)(t - 1)] + (1 - \alpha)\tilde{A}_t$, where $Q \equiv \alpha \ln \hat{s} + (1 - \alpha)[\overline{A} + \ln \hat{\ell} + \overline{N}] - \alpha(n + g)$.)

(b) Defining $\tilde{Y}_t$ as the difference between $\ln Y_t$ and the path found in (a), derive (4.40).

---

[46] The calculation of β_0 is tedious and is therefore omitted.

4.15. The derivation of the log-linearized equation of motion for capital, (4.52).
Consider the equation of motion for capital, $K_{t+1} = K_t + K_t^{\alpha}(A_t L_t)^{1-\alpha} - C_t - G_t - \delta K_t$.

(a) (i) Show that $\partial \ln K_{t+1} / \partial \ln K_t$ (holding A_t, L_t, C_t, and G_t fixed) is $(1 + r_{t+1})(K_t / K_{t+1})$.

(ii) Show that this implies that $\partial \ln K_{t+1} / \partial \ln K_t$ evaluated at the balanced growth path is $(1 + r^*)/e^{n+g}$.[47]

(b) Show that

$$\tilde{K}_{t+1} \simeq \lambda_1 \tilde{K}_t + \lambda_2 (\tilde{A}_t + \tilde{L}_t) + \lambda_3 \tilde{G}_t + (1 - \lambda_1 - \lambda_2 - \lambda_3)\tilde{C}_t,$$

where $\lambda_1 \equiv (1 + r^*)/e^{n+g}, \lambda_2 \equiv (1 - \alpha)(r^* + \delta)/\alpha e^{n+g}$, and $\lambda_3 = -(r^* + \delta)$ $(G/Y)^*/\alpha e^{n+g}$; and where $(G/Y)^*$ denotes the ratio of G to Y on the balanced growth path without shocks. (Hints: **1.** Since the production function is Cobb-Douglas, $Y^* = (r^* + \delta)K^*/\alpha$; **2.** On the balanced growth path, $K_{t+1} = e^{n+g}K_t$, which implies that $C^* = Y^* - G^* - \delta K^* - (e^{n+g} - 1)K^*$.)

(c) Use the result in (b) and equations (4.43)–(4.44) to derive (4.52), where $b_{KK} = \lambda_1 + \lambda_2 a_{LK} + (1 - \lambda_1 - \lambda_2 - \lambda_3)a_{CK}, b_{KA} = \lambda_2(1 + a_{LA}) + (1 - \lambda_1 - \lambda_2 - \lambda_3)a_{CA}$, and $b_{KG} = \lambda_2 a_{LG} + \lambda_3 + (1 - \lambda_1 - \lambda_2 - \lambda_3)a_{CG}$.

4.16. A Monte Carlo experiment, and the source of bias in OLS estimates of equation (4.56). Suppose output growth is described simply by $\Delta \ln y_t = \varepsilon_t$, where the ε's are independent, mean-zero disturbances. Normalize the initial value of $\ln y$, $\ln y_0$, to zero for simplicity. This problem asks you to consider what occurs in this situation if one estimates equation (4.56), $\Delta \ln y_t = \alpha' + b \ln y_{t-1} + \varepsilon_t$, by ordinary least squares.

(a) Suppose the sample size is 3, and suppose each ε is equal to 1 with probability $\frac{1}{2}$ and -1 with probability $\frac{1}{2}$. For each of the eight possible realizations of $(\varepsilon_1, \varepsilon_2, \varepsilon_3)((1, 1, 1), (1, 1, -1)$, and so on), what is the OLS estimate of b? What is the average of the estimates? Explain intuitively why the estimates differ systematically from the true value of $b = 0$.

(b) Suppose the sample size is 200, and suppose each ε is normally distributed with a mean of 0 and a variance of 1. Using a random-number generator on a computer, generate 200 such ε's; then generate $\ln y$'s using $\Delta \ln y_t = \varepsilon_t$ and $\ln y_0 = 0$; then estimate (4.56) by OLS; finally, record the estimate of b. Repeat this process 500 times. What is the average estimate of b? What fraction of the estimated b's are negative?

---

[47] One could express r^* in terms of the discount rate ρ. Campbell (1994) argues, however, that it is easier to discuss the model's implications in terms of r^* instead of ρ.

Chapter 5
TRADITIONAL KEYNESIAN
THEORIES OF FLUCTUATIONS

5.1 Introduction

This chapter and the next develop models of fluctuations based on the assumption that there are barriers to the instantaneous adjustment of nominal prices and wages. As we will see, sluggish nominal adjustment causes changes in the aggregate demand for goods at a given level of prices to affect the amount that firms produce. As a result, it causes purely monetary disturbances (which affect only demand) to change employment and output. In addition, many real shocks, including changes in government purchases, investment demand, and technology, affect aggregate demand at a given price level; thus sluggish price adjustment creates a channel other than the intertemporal-substitution mechanism of real-business-cycle models through which these shocks affect employment and output.

This chapter takes nominal stickiness as given. It has two main goals. The first is to investigate aggregate demand. We will examine the determinants of aggregate demand at a given price level and the effects of changes in the price level. The second is to consider alternative assumptions about the form of nominal rigidity. We will investigate different assumptions' implications for firms' willingness to change output in response to changes in aggregate demand and for the behavior of real wages, markups, and inflation. Chapter 6 then turns to the questions of why nominal prices and wages might not adjust immediately to disturbances.

The Keynesian Approach to Modeling

As will quickly become clear, Keynesian models differ from real-business-cycle models not just in substance, but also in style. Real-business-cycle models typically begin with microeconomic assumptions about households' preferences, firms' production functions, the structure of markets, and the evolution of quantities over time. Thus the models are fully specified dynamic general equilibrium models. Keynesian models, in contrast, often begin by directly specifying relationships among aggregate variables. The relationships are often static, and the models' implications for the behavior of some variables (such as the capital stock) are often omitted from the analysis. Even versions of the models that build up the behavior of some variables from microeconomic foundations often specify the behavior of others directly.

The idea behind this shortcut aggregate approach to modeling is three-fold. First, it is simple. The solutions to even relatively basic real-business-cycle models are complicated, and usually require numerical methods. Basic Keynesian models, in contrast, can be analyzed graphically.

Second, many features of the economy are likely to be robust to the details of the microeconomic environment. For example, the opportunity cost of holding non-interest-bearing money is the nominal interest rate. Thus, regardless of the precise reasons that people hold money, the quantity of money demanded is likely to be decreasing in the nominal interest rate. Building a model of money demand from microeconomic foundations would probably add little insight on this issue.

And third, by insisting on microeconomic foundations we could in fact miss important effects. In the case of money demand, for example, beginning with microeconomic foundations could lead us to a specific functional form for the money demand function; yet that functional form would probably not be robust to reasonable changes in the microeconomic assumptions. To give a more significant example, traditional Keynesian models give current income a particularly important role in consumption demand. If we build up consumer behavior from intertemporal optimization with freedom to borrow against future income, we find that current income is no more important than discounted future income in determining households' consumption. But, as we saw in the discussion of Ricardian equivalence in Section 2.9, there are microeconomic models that imply a greater role for current income. Yet these models are often complicated, and thus difficult to embed in models of the entire economy. Thus we may get greater insight by specifying directly that consumption depends particularly on current income.

Of course, there are also disadvantages to the Keynesian approach to modeling. Without microeconomic foundations, welfare analysis is not possible. More importantly, specifying aggregate relationships directly may cause us to overlook important effects. For example, stating directly that consumption depends on current disposable income neglects the possibility that temporary and permanent income movements may have different effects; similarly, it neglects the possibility of Ricardian equivalence. When consumption behavior is derived from microeconomic foundations, in contrast, these possibilities are immediately apparent.

Finally, aggregate relationships may change when the structure of the economy or the nature of policy changes. Thus, working with aggregate relationships rather than microeconomic assumptions may lead us astray in assessing the likely consequences of changes in policy. This is the basis of the *Lucas critique* of traditional macroeconomic models, which we will discuss in Chapter 6.

Overview

The remainder of the chapter consists of five sections. Sections 5.2 and 5.3 develop the aggregate demand side of the standard Keynesian model. These sections take as given that nominal prices and wages are not completely flexible, and that firms change their output in response to changes in demand. Section 5.2 assumes a closed economy, and Section 5.3 considers the open-economy case.

Sections 5.4 and 5.5 consider aggregate supply. Section 5.4 shows how different combinations of wage rigidity, price rigidity, and non-Walrasian features of the labor and goods markets yield different implications about the effect of shifts in aggregate demand on output, unemployment, the real wage, and the markup. Section 5.5 discusses short-run and long-run output-inflation tradeoffs.

Finally, Section 5.6 discusses some empirical evidence about the real effects of monetary changes.

5.2   Review of the Textbook Keynesian Model of Aggregate Demand

The textbook Keynesian model is traditionally summarized by two curves in output-price or output-inflation space, an aggregate demand (*AD*) curve and an aggregate supply (*AS*) curve.[1] The *AD* curve slopes down and the *AS* curve slopes up. These curves are shown in Figure 5.1.

The fact that the aggregate supply curve is upward-sloping rather than vertical is the critical feature of the model. If the *AS* curve is vertical, changes on the demand side of the economy affect only prices. But if it is merely upward-sloping, changes in aggregate demand affect both prices and output.

The *AD* curve summarizes the demand side of the economy. It is derived from two familiar curves in output-interest rate space, the *IS* and *LM* curves. These are shown in Figure 5.2. The curves are drawn for a given price level; as we will see shortly, considering different values of the price level allows

---

[1]Textbook treatments of the Keynesian model of aggregate demand include Abel and Bernanke (1992, Chapters 12–13); Dornbusch and Fischer (1994, Chapters 3–7); Gordon (1993, Chapters 3–6); Hall and Taylor (1991, Chapters 6–7); and Mankiw (1994, Chapters 8–10, 13). The presentation in Sections 5.2 and 5.3 is most similar to Mankiw's.

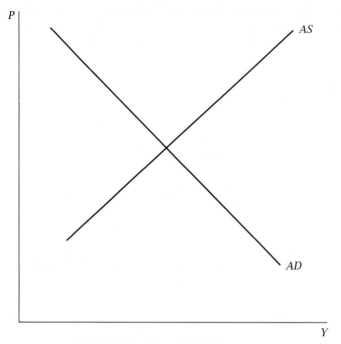

FIGURE 5.1   The *AS-AD* diagram

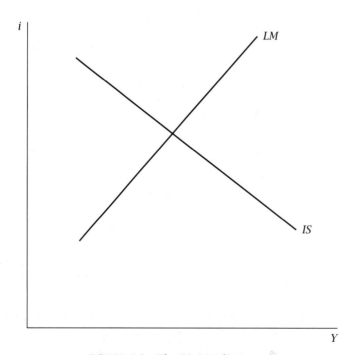

FIGURE 5.2   The *IS-LM* diagram

us to use the *IS* and *LM* curves to derive the *AD* curve. Although there are innumerable variations and extensions of the *IS*-*LM* model, here we consider a standard version.

The *LM* Curve

The *LM* curve shows the combinations of output and the interest rate that lead to equilibrium in the money market for a given price level. It is simplest to think of money as high-powered money—currency and reserves—issued by the government. Since high-powered money pays no nominal interest, the opportunity cost of holding it is the nominal interest rate. The demand for real money balances is therefore a decreasing function of the nominal interest rate. In addition, since the volume of transactions is greater when output is higher, the demand for real balances is increasing in output. The nominal money supply is set by the government. Putting all this together, the condition for the supply and demand of real balances to be equal at a given price level is

$$\frac{M}{P} = L(i, Y), \qquad L_i < 0, \quad L_Y > 0. \tag{5.1}$$

Since $L(\bullet)$ is decreasing in i and increasing in Y, the set of combinations of i and Y that satisfy (5.1) is upward-sloping. Formally, differentiating both sides of (5.1) with respect to Y,

$$0 = L_i \left(\left. \frac{di}{dY} \right|_{LM} \right) + L_Y, \tag{5.2}$$

or

$$\left. \frac{di}{dY} \right|_{LM} = -\frac{L_Y}{L_i} > 0, \tag{5.3}$$

where L_i and L_Y denote the partial derivatives of $L(\bullet)$ and $\left. \frac{di}{dY} \right|_{LM}$ denotes di/dY along the *LM* curve. Thus increases in the income elasticity of money demand, and decreases in the interest elasticity (in absolute value) make the *LM* curve steeper.

Implicitly, the *IS*-*LM* model treats all assets other than money as perfect substitutes. The market for these other assets is then suppressed by Walras's law. Specifically, total wealth in the economy equals the total value of all assets, and the total value of any individual's asset holdings must equal his or her total wealth; thus if the market for every asset but one clears, the market for the remaining asset must clear as well. In the *IS*-*LM* model there are only two assets (money and everything else), and so only one asset-market equilibrium condition is needed. Many important extensions of the

IS-LM model investigate the consequences of relaxing the assumption that all assets other than money are perfect substitutes.[2]

The *IS* Curve

The *IS* curve shows the output-interest rate combinations such that planned and actual expenditures on output are equal.[3] Planned real expenditure depends positively on real income, negatively on the real interest rate, positively on government purchases of goods and services, and negatively on taxes:

$$E = E(Y, i - \pi^e, G, T), \qquad 0 < E_Y < 1, \quad E_{i - \pi^e} < 0, \quad E_G > 0, \quad E_T < 0. \quad (5.4)$$

π^e is expected inflation, G is government purchases, and T is taxes; all of these are taken as given.[4] The negative effect of the real interest rate on planned expenditure operates through firms' investment decisions and consumers' purchases of durable goods. Planned expenditure is assumed to increase less than one-for-one with income; that is, $0 < E_Y < 1$.

In textbook treatments, E is often expressed in terms of its component parts and strong assumptions are made about how the determinants of planned expenditure enter. A standard formulation is

$$E = C(Y - T) + I(i - \pi^e) + G, \qquad (5.5)$$

where $C(\cdot)$ is consumption and $I(\cdot)$ is investment. The restrictions imposed in this specification may be highly unrealistic. For example, there is considerable evidence that the real interest rate affects consumption, and almost overwhelming evidence that income influences investment. To give another example, if Ricardian equivalence holds (see Section 2.9), taxes have no effect on demand; more generally, there is little basis for assuming that income and taxes have equal and opposite effects on spending. Since the general formulation in (5.4) is only slightly more difficult, we will use it in what follows.

If one treats goods that a firm produces and then holds as inventories as purchased by the firm, then all output is purchased by someone. Thus

---

[2] Two classic references are Tobin and Brainard (1963) and Tobin (1969). A large recent literature relaxes the assumption that assets held by banks, particularly their loans, are perfect substitutes for other interest-bearing assets. See Bernanke and Blinder (1988) and Kashyap and Stein (1994).

[3] The *IS* curve is often described as showing equilibrium in the goods market. But since supply is ignored, this is not an accurate description.

[4] Properly speaking, expected inflation should be determined within the model rather than taken as given, since the path of the price level will be determined within the model. Taking π^e as given here simplifies the discussion without altering the model's main implications, however.

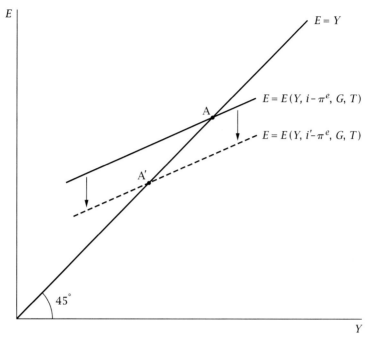

FIGURE 5.3   The Keynesian cross

actual expenditure equals the economy's output, Y. In equilibrium, planned and actual expenditures must be equal. If planned expenditure falls short of actual expenditure, for example, firms are accumulating unwanted inventories; they will respond by cutting their production. Thus equilibrium requires

$$E = Y. \tag{5.6}$$

Substituting (5.6) into (5.4) yields

$$Y = E(Y, i - \pi^e, G, T). \tag{5.7}$$

Figure 5.3, the *Keynesian cross,* depicts equations (5.4) and (5.6) in (Y, E) space for a given level of the interest rate. Equation (5.6) is just the 45-degree line. Since planned expenditure increases less than one-for-one with Y, the set of points satisfying (5.4) is less steep than the 45-degree line. The point where the planned expenditure curve crosses the 45-degree line (Point A) shows the unique level of income where actual and planned expenditures are equal for the given interest rate.[5]

---

[5]The Keynesian cross is sometimes described as a theory of income determination. But this is correct only if the interest rate can be treated as fixed, which is often inappropriate. Thus it is better to think of the Keynesian cross as an ingredient of a larger model.

An increase in the interest rate shifts the planned expenditure line down (since $E(\cdot)$ is decreasing in $i - \pi^e$), and thus reduces the level of income at which actual and planned expenditures are equal; in terms of the diagram, an increase in the interest rate from i to i' shifts the intersection of the two lines from Point A to Point A'. Thus the IS curve slopes down.

Differentiating (5.7), one can show

$$\left.\frac{dY}{di}\right|_{IS} = \frac{E_{i-\pi^e}}{1 - E_Y}. \tag{5.8}$$

Since this is an expression for dY/di (rather than di/dY), it implies that the IS curve is flatter when either $E_{i-\pi^e}$ or E_Y is larger. Intuitively, the larger the effect of the interest rate on planned expenditure, the larger the downward shift of the planned expenditure line, and thus the larger the fall in output. Similarly, the steeper the planned expenditure line, the more output must fall in response to a given downward shift of the planned expenditure line to reach a point where planned and actual expenditures are again in balance, and thus the larger the fall in output. This last effect is the famous *multiplier:* because E depends on Y, the fall in Y needed to restore the equality of E and Y is larger than the amount that E falls at a given Y.

The *AD* Curve

The intersection of the IS and LM curves shows the values of i and Y such that the money market clears and actual and planned expenditures are equal for given levels of P, π^e, G, and T. To see how the IS and LM curves imply the existence of a downward-sloping relationship between P and Y, consider the effects of assuming a higher value of P. Since the price level does not enter the planned expenditure function, $E(\cdot)$, the IS curve is unaffected. The rise in the price level reduces the supply of real money balances, however. Thus a higher interest rate is needed to clear the money market for a given level of income, and so the LM curve shifts up. As a result, i rises and Y falls. This is shown in Figure 5.4. Thus the level of output at the intersection of the IS and LM curves is a decreasing function of the price level. This is what is shown by the aggregate demand curve.

To find the slope of the AD curve, differentiate (5.1) and (5.7) with respect to P. This yields two equations in two unknowns:

$$-\frac{M}{P^2} = L_i \left.\frac{di}{dP}\right|_{AD} + L_Y \left.\frac{dY}{dP}\right|_{AD}, \tag{5.9}$$

$$\left.\frac{dY}{dP}\right|_{AD} = E_Y \left.\frac{dY}{dP}\right|_{AD} + E_{i-\pi^e} \left.\frac{di}{dP}\right|_{AD}. \tag{5.10}$$

These can be solved to obtain

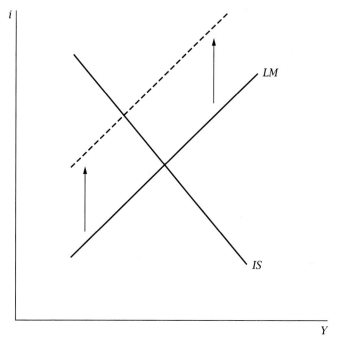

FIGURE 5.4   The effects of an increase in the price level

$$\frac{dY}{dP}\bigg|_{AD} = \frac{-M/P^2}{[(1 - E_Y)L_i/E_{i-\pi^e}] + L_Y}.$$ (5.11)

This expression is unambiguously negative, and it shows the determinants of the slope of the aggregate demand curve.

Example: The Effects of an Increase in Government Purchases

The *IS* and *LM* curves provide a simple model of aggregate demand that can be used to analyze many issues. Suppose, for example, that government purchases rise. The increase in *G* raises planned expenditure for a given level of output and the interest rate. The planned expenditure line in Figure 5.3 therefore shifts up, and so the level of *Y* such that actual and planned expenditures are equal is higher for a given level of the interest rate. Thus the *IS* curve shifts to the right; this is shown in Panel (a) of Figure 5.5. The shift in the *IS* curve raises *Y* (and *i*) for a given price level, and thus moves the *AD* curve outward; this is shown in Panel (b) of the figure.[6]

---

[6]The *IS*-*LM* diagram is drawn for a given value of *P*. Thus the amount that output increases in the *IS*-*LM* diagram is the same as the amount that the aggregate demand curve shifts to the right at the value of *P* assumed in the *IS*-*LM* diagram.

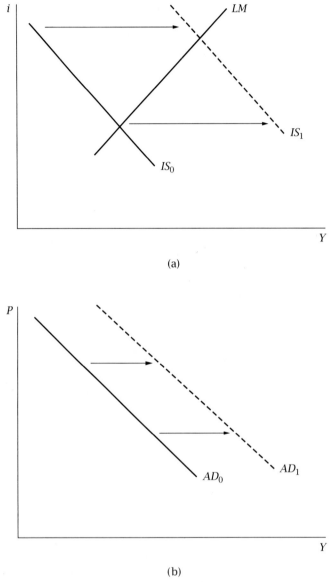

(a)

(b)

FIGURE 5.5   The effects of an increase in government purchases

The impact of this change in aggregate demand on output and the price level depends on the aggregate supply curve. If it is vertical, only the price level increases. If it is horizontal, only output increases. And if it is upward-sloping but not vertical, both output and the price level increase.

Thus, incomplete adjustment of nominal prices introduces a new channel through which shocks affect output. For some reason, which we have not yet specified, nominal prices do not adjust fully in the short run. As a result, any change in the demand for goods at a given price level affects output. In contrast, the intertemporal-substitution and wealth effects that drive employment fluctuations in real-business-cycle models would correspond to effects of government purchases on the aggregate supply curve— that is, they would affect not the quantity of output that households and firms want to buy at a given price level, but the quantity that firms want to produce at a given price level.

The Keynesian View of Fluctuations

The *IS-LM* model suggests many potential sources of fluctuations: there can be changes in monetary and fiscal policy, shocks to investment demand, shifts in the money demand function, and so on. And in the complete *IS-LM-AS* model, there can be disturbances to aggregate supply as well. Standard Keynesian accounts of macroeconomic fluctuations (such as descriptions of the macroeconomic history of the United States over the last several decades) typically assign important roles to many different kinds of shocks. Thus, in contrast to the real-business-cycle approach, Keynesian analyses typically do not attribute the bulk of fluctuations to a small number of types of disturbances.[7]

The fact that Keynesian analyses allow for many different shocks means that they generally do not deliver specific predictions about the relative magnitudes of movements in different variables or about how the movements in the variables are related: in the models, different shocks cause different patterns of changes. Because of this, Keynesian models are typically not evaluated using the calibration approach described in Section 4.9. Instead, they are usually judged by their success in describing the effects of specific kinds of shocks. For example, there is a large literature testing the models' implications concerning the effects of monetary shocks; we will discuss some of this work in Section 5.6. To give another example, the models are often judged by their success in accounting for the behavior of output and inflation in the United States over the past several decades given the major shocks that appear to have occurred. As we will see in Section 5.5, some versions of Keynesian models seem to be contradicted by this evidence, whereas others appear broadly consistent with it.

5.3   The Open Economy

In most practical applications, the exchange rate and international trade are important to short-run fluctuations. This section therefore extends the *IS-LM* model to the case of an open economy.

---

[7]An important exception is the monetarist view that monetary policy shocks are the driving force of most fluctuations.

The Real Exchange Rate and Planned Expenditure

It is simplest to think of the rest of the world as consisting of a single country. Let ε denote the nominal exchange rate—specifically, the price of a unit of foreign currency in terms of domestic currency. With this definition, a rise in the exchange rate means that foreign currency has become more expensive, and therefore corresponds to a weakening, or depreciation, of the domestic currency. Similarly, a fall in ε corresponds to an appreciation of the domestic currency. Let P^* denote the price level abroad (that is, the price of foreign goods in units of foreign currency). These definitions imply that the real exchange rate—the price of foreign goods in units of domestic goods—is $\varepsilon P^*/P$.

A higher real exchange rate implies that foreign goods have become more expensive relative to domestic goods. Both domestic residents and foreigners are therefore likely to increase their purchases of domestic goods relative to foreign ones. Thus planned expenditure rises. Mathematically, equation (5.7) becomes

$$Y = E(Y, i - \pi^e, G, T, \varepsilon P^*/P), \tag{5.12}$$

with $E(\bullet)$ increasing in $\varepsilon P^*/P$.[8] Money demand is likely to be largely unaffected by the exchange rate; thus the LM curve is the same as before.

Since any individual country is small relative to the entire rest of the world, it is reasonable to take the foreign price level as given. But it is not reasonable to take the exchange rate as given. Equations (5.1) and (5.12), together with the AS curve, are thus not a complete model.

At this point one can make different assumptions about the exchange-rate regime (floating or fixed), capital mobility (perfect or imperfect), and exchange-rate expectations (static or rational). What set of assumptions is appropriate depends on the economy being studied and the questions being asked. Here we discuss some of the most important possibilities.

The Mundell–Fleming Model

The simplest assumptions about capital movements are that there are no barriers to capital mobility and that investors are risk-neutral; we will refer to this case as *perfect capital mobility*. Barriers to foreign investment in most industrialized countries are small, and many investors appear willing to make large changes in their portfolios in response to small rate-of-return differences. As a result, perfect capital mobility is likely to be a good approximation for many purposes.

---

[8]The function is often assumed to take the specific form $C(Y - T) + I(i - \pi^e) + G + NX(\varepsilon P^*/P)$, where NX denotes net exports.

For exchange-rate expectations, the simplest assumption is that in-vestors do not expect the exchange rate to change. This assumption can be justified both on the grounds of ease and on the grounds that it is difficult to find evidence of predictable exchange-rate movements (Meese and Ro-goff, 1983). These assumptions about capital mobility and exchange-rate expectations lead to the famous Mundell–Fleming model (Mundell, 1968; Fleming, 1962).

Perfect capital mobility implies that if there were any difference in the ex-pected rate of return between domestic and foreign assets, investors would put all of their wealth into the asset with the higher yield. Since both types of assets must be held by someone, it follows that the expected rates of re-turn on the two assets must be equal. The expected rate of return on foreign assets in terms of domestic currency is the foreign interest rate plus any ex-pected increase in the price of foreign currency. With static exchange-rate expectations, the expected change in the price of foreign currency is zero. Thus the requirement that the expected rates of return are equal is simply

$$i = i^*, \tag{5.13}$$

where i^* is the foreign interest rate; i^* is taken as given.

At this point it is necessary to distinguish between floating and fixed ex-change rates. With a floating exchange rate, aggregate demand is described by the three equations (5.1), (5.12), and (5.13) in the three unknowns i, Y, and ε. Since i is determined trivially by the requirement that it equals i^*, the system immediately reduces to two equations in Y and ε:

$$\frac{M}{P} = L(i^*, Y), \tag{5.14}$$

$$Y = E(Y, i^* - \pi^e, G, T, \varepsilon P^*/P). \tag{5.15}$$

Figure 5.6 plots the sets of points satisfying (5.14) and (5.15) in output-exchange rate space. Since an increase in $\varepsilon P^*/P$ raises planned expendi-ture, the set of solutions to (5.15) is upward-sloping; this is shown as the IS^* curve in the figure. And since the exchange rate does not affect money demand, the set of solutions to (5.14) is vertical; this is shown as the LM^* curve.

The fact that the LM^* curve is vertical means that output for a given price level—that is, the position of the AD curve—is determined entirely in the money market. To take the same example as in the previous section, suppose that government purchases rise. This change shifts the IS^* curve to the right. As shown in Figure 5.7, however, at a given price level this leads only to appreciation of the exchange rate and has no effect on output. Thus the aggregate demand curve is unaffected.

Assuming a fixed rather than a floating exchange rate requires two changes to the model. First, the exchange rate is now pegged at some level $\bar{\varepsilon}$:

$$\varepsilon = \bar{\varepsilon}. \tag{5.16}$$

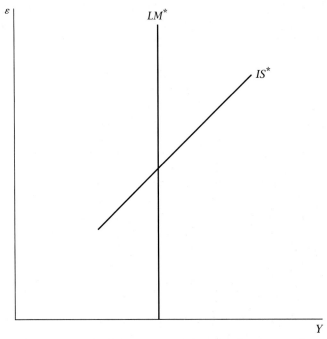

FIGURE 5.6   The Mundell–Fleming model with a floating exchange rate

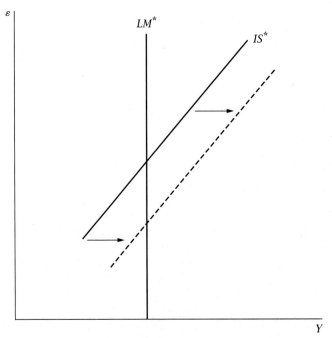

FIGURE 5.7   The effects of an increase in government purchases with a floating exchange rate

Second, the money supply becomes endogenous rather than exogenous. For the government to fix the exchange rate, it must stand ready to buy or sell domestic currency in exchange for foreign currency at the rate $\bar{\varepsilon}$. It therefore cannot independently set M, but must let it adjust to ensure that the exchange rate remains at $\bar{\varepsilon}$.

The aggregate demand side of the model with a fixed exchange rate therefore consists of the *LM* equation, (5.1); the *IS* equation, (5.12); the interest-rate equation, (5.13); and the exchange-rate equation, (5.16). Once again, we can substitute the $i = i^*$ condition into the *IS* and *LM* equations to simplify the system. This gives us the LM^* equation, (5.14); the IS^* equation, (5.15); and the exchange-rate equation, (5.16). In addition, the LM^* equation, $M/P = L(i^*, Y)$, serves only to determine M, and can therefore be neglected. Thus we are left with the IS^* equation and the exchange-rate equation. The IS^* curve is upward-sloping as before; and the exchange-rate equation is simply a horizontal line at $\bar{\varepsilon}$. Figure 5.8 depicts the solutions to these equations in output-exchange rate space.

The results for this case are the opposite of those for a floating exchange rate. Changes in planned expenditure now affect aggregate demand. A rise in government purchases, for example, shifts the IS^* curve to the right and thus raises output for a given price level. Disturbances in the money market, in contrast, have no effect on Y for a given P. A rise in the demand for money, for example, leads only to an increase in the money supply.

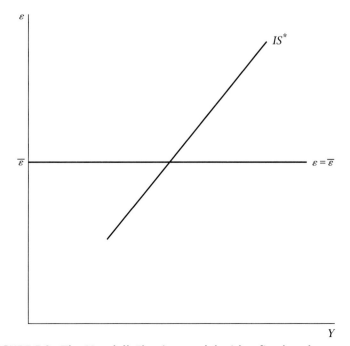

FIGURE 5.8   The Mundell–Fleming model with a fixed exchange rate

Finally, with a fixed exchange rate, the exchange rate itself is a policy instrument. For example, a devaluation—an increase in the fixed exchange rate, $\bar{\varepsilon}$—stimulates net exports and thus increases aggregate demand.

Rational Exchange-Rate Expectations and Overshooting

The Mundell–Fleming model assumes that exchange-rate expectations are static. But with a floating exchange rate, it turns out that when plausible assumptions about the dynamics of prices and output are added to the model, there are predictable changes in exchange rates. Thus static expectations are not rational: an investor with static expectations is making systematic errors in his or her exchange-rate forecasts. Such an investor can therefore earn a higher average rate of return by using information that helps to forecast exchange-rate movements. Thus it is natural to ask what happens if investors form their expectations concerning movements in the exchange rate using all of the available information—that is, if they have rational expectations. Since static expectations *are* rational when the exchange rate is fixed and likely to remain so, we focus on a floating exchange rate.[9]

When expectations are not static, perfect capital mobility no longer necessarily implies that domestic and foreign interest rates are equal. Consider an investor at some time t deciding where to hold his or her wealth. If the investor puts a dollar into a domestic asset that earns a continuously compounded rate of return of i, at time $t + \Delta t$ he or she will have $e^{i\Delta t}$ dollars. Suppose the investor instead invests in foreign assets. At t, the investor's dollar can be used to purchase foreign assets that are worth $1/\varepsilon(t)$ units of foreign currency; after Δt these assets are worth $e^{i^*\Delta t}/\varepsilon(t)$ units of foreign currency; and this foreign currency can be used to buy $\varepsilon(t + \Delta t)e^{i^*\Delta t}/\varepsilon(t)$ dollars.

Under perfect capital mobility, these two ways of investing the dollar must have the same expected payoff. $\varepsilon(t)$, i, and i^* are known, but $\varepsilon(t + \Delta t)$ may be uncertain. Thus we have

$$e^{i\Delta t} = \frac{E[\varepsilon(t + \Delta t)]}{\varepsilon(t)} e^{i^*\Delta t}. \tag{5.17}$$

Equation (5.17) holds for all values of Δt. The derivatives of both sides with respect to Δt are therefore equal:

$$e^{i\Delta t}i = \frac{E[\varepsilon(t + \Delta t)]}{\varepsilon(t)} e^{i^*\Delta t}i^* + e^{i^*\Delta t}\frac{E[\dot{\varepsilon}(t + \Delta t)]}{\varepsilon(t)}. \tag{5.18}$$

---

[9]Rational expectations may differ from static expectations under a fixed exchange rate if there is some probability of a change in the exchange rate. In addition, there are cases that fall between floating and fixed exchange rates. One that has attracted considerable attention is the *target band,* such as those used in the European Monetary System. See Krugman (1991), for example.

When this expression is evaluated at $\Delta t = 0$, it simplifies to

$$i = i^* + \frac{E[\dot{\varepsilon}(t)]}{\varepsilon(t)}. \tag{5.19}$$

Equation (5.19) states that under perfect capital mobility, interest-rate differences must be offset by expectations of exchange-rate movements. The domestic interest rate can exceed the foreign interest rate, for example, only if the domestic currency is expected to depreciate at a rate equal to the interest-rate differential. Equation (5.19) is known as *uncovered interest-rate parity.*[10]

The possibility of expected exchange-rate movements associated with interest-rate differences gives rise to the possibility of *exchange-rate overshooting* (Dornbusch, 1976). "Overshooting" refers to a situation where the initial reaction of a variable to a shock is greater than its long-run response. To see how the exchange rate can overshoot, consider an increase in the money supply starting from a situation where $i = i^*$ and where the exchange rate is not expected to change. As stressed later in the chapter, Keynesian models generally imply that monetary disturbances have no real effects in the long run. Thus the long-run effect of the shock is just to cause both the price level and the exchange rate to rise proportionally with the increase in money.

Now consider the short-run effect of the shock. If the monetary expansion reduces the interest rate, then (5.19) implies that $E[\dot{\varepsilon}]$ must be negative: if i is less than i^*, investors will hold domestic assets only if they expect the domestic currency to appreciate. But this means that the domestic currency is worth less now than it will be in the long run; that is, it must have depreciated by so much at the time of the shock that it has overshot its expected long-run value.

This leaves the question of whether the monetary expansion reduces the domestic interest rate. A particularly simple case occurs in a variant of the model where producers cannot change output in the very short run, so that the *IS* equation, (5.12), need not be satisfied at every moment. With both prices and output fixed, the only variable that can adjust to ensure that the *LM* equation, (5.1), is satisfied is the interest rate. Thus i must fall in response to an increase in M, and so there must be exchange-rate overshooting.

The intuition for this result is straightforward. If at the time of the shock the exchange rate merely depreciates to its new long-run equilibrium level, the interest-rate differential causes all investors to want to purchase foreign

---

[10]The parity is "uncovered" because although positive expected profits can be made by purchasing one country's assets and selling the other's when (5.19) fails, these profits are not riskless. The alternative is *covered interest-rate parity,* which refers to the relationship in (5.18) with the expected future exchange rate replaced by the price in futures markets of commitments to buy or sell foreign currency at a later date. Failure of covered interest-rate parity would imply a riskless profit opportunity.

currency to obtain the higher-yielding foreign assets. This cannot be an equilibrium. Instead, the price of domestic currency is bid down until it is sufficiently below its expected long-run level that the expected appreciation just balances the lower interest rate on domestic assets.

When the *IS* equation is assumed to hold continuously, an increase in *M* no longer necessarily reduces *i*. Thus in this case there can be either undershooting or overshooting. Which occurs turns out to be a complicated function of the parameters of the model (see Dornbusch, 1976, and Problem 5.10).[11]

Imperfect Capital Mobility

The assumptions that there are no barriers to capital movements between countries and that investors are risk-neutral are surely too strong. Transaction costs and the desire to diversify, for example, cause investors not to put all of their wealth into a single country's assets in response to a small difference in expected returns. It is therefore natural to consider the effects of imperfect capital mobility. We focus on the case of a floating exchange rate, and for simplicity we revert to the assumption of static exchange-rate expectations.

A simple way to model imperfect capital mobility is to assume that capital flows depend on the difference between domestic and foreign interest rates. Specifically, define the capital flow, *CF*, as foreigners' purchases of domestic assets minus domestic residents' purchases of foreign assets. Our assumption is

$$CF = CF(i - i^*), \qquad CF'(\bullet) > 0. \tag{5.20}$$

The capital flow, *CF*, and net exports, *NX*, must sum to zero. If net exports are negative, for example, this means that the country's sales of goods and services to foreigners are not sufficient to pay for its imports. The country must therefore be paying for the excess by selling assets to foreigners— that is, *CF* must be equal and opposite to *NX*. Thus:[12]

$$CF(i - i^*) + NX(Y, i - \pi^e, G, T, \varepsilon P^*/P) = 0. \tag{5.21}$$

The aggregate demand side of the model now consists of the *IS* equation, (5.12), the *LM* equation, (5.1), and the balance-of-payments equation, (5.21). If net exports are the only component of planned expenditure that is

---

[11]See Frankel (1979) and Engel and Frankel (1984) for empirical investigations of overshooting.

[12]With perfect capital mobility, *CF* is minus infinity if *i* is less than *i**, plus infinity if *i* is greater than *i**, and can take on any value—since investors are indifferent about which country's assets to hold—if *i* equals *i**. Thus (5.21) can hold in this case only if *i* = *i**.

affected by the exchange rate, the model can be analyzed graphically. With this assumption, we can write planned expenditure as the sum of domestic residents' planned expenditure (on both domestic and foreign goods) and net exports:

$$Y = E^D(Y, i - \pi^e, G, T) + NX(Y, i - \pi^e, G, T, \varepsilon P^*/P), \qquad (5.22)$$

where $E^D(\bullet)$ is domestic residents' planned expenditure. $E^D(\bullet)$ is assumed to satisfy $0 < E_Y^D < 1$, $E_{i-\pi^e}^D < 0$, $E_G^D > 0$, and $E_T^D < 0$. We can then use (5.21) to substitute for net exports, and thereby eliminate the exchange rate from the model:

$$Y = E^D(Y, i - \pi^e, G, T) - CF(i - i^*). \qquad (5.23)$$

Since $CF(i - i^*)$ is increasing in i, the set of points satisfying (5.23) is downward-sloping in (Y, i) space. This locus is shown in Figure 5.9 as the IS^{**} curve. Note that the exchange rate is implicitly changing as we move along the curve. Since the interest rate affects Y in (5.23) both through its direct effect on domestic demand and through its effect on the exchange rate and net exports, the IS^{**} is flatter than a conventional IS curve. In the extreme case of perfect capital mobility, the IS^{**} curve is flat at i^*. The LM curve is the same as before.

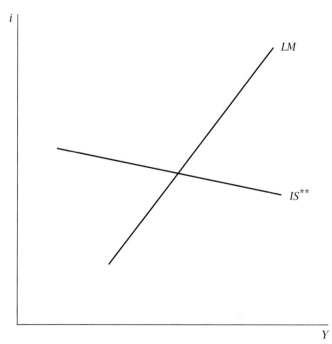

FIGURE 5.9   The case of imperfect capital mobility and a floating exchange rate

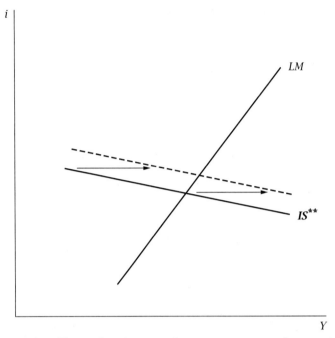

FIGURE 5.10   The effects of an increase in government purchases with imperfect capital mobility and a floating exchange rate

The results for this case typically fall between those for a closed economy and those for perfect capital mobility. Consider again the effects of an increase in government purchases. Since this increase raises expenditure for a given interest rate, the IS^{**} curve shifts to the right, as shown in Figure 5.10. Thus, in contrast to what happens with perfect capital mobility, i and Y rise for a given price level. Since the IS^{**} curve is flatter than the closed-economy IS curve, however, the effects are weaker than they are in a closed economy. The effects of other shocks can be analyzed in similar ways.

5.4   Alternative Assumptions about Wage and Price Rigidity

We now turn to the aggregate supply side of the model. This section describes various ways that a nonvertical AS curve might arise. In all of them, incomplete nominal adjustment is assumed rather than derived. Thus this section's purpose is not to discuss possible microeconomic foundations of nominal stickiness; that is the job of Chapter 6. Instead, the goal is to explore some combinations of nominal wage and price rigidity and characteristics of the labor and goods markets that give rise to a nonvertical AS

curve. The different sets of assumptions have different implications for un-employment, for the behavior of the real wage and the markup in response to aggregate demand fluctuations, and for firms' pricing behavior.

We consider four sets of assumptions. Each is of interest in its own right. Together, they illustrate the wide range of possibilities.

Case 1: Keynes's Model

The aggregate supply portion of the model in Keynes's *General Theory* (1936) begins with the assumption that the nominal wage is rigid (at least over some range):

$$W = \overline{W}. \tag{5.24}$$

Output is produced by competitive firms. Labor, L, is the only factor of production that is variable in the short run, and it is subject to decreasing returns:

$$Y = F(L), \qquad F'(\bullet) > 0, \quad F''(\bullet) < 0. \tag{5.25}$$

Since firms are competitive, they hire labor up to the point where the marginal product of labor equals the real wage:

$$F'(L) = \frac{W}{P}. \tag{5.26}$$

Equations (5.24)-(5.26) imply an upward-sloping AS curve. Since the wage is fixed, a higher price level implies a lower real wage. Firms respond by raising employment, which increases output. Thus there is a positive relationship between P and Y.

The reason that incomplete nominal adjustment causes shifts in aggregate demand to change output in this case is straightforward. With rigid nominal wages, increases in the price level reduce the real wage and therefore increase the amount that firms want to sell. As a result, increases in aggregate demand lead not just to increases in prices, but to increases in both prices and output.

Figure 5.11 shows the situation in the labor market for a given price level. Employment and the real wage are determined by labor demand at the real wage that is implied by the fixed nominal wage and the price level (Point E in the diagram). Thus there is involuntary unemployment: some workers would like to work at the prevailing wage but cannot. The amount of unemployment is the difference between supply and demand at the prevailing real wage (distance EA in the diagram).

Fluctuations in aggregate demand lead to movements of employment and the real wage along the downward-sloping labor demand curve. A decline in demand, for example, leads to a fall in the price level, a rise in the

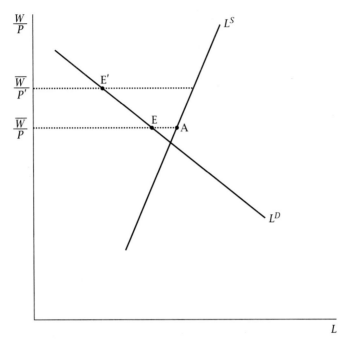

FIGURE 5.11   The labor market with sticky wages, flexible prices, and a competitive goods market

real wage, and a fall in employment. This is shown as Point E′ in the diagram. This view of aggregate supply therefore implies a countercyclical real wage in response to aggregate demand shocks. This prediction has been subject to extensive testing beginning shortly after the publication of the *General Theory*. It has found little support: most studies have found that the real wage is approximately acyclical, or moderately procyclical.[13]

Case 2: Sticky Prices, Flexible Wages, and a Competitive Labor Market

The view of aggregate supply in the *General Theory* assumes that the goods market is competitive and goods prices are completely flexible, and that the source of nominal stickiness is entirely in the labor market. This raises

---

[13]Studies of the cyclical behavior of the real wage were pioneered by Dunlop (1938) and Tarshis (1939). These papers have spawned a vast literature. See, for example, Geary and Kennan (1982); Bils (1985); Keane, Moffitt, and Runkle (1988); Beaudry and DiNardo (1991); and Solon, Barsky, and Parker (1994).

In his important paper responding to Dunlop's and Tarshis's studies, Keynes (1939) largely disavowed the specific formulation of aggregate supply in the *General Theory*, saying that he had chosen it to keep the model as classical as possible and to simplify the presentation. His 1939 view of aggregate supply is closer to Case 4, below.

the question of what occurs in the reverse case where the labor market is competitive and wages are completely flexible, and where the source of incomplete nominal adjustment is entirely in the goods market.

The assumption that goods prices are not completely flexible is almost always coupled with the assumption that there is imperfect competition in the goods market. This is done for two reasons. First, with perfect competition, at the flexible-price equilibrium firms are selling the amount they want. A rise in demand from its initial level with prices unchanged therefore causes them to ration buyers. With imperfect competition, in contrast, price exceeds marginal cost and firms are better off if they can sell more at the prevailing price. It is therefore reasonable to assume that if prices do not adjust, then over some range firms are willing to produce to satisfy demand.

Second, the eventual goal of the theory is to derive rather than assume incomplete price adjustment. To do this, it is better to have price-setters (such as the firms in a model with imperfect competition) than an outside actor who sets prices (such as the Walrasian auctioneer of competitive models).[14]

With this view, prices rather than wages are assumed rigid:

$$P = \overline{P}. \tag{5.27}$$

Wages are flexible; thus workers are on their labor supply curve, which is assumed to be upward-sloping:[15]

$$L = L^s \left(\frac{W}{P} \right), \qquad L^{s\prime}(\bullet) > 0. \tag{5.28}$$

As before, employment and output are related by the production function, $Y = F(L)$ (equation [5.25]). Finally, firms meet demand at the prevailing price as long as it does not exceed the level where marginal cost equals price; we let Y^{MAX} denote this level of output.

With these strong assumptions about price rigidity, the aggregate supply curve is not just nonvertical, but horizontal. Specifically, it is a horizontal

---

[14]An important exception to the usual pairing of incomplete price adjustment with imperfect competition is found in the *disequilibrium* literature. These models typically assume a competitive goods market, and they consider the possibility of rationing by firms. In addition, the models typically have wage rigidity as well as price rigidity and allow for rationing (of either workers or firms) in the labor market. See, for example, Barro and Grossman (1971); Solow and Stiglitz (1968); and Malinvaud (1977). Benassy (1976) extends disequilibrium models to imperfect competition.

[15]Note that by writing labor supply as a function only of the real wage, we are ignoring the intertemporal-substitution and interest-rate effects that are central to employment fluctuations in real-business-cycle models. In principle these effects can be incorporated into the model. The prevailing view among Keynesians, however, is that these effects are not large. Thus, following the general modeling strategy described in Section 5.1, they are usually simply omitted.

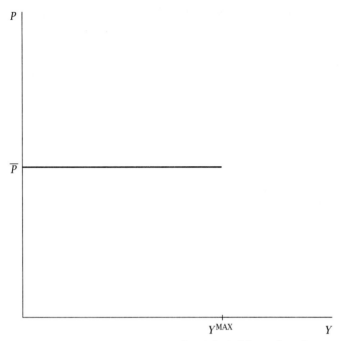

FIGURE 5.12   Aggregate supply with rigid goods prices

line at $\overline{P}$ out to Y^{MAX}; this is shown in Figure 5.12. Fluctuations in aggregate demand cause firms to change employment and output at the fixed price level, $\overline{P}$. And if aggregate demand ever becomes so large that demand at $\overline{P}$ exceeds Y^{MAX}, output equals Y^{MAX} and firms ration sales of their goods.

Figure 5.13 shows this model's implications for the labor market. Firms' demand for labor is determined by their desire to meet the demand for their goods. Thus—as long as the real wage is not so high that it is unprofitable to meet the full demand—the labor demand curve is a vertical line in employment-wage space. The term *effective labor demand* is used to describe a situation, such as this, where the quantity of labor demanded depends on the amount of goods that firms are able to sell.[16] The real wage is determined by the intersection of the effective labor demand curve and the labor supply curve (Point E). Thus workers are on their labor supply curve and there is no unemployment.

This model implies a procyclical real wage in the face of demand fluctuations. A fall in aggregate demand, for example, leads to a fall in effective labor demand, and thus to a fall in the real wage as workers move down their

---

[16]If the real wage is so high that it is not profitable for firms to meet the demand for their goods, the quantity of labor demanded is determined by the condition that the marginal product equals the real wage. Thus this portion of the labor demand curve is downward-sloping.

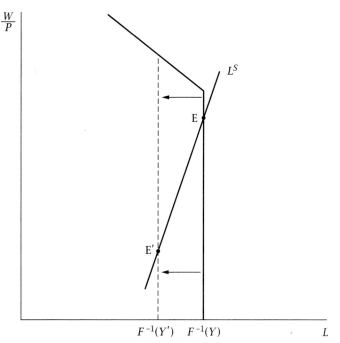

FIGURE 5.13   A competitive labor market when prices are sticky and wages are flexible

labor supply curve (to Point E′ in the diagram). If labor supply is relatively unresponsive to the real wage, the real wage varies greatly when aggregate demand changes.

Finally, this model implies a countercyclical markup (ratio of price to marginal cost) in response to demand fluctuations. A rise in demand, for example, leads to a rise in costs, both because the wage rises and because the marginal product of labor declines as output rises. Prices, however, stay fixed, and so the ratio of price to marginal cost falls.

The cyclical behavior of the markup has received much less attention than the cyclical behavior of the real wage. It plays an important role in many of the models of this chapter and the next one, however. Because of its importance to theories of fluctuations, it has begun to be the subject of intensive study. The evidence to date seems inconsistent with the view that the markup is strongly procyclical; whether it is significantly countercyclical or approximately acyclical, however, is an open question.[17]

The reason that incomplete nominal adjustment causes changes in aggregate demand to affect output is quite different in this case than in the

---

[17]See, for example, Bils (1987); Rotemberg and Woodford (1991); and Chevalier and Scharfstein (1994). Kalecki (1938) was an early advocate of the importance of the behavior of the markup for fluctuations.

previous one. A fall in aggregate demand, for example, lowers the amount that firms are able to sell at the prevailing price level; thus they reduce their production. In the previous model, in contrast, a fall in aggregate demand, by raising the real wage, reduces the amount that firms want to sell.

This model of aggregate supply is important for three reasons. First, it is the natural starting point for models in which nominal stickiness involves prices rather than wages. Second, it shows that there is no necessary connection between nominal rigidity and unemployment. And third, it is easy to use; because of this, models like it often appear in the theoretical literature.

Case 3: Sticky Prices, Flexible Wages, and Real Labor Market Imperfections

Since output fluctuations appear to be associated with unemployment fluctuations, it is natural to ask whether movements in aggregate demand can lead to changes in unemployment when it is nominal prices that adjust sluggishly. To see how this can occur, suppose that nominal wages are still flexible, but that there is some non-Walrasian feature of the labor market that causes the real wage to remain above the level that equates demand and supply. Chapter 10 investigates characteristics of the labor market that can cause this to occur and how the real wage may vary with the level of aggregate economic activity in such situations. For now, let us simply assume that firms have some "real-wage function." Thus we write

$$\frac{W}{P} = w(L), \qquad w'(\bullet) \geq 0. \tag{5.29}$$

For concreteness, one can think of firms paying more than market-clearing wages for *efficiency-wage* reasons (see Sections 10.2–10.4). As before, prices are fixed at $\overline{P}$, and output and employment are related by the production function, $Y = F(L)$.

These assumptions, like the previous ones, imply a flat aggregate supply curve up to the point where marginal cost equals $\overline{P}$; thus again changes in aggregate demand have real effects. This case's implications for the labor market are different than the previous one's, however. This is shown in Figure 5.14. Employment and the real wage are now determined by the intersection of the effective labor demand curve and the real-wage function. In contrast to the previous case, there is unemployment; the amount is given by distance EA in the diagram. Fluctuations in labor demand lead to movements along the real-wage function rather than along the labor supply curve. Thus the elasticity of labor supply no longer determines how the real wage responds to aggregate demand movements. And if the real-wage function is flatter than the labor supply curve, unemployment rises when demand falls.

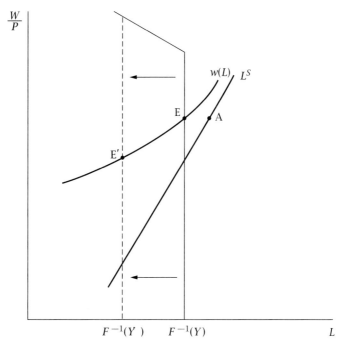

FIGURE 5.14   A non-Walrasian labor market when prices are sticky and nominal wages are flexible.

Case 4: Sticky Wages, Flexible Prices, and Imperfect Competition

Just as Case 3 extends Case 2 by introducing real imperfections in the labor market, the final case extends Case 1 by introducing real imperfections in the goods market. Specifically, assume (as in Case 1) that the nominal wage is rigid at $\overline{W}$ and that nominal prices are flexible, and continue to assume that output and employment are related by the production function. Now, however, assume that the goods market is imperfectly competitive. With imperfect competition, price is a markup over marginal cost. Paralleling our assumptions about the real wage in Case 3, we do not model the determinants of the markup, but simply assume that there is a "markup function." With these assumptions, price is given by

$$P = \mu(L)\frac{W}{F'(L)}; \tag{5.30}$$

$W/F'(L)$ is marginal cost and μ is the markup.

Equation (5.30) implies that the real wage, W/P, is given by $F'(L)/\mu(L)$. Without any restriction on $\mu(L)$, one cannot say how W/P varies with L. If

μ is constant, the real wage is countercyclical because of the diminishing marginal product of labor, just as in Case 1. Since the nominal wage is fixed, the price level must rise when output rises; thus the AS curve slopes up. Again as in Case 1, there is unemployment as long as labor supply is less than the level of employment determined by the intersection of AS and AD.

If $\mu(L)$ is sufficiently countercyclical—that is, if the markup is sufficiently lower in booms than in recoveries—the real wage can be acyclical or pro-cyclical even though the nominal rigidity is entirely in the labor market. A particularly simple case occurs when $\mu(L)$ is precisely as countercyclical as $F'(L)$. In this situation, the real wage must be constant. Since the nominal wage is constant by assumption, the price level is constant as well. Thus the AS curve is horizontal.[18] If $\mu(L)$ is more countercyclical than $F'(L)$, P must fall when L rises, and so the aggregate supply curve is actually downward-sloping. In all of these cases, employment continues to be determined by the level of output at the intersection of the AS and AD curves.

Figure 5.15 shows this case's implications for the labor market. The real wage equals $F'(L)/\mu(L)$, which can be decreasing in L (Panel [a]), constant (Panel [b]), or increasing (Panel [c]). The intersection of the AS and AD curves determines Y (and hence L) and P, and thus where on the $F'(L)/\mu(L)$ locus the economy is. Unemployment again equals the difference between labor supply and employment at the prevailing real wage.

In short, different views about the sources of incomplete nominal adjustment and the characteristics of labor and goods markets have different implications for unemployment, the real wage, and the markup. As a result, Keynesian theories do not make strong predictions about the behavior of these variables. For example, the fact that the real wage does not appear to be countercyclical is perfectly consistent with the view that the aggregate supply curve is nonvertical. The behavior of these variables can be used, however, to test specific Keynesian models. The absence of a countercyclical real wage, for example, appears to be strong evidence against the view that fluctuations are driven by changes in aggregate demand and that Keynes's original model provides a good description of aggregate supply.

5.5   Output-Inflation Tradeoffs

A Permanent Output-Inflation Tradeoff?

The models of the previous section are based on simple forms of nominal stickiness. In all of them, nominal wages or nominal prices are completely fixed in the short run. In addition, if the level at which wages or prices are fixed is determined by the previous period's wages and prices, the models imply a permanent tradeoff between output and inflation.

---

[18]Since $\mu(L)$ cannot be less than 1, it cannot be everywhere decreasing in L. Thus eventually the AS curve must turn up.

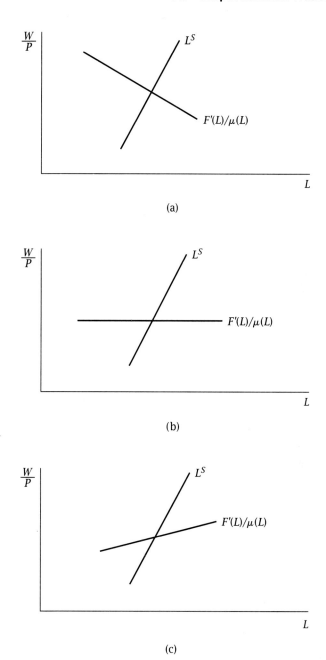

FIGURE 5.15 The labor market with sticky wages, flexible prices, and an imperfectly competitive goods market

To see this, consider, for example, our first model of aggregate supply, with fixed wages, flexible prices, and a competitive goods market. Suppose that $\overline{W}$ is proportional to the previous period's price level; that is, suppose that wages are adjusted to make up for the previous period's inflation. Thus the aggregate supply side of the economy is described by

$$W_t = AP_{t-1}, \qquad A > 0, \tag{5.31}$$

$$Y_t = F(L_t), \qquad F'(\bullet) > 0, \quad F''(\bullet) < 0, \tag{5.32}$$

$$F'(L_t) = \frac{W_t}{P_t}. \tag{5.33}$$

Assume that initially the AD and AS curves are steady, and that the price level and output are therefore constant. This situation is shown by the curves AD_0 and AS_0 in Figure 5.16. Now suppose that in some period— period 1, for convenience—policymakers use fiscal or monetary policy to shift the AD curve out to AD_1; the price level therefore rises from P_0 to P_1 and output rises from Y_0 to Y_1. Because P_1 is higher than P_0, the wage set for period 2 is higher than the one that was set for period 1. Specifically, the wage is adjusted for the previous period's inflation, and so the period-2

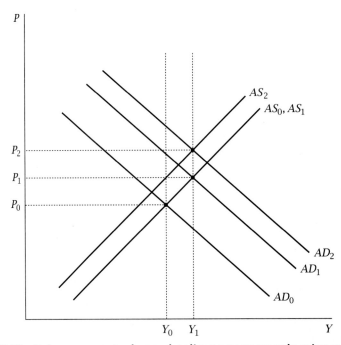

FIGURE 5.16   Using aggregate demand policy to permanently raise output under a simple model of aggregate supply

wage exceeds the period-1 wage by a factor of P_1/P_0:

$$\frac{W_2}{W_1} = \frac{AP_1}{AP_0}$$

$$= \frac{P_1}{P_0}.$$

(5.34)

This implies that if the price level in period 2 is the same as in period 1, the real wage is $AP_1/P_1 = A$, which is the same as the real wage in period 0. Thus employment and output would be the same as they were in period 0. That is, AS_2 goes through the point (Y_0, P_1); this is shown in the figure. Thus if policymakers shift the aggregate demand curve out further to AD_2, output remains at Y_1 and the price level rises further to P_2.

This process can continue indefinitely, with the price level continually rising and Y equal to Y_1 every period. And if policymakers pursue even more expansionary policies, they can keep output at an even higher level, at the cost of higher inflation. Thus the model implies a permanent output-inflation tradeoff. Since higher output is associated with lower unemployment, it also implies a permanent unemployment-inflation tradeoff.

In a famous paper, Phillips (1958) showed that there was in fact a strong and relatively stable negative relationship between unemployment and wage inflation in the United Kingdom over the previous century.[19] Subsequent researchers found a similar relationship between unemployment and price inflation—a relationship that became known as the *Phillips curve*. Thus there appeared to be both theoretical and empirical support for a stable unemployment-inflation tradeoff.

The Natural Rate

The case for this stable tradeoff was shattered in the late 1960s and early 1970s. On the theoretical side, the attack took the form of the *natural-rate hypothesis* of Friedman (1968) and Phelps (1968). Friedman and Phelps argued that the idea that nominal variables, such as the money supply or inflation, could permanently affect real variables, such as output or unemployment, was unreasonable; in the long run, they argued, the behavior of real variables is determined by real forces.

In the specific case of the output-inflation or unemployment-inflation tradeoff, Friedman's and Phelps's argument was that a shift by policymakers to permanently expansionary policy would, sooner or later, change the way that prices or wages are set. Consider again the example analyzed in Figure 5.16. When policymakers adopt permanently more expansionary polices, they permanently increase output and employment, and (with this

---

[19]See also Lipsey (1960) and Samuelson and Solow (1960).

version of the aggregate supply curve) they permanently reduce the real wage. Yet there is no reason for workers and firms to settle on different levels of employment and the real wage just because inflation is higher: if there are forces causing the employment and real wage that prevail in the absence of inflation to be an equilibrium, those same forces are present when there is inflation. Thus wages will not always be adjusted mechanically for the previous period's inflation. Sooner or later, they will be set to account for the expansionary policies that workers and firms know are going to be undertaken. Once this occurs, employment, output, and the real wage will return to the levels that prevailed in the absence of inflation.

In short, the natural-rate hypothesis states that there is some "normal" or "natural" rate of unemployment, and that monetary policy cannot keep unemployment below this level indefinitely. The precise determinants of the natural rate are unimportant. Friedman's and Phelps's argument was simply that it was determined by real rather than nominal forces. In Friedman's famous definition (1968, p. 8):

> "The natural rate of unemployment"...is the level that would be ground out by the Walrasian system of general equilibrium equations, provided there is embedded in them the actual structural characteristics of the labor and commodity markets, including market imperfections, stochastic variability in demands and supplies, the cost of gathering information about job vacancies and labor availabilities, the costs of mobility, and so on.

The empirical downfall of the stable unemployment-inflation tradeoff is illustrated by Figure 5.17, which shows the combinations of unemployment and inflation in the United States from 1961 to 1994. The points for the 1960s fall along a fairly stable downward-sloping curve. The points since then do not.

One source of the empirical failure of the Phillips curve is mundane: if there are disturbances to aggregate supply rather than aggregate demand, then even the models of the previous section imply that high inflation and high unemployment can occur together. And there certainly are plausible candidates for significant supply shocks in the 1970s. For example, there were tremendous increases in oil prices in 1973–74 and 1978–79; such increases are likely to cause firms to charge higher prices for a given level of wages. To give another example, there were large influxes of new workers into the labor force during this period; such influxes may increase unemployment for a given level of wages.

Yet these supply shocks cannot explain all of the failings of the Phillips curve in the 1970s and 1980s. In 1981 and 1982, for example, there were no identifiable large supply shocks, yet both inflation and unemployment were much higher than they were any time in the 1960s. The reason, if Friedman and Phelps are right, is that the high inflation of the 1970s changed how prices and wages were set.

Thus, the models of price and wage behavior that imply a stable relationship between inflation and unemployment do not provide even a moderately

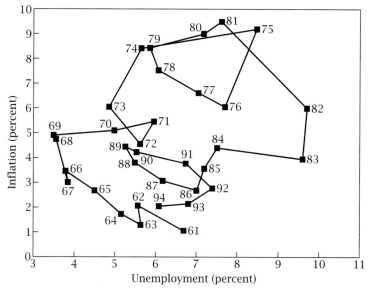

FIGURE 5.17 Unemployment and inflation in the United States, 1961-1994 (data from Citibase)

accurate description of the dynamics of inflation and the choices facing policymakers. They must therefore be modified if they are to be used to address these issues.

The Expectations-Augmented Phillips Curve

In analyzing the long run, it is easiest to state directly that prices and wages are fully flexible, so that changes in aggregate demand have no real effects. Thus the *long-run aggregate supply* (or *LRAS*) curve is vertical, and disturbances on the demand side of the economy do not affect output in the long run. The level of output at which the long-run aggregate supply curve is vertical is known as the *natural rate of output,* or *potential* or *full-employment output,* and is denoted $\overline{Y}$. This is shown in Figure 5.18.

The conclusion that the long-run aggregate supply curve is vertical does not answer the question of how to model aggregate supply in the short run. Modern Keynesian formulations of short-run aggregate supply differ from the simple models in equations (5.31)–(5.33) and in Section 5.4 in three ways. First, neither wages nor prices are assumed to be completely unresponsive to the current state of the economy. Instead, higher output is assumed to be associated with higher wages and prices. One implication is that the short-run aggregate supply curve is upward-sloping even if it is prices rather than wages that do not adjust immediately to disturbances. Second, the possibility of supply shocks is allowed for. Third, and most important, adjustment

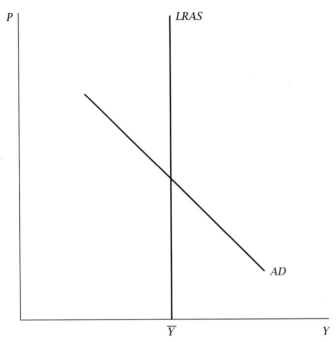

FIGURE 5.18   The long-run aggregate supply curve and the aggregate demand curve

to past and expected future inflation is assumed to be more complicated than the simple formulation in (5.31).

A typical modern Keynesian formulation of aggregate supply is

$$\ln P_t = \ln P_{t-1} + \pi_t^* + \lambda(\ln Y_t - \ln \overline{Y}_t) + \varepsilon_t^S, \qquad \lambda > 0, \qquad (5.35)$$

or

$$\pi_t = \pi_t^* + \lambda(\ln Y_t - \ln \overline{Y}_t) + \varepsilon_t^S, \qquad (5.36)$$

where $\pi_t \equiv \ln P_t - \ln P_{t-1}$ is inflation. The $\lambda(\ln Y - \ln \overline{Y})$ term implies that at any time there is an upward-sloping relationship between inflation and output; the relationship is log-linear for simplicity. Equation (5.36) takes no stand concerning whether it is nominal prices or wages, or some combination of the two, that is the source of the incomplete adjustment.[20] The ε^S term captures supply shocks.

---

[20]Equation (5.36) can be combined with Case 2 or 3 of Section 5.4 by assuming that the nominal wage is completely flexible and using the assumption in (5.36) in place of the assumption that P equals $\overline{P}$. Similarly, one can assume that wage inflation is given by an expression analogous to (5.36) and use that assumption in place of the assumption that W equals $\overline{W}$ in Case 1 or 4; this implies somewhat more complicated behavior of price inflation, however.

The key difference between (5.36) and the earlier models of aggregate supply is the π^* term. Tautologically, π^* is what inflation would be if output is equal to its natural rate and there are no supply shocks. π^* is known as *core,* or *underlying,* inflation. Equation (5.36) is referred to as the *expectations-augmented Phillips curve*—although, as we will see shortly, modern Keynesian theories do not necessarily interpret π^* as expected inflation.

A simple model of π^* that is useful for fixing ideas is that it equals the previous period's actual inflation:

$$\pi_t^* = \pi_{t-1}. \tag{5.37}$$

With this formulation, there is a tradeoff between output and the *change* in inflation, but no permanent tradeoff between output and inflation. For inflation to be held steady at any level, output must equal the natural rate. And any level of inflation is sustainable. But for inflation to fall, there must be a period when output is below the natural rate.[21]

This model is much more successful than models with a permanent output-inflation tradeoff at fitting the macroeconomic history of the United States over the past quarter-century. Consider, for example, the behavior of unemployment and inflation since 1980 shown in Figure 5.17. The model attributes the combination of high inflation and high unemployment in the early 1980s to contractionary shifts in aggregate demand with inflation starting from a high level. The high unemployment was associated with falls in inflation (and with larger falls when unemployment was higher), just as the model predicts. Once unemployment fell below the 6-7% range in the mid-1980s, inflation began to creep up. When unemployment returned to this range at the end of the decade, inflation held steady. Inflation again declined when unemployment rose above 7% in 1992, and it again held steady when unemployment fell below 7% in 1993 and 1994. All of these movements are consistent with the model.[22]

Once core inflation is added to the model, it is more convenient to describe the behavior of the economy in output-inflation space than in output-price level space. The aggregate supply curve, (5.36), implies an upward-sloping relationship between output and inflation. And the aggregate demand side of the model implies a downward-sloping relationship between the two variables. To see this, note that for a given value of the

---

[21] The standard rule of thumb is that for each percentage point that the unemployment rate exceeds the natural rate, inflation falls by one-half percentage point per year. And, as we saw in Section 4.1, for each percentage point that u exceeds $\overline{u}$, Y is roughly 2 percent less than $\overline{Y}$. Thus if each period corresponds to a year, λ in equation (5.36) is about one-quarter.

[22] One could provide similar accounts of the history of inflation and unemployment in the 1960s and 1970s, with two complications. First, some of the movements in inflation in 1973-1975 and 1978-80 would be attributed to supply shocks stemming from large oil price increases. Second, the account would posit that the natural rate of unemployment was lower in the 1960s than afterward.

previous period's price level, the price level in the current period is an in-creasing function of the inflation rate. Thus a higher value of inflation im-plies a lower level of M/P, and hence a lower level of output. These AS and AD curves are shown in Figure 5.19.

Although the model of core inflation in (5.37) is often useful, it has im-portant limitations. For example, if we interpret a period as being fairly short (such as a quarter), core inflation is likely to take more than one period to respond fully to changes in actual inflation. In this case, it is reasonable to replace the right-hand side of (5.37) with a weighted average of inflation over the previous several periods.

Perhaps the most important drawback of the model of aggregate sup-ply in (5.36)–(5.37) is that it assumes that the behavior of core inflation is independent of the economic environment. For example, if the formulation in (5.37) always held, there would be a permanent tradeoff between out-put and the change in inflation. That is, equations (5.36) and (5.37) imply that if policymakers are willing to accept ever-increasing inflation, they can push output permanently above its natural rate. But the same arguments that Friedman and Phelps make against a permanent output-inflation trade-off imply that if policymakers attempt to pursue this strategy, workers and firms will eventually stop following (5.36)–(5.37) and will adjust their behav-ior to account for the increases in inflation they know are going to occur; as a result, output will return to its natural rate.

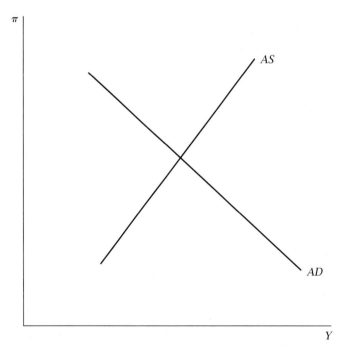

FIGURE 5.19   The AS **and** AD **curves in output-inflation space**

In his original presentation of the natural-rate hypothesis, Friedman discussed another, more realistic, example of how the behavior of core inflation may depend on the environment: how rapidly core inflation adjusts to changes in inflation is likely to depend on how long-lasting actual movements in inflation typically are. If this is right, then in a situation like the one that Phillips studied, where there are many transitory movements in inflation, core inflation will vary little; the data will therefore suggest a stable relationship between output and inflation. But in a setting like the modern United States, where there are sustained periods of high and of low inflation, core inflation will vary more, and thus there will be no consistent link between output and the level of inflation.

Carrying these criticisms of (5.36)–(5.37) to their logical extreme would suggest that we replace core inflation in (5.36) with expected inflation:

$$\pi_t = \pi_t^e + \lambda(\ln Y_t - \ln \overline{Y}_t) + \varepsilon_t^S, \tag{5.38}$$

where π_t^e is expected inflation. This formulation captures the ideas in the previous examples. For example, (5.38) implies that unless expectations are grossly irrational, no policy can permanently raise output above its natural rate, since that requires that workers' and firms' forecasts of inflation are always too low. Similarly, since expectations of future inflation respond less to current inflation when movements in inflation tend to be shorter-lived, (5.38) is consistent with Friedman's example of how the output-inflation relationship is likely to vary with the behavior of actual inflation.

Nonetheless, modern Keynesian analyses generally do not use the model of aggregate supply in (5.38). The central reason is that, as we will see in Part A of Chapter 6, if one assumes that price- and wage-setters are rational in forming their expectations, then (5.38) has strong implications—implications that, at least in the view of Keynesian economists, are not supported by the data. Alternatively, if one assumes that workers and firms do not form their expectations rationally, one is resting the theory on irrationality.

A natural compromise between the models of core inflation in (5.37) and in (5.38) is to assume that core inflation is a weighted average of past inflation and expected inflation. With this assumption, the short-run aggregate supply curve is given by

$$\pi_t = \phi\pi_t^e + (1 - \phi)\pi_{t-1} + \lambda(\ln Y_t - \ln \overline{Y}_t) + \varepsilon_t^S, \qquad 0 \le \phi \le 1. \tag{5.39}$$

Modern Keynesian theories typically allow for the possibility that ϕ is positive—that is, they let core inflation not just be a mechanical function of past inflation. But they typically also assume that ϕ is strictly less than 1. Thus the theories assume that there is some *inertia* in wage and price inflation. That is, they assume that there is some link between past and future inflation beyond effects operating through expectations.

The theories usually stop short, however, of specifying models of aggregate supply that are intended to hold generally. Instead, the models largely fall into two groups. The first group consists of models where some type of aggregate supply curve or nominal stickiness is built up from specific assumptions about the microeconomic environment. These models (such as those of Section 5.4) typically have strong forms of nominal rigidity; they are intended to illustrate particular issues but not to provide good approximations to actual behavior. We will encounter many of these models in the next chapter. The second group of models consists of specific formulations, such as the one in (5.36)–(5.37), that are intended to be useful summaries of aggregate supply behavior in specific situations but that are not intended to be universal.

The failure of modern Keynesian theory to develop a general model of aggregate supply makes the theory harder to apply in novel situations. It also, by making the models less precise, makes them harder to confront with the data—a point we will return to at the end of the next chapter.

5.6   Empirical Application: Money and Output

Perhaps the most important difference between real and Keynesian theories of fluctuations involves their predictions concerning the effects of monetary changes. In real-business-cycle models, purely monetary disturbances have no real effects. In Keynesian models, they have important effects on employment and output.

This observation suggests a natural test of real versus Keynesian theories: why not just regress output on money? Such regressions have a long history. One of the earliest and most straightforward money-output regressions was carried out by Leonall Andersen and Jerry Jordan of the Federal Reserve Bank of St. Louis (Andersen and Jordan, 1968). For that reason, the regression of output on money is known as the *St. Louis equation.*

Here we consider an example of the St. Louis equation. The left-hand-side variable is the change in the log of real GNP. The main right-hand-side variable is the change in the log of the money stock, as measured by $M1$; since any effect of money on output may occur with a lag, the contemporaneous and four lagged values are included. The other right-hand-side variables are a constant, a time trend (to account for trends in output and money growth), and seasonal dummies (to control for regular seasonal movements in the variables). The data are quarterly, and the sample period is 1948–1989.

The results are

$$\Delta \ln Y_t = \underset{(0.0022)}{0.0070} + \underset{(0.10)}{0.18} \; \Delta \ln m_t + \underset{(0.10)}{0.19} \; \Delta \ln m_{t-1}$$

$$+ \underset{(0.10)}{0.29} \; \Delta \ln m_{t-2} - \underset{(0.10)}{0.00} \; \Delta \ln m_{t-3} + \underset{(0.10)}{0.01} \; \Delta \ln m_{t-4} \quad (5.40)$$

$$- \ 0.00010t \ + \ 0.0043 \ D1_t \ + \ 0.0022 \ D2_t \ + \ 0.0029 \ D3_t,$$
$$(0.00003) \quad (0.0023) \qquad (0.0023) \qquad (0.0023)$$

$$\overline{R}^2 = 0.113, \qquad \text{D.W.} = 1.28, \qquad \text{s.e.e.} = 0.010,$$

where the numbers in parentheses are standard errors. The sum of the coefficients on the current and four lagged values of the money-growth variable is 0.66, with a standard error of 0.28. Thus the estimates suggest that a 1% increase in the money stock is associated with an increase of $\frac{2}{3}$% in output over the next year, and the null hypothesis of no association is rejected at high levels of significance.

Does this regression, then, provide powerful evidence in support of monetary over real theories of fluctuations? The answer is no. There are several basic problems with a regression like this one. First, causation may run from output to money rather than from money to output. A simple story, formalized by King and Plosser (1984), is that when firms plan to increase production, they may increase their money holdings because they will need to purchase more intermediate inputs. Similarly, households may increase their money holdings when they plan to increase their purchases. Aggregate measures of the money stock, such as $M1$, are not set directly by the Federal Reserve but are determined by the interaction of the supply of high-powered money with the behavior of the banking system and the public. Thus shifts in money demand stemming from changes in firms' and households' production plans can lead to changes in the money stock. As a result, we may see changes in the money stock in advance of output movements even if the changes in money are not causing the output movements.

The second major problem with the St. Louis equation involves the determinants of monetary policy. Suppose the Federal Reserve adjusts the money stock to try to offset other factors that influence aggregate output. Then if monetary changes have real effects and the Federal Reserve's efforts to stabilize the economy are successful, we will observe fluctuations in money without movements in output (Kareken and Solow, 1963). Thus, just as we cannot conclude from the positive correlation between money and output that money causes output, if we fail to observe such a correlation we cannot conclude that money does not cause output.[23]

The third difficulty with the St. Louis equation is that there have been a series of large shifts in the demand for money over the past two decades. At least some of the shifts are probably due to financial innovation and deregulation, but their causes are not entirely understood.[24] If the Federal Reserve

---

[23] Similarly, suppose that monetary and fiscal policy are coordinated, so that the two usually move in the same direction. Then if fiscal policy affects real output, there will be a relationship between monetary policy and output movements even if monetary changes do not have real effects.

[24] The classic reference is Goldfeld (1976).

does not adjust the money supply fully in response to these disturbances, the *IS-LM-AS* model predicts that they will lead to a negative relationship between money and output; a positive money demand shock, for example, will increase the money stock but increase the interest rate and reduce output. And even if the Federal Reserve accommodates the shifts, the fact that they are so large may cause a few observations to have a disproportionate effect on the results.

As a result of the money demand shifts, the estimated relationship between money and output is sensitive to such matters as the sample period and the measure of money. For example, if equation (5.40) is estimated using $M2$ in place of $M1$, or if it is estimated over a sample period that is slightly longer, the results change considerably.

Because of these difficulties, regressions like (5.40), or more sophisticated statistical analyses of the association between monetary and real variables, cannot be used to provide strong evidence concerning the relative merits of monetary and real theories of fluctuations.

A very different approach to testing whether monetary shocks have real effects stems from the work of Friedman and Schwartz (1963). Friedman and Schwartz undertake a careful historical analysis of the sources of movements in the money stock in the United States from the end of the Civil War to 1960. On the basis of this analysis, they argue that many of the movements in money, especially the largest ones, were mainly the result of developments in the monetary sector of the economy rather than the response of the money stock to real developments. Friedman and Schwartz demonstrate that these monetary movements were followed by output movements in the same direction. Thus, Friedman and Schwartz conclude, unless the money-output relationship in these episodes is an extraordinary fluke, it must reflect causation running from money to output rather than in the opposite direction.[25]

C. Romer and D. Romer (1989) provide more recent evidence along the same lines. They search the records of the Federal Reserve for the postwar period for evidence of policy shifts designed to lower inflation that were not motivated by developments on the real side of the economy. They identify six such shifts, and find that all of them were followed by recessions. For example, in October 1979, shortly after Paul Volcker became chairman of the Federal Reserve Board, the Federal Reserve tightened monetary policy dramatically. The change appears to have been motivated by a desire to reduce inflation, and not by the presence of other forces that would have caused output to decline in any event. Yet it was followed by one of the largest recessions in postwar U.S. history.[26]

---

[25]See especially Chapter 13 of their book—an item that every macroeconomist should read.

[26]It is possible that similar studies of open economies could provide stronger evidence concerning the importance of monetary forces. For example, shifts in monetary policy to combat high rates of inflation in small, highly open economies appear to be associated with

What Friedman and Schwartz and Romer and Romer are doing is searching for *natural experiments* to determine the effects of monetary shocks. If economies were laboratories, economists could randomly perturb the money supply and examine the subsequent output movements. Since the monetary disturbances would be chosen at random, the possibility that they were caused by output movements, or that there were other factors systematically causing the changes in both money and output, could be ruled out.

Unfortunately for economic science (though fortunately for other reasons), economies are not laboratories. The closest we can come to a laboratory experiment is to look for times when historical developments bring about monetary changes that are not caused by the behavior of output. For example, Friedman and Schwartz argue that the death in 1928 of Benjamin Strong, the president of the Federal Reserve Bank of New York, provides an example of such an independent monetary disturbance. Strong's death, Friedman and Schwartz argue, left a power vacuum in the Federal Reserve System and therefore caused monetary policy to be conducted very differently over the next several years than it otherwise would have been.[27]

Natural experiments such as Strong's death are unlikely to be as ideal as genuine randomized experiments for determining the effects of monetary changes. There is room for disagreement concerning whether any episodes are sufficiently clear-cut to be viewed as independent monetary disturbances, and if so, what set of episodes should be considered. But since randomized experiments are not possible, the evidence provided by natural experiments may be the best we can obtain.

A related approach is to use the evidence provided by specific monetary interventions to investigate the impact of monetary changes on relative prices. For example, as described in Section 9.3, Cook and Hahn (1989) confirm formally the common observation that Federal Reserve open-market

---

large changes in real exchange rates, real interest rates, and real output. Whether the evidence from such episodes in fact provides strong support for monetary nonneutrality has not been investigated systematically. The issue is complicated by the fact that the policy shifts are often accompanied by fiscal reforms and by large changes in uncertainty (see, for example, Sargent, 1982, and Dornbusch and Fischer, 1986).

[27]In effect, natural experiments provide potential instrumental variables for the St. Louis equation. The way to address the problem that there may be correlation between money growth and other factors that affect real output is to find variables that are correlated with money growth but uncorrelated with the other factors. One can then estimate the money-output regression by *instrumental variables* (or *two-stage least squares*). That is, one can examine how output growth is related to the component of money growth that is correlated with the instruments, and that is therefore uncorrelated with the omitted factors. Or, if one is interested simply in whether monetary movements affect real output but not in the precise values of the coefficients, one can estimate the *reduced form* of the model—that is, one can regress output growth directly on the instruments. In effect, Friedman and Schwartz and Romer and Romer are using historical evidence about the source of monetary developments to try to find such instruments, and then examining the reduced-form relationship between output movements and their proposed instruments.

operations are associated with changes in nominal interest rates. Given the discrete nature of the open-market operations and the specifics of how their timing is determined, it is not plausible that they occur endogenously at times when interest rates would have moved in any event. And although the issue has not been investigated formally, the fact that monetary expansions lower nominal rates strongly suggests that the changes in nominal rates represent changes in real rates as well. For example, monetary expansions lower nominal interest rates for terms as short as a day; it seems unlikely that they reduce expected inflation over such horizons.[28] Since real and Keynesian theories agree that changes in real rates affect real behavior, this evidence suggests that monetary changes have real effects.

Similarly, the exchange-rate regime appears to affect the behavior of real exchange rates. Under a fixed exchange rate, the central bank adjusts the money supply to keep the nominal exchange rate constant; under a floating exchange rate, it does not. There is strong evidence that not just nominal but also real exchange rates are much less volatile under fixed than floating exchange rates. In addition, when a central bank switches from pegging the nominal exchange rate against one currency to pegging the nominal exchange rate against another, the volatility of the two associated real exchange rates seems to change sharply as well. (See, for example, Genberg, 1978; Stockman, 1983; Mussa, 1986; and Baxter and Stockman, 1989). Since shifts between exchange-rate regimes are usually discrete, explaining this behavior of real exchange rates without appealing to real effects of monetary forces appears to require positing sudden large changes in the real shocks affecting economies. And again, both real and Keynesian theories predict that the behavior of real exchange rates has real effects.

The most significant limitation of this evidence is that the importance of these apparent effects of monetary changes on real interest rates and real exchange rates for quantities has not been determined. Baxter and Stockman (1989), for example, do not find any clear difference in the behavior of economic aggregates under floating and fixed exchange rates. Since real-business-cycle theories attribute fairly large changes in quantities to relatively modest movements in relative prices, however, a finding that the price changes were not important would be puzzling from the perspective of both real and Keynesian theories.

Problems

5.1. Consider the *IS-LM* model presented in Section 5.2. In this model, what are di/dM and dY/dM for a given value of P?

---

[28]Barro (1989) presents a model where monetary expansions lower expected inflation. The model requires that prices jump instantaneously in response to the expansions, however.

5.2. The derivation of the *LM* curve assumes that M is exogenous. But suppose instead that the Federal Reserve has some target interest rate $\bar{\imath}$ and that it adjusts M to keep i always equal to $\bar{\imath}$.

(a) With this policy, what is the slope of the "*LM* curve" (that is, the set of combinations of i and Y that cause money demand and supply to be equal)?

(b) With this policy, what is the slope of the *AD* curve?

5.3. The government budget in the standard Keynesian model.

(a) **The balanced budget multiplier.** (See Haavelmo, 1945.) Suppose that planned expenditure is given by (5.5), $E = C(Y - T) + I(i - \pi^e) + G$.

(i) How do equal increases in G and T affect the position of the *IS* curve? Specifically, what is the effect on Y for a given level of i?

(ii) How do equal increases in G and T affect the position of the *AD* curve? Specifically, what is the effect on Y for a given level of P?

(b) **Automatic stabilizers.** Suppose that tax revenues, T, instead of being exogenous, are a function of income: $T = T(Y)$, $T'(Y) > 0$. With this change, find how an increase in $T'(Y)$ affects the following:

(i) The slope of the *IS* curve.

(ii) The effects of changes in G and M on Y for a given P.

5.4. The liquidity trap and the Pigou effect. Assume that the nominal interest rate is so low that the opportunity cost of holding money is negligible. Suppose that as a result people are indifferent concerning the division of their wealth between money and other assets, and that they are therefore willing to change their money holdings without any change in the interest rate.

(a) **The liquidity trap.** (Keynes, 1936.) In this situation, what is the slope of the *AD* curve? If prices are completely flexible (so the *AS* curve is vertical), is aggregate demand irrelevant to output?

(b) **The Pigou effect.** (Pigou, 1943.) Suppose that, in addition, planned expenditure depends on real wealth as well as the variables in (5.4). Since the public's holdings of high-powered money are one component of wealth, a fall in the price level increases real wealth. If prices are completely flexible (so the *AS* curve is vertical), is aggregate demand irrelevant to output?

5.5. The Mundell effect. (Mundell, 1963.) In the *IS-LM* model, how does a fall in expected inflation, π^e, affect i, Y, and $i - \pi^e$?

5.6. The multiplier-accelerator. (Samuelson, 1939.) Consider the following model of income determination. (1) Consumption depends on the previous period's income: $C_t = a + bY_{t-1}$. (2) The desired capital stock (or inventory stock) is proportional to the previous period's output: $K_t^* = cY_{t-1}$. (3) Investment equals the difference between the desired capital stock and the stock inherited from the previous period: $I_t = K_t^* - K_{t-1} = K_t^* - cY_{t-2}$. (4) Government purchases are constant: $G_t = \overline{G}$. (5) $Y_t = C_t + I_t + G_t$.

(a) Express Y_t in terms of Y_{t-1}, Y_{t-2}, and the parameters of the model.

(b) Suppose $b = 0.9$ and $c = 0.5$. Suppose there is a one-time disturbance to government purchases; specifically, suppose that G is equal to $\overline{G} + 1$ in period t and is equal to $\overline{G}$ in all other periods. How does this shock affect output over time?

5.7. (This follows Mankiw and Summers, 1986.) Suppose that the demand for real money balances depends on the interest rate, i, and on *disposable* income $Y - T$; in other words, suppose that the correct way to write the *LM* equation is $M/P = L(i, Y - T)$.

(*a*) With this change to the *IS*-*LM*-*AS* model, can one tell whether a tax cut (that is, a fall in T) increases or decreases output? Assume a closed economy.

(*b*) Redo part (*a*) assuming an open economy under the assumptions that the exchange rate is floating, exchange-rate expectations are static, and capital is perfectly mobile.

(*c*) Redo part (*b*) assuming a fixed exchange rate.

5.8. Describe how each of the following changes affect income, the exchange rate, and net exports at a given price level under: (1) a floating exchange rate and perfect capital mobility, (2) a fixed exchange rate and perfect capital mobility, and (3) a floating exchange rate and imperfect capital mobility. Assume static exchange-rate expectations, and assume that planned expenditure is given by the expression in n. 8.

(*a*) The demand for money at a given i and Y falls.

(*b*) The foreign interest rate rises.

(*c*) The country adopts protectionist policies, so that net exports at a given real exchange rate are higher than before.

5.9. Exchange-market intervention. Suppose that the central bank intervenes in the foreign exchange market by purchasing foreign currency for dollars, and that it *sterilizes* this intervention by selling bonds for dollars to keep the money stock unchanged. With this intervention, *NX* and *CF* must sum to a positive amount rather than to zero (see equation [5.21]).

(*a*) What are the effects of this intervention on output, the exchange rate, and the price level under a floating exchange rate, static exchange-rate expectations, and imperfect capital mobility?

(*b*) How, if at all, do the results in part (*a*) change if capital is perfectly mobile?

5.10. The algebra of exchange-rate overshooting. Consider a simplified open-economy model: $m - p = hy - ki, y = b(\varepsilon - p) - a(i - \dot{p}), i = \dot{\varepsilon}, \dot{p} = \theta y$. The variables y, m, p, and ε are the logs of output, money, the price level, and the exchange rate, respectively; i is the nominal interest rate, and $\dot{p}$ is inflation. All variables are expressed as deviations from their usual values; p^* and i^* are normalized to zero, and are therefore omitted. The main changes from our usual model are that price adjustment takes a particularly simple form and that the equations are linear. h, k, b, a, and θ are all positive.

Assume that initially $y = i = \dot{p} = m = p = 0$. Now suppose that there is a permanent increase in m.

(a) Show that once prices have adjusted fully (so $\dot{p} = 0$), $y = i = 0$ and $p = \varepsilon = m$.

(b) Show that there are parameter values such that at the time of the increase in m, ε jumps immediately to exactly m and then remains constant—so that there is neither overshooting nor undershooting.[29]

5.11. Consider the model of aggregate demand in an open economy with imperfect capital mobility in Section 5.3, without the simplification assumed in equation (5.22). In addition to our usual assumptions, assume $NX_{\varepsilon P^*/P} \geq E_{\varepsilon P^*/P}$, $NX_{i-\pi^e} \geq 0$, $NX_Y \leq 0$, and $E_Y - NX_Y < 1$.

(a) Derive an expression for the slope of the IS^{**} curve (that is, the combinations of i and Y associated with the (i, Y, ε) combinations that solve [5.12] and [5.21]).

(b) Does ε rise, fall, or remain constant as we move down the IS^{**} curve?

(c) Is it still true that greater capital mobility (that is, a larger value of $CF'(\bullet)$) makes the IS^{**} curve flatter?

5.12. The analysis of Case 1 in Section 5.4 assumes that employment is determined by labor demand. A more realistic assumption may be that employment at a given real wage equals the minimum of demand and supply; this is known as the *short-side rule*.

(a) Draw diagrams showing the situation in the labor market under this assumption when

(i) P is at the level that generates the maximum possible output.

(ii) P is above the level that generates the maximum possible output.

(b) With this assumption, what does the aggregate supply curve look like?

5.13. Consider the model of aggregate supply in Case 2 of Section 5.4. Suppose that aggregate demand at $\bar{P}$ equals Y^{MAX}. Show the resulting situation in the labor market.

5.14. Suppose that the production function is $Y = AF(L)$ (where $F'(\bullet) > 0$, $F''(\bullet) < 0$, and $A > 0$), and that A falls. How does this negative technology shock affect the AS curve under each of the models of aggregate supply in Section 5.4?

5.15. Destabilizing price flexibility. (De Long and Summers, 1986b.) Consider the following closed-economy variant of the model in Problem 5.10: $y = -a(i - \dot{p})$, $m - p = -ki$, $\dot{p} = \theta y$. Assume $a > 0$, $k > 0$, $\theta > 0$, and $a\theta < 1$.

(a) Assume that initially $y = i = \dot{p} = m = p = 0$. Now suppose that at some time—time 0 for convenience—there is a permanent drop in m to some lower level, m'.

---

[29]The result that there are parameter values such that the exchange rate neither overshoots nor undershoots in response to a monetary disturbance implies that, except in unusual cases, there are perturbations of these parameter values that lead to each result. Showing this is complicated, however, and is therefore omitted.

(*i*) What are the values of y and i at time 0? (Note that p cannot jump at the time of the change.) How does an increase in θ, the speed of price adjustment, affect $y(0)$? Explain intuitively.

(*ii*) What is the path of y after time 0?

(*b*) Suppose we measure the total amount of output volatility caused by the change in m as $V = \int_{t=0}^{\infty} y(t)^2 \, dt$. How is V affected by an increase in the speed of price adjustment, θ?

5.16. Redo the regression reported in equation (5.40):

(*a*) Incorporating more recent data.

(*b*) Incorporating more recent data, and using $M2$ rather than $M1$.

Chapter **6**
MICROECONOMIC FOUNDATIONS OF INCOMPLETE NOMINAL ADJUSTMENT

This chapter is concerned with the microeconomic foundations of sluggish adjustment of nominal prices and wages. This subject is important for two reasons. First, it is central to Keynesian models. One of the models' main predictions is that monetary shocks have real effects, and the critical feature of the models that gives rise to this prediction is the presence of sluggish nominal adjustment. But, as described in the concluding section of the previous chapter, the evidence concerning whether monetary shocks have important real effects is controversial; thus the relevance of Keynesian models is not clear. One way to shed light on this issue is to investigate what microeconomic conditions are needed for nominal stickiness to arise. For example, some critics of traditional Keynesian models argue that the models' assumptions about price stickiness are inconsistent with any reasonable model of microeconomic behavior; they therefore conclude that microeconomic theory provides a strong case against the models' relevance. More generally, if the conditions needed for nominal stickiness appear implausible or inconsistent with microeconomic evidence, this would suggest that gradual nominal adjustment is unlikely to be important. If the needed conditions appear realistic, on the other hand, this would support the importance of nominal stickiness.

Second, the nature of incomplete nominal adjustment is important for policy. For example, we will see that if monetary shocks have real effects for the reasons described by the Lucas imperfect-information model (which is presented in Part A of the chapter), systematic feedback rules from economic developments to monetary policy have no effect on the real economy. Similarly, if nominal prices and wages are fully flexible, monetary policy is irrelevant to real variables. At the other extreme, if there is a stable relationship between output and inflation, then (as we saw in Chapter 5) monetary policy can raise output permanently. And as we will see, the nature of incomplete nominal adjustment also has implications for such issues as the output costs of alternative approaches to reducing inflation, the output-inflation relationship under different conditions, and the impact of stabilization policy on average output.

It is important to emphasize that the issue we are interested in is incomplete adjustment of *nominal* prices and wages. There are many reasons—involving uncertainty, information and renegotiation costs, incentives, and so on—why prices and wages may not adjust freely to equate supply and demand, or that firms may not change their prices and wages completely and immediately in response to shocks. But simply introducing some departure from perfect markets is not enough to imply that nominal disturbances matter. All of the models of unemployment in Chapter 10, for example, are real models. If one appends a monetary sector to those models without any further complications, the classical dichotomy continues to hold: monetary disturbances simply cause all nominal prices and wages to change, leaving the real equilibrium (with whatever non-Walrasian features it involves) unchanged. Any microeconomic basis for failure of the classical dichotomy requires some kind of *nominal* imperfection.

The models that follow examine three candidate nominal imperfections. In the model of Part A, which is based on the work of Lucas (1972) and Phelps (1970), the nominal imperfection is that producers do not observe the aggregate price level; as a result, they make their production decisions without full knowledge of the relative prices they will receive for their goods. In the models of staggered adjustment in Part B, monetary shocks have real effects because not all prices or wages are adjusted simultaneously. Finally, in Part C, the real effects of monetary changes stem from small costs of changing nominal prices or wages or from some other small friction in nominal adjustment.

Part A   The Lucas Imperfect-Information Model

6.1   Overview

The central idea of the Lucas–Phelps model is that when a producer observes a change in the price of his or her product, he or she does not know whether it reflects a change in the good's relative price or a change in the aggregate price level. A change in the relative price alters the optimal amount to produce. A change in the aggregate price level, on the other hand, leaves optimal production unchanged.

When the price of the producer's good increases, there is some chance that the increase reflects a rise in the price level, and some chance that it reflects a rise in the good's relative price. The rational response for the producer is to attribute part of the change to an increase in the price level and part to an increase in the relative price, and therefore to increase output somewhat. This implies that the aggregate supply curve slopes up: when the aggregate price level rises, all producers see increases in the prices of their goods, and (not knowing that the increases reflect a rise in the price level) thus raise their output.

The next two sections develop this idea in a model where individuals produce goods using their own labor, sell their output in competitive markets, and use the proceeds to buy other producers' output. The model has two types of shocks. First, there are random shifts in preferences that change the relative demands for different goods. These shocks lead to changes in relative prices and in the relative production of different goods. Second, there are disturbances to the money supply, or more generally, to aggregate demand. When these shocks are observed, they change only the aggregate price level and have no real effects. But when they are unobserved, they change both the price level and aggregate output.

As a preliminary, Section 6.2 considers the case where the money stock is publicly observed; in this situation, money is neutral. Section 6.3 then turns to the case where the money stock is not observed.

6.2   The Case of Perfect Information

Producer Behavior

There are many different goods in the economy. Consider a representative producer of a typical good, good i. The individual's production function is simply

$$Q_i = L_i, \tag{6.1}$$

where L_i is the amount that the individual works and Q_i the amount he or she produces. The individual's consumption, C_i, equals his or her real income; this equals revenue, $P_i Q_i$, divided by the price of the market basket of goods, P. P is an index of the prices of all goods (see equation [6.9], below).

Utility depends positively on consumption and negatively on the amount worked. For simplicity, it takes the form

$$U_i = C_i - \frac{1}{\gamma}L_i^{\gamma}, \qquad \gamma > 1. \tag{6.2}$$

Thus there is constant marginal utility of consumption and increasing marginal disutility of work.

When the aggregate price level P is known, the individual's maximization problem is simple. Substituting $C_i = P_i Q_i / P$ and $Q_i = L_i$ into (6.2), we can rewrite utility as

$$U_i = \frac{P_i L_i}{P} - \frac{1}{\gamma} L_i^\gamma. \tag{6.3}$$

Since markets are assumed to be competitive, the individual chooses L_i to maximize utility taking P_i and P as given. The first-order condition is

$$\frac{P_i}{P} - L_i^{\gamma-1} = 0, \tag{6.4}$$

or

$$L_i = (P_i / P)^{1/(\gamma-1)}. \tag{6.5}$$

Letting lowercase letters denote the logarithms of the corresponding upper-case variables, we can rewrite this condition as

$$\ell_i = \frac{1}{\gamma - 1}(p_i - p). \tag{6.6}$$

Thus the individual's labor supply and production are increasing in the relative price of his or her product.

Demand

Producers' behavior determines the supply curves of the various goods. Determining the equilibrium in each market requires specifying the demand curves as well. The demand for a given good is assumed to depend on three factors: real income, the good's relative price, and a random disturbance to preferences. For tractability, demand is log-linear. Specifically, the demand for good i is

$$q_i = y + z_i - \eta(p_i - p), \qquad \eta > 0, \tag{6.7}$$

where y is log aggregate real income, z_i is the shock to the demand for good i, and η is the elasticity of demand for each good. q_i is the demand per producer of good i.[1] The z_i's have a mean of zero across goods; thus they are purely relative demand shocks. y is assumed to equal the average across goods of the q_i's, and p is the average of the p_i's:

$$y = \overline{q}_i, \tag{6.8}$$

---

[1] That is, the total (log) demand for good i is $\ln N + y + z_i - \eta(p_i - p)$, where N is the number of producers of each good.

$$p = \overline{p}_i. \tag{6.9}$$

Intuitively, (6.7)–(6.9) state that the demand for a good is higher when total production (and thus total income) is higher, when its price is low relative to other prices, and when individuals have stronger preferences for it.[2]
    Finally, the aggregate demand side of the model is

$$y = m - p. \tag{6.10}$$

There are various interpretations of (6.10). The simplest, and most appropriate for our purposes, is that it is just a shortcut approach to modeling aggregate demand. Equation (6.10) implies an inverse relationship between the price level and output, which is the essential feature of aggregate demand. Since our focus is on aggregate supply, there is little point in modeling aggregate demand more fully. Under this interpretation, M should be thought of as a generic variable affecting aggregate demand rather than as money.
    It is also possible to derive (6.10) from models with more complete monetary specifications. Blanchard and Kiyotaki (1987), for example, replace C_i in the utility function, (6.2), with a Cobb–Douglas combination of C_i and the individual's real money balances, M_i/P. With an appropriate specification of how money enters the budget constraint, this gives rise to (6.10). Rotemberg (1987) derives (6.10) from a *cash-in-advance constraint.* Under Blanchard and Kiyotaki's and Rotemberg's interpretations of (6.10), it is natural to think of m as literally money; in this case the right-hand side should be modified to be $m + v - p$, where v captures aggregate demand disturbances other than shifts in money supply.

Equilibrium

Equilibrium in the market for good i requires that demand per producer equal supply. From (6.6) and (6.7), this requires

$$\frac{1}{\gamma - 1}(p_i - p) = y + z_i - \eta(p_i - p). \tag{6.11}$$

Solving this expression for p_i yields

$$p_i = \frac{\gamma - 1}{1 + \eta\gamma - \eta}(y + z_i) + p. \tag{6.12}$$

---

[2]Although (6.7)–(6.9) are intuitive, deriving these exact functional forms from individuals' preferences over the various goods requires some approximations. The difficulty is that if preferences are such that demand for each good takes the constant-elasticity form in (6.7), the corresponding (log) price index is exactly equal to the average of the individual p_i's only in the special case of $\eta = 1$. See Problem 6.2. This issue has no effect on the basic messages of the model.

Averaging the p_i's and using the fact that the average of the z_i's is zero, we obtain

$$p = \frac{\gamma - 1}{1 + \eta\gamma - \eta} y + p. \tag{6.13}$$

Equation (6.13) implies that the equilibrium value of y is simply[3]

$$y = 0. \tag{6.14}$$

Finally, (6.14) and (6.10) imply

$$m = p. \tag{6.15}$$

Not surprisingly, money is neutral in this version of the model: an increase in m leads to an equal increase in all p_i's, and hence in the overall price index, p. No real variables are affected.

6.3   The Case of Imperfect Information

We now consider the more interesting case where producers observe the prices of their own goods but not the aggregate price level.

Producer Behavior

Defining the relative price of good i by $r_i = p_i - p$, we can write

$$\begin{aligned} p_i &= p + (p_i - p) \\ &= p + r_i. \end{aligned} \tag{6.16}$$

Thus, in logs, the variable that the individual observes—the price of his or her good—equals the sum of the aggregate price level and the good's relative price.

The individual would like to base his or her production decision on r_i alone (see [6.6]). The individual does not observe r_i, but must estimate it given the observation of p_i.[4] At this point, Lucas makes two simplifying assumptions. First, he assumes that the individual finds the expectation of r_i given p_i, and then produces as much as he or she would if this estimate were certain. Thus (6.6) becomes

---

[3]The result that equilibrium log output is zero implies that the equilibrium *level* of output is 1. This results from the $1/\gamma$ term multiplying L_i^γ in the utility function, (6.2).

[4]If the individual knew others' prices as a result of making purchases, he or she could deduce p, and hence r_i. This can be ruled out in several ways. One approach is to assume that the household consists of two individuals, a "producer" and a "shopper," and that communication between them is limited. In Lucas's original model, the problem is avoided by assuming an overlapping-generations structure where individuals produce in the first period of their lives and make purchases in the second.

$$\ell_i = \frac{1}{\gamma - 1} E[r_i \mid p_i]. \tag{6.17}$$

As Problem 6.1 shows, this *certainty-equivalence* behavior is not identical to maximizing expected utility: in general, the utility-maximizing choice of ℓ_i depends not just on the individual's estimate of r_i, but also on his or her uncertainty about r_i. The assumption that individuals use certainty equivalence, however, simplifies the analysis and has no effect on the central messages of the model.

Second, and very importantly, Lucas assumes that the producer finds the expectation of r_i given p_i rationally. That is, $E[r_i \mid p_i]$ is assumed to be the true expectation of r_i given p_i and given the actual joint distribution of the two variables. Today, this assumption of *rational expectations* seems no more peculiar than the assumption that individuals maximize utility. When Lucas introduced Muth's (1960, 1961) idea of rational expectations into macroeconomics, however, it was highly controversial. As we will see, it is one source—but by no means the only one—of the strong implications of Lucas's model.

To make the computation of $E[r_i \mid p_i]$ tractable, the monetary shock (m) and the shocks to the demands for the individual goods (the z_i's) are assumed to be normally distributed. m has a mean of $E[m]$ and a variance of V_m. The z_i's have a mean of zero and a variance of V_z, and are independent of m. We will see that these assumptions imply that p and r_i are normal and independent. Since p_i equals $p + r_i$, this means that it is also normal; its mean is the sum of the means of p and r_i, and its variance is the sum of their variances. As we will see, the means of p and r_i, $E[p]$ and $E[r]$, are equal to $E[m]$ and zero, respectively; and their variances, V_p and V_r, are complicated functions of V_m and V_z and of the other parameters of the model.

The individual's problem is to find the expectation of r_i given p_i. An important result in statistics is that when two variables are jointly normally distributed (as with r_i and p_i here), the expectation of one is a linear function of the observation of the other (see, for example, Mood, Graybill, and Boes, 1974, pp. 167–168, or some other introductory statistics textbook). Thus $E[r_i \mid p_i]$ takes the form

$$E[r_i \mid p_i] = \alpha + \beta p_i. \tag{6.18}$$

In this particular case, where p_i equals r_i plus an independent variable, (6.18) takes the specific form:

$$E[r_i \mid p_i] = -\frac{V_r}{V_r + V_p} E[p] + \frac{V_r}{V_r + V_p} p_i$$

$$= \frac{V_r}{V_r + V_p} (p_i - E[p]). \tag{6.19}$$

Equation (6.19) is intuitive. First, it implies that if p_i equals its mean, the expectation of r_i equals its mean (which is zero). Second, it states that the expectation of r_i exceeds its mean if p_i exceeds its mean, and is less than its mean if p_i is less than its mean. Third, it tells us that the fraction of the departure of p_i from its mean that is estimated to be due to the departure of r_i from its mean is $V_r/(V_r + V_p)$; this is the fraction of the overall variance of p_i ($V_r + V_p$) that is due to the variance of r_i (V_r). If, for example, V_p is zero, all of the variation in p_i is due to r_i, and so $E[r_i \mid p_i]$ is $p_i - E[m]$. If V_r and V_p are equal, half of the variance in p_i is due to r_i, and so $E[r_i \mid p_i] = (p_i - E[m])/2$. And so on.[5]

Substituting (6.19) into (6.17) yields the individual's labor supply:

$$\ell_i = \frac{1}{\gamma - 1} \frac{V_r}{V_r + V_p}(p_i - E[p])$$

$$\equiv b(p_i - E[p]).$$

(6.20)

Averaging (6.20) across producers (and using the definitions of y and p) gives us an expression for overall output:

$$y = b(p - E[p]).$$

(6.21)

Equation (6.21) is the *Lucas supply curve*. It states that the departure of output from its normal level (which is zero in the model) is an increasing function of the surprise in the price level.

The Lucas supply curve is essentially the same as the expectations-augmented Phillips curve of Chapter 5 with core inflation replaced by expected inflation (see equation [5.38]). Both state that, if we neglect disturbances to supply, output is above normal only to the extent that inflation (and hence the price level) is greater than expected. Thus the Lucas model provides microeconomic foundations for this view of aggregate supply.

Equilibrium

Combining the Lucas supply curve, (6.21), with the aggregate demand equation, (6.10), and solving for p and y yields

$$p = \frac{1}{1 + b}m + \frac{b}{1 + b}E[p],$$

(6.22)

---

[5]This conditional-expectations problem is referred to as *signal extraction*. The variable that the individual observes, p_i, equals the *signal*, r_i, plus *noise*, p. Equation (6.19) shows how the individual can best extract an estimate of the signal from the observation of p_i. The ratio of V_r to V_p is referred to as the *signal-to-noise ratio*.

$$y = \frac{b}{1+b}m - \frac{b}{1+b}E[p]. \tag{6.23}$$

We can use (6.22) to find $E[p]$. Ex post, after m is determined, the two sides of (6.22) are equal. Thus it must be that ex ante, before m is determined, the *expectations* of the two sides are equal. Taking the expectations of both sides of (6.22), we obtain

$$E[p] = \frac{1}{1+b}E[m] + \frac{b}{1+b}E[p], \tag{6.24}$$

or

$$E[p] = E[m]. \tag{6.25}$$

Using (6.25) and the fact that $m = E[m] + (m - E[m])$, we can rewrite (6.22) and (6.23) as

$$p = E[m] + \frac{1}{1+b}(m - E[m]), \tag{6.26}$$

$$y = \frac{b}{1+b}(m - E[m]). \tag{6.27}$$

Equations (6.26) and (6.27) show the key implications of the model: the component of aggregate demand that is observed, $E[m]$, affects only prices, but the component that is not observed, $m - E[m]$, has real effects. Consider, for concreteness, an unobserved increase in m—that is, a higher realization of m given its distribution. This increase in the money supply raises aggregate demand, and thus produces an outward shift in the demand curve for each good. Since the increase is not observed, each supplier's best guess is that some portion of the rise in the demand for his or her product reflects a relative price shock. Thus producers increase their output.

The effects of an observed increase in m are very different. Specifically, consider the effects of an upward shift in the entire distribution of m, with the realization of $m - E[m]$ held fixed. In this case, each supplier attributes the rise in the demand for his or her product to money, and thus does not change his or her output. Of course, the taste shocks cause variations in relative prices and in output across goods (just as they do in the case of an unobserved shock), but on average real output does not rise. Thus observed changes in aggregate demand affect only prices.

To complete the model, we must express b in terms of underlying parameters rather than in terms of the variances of p and r_i. Recall that $b = [1/(\gamma-1)][V_r/(V_r+V_p)]$ (see [6.20]). Equation (6.26) implies $V_p = V_m/(1+b)^2$. The demand curve, (6.7), and the supply curve, (6.20), can be used to find V_r, the variance of $p_i - p$. Specifically, we can substitute $y = b(p - E[p])$ into

(6.7) to obtain $q_i = b(p - E[p]) + z_i - \eta(p_i - p)$, and we can rewrite (6.20) as $\ell_i = b(p_i - p) + b(p - E[p])$. Solving these two equations for $p_i - p$ then yields $p_i - p = z_i/(\eta + b)$. Thus $V_r = V_z/(\eta + b)^2$.

Substituting the expressions for V_p and V_r into the definition of b (see [6.20]) yields

$$b = \frac{1}{\gamma - 1} \left[\frac{V_z}{V_z + \dfrac{(\eta + b)^2}{(1 + b)^2} V_m} \right]. \tag{6.28}$$

Equation (6.28) implicitly defines b in terms of V_z, V_m, and γ, and thus completes the model. It is straightforward to show that b is increasing in V_z and decreasing in V_m. In the special case of $\eta = 1$, we can obtain a closed-form expression for b:

$$b = \frac{1}{\gamma - 1} \frac{V_z}{V_z + V_m}. \tag{6.29}$$

Finally, note that the results that $p = E[m] + [1/(1 + b)](m - E[m])$ and $r_i = z_i/(\eta + b)$ imply that p and r_i are linear functions of m and z_i. Since m and z_i are independent, p and r_i are independent; and since linear functions of normal variables are normal, p and r_i are normal. This confirms the assumptions made above about these variables.

6.4   Implications and Limitations

The Phillips Curve and the Lucas Critique

Lucas's model implies that unexpectedly high realizations of aggregate demand lead to both higher output and higher-than-expected prices. As a result, for reasonable specifications of the behavior of aggregate demand, the model implies a positive association between output and inflation. Suppose, for example, that m is a random walk with drift:

$$m_t = m_{t-1} + c + u_t, \tag{6.30}$$

where u is white noise. Thus the expectation of m_t is $m_{t-1} + c$, and the unobserved component of m_t is u_t. Thus, from (6.26) and (6.27),

$$p_t = m_{t-1} + c + \frac{1}{1 + b} u_t, \tag{6.31}$$

$$y_t = \frac{b}{1 + b} u_t. \tag{6.32}$$

Since the model also implies that $p_{t-1} = m_{t-2} + c + [u_{t-1}/(1 + b)]$, the rate of inflation (measured as the change in the log price level) is

$$\pi_t = (m_{t-1} - m_{t-2}) + \frac{1}{1+b}u_t - \frac{1}{1+b}u_{t-1}$$

$$= c + \frac{b}{1+b}u_{t-1} + \frac{1}{1+b}u_t.$$

(6.33)

Note that u_t appears in both (6.32) and (6.33) with a positive sign, and that u_t and u_{t-1} are uncorrelated. These facts imply that output and inflation are positively correlated. Intuitively, high unexpected money growth leads, through the Lucas supply curve, to increases in both prices and output. The model therefore implies a positive relationship between output and inflation—a Phillips curve.

But although there is a statistical output-inflation relationship, there is no exploitable tradeoff between high output and low inflation. Suppose that policymakers decide to raise average money growth (for example, by raising c in equation [6.30]). If the change is not publicly known, there is an interval when unobserved money growth is typically positive and output is therefore usually above normal. Once individuals determine that the change has occurred, however, unobserved money growth is again on average zero, and so average real output is unchanged. And if the increase in average money growth is known, expected money growth jumps immediately and there is not even a brief interval of high output. The idea that the statistical relationship between output and inflation may change if policymakers attempt to take advantage of it is not just a theoretical curiosity: as we saw in Chapter 5, when average inflation rose in the late 1960s and early 1970s, the traditional output-inflation relationship collapsed.

The central idea underlying this analysis is of wider relevance. Expectations are likely to be important to many relationships among aggregate variables, and changes in policy are likely to affect those expectations. As a result, shifts in policy can change aggregate relationships. In short, if policymakers attempt to take advantage of statistical relationships, effects operating through expectations may cause the relationships to break down. This is the famous *Lucas critique* (Lucas, 1976).

The Phillips curve is the most famous application of the Lucas critique. Another example is temporary changes in taxes. There is a close relationship between disposable income and consumption spending. Yet to some extent this relationship arises not because current disposable income determines current spending, but because current income is strongly correlated with *permanent* income (see Chapter 7)—that is, it is highly correlated with households' expectations of their disposable incomes in the future. If policymakers attempt to reduce consumption through a tax increase that is known to be temporary, the relationship between current income and expected future income, and hence the relationship between current income and spending, will change. Again this is not just a theoretical possibility. The United States enacted a temporary tax surcharge in 1968, and the impact on consumption was considerably smaller than was expected on the basis of the statistical relationship between disposable income and spending (see, for example, Dolde, 1979).

Anticipated and Unanticipated Money

The result that only unobserved aggregate demand shocks have real effects has a strong implication: monetary policy can stabilize output only if policy-makers have information that is not available to private agents. Any portion of policy that is a response to publicly available information—such as interest rates, the unemployment rate, or the index of leading indicators—is irrelevant to the real economy (Sargent and Wallace, 1975; Barro, 1976).

To see this, let aggregate demand, m, equal $m^* + v$, where m^* is a policy variable and v a disturbance outside the government's control. If the government does not pursue activist policy but simply keeps m^* constant (or growing at a steady rate), the unobserved shock to aggregate demand in some period is the realization of v less the expectation of v given the information available to private agents. If m^* is instead a function of public information, individuals can deduce m^*, and so the situation is unchanged. Thus systematic policy rules cannot stabilize output.

If the government observes variables correlated with v that are not known to the public, it can use this information to stabilize output: it can change m^* to offset the movements in v that it expects on the basis of its private information. But this is not an appealing defense of Keynesian stabilization policy, for two reasons. First, a central element of conventional stabilization policy involves reactions to general, publicly available information that the economy is in a boom or a recession. Second, if superior information is the basis for potential stabilization, there is a much easier way for the government to accomplish that stabilization than following a complex policy rule: it can simply announce the information that the public does not have.[6]

Ball (1991), building on the work of Sargent (1983), argues that the Lucas model's predictions concerning observed policy can be tested by looking at

---

[6]A large literature, pioneered by Barro (1977a, 1978) and significantly extended by Mishkin (1982, 1983), tests Lucas's predictions concerning the impacts of observed and unobserved monetary policy using the money stock as the measure of policy. In Barro's formulation, the basic idea is to regress output on measures of forecastable and unforecastable money growth and a set of control variables. Unfortunately, these tests suffer from the same difficulties as regressions of money on output (see Section 5.6). For example, a positive correlation between unexpected changes in the money stock and output movements can reflect an impact of output on money demand rather than an impact of money on output. Similarly, the absence of an association between predictable movements in money and changes in output can arise not because observed monetary changes have no real effects, but because the Federal Reserve is adjusting the money supply to offset the impact of other factors on output. See also Problem 6.3.

times of announced shifts to tighter monetary policy to combat inflation. The Lucas model predicts that there should be no systematic relationship between real variables and any publicly known information about monetary policy. Thus it implies that output growth should not be on average different from normal following such announcements. But Ball argues that when policymakers do not carry through with the announced policy, inflation typically changes little and output growth generally remains about normal, and that when they do carry through, inflation typically declines and output growth usually falls below normal. Thus, he concludes, output growth is on average below normal following the announcements, which is not consistent with Lucas's model.

Empirical Application: International Evidence on Output-Inflation Tradeoffs

In the Lucas model, suppliers' responses to changes in prices are determined by the relative importance of aggregate and idiosyncratic shocks. If aggregate shocks are large, for example, suppliers attribute most of the changes in the prices of their goods to changes in the price level, and so they alter their production relatively little in response to variations in prices (see [6.20]). The Lucas model therefore predicts that the real effect of a given aggregate demand shock is smaller in an economy where the variance of those shocks is larger.

To test this prediction, one must find a measure of aggregate demand shocks. Lucas (1973) uses the change in the log of nominal GDP. For this to be precisely correct, two conditions must be satisfied. First, the aggregate demand curve must be unit-elastic; in this case, changes in aggregate supply affect P and Y but not their product, and so nominal GDP is determined entirely by aggregate demand. Second, the change in log nominal GDP must not be predictable or observable; that is, letting x denote log nominal GDP, Δx must take the form $a + u_t$, where u_t is white noise. With this process, the change in log nominal GDP (relative to its average change) is also the unobserved change. Although these conditions are surely not satisfied exactly, they may be accurate enough to be reasonable first approximations.

Under these assumptions, the real effects of an aggregate demand shock in a given country can be estimated by regressing log real GDP (or the change in log real GDP) on the change in log nominal GDP and control variables. The specification Lucas employs is

$$y_t = c + \gamma t + \tau \Delta x_t + \lambda y_{t-1}, \tag{6.34}$$

where y is log real GDP, t is time, and Δx is the change in log nominal GDP. Lucas estimates (6.34) separately for various countries. He then asks whether the estimated τ's—the estimates of the responsiveness of output to aggregate demand movements—are related to the average size of countries' aggregate demand shocks. A simple way to do this is to estimate

$$\tau_i = \alpha + \beta \sigma_{\Delta x,i}, \tag{6.35}$$

where τ_i is the estimate of the real impact of an aggregate demand shift obtained by estimating (6.34) for country i and $\sigma_{\Delta x,i}$ is the standard deviation of the change in log nominal GDP in country i. Lucas's theory predicts that nominal shocks have smaller real effects in settings where aggregate demand is more volatile, and thus that β is negative.

Lucas employs a relatively small sample. His test has been extended to much larger samples, with various modifications in specification, in several studies. Figure 6.1, from Ball, Mankiw, and D. Romer (1988), is typical of the results. It shows a scatterplot of τ against $\sigma_{\Delta x}$ for 43 countries. The corresponding regression is

$$\tau_i = \begin{array}{cc} 0.388 & - 1.639\,\sigma_{\Delta x,i}, \\ (0.057) & (0.482) \end{array}$$

$$\overline{R}^2 = 0.201, \quad \text{s.e.e.} = 0.245, \tag{6.36}$$

where the numbers in parentheses are standard errors. Thus there is a highly statistically significant negative relationship between the variability of nominal GDP growth and the estimated effect of a given change in aggregate demand, just as the model predicts.

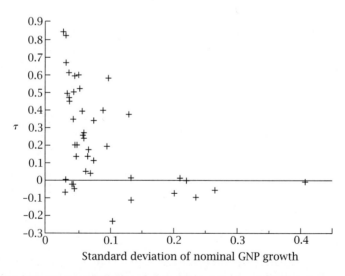

FIGURE 6.1 The output-inflation tradeoff and the variability of aggregate demand (from Ball, Mankiw, and Romer, 1988)

Difficulties

If, as suggested above, announced shifts toward disinflationary policies are on average followed by below-normal output growth, then the Lucas model does not provide a complete account of the effects of aggregate demand shifts. The more important question, however, is whether the Lucas model accounts for an important element of the effects of aggregate demand. Two major objections have been raised in this regard.

The first difficulty is that the employment fluctuations in the Lucas model, like those in real-business-cycle models, arise from changes in labor supply in response to changes in the perceived benefits of working. Thus to generate substantial employment fluctuations, the model requires a significant short-run elasticity of labor supply. But, as described in Section 4.10, there is no strong evidence of such a high elasticity.

The second difficulty concerns the assumption of imperfect information. In modern economies, high-quality information about changes in prices is released with only brief lags. Thus, other than in times of hyperinflation, individuals can estimate aggregate price movements with considerable accuracy at little cost. In light of this, it is difficult to see how they can be significantly confused between relative and aggregate price level movements.

These difficulties suggest that the specific mechanisms emphasized in the model may be relatively unimportant to fluctuations, at least in most settings.[7] But we will see in Section 6.12 that there are reasons other than intertemporal substitution that small changes in real wages or relative prices may be associated with large changes in employment and output, and that there are reasons individuals may choose not to take advantage of low-cost opportunities to acquire information relevant to their pricing decisions. Thus, as we will discuss there, it may be possible to resuscitate Lucas's central idea that unexpected monetary shocks may create confusion between relative and aggregate price changes, and thereby have important effects on aggregate output.

---

[7]In addition, the model implies that departures of output from the flexible-price level are not at all persistent. y depends only on $m - E[m]$. And by definition, $m - E[m]$ cannot have any predictable component. Thus the model implies that y is white noise—that is, that it displays no pattern of either positive or negative correlation over time. This does not appear to be a good description of actual economies. A monetary contraction—such as the Federal Reserve's decision in 1979 to disinflate—leads to abnormally low output over an extended time, not to a single period of low output followed by an immediate return to normal.

This difficulty can be addressed by introducing some reason that the economy's initial response to an unobserved monetary shock triggers dynamics that cause output to remain away for normal even after the shock has become known. Examples of such mechanisms include inventory dynamics (Blinder and Fischer, 1981), capital accumulation (Lucas, 1975), and one-time costs of recruiting and training new workers. Thus the prediction of white-noise output movements is an artifact of the simple form of the model we have been considering, and not a robust implication.

Part B   Staggered Price Adjustment

6.5   Introduction

The next source of nominal imperfections we consider is staggered adjustment of wages or prices. In one important respect, models of staggered adjustment are a reversion to traditional Keynesian models: sluggish nominal adjustment is assumed rather than derived. But the models are nonetheless important to the microeconomic foundations of nominal price and wage rigidity. There are three reasons.

First (and least important for our purposes), the Lucas model was initially perceived as showing that rational expectations alone are enough to undo many of the central results of traditional Keynesian theory, most notably the stabilizing powers of aggregate demand policy. If this were right, defending the traditional Keynesian position would require demonstrating that expectations are systematically irrational. Models of staggered adjustment show that this is unnecessary: if not all prices or wages are free to change every period, aggregate demand policy can be stabilizing even under rational expectations.

Second, the models make assumptions about imperfect adjustment at the level of individual price- or wage-setters and then aggregate individual behavior to find the implications for the macroeconomy. In that regard, the models lay the groundwork for the models of the next section, where nominal rigidity is derived from optimizing behavior at the microeconomic level.

Finally, the models show that interactions among price-setters can either magnify or dampen the effects of barriers to price adjustment. A consistent theme of the results in this section is that macroeconomic nominal rigidity is not related in any simple way to microeconomic price rigidity. We will see cases where a small amount of microeconomic rigidity leads to a large amount of rigidity in the aggregate, and others where a large amount of microeconomic rigidity yields little or no rigidity in the aggregate.

We consider three models of staggered price adjustment: the Fischer, or Fischer–Phelps–Taylor, model (Fischer, 1977a; Phelps and Taylor, 1977); the Taylor model (Taylor, 1979, 1980); and the Caplin–Spulber model (Caplin and Spulber, 1987).[8] The first two, the Fischer and Taylor models, posit that wages or prices are set by multiperiod contracts or commitments. In each period, the contracts governing some fraction of wages or prices expire and must be renewed. The central result of the models is that multiperiod contracts lead to gradual adjustment of the price level to nominal distur-

---

[8]An important earlier paper is Akerlof (1969). See also Phelps (1978) and Blanchard (1983).

bances. As a result, aggregate demand disturbances have real effects, and policy rules can be stabilizing even under rational expectations.

The Fischer and Taylor models differ in one important respect. The Fischer model assumes that prices (or wages) are *predetermined* but not *fixed*. That is, when a multiperiod contract sets prices for several periods, it can specify a *different* price for each period. In the Taylor model, in contrast, prices are fixed: a contract must specify the *same* price each period it is in effect. This distinction proves to be important.

In both the Fischer and Taylor models, the length of time that a price is in effect is determined when the price is set. Thus price adjustment is *time-dependent.* The Caplin–Spulber model provides a simple example of a model of *state-dependent* pricing. Under state-dependent pricing, price changes are triggered not by the passage of time, but by developments within the economy. As a result, the fraction of prices that change in a given time interval is endogenous. Once again, this seemingly modest change in assumptions has important consequences.[9]

6.6   A Model of Imperfect Competition and Price-Setting

Before turning to staggered adjustment, we first investigate a model of an economy of imperfectly competitive price-setters with complete price flexibility. There are two reasons for analyzing this model. First, as we will see, imperfect competition alone has interesting macroeconomic consequences. Second, the models in the rest of the chapter are concerned with the causes and effects of barriers to price adjustment. To address these issues, we will need a model of the determination of prices in the absence of barriers to adjustment, and of the effects of departures from those prices.

Assumptions

The model is a variant on the model described in Part A of this chapter. The economy consists of a large number of individuals. Each one sets the price of some good and is the good's sole producer. As in Part A, labor is

---

[9]All three models take the staggering of price changes as given. But at least for the Fischer and Taylor models, if the timing of price changes is made endogenous, the result is synchronized rather than staggered adjustment (see Problem 6.8). Staggering can arise endogenously from firms' desire to acquire information by observing other firms' prices before setting their own (Ball and Cecchetti, 1988), from firm-specific shocks (Ball and D. Romer, 1989; Caballero and Engel, 1991), and from strategic interactions among firms (Maskin and Tirole, 1988).

the only input into production. But individuals do not produce their own goods directly; instead there is a competitive labor market where they can both sell their labor and hire workers to produce their goods.[10]

As before, the demand for each good is log-linear; for simplicity, the shocks to the demands for the individual goods (the z_i's) are absent. Thus, $q_i = y - \eta(p_i - p)$ (see [6.7]). p is the (log) price level; as in Part A, it is the average of the p_i's. To ensure that a profit-maximizing price exists, η is assumed to be greater than 1. Sellers with market power set price above marginal cost; thus if they cannot adjust their prices, they are willing to produce to satisfy demand in the face of small fluctuations in demand. In the remainder of the chapter, sellers are therefore assumed not to ration customers.

As in the Lucas model, the utility of a typical individual is $U_i = C_i - L_i^{\gamma}/\gamma$ (see [6.2]); again C_i is the individual's income divided by the price index, P, and L_i is the amount that he or she works. The production function is the same as before: the output of good i equals the amount of labor employed in its production. Individual i's income is the sum of profit income, $(P_i - W)Q_i$, and labor income, WL_i, where Q_i is the output of good i and W is the nominal wage. Thus,

$$U_i = \frac{(P_i - W)Q_i + WL_i}{P} - \frac{1}{\gamma}L_i^{\gamma}. \tag{6.37}$$

Finally, the aggregate demand side of the model is again given by $y = m - p$ (equation [6.10]); y is again the average of the q_i's. In contrast to the Lucas model, the money supply is publicly observed.[11]

Individual Behavior

Converting the demand equation, $q_i = y - \eta(p_i - p)$, from logs to levels yields $Q_i = Y(P_i/P)^{-\eta}$. Substituting this into expression (6.37) gives us

$$U_i = \frac{(P_i - W)Y(P_i/P)^{-\eta} + WL_i}{P} - \frac{1}{\gamma}L_i^{\gamma}. \tag{6.38}$$

---

[10]The absence of an economy-wide labor market is critical to the Lucas model: with such a market, individuals' observation of the nominal wage would allow them to deduce the money supply, and would thus make nominal shocks neutral. In contrast, assuming a competitive labor market in the current model is not crucial to the results.

[11]As described in n. 2 and Problem 6.2, when individuals' preferences over the different goods give rise to the assumed constant-elasticity demand curves for each product, the appropriate (log) price and output indexes are not exactly equal to the averages of the p_i's and the q_i's. Problem 6.4 shows, however, that the results of this section are unchanged when the exact indexes are used.

The individual has two choice variables, the price of his or her good (P_i) and the amount he or she works (L_i). The first-order condition for P_i is

$$\frac{Y(P_i/P)^{-\eta} - (P_i - W)\eta Y(P_i/P)^{-\eta-1}(1/P)}{P} = 0. \tag{6.39}$$

Multiplying this expression by $(P_i/P)^{\eta+1}P$, dividing by Y, and rearranging yields

$$\frac{P_i}{P} = \frac{\eta}{\eta - 1}\frac{W}{P}. \tag{6.40}$$

That is, we get the standard result that a producer with market power sets price as a markup over marginal cost, with the size of the markup determined by the elasticity of demand.

Now consider labor supply. From (6.38), the first-order condition for L_i is

$$\frac{W}{P} - L_i^{\gamma-1} = 0, \tag{6.41}$$

or

$$L_i = \left(\frac{W}{P}\right)^{1/(\gamma-1)}. \tag{6.42}$$

Thus labor supply is an increasing function of the real wage; the elasticity is $1/(\gamma - 1)$.

Equilibrium

Because of the symmetry of the model, in equilibrium each individual works the same amount and produces the same amount. Equilibrium output is thus equal to the common level of labor supply. We can therefore use (6.41) or (6.42) to express the real wage as a function of output:

$$\frac{W}{P} = Y^{\gamma-1}. \tag{6.43}$$

Substituting this expression into the price equation, (6.40), yields an expression for each producer's desired relative price as a function of aggregate output:

$$\frac{P_i^*}{P} = \frac{\eta}{\eta - 1}Y^{\gamma-1}. \tag{6.44}$$

For future reference, it is useful to write this expression in logs:

$$p_i^* - p = \ln\left(\frac{\eta}{\eta - 1}\right) + (\gamma - 1)y \tag{6.45}$$

$$\equiv c + \phi y.$$

Since producers are symmetric, each charges the same price. The price index P therefore equals this common price. Equilibrium therefore requires that each producer, taking P as given, sets his or her own price equal to P; that is, each producer's desired relative price must equal 1. From (6.44), this condition is $[\eta/(\eta - 1)]Y^{\gamma-1} = 1$, or

$$Y = \left(\frac{\eta - 1}{\eta}\right)^{1/(\gamma-1)}. \tag{6.46}$$

This is the equilibrium level of output.

Finally, we can use the aggregate demand equation, $Y = M/P$, to find the equilibrium price level:

$$P = \frac{M}{Y}$$

$$= \frac{M}{\left(\dfrac{\eta - 1}{\eta}\right)^{1/(\gamma-1)}}. \tag{6.47}$$

Implications

When producers have market power, they produce less than the socially optimal amount. To see this, note that in a symmetric allocation each individual supplies some amount $\bar{L}$ of labor, and production of each good and each individual's consumption are equal to that $\bar{L}$. Thus the problem of finding the best symmetric allocation reduces to choosing $\bar{L}$ to maximize $\bar{L} - (1/\gamma)\bar{L}^\gamma$. The solution is simply $\bar{L} = 1$. As (6.46) shows, equilibrium output is less than this. Intuitively, the fact that producers face downward-sloping demand curves means that the marginal revenue product of labor is less than its marginal product. As a result, the real wage is less than the marginal product of labor: from (6.40) (and the fact that each P_i equals P in equilibrium), the real wage is $(\eta - 1)/\eta$; the marginal product of labor, in contrast, is 1. This reduces the quantity of labor supplied, and thus causes equilibrium output to be less than optimal. From (6.46), equilibrium output is $[(\eta - 1)/\eta]^{1/(\gamma-1)}$; thus the gap between the equilibrium and optimal levels of output is greater when producers have more market power (that is, when η is lower), and when labor supply is more responsive to the real wage (that is, when γ is lower).

The fact that equilibrium output is inefficiently low under imperfect competition has important implications for fluctuations. To begin with, it implies that recessions and booms have asymmetric effects on welfare (Mankiw, 1985). In practice, periods when output is unusually high are viewed as good times, and periods when output is unusually low are viewed as bad times. Now consider a model where fluctuations arise from incomplete nominal adjustment in the face of monetary shocks. If the equilibrium in the absence of shocks is optimal, both times of high output and times of low output are departures from the optimum, and thus both are undesirable. But if equilibrium output is less than optimal, a boom brings output closer to the social optimum, whereas a recession pushes it farther away.

In addition, the gap between equilibrium and optimal output implies that pricing decisions have externalities. Suppose that the economy is initially in equilibrium, and consider the effects of a marginal reduction in all prices. M/P rises, and so aggregate output rises. This affects the representative individual through two channels. First, the prevailing real wage rises (see [6.43]). But since initially the individual is neither a net purchaser nor a net supplier of labor, at the margin the increase does not affect his or her welfare. Second, because aggregate output increases, the demand curve for the individual's good, $Y(P_i/P)^{-\eta}$, shifts out. Since the individual is selling at a price that exceeds marginal cost, this change raises his or her welfare. Thus under imperfect competition, pricing decisions have externalities, and those externalities operate through the overall demand for goods. This externality is often referred to as an *aggregate demand externality* (Blanchard and Kiyotaki, 1987).

The final implication of this analysis is that imperfect competition alone does not imply monetary nonneutrality. A change in the money stock in the model leads to proportional changes in the nominal wage and all nominal prices; output and the real wage are unchanged (see [6.46] and [6.47]).

Finally, since a pricing equation of the form (6.45) is important in later sections, it is worth noting that the basic idea captured by the equation is much more general than the specific model of price-setters' desired prices we are considering here. Equation (6.45) states that $p_i^* - p$ takes the form $c + \phi y$; that is, it states that a price-setter's optimal relative price is increasing in aggregate output. In the particular model we are considering, this arises from increases in the prevailing real wage when output rises. But in a more general setting, it can also arise from increases in the costs of other inputs, from diminishing returns, or from costs of adjusting output.

The fact that price-setters' desired real prices are increasing in aggregate output is necessary for the flexible-price equilibrium to be stable. To see this, note that we can use the fact that $y = m - p$ to rewrite (6.45) as

$$p_i^* = c + (1 - \phi)p + \phi m. \tag{6.48}$$

If ϕ is negative, an increase in the price level raises each price-setter's desired price more than one-for-one. This means that if p is above the level that causes individuals to charge a relative price of 1, each individual wants to charge more than the prevailing price level; and if p is below its equilibrium value, each individual wants to charge less than the prevailing price level. Thus ϕ must be positive for the flexible-price equilibrium to be stable.

6.7   Predetermined Prices

Framework and Assumptions

We now turn to the Fischer model of staggered price adjustment. In particular, we consider a variant on the model of the previous section where price-setters cannot set their prices freely each period. Instead, each price-setter sets prices every other period for the next two periods. As emphasized in Section 6.5, the price-setter can set different prices for the two periods. In any given period, half of the individuals are setting their prices for the next two periods. Thus at any point, half of the prices in effect are those set the previous period and half are those set two periods ago.[12]

For simplicity, we normalize the constant in the equation for price-setters' desired prices, (6.45) (or [6.48]), to zero; thus the desired price of individual i in period t is $p_{it}^* = \phi m_t + (1 - \phi)p_t$. Otherwise the model is the same as that of the previous section. The behavior of m is treated as exogenous; no specific assumptions are made about the process that it follows. Thus, for example, information about m_t may be revealed gradually in the periods leading up to t; the expectation of m_t as of period $t - 1$, $E_{t-1}m_t$, may therefore differ from the expectation of m_t the period before, $E_{t-2}m_t$.

Paralleling our assumption of certainty equivalence in the Lucas model, we assume that an individual choosing his or her prices in period t for the next two periods sets the log prices equal to the expectations, given the information available through t, of the profit-maximizing log prices in the two periods. As in the Lucas model, price-setters form their expectations rationally.

Solving the Model

In any period, half of prices are ones set in the previous period, and half are ones set two periods ago. Thus the average price is

---

[12]The original versions of these models focused on staggered adjustment of wages; prices were in principle flexible but were determined as markups over wages. For simplicity, we assume instead that staggered adjustment applies directly to prices. Staggered wage adjustment has essentially the same implications.

$$p_t = \frac{1}{2}(p_t^1 + p_t^2), \tag{6.49}$$

where p_t^1 denotes the price set for t by individuals who set their prices in $t-1$, and p_t^2 the price set for t by individuals setting prices in $t-2$. Since we have assumed certainty-equivalence pricing behavior (and since all price-setters in a given period face the same problem), p_t^1 equals the expectation as of period $t-1$ of p_{it}^*, and p_t^2 equals the expectation as of $t-2$ of p_{it}^*. Thus,

$$
\begin{aligned}
p_t^1 &= E_{t-1}p_{it}^* \\
&= E_{t-1}[\phi m_t + (1-\phi)p_t] \\
&= \phi E_{t-1}m_t + (1-\phi)\frac{1}{2}(p_t^1 + p_t^2),
\end{aligned}
\tag{6.50}
$$

$$
\begin{aligned}
p_t^2 &= E_{t-2}p_{it}^* \\
&= \phi E_{t-2}m_t + (1-\phi)\frac{1}{2}(E_{t-2}p_t^1 + p_t^2),
\end{aligned}
\tag{6.51}
$$

where $E_{t-\tau}$ denotes expectations conditional on information available through period $t-\tau$. Equation (6.50) uses the fact that p_t^2 is already determined when p_t^1 is set, and thus is not uncertain.

Our goal is to find how the price level and output evolve over time given the behavior of m. To do this, we begin by solving (6.50) for p_t^1; this yields

$$p_t^1 = \frac{2\phi}{1+\phi}E_{t-1}m_t + \frac{1-\phi}{1+\phi}p_t^2. \tag{6.52}$$

We can now use the fact that expectations are rational to find the behavior of the individuals setting their prices in period $t-2$. Since the left- and right-hand sides of (6.52) are equal, and since expectations are rational, the expectation as of $t-2$ of these two expressions must be equal. Thus,

$$E_{t-2}p_t^1 = \frac{2\phi}{1+\phi}E_{t-2}m_t + \frac{1-\phi}{1+\phi}p_t^2. \tag{6.53}$$

Equation (6.53) uses the fact that $E_{t-2}E_{t-1}m_t$ is simply $E_{t-2}m_t$; otherwise price-setters would be expecting to revise their estimate of m_t either up or down, which would imply that their original estimate was not rational. The fact the current expectation of a future expectation of a variable equals the current expectation of the variable is known as the *law of iterated projections*.

We can substitute (6.53) into (6.51) to obtain

$$p_t^2 = \phi E_{t-2} m_t + (1 - \phi)\frac{1}{2}\left(\frac{2\phi}{1 + \phi}E_{t-2} m_t + \frac{1 - \phi}{1 + \phi}p_t^2 + p_t^2\right). \quad (6.54)$$

Solving this expression for p_t^2 yields simply

$$p_t^2 = E_{t-2} m_t. \quad (6.55)$$

We can now combine the results and describe the equilibrium. Substituting (6.55) into (6.52) and simplifying gives

$$p_t^1 = E_{t-2} m_t + \frac{2\phi}{1 + \phi}(E_{t-1} m_t - E_{t-2} m_t). \quad (6.56)$$

Finally, substituting (6.55) and (6.56) into the expressions for the price level and output, $p_t = (p_t^1 + p_t^2)/2$ and $y_t = m_t - p_t$, implies

$$p_t = E_{t-2} m_t + \frac{\phi}{1 + \phi}(E_{t-1} m_t - E_{t-2} m_t), \quad (6.57)$$

$$y_t = \frac{1}{1 + \phi}(E_{t-1} m_t - E_{t-2} m_t) + (m_t - E_{t-1} m_t). \quad (6.58)$$

Implications

Equation (6.58) shows the model's main implications. First, as in the Lucas model, unanticipated aggregate demand shifts have real effects; this is shown by the $m_t - E_{t-1} m_t$ term. Because price-setters are assumed not to know m_t when they set their prices, these shocks are passed one-for-one into output.

Second, and crucially, aggregate demand shifts that become anticipated after the first prices are set affect output. Consider information about aggregate demand in t that becomes available between period $t - 2$ and period $t - 1$. In practice, this might correspond to the release of survey results or other leading indicators of future economic activity, or to indications of likely shifts in monetary policy. As (6.57) and (6.58) show, proportion $1/(1 + \phi)$ of a change in m that becomes expected between $t - 2$ and $t - 1$ is passed into output, and the remainder goes into prices. The reason that the change is not neutral is straightforward: not all prices are completely flexible in the short run.

An immediate corollary is that policy rules can stabilize the economy. As in Section 6.4, suppose that m_t equals $m_t^* + v_t$, where m_t^* is controlled by policy and v_t represents other aggregate demand movements. Assume that the policymaker is subject to the same informational constraints as price-setters, and must therefore choose m_t^* before the exact value of v_t is known. Nonetheless, as long as the policymaker can adjust m_t in response to information learned between $t-2$ and $t-1$, there is a role for stabilization policy. From (6.58), when $m_t = m_t^* + v_t$, y_t depends on $(m_t^* + v_t) - E_{t-1}(m_t^* + v_t)$ and on $E_{t-1}(m_t^* + v_t) - E_{t-2}(m_t^* + v_t)$. By adjusting m_t^* to offset $E_{t-1}v_t - E_{t-2}v_t$, the policymaker can offset the effects of these changes in v on output, even if this information about v is publicly known.

An additional implication of these results is that interactions among price-setters can either increase or decrease the effects of microeconomic price stickiness. Consider an aggregate demand shift that becomes known after the first prices are set. One might expect that since half of prices are already set and the other half are free to adjust, half of the shift is passed into prices and half into output. Equations (6.57) and (6.58) show that in general this is not correct. The key parameter is ϕ: the proportion of the shift that is passed into output is not $\frac{1}{2}$ but $1/(1 + \phi)$ (see [6.58]).

Recall from equation (6.45) that ϕ is the responsiveness of price-setters' desired real prices to aggregate real output: $p_{it}^* - p_t = c + \phi y_t$. A lower value of ϕ therefore corresponds to greater *real rigidity* (Ball and D. Romer, 1990). Real rigidity alone does not cause monetary disturbances to have real effects: if prices can adjust freely, money is neutral regardless of the value of ϕ. But real rigidity magnifies the effect of nominal rigidity: given that price-setters do not adjust their prices freely, a higher degree of real rigidity (that is, a lower value of ϕ) increases the real effects of a given monetary change. The reason for this is that a low value of ϕ implies that price-setters are reluctant to allow variations in their relative prices. As a result, the price-setters that are free to adjust their prices do not allow their prices to differ greatly from the ones already set, and so the real effects of a monetary shock are large. If ϕ exceeds 1, in contrast, the later price-setters make large price changes, and the aggregate real effects of changes in m are small.[13]

Finally, the model implies that output does not depend on $E_{t-2}m_t$ (given the values of $E_{t-1}m_t - E_{t-2}m_t$ and $m_t - E_{t-1}m_t$). That is, any information about aggregate demand that all price-setters have had a chance to respond to has no effect on output.

6.8   Fixed Prices

The Model

We now change the model of the previous section by assuming that when an individual sets prices for two periods, he or she must set the same price

---

[13]Haltiwanger and Waldman (1989) show more generally how a small fraction of agents who do not respond to shocks can have a disproportionate effect on the economy.

for both periods; in the terminology introduced earlier, prices are not just predetermined, but fixed.

We make two other, less significant changes to the model. First, an individual setting a price in period t now does so for periods t and $t + 1$ rather than for periods $t + 1$ and $t + 2$. This change simplifies the model without affecting the main results. Second, the model is much easier to solve if we posit a specific process for m. A simple assumption is that m is a random walk:

$$m_t = m_{t-1} + u_t, \tag{6.59}$$

where u is white noise. The key feature of this process is that an innovation to m (the u term) has a long-lasting effect on its level (indeed, with the random-walk assumption, the effect is permanent).

Let x_t denote the price chosen by individuals who set their prices in period t. We make the usual certainty-equivalence assumption that price-setters try to get their prices as close as possible to the optimal prices. Here this implies

$$x_t = \frac{1}{2}(p_{it}^* + E_t p_{it+1}^*)$$

$$= \frac{1}{2}\left\{[\phi m_t + (1 - \phi)p_t] + [\phi E_t m_{t+1} + (1 - \phi)E_t p_{t+1}]\right\}, \tag{6.60}$$

where the second line uses the fact that $p^* = \phi m + (1 - \phi)p$.

Since half of prices are set each period, p_t is the average of x_t and x_{t-1}. In addition, since m is a random walk, $E_t m_{t+1}$ is m_t. Substituting these facts into (6.60) gives us

$$x_t = \phi m_t + \frac{1}{4}(1 - \phi)[x_{t-1} + 2x_t + E_t x_{t+1}]. \tag{6.61}$$

Solving for x_t yields

$$x_t = A(x_{t-1} + E_t x_{t+1}) + (1 - 2A)m_t,$$

$$A \equiv \frac{1}{2}\frac{1 - \phi}{1 + \phi}. \tag{6.62}$$

Equation (6.62) is the key equation of the model.

Equation (6.62) expresses x_t in terms of m_t, x_{t-1}, and the expectation of x_{t+1}. To solve the model, we need to eliminate the expectation of x_{t+1} from this expression. We will solve the model in two different ways, first using the method of undetermined coefficients and then using *lag operators*. The method of undetermined coefficients is simpler. But there are cases where it is cumbersome or intractable; in those cases the use of lag operators is often fruitful.

The Method of Undetermined Coefficients

As described in Section 4.6, the idea of the method of undetermined coefficients is to guess the general functional form of the solution and then to use the model to determine the precise coefficients. In the model we are considering, in period t two variables are given: the money stock, m_t, and the prices set the previous period, x_{t-1}. In addition, the model is linear. It is therefore reasonable to guess that x_t is a linear function of x_{t-1} and m_t:

$$x_t = \mu + \lambda x_{t-1} + \nu m_t. \tag{6.63}$$

Our goal is to determine whether there are values of μ, λ, and ν that yield a solution of the model.

Although we could now proceed to find μ, λ, and ν, it simplifies the algebra if we first use our knowledge of the model to restrict (6.63). The fact that we have normalized the constant in the expression for individuals' desired prices to zero, so that $p_{it}^* - p_t = \phi y_t$, implies that the equilibrium with flexible prices is for y to equal zero and for each price to equal m. In light of this, consider a situation where x_{t-1} and m_t are equal. If period-t price-setters also set their prices to m_t, the economy is at its flexible-price equilibrium. In addition, since m follows a random walk, the period-t price-setters have no reason to expect m_{t+1} to be on average either more or less than m_t, and hence no reason to expect x_{t+1} to depart on average from m_t. Thus in this situation p_{it}^* and $E_t p_{it+1}^*$ are both equal to m_t, and so price-setters will choose $x_t = m_t$. In sum, it is reasonable to guess that if $x_{t-1} = m_t$, then $x_t = m_t$. In terms of (6.63), this condition is

$$\mu + \lambda m_t + \nu m_t = m_t \tag{6.64}$$

for all m_t.

Two conditions are needed for (6.64) to hold. The first is $\lambda + \nu = 1$; otherwise (6.64) cannot be satisfied for all values of m_t. Second, when we impose $\lambda + \nu = 1$, (6.64) implies $\mu = 0$. Substituting these conditions into (6.63) yields

$$x_t = \lambda x_{t-1} + (1 - \lambda)m_t. \tag{6.65}$$

Our goal is now to find a value of λ that solves the model.

Since (6.65) holds each period, it implies $x_{t+1} = \lambda x_t + (1 - \lambda)m_{t+1}$. Thus the expectation as of period t of x_{t+1} is $\lambda x_t + (1 - \lambda)E_t m_{t+1}$, which equals $\lambda x_t + (1 - \lambda)m_t$. Using (6.65) to substitute for x_t then gives us

$$E_t x_{t+1} = \lambda[\lambda x_{t-1} + (1 - \lambda)m_t] + (1 - \lambda)m_t$$

$$= \lambda^2 x_{t-1} + (1 - \lambda^2)m_t. \tag{6.66}$$

Substituting this expression into (6.62) yields

$$x_t = A[x_{t-1} + \lambda^2 x_{t-1} + (1 - \lambda^2)m_t] + (1 - 2A)m_t$$

$$= (A + A\lambda^2)x_{t-1} + [A(1 - \lambda^2) + (1 - 2A)]m_t. \qquad (6.67)$$

Thus, if price-setters believe that x_t is a linear function of x_{t-1} and m_t of the form assumed in (6.65), then, acting to maximize their profits, they will indeed set their prices as a linear function of these variables. If we have found a solution of the model, these two linear equations must be the same. Comparison of (6.65) and (6.67) shows that this requires

$$A + A\lambda^2 = \lambda \qquad (6.68)$$

and

$$A(1 - \lambda^2) + (1 - 2A) = 1 - \lambda. \qquad (6.69)$$

Consider (6.68). This is a quadratic equation in λ. The solution is

$$\lambda = \frac{1 \pm \sqrt{1 - 4A^2}}{2A}. \qquad (6.70)$$

One can show that these two values of λ also satisfy (6.69). Using the definition of A in equation (6.62), one can show that the two values of λ are

$$\lambda_1 = \frac{1 - \sqrt{\phi}}{1 + \sqrt{\phi}}, \qquad (6.71)$$

$$\lambda_2 = \frac{1 + \sqrt{\phi}}{1 - \sqrt{\phi}}. \qquad (6.72)$$

Of the two values of λ, only $\lambda = \lambda_1$ gives reasonable results. When $\lambda = \lambda_1$, $|\lambda| < 1$, and so the economy is stable. When $\lambda = \lambda_2$, in contrast, $|\lambda| > 1$, and thus the economy is unstable: the slightest disturbance sends output off toward plus or minus infinity. As a result, the assumptions underlying the model—for example, that sellers do not ration buyers—break down. For that reason, we focus on $\lambda = \lambda_1$.

Thus equation (6.65) with $\lambda = \lambda_1$ solves the model: if price-setters believe that others are using that rule to set their prices, they find it in their own interests to use that same rule.

We can now describe the behavior of output. y_t equals $m_t - p_t$, which in turn equals $m_t - (x_{t-1} + x_t)/2$. With the behavior of x given by (6.65), this implies

$$y_t = m_t - \frac{1}{2}\{[\lambda x_{t-2} + (1 - \lambda)m_{t-1}] + [\lambda x_{t-1} + (1 - \lambda)m_t]\}$$

$$= m_t - [\lambda\frac{1}{2}(x_{t-2} + x_{t-1}) + (1 - \lambda)\frac{1}{2}(m_{t-1} + m_t)]. \qquad (6.73)$$

Using the facts that $m_t = m_{t-1} + u_t$ and $(x_{t-1} + x_{t-2})/2 = p_{t-1}$, we can simplify this to

$$y_t = m_{t-1} + u_t - [\lambda p_{t-1} + (1-\lambda)m_{t-1} + (1-\lambda)\frac{1}{2}u_t]$$

$$= \lambda(m_{t-1} - p_{t-1}) + \frac{1+\lambda}{2}u_t \qquad (6.74)$$

$$= \lambda y_{t-1} + \frac{1+\lambda}{2}u_t.$$

Implications

Equation (6.74) is the key result of the model. As long as λ_1 is positive (which is true if $\phi < 1$), (6.74) implies that shocks to aggregate demand have long-lasting effects on output—effects that persist *even after all price-setters have changed their prices*. Suppose the economy is initially at the equilibrium with flexible prices (so y is steady at zero), and consider the effects of a positive shock of size u^0 in some period. In the period of the shock, not all price-setters adjust their prices, and so not surprisingly, y rises; from (6.74), $y = [(1+\lambda)/2]u^0$. In the following period, even though the remaining price-setters are able to adjust their prices, y does not return to normal even in the absence of a further shock: from (6.74), y is $\lambda[(1+\lambda)/2]u^0$. Thereafter output returns slowly to normal, with $y_t = \lambda y_{t-1}$ each period.

The response of the price level to the shock is the flip side of the response of output. The price level rises by $[1 - (1+\lambda)/2]u^0$ in the initial period, and then fraction $1 - \lambda$ of the remaining distance from u^0 in each subsequent period. Thus the economy exhibits price-level inertia.

The source of the long-lasting real effects of monetary shocks is again price-setters' reluctance to allow variations in their relative prices. Recall that $p_{it}^* = \phi m_t + (1-\phi)p_t$, and that $\lambda_1 > 0$ only if $\phi < 1$. Thus there is gradual adjustment only if desired prices are an increasing function of the price level. Suppose each price-setter adjusted fully to the shock at the first opportunity. In this case, the price-setters who adjusted their prices in the period of the shock would adjust by the full amount of the shock, and the remainder would do the same in the next period. Thus y would rise by $u^0/2$ in the initial period and return to normal in the next.

To see why this rapid adjustment cannot be the equilibrium if ϕ is less than 1, consider the individuals who adjust their prices immediately. By assumption, all prices have been adjusted by the second period, and so in that period everyone is charging his or her optimal price. But since $\phi < 1$, the optimal price is lower when the price level is lower, and so the price that is optimal in the period of the shock, when not all prices have been adjusted, is less than the optimal price in the next period. Thus these individuals should not adjust their prices fully in the period of the shock. This in turn implies that it is not optimal for the remaining individuals to adjust their prices fully in the subsequent period. And the knowledge that they will not do this further dampens the initial response of the individuals who adjust their prices in the period of the shock. The end result of these forward- and backward-looking interactions is the gradual adjustment shown in equation (6.65).

Thus, as in the model with prices that are predetermined but not fixed, the extent of incomplete price adjustment in the aggregate can be larger than one might expect simply from the knowledge that not all prices are adjusted every period. Indeed, the extent of aggregate price sluggishness is even larger in this case, since it persists even after every price has changed. And again a low value of ϕ—that is, a high degree of real rigidity—is critical to this result. If ϕ is 1, then λ is 0, and so each price-setter adjusts his or her price fully to changes in m at the earliest opportunity. If ϕ exceeds 1, λ is negative, and so p moves by more than m in the period after the shock, and thereafter the adjustment toward the long-run equilibrium is oscillatory.

Lag Operators

A different, more general approach to solving the model is to use lag operators. The lag operator, which we denote by L, is a function that lags variables. That is, the lag operator applied to any variable gives the previous period's value of the variable: $Lz_t = z_{t-1}$.

To see the usefulness of lag operators, consider our model without the restriction that m follows a random walk. Equation (6.60) continues to hold. If we proceed analogously to the derivation of (6.62), but without imposing $E_t m_{t+1} = m_t$, straightforward algebra yields

$$x_t = A(x_{t-1} + E_t x_{t+1}) + \frac{1 - 2A}{2} m_t + \frac{1 - 2A}{2} E_t m_{t+1}, \qquad (6.75)$$

where A is as before. Note that (6.75) simplifies to (6.62) if $E_t m_{t+1} = m_t$.

The first step is to rewrite this expression using lag operators. x_{t-1} is the lag of x_t: $x_{t-1} = Lx_t$. In addition, if we adopt the rule that L lags the date of an expectational variable but not the date of the expectations, x_t is the lag of $E_t x_{t+1}$: $LE_t x_{t+1} = E_t x_t = x_t$.[14] Equivalently, using L^{-1} to denote the inverse lag function, $E_t x_{t+1} = L^{-1} x_t$. Similarly, $E_t m_{t+1} = L^{-1} m_t$. Thus we can rewrite (6.75) as

---

[14]Since $E_t x_{t-1} = x_{t-1}$ and $E_t m_t = m_t$, we can think of all the variables in (6.75) as being expectations as of t. Thus in the analysis that follows, the lag operator should always be interpreted as keeping all variables as expectations as of t. The *backshift operator*, B, is used to denote the function that lags both the date of the variable and the date of the expectations. Thus, for example, $BE_t x_{t+1} = E_{t-1} x_t$. Whether the lag operator or the backshift operator is more useful depends on the application; in the present case it is the lag operator.

$$x_t = A(Lx_t + L^{-1}x_t) + \frac{1 - 2A}{2}m_t + \frac{1 - 2A}{2}L^{-1}m_t, \tag{6.76}$$

or

$$(I - AL - AL^{-1})x_t = \frac{1 - 2A}{2}(I + L^{-1})m_t. \tag{6.77}$$

Here I is the identity operator (so $Iz_t = z_t$ for any z). Thus $(I + L^{-1})m_t$ is shorthand for $m_t + L^{-1}m_t$, and $(I - AL - AL^{-1})x_t$ is shorthand for $x_t - Ax_{t-1} - AE_tx_{t+1}$.

Now observe that we can "factor" $(I - AL - AL^{-1})$ as $(I - \lambda L^{-1})(I - \lambda L)(A/\lambda)$, where λ is again given by (6.70). Thus we have

$$(I - \lambda L^{-1})(I - \lambda L)x_t = \frac{\lambda}{A}\frac{1 - 2A}{2}(I + L^{-1})m_t. \tag{6.78}$$

This formulation of "multiplying" expressions involving the lag operator should be interpreted in the natural way: $(I - \lambda L^{-1})(I - \lambda L)x_t$ is shorthand for $(I - \lambda L)x_t$ minus λ times the inverse lag operator applied to $(I - \lambda L)x_t$, and thus equals $(x_t - \lambda Lx_t) - (\lambda L^{-1}x_t - \lambda^2 x_t)$. Simple algebra and the definition of λ can be used to verify that (6.78) and (6.77) are equivalent.

As before, to solve the model we need to eliminate the term involving the expectation of the future value of an endogenous variable. In (6.78), E_tx_{t+1} appears (implicitly) on the left-hand side because of the $(I - \lambda L^{-1})$ term. It is thus natural to "divide" both sides by $(I - \lambda L^{-1})$. That is, consider applying the operator $I + \lambda L^{-1} + \lambda^2 L^{-2} + \lambda^3 L^{-3} + \cdots$ to both sides of (6.78). $I + \lambda L^{-1} + \lambda^2 L^{-2} + \cdots$ times $I - \lambda L^{-1}$ is simply I; thus the left-hand side is $(I - \lambda L)x_t$. And $I + \lambda L^{-1} + \lambda^2 L^{-2} + \cdots$ times $I + L^{-1}$ is $I + (1 + \lambda)L^{-1} + (1 + \lambda)\lambda L^{-2} + (1 + \lambda)\lambda^2 L^{-3} + \cdots$.[15] Thus (6.78) becomes

$$(I - \lambda L)x_t = \frac{\lambda}{A}\frac{1 - 2A}{2}[I + (1 + \lambda)L^{-1} + (1 + \lambda)\lambda L^{-2} + (1 + \lambda)\lambda^2 L^{-3} + \cdots]m_t. \tag{6.79}$$

Rewriting this expression without lag operators yields

$$x_t = \lambda x_{t-1} + \frac{\lambda}{A}\frac{1 - 2A}{2}[m_t + (1 + \lambda)(E_t m_{t+1} + \lambda E_t m_{t+2} + \lambda^2 E_t m_{t+3} + \cdots)]. \tag{6.80}$$

Expression (6.80) characterizes the behavior of newly set prices in terms of the exogenous money supply process. To find the behavior of the

---

[15]Since the operator $I + \lambda L^{-1} + \lambda^2 L^{-2} + \cdots$ is an infinite sum, this requires that $\lim_{n \to \infty}(I + \lambda L^{-1} + \lambda^2 L^{-2} + \cdots + \lambda^n L^{-n})(I + L^{-1})m_t$ exists. This requires that $\lambda^n L^{-(n+1)}m_t$ (which equals $\lambda^n E_t m_{t+n+1}$) converges to zero. For the case where $\lambda = \lambda_1$ (so $|\lambda| < 1$) and where m is a random walk, this condition is satisfied.

aggregate price level and output, we only have to substitute this expression into the expressions for p $(p_t = (x_t + x_{t-1})/2)$ and y $(y_t = m_t - p_t)$.

In the special case when m is a random walk, all of the $E_t m_{t+i}$'s are equal to m_t. In this case, (6.80) simplifies to

$$x_t = \lambda x_{t-1} + \frac{\lambda}{A} \frac{1 - 2A}{2} \left(1 + \frac{1 + \lambda}{1 - \lambda}\right) m_t. \tag{6.81}$$

It is straightforward to show that expression (6.68), $A + A\lambda^2 = A$, implies that equation (6.81) reduces to equation (6.65), $x_t = \lambda x_{t-1} + (1 - \lambda)m_t$. Thus when m is a random walk, we obtain the same result as before. But we have also solved the model for a general process for m.

Although this use of lag operators may seem mysterious, in fact it is no more than a compact way of carrying out perfectly standard manipulations. We could have first derived (6.77) (expressed without using lag operators) by simple algebra. We could then have noted that since (6.77) holds at each date, it must be the case that

$$E_t x_{t+k} - AE_t x_{t+k-1} - AE_t x_{t+k+1} = \frac{1 - 2A}{2}(E_t m_{t+k} + E_t m_{t+k+1}) \tag{6.82}$$

for all $k \geq 0$.[16] Since the left- and right-hand sides of (6.82) are equal, it must be the case that the left-hand side for $k = 0$ plus λ times the left-hand side for $k = 1$ plus λ^2 times the left-hand side for $k = 2$ and so on equals the right-hand side for $k = 0$ plus λ times the right-hand side for $k = 1$ plus λ^2 times the right-hand side for $k = 2$ and so on. Computing these two expressions yields (6.80). Thus lag operators are not essential; they serve merely to simplify the notation and to suggest ways of proceeding that might otherwise be missed.[17]

The Taylor Model and Inflation Inertia

The solution of the Taylor model for the case where the process followed by aggregate demand need not be a random walk can be used to discuss one of the model's main limitations. As described in Chapter 5, modern Keynesian specifications of the output-inflation tradeoff assume that inflation exhibits inertia—that is, that aggregate demand policies can reduce inflation only at the cost of a period of low output and high unemployment. Such inflation inertia is central to Keynesian accounts of output behavior during many periods of disinflation, such as in the United States in the early 1980s. As

---

[16]The reason that we cannot assume that (6.82) holds for $k < 0$ is that the law of iterated projections does not apply backward: the expectation today of the expectation at some date *in the past* of a variable need not equal the expectation today of the variable.

[17]For a more thorough introduction to lag operators and their uses, see Sargent (1987a, Chapter 9).

discussed above, the Taylor model exhibits price-level inertia: the price level adjusts fully to a monetary shock only after a sustained departure of output from its normal level. As a result, it is often claimed that the Taylor model accounts for inflation inertia.

Ball (1994a) demonstrates, however, that this claim is incorrect. To see why, consider a Taylor economy with steady inflation and output equal to its flexible-price value, and consider two possible changes in policy. In the first, there is a one-time downward adjustment in the path of money; that is, money growth is low for one period but then returns to its usual value. In the second, the shift to lower money growth is permanent.

Equation (6.80) shows that the prices that individuals set depend on the entire expected future path of money. The permanent fall in money growth leads to much larger reductions in the expected future values of the money stock than does the one-time shift. As a result, the permanent change in money growth has a much larger effect on newly set prices than does the one-time reduction, and hence a much smaller short-run impact on output, $m - p$.

In fact, Ball, using a continuous-time version of the model, establishes the following result. Consider a permanent reduction in money growth achieved by reducing money growth linearly over an interval equal to the length of time between a representative individual's price changes; that is, if the initial and final money growth rates are g_0 and g_1, if prices are in effect for intervals of length τ, and if the reduction begins at time t_0, then money growth at t is $g_0 - [(t - t_0)/\tau](g_0 - g_1)$ for $t_0 \le t \le t_0 + \tau$. Ball shows that such a policy, instead of causing a recession, causes output to rise above its normal level. Thus the fact that price (and wage) changes are staggered does not account for the difficulty of reducing inflation.[18]

6.9 The Caplin–Spulber Model

The Fischer and Taylor models assume that the timing of price changes is determined solely by the passage of time. Although this is a good approximation for some prices (such as wages set by union contracts, wages that are adjusted annually, and prices in some catalogues), it is not a good description of others. Many retail stores, for example, can adjust the timing of their price changes fairly freely in response to economic developments. It is therefore natural to analyze the consequences of such state-dependent pricing. Our final model of staggered price changes, the Caplin–Spulber model, provides an example of such an analysis.

The model is set in continuous time. Each individual's optimal price at time t, $p_i^*(t)$, is again $\phi m(t) + (1 - \phi)p(t)$. Money growth is always positive; as we will see, this causes p_i^* to always be increasing. The key assumption of the model is that price-setters follow an Ss pricing policy. Specifically,

---

[18]See Problem 6.11 for a simple version of this result.

whenever a price-setter adjusts his or her price, he or she sets it so that the difference between the actual price and the optimal price at that time, $p_i - p_i^*$, equals some target level, S. The individual then keeps the nominal price fixed until money growth has raised p_i^* sufficiently that $p_i - p_i^*$ has fallen to some trigger level, s. He or she then resets $p_i - p_i^*$ to S, and the process begins anew.

Such an Ss policy is optimal when inflation is steady, aggregate output is constant, and there is a fixed cost of each nominal price change (Barro, 1972; and Sheshinski and Weiss, 1977). In addition, as Caplin and Spulber describe, it is also optimal in some cases where inflation or output is not constant. And even when it is not fully optimal, it provides a simple and tractable example of state-dependent pricing.

Two technical assumptions complete the model. First, to keep prices from overshooting s and to prevent bunching of the distribution of prices across price-setters, m changes continuously. Second, the initial distribution of $p_i - p_i^*$ across price-setters is uniform between s and S. The remaining assumptions are the same as in the Fischer and Taylor models.

Under these assumptions, money is completely neutral in the aggregate despite the price stickiness at the level of the individual price-setters. To see this, consider an increase in m of amount $\Delta m < S - s$ over some period of time. We want to find the resulting changes in the price level and output, Δp and Δy. Since $p_i^* = (1 - \phi)p + \phi m$, the rise in each price-setter's optimal price is $(1 - \phi)\Delta p + \phi \Delta m$. Price-setters change their prices if $p_i - p_i^*$ falls below s; thus price-setters with initial values of $p_i - p_i^*$ that are less than $s + [(1 - \phi)\Delta p + \phi \Delta m]$ change their prices. Since the initial values of $p_i - p_i^*$ are distributed uniformly between s and S, this means that the fraction of price-setters who change their prices is $[(1 - \phi)\Delta p + \phi \Delta m]/(S - s)$. Each price-setter who changes his or her price does so at the moment when his or her value of $p_i - p_i^*$ reaches s; thus each price increase is of amount $S - s$. Putting all of this together gives us

$$\Delta p = \frac{(1 - \phi)\Delta p + \phi \Delta m}{S - s}(S - s)$$

$$= (1 - \phi)\Delta p + \phi \Delta m.$$

(6.83)

Equation (6.83) implies that $\Delta p = \Delta m$, and thus that $\Delta y = 0$. Thus the change in money has no impact on aggregate output.[19]

To understand the intuition for this result, consider the case where $\phi = 1$, so that $p_i - p_i^*$ is just $p_i - m$. Now think of arranging the points in the interval $(s, S]$ around the circumference of a circle; this is shown in

---

[19]In addition, this result helps to justify the assumption that the initial distribution of $p_i - p_i^*$ is uniform between s and S. $p_i - p_i^*$ for each price-setter equals each value between s and S once during the interval between any two price changes; thus there is no reason to expect a concentration anywhere within the interval. Indeed, Caplin and Spulber show that under simple assumptions, a given price-setter's $p_i - p_i^*$ is equally likely to take on any value between s and S.

FIGURE 6.2   The effects of an increase in the money stock in the Caplin–Spulber model

Figure 6.2. Initially, price-setters are distributed uniformly around the circle. Now notice that an increase in m of Δm moves every price-setter around the circle counterclockwise by a distance Δm. To see this, consider first a price-setter, such as the one at Point A, with an initial value of $p_i - p_i^*$ that is greater than $s + \Delta m$. Such a price-setter does not raise his or her price when m rises by Δm; since p_i^* rises by Δm, $p_i - p_i^*$ therefore falls by Δm. Thus the price-setter moves counterclockwise by amount Δm. Now consider a price-setter, such as the one at Point C, with an initial value of $p_i - p_i^*$ that is of the form $s + k$, where k is less than Δm. For this price-setter, $p_i - p_i^*$ falls until m has risen by k; thus he or she is moving counterclockwise around the circle. At the instant that the increase in m reaches k, p_i jumps by $S - s$, and so $p_i - p_i^*$ jumps from s to S. In terms of the diagram, however, this is just an infinitesimal move around the circle. As m continues to rise, the price-setter does not change his or her price further, and thus continues to travel around the circle. Thus the total distance such a price-setter travels is also Δm.

Since the price-setters are initially distributed uniformly around the circle, and since each one moves the same distance, they end up still uniformly distributed. Thus the distribution of $p_i - m$ is unchanged. Since p is the average of the p_i's, this implies that $p - m$ is also unchanged.

The reason for the sharp difference between the results of this model and those of the Taylor model is the nature of the price-adjustment policies. In the Caplin–Spulber model, the number of price-setters changing their prices at any time is larger when the money supply is increasing more rapidly; given the specific assumptions that Caplin and Spulber make, this has the effect that the aggregate price level responds fully to changes in m. In the Taylor model, in contrast, the number of price-setters changing their prices at any time is fixed; as a result, the price level does not respond fully to changes in m.

The neutrality of money in the Caplin–Spulber model is not a robust result about settings where fixed costs of changing nominal prices cause the number of price-setters changing prices at any time to be endogenous. If, for example, inflation can be negative as well as positive, or if there are idiosyncratic shocks that sometimes cause price-setters to lower their nominal prices, the resulting extensions of Ss rules generally cause monetary shocks to have real effects (see, for example, Caplin and Leahy, 1991, and Problem 6.12). In addition, the values of S and s may change in response to changes in aggregate demand. If, for example, high money growth today signals high money growth in the future, price-setters widen their Ss bands when there is a positive monetary shock; as a result no price-setters adjust their prices in the short run (since no price-setters are now at the new, lower trigger point s), and so the positive shock raises output (Tsiddon, 1991).[20]

Thus the importance of Caplin and Spulber's model is not for its specific results about the effects of aggregate demand shocks. Rather, the model is important for two reasons. First, it introduces the idea of state-dependent price changes. Second, it demonstrates another reason that the relation between microeconomic and macroeconomic rigidity is complex. The Fischer and Taylor models show that temporary fixity of some prices can have a disproportionate effect on the response of the aggregate price level to aggregate demand disturbances. The Caplin–Spulber model, in contrast, shows that the adjustment of some prices can have a disproportionate effect: a small fraction of price-setters making large price changes can be enough to generate neutrality in the aggregate. Thus together, the Fischer, Taylor, and Caplin–Spulber models show that any complete treatment of price rigidity requires careful attention both to the nature of price-adjustment policies and to how those policies interact to determine the behavior of the aggregate price level.

Part C New Keynesian Economics

6.10 Overview[21]

The Lucas, Fischer, and Taylor models are not fully satisfactory accounts of real effects of aggregate demand disturbances. The models assume the existence of imperfections that agents could overcome easily—imperfect

---

[20]See Caballero and Engel (1991, 1993) for more detailed analyses of these issues.

[21]In places, Sections 6.10–6.12 draw on D. Romer (1993a).

knowledge of the price level in the Lucas model, and infrequent adjustment of prices or wages in the Fischer and Taylor models. Quite accurate information about movements in the price level is easily available, and the cost of much more frequent price or wage adjustments (through indexation or other means) is small. This raises the question of why agents would permit nominal disturbances to lead to substantial fluctuations in output rather than take the small measures needed to largely eliminate the nominal imperfections.

The central idea of much recent research on the real effects of nominal shocks is that this question applies not just to these particular models, but to all candidate sources of nominal imperfections. Individuals are mainly concerned with real prices and quantities: real wages, hours of work, real consumption levels, and the like. Nominal magnitudes matter to them only in ways that are minor and easily overcome. Prices and wages are quoted in nominal terms, but it costs little to change (or index) them. Individuals are not fully informed about the aggregate price level, but they can obtain accurate information at little cost. Debt contracts are usually specified in nominal terms, but they too could be indexed with little difficulty. And individuals hold modest amounts of currency, which is denominated in nominal terms, but they can change their holdings easily. There is no way in which nominal magnitudes are of great direct importance to individuals.

Thus, according to this *new Keynesian* view, if nominal imperfections are important to fluctuations in aggregate activity, it must be that nominal frictions that are small at the microeconomic level somehow have a large effect on the macroeconomy. Much of the recent research on the microeconomic foundations of nominal rigidity is devoted to addressing the question of whether this can plausibly be the case.[22]

For concreteness, most of this section addresses this question for a specific view about the nominal imperfection. In particular, we focus on a static model where firms face a *menu cost* of price adjustment—a small fixed cost of changing a nominal price. (The standard example is the cost incurred by a restaurant in printing new menus—hence the name.) But, as described at the end of Section 6.12, essentially the same issues arise with other views about the barriers to nominal adjustment. In addition, the analysis focuses on the question of whether menu costs can lead to significant nominal stickiness in response to a one-time monetary shock. As a result, the analysis is more successful in achieving the first goal of analyzing microeconomic foundations of incomplete nominal adjustment (namely, characterizing the microeconomic conditions that yield sluggish adjustment) than in achieving the second goal (namely, finding the implications of those conditions for the specifics of price adjustment, and thereby providing guidance for policy).

---

[22]The seminal papers are Mankiw (1985) and Akerlof and Yellen (1985). See also Parkin (1986); Rotemberg (1982, 1987); and Blanchard and Kiyotaki (1987).

Section 6.11 shows that introducing price-setting and menu costs into an economy that is otherwise Walrasian is probably not enough to generate substantial nominal rigidity. Section 6.12 is therefore devoted to the issue of what else is needed for menu costs to have important effects. Section 6.13 considers some relevant empirical work. Finally, Sections 6.14 and 6.15 discuss some extensions and limitations of the theory.

6.11   Are Small Frictions Enough?

General Considerations

Consider an economy of many price-setting firms. Assume that it is initially at its flexible-price equilibrium; that is, each firm's price is such that, if aggregate demand is at its expected level, marginal revenue equals marginal cost. After prices are set, aggregate demand is determined; at this point each firm can change its price by paying a menu cost. For simplicity, prices are assumed to be set afresh at the start of each period. This means that the dynamic pricing issues that are the subject of Part B of this chapter are irrelevant; it also means that if a firm pays the menu cost, it sets its price to the new profit-maximizing level.

Our focus is on the question of when firms change their prices in response to a departure of aggregate demand from its expected level. For concreteness, suppose that demand is less than expected. Since the economy is large, each firm takes the actions of other firms as given. Constant nominal prices are thus an equilibrium if, when all other firms hold their prices fixed, the maximum gain to a representative firm from changing its price is less than the menu cost of price adjustment.[23]

We can analyze this issue using the marginal revenue-marginal cost diagram in Figure 6.3. The economy begins in equilibrium; thus the representative firm is producing at the point where marginal cost equals marginal revenue (Point A in the diagram). A fall in aggregate demand with other prices unchanged reduces aggregate output, and thus shifts inward the demand curve that the firm faces—at a given price, demand for the firm's product is lower. Thus the marginal revenue curve shifts in. If the firm does not change its price, its output is determined by demand at the existing price (Point B). At this level of output, marginal revenue exceeds marginal cost, and so the firm has some incentive to lower its price and raise output.[24]

---

[23]The condition for price adjustment by all firms to be an equilibrium is not simply the reverse of this. As a result, there can be cases when both price adjustment and unchanged prices are equilibria. See Problem 6.15.

[24]The fall in aggregate output is likely to reduce the prevailing wage, and therefore to shift the marginal cost curve down. For simplicity, this effect is not shown in the figure.

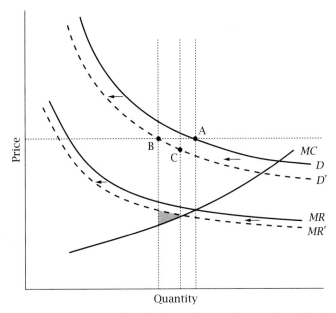

FIGURE 6.3 A representative firm's incentive to change its price in response to a fall in aggregate output (from D. Romer, 1993a)

If the firm changes its price, it produces at the point where marginal cost and marginal revenue are equal (Point C). The area of the shaded triangle in the diagram shows the additional profits to be gained from reducing price and increasing quantity produced. For the firm to be willing to hold its price fixed, the area of the triangle must be small.

The diagram reveals a crucial point: the firm's incentive to reduce its price may be small even if it is harmed greatly by the fall in demand. The firm would prefer to face the original, higher demand curve, but of course it can only choose a point on the new demand curve. This is an example of the aggregate demand externality described in Section 6.6: the representative firm is harmed by the failure of other firms to cut their prices in the face of the fall in the money supply, just as it is harmed in Section 6.6 by a decision by all firms to raise their prices. As a result, the firm may find that the gain from reducing its price is small even if the shift in its demand curve is large. Thus there is no contradiction between the view that recessions have large costs and the hypothesis that they are caused by falls in aggregate demand and small barriers to price adjustment.

It is not possible, however, to proceed further using a purely diagrammatic analysis. To answer the question of whether the firm's incentive to change its price is likely to be more or less than the menu cost for plausible cases, we must turn to a specific model and find the incentive for price adjustment for reasonable parameter values.

A Quantitative Example

As a baseline case, we use the model of imperfect competition of Section 6.6. Recall that in that model, firm i's real profit income equals the quantity sold, $Y(P_i/P)^{-\eta}$, times price minus cost, $(P_i/P) - (W/P)$ (see [6.37]). In addition, labor-market equilibrium requires that the real wage equals $Y^{1/\nu}$, where $\nu \equiv 1/(\gamma - 1)$ is the elasticity of labor supply (see [6.43]). Thus,

$$
\pi_i = Y \left(\frac{P_i}{P}\right)^{-\eta} \left(\frac{P_i}{P} - Y^{1/\nu}\right)
$$

$$
= \frac{M}{P} \left(\frac{P_i}{P}\right)^{1-\eta} - \left(\frac{M}{P}\right)^{(1+\nu)/\nu} \left(\frac{P_i}{P}\right)^{-\eta},
$$

(6.84)

where the second line uses the fact that $Y = M/P$. We know from our earlier analysis of this model that the profit-maximizing real price in the absence of the menu cost is $\eta/(\eta - 1)$ times marginal cost, or $[\eta/(\eta-1)](M/P)^{1/\nu}$ (see [6.44]). It follows that the equilibrium when prices are flexible occurs when $[\eta/(\eta - 1)](M/P)^{1/\nu} = 1$, or $M/P = [(\eta - 1)/\eta]^\nu$ (see [6.46]).

We want to find the condition for unchanged nominal prices to be a Nash equilibrium in the face of a departure of M from its expected value. That is, we want to find the condition under which, if all other firms do not adjust their prices, a representative firm will not want to pay the menu cost and adjust its own price. This condition is $\pi_{\text{ADJ}} - \pi_{\text{FIXED}} < Z$, where π_{ADJ} is the representative firm's profits if it adjusts its price to the new profit-maximizing level and other firms do not, π_{FIXED} is its profits if no prices change, and Z is the menu cost. Thus we need to find these two profit levels.

Before proceeding, it is useful to have an idea of what value of the menu cost is plausible. The flexible-price equilibrium is symmetric, with each firm's real revenue equal to aggregate output, Y. A menu cost that exceeds 1% of this quantity seems highly implausible: for most firms, the cost of a policy of much more frequent price adjustment (for example by simple indexation schemes) are almost surely much less than 1% of revenue. A menu cost of a few hundredths of a percent of revenue, on the other hand, does not seem unreasonable.

We can now turn to the profit calculations. Initially all firms are charging the same price, and by assumption, other firms do not change their prices. Thus if firm i does not adjust its price, we have $P_i = P$. Substituting this into (6.84) yields

$$
\pi_{\text{FIXED}} = \frac{M}{P} - \left(\frac{M}{P}\right)^{(1+\nu)/\nu}.
$$

(6.85)

If the firm does adjust its price, it sets it to the profit-maximizing value, $[\eta/(\eta - 1)](M/P)^{1/\nu}$. Substituting this into (6.84) yields

$$\pi_{\text{ADJ}} = \frac{M}{P}\left(\frac{\eta}{\eta-1}\right)^{1-\eta}\left(\frac{M}{P}\right)^{(1-\eta)/v} - \left(\frac{M}{P}\right)^{(1+v)/v}\left(\frac{\eta}{\eta-1}\right)^{-\eta}\left(\frac{M}{P}\right)^{-\eta/v}$$

(6.86)

$$= \frac{1}{\eta-1}\left(\frac{\eta}{\eta-1}\right)^{-\eta}\left(\frac{M}{P}\right)^{(1+v-\eta)/v}.$$

It is straightforward to check that π_{ADJ} and π_{FIXED} are equal when M/P equals its flexible-price equilibrium value, and that otherwise π_{ADJ} is greater than π_{FIXED}.

To find the firm's incentive to change its price, we need values for η and v. Since labor supply appears relatively inelastic, consider $v = 0.1$. Suppose also that $\eta = 5$, which implies that price is 1.25 times marginal cost. These parameter values imply that the flexible-price level of output is $Y^* = [(\eta-1)/\eta]^v \simeq 0.978$. Now consider a firm's incentive to adjust its price in response to a 3% fall in M with other prices unchanged. Substituting $v = 0.1$, $\eta = 5$, and $Y = 0.97Y^*$ into (6.85) and (6.86) yields $\pi_{\text{ADJ}} - \pi_{\text{FIXED}} \simeq 0.253$.

Since Y^* is about 1, this calculation implies that the representative firm's incentive to pay the menu cost in response to a 3% change in output is about a quarter of revenue. No plausible cost of price adjustment can prevent firms from changing their prices in the face of this incentive. Thus, in this setting firms adjust their prices in the face of all but the smallest shocks, and money is virtually neutral.[25]

The source of the difficulty lies in the labor market. The labor market clears, and labor supply is relatively inelastic. Thus, as in Case 2 of Section 5.4, the real wage falls considerably when aggregate output falls. Producers' costs are therefore very low, and thus they have a strong incentive to cut their prices and raise output. But this means that unchanged nominal prices cannot be an equilibrium.[26]

6.12   The Need for Real Rigidity

General Considerations

Consider again a firm that is deciding whether to change its price in the face of a fall in aggregate demand with other prices held fixed. Figure 6.4 shows

---

[25] Although $\pi_{\text{ADJ}} - \pi_{\text{FIXED}}$ is sensitive to the values of v and η, there are no remotely reasonable values that imply that the incentive for price adjustment is small. Consider, for example, $\eta = 3$ (implying a markup of 50%) and $v = 1/3$. Even with these extreme values, the incentive to pay the menu cost is 0.8% of the flexible-price level of revenue for a 3% fall in output, and 2.4% for a 5% fall. Even though these incentives are much smaller than those in the baseline calculation, they still swamp any plausible cost of changing prices.

[26] It is not possible to avoid the problem by assuming that the cost of adjustment applies to wages rather than prices. In this case, the incentive to cut prices would indeed be low. But the incentive to cut wages would be high: firms (which could greatly reduce their labor costs) and workers (who could greatly increase their hours of work) would bid wages down.

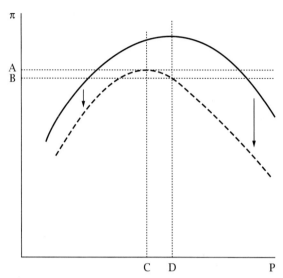

FIGURE 6.4 The impact of a fall in aggregate output on the representative firm's profits as a function of its price

the firm's profits as a function of its price. The fall in aggregate output affects this function in two ways. First, since the demand curve for the firm's good falls, the profit function shifts down. As described above, the firm cannot undo this change. Second, the firm's profit-maximizing price is less than before.[27] This the firm can do something about. If the firm does not pay the menu cost, its price remains the same, and so it is not charging the new profit-maximizing price. If the firm pays the menu cost, on the other hand, it can go to the peak of the profit function.

The firm's incentive to adjust its price is thus given by the distance AB in the diagram. This distance depends on two factors: the difference between the old and new profit-maximizing prices, and the curvature of the profit function. We consider each in turn.

Since other firms' prices are unchanged, a change in the firm's nominal price is also a change in its real price. In addition, the shift in aggregate demand with other prices held fixed changes aggregate output. Thus the difference between the firm's new and old profit-maximizing prices (distance CD in the figure) is determined by how the profit-maximizing real price depends on aggregate output—that is, by the degree of real rigidity. Greater real rigidity, holding the curvature of the profit function fixed, reduces the firm's incentive to adjust its price in response to an aggregate

---

[27]This corresponds to the assumption that the profit-maximizing relative price is increasing in aggregate output; that is, it corresponds to the assumption that $\phi > 0$ in the pricing equation, (6.45). As described in Section 6.6, this condition is needed for the equilibrium with flexible prices to be stable.

demand movement if other firms do not change their prices. The intuition is the same as the intuition for why greater real rigidity increases the real effects of nominal shocks in the Fischer and Taylor models: greater real rigidity means that firms do not want their prices to depart greatly from others' prices.

The curvature of the profit function determines the cost of a given departure of price from the profit-maximizing level. The less sensitive the profit function is to departures from the optimum, the smaller the incentive for price adjustment (for a given ϕ), and so the larger the range of shocks for which nonadjustment of prices is an equilibrium. Thus, in general terms what is needed for small costs of price adjustment to generate substantial nominal rigidity is some combination of real rigidity and of insensitivity of the profit function.

Seen in terms of real rigidity and insensitivity of the profit function, it is easy to see why the incentive for price adjustment in our baseline calculation is so large: there is immense "real flexibility" rather than real rigidity. Since the profit-maximizing real price is $[\eta/(\eta-1)]Y^{1/\nu}$, its elasticity with respect to output is $1/\nu$. If the elasticity of labor supply, ν, is small, the elasticity of $(P_i/P)^*$ with respect to Y is therefore large. A value of ν of 0.1, for example, implies an elasticity of $(P_i/P)^*$ with respect to Y of 10.

A well-known analogy may help to make clear how the combination of menu costs with either real rigidity or insensitivity of the profit function (or both) can lead to considerable nominal stickiness: monetary disturbances may have real effects for the same reasons that the switch to daylight saving time does.[28] The resetting of clocks is a purely nominal change—it simply alters the labels assigned to different times of day. But the change is associated with changes in real schedules—that is, the times of various activities relative to the sun. And in contrast to the case of monetary disturbances, there can be no doubt that the switch to daylight saving time is the cause of the changes in real schedules.

If there were literally no cost to changing nominal schedules and communicating this information to others, daylight saving time would just cause everyone to do this and would have no effect on real schedules. Thus for it to change real schedules, there must be some cost to changing nominal schedules. These costs are analogous to the menu costs of changing prices; and like the menu costs, they do not appear to be large. The reason that these small costs cause the switch to have real effects appears to be that individuals and businesses are generally much more concerned about their schedules relative to one another's than about their schedules relative to the sun. Thus, given that others do not change their scheduled hours, each individual does not wish to incur the cost of changing his or hers. This is analogous to the effects of real rigidity in the price-setting case. Finally, the

---

[28]This analogy is originally due to Friedman (1953, p. 173), in the context of exchange rates.

less concerned that individuals are about precisely what their schedules are, the less willing they are to incur the cost of changing them; this is analogous to the insensitivity of the profit function in the price-setting case.

Specific Sources of Real Rigidity

To see what types of factors can give rise to real rigidity and insensitivity of the profit function, return to the marginal revenue-marginal cost framework of Figure 6.3. On the cost side, the smaller the fall in marginal cost is as a result of the fall in aggregate output, the smaller the firm's incentive to cut its price and increase its output, and thus the more likely nominal rigidity is to be an equilibrium. This can occur in two ways. First, a smaller downward shift of the profit function in response to a fall in aggregate output implies a smaller decline in the firm's profit-maximizing price—that is, it corresponds to greater real rigidity.[29] Second, a flatter marginal cost curve implies both greater insensitivity of the profit function and greater real rigidity.

On the revenue side, the larger the fall in marginal revenue is when aggregate output falls, the smaller the gap between marginal revenue and marginal cost at the representative firm's initial price, and so the smaller the incentive for price adjustment. Specifically, a larger leftward shift of the marginal revenue curve corresponds to increased real rigidity, and so reduces the incentive for price adjustment. In addition, a steeper marginal revenue curve (for a given leftward shift) also increases the degree of real rigidity, and so again acts to reduce the incentive for adjustment.

Since there are many potential determinants of the cyclical behavior of marginal cost and marginal revenue, the hypothesis that small frictions in price adjustment result in considerable nominal rigidity is not tied to any specific view of the structure of the economy. On the cost side, factors that may make costs much less procyclical than in our baseline case include: thick-market externalities that make purchasing inputs and selling final products easier in times of high economic activity (for example, Diamond, 1982); other external economies of scale or agglomeration economies that make costs lower when other firms are producing more (for example, Hall, 1991; Caballero and Lyons, 1992; and Cooper and Haltiwanger, 1993); capital-market imperfections that make the cost of finance higher in recessions, when firms' cash flow and credit worthiness are lower (for example, Bernanke and Gertler, 1989, and Kiyotaki and Moore, 1995); and input-output linkages among firms that cause firms to face constant costs for their inputs when prices are sticky (Basu, 1993). On the revenue side, some potentially important factors are: thick-market effects that make it easier for firms to disseminate information and for consumers to acquire it when aggregate output is high, and thus make demand more elastic (Warner and

---

[29]Recall that for simplicity the marginal cost curve was not shown as shifting down in Figure 6.3 (see n. 24). There is no reason to expect it to stay fixed in general, however.

Barsky, 1995); imperfect information that makes existing customers more responsive to price increases than prospective new customers are to price decreases, and thus makes the marginal revenue curve steeper (for example, Stiglitz, 1979; Woglom, 1982; and Ball and D. Romer, 1990); capital-market imperfections that cause liquidity-constrained firms to raise prices during recessions (for example, Greenwald, Stiglitz, and Weiss, 1984, and Chevalier and Scharfstein, 1994); and the fact that higher sales increase the incentive for firms to deviate from patterns of implicit collusion by cutting their prices (for example, Rotemberg and Woodford, 1991, 1992).

Although the new Keynesian view of fluctuations does not depend on any specific source of real rigidity and insensitivity of the profit function, it almost surely requires that the cost of labor not fall nearly as dramatically as it would if labor supply is relatively inelastic and workers are on their labor supply curves. If these conditions hold, the incentive for price adjustment created by the huge swings in the cost of labor almost surely swamp the effects of other factors.

At a general level, real wages might not be highly procyclical for two reasons. First, short-run aggregate labor supply could be relatively elastic (as a result of intertemporal substitution, for example). But as described in Section 4.10, this view of the labor market has had limited empirical success.

Second, imperfections in the labor market—such as those that are the subject of Chapter 10—can cause workers to be off their labor supply curves over at least part of the business cycle. In the efficiency-wage, contracting, and search and matching models presented there, the cost of labor to firms may differ from the opportunity cost of time to workers. The models thus break the link between the elasticity of labor supply and the response of the cost of labor to demand disturbances. Indeed, Chapter 10 presents several models that imply relatively acyclical wages (or relatively acyclical costs of labor to firms) despite inelastic labor supply. If imperfections like these cause real wages to respond little to demand disturbances, they greatly reduce firms' incentive to vary their prices in response to these demand shifts.[30]

A Second Quantitative Example

To see the potential importance of labor-market imperfections, consider the following variation (from Ball and Romer, 1990) on our example of firms'

---

[30]In addition, the possibility of substantial real rigidities in the labor market suggests that small barriers to nominal adjustment may cause nominal disturbances to have substantial real effects through stickiness of nominal wages rather than of nominal prices. If wages display substantial real rigidity, a demand-driven expansion leads only to small increases in optimal real wages. As a result, just as small frictions in nominal price adjustment can lead to substantial nominal price rigidity, small frictions in nominal wage adjustment can lead to substantial nominal wage rigidity.

incentives to change prices in response to a monetary disturbance. Suppose that for some reason firms pay wages above the market-clearing level, and that the elasticity of the real wage with respect to aggregate output is β:

$$\frac{W}{P} = AY^\beta. \tag{6.87}$$

Thus, as in Case 3 of Section 5.4, the cyclical behavior of the real wage is determined by a "real-wage function" rather than by the elasticity of labor supply.

With the remainder of the model as before, firm i's profits are given by (6.37) with real wage equal to AY^β rather than $Y^{1/\nu}$. It follows that

$$\pi_i = \frac{M}{P}\left(\frac{P_i}{P}\right)^{1-\eta} - A\left(\frac{M}{P}\right)^{1+\beta}\left(\frac{P_i}{P}\right)^{-\eta} \tag{6.88}$$

(compare [6.84]). The profit-maximizing real price is again $\eta/(\eta-1)$ times the real wage; thus it is $[\eta/(\eta-1)]AY^\beta$. It follows that equilibrium output under flexible prices is $[(\eta-1)/\eta A]^{1/\beta}$. Assume that A and β are such that labor supply at the flexible-price equilibrium exceeds the amount of labor employed by firms.[31]

Now consider the representative firm's incentive to change its price in the face of a decline in aggregate demand, again assuming that other firms do not change their prices. If the firm does not change its price, then $P_i/P = 1$, and so (6.88) implies

$$\pi_{\text{FIXED}} = \frac{M}{P} - A\left(\frac{M}{P}\right)^{1+\beta}. \tag{6.89}$$

If the firm changes its price, it charges a real price of $[\eta/(\eta-1)]AY^\beta$. Substituting this expression into (6.88) yields

$$\begin{aligned}
\pi_{\text{ADJ}} &= \frac{M}{P}\left(\frac{\eta}{\eta-1}\right)^{1-\eta} A^{1-\eta}\left(\frac{M}{P}\right)^{\beta(1-\eta)} \\
&\quad - A\left(\frac{M}{P}\right)^{1+\beta}\left(\frac{\eta}{\eta-1}\right)^{-\eta} A^{-\eta}\left(\frac{M}{P}\right)^{-\beta\eta} \\
&= A^{1-\eta}\frac{1}{\eta-1}\left(\frac{\eta}{\eta-1}\right)^{-\eta}\left(\frac{M}{P}\right)^{1+\beta-\beta\eta}.
\end{aligned} \tag{6.90}$$

---

[31]When prices are flexible, each firm sets its relative price to $[\eta/(\eta-1)](W/P)$. Thus the real wage at the flexible-price equilibrium must be $(\eta-1)/\eta$, and so labor supply is $[(\eta-1)/\eta]^\nu$. Thus the condition that labor supply exceeds demand at the flexible-price equilibrium is $[(\eta-1)/\eta]^\nu > [(\eta-1)/\eta A]^{1/\beta}$.

If β, the parameter that governs the cyclical behavior of the real wage, is small, the effect of this change in the model on the incentive for price adjustment is dramatic. Suppose, for example, that $\beta = 0.1$, that $\eta = 5$ as before, and that $A = 0.806$ (so that the flexible-price level of Y is 0.928, or about 95% of its level with $\nu = 0.1$ and a clearing labor market). Substituting these parameter values into (6.89) and (6.90) implies that if the money stock falls by 3% and firms do not adjust their prices, the representative firm's gain from changing its price is approximately 0.0000168, or about 0.0018% of the revenue it gets at the flexible-price equilibrium. Even if M falls by 5% and $\beta = 0.25$ (and A is changed to 0.815, so that the flexible-price level of Y continues to be 0.928), the incentive for price adjustment is only 0.03% of the firm's flexible-price revenue. Thus *if* the labor market is such that an equation like (6.87) with a relatively small value of β correctly describes the cyclical behavior of labor costs, and if the remaining features of the model are not greatly misleading, small barriers to nominal price adjustment can give rise to substantial nominal rigidity.

Other Frictions

The barriers to complete adjustment to nominal disturbances need not be in price and wage adjustment. For example, one recent line of research examines the consequences of the fact that debt contracts are often not indexed; that is, loan agreements and bonds generally specify streams of nominal payments the borrower must make to the lender. Nominal disturbances therefore cause redistributions. A negative nominal shock, for example, increases borrowers' real debt burdens. If capital markets are perfect, such redistributions do not have any important real effects; investments continue to be made if the risk-adjusted expected payoffs exceed the costs, regardless of whether the funds for the projects can be supplied by the entrepreneurs or have to be raised in capital markets.

But actual capital markets may not be perfect. Asymmetric information between lenders and borrowers, coupled with risk aversion or limited liability, generally makes the first-best outcome unattainable. The presence of risk aversion or limited liability means that the borrowers usually do not bear the full cost of very bad outcomes of their investment projects. But if borrowers are partially insured against bad outcomes, they have an incentive to take advantage of the asymmetric information between themselves and lenders by borrowing only if they know their projects are risky (adverse selection) or by taking risks on the projects they undertake (moral hazard). These difficulties cause lenders to charge a premium on their loans. As a result, there is generally less investment, and less efficient investment, when it is financed externally than when it is funded by the entrepreneurs' own funds.

In such settings, redistributions matter: transferring wealth from entrepreneurs to lenders makes the entrepreneurs more dependent on external finance, and thus reduces investment. Thus if debt contracts are not indexed, nominal disturbances are likely to have real effects. Indeed, price and wage flexibility can increase the distributional effects of nominal shocks, and thus potentially increase their real effects. This channel for real effects of nominal shocks is known as *debt-deflation*.[32]

This view of the nature of nominal imperfections must confront the same issues that face theories based on frictions in nominal price adjustment. For example, when a decline in the money stock redistributes wealth from firms to lenders because of nonindexation of debt contracts, firms' marginal cost curves shift up. For reasonable cases, this upward shift is not large. If marginal cost falls greatly when aggregate output falls (because real wages decline sharply, for example) and marginal revenue does not, the modest increase in costs caused by the fall in the money stock leads to only a small decline in aggregate output.[33] If marginal cost changes little and marginal revenue is very responsive to aggregate output, on the other hand, the small change in costs leads to large changes in output. Thus the same kinds of forces needed to cause small barriers to price adjustment to lead to large fluctuations in aggregate output are also needed for small costs to indexing debt contracts to have this effect.

This discussion suggests an alternative interpretation of the Lucas model. Recall that Lucas's model is based on the assumptions of imperfect information about the aggregate price level and considerable intertemporal substitution in labor supply, and that neither of these assumptions appear to be good first approximations. The discussion here, however, suggests that Lucas's central results do not rest on these assumptions. Suppose that price-setters choose not to acquire current information about the price level, and that the behavior of the economy is therefore described by the Lucas model. In such a situation, price-setters' incentive to obtain information about the price level, and to adjust their pricing and output decisions accordingly, is determined by the same considerations that determine their incentive to adjust their nominal prices in menu-cost models. As we have seen, there are many possible mechanisms other than intertemporal substitution that can cause this incentive to be small. Thus neither unavail-

---

[32]The term is due to Irving Fisher (1933). For a modern treatment, see Bernanke and Gertler (1989). Gertler (1988) surveys work in this area. Section 8.7 develops a model of investment and the effects of changes in entrepreneurs' wealth when financial markets are imperfect.

[33]If a small decline in borrowers' wealth causes a discontinuous drop in their ability to borrow, the increase in costs is no longer small (see, for example, Mankiw, 1986a, and Bernanke and Gertler, 1990). But it is not clear why a small fall in borrowers' wealth would induce lenders to stop lending if at the same time labor costs (for example) had dropped sharply. In addition, it is not clear why small redistributions would have large effects on the number of entrepreneurs who can borrow.

ability of information about the price level nor intertemporal substitution is essential to the mechanism identified by Lucas. The friction in nominal adjustment may therefore be a small inconvenience or cost of obtaining information about the price level (or of adjusting one's pricing decisions in light of that information). Whether this friction is important in practice remains an open question.[34]

6.13 Empirical Applications

The Average Inflation Rate and the Output-Inflation Tradeoff

Ball, Mankiw, and D. Romer (1988) point out that if the real effects of aggregate demand movements arise from frictions in price adjustment, then the average rate of inflation is likely to influence the size of those effects. Their argument is straightforward. The higher average inflation is, the more often firms must adjust their prices to keep up with the price level. This implies that when there is an aggregate demand disturbance, firms can pass it into prices more quickly. Thus its real effects are smaller.

Ball, Mankiw, and Romer's basic test of this prediction is analogous to Lucas's test of his prediction that the variance of aggregate demand should influence the real effects of demand shocks. Following Lucas, they first estimate the real impact of aggregate demand shifts (denoted τ_i) in a large number of countries using the specification in equation (6.34). They then ask how those estimated impacts are related to average inflation.

Figure 6.5 shows a scatterplot of the estimated τ_i's against average inflation for the 43 countries considered by Ball, Mankiw, and Romer. The figure suggests a negative relationship. The corresponding regression (with a quadratic term included to account for the nonlinearity apparent in the figure) is

$$\tau_i = 0.600 - 4.835\overline{\pi}_i + 7.118\overline{\pi}_i^2$$
$$(0.079) \quad (1.074) \quad (2.088)$$

$$\overline{R}^2 = 0.388, \qquad \text{s.e.e.} = 0.215,$$

(6.91)

---

[34]Another recent line of work investigates the consequences of the fact that at any given time, not all agents are adjusting their holdings of high-powered money. Thus when the monetary authority changes the quantity of high-powered money, it cannot achieve a proportionate change in everyone's holdings. As a result, a change in the money stock generally affects real money balances even if all prices and wages are perfectly flexible. Under appropriate conditions (such as an impact of real balances on consumption), this change in real balances affects the real interest rate. And if the real interest rate affects aggregate supply, the result is that aggregate output changes. See Grossman and Weiss (1983); Rotemberg (1984); Lucas (1990b); Fuerst (1992); and Christiano and Eichenbaum (1992b).

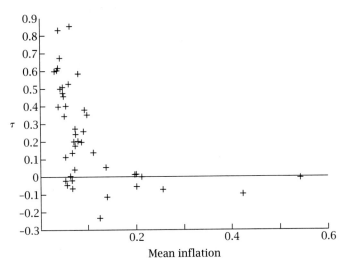

FIGURE 6.5   The output-inflation tradeoff and average inflation (from Ball, Mankiw, and Romer, 1988)

where $\bar{\pi}_i$ is average inflation in country i and the numbers in parentheses are standard errors. The point estimates imply that $\partial\tau/\partial\bar{\pi} = 4.835 - 2(7.118)\bar{\pi}$, which is negative for $\bar{\pi} < 4.835/[2(7.118)] \simeq 34\%$. Thus there is a statistically significant negative relationship between average inflation and the estimated real impact of aggregate demand movements.

Recall that the Lucas model predicts that the variance of aggregate demand shocks affects τ, and that the data appear consistent with this prediction. Moreover, countries with higher average inflation generally have more variable aggregate demand. Thus it is possible that the results in (6.91) arise not because $\bar{\pi}$ directly affects τ, but because it is correlated with the standard deviation of nominal GNP growth (σ_x), which does directly affect τ. Alternatively, it is possible that the earlier results, which appeared supportive of the Lucas model, in fact arise from the fact that σ_x and $\bar{\pi}$ are correlated.

The appropriate way to test between these two views is to include both variables in the regression. Again quadratic terms are included to allow for nonlinearities. The results are

$$\tau_i = 0.589 - 5.729\bar{\pi}_i + 8.406\bar{\pi}_i^2 + 1.241\sigma_x - 2.380\sigma_x^2$$
$$ (0.086) \quad (1.973) \quad\;\; (3.849) \quad\;\; (2.467) \quad\;\; (7.062)$$

$$\tag{6.92}$$

$$\bar{R}^2 = 0.359, \qquad \text{s.e.e.} = 0.219.$$

The coefficients on the average inflation variables are essentially the same as in the previous regression, and they remain statistically significant. The variability terms, in contrast, play little role. The null hypothesis that the coefficients on both σ_x and σ_x^2 are zero cannot be rejected at any reasonable confidence level, and the point estimates imply that reasonable changes in σ_x have quantitatively small effects on τ; for example, a change in σ_x from 0.05 to 0.10 changes τ by only 0.04. Thus the results appear to favor the new Keynesian view over the Lucas model.[35]

Supply Shocks

Ball and Mankiw (1995) use the observation that large disturbances are more likely than small disturbances to cause firms to adjust their prices to develop and test a theory of supply shocks arising from costs of price adjustment. To understand their idea, consider an economy where there are costs of price adjustment, where firms are subject to relative cost shocks, and where aggregate demand is constant. In such a setting, only firms subject to unusually large relative cost shocks, either positive or negative, adjust their prices. The average relative cost shock is zero by definition. But if the shocks' distribution across firms is skewed, there may be more large positive shocks than large negative ones, or vice versa. If, for example, the distribution is positively skewed, as in Figure 6.6, more firms raise their prices than lower them. Thus the average price level rises, and output falls. In a period when the distribution is negatively skewed, on the other hand, the price level falls and output rises. Thus changes in the skewness of the distribution of relative cost shocks act as aggregate supply shocks.

    To test this idea, Ball and Mankiw proxy the distribution of relative cost shocks with the distribution of relative price movements in disaggregated U.S. Producer Price Index data. They consider various measures of the asymmetry of this distribution. Their simplest measure is a weighted average of relative price movements that are greater in absolute value than some cutoff. That is, their measure is

$$S_t = \int_{r=-\infty}^{-X} rf_t(r)dr + \int_{r=X}^{\infty} rf_t(r)dr, \qquad (6.93)$$

where $f_t(r)$ is the density function of relative price changes in period t and X is the cutoff. Note that if $X = 0$, S is simply the average relative price movement, which is zero by definition. Loosely speaking, S is the change in the aggregate price level caused by the price changes of industries whose relative prices change by more than X. Thus if price adjustment is described

---

[35]The lack of a discernible link between σ_x and τ, however, is a puzzle not only for the Lucas model but also for models based on small frictions: an increase in the variability of shocks should make firms change their prices more often, and should therefore reduce the real impact of a change in aggregate demand.

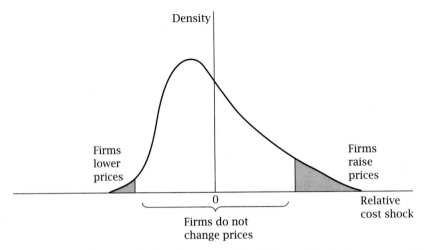

FIGURE 6.6   The impact of the skewness of relative cost shocks on average prices

precisely by the view shown in Figure 6.6, S is the appropriate measure of supply shocks.

Ball and Mankiw compute S annually for the United States for the period 1948–1989. They focus on the case of $X = 10\%$, although their findings are robust to reasonable changes in this value. The resulting series for S exhibits large fluctuations over time. Some of the extreme observations correspond to well-known supply shocks; for example, S is large and positive in 1973 and 1979, years when there were large increases in the relative price of oil. But other cases do not correspond to previously identified supply shocks; for example, S is large and negative in 1952 and 1953.

Ball and Mankiw test their theory in three ways. The first is to investigate whether S is associated with inflation. Regressing inflation on a constant, lagged inflation, and S yields

$$\pi_t = 0.015 + 0.252\,\pi_{t-1} + 7.33S_t,$$
$$(0.004)\;\;(0.082)\qquad(0.80)$$

$$(6.94)$$

$$\overline{R}^2 = 0.765, \qquad \text{D.W.} = 2.01, \qquad \text{s.e.e.} = 0.023.$$

Thus there is an overwhelmingly statistically significant relationship between the distribution of relative price movements and overall inflation.

The second test is to ask whether the skewness of relative price shocks affects the inflation-unemployment tradeoff. In other words, Ball and Mankiw ask whether S shifts the Phillips curve. Adding detrended unemployment, U, to the previous regression yields

$$\pi_t = 0.015 + 0.283\,\pi_{t-1} - 1.15U_t + 6.84S_t,$$
$$(0.004)\ (0.077)\qquad (0.44)\quad (0.77)$$

(6.95)

$$\overline{R}^2 = 0.796, \qquad \text{D.W.} = 2.12, \qquad \text{s.e.e.} = 0.021.$$

Thus this change does not noticeably weaken the results.

Ball and Mankiw's final test is the most demanding of their theory. The conventional view is that the prices of oil and other raw materials are more flexible than other prices; as a result, disturbances to these goods' relative prices affect the price level for a given level of output. In Ball and Mankiw's model, in contrast, large shocks to the prices of these goods are supply shocks simply because they are large; which specific goods are involved is irrelevant.

To test between these two views, Ball and Mankiw add the change in the relative price of raw materials to their equation. Their model predicts that this relative-price measure should provide no information about aggregate supply once the overall skewness of relative price movements is accounted for; the conventional view predicts the reverse.

The results are[36]

$$\pi_t = 0.018 + 0.257\,\pi_{t-1} - 1.35U_t + 6.84S_t + 0.133R_t$$
$$(0.004)\ (0.096)\qquad (0.43)\quad (0.77)\quad (0.136)$$

(6.96)

$$\overline{R}^2 = 0.812, \qquad \text{D.W.} = 2.25, \qquad \text{s.e.e.} = 0.020,$$

where R is the change in the relative price of raw materials. The coefficient on R is small and insignificant; in addition, it is only about one-fifth as large as it is in a regression that does not include the skewness measure. The coefficient on S, in contrast, is little changed by the inclusion of R. In sum, the menu-cost model's predictions about aggregate supply appear to be strongly supported.

Microeconomic Evidence on Price Adjustment

The central assumption of the analysis of this part of the chapter is that there is some kind of barrier to complete price adjustment at the level of individual firms. It is therefore natural to investigate pricing policies at the microeconomic level. By doing so, one can hope to learn both whether there are barriers to price adjustment, and if so, what form they take.

Prominent examples of such studies include Carlton (1986), Cecchetti (1986), Lach and Tsiddon (1992), Blinder (1994), and Kashyap (1995). There are two general themes to the results. First, infrequent price adjustment is

---

[36]The regression also includes a dummy variable for the Nixon wage and price controls; the dummy is not important for the results, however.

common. For example, the two studies of price adjustment that examine the broadest ranges of goods, Carlton's and Blinder's, find that intervals between price changes are typically about a year. And price changes for some goods are much less frequent. Cecchetti, for example, finds that the newsstand prices of magazines are changed on average only every three years.

The second theme of these studies is that the price adjustments do not follow any simple pattern. The behavior of L.L. Bean catalog prices, documented by Kashyap, is representative. As in the other studies, the frequency of price changes is low: on average, the price of a good is changed only after inflation has eroded its real price by about 10%. Only an extremely large cost of price adjustment, or an extremely small cost of failing to charge the price that is optimal in the absence of adjustment costs, can reconcile this finding with a menu-cost view. In addition, although Bean issues over 20 catalogs a year, prices are changed in only two of the catalogs (fall and spring). Even in these catalogs, most prices are usually not changed. Neither fact supports the view that the barrier to price adjustment is the cost of printing and posting a new price. In addition, the spacing of the changes is highly irregular; thus the results are not at all consistent with the assumption of the Fischer and Taylor models that there is a fixed interval between changes. Finally, the size of changes varies tremendously, and small changes are as likely as large changes to be followed quickly by an additional change; if the barrier to price adjustment is some kind of fixed cost, then under reasonable assumptions the changes would be fairly uniform in size, and the firm would make a relatively small change only if it expected the new price to be in effect for a relatively long time. In sum, the microeconomic evidence on price stickiness is puzzling.

6.14 Coordination-Failure Models and Real Non-Walrasian Theories

Coordination-Failure Models

All the models of fluctuations we have examined imply that when prices are flexible, the economy has a unique equilibrium. Thus fluctuations arise only from changes in the flexible-price equilibrium (as in real-business-cycle models) or from departures of the economy from that equilibrium (as in models with nominal stickiness). If more than one level of output is a flexible-price equilibrium, however, fluctuations can also arise from movements of the economy among different equilibria.

Cooper and John (1988) present a simple framework for analyzing multiple equilibria in aggregate activity. The economy consists of many identical agents. Each agent chooses the value of some variable, which we call output for concreteness, taking others' choices as given. Let $U_i = V(y_i, y)$ be

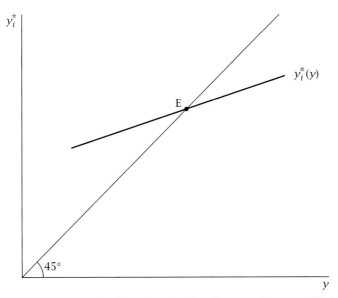

FIGURE 6.7   A reaction function that implies a unique equilibrium

agent i's payoff when he or she chooses output y_i and all others choose y. (We will consider only symmetric equilibria; thus we do not need to specify what happens when others' choices are heterogeneous.) Let $y_i^*(y)$ denote the representative agent's optimal choice of y_i given y. Assume that $V(\bullet)$ is sufficiently well behaved that $y_i^*(y)$ is uniquely defined for any y, is continuous, and is always between zero and some upper bound $\bar{y}$. $y_i^*(y)$ is referred to as the *reaction function.*

Equilibrium occurs when $y_i^*(y) = y$. In such a situation, if each agent believes that other agents will produce y, each agent in fact chooses to produce y.

Figure 6.7 shows an economy without multiple equilibria. The figure plots the reaction function, $y_i^*(y)$. Equilibrium occurs when the reaction function crosses the 45-degree line. Since there is only one crossing, the equilibrium is unique.

Figure 6.8 shows a case with multiple equilibria. Since $y_i^*(y)$ is bounded between zero and $\bar{y}$, it must begin above the 45-degree line and end up below. And since it is continuous, it must cross the 45-degree line an odd number of times (if we ignore the possibility of tangencies). The figure shows a case with three crossings, and thus three equilibrium levels of output. Under plausible assumptions, the equilibrium at Point A is unstable. If, for example, agents expect output to be slightly above the level at A, they produce slightly more than they expect others to produce. With natural assumptions about dynamics, this causes the economy to move away from A. The equilibria at B and C, however, are stable.

With multiple equilibria, fundamentals do not fully determine outcomes. If agents expect the economy to be at C, it ends up there; if they expect it to

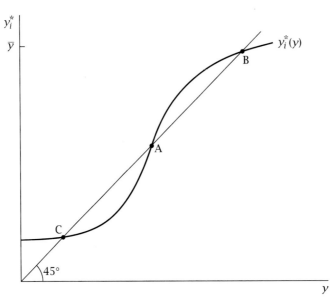

FIGURE 6.8   A reaction function that implies multiple equilibria

be at B, it ends up there instead. Thus *animal spirits, self-fulfilling prophecies,* and *sunspots* can affect aggregate outcomes.[37]

It is plausible that $V(y_i, y)$ is increasing in y—that is, that a typical individual is better off when aggregate output is higher. In the model of Section 6.6, for example, higher aggregate output shifts the demand curve that the representative firm faces out, and thus increases the real price the firm obtains for a given level of its output. If this condition holds, equilibria with higher output involve higher welfare. To see this, consider two equilibrium levels of output, y_1 and y_2, with $y_2 > y_1$. Since $V(y_i, y)$ is increasing in y, $V(y_1, y_2)$ is greater than $V(y_1, y_1)$. And since y_2 is an equilibrium, $y_i = y_2$ maximizes $V(y_i, y)$ given $y = y_2$, and so $V(y_2, y_2)$ exceeds $V(y_1, y_2)$. Thus the representative agent is better off at the higher-output equilibrium.[38]

---

[37]A sunspot equilibrium occurs when some variable that has no inherent effect on the economy matters because agents believe that it does. Any model with multiple equilibria has the potential for sunspots: if agents believe that the economy will be at one equilibrium when the extraneous variable takes on a high value and at another when it takes on a low value, they behave in ways that validate this belief. For more on these issues, see Cass and Shell (1983); Woodford (1990, 1991); and Farmer (1993).

[38]There is no necessary connection between the slope of the reaction function and the welfare properties of equilibria. If agents' maximization problem has an interior solution, $y_i^*(y)$ is defined by $V_1(y_i^*(y), y) = 0$, where subscripts denote partial derivatives. Differentiating this condition with respect to y yields $y_i^{*\prime}(y) = V_{12}/(-V_{11})$. Since V_{11} must be negative for $y_i^*(y)$ to be an interior maximum, the sign of $y_i^{*\prime}(y)$ is given by the sign of V_{12}. Relative welfare in different equilibria, on the other hand, is determined by V_2. Thus the issues of whether there are multiple equilibria and whether a high-output equilibrium is preferable to a low-output one are distinct.

Models with multiple, Pareto-ranked equilibria are known as *coordination-failure* models. The possibility of coordination failure implies that the economy can get stuck in an underemployment equilibrium. That is, output can be inefficiently low just because everyone believes that it will be. In such a situation, there is no force tending to restore output to normal. As a result, there may be scope for government policies that coordinate expectations on a high-output equilibrium; for example, a temporary stimulus might permanently move the economy to a better equilibrium.

There is an important link between multiple equilibria and our earlier discussion of real rigidity. Recall that there is a high degree of real rigidity when, in response to an increase in the price level and the consequent decline in aggregate output, the representative firm wants to reduce its relative price only slightly. In terms of output, this corresponds to a reaction function with a slope slightly less than 1: when aggregate output falls, the representative firm wants its sales to decline almost as much as others'. The existence of multiple equilibria requires that over some range, declines in aggregate output cause the representative firm to want to *raise* its price and thus *reduce* its sales relative to others'; that is, what is needed is that the reaction function have a slope greater than 1 over some range. In short, coordination failure requires that real rigidity be very strong over some range.

One implication of this observation is that, since there are many potential sources of real rigidity, there are many potential sources of coordination failure. Thus there are many possible models that fit Cooper and John's general framework. Examples include Bryant (1983); Heller (1986); Kiyotaki (1988); Shleifer (1986); Murphy, Shleifer, and Vishny (1989b, 1989c); Durlauf (1993); and Lamont (1994).

Empirical Application: Experimental Evidence on Coordination-Failure Games

Coordination-failure models have more than one Nash equilibrium. Traditional game theory predicts that such economies will arrive at one of their equilibria, but does not predict which one. Various theories of equilibrium refinements make predictions about which equilibrium will be reached. For example, a common view is that Pareto-superior equilibria are focal, and that economies where there is the potential for coordination failure therefore attain the best possible equilibrium. There are other possibilities as well. For example, it may be that each agent is unsure about what rule others are using to choose among the possible outcomes, and that as a result such economies do not reach any of their equilibria.

One approach to testing theories that has been pursued extensively in recent years, especially in game theory, is the use of experiments. Experiments have the advantage that they allow researchers to control the economic environment precisely. They have the disadvantages, however, that they are often not feasible and that behavior may be different in the laboratory than in similar situations in practice.

Van Huyck, Battalio, and Beil (1990, 1991) and Cooper, DeJong, Forsythe, and Ross (1990, 1992) test coordination-failure theories experimentally. Van Huyck, Battalio, and Beil (1990) consider the coordination-failure game proposed by Bryant (1983). In Bryant's game, each of N agents chooses an effort level over the range $[0, \bar{e}]$. The payoff to agent i is

$$U_i = \alpha \min[e_1, e_2, \ldots, e_N] - \beta e_i, \qquad \alpha > \beta > 0. \qquad (6.97)$$

The best equilibrium is for every agent to choose the maximum effort level, $\bar{e}$; this gives each agent a payoff of $(\alpha - \beta)\bar{e}$. But any common effort level in $[0, \bar{e}]$ is also a Nash equilibrium: if every agent other than agent i sets his or her effort to some level $\hat{e}$, i also wants to choose effort of $\hat{e}$. Since each agent's payoff is increasing in the common effort level, Bryant's game is a coordination-failure model with a continuum of equilibria.

Van Huyck, Battalio, and Beil consider a version of Bryant's game with effort restricted to the integers 1 through 7, $\alpha = \$0.20, \beta = \$0.10$, and N between 14 and 16.[39] They report several main results. The first concerns the first time a group plays the game; since Bryant's model is not one of repeated play, this situation may correspond most closely to the model. Van Huyck, Battalio, and Beil find that in the first play, the players do not reach any of the equilibria. The most common levels of effort are 5 and 7, but there is a great deal of dispersion. Thus, no deterministic theory of equilibrium selection successfully describes behavior.

Second, repeated play of the game results in rapid movement toward low effort. Among five of the seven experimental groups, the minimum effort in the first period is more than 1. But in all seven groups, by the fourth play the minimum level of effort reaches 1 and remains there in every subsequent round. Thus there is strong coordination failure.

Third, the game fails to converge to any equilibrium. Each group played the game 10 times, for a total of 70 trials. Yet in none of the 70 trials do all of the players choose the same effort. Even in the last several trials, which are preceded in every group by a string of trials where the minimum effort is 1, over a quarter of players choose effort greater than 1.

Finally, even modifying the payoff function to induce "coordination successes" does not prevent reversion to inefficient outcomes. After the initial 10 trials, each group played 5 trials with the parameter β in (6.97) set to zero. With $\beta = 0$, there is no cost to higher effort; as a result, most (though not all) of the groups converge to the Pareto-efficient outcome of $e_i = 7$ for all players. But when β is changed back to $\$0.10$, there is rapid reversion to the situation where most players choose the minimum effort.

---

[39]In addition, they add a constant of $0.60 to the payoff function so that no one can lose money.

Van Huyck, Battalio, and Beil's results suggest that predictions from deductive theories of behavior should be treated with caution: even though Bryant's game is fairly simple, actual behavior does not correspond well with the predictions of any standard theory. The results also suggest that coordination-failure models can give rise to complicated behavior and dynamics.

Real Non-Walrasian Theories

Substantial real rigidity, even if it is not strong enough to cause multiple equilibria, can make the equilibrium highly sensitive to disturbances. Consider the case where the reaction function is upward-sloping with a slope slightly less than 1. As shown in Figure 6.9, this leads to a unique equilibrium. Now let x be some variable that shifts the reaction function; thus we now write the reaction function as $y_i = y_i^*(y, x)$. The equilibrium level of y for a given x, denoted $\hat{y}(x)$, is defined by the condition $y_i^*(\hat{y}(x), x) = \hat{y}(x)$. Differentiating this condition with respect to x yields

$$\frac{\partial y_i^*}{\partial y}\hat{y}'(x) + \frac{\partial y_i^*}{\partial x} = \hat{y}'(x), \tag{6.98}$$

or

$$\hat{y}'(x) = \frac{1}{1 - (\partial y_i^*/\partial y)}\frac{\partial y_i^*}{\partial x}. \tag{6.99}$$

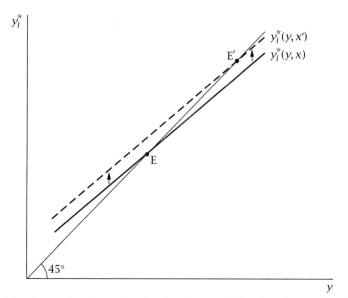

FIGURE 6.9   A reaction function that implies a unique but fragile equilibrium

Equation (6.99) shows that when the reaction function slopes up, there is a "multiplier" that magnifies the effect of the shift of the reaction function at a given level of y, $\partial y_i^* / \partial x$. In terms of the diagram, the impact on the equilibrium level of y is much larger than the upward shift of the reaction function. The closer the slope is to 1, the larger the multiplier is.

In a situation like this, any factor that affects the reaction function has a large impact on overall economic activity. In the terminology of Summers (1988), the equilibrium is *fragile.* Thus it is possible that there is substantial real rigidity but that fluctuations are driven by real rather than nominal shocks. When there is substantial real rigidity, technology shocks, credit-market disruptions, changes in government spending and tax rates, shifts in uncertainty about future policies, and other real disturbances can all be important sources of output movements. Since, as we have seen, there is unlikely to be substantial real rigidity in a Walrasian model, we refer to theories of fluctuations based on real rigidities and real disturbances as *real non-Walrasian theories.* Just as there are many candidate real rigidities, there are many possible theories of this type.[40]

This discussion suggests that whether there are multiple flexible-price equilibria or merely a unique but fragile equilibrium is not crucial to fluctuations. Suppose first that (as we have been assuming throughout this section) there are no barriers to nominal adjustment. If there are multiple equilibria, fluctuations can occur without any disturbances at all as the economy moves among the different equilibria. With a unique but fragile equilibrium, on the other hand, fluctuations can occur in response to small disturbances as the equilibrium is greatly affected by the shocks.

The situation is similar with small barriers to price adjustment. Strong real rigidity (plus appropriate insensitivity of the profit function) causes firms' incentives to adjust their prices in response to a nominal disturbance to be small; whether the real rigidity is strong enough to create multiple equilibria when prices are flexible is not important.

6.15 Limitations

Real-business-cycle research has developed precisely specified models that take strong stands concerning the sources of shocks and how they are transmitted to the aggregate economy. As a result, it is often easy to confront the

---

[40]Accepting that there is substantial real rigidity does not require adopting the view that many types of shocks are important to fluctuations. In the daylight-saving-time example, for instance, although there appears to be considerable real rigidity in individuals' preferences about their schedules, we do not observe sharp short-run variations in economy-wide real schedules arising from sources other than changes in the time standard. Finally, an intermediate possibility is that when there are large real rigidities, many kinds of shocks, both real and nominal, are important to fluctuations (see, for example, Greenwald and Stiglitz, 1988).

models with the data and to identify ways in which they are unsuccessful. Keynesian theory, in contrast, encompasses a wide range of models, most of which are intended to address specific issues rather than to approximate the behavior of the economy as a whole. In addition, Keynesian accounts of fluctuations usually ascribe important roles to many different kinds of shocks and many different types of market imperfections.

These features of the Keynesian approach form the basis for the major criticism that can be made against it: Keynesian models are so vague and so flexible that they are almost impossible to refute. Like Ptolemaic astronomers with their epicycles to explain every new observation, Keynesian macroeconomists can modify their theories and postulate unobserved shocks to fit the data in almost any situation.

It is easy to find examples of the flexibility of Keynesian analysis, involving issues ranging from the basic assumptions of the models to the specifics of individual episodes. Shortly after the publication of the *General Theory,* Dunlop (1938) and Tarshis (1939) provided strong evidence against its prediction of a countercyclical real wage. Rather than abandoning his theory, Keynes (1939) merely argued that its description of price-setting behavior should be changed. To give another example, the Keynesian response to the breakdown of the output-inflation relationship in the late 1960s and early 1970s was simply to modify the models to include supply shocks and core inflation. Similarly, confronted with clear evidence that the microeconomics of nominal adjustment differ greatly from what one would expect if the only barriers to adjustment are small fixed costs of changing prices, new Keynesians did not discard their theories; instead they argued that the actual barriers to nominal flexibility are a complicated combination of adjustment costs and other factors (D. Romer, 1993a), or that menu costs are just a metaphor that is no more intended to describe reality than is the Walrasian auctioneer of competitive models (Ball and Mankiw, 1994). And so on.

The same flexibility characterizes not just Keynesian models, but Keynesian accounts of specific episodes. The models allow for disturbances in essentially every sector of the economy—money supply, money demand, fiscal policy, consumption, investment, price-setting, wage-setting, and international trade—and thus are consistent with almost any combination of movements in the different variables. For example, conventional Keynesian accounts attribute the 1981–82 U.S. recession to tight monetary policy. The fact that most measures of money growth did not decline sharply is not viewed as an important problem for this view, but is accounted for by postulating a shift in money demand that was only partly accommodated by the Federal Reserve. Similarly, conventional Keynesian accounts attribute a large part of the 1990–91 U.S. recession to an unexplained fall in "consumer confidence."

Of course, it is possible that the economy is complicated, that there are many types of shocks, and that the modifications of Keynesian models reflect gradual progress in our understanding of the economy. But a theory that is so flexible that it cannot be contradicted by any set of observations is devoid of content. Thus if Keynesian theory is to be useful, there must be some questions about which it delivers clear predictions.

One view is that the central issue on which Keynesian theory must stand or fall is the real effects of nominal disturbances. A central element of all Keynesian models is that nominal prices or wages do not adjust immediately. As a result, the models predict that independent monetary disturbances affect real activity. If this prediction is contradicted by the data, it appears that the models would have to be abandoned rather than modified, and that the study of fluctuations would have to pursue the real-business-cycle models of Chapter 4 or the real non-Walrasian theories of the previous section. If this view of the defining element of Keynesian theory is right, evaluating and extending the evidence described in Section 5.6 concerning the effects of monetary shocks is critical to business-cycle research.

Problems

6.1. Consider the problem facing an individual in the Lucas model when P_i/P is unknown. The individual chooses L_i to maximize the expectation of U_i; U_i continues to be given by equation (6.3).

(a) Find the first-order condition for L_i, and rearrange it to obtain an expression for L_i in terms of $E[P_i/P]$. Take logs of this expression to obtain an expression for ℓ_i.

(b) How does the amount of labor the individual supplies if he or she follows the certainty-equivalence rule in (6.17) compare with the optimal amount derived in part (a)? (Hint: how does $E[\ln(P_i/P)]$ compare with $\ln(E[P_i/P])$?)

(c) Suppose that (as in the Lucas model) $\ln(P_i/P) = E[\ln(P_i/P) \mid P_i] + u_i$, where u_i is normal with a mean of zero and a variance that is independent of P_i. Show that this implies that $\ln\{E[(P_i/P) \mid P_i]\} = E[\ln(P_i/P) \mid P_i] + C$, where C is a constant whose value is independent of P_i. (Hint: note that $P_i/P = \exp\{E[\ln(P_i/P) \mid P_i]\} \exp\{u_i\}$, and show that this implies that the ℓ_i that maximizes expected utility differs from the certainty-equivalence rule in (6.17) only by a constant.)

6.2. (This follows Dixit and Stiglitz, 1977.) Suppose that the consumption index C_i in equation (6.2) is $C_i = [\int_{j=0}^{1} Z_j^{1/\eta} C_{ij}^{(\eta-1)/\eta} \, dj]^{\eta/(\eta-1)}$, where C_{ij} is the individual's consumption of good j and Z_j is the taste shock for good j. Suppose the individual has amount Y_i to spend on goods. Thus the budget constraint is $\int_{j=0}^{1} P_j C_{ij} \, dj = Y_i$.

(a) Find the first-order condition for the problem of maximizing C_i subject to the budget constraint. Solve for C_{ij} in terms of Z_j, P_j, and the Lagrange multiplier on the budget constraint.

(b) Use the budget constraint to find C_{ij} in terms of Z_j, P_j, Y_i, and the Z's and P's.

(c) Substitute your result in part (b) into the expression for C_i and show that $C_i = Y_i/P$, where $P \equiv [\int_{j=0}^{1} Z_j P_j^{1-\eta} \, dj]^{1/(1-\eta)}$.

(d) Use the results in part (b) and part (c) to show that $C_{ij} = Z_j(P_j/P)^{-\eta}(Y_i/P)$.

(e) Compare your results with (6.7) and (6.9) in the text.

6.3. Observational equivalence. (Sargent, 1976.) Suppose that the money supply is determined by $m_t = c'z_{t-1} + e_t$, where c and z are vectors and e_t is an i.i.d. disturbance uncorrelated with z_{t-1}. e_t is unpredictable and unobservable. Thus the expected component of m_t is $c'z_{t-1}$, and the unexpected component is e_t. In setting the money supply, the Federal Reserve responds only to variables that matter for real activity; that is, the variables in z directly affect y.

Now consider the following two models: (i) Only unexpected money matters, so $y_t = a'z_{t-1} + be_t + v_t$; (ii) all money matters, so $y_t = \alpha'z_{t-1} + \beta m_t + v_t$. In each specification, the disturbance is i.i.d. and uncorrelated with z_{t-1} and e_t.

(a) Is it possible to distinguish between these two theories? That is, given a candidate set of parameter values under, say, Model (i), are there parameter values under Model (ii) that have the same predictions? Explain.

(b) Suppose that the Federal Reserve also responds to some variables that do not directly affect output; that is, suppose $m_t = c'z_{t-1} + \gamma'w_{t-1} + e_t$ and that Models (i) and (ii) are as before (with their distubances now uncorrelated with w_{t-1} as well as with z_{t-1} and e_t). In this case, is it possible to distinguish between the two theories? Explain.

6.4. Suppose the economy is described by the model of Section 6.6. Assume, however, that P is the price index described in part (c) of Problem 6.2 (with all the Z_j's equal to 1 for simplicity). In addition, assume that money-market equilibrium requires that total spending in the economy equal M. With these changes, is it still the case that in equilibrium, output of each good is given by (6.46) and that the price of each good is given by (6.47)?

6.5. Indexation. (See Gray, 1976, 1978, and Fischer, 1977b. This problem follows Ball, 1988.) Suppose production at firm i is given by $Y_i = SL_i^\alpha$, where S is a supply shock and $0 < \alpha \leq 1$. Thus in logs, $y_i = s + \alpha\ell_i$. Prices are flexible; thus (setting the constant term to zero for simplicity), $p_i = w_i + (1 - \alpha)\ell_i - s$. Aggregating the output and price equations yields $y = s + \alpha\ell$ and $p = w + (1 - \alpha)\ell - s$. Wages are partially indexed to prices: $w = \theta p$, where $0 \leq \theta \leq 1$. Finally, aggregate demand is given by $y = m - p$. s and m are independent, mean-zero random variables with variances V_s and V_m.

(a) What are p, y, ℓ, and w as functions of m and s and the parameters α and θ? How does indexation affect the response of employment to monetary shocks? How does it affect the response to supply shocks?

(b) What value of θ minimizes the variance of employment?

(c) Suppose the demand for a single firm's output is $y_i = y - \eta(p_i - p)$. Suppose all firms other than firm i index their wages to the price level by $w = \theta p$ as before, but that firm i indexes its wage to the price level by $w_i = \theta_i p$. Firm i continues to set its price as $p_i = w_i + (1 - \alpha)\ell_i - s$. The production function and the pricing equation then imply that $y_i = y - \phi(w_i - w)$, where $\phi \equiv \alpha\eta/[\alpha + (1 - \alpha)\eta]$.

(*i*) What is employment at firm i, ℓ_i, as a function of $m, s, \alpha, \eta, \theta$, and θ_i?

(*ii*) What value of θ_i minimizes the variance of ℓ_i?

(*iii*) Find the Nash equilibrium value of θ. That is, find the value of θ such that if aggregate indexation is given by θ, the representative firm minimizes the variance of ℓ_i by setting $\theta_i = \theta$. Compare this value with the value found in part (*b*).

6.6. Synchronized price-setting. Consider the Taylor model. Suppose, however, that every other period all of the individuals set their prices for that period and the next. That is, in period t prices are set for t and $t + 1$; in $t + 1$, no prices are set; in $t + 2$, prices are set for $t + 2$ and $t + 3$; and so on. As in the Taylor model, prices are both predetermined and fixed, and individuals set their prices according to (6.60). Finally, assume that m follows a random walk.

(*a*) What is the representative individual's price in period t, x_t, as a function of m_t, $E_t m_{t+1}$, p_t, and $E_t p_{t+1}$?

(*b*) Use the fact that synchronization implies that p_t and p_{t+1} are both equal to x_t to solve for x_t in terms of m_t and $E_t m_{t+1}$.

(*c*) What are y_t and y_{t+1}? Does the central result of the Taylor model—that nominal disturbances continue to have real effects after all prices have been changed—still hold? Explain intuitively.

6.7. The Fischer model with unbalanced price-setting. Suppose the economy is as described by the model of Section 6.7, except that instead of half of the individuals setting their prices each period, fraction f set their prices in odd periods and fraction $1 - f$ set their prices in even periods. Thus the price level is $fp_t^1 + (1 - f)p_t^2$ if t is even and $(1 - f)p_t^1 + fp_t^2$ if t is odd. Derive expressions analogous to (6.57) and (6.58) for p_t and y_t for even and odd periods.

6.8. The instability of staggered price-setting. (See Fethke and Policano, 1986; Ball and Cecchetti, 1988; and Ball and D. Romer, 1989.) Suppose the economy is described as in Problem 6.7, and assume for simplicity that m is a random walk (so $m_t = m_{t-1} + u_t$, where u is white noise and has a constant variance). Assume that the amount of profits an individual loses over two periods relative to always having $p_i = p_i^*$ is proportional to $(p_{it} - p_{it}^*)^2 + (p_{it+1} - p_{it+1}^*)^2$. If $f < \frac{1}{2}$ and $\phi < 1$, is the expected value of this loss larger for the individuals who set their prices in odd periods or for the individuals who set their prices in even periods? In light of this, would you expect to see staggered price-setting if $\phi < 1$?

6.9. Consider the Taylor model with the money stock white noise rather than a random walk; that is, $m_t = \varepsilon_t$, where ε_t is serially uncorrelated. Solve the model using the method of undetermined coefficients. (Hint: in the equation analogous to (6.63), is it still reasonable to impose $\lambda + \nu = 1$?)

6.10. Repeat Problem 6.9 using lag operators.

6.11. (This follows Ball, 1994a.) Consider a continuous-time version of the Taylor model, so that $p(t) = (1/T)\int_{\tau=0}^{T} x(t - \tau)d\tau$, where T is the interval between each individual's price changes and $x(t - \tau)$ is the price set by individuals who set their prices at time $t - \tau$. Assume that $\phi = 1$, so that $p_i^*(t) = m(t)$; thus $x(t) = (1/T) \int_{\tau=0}^{T} E_t m(t + \tau) d\tau$.

(a) Suppose that initially $m(t) = gt$ $(g > 0)$, and that $E_t m(t + \tau)$ is therefore $(t + \tau)g$. What are $x(t)$, $p(t)$, and $y(t) = m(t) - p(t)$?

(b) Suppose that at time zero the government announces that it is steadily reducing money growth to zero over the next interval T of time. Thus $m(t) = t[1 - (t/2T)]g$ for $0 < t < T$, and $m(t) = gT/2$ for $t \geq T$. The change is unexpected, so that prices set before $t = 0$ are as in part (a).

　(i) Show that if $x(t) = gT/2$ for all $t > 0$, then $p(t) = m(t)$ for all $t > 0$, and thus that output is the same as it would be without the change in policy.

　(ii) For $0 < t < T$, are the prices that firms set more than, less than, or equal to $gT/2$? What about for $T \leq t \leq 2T$? Given this, how does output during the period $(0, 2T)$ compare with what it would be without the change in policy?

6.12. State-dependent pricing with both positive and negative inflation. (This follows Caplin and Leahy, 1991.) Consider an economy like that of the Caplin–Spulber model. Suppose, however, that m can either rise or fall, and that firms therefore follow a two-sided Ss policy: if $p_i - p_i^*(t)$ reaches either S or $-S$, firm i changes p_i so that $p_i - p_i^*(t)$ equals zero. As in the Caplin–Spulber model, changes in m are continuous.

　Assume for simplicity that $p_i^*(t) = m(t)$. In addition, assume that $p_i - p_i^*(t)$ is initially distributed uniformly over some interval of width S; that is, $p_i - p_i^*(t)$ is distributed uniformly on $[X, X + S]$ for some X between $-S$ and 0. This is shown in Figure 6.10: the distribution of $p_i - p_i^*(t)$ is an "elevator" of height S in a "shaft" of height $2S$.

(a) Explain why, given these assumptions, $p_i - p_i^*(t)$ continues to be distributed uniformly over some interval of width S. (In terms of the diagram, this means that although the elevator may move in the shaft, it remains of height S.)

(b) Are there any positions of the elevator (that is, any values of X) where an infinitesimal increase in m of dm raises average prices by less than dm? by more than dm? by exactly dm? Thus, what does this model imply about the real effects of monetary shocks?

6.13. Consider an economy consisting of some firms with flexible prices and some with rigid prices. Let p^f denote the price set by a representative flexible-price firm and p^r the price set by a representative rigid-price firm. Flexible-price firms set their prices after m is known; rigid-price firms set their prices before m is known. Thus flexible-price firms set $p^f = p_i^* = (1 - \phi)p + \phi m$, and rigid-price firms set $p^r = Ep_i^* = (1 - \phi)Ep + \phi Em$, where E denotes the expectation of a variable as of when the rigid-price firms set their prices.

　Assume that fraction q of firms have rigid prices, so that $p = qp^r + (1 - q)p^f$.

(a) Find p^f in terms of p^r, m, and the parameters of the model (ϕ and q).

(b) Find p^r in terms of Em and the parameters of the model.

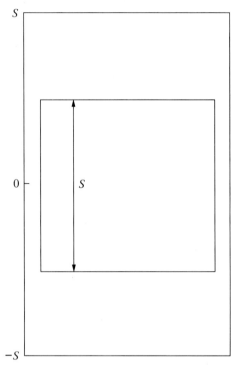

FIGURE 6.10   The distribution of $p_i - p_i^*(t)$ in the Caplin–Leahy model

(c) (i) Do anticipated changes in m (that is, changes that are expected as of when rigid-price firms set their prices) affect y? Why or why not?

   (ii) Do unanticipated changes in m affect y? Why or why not?

6.14. Consider an economy consisting of many imperfectly competitive, price-setting firms. The profits of the representative firm, firm i, depend on aggregate output, y, and the firm's real price, r_i: $\pi_i = \pi(y, r_i)$, where $\pi_{22} < 0$ (subscripts denote partial derivatives). Let $r^*(y)$ denote the profit-maximizing price as a function of y; note that $r^*(y)$ is characterized by $\pi_2(y, r^*(y)) = 0$.

   Assume that output is at some level y_0, and that firm i's real price is $r^*(y_0)$. Now suppose there is a change in the money supply, and suppose that other firms do not change their prices and that aggregate output therefore changes to some new level, y_1.

(a) Explain why firm i's incentive to adjust its price is given by $G = \pi(y_1, r^*(y_1)) - \pi(y_1, r^*(y_0))$.

(b) Use a second-order Taylor approximation of this expression in y_1 around $y_1 = y_0$ to show that $G \simeq -\pi_{22}(y_0, r^*(y_0))[r^{*\prime}(y_0)]^2(y_1 - y_0)^2/2$.

(c) What component of this expression corresponds to the degree of real rigidity? What component corresponds to the degree of insensitivity of the profit function?

6.15. Multiple equilibria with menu costs. (This follows Ball and D. Romer, 1991.) Consider an economy consisting of many imperfectly competitive firms. The profits that a firm loses relative to what it obtains with $p_i = p^*$ are $K(p_i - p^*)^2, K > 0$. As usual, $p^* = p + \phi y$ and $y = m - p$. Each firm faces a fixed cost Z of changing its nominal price.

Initially m is zero and the economy is at its flexible-price equilibrium, which is $y = 0$ and $p = m = 0$. Now suppose m changes to m'.

(a) Suppose that fraction f of firms change their prices. Since the firms that change their prices charge p^* and the firms that do not charge zero, this implies $p = fp^*$. Use this fact to find p, y, and p^* as functions of m' and f.

(b) Plot a firm's incentive to adjust its price, $K(0 - p^*)^2 = K p^{*2}$, as a function of f. Be sure to distinguish the cases $\phi < 1$ and $\phi > 1$.

(c) A firm adjusts its price if the benefit exceeds Z, does not adjust if the benefit is less than Z, and is indifferent if the benefit is exactly Z. Given this, can there be a situation where both adjustment by all firms and adjustment by no firms are equilibria? Can there be a situation where neither adjustment by all firms nor adjustment by no firms are equilibria?

6.16. (This follows Diamond, 1982.)[41] Consider an island consisting of N people and many palm trees. Each person is in one of two states, not carrying a coconut and looking for palm trees (state P) or carrying a coconut and looking for other people with coconuts (state C). If a person without a coconut finds a palm tree, he or she can climb the tree and pick a coconut; this has a cost (in utility units) of c. If a person with a coconut meets another person with a coconut, they trade and eat each other's coconuts; this yields $\bar{u}$ units of utility for each of them. (People cannot eat coconuts that they have picked themselves.)

A person looking for coconuts finds palm trees at rate b per unit time. A person carrying a coconut finds trading partners at rate aL per unit time, where L is the total number of people carrying coconuts. a and b are exogenous.

Individuals' discount rate is r. Focus on steady states; that is, assume that L is constant.

(a) Explain why, if everyone in state P climbs a palm tree whenever he or she finds one, then $rV_P = b(V_C - V_P - c)$, where V_P and V_C are the values of being in the two states.

(b) Find the analogous expression for V_C.

(c) Solve for $V_C - V_P, V_C$, and V_P in terms of $r, b, c, \bar{u}, a$, and L.

(d) What is L, still assuming that anyone in state P climbs a palm tree whenever he or she finds one? Assume for simplicity that $aN = 2b$.

---

[41] The solution to this problem requires dynamic programming (see Section 10.4).

(e) For what values of c is it a steady-state equilibrium for anyone in state P to climb a palm tree whenever he or she finds one? (Continue to assume $aN = 2b$.)

(f) For what values of c is it a steady-state equilibrium for no one who finds a tree to climb it? Are there values of c for which there is more than one steady-state equilibrium? If there are multiple equilibria, does one involve higher welfare than the other? Explain intuitively.

Chapter 7
CONSUMPTION

This chapter and the next investigate households' consumption choices and firms' investment decisions in more detail. Consumption and investment are important to both growth and fluctuations. With regard to growth, the division of society's resources between current consumption and various types of investment—in physical capital, human capital, and research and development—is central to standards of living in the long run. That division is determined by the interaction of households' allocation of their incomes between consumption and saving given the rates of return and other constraints they face, and firms' investment demand given the interest rates and other constraints they face. With regard to fluctuations, consumption and investment make up the vast majority of the demand for goods. Thus if we wish to understand how such forces as government purchases, technology, and monetary policy affect aggregate output, we must understand how consumption and investment are determined.

There are two other reasons for studying consumption and investment. First, they introduce some important issues involving financial markets. Financial markets affect the macroeconomy mainly through their impact on consumption and investment. In addition, consumption and investment have important feedback effects on financial markets. We will investigate the interaction between financial markets and consumption and investment both in cases where financial markets function perfectly and in cases where they do not.

Second, much of the most insightful empirical work in macroeconomics over the past twenty years has been concerned with consumption and investment. These two chapters therefore have an unusually intensive empirical focus.

7.1   Consumption under Certainty: The Life-Cycle/Permanent-Income Hypothesis

Assumptions

Although we have already examined aspects of individuals' consumption decisions in our investigations of the Ramsey and Diamond models in Chapter 2 and of real-business-cycle theory in Chapter 4, here we start with a simple case. Consider an individual who lives for T periods whose lifetime utility is

$$U = \sum_{t=1}^{T} u(C_t), \qquad u'(\bullet) > 0, \quad u''(\bullet) < 0, \tag{7.1}$$

where $u(\bullet)$ is the instantaneous utility function and C_t is consumption in period t. The individual has initial wealth of A_0 and labor incomes of $Y_1, Y_2, \ldots, Y_T$ in the T periods of his or her life; the individual takes these as given. The individual can save or borrow at an exogenous interest rate, subject only to the constraint that any outstanding debt must be repaid at the end of his or her life. For simplicity, this interest rate is set to zero.[1] Thus the individual's budget constraint is

$$\sum_{t=1}^{T} C_t \le A_0 + \sum_{t=1}^{T} Y_t. \tag{7.2}$$

Behavior

Since the marginal utility of consumption is always positive, the individual satisfies the budget constraint with equality. The Lagrangian for his or her maximization problem is therefore

$$\mathcal{L} = \sum_{t=1}^{T} u(C_t) + \lambda \left(A_0 + \sum_{t=1}^{T} Y_t - \sum_{t=1}^{T} C_t \right). \tag{7.3}$$

The first-order condition for C_t is

$$u'(C_t) = \lambda. \tag{7.4}$$

---

[1] Note that we have also assumed that the individual's discount rate is zero (see [7.1]). Assuming that the interest rate and the discount rate are equal but not necessarily zero would have almost no effect on the analysis in this section and the next. And assuming that they need not be equal would have only modest effects.

Since (7.4) holds in every period, the marginal utility of consumption is constant. And since the level of consumption uniquely determines its marginal utility, this means that consumption must be constant. Thus $C_1 = C_2 = \cdots = C_T$. Substituting this fact into the budget constraint yields

$$C_t = \frac{1}{T}\left(A_0 + \sum_{\tau=1}^{T} Y_\tau\right) \qquad \text{for all } t. \tag{7.5}$$

The term in parentheses is the individual's total lifetime resources. Thus (7.5) states that the individual divides his or her lifetime resources equally among each period of life.

Implications

This analysis implies that the individual's consumption in a given period is determined not by income that period, but by income over his or her entire lifetime. In the terminology of Friedman (1957), the right-hand side of (7.5) is *permanent income,* and the difference between current and permanent income is *transitory income.* Equation (7.5) implies that consumption is determined by permanent income.

To see the importance of the distinction between permanent and transitory income, consider the effect of a windfall gain of amount Z in the first period of life. Although this windfall raises current income by Z, it raises permanent income by only Z/T. Thus if the individual's horizon is fairly long, the windfall's impact on current consumption is small. One implication is that a temporary tax cut may have little impact on consumption; as described in Chapter 6, this appears to be the case in practice.

Our analysis also implies that although the time pattern of income is not important to consumption, it is critical to saving. The individual's saving in period t is the difference between income and consumption:

$$S_t = Y_t - C_t$$
$$= \left(Y_t - \frac{1}{T}\sum_{\tau=1}^{T} Y_\tau\right) - \frac{1}{T}A_0, \tag{7.6}$$

where the second line uses (7.5) to substitute for C_t. Thus saving is high when income is high relative to its average—that is, when transitory income is high. Similarly, when current income is less than permanent income, saving is negative. Thus the individual uses saving and borrowing to smooth the path of consumption. This is the key idea of the life-cycle/permanent-income hypothesis of Modigliani and Brumberg (1954) and Friedman (1957).

What Is Saving?

At a more general level, the basic idea of the life-cycle/permanent-income hypothesis is a simple insight about saving: saving is future consumption. As long as an individual does not save just for the sake of saving, he or she saves to consume in the future. The saving may be used for conventional consumption later in life, or bequeathed to the individual's children for their consumption, or even used to erect monuments to the individual upon his or her death. But as long as the individual does not value saving in itself, the decision about the division of income between consumption and saving is driven by preferences between present and future consumption and information about future consumption prospects.

This observation suggests that many common statements about saving may be incorrect. For example, it is often asserted that poor individuals save a smaller fraction of their incomes than the wealthy do because their incomes are little above the level needed to provide a minimal standard of living. But this claim overlooks the fact that individuals who have trouble obtaining even a low standard of living today may also have trouble obtaining that standard in the future. Thus their saving is likely to be determined by the time pattern of their income, just as it is for the wealthy.

To take another example, consider the common assertion that individuals' concern about their consumption relative to others' tends to raise their consumption as they try to "keep up with the Joneses." Again, this claim fails to recognize what saving is: since saving represents future consumption, saving less implies consuming less in the future, and thus falling further behind the Joneses. Thus one can just as well argue that concern about relative consumption causes individuals to try to catch up with the Joneses in the future, and thus lowers rather than raises current consumption.[2]

Empirical Application: Understanding Estimated Consumption Functions

The traditional Keynesian consumption function posits that consumption is determined by current disposable income. Keynes (1936) argued that "the amount of aggregate consumption mainly depends on the amount of aggregate income," and that this relationship "is a fairly stable function." He claimed further that "it is also obvious that a higher absolute level of income...will lead, as a rule, to a greater *proportion* of income being saved" (Keynes, 1936, pp. 96–97; emphasis in original).

The importance of the consumption function to Keynes's analysis of fluctuations led many researchers to estimate the relationship between

---

[2]See Abel (1990) and Campbell and Cochrane (1995) for more on how individuals' concern about their consumption relative to others' affects saving once one recognizes that saving represents future consumption.

consumption and current income. Contrary to Keynes's claims, these studies did not demonstrate a consistent, stable relationship. Across households at a point in time, the relationship is indeed of the type that Keynes postulated; an example of such a relationship is shown in Panel (a) of Figure 7.1. But within a country over time, aggregate consumption is essentially proportional to aggregate income; that is, one sees a relationship like that in Panel (b) of the figure. Further, the cross-section consumption function differs across groups. For example, the slope of the estimated consumption function is similar for whites and blacks, but the intercept is higher for whites. This is shown in Panel (c) of the figure.

As Friedman (1957) demonstrates, the permanent-income hypothesis provides a straightforward explanation of all of these findings. Suppose that consumption is in fact determined by permanent income: $C = Y^P$. Current income equals the sum of permanent and transitory income: $Y = Y^P + Y^T$. And since transitory income reflects departures of current income from permanent income, in most samples it has a mean near zero and is roughly uncorrelated with permanent income.

Now consider a regression of consumption on current income:

$$C_i = a + bY_i + e_i. \tag{7.7}$$

In a univariate regression, the estimated coefficient on the independent variable is the ratio of the covariance of the independent and dependent variables to the variance of the independent variable. In this case, this implies

$$\hat{b} = \frac{\text{Cov}(Y, C)}{\text{Var}(Y)}$$

$$= \frac{\text{Cov}(Y^P + Y^T, Y^P)}{\text{Var}(Y^P + Y^T)} \tag{7.8}$$

$$= \frac{\text{Var}(Y^P)}{\text{Var}(Y^P) + \text{Var}(Y^T)};$$

here the second line uses the facts that current income equals the sum of permanent and transitory income and that consumption equals permanent income, and the last line uses the assumption that permanent and temporary income are uncorrelated. In addition, the estimated constant equals the mean of the dependent variable minus the estimated slope coefficient times the mean of the independent variable. Thus,

$$\hat{a} = \overline{C} - \hat{b}\overline{Y}$$

$$= \overline{Y}^P - \hat{b}(\overline{Y}^P + \overline{Y}^T) \tag{7.9}$$

$$= (1 - \hat{b})\overline{Y}^P,$$

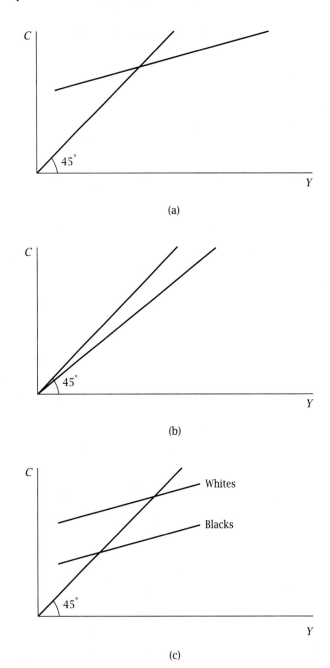

FIGURE 7.1   Some different forms of the relationship between current income and consumption

where the last line uses the assumption that the mean of transitory income is zero.

Thus the permanent-income hypothesis predicts that the key determinant of the slope of an estimated consumption function, $\hat{b}$, is the relative variation in permanent and transitory income. Intuitively, an increase in current income is associated with an increase in consumption only to the extent that it reflects an increase in permanent income. When the variation in permanent income is much greater than the variation in transitory income, almost all differences in current income reflect differences in permanent income; thus consumption rises nearly one-for-one with current income. But when the variation in permanent income is small relative to the variation in transitory income, little of the variation in current income comes from variation in permanent income, and so consumption rises little with current income.

This analysis can be used to understand the estimated consumption functions in Figure 7.1. Across households, much of the variation in income reflects such factors as unemployment and the fact that households are at different points in their life cycles. As a result, the estimated slope coefficient is substantially less than 1, and the estimated intercept is positive. Over time, in contrast, almost all of the variation in aggregate income reflects long-run growth—that is, permanent increases in the economy's resources. Thus the estimated slope coefficient is close to 1, and the estimated intercept is close to zero.[3]

Now consider the differences between blacks and whites. The relative variances of permanent and transitory income are similar in the two groups, and so the estimates of b are similar. But blacks' average incomes are lower than whites'; as a result, the estimate of a for blacks is lower than the estimate for whites (see [7.9]).

To see the intuition for this result, consider a member of each group whose income equals the average income among whites. Since there are many more blacks with permanent incomes below this level than there are with permanent incomes above it, the black's permanent income is much more likely to be less than his or her current income than more. As a result, blacks with this current income have on average lower permanent income; thus on average they consume less than their income. For the white, in contrast, his or her permanent income is about as likely to be more than current income as it is to be less; as a result, whites with this current income on average have the same permanent income, and thus on average they consume

---

[3]In this case, although consumption is approximately proportional to income, the constant of proportionality is less than 1; that is, consumption is on average less than permanent income. As Friedman describes, there are various ways of extending the basic theory to make it consistent with this result. One is to account for turnover among generations and long-run growth: if the young generally save and the old generally dissave, the fact that each generation is wealthier than the previous one implies that the young's saving is greater than the old's dissaving.

their income. In sum, the permanent-income hypothesis attributes the different consumption patterns of blacks and whites to the different average incomes of the two groups, and not to any differences in tastes or culture.

7.2 Consumption under Uncertainty: The Random-Walk Hypothesis

Individual Behavior

We now extend our analysis to account for uncertainty. Continue to assume that both the interest rate and the discount rate are zero. In addition, suppose that the instantaneous utility function, $u(\cdot)$, is quadratic. Thus the individual maximizes

$$E[U] = E\left[\sum_{t=1}^{T} C_t - \frac{a}{2} C_t^2 \right], \qquad a > 0. \tag{7.10}$$

We will assume that the individual's wealth is such that consumption is always in the range where marginal utility is positive. As before, the individual must pay off any outstanding debts at the end of his or her life. Thus the budget constraint is again given by equation (7.2), $\sum_{t=1}^{T} C_t \leq A_0 + \sum_{t=1}^{T} Y_t$.

To describe the individual's behavior, we use the Euler-equation approach that we employed in Chapters 2 and 4. Specifically, suppose that the individual has chosen first-period consumption optimally given the information available, and suppose that he or she will choose consumption in each future period optimally given the information then available. Now consider a reduction in C_1 of dC from the value the individual has chosen and an equal increase in consumption at some future date from the value he or she would have chosen. If the individual is optimizing, a marginal change of this type does not affect expected utility. Since the marginal utility of consumption in period 1 is $1 - aC_1$, the change has a utility cost of $(1 - aC_1)dC$. And since the marginal utility of period-t consumption is $1 - aC_t$, the change has an expected utility benefit of $E_1[1 - aC_t]dC$, where $E_1[\cdot]$ denotes expectations conditional on the information available in period 1. Thus if the individual is optimizing,

$$1 - aC_1 = E_1[1 - aC_t], \qquad \text{for } t = 2, 3, \ldots, T. \tag{7.11}$$

Since $E_1[1 - aC_t]$ equals $1 - aE_1[C_t]$, this implies

$$C_1 = E_1[C_t], \qquad \text{for } t = 2, 3, \ldots, T. \tag{7.12}$$

The individual knows that his or her lifetime consumption will satisfy the budget constraint, (7.2), with equality. Thus the expectations of the two sides of the constraint must be equal:

$$\sum_{t=1}^{T} E_1[C_t] = A_0 + \sum_{t=1}^{T} E_1[Y_t]. \tag{7.13}$$

Equation (7.12) implies that the left-hand side of (7.13) is TC_1. Substituting this into (7.13) and dividing by T yields

$$C_1 = \frac{1}{T}\left(A_0 + \sum_{t=1}^{T} E_1[Y_t]\right). \tag{7.14}$$

That is, the individual consumes $1/T$ of his or her expected lifetime resources.

Implications

Equation (7.12) implies that $E_1[C_2]$ equals C_1. More generally, reasoning analogous to what we have just done implies that in each period, expected next-period consumption equals current consumption. This implies that changes in consumption are unpredictable. By the definition of expectations, we can write

$$C_t = E_{t-1}[C_t] + e_t, \tag{7.15}$$

where e_t is a variable whose expectation as of period $t - 1$ is zero. Thus, since $E_{t-1}[C_t] = C_{t-1}$, we have

$$C_t = C_{t-1} + e_t. \tag{7.16}$$

This is Hall's famous result that the life-cycle/permanent-income hypothesis implies that consumption follows a random walk (Hall, 1978). The intuition for this result is straightforward: if consumption is expected to change, the individual can do a better job of smoothing consumption. Suppose, for example, that consumption is expected to rise. This means that the current marginal utility of consumption is greater than the expected future marginal utility of consumption, and thus that the individual is better off raising current consumption. Thus the individual adjusts his or her current consumption to the point where consumption is not expected to change.

In addition, our analysis can be used to find what determines the change in consumption, e. Consider for concreteness the change from period 1 to period 2. Reasoning parallel to that used to derive (7.14) implies that C_2 equals $1/(T - 1)$ of the individual's expected remaining lifetime resources:

$$C_2 = \frac{1}{T-1} \left(A_1 + \sum_{t=2}^{T} E_2[Y_t] \right)$$

$$= \frac{1}{T-1} \left(A_0 + Y_1 - C_1 + \sum_{t=2}^{T} E_2[Y_t] \right),$$

(7.17)

where the second line uses the fact that $A_1 = A_0 + Y_1 - C_1$. We can rewrite the expectation as of period 2 of income over the remainder of life, $\sum_{t=2}^{T} E_2[Y_t]$, as the expectation of this quantity as of period 1, $\sum_{t=2}^{T} E_1[Y_t]$, plus the information learned between period 1 and period 2, $\sum_{t=2}^{T} E_2[Y_t] - \sum_{t=2}^{T} E_1[Y_t]$. Thus we can rewrite (7.17) as

$$C_2 = \frac{1}{T-1} \left\{ A_0 + Y_1 - C_1 + \sum_{t=2}^{T} E_1[Y_t] + \left(\sum_{t=2}^{T} E_2[Y_t] - \sum_{t=2}^{T} E_1[Y_t] \right) \right\}.$$ (7.18)

From (7.14), $A_0 + Y_1 + \sum_{t=2}^{T} E_1[Y_t]$ equals TC_1. Thus (7.18) becomes

$$C_2 = \frac{1}{T-1} \left\{ TC_1 - C_1 + \left(\sum_{t=2}^{T} E_2[Y_t] - \sum_{t=2}^{T} E_1[Y_t] \right) \right\}$$

$$= C_1 + \frac{1}{T-1} \left(\sum_{t=2}^{T} E_2[Y_t] - \sum_{t=2}^{T} E_1[Y_t] \right).$$

(7.19)

Equation (7.19) states that the change in consumption between period 1 and period 2 equals the change in the individual's estimate of his or her lifetime resources divided by the number of periods of life remaining.

Finally, note that the individual's behavior exhibits certainty equivalence: as (7.14) shows, the individual consumes the amount he or she would if his or her future incomes were certain to equal their means; that is, uncertainty about future income has no impact on consumption.

To see the intuition for this certainty-equivalence behavior, consider the Euler equation relating consumption in periods 1 and 2. With a general instantaneous utility function, this condition is

$$u'(C_1) = E_1[u'(C_2)].$$ (7.20)

When utility is quadratic, marginal utility is linear. Thus the expected marginal utility of consumption is the same as the marginal utility of expected consumption. That is, since $E_1[1 - aC_2] = 1 - aE_1[C_2]$, for quadratic utility (7.20) is equivalent to

$$u'(C_1) = u'(E_1[C_2]).$$ (7.21)

This implies $C_1 = E_1[C_2]$.

This analysis shows that quadratic utility is the source of certainty-equivalence behavior: if utility is not quadratic, marginal utility is not linear, and so (7.21) does not follow from (7.20). We return to this point in Section 7.6.[4]

7.3   Empirical Application: Two Tests of the Random-Walk Hypothesis

Hall's random-walk result ran strongly counter to existing views about consumption.[5] The traditional view of consumption over the business cycle implies that when output declines, consumption declines but is expected to recover; thus it implies that there are predictable movements in consumption. Hall's extension of the permanent-income hypothesis, in contrast, predicts that when output declines unexpectedly, consumption declines only by the amount of the fall in permanent income; as a result, it is not expected to recover.

Because of this divergence in the predictions of the two views, a great deal of effort has been devoted to testing whether predictable changes in income produce predictable changes in consumption. The hypothesis that consumption responds to predictable income movements is referred to as *excess sensitivity* of consumption (Flavin, 1981).[6]

Campbell and Mankiw's Test Using Aggregate Data

The random-walk hypothesis implies that the change in consumption is unpredictable; thus it implies that no information available at time $t - 1$ can

---

[4]Although the specific result that the change in consumption has a mean of zero and is unpredictable (equation [7.16]) depends on the assumption of quadratic utility (and on the assumption that the discount rate and the interest rate are equal), the result that departures of consumption growth from its average value are not predictable arises under more general assumptions. See, for example, Problem 7.3.

[5]Indeed, it is said that when Hall first presented the paper deriving and testing the random-walk result, one prominent macroeconomist told him that he must have been on drugs when he wrote the paper.

[6]The permanent-income hypothesis also makes predictions about how consumption responds to unexpected changes in income. In the model of Section 7.2, for example, the response to news is given by equation [7.19]. The hypothesis that consumption responds less than the permanent-income hypothesis predicts to unexpected changes in income is referred to as *excess smoothness* of consumption. Since excess sensitivity concerns expected changes in income and excess smoothness concerns unexpected changes, it is possible for consumption to be excessively sensitive and excessively smooth at the same time. For more on excess smoothness, see Campbell and Deaton (1989); West (1988); Flavin (1993); and Problem 7.4.

be used to forecast the change in consumption from $t - 1$ to t. Thus one approach to testing the random-walk hypothesis is to regress the change in consumption on variables that are known at $t - 1$. If the random-walk hypothesis is correct, the coefficients on the variables should not differ systematically from zero.

This is the approach that Hall took in his original work. He was unable to reject the hypothesis that lagged values of either income or consumption cannot predict the change in consumption. He did find, however, that lagged stock-price movements have statistically significant predictive power for the change in consumption.

The disadvantage of this approach is that the results are hard to interpret. Hall's result that lagged income does not have strong predictive power for consumption, for example, could arise not because predictable changes in income do not produce predictable changes in consumption, but because lagged values of income are of little use in predicting income movements. Similarly, it is hard to gauge the importance of the rejection of the random-walk prediction using stock-price data.

Campbell and Mankiw (1989a) therefore use an instrumental-variables approach to test Hall's hypothesis against a specific alternative. The alternative they consider is that some fraction of consumers simply spend their current income, and the remainder behave according to Hall's theory. This alternative implies that the change in consumption from period $t - 1$ to period t equals the change in income between $t - 1$ and t for the first group of consumers, and equals the change in estimated permanent income between $t - 1$ and t for the second group. Thus if we let λ denote the fraction of consumption that is done by consumers in the first group, the change in aggregate consumption is

$$C_t - C_{t-1} = \lambda(Y_t - Y_{t-1}) + (1 - \lambda)e_t,$$

$$\equiv \lambda Z_t + v_t,$$

(7.22)

where e_t is the change in consumers' estimate of their permanent income from $t - 1$ to t.

Z_t and v_t are almost surely correlated. Times when income increases greatly are usually also times when households receive favorable news about their total lifetime incomes. But this means that the right-hand-side variable in (7.22) is positively correlated with the error term. Thus estimating (7.22) by ordinary least squares (OLS) leads to estimates of λ that are biased upward.

The solution to correlation between the right-hand-side variable and the error term is to use instrumental variables (IV) rather than OLS. The intuition behind IV estimation is easiest to see using the two-stage least squares interpretation of instrumental variables. What one needs are variables correlated with the right-hand-side variables but uncorrelated with the residual. Once one has such *instruments,* the first-stage regression is a regression of the right-hand-side variable, Z_t, on the instruments. The second-stage regression is then a regression of the left-hand-side variable, $C_t - C_{t-1}$, on the fitted value of Z_t from the first-stage regression, $\hat{Z}_t$. That is, we estimate:

$$C_t - C_{t-1} = \lambda\hat{Z}_t + \lambda(Z_t - \hat{Z}_t) + v_t$$

$$\equiv \lambda\hat{Z}_t + \tilde{v}_t. \tag{7.23}$$

The residual in (7.23), $\tilde{v}_t$, consists of two terms, v_t and $\lambda(Z_t - \hat{Z}_t)$. By assumption, the instruments used to construct $\hat{Z}$ are not systematically correlated with v_t. And since $\hat{Z}$ is the fitted value from a regression, by construction it is uncorrelated with the residual from that regression, $Z - \hat{Z}$. Thus regressing $C_t - C_{t-1}$ on $\hat{Z}$ yields a valid estimate of λ.[7]

The usual problem in using instrumental variables is finding valid instruments: it is often hard to find variables that one can be confident are uncorrelated with the residual. But in cases where the residual reflects new information between $t - 1$ and t, theory tells us that there are many candidate instruments: any variable that is known as of time $t - 1$ is uncorrelated with the residual.

We can now turn to the specifics of Campbell and Mankiw's test. They measure consumption as real purchases of consumer nondurables and services per person, and income as real disposable income per person. The data are quarterly, and the sample period is 1953–1986. They consider various sets of instruments. They find that lagged changes in income have almost no predictive power for future changes. This suggests that Hall's failure to find predictive power of lagged income movements for consumption is not strong evidence against the traditional view of consumption. As a base case, they therefore use lagged values of the change in consumption as instruments. When three lags are used, the estimate of λ is 0.42, with a standard error of 0.16; when five lags are used, the estimate is 0.52, with a standard error of 0.13. Other specifications yield similar results.

Thus Campbell and Mankiw's estimates suggest quantitatively large and statistically significant departures from the predictions of the random-walk model: consumption appears to increase by about fifty cents in response to an anticipated 1-dollar increase in income, and the null hypothesis of no effect is strongly rejected. At the same time, the estimates of λ are far below

---

[7]The fact that $\hat{Z}$ is based on estimated coefficients causes two complications. First, the uncertainty about the estimated coefficients must be accounted for in finding the standard error of the estimate of λ; this is done in the usual formulas for the standard errors of instrumental-variables estimates. Second, the fact that the first-stage coefficients are estimated introduces some correlation between $\hat{Z}$ and v in the same direction as the correlation between Z and v. This correlation disappears as the sample size becomes large; thus IV is consistent but not unbiased. If the instruments are only moderately correlated with the right-hand-side variable, however, the bias in finite samples can be substantial. See, for example, Nelson and Startz (1990).

1. Thus the results also suggest that the permanent-income hypothesis is important to understanding consumption.[8]

Shea's Test Using Household Data

Testing the random-walk hypothesis with aggregate data has several disadvantages. Most obviously, the number of observations is small. In addition, it is difficult to find variables with much predictive power for changes in income; it is therefore hard to test the key prediction of the random-walk hypothesis that predictable changes in income are not associated with predictable changes in consumption. Finally, the theory concerns individuals' consumption, and additional assumptions are needed for the predictions of the model to apply to aggregate data. Entry and exit of households from the population, for example, can cause the predictions of the theory to fail in the aggregate even if they hold for each household individually.

Because of these considerations, many investigators have examined consumption behavior using data on individual households. Shea (1995) takes particular care to identify predictable changes in income. He focuses on households in the Panel Study of Income Dynamics (commonly referred to as the PSID) with wage-earners covered by long-term union contracts. For these households, the wage increases and cost-of-living provisions in the contracts cause income growth to have an important predictable component.

Shea constructs a sample of 647 observations where the union contract provides clear information about the household's future earnings. A regression of actual real wage growth on the estimate constructed from the union contract and some control variables produces a coefficient on the constructed measure of 0.86, with a standard error of 0.20. Thus the union contract has important predictive power for changes in earnings.

Shea then regresses consumption growth on this measure of expected wage growth; the permanent-income hypothesis predicts that the coeffi-

---

[8]In addition, the instrumental-variables approach has *overidentifying restrictions* that can be tested. If the lagged changes in consumption are valid instruments, they are uncorrelated with v. This implies that once we have extracted all of the information in the instruments about income growth, they should have no additional predictive power for the left-hand-side variable: if they do, that means that they are correlated with v, and thus that they are not valid instruments. This implication can be tested by regressing the estimated residuals from (7.22) on the instruments and testing whether the instruments have any explanatory power. Specifically, one can show that under the null hypothesis of valid instruments, the R^2 of this regression times the number of observations is asymptotically distributed χ^2 with degrees of freedom equal to the number of overidentifying restrictions—that is, the number of instruments minus the number of endogenous variables.

In Campbell and Mankiw's case, this TR^2 statistic is distributed χ^2_2 when three lags of the change in consumption are used, and χ^2_4 when five lags are used. The values of the test statistic in the two cases are only 1.83 and 2.94; these are only in the 59th and 43rd percentiles of the relevant χ^2 distributions. Thus the hypothesis that the instruments are valid cannot be rejected.

cient should be zero.[9] The estimated coefficient is in fact 0.89, with a standard error of 0.46. Thus Shea also finds a quantitatively large (though only marginally statistically significant) departure from the random-walk prediction.

Recall that in our analysis in Sections 7.1 and 7.2, we assumed that households can borrow without limit as long as they eventually repay their debts. One reason that consumption might not follow a random walk is that this assumption might fail—that is, that households might face *liquidity constraints.* If households are unable to borrow and their current income is less than their permanent income, their consumption is determined by their current income. In this case, predictable changes in income produce predictable changes in consumption.

Shea tests for liquidity constraints in two ways. First, following Zeldes (1989) and others, he divides the households according to whether they have liquid assets. Households with liquid assets can smooth their consumption by running down these assets rather than by borrowing. Thus if liquidity constraints are the reason that predictable wage changes affect consumption growth, the prediction of the permanent-income hypothesis will fail only among the households with no assets. Shea finds, however, that the estimated effect of expected wage growth on consumption is essentially the same in the two groups.

Second, following Altonji and Siow (1987), Shea splits the low-wealth sample according to whether the expected change in the real wage is positive or negative. Individuals facing expected declines in income need to save rather than borrow to smooth their consumption. Thus if liquidity constraints are important, predictable wage increases produce predictable consumption increases, but predictable wage decreases do not produce predictable consumption decreases.

Shea's findings are the opposite of this. For the households with positive expected income growth, the estimated impact of the expected change in the real wage on consumption growth is 0.06 (with a standard error of 0.79); for the households with negative expected growth, the estimated effect is 2.24 (with a standard error of 0.95). Thus there is no evidence that liquidity constraints are the source of Shea's results.

7.4 The Interest Rate and Saving

An important issue concerning consumption involves its response to rates of return. For example, many economists have argued that more favorable

---

[9]An alternative would be to follow Campbell and Mankiw's approach and regress consumption growth on actual income growth by instrumental variables, using the constructed wage growth measure as an instrument. Given the almost one-for-one relationship between actual and constructed earnings growth, this approach would be likely to produce similar results.

tax treatment of interest income would increase saving, and thus increase growth. But if consumption is relatively unresponsive to the rate of return, such policies would have little effect. Understanding the impact of rates of return on consumption is thus important.

The Interest Rate and Consumption Growth

We begin by extending the analysis of consumption under certainty in Section 7.1 to allow for a nonzero interest rate. This largely repeats material in Section 2.2; for convenience, however, we quickly repeat that analysis here.

Once we allow for a nonzero interest rate, the individual's budget constraint is that the present value of lifetime consumption cannot exceed initial wealth plus the present value of lifetime labor income. For the case of a constant interest rate and a lifetime of T periods, this constraint is

$$\sum_{t=1}^{T} \frac{1}{(1+r)^t} C_t \le A_0 + \sum_{t=1}^{T} \frac{1}{(1+r)^t} Y_t, \tag{7.24}$$

where r is the interest rate and where all variables are discounted to period 0.

When we allow for a nonzero interest rate, it is also useful to allow for a nonzero discount rate. In addition, it simplifies the analysis to assume that the instantaneous utility function takes the constant-relative-risk-aversion form used in Chapter 2: $u(C_t) = C_t^{1-\theta}/(1-\theta)$, where θ is the coefficient of relative risk aversion (the inverse of the elasticity of substitution between consumption at different dates). Thus the utility function, (7.1), becomes

$$U = \sum_{t=1}^{T} \frac{1}{(1+\rho)^t} \frac{C_t^{1-\theta}}{1-\theta}, \tag{7.25}$$

where ρ is the discount rate.

Now consider our usual experiment of a decrease in consumption in some period, period t, accompanied by an increase in consumption in the next period by $1+r$ times the amount of the decrease. Optimization requires that a marginal change of this type has no effect on lifetime utility. Since the marginal utilities of consumption in periods t and $t+1$ are $C_t^{-\theta}/(1+\rho)^t$ and $C_{t+1}^{-\theta}/(1+\rho)^{t+1}$, this condition is

$$\frac{1}{(1+\rho)^t} C_t^{-\theta} = (1+r)\frac{1}{(1+\rho)^{t+1}} C_{t+1}^{-\theta}. \tag{7.26}$$

We can rearrange this condition to obtain

$$\frac{C_{t+1}}{C_t} = \left(\frac{1+r}{1+\rho}\right)^{1/\theta}. \tag{7.27}$$

This analysis implies that once we allow for the possibility that the real interest rate and the discount rate are not equal, consumption need not be a random walk: consumption is rising over time if r exceeds ρ and falling if r is less than ρ. In addition, if there are variations in the real interest rate, there are variations in the predictable component of consumption growth. Mankiw (1981), Hansen and Singleton (1983), Hall (1988b), Campbell and Mankiw (1989a), and others therefore examine how much consumption growth responds to variations in the real interest rate. For the most part they find that it responds relatively little, which suggests that the intertemporal elasticity of substitution is low (that is, that θ is high).

The Interest Rate and Saving in the Two-Period Case

Although an increase in the interest rate causes the path of consumption to be more steeply sloped, it does not necessarily follow that the increase reduces initial consumption and thereby raises saving. The complication is that the change in the interest rate has not only a substitution effect, but also an income effect. Specifically, if the individual is a net saver, the increase in the interest rate allows him or her to attain a higher path of consumption than before.

The qualitative issues can be seen in the case where the individual lives for only two periods. For this case, we can use the standard indifference-curve diagram shown in Figure 7.2. Assume, for simplicity, that the individual has no initial wealth. Thus in (C_1, C_2) space, the individual's budget constraint goes through the point (Y_1, Y_2): the individual can choose to consume his or her income each period. And the slope of the budget constraint is $-(1 + r)$: giving up one unit of first-period consumption allows the individual to increase second-period consumption by $1 + r$. When r rises, the budget constraint continues to go through (Y_1, Y_2) but becomes steeper; thus it pivots clockwise around (Y_1, Y_2).

In Panel (a), the individual is initially at the point (Y_1, Y_2); that is, saving is initially zero. In this case the increase in r has no income effect—the individual's initial consumption bundle continues to be on the budget constraint. Thus first-period consumption necessarily falls, and so saving necessarily rises.

In Panel (b), C_1 is initially less than Y_1, and thus saving is positive. In this case the increase in r has a positive income effect—the individual can now afford strictly more than his or her initial bundle. The income effect acts to decrease saving, whereas the substitution effect acts to increase it. The overall effect is ambiguous; in the case shown in the figure, saving does not change.

Finally, in Panel (c) the individual is initially borrowing. In this case both the substitution and income effects reduce first-period consumption, and so saving necessarily rises.

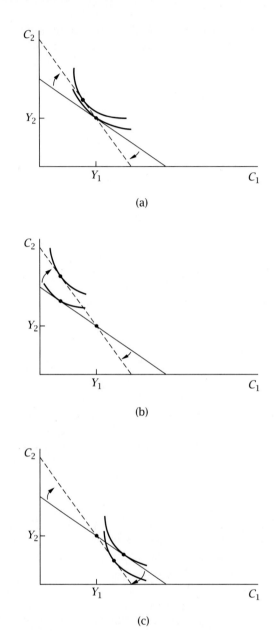

(a)

(b)

(c)

FIGURE 7.2   The interest rate and consumption choices in the two-period case

Since the stock of wealth in the economy is positive, individuals are on average savers rather than borrowers. Thus the overall income effect of a rise in the interest rate is positive. An increase in the interest rate thus has two competing effects on overall saving, a positive one through the substitution effect and a negative one through the income effect.

Complications

This discussion appears to imply that, unless the elasticity of substitution between consumption in different periods is large, increases in the interest rate are unlikely to bring about substantial increases in saving. There are two reasons, however, that the importance of this conclusion is limited.

First, many of the changes we are interested in do not involve just changes in the interest rate. For tax policy, the relevant experiment is usually a change in composition between taxes on interest income and other taxes that leaves government revenue unchanged. As Problem 7.5 shows, such a change has only a substitution effect, and thus necessarily shifts consumption toward the future.

Second, and more subtly, if individuals have long horizons, small changes in saving can accumulate over time into large changes in wealth (Summers, 1981a). To see this, first consider an individual with an infinite horizon and constant labor income. Suppose that the interest rate equals the individual's discount rate. From (7.27), this means that the individual's consumption is constant. The budget constraint then implies that the individual consumes the sum of interest and labor incomes: any higher steady level of consumption implies violating the budget constraint, and any lower level implies failing to satisfy the constraint with equality. That is, the individual maintains his or her initial wealth level regardless of its value: the individual is willing to hold any amount of wealth if $r = \rho$. A similar analysis shows that if $r > \rho$, the individual's wealth grows without bound, and that if $r < \rho$, his or her wealth falls without bound. Thus the long-run supply of capital is perfectly elastic at $r = \rho$.

Summers shows that similar, though less extreme, results hold in the case of long but finite lifetimes. Suppose, for example, that r is slightly larger than ρ, that the intertemporal elasticity of substitution is small, and that labor income is constant. The facts that r exceeds ρ and that the elasticity of substitution is small imply that consumption rises slowly over the individual's lifetime. But with a long lifetime, this means that consumption is much larger at the end of life than at the beginning. But since labor income is constant, this in turn implies that the individual gradually builds up considerable savings over the first part of his or her life and gradually decumulates them over the remainder. As a result, when horizons are finite but long, wealth holdings may be highly responsive to the interest rate in the long run even if the intertemporal elasticity of substitution is small.[10]

7.5 Consumption and Risky Assets

In practice, individuals can invest in many assets, almost all of which have uncertain returns. Extending our analysis to account for multiple assets and risk raises some new issues concerning both household behavior and asset markets.

The Conditions for Individual Optimization

Consider our usual experiment of an individual reducing consumption in period t by an infinitesimal amount and using the resulting saving to raise consumption in period $t + 1$. If the individual is optimizing, this change leaves expected utility unchanged regardless of which asset the increased saving is invested in. Thus optimization requires

$$u'(C_t) = \frac{1}{1 + \rho} E_t[(1 + r^i_{t+1})u'(C_{t+1})] \qquad \text{for all } i, \qquad (7.28)$$

where r^i is the return on asset i. Since the expectation of the product of two variables equals the product of their expectations plus their covariance, we can rewrite this expression as

$$u'(C_t) = \frac{1}{1 + \rho}\{E_t[1 + r^i_{t+1}]E_t[u'(C_{t+1})] + \text{Cov}_t(1 + r^i_{t+1}, u'(C_{t+1})\} \qquad \text{for all } i,$$

$$(7.29)$$

where $\text{Cov}_t(\bullet)$ is covariance conditional on information available at time t.

If we assume that utility is quadratic, $u(C) = C - aC^2/2$, then the marginal utility of consumption is $1 - aC$. Using this to substitute for the covariance term in (7.29), we obtain

$$u'(C_t) = \frac{1}{1 + \rho}\left\{E_t[1 + r^i_{t+1}]E_t[u'(C_{t+1})] - a\text{Cov}_t(1 + r^i_{t+1}, C_{t+1})\right\}. \qquad (7.30)$$

Equation (7.30) implies that in deciding whether to hold more of an asset, the individual is not concerned with how risky the asset is: the variance of the asset's return does not appear in (7.30). Intuitively, a marginal increase in holdings of an asset that is risky, but whose risk is not correlated with

---

[10]Carroll (1992) shows, however, that the presence of uncertainty weakens this conclusion somewhat.

the overall risk the individual faces, does not increase the variance of the individual's consumption. Thus in evaluating that marginal decision, the individual considers only the asset's expected return.

Equation (7.30) implies that the aspect of riskiness that matters to the decision of whether to hold more of an asset is the relation between the asset's payoff and consumption. Suppose, for example, that the individual is given an opportunity to buy a new asset whose expected return equals the rate of return on a risk-free asset that the individual is already able to buy. If the payoff to the new asset is typically high when the marginal utility of consumption is high (that is, when consumption is low), buying one unit of the asset raises expected utility by more than buying one unit of the risk-free asset does. Thus (since the individual was previously indifferent about buying more of the risk-free asset), the individual can raise his or her expected utility by buying the new asset. As the individual invests more in the asset, his or her consumption comes to depend more on the asset's payoff, and so the covariance between consumption and the asset's return becomes less negative. In the example we are considering, since the asset's expected return equals the risk-free rate, the individual invests in the asset until the covariance of its return with consumption reaches zero.

This discussion implies that hedging risks is crucial to optimal portfolio choices. A steel worker whose future labor income depends on the health of the American steel industry should avoid—or better yet, sell short—assets whose returns are positively correlated with the fortunes of the steel industry, such as shares in American steel companies. Instead the worker should invest in assets whose returns move inversely with the health of the U.S. steel industry, such as foreign steel companies or American aluminum companies.

The Consumption CAPM

This discussion takes assets' expected returns as given. But individuals' demands for assets determine these expected returns. If, for example, an asset's payoff is highly correlated with consumption, its price must be driven down to the point where its expected return is high for individuals to hold it.

To see the implications of this observation, suppose that all individuals are the same, and return to the first-order condition in (7.30). Solving this expression for the expected return on the asset yields

$$E_t[1 + r_{t+1}^i] = \frac{1}{E_t[u'(C_{t+1})]}[(1 + \rho)u'(C_t) + a\operatorname{Cov}_t(1 + r_{t+1}^i, C_{t+1})]. \quad (7.31)$$

Equation (7.31) states that the higher the covariance of an asset's payoff with consumption, the higher its expected return must be.

We can simplify (7.31) by considering the return on a risk-free asset. If the payoff to an asset is certain, then the covariance of its payoff with consumption is zero. Thus the risk-free rate, $\overline{r}_{t+1}$, satisfies

$$1 + \overline{r}_{t+1} = \frac{(1 + \rho)u'(C_t)}{E_t[u'(C_{t+1})]}. \tag{7.32}$$

Subtracting (7.32) from (7.31) then gives us

$$E_t[r_{t+1}^i] - \overline{r}_{t+1} = \frac{a\,\mathrm{Cov}_t(1 + r_{t+1}^i, C_{t+1})}{E_t[u'(C_{t+1})]}. \tag{7.33}$$

Equation (7.33) states that the expected-return premium an asset must offer relative to the risk-free rate is proportional to the covariance of its return with consumption.

This model of the determination of expected asset returns is known as the *consumption capital-asset pricing model,* or *consumption CAPM.* The covariance between an asset's return and consumption is known as its *consumption beta.* Thus the central prediction of the consumption CAPM is that the premiums that assets offer are proportional to their consumption betas (Breeden, 1979; see also Merton, 1973, and Rubinstein, 1976).[11]

Empirical Application: The Equity-Premium Puzzle

One of the most important implications of this analysis of assets' expected returns concerns the case where the risky asset is a broad portfolio of stocks. To see the issues involved, it is easiest to return to the Euler equation, (7.28), and to assume that individuals have constant-relative-risk-aversion utility rather than quadratic utility. With this assumption, the Euler equation becomes

$$C_t^{-\theta} = \frac{1}{1 + \rho} E_t[(1 + r_{t+1}^i)C_{t+1}^{-\theta}], \tag{7.34}$$

where θ is the coefficient of relative risk aversion. If we divide both sides by $C_t^{-\theta}$ and multiply both sides by $1 + \rho$, this expression becomes

$$1 + \rho = E_t\left[(1 + r_{t+1}^i)\frac{C_{t+1}^{-\theta}}{C_t^{-\theta}}\right]. \tag{7.35}$$

Finally, it is convenient to let g_{t+1}^c denote the growth rate of consumption from t to $t + 1$, $(C_{t+1}/C_t) - 1$, and to omit the time subscripts. Thus we have

---

[11]The original CAPM assumes that investors are concerned with the mean and variance of the return on their portfolio rather than the mean and variance of consumption. That version of the model therefore focuses on *market betas*—that is, the covariances of assets' returns with the returns on the market portfolio—and predicts that expected-return premia are proportional to market betas (Lintner, 1965; Sharpe, 1964).

$$E[(1 + r^i)(1 + g^c)^{-\theta}] = 1 + \rho. \tag{7.36}$$

To see the implications of (7.36), we take a second-order Taylor approximation of the left-hand side around $r = g = 0$. Computing the relevant derivatives yields

$$(1 + r)(1 + g)^{-\theta} \simeq 1 + r - \theta g - \theta gr + \frac{1}{2}\theta(\theta + 1)g^2. \tag{7.37}$$

Thus we can rewrite (7.36) as

$$E[r^i] - \theta E[g^c] - \theta\{E[r^i]E[g^c] + \text{Cov}(r^i, g^c)\}$$
$$+ \frac{1}{2}\theta(\theta + 1)\{(E[g^c])^2 + \text{Var}(g^c)\} \simeq \rho. \tag{7.38}$$

When the time period involved is short, the $E[r^i]E[g^c]$ and $(E[g^c])^2$ terms are small relative to the others.[12] Omitting these terms and solving the resulting expression for $E[r^i]$ yields

$$E[r^i] \simeq \rho + \theta E[g^c] + \theta\text{Cov}(r^i, g^c) - \frac{1}{2}\theta(\theta + 1)\text{Var}(g^c). \tag{7.39}$$

Again, it is helpful to consider a risk-free asset. For such an asset, (7.39) simplifies to

$$\bar{r} \simeq \rho + \theta E[g^c] - \frac{1}{2}\theta(\theta + 1)\text{Var}(g^c). \tag{7.40}$$

Finally, subtracting (7.40) from (7.39) yields

$$E[r^i] - \bar{r} \simeq \theta\text{Cov}(r^i, g^c). \tag{7.41}$$

In a famous paper, Mehra and Prescott (1985) show that it is difficult to reconcile observed asset returns with equation (7.41). Mankiw and Zeldes (1991) report a simple calculation that shows the essence of the problem. For the United States during the period 1890–1979 (which is the sample that Mehra and Prescott consider), the difference between the average return on the stock market and the return on short-term government debt—the *equity premium*—is about six percentage points. Thus if we take the average return on short-term government debt as an approximation to the average risk-free rate, the quantity $E[r^i] - \bar{r}$ is about 0.06. Over the same period, the standard deviation of the growth of consumption (as measured by real purchases of nondurables and services) is 3.6 percentage points, and the standard deviation of the return on the market is 16.7 percentage points; the

---

[12]Indeed, for the continuous-time case, one can derive equation (7.39) without any approximations.

correlation between these two quantities is 0.40. These figures imply that the covariance of consumption growth and the return on the market is 0.40(0.036)(0.167), or 0.0024.

Equation (7.41) therefore implies that the coefficient of relative risk aversion needed to account for the equity premium is the solution to $0.06 = \theta(0.0024)$, or $\theta = 25$. This is an extraordinary level of risk aversion; it implies, for example, that individuals prefer a 17% reduction in consumption with certainty to a 1-in-2 chance of a 20% reduction. As Mehra and Prescott describe, other evidence suggest that risk aversion is much lower than this. Among other things, such a high degree of aversion to variations in consumption makes it puzzling that the average risk-free rate is close to zero despite the fact that consumption is growing over time.

In addition, the problem becomes even more severe if we focus on the postwar period. Mankiw and Zeldes report that for the 1948–1988 period, the average equity premium is 8 percentage points, the standard deviation of consumption growth is 1.4 percentage points, the standard deviation of the market return is 14.0 percentage points, and the correlation of consumption growth and the market return is 0.45. These numbers imply a value of θ of $0.08/[0.45(0.014)(0.140)] \simeq 91$.

The large equity premium, particularly when coupled with the low risk-free rate, is thus difficult to reconcile with household optimization. This *equity-premium puzzle* has stimulated a large amount of research, and many explanations for it have been proposed. No clear resolution of the puzzle has been provided, however.[13]

7.6   Alternative Views of Consumption

The permanent-income hypothesis provides appealing explanations of many important features of consumption. For example, it explains why temporary tax cuts appear to have much smaller effects than permanent ones, and it accounts for many features of the relationship between current income and consumption, such as those described in Section 7.1.

Yet there are also important features of consumption that appear inconsistent with the permanent-income hypothesis. For example, as described in Section 7.3, both macroeconomic and microeconomic evidence suggest that consumption responds to predictable changes in income. And as we just saw, simple models of consumer optimization cannot account for the equity premium.

---

[13]Cochrane and Hansen (1992) provide an overview of work on the puzzle and a framework for thinking about proposed explanations. For some proposed explanations, see Mankiw (1986b); Mankiw and Zeldes (1991); Constantinides (1990); Campbell and Cochrane (1995); Weil (1989b); Epstein and Zin (1991); and Problem 7.10.

Because of these and other difficulties, there has been considerable work on extensions or alternatives to the permanent-income hypothesis. This section touches on some of the issues raised by these theories.[14]

Precautionary Saving and the Growth of Consumption

Recall that our derivation of the random-walk result in Section 7.2 was based on the assumption that utility is quadratic. Quadratic utility requires, however, that marginal utility reaches zero at some finite level of consumption and then becomes negative. It also implies that the utility cost of a given variance of consumption is independent of the level of consumption. Since the marginal utility of consumption is declining, individuals have increasing absolute risk aversion: the amount of consumption they are willing to give up to avoid a given amount of uncertainty about the level of consumption rises as they become wealthier. These difficulties with quadratic utility suggest that marginal utility falls more slowly as consumption rises; that is, the third derivative of utility is probably positive rather than zero.

To see the effects of a positive third derivative, assume that both the real interest rate and the discount rate are zero, and consider again the Euler equation relating consumption in consecutive periods, equation (7.20): $u'(C_t) = E_t[u'(C_{t+1})]$. As described in Section 7.2, if utility is quadratic, marginal utility is linear, and so $E_t[u'(C_{t+1})]$ equals $u'(E_t[C_{t+1}])$; thus in this case, the Euler equation reduces to $C_t = E_t[C_{t+1}]$. But if $u'''(\bullet)$ is positive, then $u'(C)$ is a convex function of C. Thus in this case $E_t[u'(C_{t+1})]$ exceeds $u'(E_t[C_{t+1}])$. But this means that if C_t and $E_t[C_{t+1}]$ are equal, $E_t[u'(C_{t+1})]$ is greater than $u'(C_t)$, and so a marginal reduction in C_t increases expected utility. Thus the combination of a positive third derivative of the utility function and uncertainty about future income reduces current consumption, and thus raises saving. This saving is known as *precautionary saving* (Leland, 1968).

Panel (a) of Figure 7.3 shows the impact of uncertainty and a positive third derivative of the utility function on the expected marginal utility of consumption. Since $u''(C)$ is negative, $u'(C)$ is decreasing in C. And since $u'''(C)$ is positive, $u'(C)$ declines less rapidly as C rises—that is, $u'(C)$ is convex. If consumption takes on only two possible values, C_A and C_B, each with probability $\frac{1}{2}$, the expected marginal utility of consumption is the average of marginal utility at these two values. In terms of the diagram, this is shown by the midpoint of the line connecting $u'(C_A)$ and $u'(C_B)$. As the

---

[14]Three extensions of the permanent-income hypothesis that we will not discuss are durability of consumption goods, habit formation, and nonexpected utility. For durability, see Mankiw (1982); Caballero (1990a, 1993); Eberly (1994); and Problem 7.6. For habit formation, see Deaton (1992, pp. 29–34, 99–100) and Campbell and Cochrane (1995). For nonexpected utility, see Weil (1989b, 1990) and Epstein and Zin (1989, 1991).

(a)

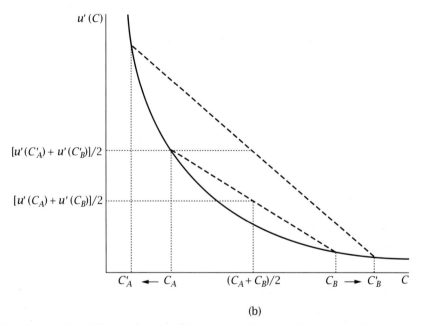

(b)

FIGURE 7.3   The effects of a positive third derivative of the utility function on the expected marginal utility of consumption

diagram shows, the fact that $u'(C)$ is convex implies that this quantity is larger than marginal utility at the average value of consumption, $(C_A+C_B)/2$.

Panel (b) shows the effects of an increase in uncertainty. When the high value of consumption rises, the fact that $u'''(C)$ is positive means that marginal utility falls relatively little; but when the low value falls, the positive third derivative magnifies the rise in marginal utility. As a result, the increase in uncertainty raises expected marginal utility for a given value of expected consumption. Thus the increase in uncertainty raises the incentive to save.

An important question, of course, is whether precautionary saving is quantitatively important. To address this issue, recall that in our analysis of the equity premium we found that the Euler equation for the risk-free asset is $\bar{r} \simeq \rho + \theta E[g^c] - \theta(\theta + 1)\text{Var}(g^c)/2$ (see [7.40]). For the case of $\bar{r} = \rho$, this becomes

$$E[g^c] \simeq \frac{1}{2}(\theta + 1)\text{Var}(g^c). \tag{7.42}$$

Thus the impact of precautionary saving on expected consumption growth depends on the variance of consumption growth and the coefficient of relative risk aversion.[15] If both are substantial, precautionary saving can have a large effect on expected consumption growth. If the coefficient of relative risk aversion is 4 (which is toward the high end of values that are viewed as plausible), and the standard deviation of households' uncertainty about their consumption a year ahead is 0.1 (which is consistent with the evidence in Dynan, 1993, and Carroll, 1992), (7.42) implies that precautionary saving raises expected consumption growth by $(1/2)(4 + 1)(0.1)^2$, or 2.5 percentage points.[16]

Finally, the presence of precautionary saving implies that not just expectations of future income but also uncertainty about that income affects consumption. C. Romer (1990), for example, argues that the tremendous uncertainty generated by the stock-market crash of 1929 and by the subsequent gyrations of the stock market was a major force behind the sharp fall in consumption spending in 1930, and thus behind the onset of the Great Depression. To give another example, Barsky, Mankiw, and Zeldes (1986) show that the combination of a current tax cut and an offsetting increase in future tax rates reduces households' uncertainty about their lifetime after-tax resources. Thus when there is precautionary saving, this change raises current consumption. More generally, Caballero (1990b) observes that, for a given level of expected lifetime resources, uncertainty is likely to be larger when

---

[15]For a general utility function, the $\theta + 1$ term is replaced by $-Cu'''(C)/u''(C)$. In analogy to the coefficient of relative risk aversion, $-Cu''(C)/u'(C)$, Kimball (1990) refers to $-Cu'''(C)/u''(C)$ as the coefficient of relative prudence.

[16]For more on the impact of precautionary saving on the level of aggregate consumption, see Skinner (1988); Caballero (1991); and Aiyagari (1994).

more of those resources are expected to come in the future. As a result, precautionary saving can help to account for the fact that when income is expected to rise, consumption is also expected to rise. Finally, Dynan (1993) and Carroll (1994) investigate the empirical relationship between households' uncertainty about their future income and consumption growth; they reach conflicting conclusions, however.

Liquidity Constraints

The permanent-income hypothesis assumes that individuals can borrow at the same interest rate at which they can save as long as they eventually repay their loans. Yet the interest rates that households pay on credit-card debt, automobile loans, and other borrowing are often much higher than the rates they obtain on their saving. In addition, some individuals are unable to borrow more at any interest rate.

A large literature investigates the causes, extent, and effects of such liquidity constraints. They are potentially important for many aspects of consumption. As described in Section 7.3, they can produce excess sensitivity of consumption to predictable changes in income. If individuals face high interest rates for borrowing, they may choose not to borrow to smooth their consumption when their current resources are low. And if they cannot borrow at all, they have no choice but to have low consumption when their current resources are low. Thus liquidity constraints can cause current income to be more important to consumption than is predicted by the permanent-income hypothesis.

This chapter will not provide a thorough treatment of liquidity constraints.[17] Instead, as with our discussion of precautionary saving, we will focus on the potential effects of liquidity constraints on the level of consumption.

Liquidity constraints can raise saving in two ways. First, and most obviously, whenever a liquidity constraint is binding, it causes the individual to consume less than he or she otherwise would. Second, as Zeldes (1989) emphasizes, even if the constraints are not currently binding, the fact that they may bind in the future reduces current consumption. Suppose, for example, that there is some chance of low income in the next period. If there are no liquidity constraints, and if income in fact turns out to be low, the individual can borrow to avoid a sharp fall in consumption. If there are liquidity constraints, however, the fall in income causes a large fall in consumption unless the individual has savings. Thus the presence of liquidity constraints

---

[17] See Deaton (1992, pp. 194–213) for a general introduction to liquidity constraints. In addition, Section 8.7 presents a model of capital-market imperfections in the context of loans to firms rather than to households.

causes individuals to save as insurance against the effects of future falls in income.

These points can be seen in a three-period model. To distinguish the effects of liquidity constraints from precautionary saving, assume that the instantaneous utility function is quadratic. In addition, continue to assume that the real interest rate and the discount rate are zero.

Begin by considering the individual's behavior in period 2. Let A_t denote assets at the end of period t. Since the individual lives for only three periods, C_3 equals $A_2 + Y_3$, which in turn equals $A_1 + Y_2 + Y_3 - C_2$. The individual's expected utility over the last two periods of life as a function of his or her choice of C_2 is therefore

$$U = (C_2 - \frac{1}{2}aC_2^2) + E_2[(A_1 + Y_2 + Y_3 - C_2) - \frac{1}{2}a(A_1 + Y_2 + Y_3 - C_2)^2]. \quad (7.43)$$

The derivative of this expression with respect to C_2 is

$$\frac{\partial U}{\partial C_2} = 1 - aC_2 - (1 - aE_2[A_1 + Y_2 + Y_3 - C_2]) \quad (7.44)$$

$$= a(A_1 + Y_2 + E_2[Y_3] - 2C_2).$$

This expression is positive for $C_2 < (A_1 + Y_2 + E_2[Y_3])/2$, and negative thereafter. Thus, as we know from our earlier analysis, if the liquidity constraint does not bind, the individual chooses $C_2 = (A_1 + Y_2 + E_2[Y_3])/2$. But if it does bind, he or she sets consumption to the maximum attainable level, which is $A_1 + Y_2$. Thus,

$$C_2 = \min\left[\frac{A_1 + Y_2 + E_2[Y_3]}{2}, A_1 + Y_2\right]. \quad (7.45)$$

Thus the liquidity constraint reduces current consumption if it is binding.

Now consider the first period. If the liquidity constraint is not binding that period, the individual has the option of marginally raising C_1 and paying for this by reducing C_2. Thus if the individual's assets are not literally zero, the usual Euler equation holds. With the specific assumptions we are making here, this means that C_1 equals the expectation of C_2.

But the fact that the Euler equation holds does not mean that the liquidity constraints do not affect consumption. Equation (7.45) implies that if the probability that the liquidity constraint will bind in the second period is strictly positive, the expectation of C_2 as of period 1 is strictly less than the expectation of $(A_1 + Y_2 + E_2[Y_3])/2$. A_1 is given by $A_0 + Y_1 - C_1$, and the law of iterated projections implies that $E_1[E_2[Y_3]]$ equals $E_1[Y_3]$. Thus,

$$C_1 < \frac{A_0 + Y_1 + E_1[Y_2] + E_1[Y_3] - C_1}{2}. \quad (7.46)$$

Adding $C_1/2$ to both sides of this expression and then dividing by $3/2$ yields

$$C_1 < \frac{A_0 + Y_1 + E_1[Y_2] + E_1[Y_3]}{3}. \tag{7.47}$$

Thus even when the liquidity constraint does not bind currently, the possibility that it will bind in the future reduces consumption.

Finally, if the value of C_1 that satisfies $C_1 = E_1[C_2]$ (given that C_2 is determined by [7.45]) is greater than the individual's period-1 resources, $A_0 + Y_1$, the first-period liquidity constraint is binding; in this case the individual consumes $A_0 + Y_1$.[18]

Empirical Application: Liquidity Constraints and Aggregate Saving

As we have just seen, liquidity constraints can raise saving. Jappelli and Pagano (1994) investigate empirically whether cross-country differences in liquidity constraints are important to cross-country differences in aggregate saving.

Jappelli and Pagano begin by arguing that there are important differences in the extent of liquidity constraints across countries. In Spain and Japan, for example, home purchases generally require down payments of 40% of the purchase price, whereas in the United States and France they require 20% or less. Similarly, Korea strongly restricts the availability of consumer credit, but the Scandinavian countries do not. Bankruptcy and foreclosure laws also vary greatly. In Belgium and Spain, for example, it takes two years or more to foreclose on a mortgage, whereas in Denmark and the Netherlands it takes less than six months. Greater legal barriers to foreclosure are likely to discourage lending.

Jappelli and Pagano then ask whether these differences in credit availability are associated with differences in saving rates. They first examine the relationship between the loan-to-value ratio for home purchases (that is, one minus the required down payment) and the saving rate. As Figure 7.4 shows, there is a clear negative association. They then add the loan-to-value ratio to a regression of saving rates on measures of government saving, the demographic composition of the population, and income growth. The loan-to-value ratio enters negatively and significantly. In a typical specification, the point estimates imply that an increase in the required down payment of 10 percent of the purchase price is associated with a rise in the saving rate of 2 percent of NNP. They also find that using a measure of the availability of consumer credit in place of the loan-to-value ratio yields similar results.

---

[18]Because both present and future liquidity constraints potentially affect behavior, complete solutions of models with liquidity constraints usually require the use of numerical methods (see, for example, Deaton, 1992, pp. 180–189).

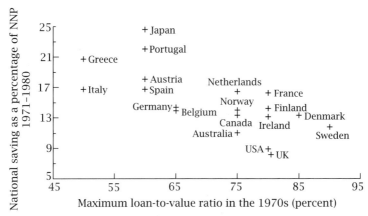

FIGURE 7.4   The loan-to-value ratio for home purchases and the saving rate (from Jappelli and Pagano, 1994; used with permission)

In sum, their evidence suggests that liquidity constraints are important to aggregate saving.[19]

Empirical Application: Buffer-Stock Saving

A central prediction of the permanent-income hypothesis is that there should be no relation between the expected growth of an individual's income over his or her lifetime and the expected growth of his or her consumption: consumption growth is determined by the real interest rate and the discount rate, not by the time pattern of income.

Carroll and Summers (1991) present extensive evidence that this prediction of the permanent-income hypothesis is incorrect. For example, individuals in countries where income growth is high typically have high rates of consumption growth over their lifetimes, and individuals in slowly growing countries typically have low rates of consumption growth. Similarly, typical lifetime consumption patterns of individuals in different occupations tend to match typical lifetime income patterns in those occupations. Managers and professionals, for example, generally have earnings profiles that rise steeply until middle age and then level off; their consumption profiles follow a similar pattern.

More generally, most households have little wealth (see, for example, Deaton, 1991, and Hubbard, Skinner, and Zeldes, 1994a). Their consumption

---

[19] Jappelli and Pagano go on to investigate the relationship between liquidity constraints and aggregate growth. They find that even when they control for investment, liquidity constraints are positively related to growth. Given that the way that liquidity constraints most plausibly affect growth is through their effect on saving (and hence investment), this finding is difficult to interpret.

approximately tracks their income, but they have a small amount of saving that they use in the event of sharp falls in income or emergency spending needs. In the terminology of Deaton (1991), most households exhibit *buffer-stock* saving behavior. As a result, a small fraction of households hold the vast majority of wealth.

At least three explanations of buffer-stock saving have been proposed. First, Shefrin and Thaler (1988) argue that consumption behavior is not well described by complete intertemporal optimization (see also Laibson, 1993). Instead, individuals have a set of rules of thumb that they use to guide their consumption behavior. Examples of these rules of thumb are that it is usually reasonable to spend one's current income, but that assets should be dipped into only in exceptional circumstances. Such rules of thumb may lead consumers to use saving and borrowing to smooth short-run income fluctuations, and thus cause consumption to follow the predictions of the permanent-income hypothesis reasonably well at short horizons. But they may also cause consumption to track income fairly closely over long horizons.

Second, Deaton (1991) and Carroll (1992) argue that buffer-stock saving arises from a combination of a high discount rate, a precautionary-saving motive, and some reason that households do not go heavily into debt. In Deaton's analysis, the reason for the absence of debt is the presence of liquidity constraints. In Carroll's, it is that the marginal utility of consumption approaches infinity as consumption becomes sufficiently low; as a result, households are unwilling to risk the very low consumption that would occur if they were in debt and their future income turned out to be low. The combination of the high discount rate and the inability or unwillingness to go into debt causes households' wealth to be approximately zero, and thus causes consumption to approximately track income. But even with a relatively high discount rate, the positive third derivative of the utility function causes households to view the risks of sharp falls in consumption and sharp rises as asymmetric; as a result, they typically keep a small amount of savings to use in the event of large falls in income.

Third, Hubbard, Skinner, and Zeldes (1994a, 1994b) suggest an explanation of buffer-stock saving that is close in spirit to the permanent-income hypothesis. The key elements of their explanation, aside from intertemporal optimization, are a precautionary-saving motive and the fact that welfare programs provide insurance against very low levels of consumption. For households that face a nonnegligible probability of going on welfare, the presence of welfare discourages saving in two ways: it directly provides insurance against unfavorable realizations of income, and it imposes extremely high implicit tax rates on asset holdings. Nonetheless, the precautionary-saving motive causes these households to typically hold some assets when their consumption is above the guaranteed floor. For households whose income prospects are favorable enough that the possibility of going on welfare is negligible, on the other hand, consumption is determined by conventional intertemporal optimization; thus they exhibit conventional life-cycle saving. Hubbard, Skinner, and Zeldes therefore argue that the different patterns of wealth accumulation of the poor and the rich can be explained without appealing to differences in their preferences.

Problems

7.1. The average income of farmers is less than the average income of non-farmers, but fluctuates more from year to year. Given this, how does the permanent-income hypothesis predict that estimated consumption functions for farmers and nonfarmers differ?

7.2. The time-averaging problem. (Working, 1960.) Actual data do not give consumption at a point in time, but average consumption over an extended period, such as a quarter. This problem asks you to examine the effects of this fact.

Suppose that consumption follows a random walk: $C_t = C_{t-1} + e_t$, where e is white noise. Suppose, however, that the data provide average consumption over two-period intervals; that is, one observes $(C_t + C_{t+1})/2$, $(C_{t+2} + C_{t+3})/2$, and so on.

(a) Find an expression for the change in measured consumption from one two-period interval to the next in terms of the e's.

(b) Is the change in measured consumption uncorrelated with the previous value of the change in measured consumption? In light of this, is measured consumption a random walk?

(c) Given your result in part (a), is the change in consumption from one two-period interval to the next necessarily uncorrelated with anything known as of the first of these two-period intervals? Is it necessarily uncorrelated with anything known as of the two-period interval immediately preceding the first of the two-period intervals?

(d) Suppose that measured consumption for a two-period interval is not the average over the interval, but consumption in the second of the two periods. That is, one observes C_{t+1}, C_{t+3}, and so on. In this case, is measured consumption a random walk?

7.3. (This follows Hansen and Singleton, 1983.) Suppose instantaneous utility is of the constant-relative-risk-aversion form, $u(C_t) = C_t^{1-\theta}/(1-\theta)$, $\theta > 0$. Assume that the real interest rate, r, is constant but not necessarily equal to the discount rate, ρ.

(a) Find the Euler equation relating C_t to expectations concerning C_{t+1}.

(b) Suppose that the log of income is distributed normally, and that as a result the log of C_{t+1} is distributed normally; let σ^2 denote its variance conditional on information available at time t. Rewrite the expression in part (a) in terms of $\ln C_t$, $E_t[\ln C_{t+1}]$, σ^2, and the parameters r, ρ, and θ. (Hint: if a variable x is distributed normally with mean μ and variance V, $E[e^x] = e^\mu e^{V/2}$.)

(c) Show that if r and σ^2 are constant over time, the result in part (b) implies that the log of consumption follows a random walk with drift: $\ln C_{t+1} = a + \ln C_t + u_{t+1}$, where u is white noise.

(d) How do changes in each of r and σ^2 affect expected consumption growth, $E_t[\ln C_{t+1} - \ln C_t]$? Interpret the effect of σ^2 on expected consumption growth in light of the discussion of precautionary saving in Section 7.6.

7.4. A framework for investigating excess smoothness. Suppose that C_t equals $[r/(1+r)][A_t + \sum_{s=0}^{\infty} E_t[Y_{t+s}]/(1+r)^s]$, and that $A_{t+1} = (1+r)(A_t + Y_t - C_t)$.

(a) Show that these assumptions imply that $E_t[C_{t+1}] = C_t$ (and thus that consumption follows a random walk) and that $\sum_{s=0}^{\infty} E_t[C_{t+s}]/(1+r)^s = A_t + \sum_{s=0}^{\infty} E_t[Y_{t+s}]/(1+r)^s$.

(b) Suppose that $\Delta Y_t = \phi \Delta Y_{t-1} + u_t$, where u is white noise. Suppose that Y_t exceeds $E_{t-1}[Y_t]$ by one unit (that is, suppose $u_t = 1$). By how much does consumption increase?

(c) For the case of $\phi > 0$, which has a larger variance, the innovation in income, u_t, or the innovation in consumption, $C_t - E_{t-1}[C_t]$? Do consumers use saving and borrowing to smooth the path of consumption relative to income in this model? Explain.

7.5. Consider the two-period setup analyzed in Section 7.4. Suppose that the government initially raises revenue only by taxing interest income. Thus the individual's budget constraint is $C_1 + C_2/[1 + (1-\tau)r] \leq Y_1 + Y_2/[1 + (1-\tau)r]$, where τ is the tax rate. The government's revenue is zero in period 1 and $\tau r(Y_1 - C_1^0)$ in period 2, where C_1^0 is the individual's choice of C_1 given this tax rate. Now suppose the government eliminates the taxation of interest income and instead institutes lump-sum taxes of amounts T_1 and T_2 in the two periods; thus the individual's budget constraint is now $C_1 + C_2/(1+r) \leq (Y_1 - T_1) + (Y_2 - T_2)/(1+r)$. Assume that Y_1, Y_2, and r are exogenous.

(a) What condition must the new taxes satisfy so that the change does not affect the present value of government revenues?

(b) If the new taxes satisfy the condition in part (a), is the old consumption bundle, (C_1^0, C_2^0), not affordable, just affordable, or affordable with room to spare?

(c) If the new taxes satisfy the condition in part (a), does first-period consumption rise, fall, or stay the same?

7.6. Consumption of durable goods. (Mankiw, 1982.) Suppose that, as in Section 7.2, the instantaneous utility function is quadratic and the interest rate and the discount rate are zero. Suppose, however, that goods are durable; specifically, $C_t = (1-\delta)C_{t-1} + E_t$, where E_t is purchases in period t and $0 \leq \delta < 1$.

(a) Consider a marginal reduction in purchases in period t of dE_t. Find values of dE_{t+1} and dE_{t+2} such that the combined changes in E_t, E_{t+1}, and E_{t+2} leave the present value of spending unchanged (so $dE_t + dE_{t+1} + dE_{t+2} = 0$) and leave C_{t+2} unchanged (so $(1-\delta)^2 dE_t + (1-\delta)dE_{t+1} + dE_{t+2} = 0$).

(b) What is the effect of the change in part (a) on C_t and C_{t+1}? What is the effect on expected utility?

(*c*) What condition must C_t and $E_t[C_{t+1}]$ satisfy for the change in part (*a*) not to affect expected utility? Does C follow a random walk?

(*d*) Does E follow a random walk? (Hint: write $E_t - E_{t-1}$ in terms of $C_t - C_{t-1}$ and $C_{t-1} - C_{t-2}$.) Explain intuitively. If $\delta = 0$, what is the behavior of E?

7.7. Consider a stock that pays dividends of D_t in period t and whose price in period t is P_t. Assume that consumers are risk-neutral and have a discount rate of r; thus they maximize $E[\sum_{t=0}^{\infty} C_t /(1 + r)^t]$.

(*a*) Show that equilibrium requires $P_t = E_t[(D_{t+1} + P_{t+1})/(1 + r)]$ (assume that if the stock is sold, this happens after that period's dividends have been paid).

(*b*) Assume that $\lim_{s \to \infty} E_t[P_{t+s}/(1+r)^s] = 0$ (this is a *no-bubbles* condition; see the next problem). Iterate the expression in part (*a*) forward to derive an expression for P_t in terms of expectations of future dividends.

7.8. Bubbles. Consider the setup of the previous problem without the assumption that $\lim_{s \to \infty} E_t[P_{t+s}/(1 + r)^s] = 0$.

(*a*) **Deterministic bubbles.** Suppose that P_t equals the expression derived in part (*b*) of Problem 7.7 plus $(1 + r)^t b, b > 0$.

   (*i*) Is consumers' first-order condition derived in part (*a*) of Problem 7.7 still satisfied?

   (*ii*) Can b be negative? (Hint: consider the strategy of never selling the stock.)

(*b*) **Bursting bubbles.** (Blanchard, 1979.) Suppose that P_t equals the expression derived in part (*b*) of Problem 7.7 plus q_t, where q_t equals $(1+r)q_{t-1}/\alpha$ with probability α and equals zero with probability $1 - \alpha$.

   (*i*) Is consumers' first-order condition derived in part (*a*) of Problem 7.7 still satisfied?

   (*ii*) If there is a bubble at time t (that is, if $q_t > 0$), what is the probability that the bubble has burst by time $t + s$ (that is, that $q_{t+s} = 0$)? What is the limit of this probability as s approaches infinity?

(*c*) **Intrinsic bubbles.** (Froot and Obtsfeld, 1991.) Suppose that dividends follow a random walk: $D_t = D_{t-1} + e_t$, where e is white noise.

   (*i*) In the absence of bubbles, what is the price of the stock in period t?

   (*ii*) Suppose that P_t equals the expression derived in (*i*) plus b_t, where $b_t = (1 + r)b_{t-1} + ce_t, c > 0$. Is consumers' first-order condition derived in part (*a*) of Problem 7.7 still satisfied? In what sense do stock prices overreact to changes in dividends?

7.9. The Lucas asset-pricing model. (Lucas, 1978.) Suppose the only assets in the economy are infinitely-lived trees. Output equals the fruit of the trees, which is exogenous and cannot be stored; thus $C_t = Y_t$, where Y_t is the exogenously determined output per person and C_t is consumption per person. Assume that initially each consumer owns the same number of trees. Since all consumers are assumed to be the same, this means that, in equilibrium, the behavior of the price of trees must be such that, each period, the representative consumer does not want to either increase or decrease his or her holdings of trees.

Let P_t denote the price of a tree in period t (assume that if the tree is sold, the sale occurs after the existing owner receives that period's output). Finally, assume that the representative consumer maximizes $E[\sum_{t=0}^{\infty} \ln C_t / (1 + \rho)^t]$.

(a) Suppose the representative consumer reduces his or her consumption in period t by an infinitesimal amount, uses the resulting saving to increase his or her holdings of trees, and then sells these additional holdings in period $t + 1$. Find the condition that C_t and expectations involving Y_{t+1}, P_{t+1}, and C_{t+1} must satisfy for this change not to affect expected utility. Solve this condition for P_t in terms of Y_t and expectations involving Y_{t+1}, P_{t+1}, and C_{t+1}.

(b) Assume that $\lim_{s \to \infty} E_t[(P_{t+s}/Y_{t+s})/(1 + \rho)^s] = 0$. Given this assumption, iterate your answer to part (a) forward to solve for P_t. (Hint: use the fact that $C_{t+s} = Y_{t+s}$ for all s.)

(c) Explain intuitively why an increase in expectations of future dividends does not affect the price of the asset.

(d) Does consumption follow a random walk in this model?

7.10. **The equity premium and the concentration of aggregate shocks.** (Mankiw, 1986b.) Consider an economy with two possible states, each of which occurs with probability $\frac{1}{2}$. In the good state, each individual's consumption is 1. In the bad state, fraction λ of the population consumes $1 - (\phi/\lambda)$ and the remainder consumes 1, where $0 < \phi < 1$ and $\phi \le \lambda \le 1$. ϕ measures the reduction in average consumption in the bad state, and λ measures how broadly that reduction is shared.

Consider two assets, one that pays off 1 unit in the good state and one that pays off 1 unit in the bad state. Let p denote the relative price of the bad-state asset to the good-state asset.

(a) Consider an individual whose initial holdings of the two assets are zero, and consider the experiment of the individual marginally reducing (that is, selling short) his or her holdings of the good-state asset and using the proceeds to purchase more of the bad-state asset. Derive the condition for this change not to affect the individual's expected utility.

(b) Since consumption in the two states is exogenous and individuals are ex ante identical, p must adjust to the point where it is an equilibrium for individuals' holdings of both assets to be zero. Solve the condition derived in part (a) for this equilibrium value of p in terms of ϕ, λ, $U'(1)$, and $U'(1 - (\phi/\lambda))$.

(c) Find $\partial p / \partial \lambda$.

(d) Show that if utility is quadratic, $\partial p / \partial \lambda = 0$.

(e) Show that if $U'''(\bullet)$ is everywhere positive, $\partial p / \partial \lambda < 0$.

Chapter 8

INVESTMENT

This chapter investigates the demand for investment. As described at the beginning of Chapter 7, there are two main reasons for studying investment. First, the combination of firms' investment demand and households' saving supply determines how much of an economy's output is invested; as a result, investment demand is potentially important to the behavior of standards of living over the long run. Second, investment is highly volatile; thus investment demand may be important to short-run fluctuations.

Section 8.1 presents a baseline model of investment where firms face a perfectly elastic supply of capital goods and can adjust their capital stocks costlessly. We will see that this model, even though it is a natural one to consider, provides little insight into actual investment. It implies, for example, that discrete changes in the economic environment (such as discrete changes in interest rates) produce infinite rates of investment or disinvestment.

Sections 8.2 through 8.5 therefore develop and analyze the *q theory* model of investment. The model's key assumption is that firms face costs of adjusting their capital stocks. As a result, the model avoids the unreasonable implications of the baseline case and provides a useful framework for analyzing the effects that expectations and current conditions have on investment.

Sections 8.6 and 8.7 introduce two important extensions of the model: Section 8.6 considers uncertainty, and Section 8.7 investigates financial-market imperfections. Finally, Section 8.8 presents some empirical tests and applications of the models.

8.1 Investment and the Cost of Capital

The Desired Capital Stock

Consider a firm that can rent capital at a price of r_K. The firm's profits at a point in time are given by $\pi(K, X_1, X_2, \ldots, X_n) - r_K K$, where K is the amount of capital the firm rents and the X's are variables that it takes as given. In the case of a perfectly competitive firm, for example, the X's include the price of the firm's product and the costs of other inputs. $\pi(\cdot)$ is assumed to account for whatever optimization the firm can do on dimensions other than its choice of K. For a competitive firm, for example, $\pi(K, X_1, \ldots, X_n) - r_K K$ gives the firm's profits at the profit-maximizing choices of inputs other than capital given K and the X's. We assume that $\pi_K > 0$ and $\pi_{KK} < 0$, where subscripts denote partial derivatives.

The first-order condition for the profit-maximizing choice of K is

$$\pi_K(K, X_1, \ldots, X_n) = r_K. \tag{8.1}$$

That is, the firm rents capital up to the point where its marginal revenue product equals its rental price.

Equation (8.1) implicitly defines the firm's desired capital stock as a function of r_K and the X's. We can differentiate this condition to find the impact of a change in one of these exogenous variables on the desired capital stock. Consider, for example, a change in the rental price of capital, r_K. By assumption, the X's are exogenous; thus they do not change when r_K changes. K, however, is chosen by the firm. Thus it adjusts so that (8.1) continues to hold. Differentiating both sides of (8.1) with respect to r_K shows that this requires

$$\pi_{KK}(K, X_1, \ldots, X_n) \frac{\partial K(r_K, X_1, \ldots, X_n)}{\partial r_K} = 1. \tag{8.2}$$

Solving this expression for $\partial K / \partial r_K$ yields

$$\frac{\partial K(r_K, X_1, \ldots, X_n)}{\partial r_K} = \frac{1}{\pi_{KK}(K, X_1, \ldots, X_n)}. \tag{8.3}$$

Since π_{KK} is negative, (8.3) implies that K is decreasing in r_K. A similar analysis can be used to find the effects of changes in the X's on K.

The User Cost of Capital

Most capital is not rented but is owned by the firms that use it. Thus there is no clear empirical counterpart of r_K. This difficulty has given rise to a large literature on the *user cost of capital.*

Consider a firm that owns a unit of capital. Suppose the real market price of the capital at time t is $p_K(t)$, and consider the firm's choice between selling the capital and continuing to use it. Keeping the capital has three costs to the firm. First, the firm forgoes the interest it would receive if it sold the capital and saved the proceeds; this has a real cost of $r(t)p_K(t)$ per unit time, where $r(t)$ is the real interest rate. Second, the capital is depreciating; this has a cost of $\delta p_K(t)$ per unit time, where δ is the depreciation rate. And third, the price of the capital may be changing. This increases the cost of using the capital if the price is falling (since the firm obtains less if it waits to sell the capital), and decreases the cost if the price is rising. This has a cost of $-\dot{p}_K(t)$ per unit time. Putting the three components together yields the real user cost of capital:

$$r_K(t) = r(t)p_K(t) + \delta p_K(t) - \dot{p}_K(t)$$

$$= \left[r(t) + \delta - \frac{\dot{p}_K(t)}{p_K(t)} \right] p_K(t). \tag{8.4}$$

This analysis ignores the existence of taxes. In practice, however, the tax treatments of investment and of capital income have large effects on the user cost of capital. To give an idea of these effects, consider an investment tax credit. Specifically, suppose the firm's income that is subject to the corporate income tax is reduced by fraction f of its investment expenditures; for symmetry, suppose also that its taxable income is increased by fraction f of any receipts from selling capital goods. Such an investment tax credit implies that the effective price of a unit of capital to the firm is $(1 - f\tau)p_K(t)$, where τ is the marginal corporate income tax rate. The user cost of capital is therefore

$$r_K(t) = \left[r(t) + \delta - \frac{\dot{p}_K(t)}{p_K(t)} \right] (1 - f\tau)p_K(t). \tag{8.5}$$

Thus the investment tax credit reduces the user cost of capital, and hence increases firms' desired capital stocks. One can also investigate the effects of depreciation allowances, the tax treatment of interest, and many other features of the tax code on the user cost of capital and the desired capital stock.[1]

Difficulties with the Baseline Model

This simple model of investment has at least two major failings as a description of actual behavior. The first concerns the impact of changes in the exogenous variables. Our model concerns firms' demand for capital, and it implies that firms' desired capital stocks are smooth functions of the exogenous variables. As a result, a discrete change in one of the exogenous variables leads to a discrete change in the desired capital stock. Suppose, for example, that the Federal Reserve reduces interest rates by a discrete amount; as the analysis above shows, this discretely reduces the cost of capital, r_K. This in turn means that the capital stock that satisfies (8.1) rises discretely.

The problem with this implication is that, since the rate of change of the capital stock equals investment minus depreciation, a discrete change

---

[1]The seminal paper is Hall and Jorgenson (1967). See also Problems 8.2 and 8.3.

in the capital stock requires an infinite rate of investment. For the economy as a whole, however, investment is limited by the economy's output; thus aggregate investment cannot be infinite.

The second problem with the model is that it does not identify any mechanism through which expectations affect investment demand. The model implies that firms equate the current marginal revenue product of capital with its current user cost, without regard to what they expect future marginal revenue products or user costs to be. Yet it is clear that in practice, expectations about demand and costs are central to investment decisions: firms expand their capital stocks when they expect their sales to be growing and the cost of capital to be low, and they contract them when they expect their sales to be falling and the cost of capital to be high.

Thus we need to modify the model if we are to obtain even a remotely reasonable picture of actual investment decisions. The standard theory that does this emphasizes the presence of costs to changing the capital stock. Those adjustment costs come in two forms, internal and external (Mussa, 1977). *Internal adjustment costs* arise when firms face direct costs of changing their capital stocks (Eisner and Strotz, 1963; Lucas, 1967; Gould, 1968). Examples of such costs are the costs of installing the new capital and training workers to operate the new machines. Consider again a discrete cut in interest rates. If the adjustment costs approach infinity as the rate of change of the capital stock approaches infinity, the fall in interest rates causes investment to increase but not to become infinite. As a result, the capital stock moves gradually toward the new desired level.

External adjustment costs arise when each firm, as in our baseline model, faces a perfectly elastic supply of capital, but where the price of capital goods relative to other goods adjusts so that firms do not wish to invest or disinvest at infinite rates (Foley and Sidrauski, 1970). When the supply of capital is not perfectly elastic, a discrete change that increases firms' desired capital stocks bids up the price of capital goods. Under plausible assumptions, the result is that the rental price of capital does not change discontinuously but merely begins to adjust, and that again investment increases but does not become infinite.

8.2   A Model of Investment with Adjustment Costs

We now turn to a model of investment with adjustment costs. For concreteness, the adjustment costs are assumed to be internal; it is straightforward, however, to reinterpret the model as one of external adjustment costs.[2] The model is known as the q theory model of investment.

---

[2] See n. 11 and Problem 8.7. The model presented here is developed by Abel (1982); Hayashi (1982); and Summers (1981b).

Assumptions

Consider an industry with N firms. A representative firm's real profits at time t, neglecting any costs of acquiring and installing capital, are proportional to its capital stock, $\kappa(t)$, and decreasing in the industry-wide capital stock, $K(t)$; thus they take the form $\pi(K(t))\kappa(t)$, where $\pi'(\bullet) < 0$. The assumption that the firm's profits are proportional to its capital is appropriate if the production function has constant returns to scale, output markets are competitive, and the supply of all factors other than capital is perfectly elastic. Under these assumptions, if one firm has, for example, twice as much capital as another, it employs twice as much of all inputs; as a result both its revenues and its costs are twice as high as the other's.[3] And the assumption that profits are decreasing in the industry's capital stock is appropriate if the demand curve for the industry's product is downward-sloping.

The key assumption of the model is that firms face costs of adjusting their capital stocks. The adjustment costs are a convex function of the rate of change of the firm's capital stock, $\dot{\kappa}$. Specifically, the adjustment costs, $C(\dot{\kappa})$, satisfy $C(0) = 0$, $C'(0) = 0$, and $C''(\bullet) > 0$. These assumptions imply that it is costly for a firm to increase or decrease its capital stock, and that the marginal adjustment cost is increasing in the size of the adjustment.

The purchase price of capital goods is constant and equal to 1; thus there are only internal adjustment costs. Finally, for simplicity, the depreciation rate is assumed to be zero; thus $\dot{\kappa}(t) = I(t)$, where I is the firm's investment.

A Discrete-Time Version of the Firm's Problem

These assumptions imply that the firm's profits at a point in time are $\pi(K)\kappa - I - C(I)$. The firm maximizes the present value of these profits,

$$\Pi = \int_{t=0}^{\infty} e^{-rt} \left[\pi(K(t))\kappa(t) - I(t) - C(I(t)) \right] dt, \tag{8.6}$$

where we assume for simplicity that the real interest rate is constant. Each firm takes the path of the industry-wide capital stock, K, as given, and chooses its investment over time to maximize Π given this path.

To solve the firm's maximization problem, we need to employ the *calculus of variations*. To understand this method, it is helpful to first consider a discrete-time version of the firm's problem.[4] The evolution of the firm's capital stock is now given by $\kappa_{t+1} = \kappa_t + I_t$, and the adjustment costs are

---

[3]Note that these assumptions imply that in the model of Section 8.1, $\pi(K, X_1, \ldots, X_n)$ takes the form $\tilde{\pi}(X_1, \ldots, X_n)K$, and so the assumption that $\pi_{KK} < 0$ fails. Thus in this case, in the absence of adjustment costs, the firm's demand for capital is not well defined: it is infinite if $\tilde{\pi}(X_1, \ldots, X_n) > 0$, zero if $\tilde{\pi}(X_1, \ldots, X_n) < 0$, and not defined if $\tilde{\pi}(X_1, \ldots, X_n) = 0$.

[4]For more thorough and formal introductions to the calculus of variations, see Kamien and Schwartz (1991) and Dixit (1990, Chapter 10).

given by $C(I_t)$. The firm's objective function is therefore

$$\tilde{\Pi} = \sum_{t=0}^{\infty} \frac{1}{(1+r)^t} [\pi(K_t)\kappa_t - I_t - C(I_t)]. \tag{8.7}$$

We can think of the firm as choosing its investment and capital stock each period subject to the constraint that they are related by $\kappa_{t+1} = \kappa_t + I_t$ for each t. Since there are infinitely many periods, there are infinitely many constraints. The Lagrangian for the firm's maximization problem is

$$\mathcal{L} = \sum_{t=0}^{\infty} \frac{1}{(1+r)^t} [\pi(K_t)\kappa_t - I_t - C(I_t)]$$

$$+ \sum_{t=0}^{\infty} \lambda_t(\kappa_t + I_t - \kappa_{t+1}). \tag{8.8}$$

λ_t is the Lagrange multiplier associated with the constraint relating κ_{t+1} and κ_t. It therefore gives the marginal value of relaxing the constraint; that is, it gives the marginal impact of an exogenous increase in κ_{t+1} on the lifetime value of the firm's profits discounted to time zero. If we define $q_t = (1+r)^t \lambda_t$, q_t therefore shows the value to the firm of an additional unit of capital at time $t+1$ in time-t dollars.[5] With this definition, we can rewrite the Lagrangian as

$$\mathcal{L}' = \sum_{t=0}^{\infty} \frac{1}{(1+r)^t} [\pi(K_t)\kappa_t - I_t - C(I_t) + q_t(\kappa_t + I_t - \kappa_{t+1})]. \tag{8.9}$$

The first-order condition for the firm's investment in period t is therefore

$$\frac{1}{(1+r)^t}[-1 - C'(I_t) + q_t] = 0. \tag{8.10}$$

Multiplying both sides by $(1+r)^t$, we obtain

$$1 + C'(I_t) = q_t. \tag{8.11}$$

To interpret this condition, observe that the cost of acquiring a unit of capital equals the purchase price (which is fixed at 1) plus the marginal adjustment cost. Thus (8.11) states that the firm invests to the point where the cost of acquiring capital equals the value of the capital.

Now consider the first-order condition for capital in period t. The term for period t in the Lagrangian, (8.9), involves both κ_t and κ_{t+1}. Thus the

---

[5]The awkward fact that λ and q in period t concern the value of capital in period $t + 1$ will disappear when we consider the continuous-time case.

capital stock in period t, κ_t, appears in both the term for period t and the term for period $t - 1$. The first-order condition for κ_t is therefore

$$\frac{1}{(1 + r)^t}[\pi(K_t) + q_t] - \frac{1}{(1 + r)^{t-1}}q_{t-1} = 0. \tag{8.12}$$

Multiplying this expression by $(1 + r)^t$ and rearranging yields

$$\pi(K_t) = (1 + r)q_{t-1} - q_t. \tag{8.13}$$

If we define $\Delta q_t = q_t - q_{t-1}$, we can rewrite the right-hand side of (8.13) as $(1 + r)(q_t - \Delta q_t) - q_t$, or $rq_t - \Delta q_t - r\Delta q_t$. Thus we have

$$\pi(K_t) = rq_t - \Delta q_t - r\Delta q_t. \tag{8.14}$$

The left-hand side of (8.14) is the marginal revenue product of capital. And the right-hand side is the opportunity cost of a unit of capital. Intuitively, owning a unit of capital for a period requires forgoing rq_t of real interest and involves offsetting capital gains of Δq_t (see [8.4] with the depreciation rate assumed to be zero; in addition, there is an interaction term involving r and Δq that will disappear in the continuous-time case.) For the firm to be optimizing, the returns to capital must equal this opportunity cost. This is what is stated by (8.14). This condition is thus analogous to the condition in the model without adjustment costs that the firm rents capital to the point where its marginal revenue product equals its rental price.

The final condition characterizing the firm's behavior concerns what happens as t approaches infinity. If the firm has a finite horizon, T, and if it cannot have a negative capital stock, optimality requires that the value of its terminal capital stock is zero. If not, the firm would be better off reducing its terminal capital holdings. The condition that the value of the firm's terminal capital holdings is zero is

$$\frac{1}{(1 + r)^T}q_T\kappa_T = 0. \tag{8.15}$$

The infinite-horizon analogue of this condition is

$$\lim_{t\to\infty}\frac{1}{(1 + r)^t}q_t\kappa_t = 0. \tag{8.16}$$

Equation (8.16) is known as the *transversality condition.* It states that the value of the capital stock must approach zero. If this condition fails, then, loosely speaking, the firm is holding valuable capital forever, and so it can increase the present value of its profits by reducing its capital stock.[6]

---

[6]See Section 8.4 for more on the interpretation of this condition.

The Continuous-Time Case

We can now consider the case when time is continuous. The firm's profit-maximizing behavior in this case is characterized by three conditions that are analogous to the three conditions that characterize its behavior in discrete time, (8.11), (8.14), and (8.16). Indeed, the optimality conditions for continuous time can be derived by considering the discrete-time problem where the time periods are separated by intervals of length Δt and then taking the limit as Δt approaches zero. We will not use this method, however; instead we will simply describe how to find the optimality conditions, and justify them as necessary by way of analogy to the discrete-time case.

The firm's problem is now to maximize the continuous-time objective function, (8.6), rather than the discrete-time objective function, (8.7). The first step in analyzing this problem is to set up the *current-value Hamiltonian:*

$$H(\kappa(t), I(t)) = \pi(K(t))\kappa(t) - I(t) - C(I(t))$$
$$+ q(t)[I(t) - \dot{\kappa}(t)].$$

$$(8.17)$$

This expression is analogous to the period-t term in the Lagrangian for the discrete-time case (see [8.9]). There is some standard terminology associated with this type of problem. The variable that can be controlled freely (I) is the *control variable;* the variable whose value at any time is determined by past decisions (κ) is the *state variable;* and the shadow value of the state variable (q) is the *costate variable.*

The first condition characterizing the optimum is that the derivative of the Hamiltonian with respect to the control variable at each point in time is zero; this is analogous to the condition in the discrete-time problem that the derivative of the Lagrangian with respect to I for each t is zero. This condition is

$$1 + C'(I(t)) = q(t). \qquad (8.18)$$

This condition is analogous to (8.11) in the discrete-time case.

The second condition is that the derivative of the Hamiltonian with respect to the state variable equals the discount rate times the costate variable minus the derivative of the costate variable with respect to time. In our case, this condition is

$$\pi(K(t)) = rq(t) - \dot{q}(t). \qquad (8.19)$$

This condition is analogous to (8.14) in the discrete-time problem.[7]

---

[7]An alternative approach is to formulate the *present-value Hamiltonian,* $\tilde{H}(\kappa(t), I(t)) = e^{-rt}[\pi(K(t))\kappa(t) - I(t) - C(I(t))] + \lambda(t)[I(t) - \dot{\kappa}(t)]$. This is analogous to using the Lagrangian (8.8) rather than (8.9). With this formulation, (8.19) is replaced by $e^{-rt}\pi(K(t)) = -\dot{\lambda}(t)$. It is straightforward to check that, since $q(t) = \lambda(t)e^{rt}$, these two conditions are equivalent.

The final condition is the continuous-time version of the transversality condition. This condition is

$$\lim_{t \to \infty} e^{-rt} q(t) \kappa(t) = 0. \tag{8.20}$$

Equations (8.18), (8.19), and (8.20) characterize the firm's behavior.

Finally, it is useful to note that we can express q, the value of capital, in terms of capital's future marginal revenue products. Equation (8.19) implies

$$q(t) = \int_{\tau=t}^{T} e^{-r(\tau-t)} \pi(K(\tau)) d\tau + e^{-r(T-t)} q(T) \tag{8.21}$$

for any $T > t$.[8] One can show that the transversality condition implies that the second term approaches zero as T approaches infinity. Thus we have

$$q(t) = \int_{\tau=t}^{\infty} e^{-r(\tau-t)} \pi(K(\tau)) d\tau. \tag{8.22}$$

Expression (8.22) states that the value of a unit of capital at a given time equals the discounted value of its future marginal revenue products.

8.3 Tobin's q

Our analysis implies that q summarizes all information about the future that is relevant to a firm's investment decision. q shows how an additional dollar of capital affects the present value of profits. Thus the firm wants to increase its capital stock if q is high and reduce it if q is low; it does not need to know anything about the future other than the information that is summarized in q in order to make this decision (see [8.18]).

q has a natural economic interpretation. A one-unit increase in the firm's capital stock increases the present value of the firm's profits by q, and thus raises the value of the firm by q. Thus q is the market value of a unit of capital. If there is a market for shares in firms, for example, the total value of a firm with one more unit of capital than another firm exceeds the value of the other by q. And since we have assumed that the purchase price of capital is fixed at 1, q is also the ratio of the market value of a unit of capital to its replacement cost. Thus equation (8.18) states that a firm increases its capital stock if the market value of capital exceeds what it costs to acquire it, and that it decreases its capital stock if the market value of the capital is less than what it costs to acquire it.

The ratio of the market value to the replacement cost of capital is known as *Tobin's q* (Tobin, 1969); it is because of this terminology that we used q

---

[8]To verify that (8.21) follows from (8.19), differentiate (8.21) with respect to t, and then rearrange the resulting expression to obtain (8.19).

to denote the value of capital in the previous section. Our analysis implies that what is relevant to investment is *marginal q*—the ratio of the market value of a marginal unit of capital to its replacement cost. Marginal q is likely to be harder to measure than *average q*—the ratio of the total value of the firm to the replacement cost of its total capital stock. Thus it is important to know how marginal q and average q are related.

One can show that in our model, marginal q is less than average q. The reason is that when we assumed that adjustment costs depend only on $\dot{\kappa}$, we implicitly assumed diminishing returns to scale in adjustment costs. Our assumptions imply, for example, that it is more than twice as costly for a firm with 20 units of capital to add 2 more than it is for a firm with 10 units to add 1 more. Because of this assumption of diminishing returns, firms' lifetime profits, Π, rise less than proportionally with their capital stocks, and so marginal q is less than average q.

One can also show that if we modify the model to have constant returns in the adjustment costs, average and marginal q are equal (Hayashi, 1982).[9] The source of this result is that the constant returns in the costs of adjustment imply that q determines the growth rate of a firm's capital stock. As a result, all firms choose the same growth rate of their capital stocks. Thus if, for example, one firm initially has twice as much capital as another and if both firms optimize, the larger firm will have twice as much capital as the other at every future date. In addition, profits are linear in a firm's capital stock. This implies that the present value of a firm's profits—the value of Π when it chooses the path of its capital stock optimally—is proportional to its initial capital stock. Thus average q and marginal q are equal.

In other models, there are potentially more significant reasons than the degree of returns to scale in adjustment costs that average q may differ from marginal q. If a firm faces a downward-sloping demand curve for its product, for example, doubling its capital stock is likely to less than double the present value of its profits; thus marginal q is less than average q. If the firm owns a large amount of outmoded capital, on the other hand, its marginal q may exceed its average q.

8.4   Analyzing the Model

We will analyze the model using a phase diagram similar to the one we used in Chapter 2 to analyze the Ramsey model. The two variables we will focus on are the aggregate quantity of capital, K, and its value q. As with k and c in the Ramsey model, the initial value of one of these variables is given, but

---

[9]Constant returns can be introduced by assuming that the adjustment costs take the form $C(\dot{\kappa}/\kappa)\kappa$, with $C(\cdot)$ having the same properties as before. With this assumption, doubling both $\dot{\kappa}$ and κ doubles the adjustment costs. Changing our model in this way implies that κ affects profits not only directly, but also through its impact on adjustment costs for a given level of investment. As a result, it complicates the analysis. The basic messages are the same, however. See Problem 8.8 and Sala-i-Martin (1991a).

the other must be determined: the quantity of capital is something that the industry inherits from the past, but its price adjusts freely in the market.

Equation (8.18) states that each firm invests to the point where the purchase price of capital plus the marginal adjustment cost equals the value of capital: $1 + C'(I) = q$. Since $C'(I)$ is increasing in I, this condition implies that I is increasing in q. And since $C'(0)$ is zero, it also implies that I is zero when q is 1. Finally, since q is the same for all firms, all firms choose the same value of I. Thus the rate of change of the aggregate capital stock, $\dot{K}$, is given by the number of firms, N, times the value of I that satisfies (8.18).

Putting this information together, we can write

$$\dot{K}(t) = f(q(t)), \qquad f(1) = 0, \quad f'(\bullet) > 0, \qquad (8.23)$$

where $f(q) \equiv NC'^{-1}(q-1)$. Equation (8.23) implies that K is increasing when $q > 1$, decreasing when $q < 1$, and constant when $q = 1$. This information is summarized in Figure 8.1.

Equation (8.19) states that the marginal revenue product of capital equals its user cost, $rq - \dot{q}$. Rewriting this as an equation for $\dot{q}$ yields

$$\dot{q}(t) = rq(t) - \pi(K(t)). \qquad (8.24)$$

This expression implies that q is constant when $rq = \pi(K)$, or $q = \pi(K)/r$. Since $\pi(K)$ is decreasing in K, the set of points satisfying this condition

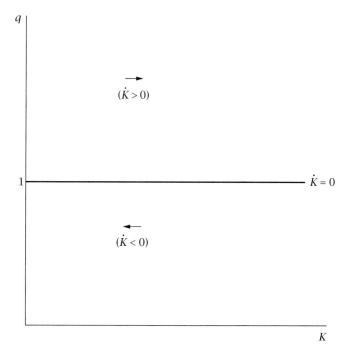

FIGURE 8.1   The dynamics of the capital stock

is downward-sloping in (K, q) space. In addition, (8.24) implies that $\dot{q}$ is increasing in K; thus $\dot{q}$ is positive to the right of the $\dot{q} = 0$ locus, and negative to the left. This information is summarized in Figure 8.2.

The Phase Diagram

Figure 8.3 combines the information in Figures 8.1 and 8.2. The diagram shows how K and q must behave to satisfy (8.23) and (8.24) at every point in time given their initial values. Suppose, for example, that K and q begin at Point A. Then, since q is more than 1, firms increase their capital stocks; thus $\dot{K}$ is positive. And since K is high and profits are therefore low, q can only be high if it is expected to rise; thus $\dot{q}$ is also positive. Thus K and q move up and to the right in the diagram.

As in the Ramsey model, the initial level of the capital stock is given. But the level of the other variable—consumption in the Ramsey model, the market value of capital in this model—is free to adjust. Thus its initial level must be determined. As in the Ramsey model, for a given level of K there is a unique level of q that produces a stable path. Specifically, there is a unique level of q such that K and q converge to the point where they are stable (Point E in the diagram). If q starts below this level, the industry eventually crosses into the region where both K and q are falling, and they

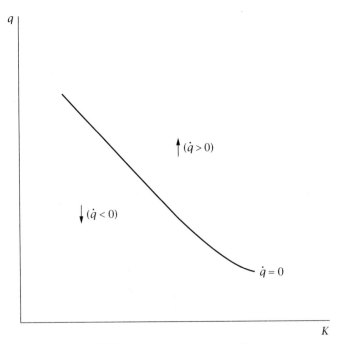

FIGURE 8.2   The dynamics of q

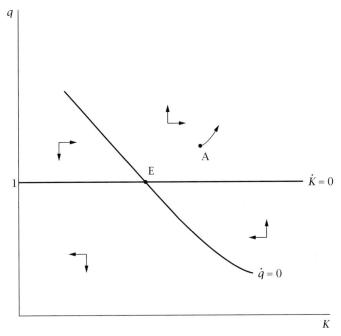

FIGURE 8.3   The phase diagram

then continue to fall indefinitely. Similarly, if q starts too high, the industry eventually moves into the region where both K and q are rising and remains there. One can show that the transversality condition fails for these paths, and thus that they can be ruled out.[10]

This discussion suggests why a firm's optimal policy must satisfy the transversality condition. Along the path starting at A, for example, the representative firm is continually building up capital because the value it attaches to the capital is always high. This high value is justified not by large marginal revenue products, but by further increases in the value the firm attaches to the capital (that is, equation [8.19], $\pi(K) = rq - \dot{q}$, holds with a high value of q not because $\pi(K)$ is high, but because $\dot{q}$ is high). But attaching this high and rising value to capital makes sense only if at some point the capital actually makes large contributions to the firm's profits. On the path starting at A, this time never comes. As a result, one can show that the firm can raise the present value of its lifetime profits by lowering the path of its capital holdings. An analogous argument applies to paths where K and q are continually falling.

Thus the unique equilibrium, given the initial value of K, is for q to equal the value that puts the industry on the saddle path, and for K and q to then move along this saddle path to E. This saddle path is shown in Figure 8.4.

---

[10]For formal demonstrations of this, see Abel (1982) and Hayashi (1982).

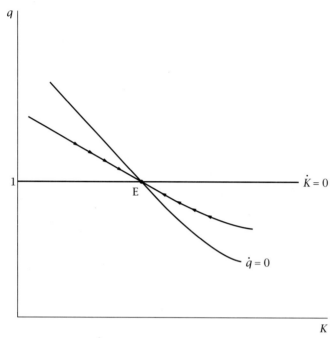

FIGURE 8.4   The saddle path

The long-run equilibrium, Point E, is characterized by $q = 1$ (which implies $\dot{K} = 0$) and $\dot{q} = 0$. The fact that q equals 1 means that the market and replacement values of capital are equal; thus firms have no incentive to increase or decrease their capital stocks. And from (8.19), for $\dot{q}$ to equal zero when q is 1, the marginal revenue product of capital must equal r. This means that the profits from holding a unit of capital just offset the forgone interest, and thus that investors are content to hold capital without the prospect of either capital gains or losses.[11]

8.5   Implications

The model developed in the previous section can be used to address many issues. This section examines its implications for the effects of changes in output, interest rates, and tax policies.

---

[11]It is straightforward to modify the model to be one of external rather than internal adjustment costs. The key change is to replace the adjustment-cost function with a supply curve for new capital goods, $\dot{K} = g(p_K)$, where $g'(\bullet) > 0$ and where p_K is the relative price of capital. With this change, the market value of firms always equals the replacement cost of their capital stocks; the role played by q in the model with internal adjustment costs is played instead by the relative price of capital. See Foley and Sidrauski (1970) and Problem 8.7.

The Effects of Output Movements

An increase in aggregate output raises the demand for the industry's product, and thus raises profits for a given capital stock. Thus the natural way to model an increase in aggregate output is as an upward shift of the $\pi(\cdot)$ function.

For concreteness, assume that the industry is initially in long-run equilibrium, and that there is an unanticipated, permanent upward shift of the $\pi(\cdot)$ function. The effects of this change are shown in Figure 8.5. The upward shift of the $\pi(\cdot)$ function shifts the $\dot{q} = 0$ locus up: since profits are higher for a given capital stock, smaller capital gains are needed for investors to be willing to hold shares in firms (see [8.24]). From our analysis of phase diagrams in Chapter 2, we know what the effects of this change are. q jumps immediately to the point on the new saddle path for the given capital stock; K and q then move down that path to the new long-run equilibrium at Point E'. Since the rate of change of the capital stock is an increasing function of q, this implies that $\dot{K}$ jumps at the time of the change and then gradually returns to zero. Thus a permanent increase in output leads to a temporary increase in investment.

The intuition behind these responses is straightforward. The increase in output raises the demand for the industry's product. Since the capital stock cannot adjust instantly, existing capital in the industry earns rents, and so

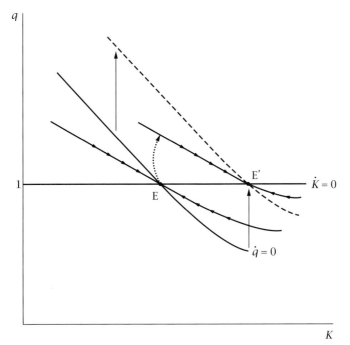

FIGURE 8.5   The effects of a permanent increase in output

its market value rises. The higher market value of capital attracts investment, and so the capital stock begins to rise. As it does so, the industry's
output rises, and thus the relative price of its product declines; thus profits
and the value of capital fall. The process continues until the value of the
capital returns to normal; at this point there are no incentives for further
investment.

Now consider an increase in output that is known to be temporary.
Specifically, the industry begins in long-run equilibrium. There is then an unexpected upward shift of the profit function; when this happens, it is known
that the function will return to its initial position at some later time, T.

The key insight needed to find the effects of this change is that there
cannot be an anticipated jump in q. If, for example, there is an anticipated
downward jump in q, the owners of shares in firms will suffer capital losses
at an infinite rate with certainty at that moment. But that means that no one
will hold shares at that moment.

Thus at time T, K and q must be on the saddle path leading back to
the initial long-run equilibrium: if they were not, q would have to jump for
the industry to get back to its long-run equilibrium. Between the time
of the upward shift of the profit function and T, the dynamics of K and q
are determined by the temporarily high profit function. Finally, the initial
value of K is given, but (since the upward shift of the profit function is
unexpected) q can change discretely at the time of the initial shock.

Together, these facts tell us how the industry responds. At the time of
the change, q jumps to the point such that, with the dynamics of K and q
given by the new profit function, they reach the old saddle path at exactly
time T. This is shown in Figure 8.6. q jumps from Point E to Point A at the
time of the shock. q and K then move gradually to Point B, arriving there
at time T. Finally, they then move up the old saddle path to E.

This analysis has several implications. First, the temporary increase in
output raises investment: since output is higher for a period, firms increase
their capital stocks to take advantage of this. Second, comparing Figure 8.6
with Figure 8.5 shows that q rises less than it does if the increase in output
is permanent; thus, since q determines investment, investment responds
less. Intuitively, since it is costly to reverse increases in capital, firms respond less to a rise in profits when they know they will reverse the increases.
And third, Figure 8.6 shows that the path of K and q crosses the $\dot{K} = 0$ line
before it reaches the old saddle path—that is, before time T. Thus the capital stock begins to decline before output returns to normal. To understand
this intuitively, consider the time just before time T. The profit function is
just about to return to its initial level; thus firms are about to want to have
smaller capital stocks. And since it is costly to adjust the capital stock and
since there is only a brief period of high profits left, there is a benefit and
almost no cost to beginning the reduction immediately.

These results imply that it is not just current output but its entire
path over time that affects investment. The comparison of permanent and
temporary output movements shows that investment is higher when output

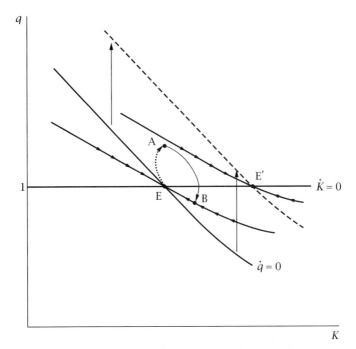

FIGURE 8.6 The effects of a temporary increase in output

is expected to be higher in the future than when it is not. Thus expectations of high output in the future raise current demand. In addition, as the example of a permanent increase in output shows, investment is higher when output has recently risen than when it has been high for an extended period. This impact of the change in output on the level of investment demand is known as the *accelerator.*

The Effects of Interest-Rate Movements

Recall that the equation of motion for q is $\dot{q} = rq - \pi(K)$ (equation [8.24]). Thus interest-rate movements, like shifts of the profit function, affect investment through their impact on the equation for $\dot{q}$. Their effects are therefore similar to the effects of output movements. A permanent decline in the interest rate, for example, shifts the $\dot{q} = 0$ locus up. In addition, since r multiplies q in the equation for $\dot{q}$, the decline also makes the locus steeper. This is shown in Figure 8.7.

The figure can be used to analyze the effects of permanent and temporary changes in the interest rate along the lines of our analysis of the effects of permanent and temporary output movements. A permanent fall in the interest rate, for example, causes q to jump to the point on the new saddle path (Point A in the diagram). K and q then move down to the new long-run equilibrium (Point E'). Thus the permanent decline in the interest

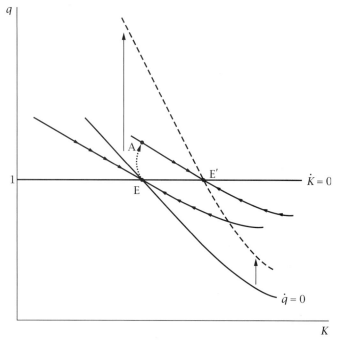

FIGURE 8.7   The effects of a permanent decrease in the interest rate

rate produces a temporary boom in investment as the industry moves to a permanently higher capital stock.

Thus, just as with output, both past and expected future interest rates affect investment. The interest rate in our model, r, is the instantaneous rate of return; thus it corresponds to the short-term interest rate. One implication of this analysis is that the short-term rate does not reflect all the information about interest rates that is relevant for investment. As we will see in more detail in Section 9.3, long-term interest rates are likely to reflect expectations of future short-term rates. If long-term rates are less than short-term rates, for example, it is likely that investors are expecting short-term rates to fall; if not, they are better off buying a series of short-term bonds than buying a long-term bond, and so no one is willing to hold long-term bonds. Thus, since our model implies that increases in expected future short-term rates reduce investment, it implies that, for a given level of current short-term rates, investment is lower when long-term rates are higher. Thus the model supports the standard view that long-term interest rates are important to investment.

The Effects of Taxes: An Example

A temporary investment tax credit is often proposed as a way to stimulate aggregate demand during recessions. The argument is that an investment tax credit that is known to be temporary gives firms a strong incentive to invest while the credit is in effect. Our model can be used to investigate this argument.

For simplicity, assume that the investment tax credit takes the form of a direct rebate to the firm of fraction θ of the price of capital, and assume that the rebate applies to the purchase price but not to the adjustment costs. When there is a credit of this form, the firm invests as long as the value of the capital plus the rebate exceeds the capital's cost. Thus the first-order condition for current investment, (8.18), becomes

$$q(t) + \theta(t) = 1 + C'(I(t)), \qquad (8.25)$$

where $\theta(t)$ is the credit at time t. The equation for $\dot{q}$, (8.24), is unchanged.

Equation (8.25) implies that the capital stock is constant when $q + \theta = 1$. An investment tax credit of θ therefore shifts the $\dot{K} = 0$ locus down by θ; this is shown in Figure 8.8. If the credit is permanent, q jumps down to the new saddle path at the time it is announced. Intuitively, because the credit increases investment, it means that the industry's profits (neglecting the credit) will be lower, and thus that existing capital is less valuable. K and q then move along the saddle path to the new long-run equilibrium, which involves higher K and lower q.

Now consider a temporary credit. From our earlier analysis of a temporary change in output, we know that the announcement of the credit causes q to fall to a point where the dynamics of K and q, given the credit, bring

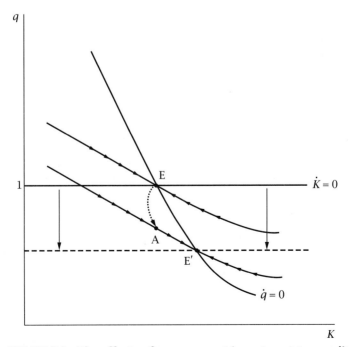

FIGURE 8.8   The effects of a permanent investment tax credit

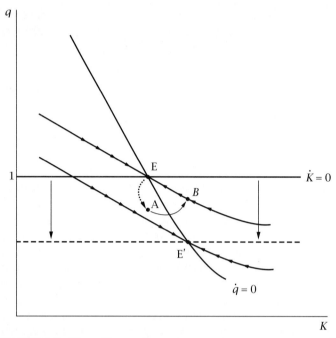

FIGURE 8.9   The effects of a temporary investment tax credit

them to the old saddle path just as the credit expires. They then move up that saddle path back to the initial long-run equilibrium.

This is shown in Figure 8.9. As the figure shows, q does not fall all the way to its value on the new saddle path; thus the temporary credit reduces q by less than a comparable permanent credit does. The reason is that, because the temporary credit does not lead to a permanent increase in the capital stock, it causes a smaller reduction in the value of existing capital. Now recall that the change in the capital stock, $\dot{K}$, depends on $q + \theta$ (see [8.25]). q is higher under the temporary credit than under the permanent one; thus, just as the informal argument suggests, the temporary credit has a larger effect on investment than the permanent credit does. Finally, note that the figure shows that under the temporary credit, q is rising in the later part of the period that the credit is in effect. Thus, after a point, the temporary credit leads to a growing investment boom as firms try to invest just before the credit goes out of effect. Under the permanent credit, in contrast, the rate of change of the capital stock declines steadily as the industry moves towards its new long-run equilibrium.

8.6   The Effects of Uncertainty: An Introduction

Our analysis so far assumes that firms are certain about future profitability, interest rates, and tax policies. In practice, they face uncertainty about all of these. This section therefore introduces some of the issues raised by uncertainty.

Uncertainty about Future Profitability

We begin with the case where there is no uncertainty about the path of the interest rate; for simplicity it is assumed to be constant. Thus the uncertainty concerns only future profitability. In the case, the value of one unit of capital is given by

$$q(t) = \int_{\tau=t}^{\infty} e^{-r(\tau-t)} E_t[\pi(K(\tau))]\, d\tau \tag{8.26}$$

(see [8.22]).

This expression can be used to find how q is expected to evolve over time. Since (8.26) holds at all times, it implies that the expectation as of time t of q at some later time, $t + \Delta t$, is given by

$$E_t[q(t + \Delta t)] = E_t\left[\int_{\tau=t+\Delta t}^{\infty} e^{-r[\tau-(t+\Delta t)]} E_{t+\Delta t}[\pi(K(\tau))]\, d\tau\right]$$

$$= \int_{\tau=t+\Delta t}^{\infty} e^{-r[\tau-(t+\Delta t)]} E_t[\pi(K(\tau))]\, d\tau, \tag{8.27}$$

where the second line uses the fact that the law of iterated projections implies that $E_t[E_{t+\Delta t}[\pi(K(\tau))]]$ is just $E_t[\pi(K(\tau))]$. Differentiating (8.27) with respect to Δt and evaluating the resulting expression at $\Delta t = 0$ gives us

$$E_t[\dot{q}(t)] = rq(t) - \pi(K(t)). \tag{8.28}$$

Except for the presence of the expectations term, this expression is identical to the equation for $\dot{q}$ in the model with certainty (see [8.24]).

As before, each firm invests to the point where the cost of acquiring new capital equals the market value of capital. Thus equation (8.23), $\dot{K}(t) = f(q(t))$, continues to hold.

Our analysis so far appears to imply that uncertainty has no direct effect on investment: firms invest as long as the value of new capital exceeds the cost of acquiring it, and the value of that capital depends only on its expected payoffs. But this analysis neglects the fact that it is not quite correct to assume that there is exogenous uncertainty about the future values of $\pi(K)$. Since the path of K is determined within the model, what can be taken as exogenous is uncertainty about the position of the $\pi(\cdot)$ function; the combination of that uncertainty and firms' behavior then determines uncertainty about the values of $\pi(K)$.

In one natural baseline case, this subtlety proves to be unimportant: if $\pi(\cdot)$ is linear and $C(\cdot)$ is quadratic and if the uncertainty concerns the intercept of the $\pi(\cdot)$ function, then the uncertainty does not affect invest-ment. That is, one can show that in this case, investment at any time is the same as it is if the future values of the intercept of the $\pi(\cdot)$ function are certain to equal their expected values (see Problems 8.9 and 8.10).

An Example

To see the effects of uncertainty about profitability, consider the following example. Suppose that the assumptions of our baseline case are satisfied, and that initially the $\pi(\cdot)$ function is constant and the industry is in long-run equilibrium. It then becomes known that the government is considering a change in the tax code that would raise the intercept of the $\pi(\cdot)$ function. The proposal will be voted on after time T, and it has a 50 percent chance of passing. There is no other source of uncertainty.

The effects of this development are shown in Figure 8.10. The figure shows the $\dot{K} = 0$ locus and the $\dot{q} = 0$ loci and the saddle paths with the initial $\pi(\cdot)$ function and the potential new, higher function. Given our as-sumptions, all of these loci are straight lines (see Problem 8.9). Initially, K and q are at Point E. After the proposal is voted on, they will move along the appropriate saddle path to the relevant long-run equilibrium (Point E' if the proposal is passed, E if it is defeated). There cannot be an expected capital gain or loss at the time the proposal is voted on. Thus, since the proposal has a 50 percent chance of passing, q must be midway between the points on the two saddle paths at the time of the vote; that is, it must be on the dotted line in the figure. Finally, before the vote the dynamics of K and q are given by (8.28) and (8.23) with the initial $\pi(\cdot)$ function and no uncertainty about $\dot{q}$.

Thus at the time it becomes known that the government is considering the proposal, q jumps up to the point such that the dynamics of K and q carry them to the dashed line after time T. q then jumps up or down depending on the outcome of the vote, and K and q then converge to the relevant long-run equilibrium.

Irreversible Investment

If $\pi(\cdot)$ is not linear or $C(\cdot)$ is not quadratic, uncertainty about the $\pi(\cdot)$ func-tion can affect expectations of future values of $\pi(K)$, and thus can affect current investment. Suppose, for example, that it is more costly for firms to reduce their capital stocks than to increase them. Then if $\pi(\cdot)$ shifts up, the industry-wide capital stock will rise rapidly, and so the increase in $\pi(K)$ will be brief; but if $\pi(\cdot)$ shifts down, K will fall only slowly, and so the decrease in $\pi(K)$ will be long-lasting. Thus with asymmetry in adjustment costs, un-certainty about the position of the profit function reduces expectations of future profitability, and thus reduces investment.

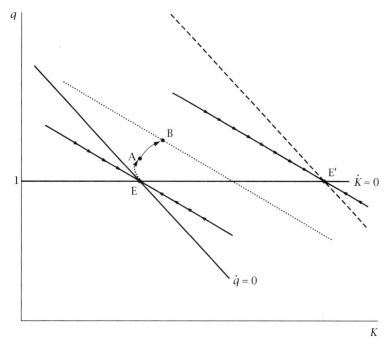

FIGURE 8.10   The effects of uncertainty about future tax policy when adjust-ment costs are symmetric

This type of asymmetry in adjustment costs means that investment is somewhat *irreversible:* it is easier to increase the capital stock than to reverse the increase. In the phase diagram, irreversibility causes the saddle path to be curved. If K exceeds its long-run equilibrium value, it falls only slowly; thus profits are depressed for an extended period, and so q is much less than 1. If K is less than its long-run equilibrium value, on the other hand, it rises rapidly, and so q is only slightly more than 1.

To see the effects of irreversibility, consider our previous example, but now with the assumption that the costs of adjusting the capital stock are asymmetric. This situation is analyzed in Figure 8.11. As before, at the time the proposal is voted on, q must be midway between the two saddle paths, and again the dynamics of K and q before the vote are given by (8.28) and (8.23) with the initial $\pi(\cdot)$ function and no uncertainty about $\dot{q}$.

Thus, as before, when it becomes known that the government is consid-ering the proposal, q jumps up to the point such that the dynamics of K and q carry them to the dashed line after time T. As the figure shows, however, the asymmetry of the adjustment costs causes this jump to be smaller than it is under symmetric costs. Specifically, the fact that it is costly to reduce capital holdings means that if firms build up large capital stocks before the vote and the proposal is then defeated, the fact that it is hard to reverse the increase causes q to be quite low. This acts to reduce the value of capital before the vote, and thus reduces investment. Intuitively, when investment

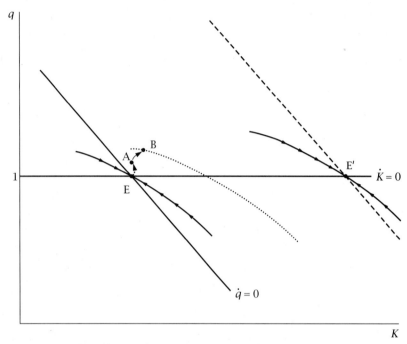

FIGURE 8.11   The effects of uncertainty about future tax policy when adjust-ment costs are asymmetric

is irreversible, there is an *option value* to waiting rather than investing. If a firm does not invest, it retains the possibility of keeping its capital stock low; if it invests, on the other hand, it commits itself to a high capital stock.

A large recent literature investigates the effects of irreversibility in more detail.[12] Realistically, adjustment costs are likely to be more complicated than just taking some asymmetric form around $\dot{\kappa} = 0$. For example, the marginal cost of both the first unit of investment and the first unit of disin-vestment may be strictly positive (so that $C(\dot{\kappa})$ is not differentiable at $\dot{\kappa} = 0$). In this case, there is a range of values of q around 1 for which the firm leaves its capital stock unchanged. The firm increases its capital only if q exceeds some threshold that is strictly greater than 1, and decreases it only if q is below some threshold that is strictly less than 1 (Abel and Eberly, 1994).

In addition, there may be a fixed cost to undertaking any nonzero amount of investment (so that $C(\dot{\kappa})$ is discontinuous at $\dot{\kappa} = 0$). Such a fixed cost increases the range of values of q for which the firm leaves its capital stock unchanged (again, see Abel and Eberly). Investment in the presence of fixed costs and uncertainty is most usefully analyzed using the tools of option-pricing theory from finance; Dixit and Pindyck (1994) develop this approach in detail.

---

[12]Bernanke (1983a) is an important early paper on irreversibility.

Uncertainty about Discount Factors

Firms are uncertain not only about what their future profits will be, but also about how those payoffs will be valued. To see the effects of this uncertainty, suppose the firm is owned by a representative consumer. As we saw in Section 7.5, the consumer values future payoffs not according to a constant interest rate, but according to the marginal utility of consumption. The discounted marginal utility of consumption at time τ, relative to the marginal utility of consumption at t, is $e^{-\rho(\tau-t)}u'(C(\tau))/u'(C(t))$, where ρ is the consumer's discount rate, $u(\bullet)$ is the instantaneous utility function, and C is consumption. Thus our expression for the value of a unit of capital, (8.26), becomes

$$q(t) = \int_{\tau=t}^{\infty} e^{-\rho(\tau-t)} E_t \left[\frac{u'(C(\tau))}{u'(C(t))} \pi(K(\tau)) \right] d\tau. \tag{8.29}$$

As Craine (1989) emphasizes, (8.29) implies that the impact of a project's riskiness on investment in the project depends on the same considerations that determine the impact of assets' riskiness on their values in the consumption CAPM. Idiosyncratic risk—that is, randomness in $\pi(K)$ that is uncorrelated with $u'(C)$—has no impact on the market value of capital, and thus no impact on investment. But uncertainty that is positively correlated with aggregate risk—that is, positive correlation of $\pi(K)$ and C, and thus negative correlation of $\pi(K)$ and $u'(C)$—lowers the value of capital and hence reduces investment. And uncertainty that is negatively correlated with aggregate risk raises investment.

8.7   Financial-Market Imperfections

Introduction

When firms and investors are equally well informed, financial markets function efficiently. Investments are valued according to their expected payoffs and riskiness; as a result, they are undertaken if their value exceeds the cost of acquiring and installing the necessary capital. These are the assumptions underlying our analysis so far. In particular, we have assumed that firms make investments if they raise the present value of profits evaluated using the prevailing economy-wide interest rate; thus we have implicitly assumed that firms can borrow at that interest rate.

In practice, however, firms are much better informed about their investment projects than potential outside investors are. Outside financing must ultimately come from individuals. These individuals usually have little contact with the firm and little expertise concerning the firm's activities. In addition, their stakes in the firm are usually low enough that their incentive to acquire relevant information is small.

Because of these problems, institutions such as banks, mutual funds, and bond-rating agencies that specialize in acquiring and transmitting information play central roles in financial markets. But even they are much less informed than the firms or individuals in whom they are investing their funds. The issuer of a credit card, for example, is usually much less informed than the holder of the card about the holder's financial circumstances and spending habits. In addition, the existence of intermediaries between the ultimate investors and firms means that there is a two-level problem of asymmetric information: there is asymmetric information not just between the intermediaries and the firms, but also between the individuals and the intermediaries (Diamond, 1984).

Asymmetric information creates *agency problems* between investors and firms. Some of the risk in the payoff to investment is usually borne by the investors rather than by the firm; this occurs, for example, in any situation where there is a possibility that the firm may go bankrupt. When this is the case, the firm can change its behavior to take advantage of its superior information. It can only borrow if it knows that its project is particularly risky, for example, or it can choose a high-risk strategy over a low-risk one even if this reduces expected returns. Thus asymmetric information can distort investment choices away from the most efficient projects. In addition, the presence of asymmetric information can lead the investors to expend resources monitoring the firms' activities; thus again it imposes costs.

This section presents a simple model of asymmetric information and the resulting agency problems, and discusses some of their effects. We will find that when there is asymmetric information, investment depends on more than just interest rates and profitability; such factors as investors' ability to monitor firms and firms' ability to finance their investment using internal funds also matter. We will also see that asymmetric information changes how interest rates and profitability affect investment.

Assumptions

An entrepreneur has the opportunity to undertake a project that requires 1 unit of resources. The entrepreneur has wealth of W, which is less than 1; thus he or she must obtain $1 - W$ units of outside financing to undertake the project. If the project is undertaken, it has an expected output of γ, which is positive. γ is heterogeneous across entrepreneurs, and is publicly observable. Actual output can differ from expected output, however; specifically, the actual output of a project with an expected output of γ is distributed uniformly on $[0, 2\gamma]$. Since the entrepreneur's wealth is all invested in the project, his or her payment to the outside investors cannot exceed the project's output. This limit on the amount that the entrepreneur can pay to outside investors means that the investors must bear some of the project's risk.

If the entrepreneur does not undertake the project, he or she can invest at the risk-free interest rate, r. The entrepreneur is risk-neutral; thus he or she undertakes the project if the difference between γ and the expected payments to the outside investors is greater than $(1 + r)W$.

The outside investors, like the entrepreneur, are risk-neutral and can invest their wealth at the risk-free rate. In addition, the outside investors are competitive; thus in equilibrium their expected rate of return on any financing they provide to entrepreneurs must be r.

The key assumption of the model is that entrepreneurs are better informed than outside investors about their projects' actual output. Specifically, an entrepreneur observes his or her output costlessly; an outside investor, however, must pay a cost c to observe output. c is assumed to be positive; for convenience, it is also assumed to be less than expected output, γ.

This type of asymmetric information is known as *costly state verification* (Townsend, 1979). We focus on this type of asymmetric information between entrepreneurs and investors not because it is the most important type in practice, but because it is relatively straightforward to analyze. Other types of information asymmetries, such as asymmetric information about the riskiness of projects or entrepreneurs' actions, have broadly similar effects.

The Equilibrium under Symmetric Information

In the absence of the cost to outside investors of observing the project's output, the equilibrium is straightforward. Entrepreneurs whose projects have an expected payoff that exceeds $1 + r$ obtain financing and undertake their projects; entrepreneurs whose projects have an expected output less than $1 + r$ do not. For the projects that are undertaken, the contract between the entrepreneur and the outside investors provides the investors with expected payments of $(1 - W)(1 + r)$. There are many contracts that do this. One example is a contract that gives to investors the fraction $(1 - W)(1 + r)/\gamma$ of whatever output turns out to be; since expected output is γ, this yields an expected payment of $(1 - W)(1 + r)$. The entrepreneur's expected income is then $\gamma - (1 - W)(1 + r)$, which equals $W(1 + r) + \gamma - (1 + r)$. Since γ exceeds $1 + r$ by assumption, this is greater than $W(1 + r)$. Thus the entrepreneur is made better off by undertaking the project.

The Form of the Contract under Asymmetric Information

Let us now reintroduce the assumption that it is costly for outside investors to observe a project's output. In addition, assume that each outsider's wealth is greater than $1 - W$. Thus we can focus on the case where, in equilibrium, each project has only a single outside investor. This allows us to avoid dealing with the complications that arise when there is more than one outside investor who may want to observe a project's output.

Since outside investors are risk-neutral and competitive, an entrepreneur's expected payment to the investor must equal $(1 + r)(1 - W)$ plus the investor's expected spending on verifying output. The entrepreneur's expected income equals the project's expected output, which is exogenous, minus the expected payment to the investor. Thus the optimal contract is the one that minimizes the fraction of the time that the investor verifies output while providing the outside investor with the required rate of return.

Given our assumptions, the contract that accomplishes this takes a simple form. If the payoff to the project exceeds some critical level D, then the entrepreneur pays the investor D and the investor does not verify output. But if the payoff is less than D, the entrepreneur pays the verification cost and takes all of output. Thus the contract is a debt contract. The entrepreneur borrows $1 - W$ and promises to pay back D if that is possible. If the entrepreneur's output exceeds the amount that is due, he or she pays off the loan and keeps the surplus. And if the entrepreneur cannot make the required payment, all of his or her resources go to the lender. This payment function is shown in Figure 8.12.

The argument that the optimal contract takes this form has several steps. First, when the investor does not verify output, the payment cannot depend on actual output. To see this, suppose that the payment is supposed to be Q_1 when output is Y_1 and Q_2 when output is Y_2, with $Q_2 > Q_1$, and that the investor does not verify output in either of these cases. Since the investor does not know output, when output is Y_2 the entrepreneur

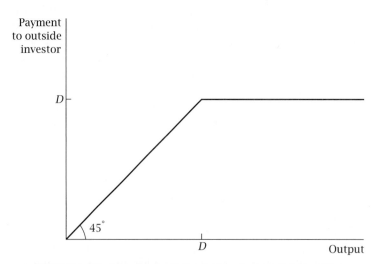

FIGURE 8.12   The form of the optimal payment function

pretends that it is Y_1, and therefore pays Q_1. Thus the contract cannot make the payment when output is Y_2 exceed the payment when it is Y_1.

Second, and similarly, the payment with verification can never exceed the payment without verification, D; otherwise the entrepreneur always pretends that output is not equal to the values of output that yield a payment greater than D. In addition, the payment with verification cannot equal D; otherwise it is possible to reduce expected expenditures on verification by not verifying whenever the entrepreneur pays D.

Third, the payment is D whenever output exceeds D. To see this, note that if the payment is ever less than D when output is greater than D, it is possible to increase the investor's expected receipts and reduce expected verification costs by changing the payment to D for these levels of output; as a result, it is possible to construct a more efficient contract.

Fourth, the entrepreneur cannot pay D if output is less than D; thus in these cases the investor must verify output.

Finally, if the payment is less than all of output when output is less than D, increasing the payment in these situations raises the investor's expected receipts without changing expected verification costs. But this means that it is possible to reduce D, and thus to save on verification costs.

Together, these facts imply that the optimal contract is a debt contract.[13]

The Equilibrium Value of D

The next step of the analysis is to determine what value of D is specified in the contract. Investors are risk-neutral and competitive, and the risk-free interest rate is r. Thus the expected payments to the investor, minus his or her expected spending on verification, must equal $1 + r$ times the amount of the loan, $1 - W$. To find the equilibrium value of D, we must therefore determine how the investor's expected receipts net of verification costs vary with D, and then find the value of D that provides the investor with the required expected net receipts.

To find the investor's expected net receipts, suppose first that D is less than the project's maximum possible output, 2γ. In this case, actual output can be either more or less than D. If output is more than D, the investor does not pay the verification cost and receives D. Since output is distributed

---

[13]For formal proofs, see Townsend (1979) and Gale and Hellwig (1985). This analysis neglects two subtleties. First, it assumes that verification must be a deterministic function of the state. One can show, however, that a contract that makes verification a random function of the entrepreneur's announcement of output can improve on the contract shown in Figure 8.12 (Bernanke and Gertler, 1989). Second, the analysis assumes that the investor can commit to verification if the entrepreneur announces that output is less than D. For any announced level of output less than D, the investor prefers to receive that amount without verifying than with verifying. But if the investor can decide ex post not to verify, the entrepreneur has an incentive to announce low output. Thus the contract is not *renegotiation-proof*. For simplicity, we ignore these complications.

uniformly on $[0, 2\gamma]$, the probability of this occurring is $(2\gamma - D)/2\gamma$. If output is less than D, the investor pays the verification cost and receives all of output. The assumption that output is distributed uniformly implies that the probability of this occurring is $D/2\gamma$, and that average output conditional on this event is $D/2$.

If D exceeds 2γ, on the other hand, then output is always less than D. Thus in this case the investor always pays the verification cost and receives all of output. In this case the expected payment is γ.

Thus the investor's expected receipts minus verification costs are

$$R(D) = \begin{cases} \dfrac{2\gamma - D}{2\gamma}D + \dfrac{D}{2\gamma}\left(\dfrac{D}{2} - c\right) & \text{if } D \le 2\gamma \\[2ex] \gamma - c & \text{if } D > 2\gamma. \end{cases} \tag{8.30}$$

Equation (8.30) implies that when D is less than 2γ, $R'(D) = [1-(c/2\gamma)]-(D/2\gamma)$. Thus R increases until $D = 2\gamma - c$ and then decreases. The reason that R is eventually decreasing in D is that when D is close to the maximum possible payoff, raising it further mainly means that the investor must verify output more often, and thus reduces his or her expected net receipts. At the maximum, the investor's expected net revenues are $R(2\gamma-c) = [(2\gamma-c)/2\gamma]^2\gamma \equiv R^{\text{MAX}}$. Thus the maximum expected net revenues equal expected output when c is zero, but are less than this when c is greater than zero. Finally, R declines to $\gamma - c$ at $D = 2\gamma$; thereafter further increases in D do not affect $R(D)$. The $R(D)$ function is plotted in Figure 8.13.

Figure 8.14 shows three possible values of the investor's required net revenues, $(1 + r)(1 - W)$. If the required net revenues equal V_1—more generally, if they are less than $\gamma - c$—there is a unique value of D that yields

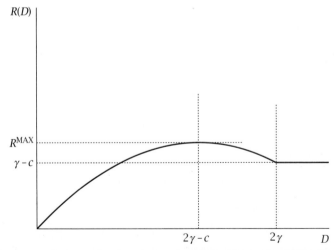

FIGURE 8.13   The investor's expected revenues net of verification costs

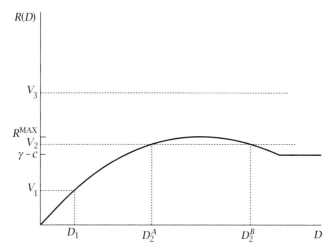

FIGURE 8.14 **The determination of the entrepreneur's required payment to the investor**

the investor the required net revenues. The contract therefore specifies this value of D. For the case when the required payment equals V_1, the equilibrium value of D is given by D_1 in the figure.

If the required net revenues exceed R^{MAX}—if they equal V_3, for example— there is no value of D that yields the necessary revenues for the investor. Thus in this situation there is *credit rationing:* investors refuse to lend $1 - W$ to the entrepreneur at any interest rate.

Finally, if the required net revenues are between $\gamma - c$ and R^{MAX}, there are two possible values of D. For example, the figure shows that a D of either D_2^A or D_2^B yields $R(D) = V_2$. The higher of these two D's (D_2^B in the figure) is not a competitive equilibrium, however: if an investor is making a loan to an entrepreneur with a required payment of D_2^B, other investors can profitably lend on more favorable terms. Thus competition drives D down to D_2^A. The equilibrium value of D is thus the smaller solution to $R(D) = (1 + r)(1 - W)$. Expression (8.30) implies that this solution is[14]

$$D^* = 2\gamma - c - \sqrt{(2\gamma - c)^2 - 4\gamma(1 + r)(1 - W)} \qquad \text{for } (1 + r)(1 - W) \le R^{\text{MAX}}.$$

$$(8.31)$$

Equilibrium Investment

The final step of the analysis is to determine when the entrepreneur undertakes the project. Clearly a necessary condition is that he or she can

---

[14]Note that the condition for the expression under the square root sign, $(2\gamma - c)^2 - 4\gamma(1 + r)(1 - W)$, to be negative is that $[(2\gamma - c)/2\gamma]^2\gamma < (1 + r)(1 - W)$—that is, that R^{MAX} is less than required net revenues. Thus the case where the expression in (8.31) is not defined corresponds to the case where there is no value of D at which investors are willing to lend.

obtain financing at some interest rate. But this is not sufficient: some entrepreneurs who can obtain financing may be better off investing in the safe
asset.

An entrepreneur who invests in the safe asset obtains $(1+r)W$. If the entrepreneur instead undertakes the project, his or her expected receipts are
expected output, γ, minus expected payments to the outside investor. If the
entrepreneur can obtain financing, the expected payments to the investor
are the opportunity cost of the investor's funds, $(1+r)(1-W)$, plus the investor's expected spending on verification costs. Thus to determine when
a project is undertaken, we need to determine these expected verification
costs.

These can be found from equation (8.31). The investor verifies when output is less than D^*; this occurs with probability $D^*/2\gamma$. Thus expected verification costs are

$$A = \frac{D^*}{2\gamma}c$$

$$= \left[\frac{2\gamma - c}{2\gamma} - \sqrt{\left(\frac{2\gamma - c}{2\gamma}\right)^2 - \frac{(1+r)(1-W)}{\gamma}} \right] c. \tag{8.32}$$

Straightforward differentiation shows that A is increasing in c and r and
decreasing in γ and W. We can therefore write

$$A = A(c, r, W, \gamma), \qquad A_c > 0, \quad A_r > 0, \quad A_W < 0, \quad A_\gamma < 0. \tag{8.33}$$

The entrepreneur's expected payments to the investor are $(1+r)(1-W)+$
$A(c, r, W, \gamma)$. Thus the project is undertaken if $(1+r)(1-W) \le R^{\text{MAX}}$ and

$$\gamma - (1+r)(1-W) - A(c, r, W, \gamma) > (1+r)W. \tag{8.34}$$

Although we have derived these results from a particular model of asymmetric information, the basic ideas are general. Suppose, for example, that
there is asymmetric information about how much risk the entrepreneur is
taking. In such a situation, if the investor bears some of the cost of poor
outcomes, the entrepreneur has an incentive to increase the riskiness of his
or her activities beyond the point that maximizes the expected return to
the project; thus there is *moral hazard*. As a result, asymmetric information again reduces the total expected returns to the entrepreneur and the
investor, just as it does in our model of costly state verification. Under plausible assumptions, these agency costs are decreasing in the amount of financing that the entrepreneur can provide (W), increasing in the amount
that the investor must be paid for a given amount of financing (r), decreasing in the expected payoff to the project (γ), and increasing in the magnitude of the asymmetric information (c when there is costly state verification,
and the entrepreneur's ability to take high-risk actions when there is moral
hazard).

Similarly, suppose that entrepreneurs are heterogeneous in terms of how risky their projects are, and that risk is not publicly observable—that is, that there is *adverse selection*. Then again there are agency costs of outside finance, and again those costs are determined by the same types of considerations as in our model. Thus the qualitative results of this model apply to many other models of asymmetric information in financial markets.

Implications

This model has many implications. As the preceding discussion suggests, most of the major ones arise from financial-market imperfections in general rather than from our specific model. Here we discuss four of the most important.

First, the agency costs arising from asymmetric information raise the cost of external finance, and therefore discourage investment. Under symmetric information, investment occurs in our model if $\gamma > 1 + r$. But when there is asymmetric information, investment occurs only if $\gamma > 1 + r + A(c, r, W, \gamma)$. Thus the agency costs reduce investment at a given safe interest rate.

Second, because financial-market imperfections create agency costs that affect investment, they alter the impact of output and interest-rate movements on investment. Recall from Section 8.5 that when financial markets are perfect, output movements affect investment through their effect on future profitability. Financial-market imperfections create a second channel: because output movements affect firms' current profitability, they affect firms' ability to provide internal finance. In the context of our model, we can think of a fall in current output as lowering entrepreneurs' wealth, W; since a reduction in wealth increases agency costs, the fall in output reduces investment even if the profitability of investment projects (the distribution of the γ's) is unchanged.

Similarly, interest-rate movements affect investment not only through the conventional channel, but also through their impact on agency costs: an increase in interest rates raises agency costs, and thus discourages investment. Intuitively, an increase in r raises the total amount the entrepreneur must pay the investor. This means that the probability that the investor is unable to make the required payment is higher, and thus that agency costs are higher. Specifically, since the investor's required net revenues are $(1 + r)(1 - W)$, an increase in r of Δr increases these required revenues by $(1 - W)\Delta r$; thus it has the same effect on the required net revenues as does a fall in W of $[(1 - W)/(1 + r)]\Delta r$. As a result, as equation (8.32) shows, these two changes have the same effect on agency costs.

In addition, the model implies that the effects of changes in output and interest rates on investment do not all occur through their impact on entrepreneurs' decisions of whether to borrow at the prevailing interest rate;

instead some of the impact comes from changes in the set of entrepreneurs who are able to borrow.

The third implication of our analysis is that many variables that do not affect investment when capital markets are perfect matter when capital markets are imperfect. Entrepreneurs' wealth provides a simple example. Suppose that γ and W are heterogenous across entrepreneurs. With perfect financial markets, whether a project is funded depends only on γ. Thus the projects that are undertaken are the most productive ones. This is shown in Panel (a) of Figure 8.15. With asymmetric information, in contrast, since W affects the agency costs, whether a project is funded depends on both γ and W. Thus a project with a lower expected payoff than another can be funded if the entrepreneur with the less productive project is wealthier. This is shown in Panel (b) of the figure.

The fact that financial-market imperfections cause entrepreneurs' wealth to affect investment implies that these imperfections can magnify the effects of shocks that occur outside the financial system. Declines in output arising from other sources act to reduce entrepreneurs' wealth; these reductions in wealth reduce investment, and thus increase the output declines (Bernanke and Gertler, 1989; Kiyotaki and Moore, 1995).

Two other examples of variables that affect investment only when capital markets are imperfect are average tax rates and idiosyncratic risk. If taxes are added to the model, the average rate (rather than just the marginal rate) affects investment through its impact on firms' ability to use internal finance. And risk, even if it is uncorrelated with consumption, affects investment through its impact on agency costs. Outside finance of a project whose payoff is certain, for example, involves no agency costs, since there is no possibility that the entrepreneur will be unable to repay the investor. But, as our model shows, outside finance of a risky project involves agency costs.

Fourth, and potentially most important, our analysis implies that the financial system itself can be important to investment. The model implies that increases in c, the cost of verification, reduce investment. More generally, the existence of agency costs suggests that the efficiency of the financial system in processing information and monitoring borrowers is a potentially important determinant of investment.

This observation has implications for both short-run fluctuations and long-run growth. For short-run fluctuations, it implies that disruptions to the financial system can affect investment, and thus aggregate output. For example, Bernanke (1983b) argues that the collapse of the U.S. banking system in the early 1930s contributed to the severity of the Great Depression by reducing the effectiveness of the financial system in evaluating and funding investment projects. Similarly, many observers argue that an important factor in the 1990–91 recession in the United States was a "capital crunch" at banks that reduced their ability to make loans. Their argument is that because banks had little capital of their own in this period, they were

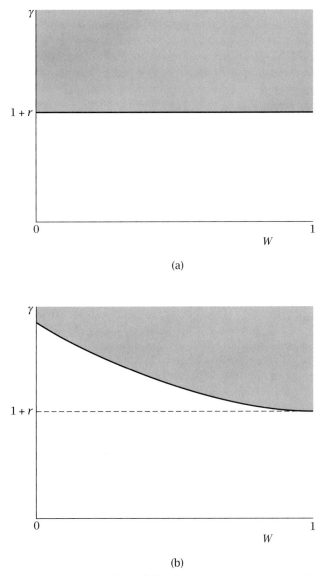

FIGURE 8.15   The determination of the projects that are undertaken under symmetric and asymmetric information

unusually dependent on external finance; this raised the opportunity cost of funds to them, and thus made them less willing to lend (see, for example, Bernanke and Lown, 1991).

With regard to long-run growth, McKinnon (1973) and others argue that the financial system has important effects on overall investment and on the quality of the investment projects that are undertaken, and thus on economies' growth over extended periods. Because the development of the financial system may be a by-product, rather than a cause, of growth, this argument is difficult to test. Nonetheless, King and Levine (1993a, 1993b) present some evidence that financial development is important to growth.

8.8 Empirical Applications

The Investment Tax Credit and the Price of Capital Goods

As we saw in Section 8.1, the costs of adjusting the capital stock can be either external or internal to firms. If they are external, they take the form of an increase in the relative price of capital goods when firms' desired capital stocks rise. Since there are data on the relative price of capital goods, it is possible to test for this effect.

Such a test is carried out by Goolsbee (1994). He focuses on how the investment tax credit affects capital-goods prices. His basic specification is

$$\ln P_{it} = b\tau_{it} + c_i' X_{it} + e_{it}, \tag{8.35}$$

where P_{it} is the relative price of capital of type i in year t, τ_{it} is a measure of the investment tax credit's subsidy to the purchase of capital good i in year t (as a percentage of the purchase price), and X_{it} is a vector of control variables whose effects are allowed to vary across the goods. Goolsbee argues that the government may have a tendency to increase the investment tax credit in times, such as recessions, when investment demand is otherwise weak. If this is correct, the estimate of b will tend to understate the true effect of the investment tax credit on capital-goods prices. To address this problem, Goolsbee includes dummy variables for each year in some specifications; when he does this, he is controlling for the variation over time in the overall investment tax credit and focusing only on the differences in the credit across different types of capital.

Goolsbee considers 22 capital goods over the period 1962–1988. His basic regression includes dummy variables for each capital good, a time trend, and dummy variables for the years of the Nixon price controls. This specification yields an estimate of b of 0.55, with a standard error of 0.12. Thus the results provide strong evidence of external adjustment costs, and they suggest that about half of the investment tax credit's subsidy to investment is passed into capital-goods prices.

When dummy variables for each year and time trends for each good are included, the estimate of b rises, which is consistent with Goolsbee's argument that leaving out the year dummies biases the estimate of b downward. The estimate of b is now 0.95 (with a standard error of 0.35); thus this specification suggests that the investment tax credit is reflected essentially one-for-one in prices and has essentially no effect on firms' incentives to invest.

The theory predicts that the effect of an increase in the credit on the relative price of capital goods should disappear over time as firms gradually increase their capital stocks; in addition, Goolsbee argues that capital-goods suppliers' adjustment of their capacity also contributes to the adjustment process. To investigate whether the impact of the credit is temporary, Goolsbee examines its effect on the relative price of capital goods over various horizons. The estimated effect is 0.55 (with a standard error of 0.18) after one year, 0.60 (0.19) after two, and 0.45 (0.36) after three.

It is tempting to interpret these results as supporting the predictions of the theory: the estimated effect is significantly different from zero in the first two years but not significantly different in the third. This interpretation, however, commits the classic error of equating the failure to reject a hypothesis with accepting it. The hypothesis that the impact after three years is zero cannot be rejected only because the effect is estimated imprecisely: although one cannot reject the hypothesis that the effect is zero, one also cannot reject the hypothesis that it is 1. Thus the results' support for the theory is slight: they suggest only a small decline in the effect over time, and they are more consistent with the view that the effect is constant than with the view that it disappears after three years.

Finally, returning to the contemporaneous effect of the investment tax credit, Goolsbee examines the variation in the effect across capital goods; specifically, he estimates a separate b for each type of capital. He finds that the price responses are large for goods that are purchased almost entirely by firms, such as mining machinery and railroad equipment, and small for goods that are purchased mainly by households, such as personal computers and furniture. Since households are not eligible for the investment tax credit, this suggests that the price effect of the credit is larger when it affects more of the buyers of a good. To investigate this idea, Goolsbee constructs estimates of the fractions of the purchasers of each good who are eligible for the credit. He then includes in the regression not just the credit, but the product of the credit and his eligibility estimate. If the reason that the credit is associated with increases in the price of capital is through its impact on demand, then under plausible assumptions the association should depend on only this interaction term.

The results support this prediction. When the interaction term is included, the coefficient on the credit falls to -0.02, with a standard error of 0.27. Thus not only can the hypothesis of no effect not be rejected, but the point estimate suggests a negligible impact. The coefficient on the interaction term is 0.80, with a standard error of 0.35; thus the estimated effect of the interaction is quantitatively large and statistically significant.

Cash Flow and Investment

Theories of financial-market imperfections imply that internal finance is less costly than external finance. They therefore imply that, for a given level of interest rates, firms with higher profits invest more.

A naive way to test this prediction is to regress investment on measures of the cost of capital and on *cash flow*—loosely speaking, current revenues minus expenses and taxes. Such regressions can use either firm-level data at a point in time or aggregate data over time. In either form, they typically find a strong link between cash flow and investment.

There is a problem with this test, however. The regression does not control for the future profitability of capital, and cash flow is likely to be correlated with future profitability. We saw in Section 8.5, for example, that our model of investment without financial-market imperfections predicts that a rise in output that is not immediately reversed raises investment. The reason is not that higher current output reduces firms' need to rely on outside finance, but that higher future output means that capital is more valuable. A similar relationship is likely to hold across firms at a point in time: firms with high cash flow probably have successful products or low costs, and thus have strong incentives to expand output. Because of this potential correlation between cash flow and current profitability, the regression may show a relationship between cash flow and investment even if financial markets are perfect.

A large literature, begun by Fazzari, Hubbard, and Petersen (1988), addresses this problem by comparing the investment behavior of different types of firms. Specifically, Fazzari, Hubbard, and Petersen's idea is to divide firms into those that are likely to face significant costs of obtaining outside funds and those that are not (see also Hoshi, Kashyap, and Scharfstein, 1991). There is likely to be an association between cash flow and investment among both types of firms even if financial-market imperfections are not important. But the theory that financial-market imperfections have large effects on investment predicts that the association will be stronger among the firms that face greater barriers to external finance. And unless the association between current cash flow and future profitability is for some reason stronger for the firms with less access to financial markets, the view that financial-market imperfections are not important predicts no difference in the cash flow–investment link for the two groups. Thus, Fazzari, Hubbard, and Petersen argue, the difference in the cash flow–investment relationship between the two groups can be used to test for the importance of financial-market imperfections to investment.

The specific way that Fazzari, Hubbard, and Petersen divide their firms is according to their dividend payments as a fraction of income. Firms that pay high dividends can finance additional investment by reducing their dividends. Firms that pay low dividends, in contrast, must rely on external finance.[15]

---

[15] One complication to this argument is that it may be costly for high-dividend firms to reduce their dividends: there is evidence that reductions in dividends are interpreted by the stock market as a signal of lower future profitability, and that the reductions therefore lower the value of firms' shares. Thus it is possible that the test could fail to find differences between the two groups of firms not because financial-market imperfections are unimportant, but because they are important to both groups.

The basic regression is a pooled time series–cross section regression of investment as a fraction of firms' capital stock on the ratio of cash flow to the capital stock, an estimate of q, and dummy variables for each firm and each year. The regression is estimated separately for the two groups of firms. The sample consists of 422 relatively large U.S. firms over the period 1970–1984. Low-dividend firms are defined as those with ratios of dividends to income consistently under 10%, and high-dividend firms are defined as those with dividend-income ratios consistently over 20% (Fazzari, Hubbard, and Petersen also consider an intermediate-dividend group).

For the high-dividend firms, the coefficient on cash flow is 0.230, with a standard error of 0.010; for the low-dividend firms, it is 0.461, with a standard error of 0.027. The t-statistic for the hypothesis that the two coefficients are equal is 12.1; thus the hypothesis is overwhelmingly rejected. The point estimates imply that low-dividend firms invest 23 cents more of each extra dollar of cash flow than the high-dividend firms do. Thus even if we interpret the estimate for the high-dividend firms as reflecting only the correlation between cash flow and future profitability, the results still suggest that financial-market imperfections have a large effect on investment by low-dividend firms.

Many authors have used variations on Fazzari, Hubbard, and Petersen's approach. Lamont (1993), for example, compares the investment behavior of the non-oil subsidiaries of oil companies after the collapse in oil prices in 1986 with the investment behavior of comparable companies that are not connected with oil companies. The view that internal finance is cheaper than external finance predicts that a decline in oil prices, by reducing the availability of internal funds, should reduce the subsidiaries' investment; the view that financial-market imperfections are unimportant predicts that it should have no effect. Lamont finds a statistically significant and quantitatively large difference in the behavior of the two groups; the point estimates imply that each dollar of lower income of a parent oil company reduces investment of the company's non-oil subsidiaries by 10 cents. Thus his results suggest that the barriers to outside finance are considerably larger than the barriers to finance between different parts of a company.

Gertler and Gilchrist (1994) carry out a test that is in the same spirit as these but that focuses on the effects of monetary policy (see also Kashyap, Lamont, and Stein, 1994, and Oliner and Rudebusch, 1994). They begin by arguing that small firms are likely to face larger barriers to outside finance than large firms do; for example, the fixed costs associated with issuing publicly traded bonds may be more important for small firms. They then compare the behavior of small and large firms' inventories and sales following moves to tighter monetary policy. Again the results support the importance of imperfect financial markets. Small firms account for a highly disproportionate share of the declines in sales, inventories, and short-term debt following monetary tightening. Indeed, large firms' borrowing increases after a monetary tightening, whereas small firms' borrowing declines sharply.

These papers' findings are representative of the findings in this litera-ture: the evidence consistently suggests that financial-market imperfections are important to investment. Precisely what form those imperfections take, and how important they are quantitatively, remain open questions.

Problems

8.1. Consider a firm that produces output using a Cobb–Douglas combination of capital and labor: $Y = K^\alpha L^{1-\alpha}, 0 < \alpha < 1$. Suppose that the firm's price is fixed in the short run; thus it takes both the price of its product, P, and the quantity, Y, as given. Finally, input markets are competitive; thus the firm takes the wage, W, and the rental price of capital, r_K, as given.

(a) What is the firm's choice of L given P, Y, W, and K?

(b) Given this choice of L, what are profits as a function of P, Y, W, and K?

(c) Find the first-order condition for the profit-maximizing choice of K. Is the second-order condition satisfied?

(d) Solve the first-order condition in part (c) for K as a function of P, Y, W, and r_K. How, if at all, do changes in each of these variables affect K?

8.2. Corporations in the United States are allowed to subtract depreciation al-lowances from their taxable income. The depreciation allowances are based on the purchase price of the capital; a corporation that buys a new capital good at time t can deduct fraction $D(s)$ of the purchase price from its taxable income at time $t + s$. Depreciation allowances often take the form of *straight-line de-preciation*: $D(s)$ equals $1/T$ for $s \varepsilon [0, T]$, and equals zero for $s > T$, where T is the *tax life* of the capital good.

(a) Assume straight-line depreciation. If the marginal corporate income tax rate is constant at τ and the interest rate is constant at i, by how much does purchasing a unit of capital at a price of P_K reduce the present value of the firm's corporate tax liabilities as a function of T, τ, i, and P_K? Thus, what is the after-tax price of the capital good to the firm?

(b) Suppose that $i = r + \pi$, and that π increases with no change in r. How does this affect the after-tax price of the capital good to the firm?

8.3. The major feature of the tax code that affects the user cost of capital in the case of owner-occupied housing in the United States is that nominal interest payments are tax deductible. Thus the after-tax real interest rate relevant to home ownership is $r - \tau i$, where r is the pretax real interest rate, i is the nominal interest rate, and τ is the marginal tax rate. In this case, how does an increase in inflation for a given r affect the user cost of capital and the desired capital stock?

8.4. **Using the calculus of variations to solve the social planner's problem in the Ramsey model.** Consider the social planner's problem that we analyzed in Section 2.4: the planner wants to maximize $\int_{t=0}^{\infty} e^{-\beta t}[c(t)^{1-\theta}/(1 - \theta)]\, dt$ subject to $\dot{k}(t) = f(k(t)) - c(t) - (n + g)k(t)$.

(a) What is the current-value Hamiltonian? What variables are the control variable, the state variable, and the costate variable?

(b) Find the three conditions that characterize optimal behavior analogous to equations (8.18), (8.19), and (8.20), in Section 8.2.

(c) Show that the first two conditions in part (b), together with the fact that $f'(k(t)) = r(t)$, imply the Euler equation (equation [2.19]).

(d) Let μ denote the costate variable. Show that $[\dot{\mu}(t)/\mu(t)] - \beta = (n + g) - r(t)$, and thus that $e^{-\beta t}\mu(t)$ is proportional to $e^{-R(t)}e^{(n+g)t}$. Show that this implies that the transversality condition in part (b) holds if and only if the budget constraint, equation (2.12), holds with equality.

8.5. Consider the model of investment in Sections 8.2–8.5. Describe the effects of each of the following changes on the $\dot{K} = 0$ and $\dot{q} = 0$ loci, on K and q at the time of the change, and on their behavior over time. In each case, assume that K and q are initially at their long-run equilibrium values.

(a) A war destroys half of the capital stock.

(b) The government taxes returns from owning firms at rate τ.

(c) The government taxes investment. Specifically, firms pay the government γ for each unit of capital they acquire, and receive a subsidy of γ for each unit of disinvestment.

8.6. Consider the model of investment in Sections 8.2–8.5. Suppose it becomes known at some date that there will be a one-time capital levy; specifically, capital holders will be taxed an amount equal to fraction f of the value of their capital holdings after time T. Assume the industry is initially in long-run equilibrium. What happens at the time of this news? How do K and q behave between the time of the news and the time the levy is imposed? What happens to K and q at the time of the levy? How do they behave thereafter? (Hint: is q anticipated to change discontinuously at the time of the levy?)

8.7. A model of the housing market. (This follows Poterba, 1984.) Let H denote the stock of housing, I the rate of investment, p_H the real price of housing, and R the rent. Assume that I is increasing in p_H, so that $I = I(p_H)$, with $I'(\bullet) > 0$, and that $\dot{H} = I - \delta H$. Assume also that the rent is a decreasing function of H: $R = R(H), R'(\bullet) < 0$. Finally, assume that rental income plus capital gains must equal the exogenous required rate of return, r: $(R + \dot{p}_H)/p_H = r$.

(a) Sketch the set of points in (H, p_H) space such that $\dot{H} = 0$. Sketch the set of points such that $\dot{p}_H = 0$.

(b) What are the dynamics of H and p_H in each region of the resulting diagram? Sketch the saddle path.

(c) Suppose the market is initially in long-run equilibrium, and that there is an unexpected permanent increase in r. What happens to H and p_H at the time of the change? How do H, p_H, I, and R behave over time following the change?

(d) Suppose the market is initially in long-run equilibrium, and that it becomes known that there will be a permanent increase in r time T in the future. What happens to H and p_H at the time of the news? How do H, p_H, I, and R behave between the time of the news and the time of the increase? What happens to them when the increase occurs? How do they behave after the increase?

(e) Are adjustment costs internal or external in this model? Explain.

(f) Why is the $\dot{H} = 0$ locus not horizontal in this model?

8.8. Suppose that the costs of adjustment exhibit constant returns in $\dot{\kappa}$ and κ. Specifically, suppose they are given by $C(\dot{\kappa}/\kappa)\kappa$, where $C(0) = 0$, $C'(0) = 0$, $C''(\bullet) > 0$. In addition, suppose capital depreciates at rate δ; thus $\dot{\kappa}(t) = I(t) - \delta\kappa(t)$. Consider the representative firm's maximization problem.

(a) What is the current-value Hamiltonian?

(b) Find the three conditions that characterize optimal behavior analogous to equations (8.18), (8.19), and (8.20), in Section 8.2.

(c) Show that the condition analogous to (8.18) implies that the growth rate of each firm's capital stock, and thus the growth rate of the aggregate capital stock, is determined by q. In (K, q) space, what is the $\dot{K} = 0$ locus?

(d) Substitute your result in part (c) into the condition analogous to (8.19) to express $\dot{q}$ in terms of K and q.

(e) In (K, q) space, what is the slope of the $\dot{q} = 0$ locus at the point where $q = 1$?

8.9. Suppose that $\pi(K) = a - bK$ and $C(I) = \alpha I^2/2$.

(a) What is the $\dot{q} = 0$ locus? What is the long-run equilibrium value of K?

(b) What is the slope of the saddle path? (Hint: use the approach in Section 2.6.)

8.10. Consider the model of investment under uncertainty with a constant interest rate in Section 8.6. Suppose that, as in Problem 8.9, $\pi(K) = a - bK$ and that $C(I) = \alpha I^2/2$; in addition, suppose that what is uncertain is future values of a. This problem asks you to show that it is an equilibrium for $q(t)$ and $K(t)$ to have the values at each point in time that they would if there were no uncertainty about the path of a. Specifically, let $\hat{q}(t + \tau, t)$ and $\hat{K}(t + \tau, t)$ be the paths q and K would take after time t if $a(t + \tau)$ were certain to equal $E_t[a(t + \tau)]$ for all $\tau \geq 0$.

(a) Show that if $E_t[q(t+\tau)] = \hat{q}(t+\tau, t)$ for all $\tau \geq 0$, then $E_t[K(t+\tau)] = \hat{K}(t+\tau, t)$ for all $\tau \geq 0$.

(b) Use equation (8.26) to show that this implies that if $E_t[q(t+\tau)] = \hat{q}(t+\tau, t)$, then $q(t) = \hat{q}(t, t)$, and thus that $\dot{K}(t) = N[\hat{q}(t, t) - 1]/\alpha$, where N is the number of firms.

8.11. (This follows Bernanke, 1983a, and Dixit and Pindyck, 1994.) Consider a firm that is contemplating undertaking an investment with a cost of I. There are two periods. The investment will pay off π_1 in period 1 and π_2 in period 2. π_1

is certain, but π_2 is uncertain. The firm maximizes expected profits and, for simplicity, the interest rate is zero.

(a) Suppose the firm's only choices are to undertake the investment in period 1 or not to undertake it at all. Under what condition will the firm undertake the investment?

(b) Suppose the firm also has the possibility of undertaking the investment in period 2, after the value of π_2 is known; in this case the investment pays off only π_2. Is it possible for the firm's expected profits to be higher if it does not invest in period 1 than if it does even if the condition in (a) is satisfied?

(c) Define the cost of waiting as π_1, and define the benefit of waiting as $\text{Prob}(\pi_2 < I)E[I - \pi_2 \mid \pi_2 < I]$. Explain why these represent the cost and the benefit of waiting. Show that the difference in the firm's expected profits between not investing in period 1 and investing in period 1 equals the benefit of waiting minus the cost.

8.12. The Modigliani–Miller theorem. (Modigliani and Miller, 1958.) Consider the analysis of the effects of uncertainty about discount factors in Section 8.6. Suppose, however, that the firm finances its investment using a mix of equity and risk-free debt. Specifically, consider the financing of the marginal unit of capital. The firm issues quantity b of bonds; each bond pays one unit of output with certainty at time $t + \tau$ for all $\tau \geq 0$. Equity holders are the residual claimant; thus they receive $\pi(K(t + \tau)) - b$ at $t + \tau$ for all $\tau \geq 0$.

(a) Let $P(t)$ denote the value of a unit of debt at t, and $V(t)$ the value of the equity in the marginal unit of capital. Find expressions analogous to (8.29) for $P(t)$ and $V(t)$.

(b) How, if at all, does the division of financing between bonds and equity affect the market value of the claims on the unit of capital, $P(t)b + V(t)$? Explain intuitively.

(c) More generally, suppose the firm finances the investment by issuing n financial instruments. Let $d_i(t + \tau)$ denote the payoff to instrument i at time $t + \tau$; the payoffs satisfy $d_1(t + \tau) + \cdots + d_n(t + \tau) = \pi(K(t + \tau))$, but are otherwise unrestricted. How, if at all, does the total value of the n assets depend on how the total payoff is divided among the assets?

(d) Return to the case of debt and equity finance. Suppose, however, that the firm's profits are taxed at rate θ, and that interest payments are tax deductible. Thus the payoff to bond holders is the same as before, but the payoff to equity holders at time $t + \tau$ is now $(1 - \theta)[\pi(K(t + \tau)) - b]$. Does the result in part (b) still hold? Explain.

Chapter 9
INFLATION AND MONETARY POLICY

9.1 Introduction

Inflation and unemployment are two of the main subjects of macroeconomics. They are among the principal concerns of policymakers and the public, and they have been the subject of large amounts of research. In our investigations of fluctuations in Chapters 4 through 6, we encountered various possible sources of short-run movements in both variables. Yet we said little about what determines their average levels over longer periods. This is the focus of the final two chapters. This chapter considers inflation, and Chapter 10 considers unemployment.

Inflation varies greatly both across countries and over time. In Germany and Japan, for example, the price level has risen an average of just a few percent per year over the past few decades, whereas in Italy and the United Kingdom it has risen an average of over 10% per year. In the United States during this period, annual inflation increased slowly and irregularly from around 1% in the late 1950s to almost 10% at the end of the 1970s; it then fell rapidly to less than 5%, and has remained between 2% and 5% since then.

If we consider periods before the past few decades and countries outside the industrialized world, there is even more variation in inflation. Many countries experienced large deflations—that is, declines in prices—after World War I and at the beginning of the Great Depression. And some developing countries, such as Bahrain, Burma, and Singapore, have average inflation rates in recent decades that are similar to Germany's and Japan's. At the other extreme, several countries have recently experienced hyperinflations (traditionally defined as inflation greater than 50% per month). In Argentina, for example, prices rose by a factor of 600 between May 1989 and March 1990, and in some months the price level almost tripled. And many other countries have undergone episodes of triple-digit annual inflation. Yet many of the countries that have experienced hyperinflations or very high inflations have also had extended periods of low inflation.[1]

This chapter's main subject is the causes of inflation. Sections 9.2 and 9.3 explain why inflation is almost always the result of rapid growth of the money supply; they also investigate the effects of money growth on inflation, real balances, and interest rates.

We then turn to the deeper question of what causes growth of the money supply. Most economists believe that average rates of inflation in most countries in the postwar period have been higher than is socially optimal. Since inflation stems mainly from money growth, this suggests that there is some type of *inflationary bias* in monetary policy. There are two main sets of explanations for such a bias.

The first set emphasizes the output-inflation tradeoff. If monetary policy has real effects (or if policymakers believe that it does), policymakers may increase the money supply in an effort to increase output. Theories of how inflation can arise from this tradeoff—particularly theories that emphasize the *dynamic inconsistency* of low-inflation policy—are discussed in Sections 9.4 through 9.6. Section 9.6 also considers several related policy questions that arise when monetary policy has real effects, particularly the issues of how much importance policymakers should attach to stabilizing real output versus keeping inflation low and of how monetary policy should be conducted when the economy is subject to shocks.

The second set of explanations of rapid money growth focuses on *seignorage*—the revenue the government gets from printing money. These theories, which are more relevant to less-developed countries than to industrialized ones, and which are at the heart of hyperinflations, are the subject of Section 9.7.

All of this analysis presumes that we understand why inflation is costly and how large its costs are. In fact, however, these are difficult issues. Section 9.8 is therefore devoted to the costs of inflation. This section not only describes the various potential costs of inflation, but also attempts to understand the basis for the intense concern about inflation among policymakers, the business community, and the public.

9.2 Inflation, Money Growth, and Interest Rates

Inflation and Money Growth

The simple diagram from Chapter 5 showing aggregate supply and aggregate demand, which is reproduced as Figure 9.1, provides a framework

---

[1] The all-time record inflation appears to have occurred in Hungary between August 1945 and July 1946, when the price level rose by a factor of approximately 10^{27}. During the peak month of this inflation, prices on average tripled daily (Sachs and Larrain, 1993).

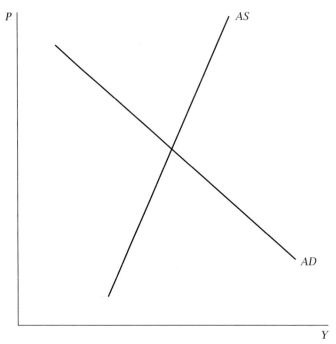

FIGURE 9.1   The aggregate demand and aggregate supply curves

for identifying potential sources of inflation. Since our interest is in prices rather than output, the issue of whether the aggregate supply curve is vertical or merely upward-sloping is not important: in either case, both expansions of aggregate demand and contractions of aggregate supply raise the price level. Thus there are many potential sources of inflation. Negative technology shocks, downward shifts in labor supply, upwardly skewed relative-cost shocks, and other factors that shift the aggregate supply curve to the left cause inflation; the same is true of increases in the money stock, downward shifts in money demand, increases in government purchases, and other factors that shift the aggregate demand curve to the right.[2] Since all of these types of shocks occur to some extent, there are many factors that affect inflation.

Nonetheless, when it comes to understanding inflation over the longer term, economists typically emphasize just one factor: growth of the money supply. The reason for this emphasis is that no other factor is likely to lead to persistent increases in the price level. Repeated increases in prices require either repeated falls in aggregate supply or repeated rises in aggregate demand. Given technological progress, repeated falls in aggregate

---

[2]Many shocks affect both curves. A rise in government purchases, for example, may not only shift the aggregate demand curve, but also move the aggregate supply curve through its impact on labor supply. The overall effect of any shock on the price level depends on how it affects both curves.

supply are unlikely. And although there are many factors that can increase aggregate demand, most of them are limited in scope. For example, there cannot be repeated large increases in aggregate demand coming from increases in government purchases or reductions in taxes, because there are practical limits on these variables; for instance, we never observe government purchases that are larger than total output, or total taxes that are negative. The money supply, in contrast, can grow at almost any rate, and we observe huge variations in money growth—from large and negative during some deflations to immense and positive during hyperinflations.

To see more clearly why money is crucial to inflation, consider the money market. With the specification of money demand from Chapter 5, the condition for equilibrium in the money market is

$$\frac{M}{P} = L(i, Y), \tag{9.1}$$

where M is the money stock, P the price level, i the nominal interest rate, Y real income, and $L(\cdot)$ the demand for real money balances. This condition implies that the price level is given by

$$P = \frac{M}{L(i, Y)}. \tag{9.2}$$

Conventional estimates of money demand suggest that the income elasticity of money demand is about 1 and the interest elasticity is about −0.2 (see Goldfeld and Sichel, 1990, for example). Thus for the price level to double over some period of time without a change in the money supply, income must fall roughly in half or the interest rate must rise by a factor of about 32. Alternatively, the demand for real balances at a given interest rate and income must fall in half. All of these possibilities are essentially unheard of. In contrast, a doubling of the money supply, either over several years in a moderate inflation or over a few days at the height of a hyperinflation, is not uncommon.

Thus money growth plays a special role in determining inflation not because money affects prices more directly than other factors do, but because empirically variations in money growth account for most of the variation in the growth of aggregate demand. Figure 9.2 provides powerful confirmation of the importance of money growth to inflation. The figure plots average inflation against average money growth in the 1980s for a sample of 65 countries; there is a clear and strong relationship between the two variables.

Money Growth and Interest Rates

Since money growth is the main determinant of inflation, it is natural to examine its effects in more detail. As we will see, there are interesting links between the growth of the nominal money stock and the behavior of inflation, real and nominal interest rates, and real balances.

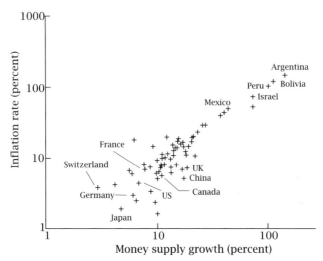

FIGURE 9.2   Money growth and inflation (data from International Financial Statistics)

We begin with the case where prices are completely flexible; this is presumably a good description of the long run. As we know from our analysis of fluctuations, this assumption implies that the money supply does not affect real output or the real interest rate. For simplicity, we assume that these are constant at $\overline{Y}$ and $\overline{r}$, respectively.

By definition, the real interest rate is the difference between the nominal interest rate and expected inflation. That is, $r \equiv i - \pi^e$, or

$$i \equiv r + \pi^e. \tag{9.3}$$

Equation (9.3) is known as the *Fisher identity.*

Using (9.3) and our assumption that r and Y are constant, we can rewrite (9.2) as

$$P = \frac{M}{L(\overline{r} + \pi^e, \overline{Y})}. \tag{9.4}$$

Assume that initially M and P are growing together at some steady rate (so that M/P is constant), and that π^e equals actual inflation. Now suppose that at some time, time t_0, there is a permanent increase in money growth. The resulting path of the money stock is shown in the top panel of Figure 9.3. After the change, since M is growing at a new steady rate and r and Y are constant by assumption, M/P is constant; that is, (9.4) is satisfied with P growing at the same rate as M and with π^e equal to the new rate of money growth.

But what happens at the time of the change? Since the price level rises faster after the change than before, expected inflation jumps up when the change occurs. Thus the nominal interest rate jumps up, and so the quantity

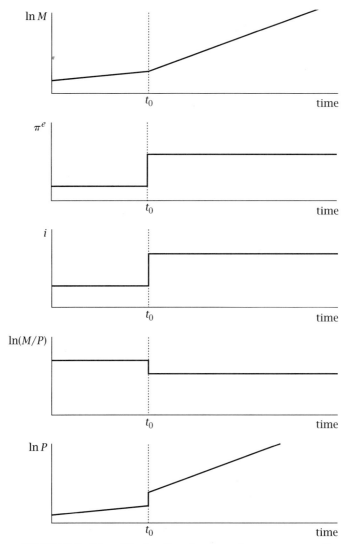

FIGURE 9.3 The effects of an increase in money growth

of real balances demanded falls discontinuously. Since M does not change discontinuously, it follows that P must jump up at the time of the change. This information is summarized in the remaining panels of Figure 9.3.[3]

This analysis has two messages. First, the change in inflation resulting from the change in money growth is reflected one-for-one in the nominal interest rate. The hypothesis that inflation affects the nominal rate

---

[3]In addition to the path of P described here, there may also be *bubble paths* that satisfy (9.4). Along these paths, P rises at an increasing rate, thereby causing π^e to be rising and the quantity of real balances demanded to be falling. See, for example, Problem 2.20 and Blanchard and Fischer (1989, Chapter 5, Section 3).

one-for-one is known as the *Fisher effect;* it follows from the Fisher identity and the assumption that inflation does not affect the real rate.

Second, a higher growth rate of the *nominal* money stock reduces the *real* money stock. The rise in money growth increases expected inflation, thereby increasing the nominal interest rate. This increase in the opportunity cost of holding money reduces the quantity of real balances that individuals want to hold. Thus equilibrium requires that P rises more than M does. That is, there must be a period when inflation exceeds the rate of money growth. In our model, this occurs at the moment that money growth increases. In models where prices are not completely flexible or individuals cannot adjust their real money holdings costlessly, in contrast, it occurs over a longer period.

A corollary is that a reduction in inflation can be accompanied by a temporary period of unusually high money growth. Rather than taking the path of the money stock as fixed, consider the problem of choosing the path of the money stock to yield some desired path of the price level. Specifically, suppose that policymakers want to reduce inflation and that they do not want the price level to change discontinuously. What path of M is needed to do this? The decline in inflation will reduce expected inflation, and thus lower the nominal interest rate and raise the quantity of real balances demanded. Writing the money market equilibrium condition as $M = PL(i, Y)$, it follows that—since $L(i, Y)$ increases discontinuously and P does not jump—M must jump up. Of course, to keep inflation low, the money stock must then grow slowly from this higher level.

Thus, the monetary policy that is consistent with a permanent drop in inflation is a sudden upward jump in the money supply, followed by low growth. And, in fact, the clearest examples of declines in inflation—the ends of hyperinflations—are accompanied by spurts of very high money growth that continue for a time after prices have stabilized (Sargent, 1982).[4]

The Case of Incomplete Price Flexibility

In the preceding analysis, an increase in money growth increases nominal interest rates. In practice, however, the immediate effect of a monetary expansion is to lower short-term nominal rates. This negative effect of monetary expansions on nominal rates is known as the *liquidity effect.*

The conventional explanation of the liquidity effect is that monetary expansions reduce real rates. If prices are not completely flexible, an increase in the money stock raises output, which requires a decline in the real interest rate; in terms of the *IS-LM* framework of Chapter 5, the *LM* curve shifts to the right along the downward-sloping *IS* curve. If the decline in

---

[4]This analysis raises the question of why expected inflation falls when the money supply is exploding. We return to this issue in Section 9.7.

the real rate is large enough, it more than offsets the effect of the increase in expected inflation.[5]

If prices are fully flexible in the long run, then the real rate eventually returns to normal following a shift to higher money growth. Thus if the real-rate effect dominates the expected-inflation effect in the short run, the shift depresses the nominal rate in the short run but increases it in the long run. As Friedman (1969) pointed out, this appears to provide an accurate description of the effects of monetary policy in practice. The Federal Reserve's expansionary policies in the late 1960s, for example, seem to have lowered nominal rates for several years, but, by generating inflation, to have raised them over the longer term.

9.3 Monetary Policy and the Term Structure of Interest Rates

In many situations, we are interested in the behavior not just of short-term interest rates, but also of long-term rates. To understand how monetary policy affects long-term rates, we must consider the relationship between short-term and long-term rates. The relationship among interest rates over different horizons is known as the *term structure of interest rates*, and the standard theory of that relationship is known as the *expectations theory of the term structure*. This section describes this theory and considers its implications for the effects of monetary policy.

The Expectations Theory of the Term Structure

Consider the problem of an investor deciding how to invest a dollar over the next n periods; assume for simplicity that there is no uncertainty about future interest rates. Suppose first the investor puts the dollar in an n-period zero-coupon bond (that is, a bond whose entire payoff comes after n periods). If the bond has a continuously compounded return of i_t^n per period, the investor has $\exp(ni_t^n)$ dollars after n periods. Now consider what happens if he or she puts the dollar into a sequence of 1-period bonds paying continuously compounded rates of return of $i_t^1, i_{t+1}^1, \ldots, i_{t+n-1}^1$ over the n periods. In this case, he or she ends up with $\exp(i_t^1 + i_{t+1}^1 + \cdots + i_{t+n-1}^1)$ dollars.

Equilibrium requires that investors are willing to hold both 1-period and n-period bonds. Thus the returns on the investor's two strategies must be the same. This requires

---

[5] See Problem 9.2. In addition, if inflation is completely unresponsive to monetary policy for any interval of time, then expectations of inflation over that interval do not rise; thus in this case short-term nominal rates necessarily fall.

$$i_t^n = \frac{i_t^1 + i_{t+1}^1 + \cdots + i_{t+n-1}^1}{n}. \tag{9.5}$$

That is, the interest rate on the long-term bond must equal the average of the interest rates on short-term bonds over its lifetime.

In this example, since there is no uncertainty, rationality alone implies that the term structure is determined by the path that short-term interest rates will take. With uncertainty, under plausible assumptions expectations concerning future short-term rates continue to play an important role in the determination of the term structure. A typical formulation is

$$i_t^n = \frac{i_t^1 + E_t i_{t+1}^1 + \cdots + E_t i_{t+n-1}^1}{n} + \theta_t, \tag{9.6}$$

where E_t denotes expectations as of period t. With uncertainty, the strategies of buying a single n-period bond and a sequence of 1-period bonds generally involve different risks. Thus rationality does not imply that the expected returns on the two strategies must be equal. This is reflected by the inclusion of θ, the *term premium* to holding the long-term bond, in (9.6).

The expectations theory of the term structure is the hypothesis that changes in the term structure are determined by changes in expectations of future interest rates (rather than by changes in the term premium). Typically, though not always, the expectations are assumed to be rational.[6]

As described at the end of Section 9.2, even if prices are not completely flexible, a permanent increase in money growth eventually increases the short-term nominal interest rate permanently. Thus even if short-term rates fall for some period, (9.5) implies that interest rates for sufficiently long maturities (that is, for sufficiently large n) immediately rise. Thus our analysis implies that a monetary expansion is likely to reduce short-term rates but increase long-term ones.

Empirical Application: The Response of the Term Structure to Changes in the Federal Reserve's Federal-Funds-Rate Target

In many periods, the Federal Reserve has had a target level of a particular interest rate, the Federal funds rate, and has implemented monetary policy through discrete changes in that target. The Federal funds rate is the interest rate that banks charge each other on one-day loans of reserves; thus it is a very short-term rate. Because changes in the Federal Reserve's target are discrete, it is usually clear what the target is and when it changes. Cook and Hahn (1989) use this fact to investigate the impact that monetary policy has

---

[6]See Shiller (1990) for an overview of the study of the term structure.

on interest rates on bonds of different maturities. They focus on the period 1974–1979, which was a time when the Federal Reserve was targeting the funds rate.

Cook and Hahn begin by compiling a record of the changes in the Federal Reserve's target over this period. They examine both the records of the Federal Reserve Bank of New York (which implemented the changes) and the reports of the changes in the *Wall Street Journal*. They find that the *Journal*'s reports are almost always correct; thus it is reasonable to think of the changes in the target reported by the *Journal* as publicly observed.

As Cook and Hahn describe, the actual Federal funds rate moves closely with the Federal Reserve's target. Moreover, it is highly implausible that the Federal Reserve is changing the target in response to factors that would have moved the funds rate in the absence of the policy changes. For example, it is unlikely that, absent the Federal Reserve's actions, the funds rate would move by discrete amounts. In addition, there is often a lag of several days between the Federal Reserve's decision to change the target and the actual change; thus arguing that the Federal Reserve is responding to forces that would have moved the funds rate in any event requires arguing that the Federal Reserve has advance knowledge of those forces.

The close link between the actual funds rate and the Federal Reserve's target thus provides strong evidence that monetary policy affects short-term interest rates. As Cook and Hahn describe, earlier investigations of this issue mainly regressed changes in interest rates over periods of a month or a quarter on changes in the money supply over those periods; the regressions produced no clear evidence of the Federal Reserve's ability to influence interest rates. The reason appears to be that the regressions are complicated by the same types of issues that complicate the money-output regressions discussed in Section 5.6: the money supply is not determined solely by the Federal Reserve, the Federal Reserve adjusts policy in response to information about the economy, and so on.

Cook and Hahn then examine the impact of changes in the Federal Reserve's target on longer-term interest rates. Specifically, they estimate regressions of the form

$$\Delta R_t^i = b_1^i + b_2^i \, \Delta FF_t + u_t^i, \tag{9.7}$$

where ΔR_t^i is the change in the nominal interest rate on a bond of maturity i on day t, and ΔFF_t is the change in the target Federal funds rate on that day.

Cook and Hahn find, contrary to the predictions of the analysis in the first part of this section, that increases in the Federal-funds-rate target raise nominal interest rates at all horizons. An increase in the target of 100 basis points (that is, one percentage point) is associated with increases in the 3-month interest rate of 55 basis points (with a standard error of 6.8 basis points), in the 1-year rate of 50 basis points (5.2), in the 5-year rate of 21 basis points (3.2), and the 20-year rate of 10 basis points (1.8).

The idea that contractionary monetary policy should immediately lower long-term nominal interest rates is intuitive: contractionary policy is likely to raise real interest rates only briefly and is likely to lower inflation over the longer term. Yet, as Cook and Hahn's results show, the evidence does not support this prediction.

There are at least four possible explanations of this anomaly. First, the response of the real rate to monetary policy may be so persistent, and the response of inflation so slow, that the real-interest-rate effect dominates the expected-inflation effect even at fairly long horizons. Second, the Federal Reserve may be changing policy on the basis of information that it has, and that market participants do not have, concerning future inflation. If this is correct, when market participants observe a shift to tighter policy, they revise up their estimates of future inflation, and so long-term rates rise. Third, the behavior of the money supply may be sufficiently complicated that lower current money growth is on average associated with higher rather than lower money growth in the future (Barro, 1989).[7] And finally, rational expectations of future short-term rates may not be the main determinant of the response of long-term rates to changes in monetary policy. For example, term premia may change systematically, or market participants may form their expectations partly on the basis of rules of thumb. Some support for this possibility is provided by the fact that the rational-expectations theory of the term structure does not seem to fit the data particularly well (see, for example, Mankiw and Miron, 1986). Whether it fails as a description of how longer-term rates react to changes in monetary policy is an open question, however.

9.4   The Dynamic Inconsistency of Low-Inflation Monetary Policy

Our analysis thus far suggests that money growth is the key determinant of inflation. Thus to understand what causes high inflation, we need to understand what causes high money growth. For the major industrialized countries, where government revenue from money creation does not appear important, the leading candidate is the existence of a perceived output-inflation tradeoff. If policymakers believe that aggregate demand movements affect real output, they may increase the money supply to try to push output above its normal level. Or, if they are faced with inflation that they believe is too high, they may be reluctant to undergo a recession to reduce it.

Any theory of how an output-inflation tradeoff can lead to inflation must confront the fact that there is no tradeoff in the long run. Since average inflation has no effect on average output, it might seem that the existence

---

[7] This explanation also implies that contractionary monetary policy can raise the short-term nominal rate without increasing the real rate.

of a short-run tradeoff is irrelevant to the determination of average inflation. Consider, for example, two monetary policies that differ only because money growth is lower by a constant amount in every situation under one policy than the other. If the public is aware of the difference, there is no reason for output to behave differently under the low-inflation policy than under the high-inflation one.

In a famous paper, however, Kydland and Prescott (1977) show that the inability of policymakers to commit themselves to such a low-inflation policy can give rise to excessive inflation despite the absence of a long-run tradeoff (see also Barro and Gordon, 1983a). Kydland and Prescott's basic observation is that if expected inflation is low, so that the marginal cost of additional inflation is low, policymakers will pursue expansionary policies to push output temporarily above its normal level. But the public's knowledge that policymakers have this incentive means that they will not in fact expect low inflation. The end result is that policymakers' ability to pursue discretionary policy results in inflation without any increase in output. This section presents a simple model that formalizes this idea.

Assumptions

Kydland and Prescott consider an economy where aggregate demand disturbances have real effects and expectations concerning inflation affect aggregate supply. We can capture both of these effects by assuming that aggregate supply is given by the Lucas supply curve (see equations [5.38] and [6.21]):

$$y = \bar{y} + b(\pi - \pi^e), \qquad b > 0, \tag{9.8}$$

where y is the log of output and $\bar{y}$ is the log of its flexible-price level.[8] Kydland and Prescott assume that the flexible-price level of output is less than the socially optimal level. This could arise from positive marginal tax rates (so that individuals do not capture the full benefits of additional labor supply), or from imperfect competition (so that firms do not capture the full benefits of additional output). In addition, they assume that inflation above some level is costly, and that the marginal cost of inflation increases as inflation rises. A simple way to capture these assumptions is to make social welfare quadratic in both output and inflation. Thus the policymaker minimizes:

$$L = \frac{1}{2}(y - y^*)^2 + \frac{1}{2}a(\pi - \pi^*)^2, \qquad y^* > \bar{y}, \quad a > 0. \tag{9.9}$$

---

[8]The assumption that only unexpected inflation matters is not essential. For example, a model along the lines of equation (5.39), in Section 5.5, where core inflation is given by a weighted average of past inflation and expected inflation, has similar implications.

The parameter a reflects the relative importance of output and inflation in social welfare.[9]

Finally, the policymaker controls money growth, which determines the behavior of aggregate demand. Since there is no uncertainty, we can think of the policymaker as choosing inflation directly, subject to the constraint that inflation and output are related by the aggregate supply curve, (9.8).

Analyzing the Model

To see the model's implications, consider two ways that monetary policy and expected inflation could be determined. In the first, the policymaker makes a binding commitment about what inflation will be before expected inflation is determined. Since the commitment is binding, expected inflation equals actual inflation, and so (by [9.8]) output equals its natural rate. Thus the policymaker's problem is to choose π to minimize $(\bar{y} - y^*)^2/2 + a(\pi - \pi^*)^2/2$. The solution is simply $\pi = \pi^*$.

In the second situation, the policymaker chooses inflation taking expectations of inflation as given. This could occur either if expected inflation is determined before money growth is, or if π and π^e are determined simultaneously. Substituting (9.8) into (9.9) implies that the policymaker's problem is

$$\min_{\pi} \frac{1}{2}[\bar{y} + b(\pi - \pi^e) - y^*]^2 + \frac{1}{2}a(\pi - \pi^*)^2. \tag{9.10}$$

The first-order condition is

$$[\bar{y} + b(\pi - \pi^e) - y^*]b + a(\pi - \pi^*) = 0. \tag{9.11}$$

Solving (9.11) for π yields

$$\pi = \frac{b^2\pi^e + a\pi^* + b(y^* - \bar{y})}{a + b^2}$$

$$= \pi^* + \frac{b}{a + b^2}(y^* - \bar{y}) + \frac{b^2}{a + b^2}(\pi^e - \pi^*). \tag{9.12}$$

---

[9]Equation (9.9) is intended to reflect not just the policymaker's preferences, but also the representative individual's. The reason that the decentralized equilibrium with flexible prices does not achieve the first-best level of output is that (because of the taxes or imperfect competition) there are positive externalities from higher output. That is, neglecting inflation for the moment, we can think of the representative individual's welfare as depending on his or her own output (or labor supply), y_i, and average economy-wide output, y: $U_i = V(y_i, y)$. The assumption underlying (9.9) is that $\bar{y}$ is the Nash equilibrium (so $V_1(\bar{y}, \bar{y}) = 0$ and $V_{11}(\bar{y}, \bar{y}) < 0$, where subscripts denote partial derivatives), but is less than the social optimum (so $V_2(\bar{y}, \bar{y}) > 0$).

Figure 9.4 plots the policymaker's choice of π as a function of π^e. The relationship is upward sloping with a slope less than 1. The figure and equation (9.12) show the policymaker's incentive to pursue expansionary policy. If the public expects the policymaker to choose the optimal rate of inflation, π^*, the marginal cost of slightly higher inflation is zero, and the marginal benefit of the resulting higher output is positive. Thus in this situation the policymaker chooses an inflation rate greater than π^*.

Since there is no uncertainty, equilibrium requires that expected and actual inflation are equal. As Figure 9.4 shows, there is a unique inflation rate for which this is true. If we impose $\pi = \pi^e$ in (9.12) and then solve for this inflation rate, we obtain

$$\pi^e = \pi^* + \frac{b}{a}(y^* - \overline{y})$$

$$\equiv \pi^{EQ}.$$

(9.13)

If expected inflation exceeds this level, actual inflation is less than individuals expect, and thus the economy is not in equilibrium. Similarly, if π^e is less than π^{EQ}, π exceeds π^e.

Thus the only equilibrium is for π and π^e to equal π^{EQ}, and for y to therefore equal $\overline{y}$. Intuitively, expected inflation rises to the point where the policymaker, taking π^e as given, chooses to set π equal to π^e. In short,

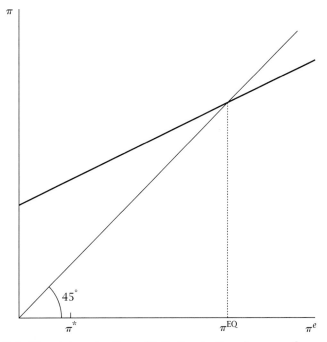

FIGURE 9.4 **The determination of inflation in the absence of commitment**

all that the policymaker's discretion does is to increase inflation without affecting output.[10]

Discussion

The reason that the ability to choose inflation after expected inflation is de-termined makes the policymaker worse off is that the policy of announcing that inflation will be π^*, and then producing that inflation rate after ex-pected inflation is determined, is not *dynamically consistent* (equivalently, it is not *subgame-perfect*). If the policymaker announces that inflation will equal π^* and the public forms its expectations accordingly, the policymaker will deviate from the policy once expectations are formed. The public's knowledge that the policymaker would do this causes it to expect inflation greater than π^*; this expected inflation worsens the menu of choices that the policymaker faces.

To see that it is the knowledge that the policymaker has discretion, rather than just the discretion itself, that is the source of the problem, con-sider what happens if the public believes the policymaker can commit but he or she in fact has discretion. In this case, the policymaker can announce that inflation will equal π^*, and thereby cause expected inflation to equal π^*. But the policymaker can then set inflation according to (9.12). Since (9.12) is the solution to the problem of minimizing the social loss function given expected inflation, this "reneging" on the commitment raises social welfare.[11]

Dynamic inconsistency arises in many other situations. Policymakers choosing how to tax capital may want to encourage capital accumulation by adopting a low tax rate. Once the capital has been accumulated, however, taxing it is nondistortionary; thus it is optimal for policymakers to tax it at high rates. As a result, the low tax rate is not dynamically consistent.[12] To give another example, policymakers who want individuals to obey a law may

---

[10]None of these results depend on the use of specific functional forms. With general functional forms, the equilibrium is for expected and actual inflation to rise to the point where the marginal cost of inflation just balances its marginal benefit through higher output. Thus output equals its natural rate and inflation is above the optimal level. The equilibrium if the policymaker can make a binding commitment is still for inflation to equal its optimal level and output to equal its natural rate.

[11]In fact, the policymaker can do even better by announcing that inflation will equal $\pi^* - (y^* - \bar{y})/b$ and then setting $\pi = \pi^*$; this yields $y = y^*$ and $\pi = \pi^*$.

[12]A corollary of this observation is that low-inflation policy can be dynamically incon-sistent not because of an output-inflation tradeoff, but because of government debt. Since government debt is denominated in nominal terms, unanticipated inflation is a lump-sum tax on debt holders. As a result, even if monetary shocks do not have real affects, a policy of setting $\pi = \pi^*$ is not dynamically consistent as long as the government has nominally denominated debt (Calvo, 1978b).

want to promise that violators will be punished harshly. Once individuals have decided whether to comply, however, there is no benefit to punishing violators. Thus again the optimal policy is not dynamically consistent.

9.5 Addressing the Dynamic-Inconsistency Problem

Kydland and Prescott's analysis shows that under fairly mild conditions, discretionary monetary policy gives rise to inefficiently high inflation. This naturally raises the question of what can be done to avoid, or at least mitigate, this possibility.

One approach, of course, is to have monetary policy determined by rules rather than discretion. It is important to emphasize, however, that the rules must be binding. Suppose the policymaker just announces that he or she is going to determine monetary policy according to some procedure, such as pegging the exchange rate or making the money stock grow at a constant rate. If the public believes this announcement and therefore expects low inflation, the policymaker can raise social welfare by departing from the announced policy and choosing a higher rate of money growth. Thus the public will not believe the announcement. Only if the monetary authority relinquishes the ability to determine the money supply does a rule solve the problem.

There are two problems, however, with using binding rules to overcome the dynamic-inconsistency problem. One is normative, the other positive. The normative problem is that rules cannot account for completely unexpected circumstances. There is no difficulty in constructing a rule that makes money growth respond to normal economic developments (such as changes in unemployment and movements in indexes of leading indicators). But sometimes there are events that could not plausibly have been expected. In the 1980s, for example, the United States experienced a major stock market crash that caused a severe liquidity crisis, a "capital crunch" that may have significantly affected banks' lending, and a collapse of the relationships between economic activity and many standard measures of the money stock. It is almost inconceivable that a binding rule would have anticipated all of these possibilities.

The positive problem with binding rules as the solution to the dynamic-inconsistency problem is that we observe low rates of inflation in many situations (such as the United States in the 1950s and in recent years, and Germany over most of the postwar period) where policy is not made according to fixed rules. Thus there must be ways of alleviating the dynamic-inconsistency problem that do not involve binding commitments.

Because of considerations like these, there has been considerable interest in other ways of dealing with dynamic inconsistency. The two approaches that have received the most attention are reputation and delegation.[13]

A Model of Reputation

Reputation can be used to address the dynamic-inconsistency problem if policymakers are in office for more than one period and the public is unsure of their characteristics. For example, the public may not know policymakers' preferences between output and inflation or their beliefs about the output-inflation tradeoff, or whether their announcements about future policy are binding. In such situations, policymakers' behavior conveys information about their characteristics, and thus affects the public's expectations of inflation in subsequent periods. Since policymakers face a more favorable menu of output-inflation choices when expected inflation is lower, this gives them an incentive to pursue low-inflation policies.

To see this formally, consider the following model, which is based on Backus and Driffill (1985) and Barro (1986). Policymakers are in office for two periods, and the output-inflation relationship is given by (9.8) each period; thus $y_t = \bar{y} + b(\pi_t - \pi_t^e)$. It simplifies the algebra to assume that social welfare is linear rather than quadratic in output, and that π^* is zero. Thus social welfare in period t is

$$
\begin{aligned}
w_t &= (y_t - \bar{y}) - \frac{1}{2}a\pi_t^2 \\
&= b(\pi_t - \pi_t^e) - \frac{1}{2}a\pi_t^2.
\end{aligned}
$$

(9.14)

There are two possible types of policymaker; the public does not know in advance which type it is dealing with. A Type-1 policymaker, which occurs with probability p, shares the public's preferences concerning output and inflation. He or she therefore maximizes

$$
W = w_1 + \beta w_2, \qquad 0 < \beta \le 1,
$$

(9.15)

---

[13]Two other possibilities are punishment equilibria and incentive contracts. Punishment equilibria (which are often described as models of reputation, but which differ fundamentally from the models considered below) arise in infinite-horizon models. These models typically have multiple equilibria, including ones where inflation stays below the one-time discretionary level (that is, below π^{EQ}). Low inflation is sustained by beliefs that if the policymaker were to choose high inflation, the public would "punish" him or her by expecting high inflation in subsequent periods; the punishments are structured so that the expectations of high inflation would in fact be rational if that situation ever arose. See, for example, Barro and Gordon (1983b); Rogoff (1987); and Problems 9.8–9.10. Incentive contracts are arrangements in which the central banker is penalized (either financially or through loss of prestige) for inflation. In simple models, the appropriate choice of penalties produces the optimal policy (Persson and Tabellini, 1993; Walsh, 1995). The empirical relevance of such contracts is not clear, however.

where β reflects the importance of the second period in social welfare. A Type-2 policymaker, which occurs with probability $1 - p$, cares only about inflation, and therefore sets inflation to zero in both periods.[14]

Analyzing the Model

Since a Type-2 policymaker always sets inflation to zero, we focus on the behavior of a Type-1 policymaker. In the second period, he or she takes π_2^e as given, and therefore chooses π_2 to maximize $b(\pi_2 - \pi_2^e) - a\pi_2^2/2$. The solution is $\pi_2 = b/a$.

The policymaker's first-period problem is more complicated, because his or her choice of inflation affects expected inflation in the second period. If the policymaker chooses any value of π_1 other than zero, the public learns that it is facing a Type-1 policymaker, and therefore expects inflation of b/a in the second period. Conditional on π_1 not equaling 0, the choice of π_1 has no effect on π_2^e. Thus if the policymaker chooses a nonzero first-period inflation rate, he or she chooses it to maximize $b(\pi_1 - \pi_1^e) - a\pi_1^2/2$, and therefore sets $\pi_1 = b/a$. π_2^e and π_2 are then both equal to b/a, and y_2 equals $\bar{y}$. The value of the objective function for the two periods in this case is thus

$$
W_{\text{INF}} = \left[b\left(\frac{b}{a} - \pi_1^e\right) - \frac{1}{2}a\left(\frac{b}{a}\right)^2 \right] - \beta\frac{1}{2}a\left(\frac{b}{a}\right)^2
$$

$$
= \frac{b^2}{a}\frac{1}{2}(1 - \beta) - b\pi_1^e.
$$

(9.16)

The Type-1 policymaker's other possibility is to set π_1 to 0. It turns out that in equilibrium, he or she may randomize between $\pi_1 = b/a$ and $\pi_1 = 0$. Thus, let q denote the probability that the Type-1 policymaker chooses $\pi_1 = 0$. Now consider the public's inference problem if it observes zero inflation. It knows that this means either that the policymaker is a Type 2 (which occurs with probability $1 - p$), or that the policymaker is a Type 1 but chose zero inflation (which occurs with probability pq). Thus, by Bayes's law, its estimate of the probability that the policymaker is a Type 1 is $qp/[(1 - p) + qp]$. Its expectation of π_2 is therefore $\{qp/[(1-p)+qp]\}(b/a)$, which is less than b/a.

This analysis implies that the value of the objective function when the policymaker chooses $\pi_1 = 0$ is

$$
W_0(q) = b(-\pi_1^e) + \beta\left\{b\left[\frac{b}{a} - \frac{qp}{(1 - p) + qp}\frac{b}{a}\right] - \frac{1}{2}a\left(\frac{b}{a}\right)^2\right\}.
$$

(9.17)

$$
= \frac{b^2}{a}\beta\left[\frac{1}{2} - \frac{qp}{(1 - p) + qp}\right] - b\pi_1^e.
$$

---

[14]The key assumption is that the two types have different preferences, not that one type always chooses zero inflation.

Note that $W_0(q)$ is decreasing in q, the probability that the Type-1 policy-maker chooses zero inflation in the first period: a higher q implies a higher value of π_2^e if $\pi_1 = 0$, and thus a smaller value to the policymaker of choosing $\pi_1 = 0$.

The equilibrium of the model can take three possible forms. The first possibility occurs if $W_0(0)$ is less than W_{INF}. In this case, even if the Type-1 policymaker can cause the public to be certain that it is facing a Type-2 policymaker by setting $\pi_1 = 0$, he or she will not want to do so. Thus in this case the Type-1 policymaker always chooses $\pi_1 = b/a$. Equations (9.16) and (9.17) imply that $W_0(0)$ is less than W_{INF} when

$$\frac{b^2}{a}\beta\frac{1}{2} - b\pi_1^e < \frac{b^2}{a}\frac{1}{2}(1 - \beta) - b\pi_1^e, \tag{9.18}$$

or simply

$$\beta < \frac{1}{2}. \tag{9.19}$$

Thus if the weight on the second period is sufficiently small, the public's uncertainty about the policymaker's type has no effects.

The second possibility arises when $W_0(1)$ is greater than W_{INF}. In this situation, the Type-1 policymaker always chooses $\pi_1 = 0$: even if the public learns nothing about the policymaker's type from observing $\pi_1 = 0$, the cost of revealing that he or she is a Type-1 is enough to dissuade the policymaker from choosing positive inflation. Equations (9.16) and (9.17) imply that $W_0(1)$ exceeds W_{INF} when

$$\frac{b^2}{a}\beta\left(\frac{1}{2} - p\right) - b\pi_1^e > \frac{b^2}{a}\frac{1}{2}(1 - \beta) - b\pi_1^e. \tag{9.20}$$

This condition simplifies to

$$\beta > \frac{1}{2}\frac{1}{1 - p}. \tag{9.21}$$

The final possibility arises when $W_0(0) > W_{INF} > W_0(1)$; the preceding analysis implies that this occurs when $1/2 < \beta < (1/2)[1/(1 - p)]$. In this case, Type-1 policymakers would choose zero first-period inflation if the public believes they would choose positive inflation, and would choose positive inflation if the public believes they would choose zero. As a result, the economy can be in equilibrium only if the Type-1 policymakers sometimes choose positive inflation and sometimes choose zero. Specifically, q must adjust to the point where the Type-1 policymakers are indifferent between $\pi_1 = 0$ and $\pi_1 = b/a$. Equating (9.16) and (9.17) and solving for q shows that this requires

$$q = \frac{1 - p}{p}(2\beta - 1) \qquad \text{if } \frac{1}{2} < \beta < \frac{1}{2}\frac{1}{1 - p}. \tag{9.22}$$

Discussion

Although this model is highly stylized, the basic idea is simple. The public is unsure about what policies the government will follow in future periods. Under plausible assumptions, the lower the inflation it observes today, the lower its expectations of inflation in future periods. This gives policymakers an incentive to keep inflation low. Because of the simplicity of the central idea, the basic result that uncertainty about policymakers' characteristics reduces inflation is highly robust (see, for example, Vickers, 1986; Cukierman and Meltzer, 1986; Rogoff, 1987; and Problem 9.11).

This analysis implies that the impact of reputational considerations on inflation is greater when policymakers place more weight on future periods. Specifically, q—the probability that a Type-1 policymaker chooses $\pi_1 = 0$— is increasing in β for $1/2 < \beta < (1/2)[1/(1 - p)]$, and is independent of β elsewhere. Similarly, one can show that the impact of the reputational considerations is greater when there are more periods.

The model also implies that the impact on inflation is greater when there is more uncertainty about policymakers' characteristics. To see this, consider, for simplicity, the case of $\beta = 1$. If the policymaker's type is publicly observed, the Type 1's always set $\pi_1 = b/a$ and the Type 2's always set $\pi_1 = 0$. Under imperfect information, however, the Type 1's set $\pi_1 = 0$ with probability q. Thus the uncertainty lowers average first-period inflation by $pq(b/a)$. With $\beta = 1$, (9.21) implies that $q = 1$ when $p < 1/2$; thus for these values of p, the reduction in average first-period inflation is pb/a. And (9.22) implies that $q = (1 - p)/p$ when $p > 1/2$; thus for these values, the reduction is $(1 - p)b/a$. The maximum reduction thus occurs at $p = 1/2$, and equals $b/2a$. In short, the impact of the reputational considerations is greater when the difference between the two types' preferred inflation rates is larger (that is, when b/a is larger) and when there is more uncertainty about the policymaker's type (that is, when p is closer to $1/2$).[15]

The idea that reputational considerations cause policymakers to pursue less expansionary policies seems not only theoretically robust, but also realistic. Central bankers appear to be very concerned with establishing reputations as being tough on inflation and as being credible. If the public were certain of policymakers' preferences and beliefs, there would be no reason for this. Only if the public is uncertain and if expectations matter is this concern appropriate.

Delegation

A second way to overcome the dynamic inconsistency of low-inflation monetary policy is to delegate policy to individuals who do not share the public's

---

[15]For a general value of $\beta > 1/2$, one can show that the maximum effect occurs at $p = (2\beta - 1)/2\beta$, and equals $[(2\beta - 1)/2\beta]b/a$. For $\beta < 1/2$, there is no effect.

view about the relative importance of output and inflation. The idea, due to Rogoff (1985), is simple: inflation—and hence expected inflation—is lower when monetary policy is controlled by someone who is known to be espe- cially averse to inflation.

To see how delegation can address the dynamic-inconsistency prob- lem, suppose that the output-inflation relationship and social welfare are given by (9.8) and (9.9); thus $y = \bar{y} + b(\pi - \pi^e)$ and $L = [(y - y^*)^2/2] + [a(\pi - \pi^*)^2/2]$. Suppose, however, that monetary policy is determined by an individual whose objective function is

$$L' = \frac{1}{2}(y - y^*)^2 + \frac{1}{2}a'(\pi - \pi^*)^2, \qquad y^* > \bar{y}, \quad a' > 0. \qquad (9.23)$$

a' may differ from a, the weight that society as a whole places on inflation. Solving the policymaker's maximization problem along the lines of (9.10) implies that his or her choice of π, given π^e, is given by (9.12) with a' in place of a. Thus,

$$\pi = \pi^* + \frac{b}{a' + b^2}(y^* - \bar{y}) + \frac{b^2}{a' + b^2}(\pi^e - \pi^*). \qquad (9.24)$$

Figure 9.5 shows the effects of delegating policy to an individual with a value of a' greater than a. Because the policymaker puts more weight on inflation

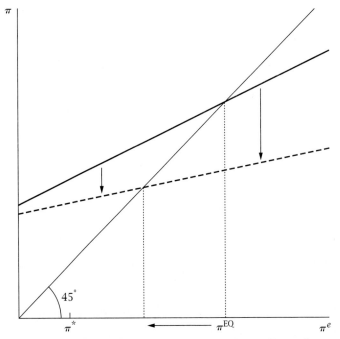

FIGURE 9.5   The effect of delegation to a conservative policymaker on equilib- rium inflation

than before, he or she chooses a lower value of inflation for a given level of expected inflation (at least over the range where $\pi^e \geq \pi^*$); in addition, his or her response function is flatter.

As before, the public knows how inflation is determined. Thus equilibrium again requires that expected and actual inflation are equal. As a result, when we solve for expected inflation we find that it is given by (9.13) with a' in place of a:

$$\pi^{EQ} = \pi^* + \frac{b}{a'}(y^* - \overline{y}). \tag{9.25}$$

The equilibrium is for both actual and expected inflation to be given by (9.25), and for output to equal its natural rate.

Now consider social welfare, which is higher the lower is $(y - y^*)^2/2 + a(\pi - \pi^*)^2/2$. Output is equal to $\overline{y}$ regardless of a'. But the higher a' is, the closer π is to π^*. Thus the higher a' is, the higher social welfare is. Intuitively, when monetary policy is controlled by someone who cares strongly about inflation, the public realizes that the policymaker has little desire to pursue expansionary policy; the result is that expected inflation is low.

Rogoff extends this analysis to the case where the economy is affected by shocks. Under plausible assumptions, a policymaker whose preferences between output and inflation differ from society's does not respond optimally to shocks. Thus in choosing whom to delegate monetary policy to, there is a tradeoff: choosing someone with a stronger dislike of inflation produces a better performance in terms of average inflation, but a worse one in terms of responses to disturbances. As a result, there is some optimal level of "conservatism" for central bankers.[16]

Again, the idea that societies can address the dynamic-inconsistency problem by letting individuals who particularly dislike inflation control monetary policy appears realistic. In many countries, monetary policy is determined by independent central banks rather than by the central government. And the central government often seeks out individuals who are known to be particularly averse to inflation to run those banks. The result is that those who control monetary policy are often known for being more concerned about inflation than society as a whole, and only rarely for being less concerned.

Empirical Application: Central-Bank Independence and Inflation

Theories that attribute inflation to the dynamic inconsistency of low-inflation monetary policy are difficult to test. The theories suggest that inflation is related to such variables as the costs of inflation, policymakers' ability to commit, their ability to establish reputations, and the extent to

---

[16]This idea is developed in Problem 9.12.

which policy is delegated to individuals who particularly dislike inflation. All of these are hard to measure.

One variable that has received considerable attention is the independence of the central bank. Alesina (1988) argues that central-bank independence provides a measure of the delegation of policymaking to conservative policymakers. Intuitively, the greater the independence of the central bank, the greater the government's ability to delegate policy to individuals who especially dislike inflation. Empirically, central-bank independence is generally measured by qualitative indexes based on such factors as how its governor and board are appointed and dismissed, whether there are government representatives on the board, and the government's ability to veto or directly control the bank's decisions.

Investigations of the relation between these measures of independence and inflation produce a consistent result: independence and inflation are strongly negatively related (Alesina, 1988; Grilli, Masciandaro, and Tabellini, 1991; Cukierman, Webb, and Neyapti, 1992). Figure 9.6 is representative of the results. Thus it appears that delegation is an important determinant of inflation.

There are two limitations to this finding, however. First, the fact that there is a negative relation between central-bank independence and inflation does not mean that the independence is the source of the low inflation. As Posen (1993) observes, countries whose citizens are particularly averse to inflation are likely to try to insulate their central banks from political pressure. For example, it is widely believed that Germans especially dislike inflation, perhaps because of the hyperinflation that Germany experienced after World War I. And the institutions governing Germany's central bank appear to have been created largely because of this desire to avoid inflation. Thus some of Germany's low inflation is almost surely the result of the general aversion to inflation, rather than of the independence of its central bank.

Second, it is not clear that theories of dynamic inconsistency and delegation predict that greater central-bank independence will produce lower inflation. The argument that they do predict this implicitly assumes that both central bankers' and government policymakers' preferences do not vary systematically with central-bank independence. But the delegation hypothesis implies that they will. Suppose, for example, that monetary policy depends on the central bank's and the government's preferences, with the weight on the bank's preferences increasing in its independence. Then when the bank is less independent, government officials should compensate by appointing more inflation-averse individuals to the bank. Similarly, when the government is less able to delegate policy to the bank, voters should elect more inflation-averse governments. These effects will mitigate, and might even offset, the effects of reduced central-bank independence.[17] In short,

---

[17]In addition, the usual measures of central-bank independence appear to be biased in favor of finding a link between independence and low inflation. For example, the measures often put some weight on whether the bank's charter gives low inflation as its principal goal (Pollard, 1993).

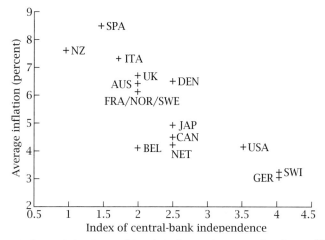

FIGURE 9.6   Central-bank independence and inflation[18]

although the relationship between central-bank independence and inflation is striking, its ultimate implications remain to be determined.

Limitations of Dynamic-Inconsistency Theories of Inflation

Theories based on dynamic inconsistency provide a simple and appealing explanation of inflation. Unfortunately, it is not clear that their explanation is important to actual inflation, particularly for the industrialized countries. There are two problems. First, the importance of forward-looking expectations to aggregate supply, which is central to the dynamic-inconsistency explanation, is not well established. For example, Canada and New Zealand have recently taken strong measures to commit themselves to low-inflation monetary policies. New Zealand, for instance, has modified the central bank's charter to make price stability the sole objective of policy and to provide for the dismissal of the bank's governor if inflation falls outside a target range. Yet, contrary to the predictions of dynamic-inconsistency models, these measures do not appear to have had a major impact on the output-inflation relationship in these countries (Debelle, 1994).

Second, there is a great deal of variation in inflation that the dynamic-inconsistency models have difficulty accounting for. In the United States, for example, policymakers were able to reduce inflation from about 10% at the end of the 1970s to under 5% just a few years later, and to maintain the lower inflation, without any significant change in the institutions or

---

[18] Figure 9.6, from "Central Bank Independence and Macroeconomic Performance" by Alberto Alesina and Lawrence H. Summers, *Journal of Money, Credit, and Banking,* Vol. 25, No. 2 (May 1993), is reprinted by permission. Copyright 1993 by the Ohio State University Press. All rights reserved.

rules governing monetary policy. Similarly, Japan has had consistently low inflation despite the fact that its central bank is not particularly independent. Indeed, if one is not willing to interpret the correlation between central-bank independence and inflation as reflecting the effects of dynamic inconsistency and delegation, it is hard to identify any important part of either the time-series or cross-section variations in inflation in the industrialized countries that is due to dynamic-inconsistency considerations.[19]

These weaknesses of dynamic-inconsistency theories suggest that we should consider other ways that inflation could come about. In addition, there are a variety of important issues concerning how monetary policy should be conducted that do not involve dynamic inconsistency. The next section discusses some of those issues and considers several ways that inflation could arise from other sources.

9.6   Some Macroeconomic Policy Issues

The discussion in the previous two sections makes it appear that monetary policymakers face a single problem: they must find a way of getting inflation to its optimal level. Actual policymaking is much more complicated. There are two issues. First, it is not clear what the optimal rate of inflation is; this issue is addressed in Section 9.8. Second, various kinds of disturbances are continually affecting the economy. This section addresses some of the issues that are raised by the presence of these shocks.

What Can Policy Accomplish? A Baseline Case

How much weight should policymakers put on stabilizing output as opposed to other objectives, such as keeping inflation low and predictable? To address this issue, it is useful to begin with a simple case. Suppose that aggregate supply relates the change in inflation linearly to the departure of the unemployment rate from the natural rate, and that it has no forward-looking element (see equations [5.36]–[5.37]):

$$\pi_t = \pi_{t-1} - \alpha(u_t - \overline{u}) + \varepsilon_t^S, \qquad \alpha > 0, \tag{9.26}$$

---

[19]D. Romer (1993b) argues that dynamic-inconsistency models predict that more open economies will have lower inflation, and that the evidence from outside the industrialized world strongly supports this prediction. He does not find any relation between openness and inflation among industrialized countries, however. Similarly, Cukierman, Edwards, and Tabellini (1992) find that inflation is higher in countries that are less politically stable, and they observe that this may reflect the diminished importance of reputation when policymakers' horizons are shorter. The variation in instability among industrialized countries is small, however, and thus this variable also fails to account for much of the differences in inflation among these countries.

where ε_t^S represents supply shocks. In addition, suppose that social welfare depends on unemployment and inflation, and that the dependence on unemployment is linear:

$$W_t = -cu_t - f(\pi_t), \qquad c > 0, \quad f''(\bullet) > 0. \tag{9.27}$$

This simple model has strong implications for policy. First, the aggregate supply curve, (9.26), implies that policy has no control over average unemployment unless policymakers are willing to accept ever-increasing (or ever-decreasing) inflation. Equation (9.26) implies that the average change in inflation is determined by average unemployment and average supply shocks. Thus altering average unemployment alters the average change in inflation. But if the average change in inflation is anything other than zero, the level of inflation grows (or falls) without bound.[20]

This result, coupled with the assumption that social welfare is linear in unemployment, implies that policy should put essentially no weight on unemployment. Suppose that policymakers' discount rate is zero, and consider the first-order condition for π_t.[21] Raising π_t by a small amount $d\pi$ changes current-period social welfare by both its direct effect, $-f'(\pi_t)d\pi$, and its effect via unemployment, $c\alpha d\pi$. In addition, the increase in current inflation means (for given next-period inflation) higher unemployment next period; this contributes $-c\alpha d\pi$ to social welfare. Thus the first-order condition for π_t is simply $f'(\pi_t) = 0$: policymakers should keep inflation at its optimal level and pay no attention to unemployment. This is true regardless of the importance of unemployment (that is, regardless of c), and regardless of what supply shocks are buffeting the economy. Intuitively, any change in the path of inflation that does not permanently raise inflation can only rearrange the timing of unemployment, which has no effect on welfare. And with a discount rate of zero, any policy that permanently raises inflation above the optimal level has infinite costs regardless of how small inflation's costs are.

With discounting, one can show that the first-order condition for π_t is

$$\frac{1+\rho}{\rho}f'(\pi_t) = c\alpha, \tag{9.28}$$

where ρ is policymakers' discount rate.[22] Thus inflation should be set at the level where the cost of a permanent increase in inflation just balances the benefit of the associated one-time decrease in unemployment. Even with discounting, there is little scope for sophisticated stabilization policy:

---

[20]In addition, as described in Chapter 5, if policymakers allow inflation to grow without bound, the aggregate supply curve (9.26) will almost surely break down. This is not relevant to the point made here, however.

[21]We are assuming for the moment that policymakers can control inflation perfectly, subject to (9.26).

[22]That is, policymakers maximize $\sum_{t=0}^{\infty}(1+\rho)^{-t}W_t$.

because the first-order condition does not depend on π_{t-1} or ε_t^S, the optimal policy is to go directly to the inflation rate that satisfies (9.28) regardless of the current state of the economy. Indeed, if policymakers respond to high inflation by creating an extended recession that brings inflation down to the level satisfying (9.28) only slowly, the total amount of unemployment will be no different than it would have been if they had reduced inflation all at once. Thus they will have subjected the economy to an extended period of above-normal inflation for no benefit.

This baseline case implies that policymakers should not attempt to stabilize unemployment in the face of supply shocks. It also implies that the benefits of using policy to offset aggregate demand shocks come only from reducing the variability of inflation. The linearity of aggregate supply implies that if policymakers allow demand shocks to cause fluctuations in unemployment and inflation, average unemployment is unaffected; and the linearity of social welfare implies that fluctuations in unemployment do not affect welfare. Thus the only costs of the fluctuations come from the costs of the variation in inflation. If inflation variability has low costs over the relevant range, policymakers should attach little importance to offsetting demand shocks.

Is There a Case for Stabilization Policy?

The key assumptions behind these results are the linearity of the social welfare function, (9.27), and of the aggregate supply curve, (9.26). Thus for there to be a substantial benefit to stabilization policy, one of these functions must be significantly nonlinear.[23]

Consider first social welfare. Lucas (1987) shows that in a representative-agent setting, the potential welfare gain from stabilizing consumption around its mean is small; that is, he suggests that social welfare is not sufficiently nonlinear in output for there to be a significant gain from stabilization. His argument is straightforward. Suppose that utility takes the constant-relative-risk-aversion form:

$$U(C) = \frac{C^{1-\theta}}{1 - \theta}, \qquad \theta > 0, \tag{9.29}$$

where θ is the coefficient of relative risk aversion (see Section 2.1). Since $U''(C) = -\theta C^{-\theta-1}$, a second-order Taylor expansion of $U(\cdot)$ around the mean of consumption implies

$$E[U(C)] \simeq \frac{\overline{C}^{1-\theta}}{1 - \theta} - \frac{\theta}{2}\overline{C}^{-\theta-1}\sigma_C^2, \tag{9.30}$$

---

[23]For demand shocks, this assumes that the costs of moderate inflation variability is low.

where $\overline{C}$ and σ_C^2 are the mean and variance of consumption. Thus eliminating consumption variability would raise expected utility by approximately $(\theta/2)\overline{C}^{-\theta-1}\sigma_C^2$. Similarly, doubling consumption variability would lower welfare by approximately that amount.

To translate this into units that can be interpreted, note that the marginal utility of consumption at $\overline{C}$ is $\overline{C}^{-\theta}$. Thus setting σ_C^2 to zero would raise expected utility by approximately as much as would raising average consumption by $(\theta/2)\overline{C}^{-\theta-1}\sigma_C^2/\overline{C}^{-\theta} = (\theta/2)\overline{C}^{-1}\sigma_C^2$. As a fraction of average consumption, this equals $(\theta/2)\overline{C}^{-1}\sigma_C^2/\overline{C}$, or $(\theta/2)(\sigma_C/\overline{C})^2$.

Lucas argues that a generous estimate of the standard deviation of consumption due to short-run fluctuations is 1.5% of its mean, and that a generous estimate of the coefficient of relative risk aversion is 5. Thus, he concludes, an optimistic figure for the maximum possible welfare gain from more successful stabilization policy is equivalent to $(5/2)(0.015)^2$, or 0.06%, of average consumption—a very small amount.

At first glance, it appears that Lucas's conclusion rests critically on his assumption that there is a representative agent. Actual recessions do not reduce everyone's consumption by a small amount, but reduce the consumption of a small fraction of the population by a large amount; thus their welfare costs are larger than they would be in a representative-agent setting. Atkeson and Phelan (1994) show, however, that accounting for the dispersion of consumption decreases rather than increases the potential gain from stabilization. Indeed, their analysis suggests a basis for the linear social welfare function, (9.27), where there is no gain at all from stabilizing unemployment. Suppose that individuals have one level of consumption, C_E, when they are employed, and another level, C_U, when they are unemployed, and suppose that C_E and C_U do not depend on the state of the economy. Since u is the fraction of individuals who are unemployed, average utility from consumption is $uU(C_U) + (1 - u)U(C_E)$. Thus expected social welfare from consumption is $E[u]U(C_U) + (1 - E[u])U(C_E)$: social welfare is independent of the variance of unemployment. Intuitively, in this case stabilizing unemployment has no effect on the variance of individuals' consumption; individuals have consumption C_E fraction $1 - E[u]$ of the time, and C_U fraction $E[u]$ of the time.

Consumption variability is not the only cost of fluctuations, however. The variability of hours of work may have much larger costs than the variability of consumption. The cyclical variability of hours is much larger than that of consumption; and if labor supply is relatively inelastic, utility may be much more sharply curved in hours than in consumption. Ball and D. Romer (1990) find that as a result, it is possible (though by no means clear-cut) that the cost of fluctuations through hours variability is substantial. Intuitively, the utility benefit of the additional leisure during periods of below-normal output may not nearly offset the utility cost of the reduced consumption, whereas the disutility from the additional hours during booms may nearly offset the benefit of the higher consumption.[24] Thus if there is a substantial direct welfare gain from reducing the variance of output, it is likely to be through the impact on hours rather than on consumption.

It is also possible that stabilization policy has important indirect benefits. One natural mechanism is through investment: investment may be higher when the economy is more stable. As a result, stabilization policy could raise income substantially over the long run (see, for example, Meltzer, 1988). As Section 8.6 describes, however, the effect of uncertainty on investment is complicated and not necessarily negative. Thus whether stabilization policy has important benefits through this channel is not known.

There has been little work on nonlinearities in the aggregate supply curve. Many textbook formulations assume that the increase in inflation triggered by a fall in unemployment below the natural rate is larger than the decrease in inflation caused by a comparable rise in unemployment above the natural rate. If this is correct, reducing the variance of unemployment reduces the average increase in inflation, and thus makes a lower average unemployment rate feasible.

In fact, however, most researchers working on aggregate supply have found that a linear specification provides an adequate description of the data (see, for example, Gordon, 1990, and Ball and Mankiw, 1995). There is certainly no strong evidence of any large nonlinearity over the relevant range.[25]

If social welfare or aggregate supply is nonlinear in output, the optimal response to an unfavorable supply shock that raises inflation is to reduce inflation gradually rather than all at once. Thus a supply shock could give rise to an extended period of inflation. At the same time, however, such nonlinearities would also imply that the optimal response to a positive supply shock is to bring inflation back up to its initial level only gradually. Thus although nonlinearities may provide grounds for stabilization policy, they do not provide a simple explanation of high average inflation.

Targets, Indicators, and Instruments

Policy actions affect the economy with a lag. In addition, policymakers have imperfect information about the current condition of the economy, about the path it would follow if policy did not change, and about the effects

---

[24] Just as with the argument for the cost from consumption variability, Ball and Romer's argument concerning the cost from hours variability requires that not all of the variation in aggregate hours take the form of movements between employment and unemployment.

[25] See De Long and Summers (1989) for one attempt to argue for important nonlinearity of the form that makes stabilization policy beneficial. Ball (1994b), on the other hand, finds evidence of nonlinearity of the opposite form, which implies that stabilization policy could actually increase average unemployment.

a change in policy would have. This naturally raises the issue of how these lags and uncertainties should affect policy.

The traditional analysis of policymaking under uncertainty distinguishes among objectives, instruments, intermediate targets, and indicators of policy.[26] The objectives are the ultimate goals of policy, such as inflation and unemployment. The instruments are the variables that policymakers can control directly, such as open-market operations, reserve requirements, tax rates, and government purchases.

Indicators and intermediate targets fall between the instruments and the objectives. Indicators are variables that provide information about the current or future behavior of the objectives. Some examples are orders for new goods, prices of raw materials, and measures of money and lending. As policymakers obtain new information about the likely behavior of the objectives by observing the indicators, they may adjust the settings of the instruments. Intermediate targets, in contrast, are variables that policymakers choose to focus on in place of the ultimate objectives. The most famous candidate target is the money stock. Many economists have argued that it is better to instruct policymakers to try to keep the growth rate of a measure of the money stock (such as $M1$ or $M2$) as close as possible to some steady, low rate (such as 3% per year) rather than to try to maximize some broader objective function (see, for example, Friedman, 1960).

To see how instruments, indicators, targets, and objectives are used in practice, consider the following stylized description of U.S. monetary policy in recent years. The main ultimate objectives of policy are the behavior of unemployment (or real output) and inflation. Policymakers appear to want inflation to be around 2% or 3% per year and to avoid large swings in unemployment.[27] Thus, for example, when inflation is above the 2–3% range, policymakers have sought to reduce it gradually. Other objectives, such as keeping exchange rates and interest rates moderately stable, also appear to get some weight in policymakers' objective function.

Over the short term (say, day-to-day and week-to-week), the key intermediate target of policy is the Federal funds rate. The Federal Reserve conducts its daily open-market operations to try to keep the funds rate close to its current target level.[28] Although on a day-to-day basis there are noticeable departures of the funds rate from the target, on a weekly or longer-term basis the Federal Reserve usually hits the target quite accurately.

Over the slightly longer term (say, month-to-month), the Federal Reserve does not focus on any single intermediate target. Instead, it adjusts the target level of the funds rate in response to many variables that can provide information about the future paths of real activity and inflation.

---

[26]This analysis was pioneered by Tinbergen (1952).

[27]As the discussion earlier in this section suggests, it is not clear that this is what policymakers should in fact be trying to achieve.

[28]Meulendyke (1990) describes the specifics of the Federal Reserve's operating procedures.

Finally, over the medium term (say, quarter-to-quarter), there usually is clearer information about how real output and unemployment are likely to behave than about inflation. Thus over this horizon, real output and unemployment are not only among the main objectives of policy, but are also the main indicators or intermediate targets. When inflation is above the desired range, for example, policymakers typically aim to keep unemployment moderately above the natural rate; when inflation is in the desired range, they usually try to maintain unemployment roughly at the natural rate.[29] In either situation, policymakers adjust the target as they obtain more information about the behavior of inflation.

The Traditional Argument for Rules

A natural question about indicators and intermediate targets is why policymakers would ever adopt an intermediate target. It seems that policymakers should take all relevant information into account in their efforts to achieve their ultimate goals. A particular indicator, such as a measure of the money stock, may turn out to be particularly informative; but even then, it appears that there is a cost and no benefit to targeting that variable.

One possible answer involves the dynamic-inconsistency issue, discussed in Sections 9.4 and 9.5: adopting a binding rule about the behavior of an intermediate target can overcome the dynamic-inconsistency problem, and can therefore lead to lower average inflation. But support for money-stock rules and other intermediate targets long predates concern about dynamic inconsistency. Moreover, many proposed ways of adopting intermediate targets do not involve binding commitments, and thus would not overcome the problem.

The basis for the traditional argument for instructing policymakers to target some intermediate variable is twofold. Consider for concreteness a money-stock target. The first, and less important, part of the argument for targeting the money stock is that the relation between the money stock and the ultimate objectives of policy is strong enough, and the uncertainty about the effects of departures of the money stock from a path of steady growth large enough, that the potential for improvement over a money-stock rule is small. And since the rule would not be completely binding, in the event of a calamitous breakdown it could be abandoned.

The second, and more important, part of the argument is that instructing policymakers to try to achieve the ultimate goals of policy to the best of their ability may lead to systematic errors in policy. Those potential errors have several sources.

---

[29]For the United States today, estimates of the natural rate range from under 6% to almost 7%. Obviously where in this range the true figure lies has important implications for policy.

First, policymakers are subject to political pressures. Policymakers outside the Federal Reserve, and the public, may place too much weight on the short-run cost of lower unemployment relative to the long-run cost of higher inflation. This could arise from a higher discount rate than is appropriate, or from a failure to understand how the economy operates. Some evidence for this view is provided by the fact that during periods (such as 1979–1982) when the Federal Reserve has pursued policies that involved very high interest rates, it has not explicitly acknowledged that it was doing so. Instead, policymakers have characterized policy as focusing on some intermediate target (such as *nonborrowed reserves* in 1979–1982) and as not being directly concerned with interest rates.

Second, monetary policymakers may have objectives other than maximizing social welfare, and providing them with only vague instructions about how to conduct policy may increase their ability to pursue those objectives. For example, they may wish to improve the President's chances of being reelected, or to increase seignorage revenues.[30]

Finally, policymakers may genuinely try to maximize social welfare but may nonetheless make systematic errors. Individuals are often overconfident in their judgments (of the state of the economy, or of the likely effects of policy, for example). In addition, they may be reluctant to admit that, given the lags and uncertainties in the effects of policies, the best reaction to a problem may be to do little or nothing. As a result, policy may systematically overreact, easing too much in recessions and thereby causing the subsequent expansions to be too strong, and tightening too much in expansions and thereby causing recessions (see, for example, Friedman, 1960). Similarly, given the suffering associated with unemployment, policymakers may have a tendency to read the evidence about the natural rate optimistically. This can generate an inflationary bias in policy. And, as with the tendency to overreact, it can generate fluctuations. Policymakers may first, out of concern about unemployment and in hopes that the natural rate is low, push unemployment below the natural rate; then, when signs of rising inflation become clear, they may tighten and cause a recession.[31]

This discussion suggests several potential sources of inflation other than dynamic inconsistency: political pressures on policymakers, policymakers' pursuit of objectives other than social welfare, and overoptimism about the

---

[30]The possibility of the Federal Reserve pursuing objectives other than social welfare (either because of its own preferences or because of political pressures) suggests that fluctuations can arise from political forces rather than exogenous disturbances. For examples of theories of such *political business cycles,* see Nordhaus (1975); Alesina and Sachs (1988); Rogoff and Sibert (1988); and Harrington (1993).

[31]Karamouzis and Lombra (1989) present one piece of evidence of a tendency for overoptimism among policymakers: during the 1970s, the Federal Open Market Committee tended to adopt combinations of interest-rate and money-growth targets that were systematically off the frontier (in the direction of lower money growth and lower interest rates) of possibilities presented by the staff as being feasible.

level of unemployment that is sustainable.[32] None of these theories, however, have yet been formulated rigorously or tested empirically.

9.7   Seignorage and Inflation

The existence of an output-inflation tradeoff cannot plausibly lead to hyperinflations, or even to very high rates of inflation that fall short of hyperinflation. By the time inflation reaches triple digits, the costs of inflation are
almost surely large, and the real effects of monetary changes are almost
surely small. No reasonable policymaker would choose to subject an economy to such large costs out of a desire to obtain such modest output gains.

The underlying cause of most, if not all, episodes of high inflation and
hyperinflation is government's need to obtain seignorage—that is, revenue
from printing money (Bresciani-Turroni, 1937; Cagan, 1956). Wars, falls in
export prices, tax evasion, and political stalemate frequently leave governments with large budget deficits. And often investors do not have enough
confidence that the government will honor its debts to be willing to buy its
bonds. Thus the government's only choice is to resort to seignorage.[33]

This section therefore investigates the interactions among seignorage
needs, money growth, and inflation. We begin by considering a situation
where seignorage needs are sustainable, and see how this can lead to high
inflation. We then consider what happens when the seignorage needs are
unsustainable, and see how that can lead to hyperinflation.

The Inflation Rate and Seignorage

As in Section 9.2, assume that real money demand depends negatively on
the nominal interest rate and positively on real income (see equation [9.1]):

$$\frac{M}{P} = L(i, Y)$$

$$= L(r + \pi^e, Y), \qquad L_i < 0, \quad L_Y > 0.$$

(9.31)

Since we are interested in the government's revenue from money creation,

---

[32]Inflation can also arise if policymakers do not know the correct model of the economy.
Suppose that policymakers believe that the costs of moderate inflation are small and that
there is (or that there may be) a permanent output-inflation tradeoff. Then they are likely to
pursue expansionary policies, and to be slow to disinflate when inflation sets in. This may
be a good description of what happened in the United States in the 1960s and 1970s (see,
for example, Freedman, 1993).

[33]An important question is how the political process leads to situations that require
such large amounts of seignorage. The puzzle is that given the apparent high costs of the
resulting inflation, there appear to be alternatives that all parties prefer. See Alesina and
Drazen (1991) for one attempt to answer this question.

M should be interpreted as high-powered money (that is, currency and reserves issued by the government). Thus $L(\cdot)$ is the demand for high-powered money.

For the moment we focus on steady states. It is therefore reasonable to assume that output and the real interest rate are unaffected by the rate of money growth, and that actual inflation and expected inflation are equal. If we neglect output growth for simplicity, then in steady state the quantity of real balances is constant. This implies that inflation equals the rate of money growth. Thus we can rewrite (9.31) as

$$\frac{M}{P} = L(\bar{r} + g_M, \overline{Y}), \tag{9.32}$$

where $\bar{r}$ and $\overline{Y}$ are the real interest rate and output and where g_M is the rate of money growth, $\dot{M}/M$.

The quantity of real purchases per unit time that the government finances from money creation equals the increase in the nominal money stock per unit time divided by the price level:

$$S = \frac{\dot{M}}{P}$$

$$= \frac{\dot{M}}{M}\frac{M}{P} \tag{9.33}$$

$$= g_M \frac{M}{P}.$$

Equation (9.33) shows that in steady state, real seignorage equals the growth rate of the money stock times the quantity of real balances. The growth rate of money is equal to the rate at which nominal money holdings lose real value, π. Thus, loosely speaking, seignorage equals the "tax rate" on real balances, π, times the amount being taxed, M/P. For this reason, seignorage revenues are often referred to as *inflation-tax* revenues.[34]

Substituting (9.32) into (9.33) yields

$$S = g_M L(\bar{r} + g_M, \overline{Y}). \tag{9.34}$$

Equation (9.34) shows that an increase in g_M increases seignorage by raising the rate at which real money holdings are taxed, but decreases it by reducing the tax base. Formally,

---

[34]Phelps (1973) shows that it is more natural to think of the tax rate on money balances as the nominal interest rate, since the nominal rate is the difference between the cost to agents of holding money (which is the nominal rate itself) and the cost to the government of producing it (which is essentially zero). In our framework, where the real rate is fixed and the nominal rate therefore moves one-for-one with inflation, this distinction is not important.

$$\frac{dS}{dg_M} = L(\bar{r} + g_M, \bar{Y}) + g_M L_1(\bar{r} + g_M, \bar{Y}), \tag{9.35}$$

where $L_1(\bullet)$ denotes the derivative of $L(\bullet)$ with respect to its first argument.

The first term of (9.35) is positive and the second is negative. The second term approaches zero as g_M approaches zero (unless $L_1(\bar{r} + g_M, \bar{Y})$ approaches minus infinity as g_M approaches zero). Since $L(\bar{r}, \bar{Y})$ is strictly positive, it follows that dS/dg_M is positive for sufficiently low values of g_M. That is, at low tax rates, seignorage is increasing in the tax rate. It is plausible, however, that as g_M becomes large, the second term eventually dominates; that is, it is reasonable to suppose that when the tax rate becomes extreme, further increases in the rate reduce revenue. The resulting "inflation-tax Laffer curve" is shown in Figure 9.7.

As a concrete example of the relation between inflation and steady-state seignorage, consider the money-demand function proposed by Cagan (1956). Cagan suggests that a good description of money demand, particularly under high inflation, is given by

$$\ln \frac{M}{P} = a - bi + \ln Y, \qquad b > 0. \tag{9.36}$$

Converting (9.36) from logs to levels and substituting the resulting expression into (9.34) yields

$$S = g_M e^a \bar{Y} e^{-b(\bar{r}+g_M)}$$
$$= C g_M e^{-bg_M}, \tag{9.37}$$

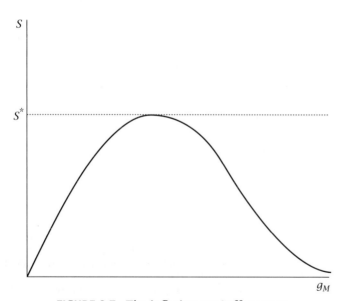

FIGURE 9.7 The inflation-tax Laffer curve

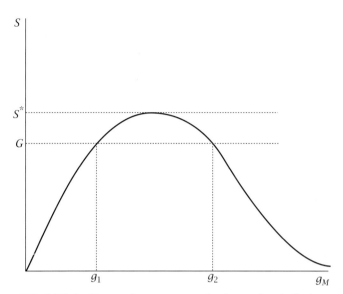

FIGURE 9.8   How seignorage needs determine inflation

where $C \equiv e^{a}\overline{Y}e^{-b\overline{r}}$. The impact of a change in money growth on seignorage is therefore given by

$$\frac{dS}{dg_{M}} = Ce^{-bg_{M}} - bCg_{M}e^{-bg_{M}}$$

$$= (1 - bg_{M})Ce^{-bg_{M}}.$$

(9.38)

This expression is positive for $g_{M} < 1/b$ and negative thereafter.

Cagan's estimates suggest that b is between $\frac{1}{3}$ and $\frac{1}{2}$. This implies that the peak of the inflation-tax Laffer curve occurs when g_{M} is between 2 and 3. This corresponds to a continuously compounded rate of money growth of 200% to 300% per year, which implies an increase in the money stock by a factor of between $e^{2} \simeq 7.4$ and $e^{3} \simeq 20$ per year. Cagan, Sachs and Larrain (1993), and others suggest that for most countries, seignorage at the peak of the Laffer curve is about 10% of GDP.

Now consider a government that has some amount of real purchases, G, that it needs to finance with seignorage. Assume that G is less than the maximum feasible amount of seignorage, denoted S^{*}. Then, as Figure 9.8 shows, there are two rates of money growth that can finance the purchases.[35] With one, inflation is low and real balances high; with the

---

[35]Figure 9.8 implicitly assumes that the seignorage needs are independent of the inflation rate. This assumption omits an important effect of inflation: because taxes are usually specified in nominal terms and collected with a lag, an increase in inflation typically reduces real tax revenues. As a result, seignorage needs are likely to be greater at higher inflation rates. This *Tanzi* (or *Olivera-Tanzi*) effect does not require any basic change in our analysis;

other, inflation is high and real balances low. The high-inflation equilibrium has peculiar comparative-statics properties; for example, a decrease in the government's seignorage needs raises inflation. Since we do not appear to observe such situations in practice, we focus on the low-inflation equilibrium. Thus the rate of money growth—and hence the rate of inflation—is given by g_1.

This analysis provides an explanation of high inflation: it stems from governments' need for seignorage. Suppose, for example, that $b = \frac{1}{3}$ and that seignorage at the peak of the Laffer curve, S^*, is 10% of GDP. Since seignorage is maximized when $g_M = 1/b$, (9.37) implies that S^* is Ce^{-1}/b. Thus for S^* to equal 10% of GDP when b is $\frac{1}{3}$, C must be about 9% of GDP. Straightforward calculations then show that raising 2% of GDP from seignorage requires $g_M \simeq 0.24$, raising 5% requires $g_M \simeq 0.70$, and raising 8% requires $g_M \simeq 1.42$. Thus moderate seignorage needs give rise to substantial inflation, and large seignorage needs produce high inflation.

Seignorage and Hyperinflation

This analysis seems to imply that even governments' need for seignorage cannot account for hyperinflations: if seignorage revenue is maximized at inflation rates of several hundred percent, why do governments ever let inflation go higher? The answer is that the preceding analysis holds only in steady state. If the public does not immediately adjust its money holdings or its expectations of inflation to changes in the economic environment, then in the short run seignorage is always increasing in money growth, and the government can obtain more seignorage than the maximum sustainable amount, S^*. Thus hyperinflations arise when the government's seignorage needs exceed S^* (Cagan, 1956).

Gradual adjustment of money holdings and gradual adjustment of expected inflation have similar implications for the dynamics of inflation. We focus on the case of gradual adjustment of money holdings. Specifically, assume that individuals' desired money holdings are given by the Cagan money-demand function, (9.36). In addition, continue to assume that the real interest rate and output are fixed at $\overline{r}$ and $\overline{Y}$: although both variables are likely to change somewhat over time, the effects of those variations are likely to be small relative to the effects of changes in inflation.

Thus desired real money holdings are

$$m^*(t) = Ce^{-b\pi(t)}. \tag{9.39}$$

The key assumption of the model is that actual money holdings adjust gradually toward desired holdings. Specifically, our assumption is

$$\ln{}^{\cdot}m(t) = \beta[\ln m^*(t) - \ln m(t)], \tag{9.40}$$

---

we only have to replace the horizontal line at G with an upward-sloping line. But the effect can be quantitatively significant, and is therefore important to understanding high inflation in practice.

or

$$\frac{\dot{m}(t)}{m(t)} = \beta[\ln m^*(t) - \ln m(t)]$$

(9.41)

$$= \beta[\ln C - b\pi(t) - \ln m(t)],$$

where the second line uses (9.39) to substitute for $\ln m^*(t)$. The idea behind this assumption of gradual adjustment is that it is difficult for individuals to adjust their money holdings; for example, they may have made arrangements to make certain types of purchases using money. As a result, they adjust their money holdings toward the desired level only gradually. The specific functional form is chosen for convenience. Finally, β is assumed to be positive but less than $1/b$—that is, adjustment is assumed not to be too rapid.[36]

As before, seignorage equals $\dot{M}/P$, or $(\dot{M}/M)(M/P)$; thus

$$S(t) = g_M(t)m(t).$$

(9.42)

Suppose that this economy is initially in steady state with G less than S^*, and that G then increases to a value greater than S^*. If adjustment is instantaneous, there is no equilibrium with positive money holdings. Since S^* is the maximum amount of seignorage the government can obtain when individuals have adjusted their real money holdings to their desired level, the government cannot obtain more than this with instantaneous adjustment. As a result, the only possibility is for money to immediately become worthless and for the government to be unable to obtain the seignorage it needs.

With gradual adjustment, on the other hand, the government can obtain the needed seignorage through increasing money growth and inflation. With rising inflation, real money holdings are falling. But because the adjustment is not immediate, the real money stock exceeds $Ce^{-b\pi}$; as a result (as long as the adjustment is not too rapid), the government is able to obtain more than S^*. But with the real money stock falling, the required rate of money growth is rising. The result is explosive inflation.

To see the dynamics of the economy formally, it is easiest to focus on the dynamics of the real money stock, m. Equation (9.41) gives $\dot{m}/m$ in terms of π and m. Thus to characterize the behavior of m, we need to eliminate π from this equation.

To do this, note that the growth rate of real money, $\dot{m}/m$, equals the growth rate of nominal money, g_M, minus the rate of inflation, π. Rewriting

---

[36]The assumption that the change in real money holdings depends only on the current values of m^* and m implies that individuals are not forward-looking. A more appealing assumption, along the lines of the q model of investment in Chapter 8, is that individuals consider the entire future path of inflation in deciding how to adjust their money holdings. This assumption complicates the analysis greatly without changing the implications for most of the issues we are interested in (but see n. 39, below).

this as an equation for inflation gives us

$$\pi(t) = g_M(t) - \frac{\dot{m}(t)}{m(t)}$$

$$= \frac{G}{m(t)} - \frac{\dot{m}(t)}{m(t)},$$

(9.43)

where the second line uses the fact that $m(t)g_M(t) = G$ (see [9.42]). Substituting this expression into (9.41) yields

$$\frac{\dot{m}(t)}{m(t)} = \beta \left\{ \ln C - b \left[\frac{G}{m(t)} - \frac{\dot{m}(t)}{m(t)} \right] - \ln m(t) \right\}.$$

(9.44)

We can now solve this expression for $\dot{m}(t)/m(t)$; this yields

$$\frac{\dot{m}(t)}{m(t)} = \frac{\beta}{1 - b\beta} \left[\ln C - b\frac{G}{m(t)} - \ln m(t) \right].$$

$$= \frac{\beta}{1 - b\beta} \frac{b}{m(t)} \left[\frac{\ln C - \ln m(t)}{b} m(t) - G \right].$$

(9.45)

Our assumption that G is greater than S^* implies that the expression in brackets is negative for all values of m. To see this, note first that the rate of inflation needed to make desired money holdings equal m is the solution to $Ce^{-b\pi} = m$; taking logs and rearranging the resulting expression shows

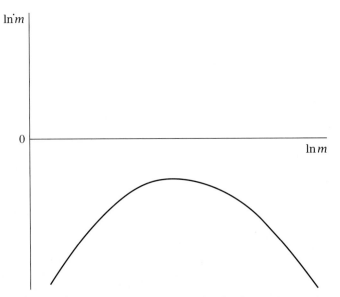

FIGURE 9.9   The dynamics of the real money stock when seignorage needs are unsustainable

that this inflation rate is $(\ln C - \ln m)/b$. Next, recall that if real money holdings are steady, seignorage is πm; thus the sustainable level of seignorage associated with real money balances of m is $[(\ln C - \ln m)/b]m$. Finally, recall that S^* is defined as the maximum sustainable level of seignorage. Thus the assumption that S^* is less than G implies that $[(\ln C - \ln m)/b]m$ is less than G for all values of m. But this means that the expression in brackets in (9.45) is negative.

Thus, since $b\beta$ is less than 1, the right-hand side of (9.45) is everywhere negative: regardless of where it starts, the real money stock continually falls. The associated phase diagram is shown in Figure 9.9.[37] With the real money stock continually falling, money growth must be continually rising for the government to obtain the seignorage it needs (see [9.42]). In short, the government can obtain seignorage greater than S^*, but only at the cost of explosive inflation.

This analysis can also be used to understand the dynamics of the real money stock and inflation under gradual adjustment of money holdings when G is less than S^*. Consider the situation depicted in Figure 9.8. Sustainable seignorage, πm^*, equals G if inflation is either g_1 or g_2; it is greater than G if inflation is between g_1 and g_2; and it is less than G otherwise. The resulting dynamics of the real money stock implied by (9.45) for this case are shown in Figure 9.10. The steady state with the higher real money stock (and thus with the lower inflation rate) is stable, and the steady state with the lower money stock is unstable.[38]

This analysis of the relation between seignorage and inflation explains many of the main characteristics of high inflations and hyperinflations. Most basically, the analysis explains the puzzling fact that inflation often reaches

---

[37]By differentiating (9.45) twice, it is straightforward to show that $d^2 \ln \dot{m}/(d \ln m)^2 < 0$, and thus that the phase diagram has the shape shown.

[38]Recall that this analysis depends on the assumption that $\beta < 1/b$. If this assumption fails, the denominator of (9.45) is negative. The stability and dynamics of the model are peculiar in this case. If $G < S^*$, the high-inflation equilibrium is stable and the low-inflation equilibrium is unstable; if $G > S^*$, $\dot{m} < 0$ everywhere, and thus there is explosive deflation. And with G in either range, an increase in G leads to a downward jump in inflation (to see this, note that [9.45] implies that the increase leads to an upward jump in $\dot{m}/m$; from [9.41], this means that π must jump down).

One interpretation of these results is that it is only because parameter values happen to fall in a particular range that we do not observe such unusual outcomes in practice. A more appealing interpretation, however, is that these results suggest that the model omits important features of actual economies. For example, if there is gradual adjustment of both real money holdings and expected inflation, then the stability and dynamics of the model are reasonable regardless of the adjustment speeds. More importantly, Ball (1993) and Cardoso (1991) argue that the assumption that Y is fixed at $\overline{Y}$ omits crucial features of the dynamics of high inflations (though not necessarily of hyperinflations). Ball and Cardoso develop models that combine seignorage-driven monetary policy with the standard Keynesian assumption that aggregate demand policies can reduce inflation only by temporarily depressing real output. They show that with this assumption, only the low-inflation steady state is stable. They then use their models to analyze a variety of aspects of high-inflation economies.

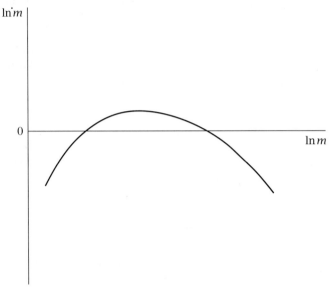

FIGURE 9.10   The dynamics of the real money stock when seignorage needs are sustainable

extremely high levels. The analysis also explains why inflation can reach some level—empirically, in the triple-digit range—without becoming explosive, but that beyond this level it degenerates into hyperinflation. In addition, the model explains the central role of fiscal problems in causing high inflations and hyperinflations, and of fiscal reforms in ending them (Sargent, 1982; Dornbusch and Fischer, 1986).

Finally, the central role of seignorage in hyperinflations explains how the hyperinflations can end before money growth stabilizes. As described in Section 9.2, the increased demand for real money balances after hyperinflations end is satisfied by continued rapid growth of the nominal money stock rather than by declines in the price level. But this leaves the question of why the public expects low inflation when there is still rapid money growth. The answer is that the hyperinflations end when fiscal and monetary reforms eliminate either the deficit or the government's ability to use seignorage to finance it, or both. At the end of the German hyperinflation of 1922–23, for example, Germany's World War I reparations were reduced, and the existing central bank was replaced by a new institution with much greater independence. Because of reforms like these, the public knows that the burst of money growth is only temporary (Sargent, 1982).[39]

---

[39]To incorporate the effects of the knowledge that the money growth is temporary into our formal analysis, we would have to let the change in real money holdings at a given time depend not just on current holdings and current inflation, but on current holdings and the entire expected path of inflation. See n. 36.

9.8   The Costs of Inflation

All of the analysis so far in this chapter assumes that inflation is costly, and that policymakers know what those costs are and how they vary with inflation. In fact, however, inflation's costs are not well understood.[40] There is a wide gap between the popular view of inflation and the costs of inflation that economists can identify. Inflation is intensely disliked. In periods when inflation is moderately high in the United States, for example, it is often cited in opinion polls as the most important problem facing the country. It appears to have an important effect on the outcome of Presidential elections, and it is blamed for a wide array of problems. Yet economists have difficulty in identifying substantial costs of inflation.

Easily Identifiable Costs of Inflation

In many models, steady inflation just adds an equal amount to the growth rate of all prices and wages and to the nominal interest rate on all assets; it therefore has no effects on relative prices, real wages, or real interest rates. It is this fact that makes it hard to identify large costs of inflation.

The only exception to the statement that steady inflation has no real effects in simple models is that, since high-powered money's nominal return is fixed at zero, inflation necessarily reduces its real return. This gives rise to the most easily identified cost of inflation. The increased gap between the rates of return on money and on other assets causes people to exert effort to reduce their holdings of high-powered money; for example, they make smaller and more frequent conversions of other assets into currency. Since high-powered money is essentially costless for the government to produce, these efforts have no social benefit. Thus they represent a cost of inflation.

These socially unproductive efforts to conserve on money holdings can be eliminated if inflation is chosen so that the nominal interest rate—and hence the opportunity cost of holding money—is zero. Since real interest rates are typically modestly positive, this requires slight deflation.[41]

It seems unlikely, however, that this is all there is to the costs of inflation. Most obviously, the *shoe-leather* costs associated with a positive nominal interest rate are surely small for almost all inflation rates observed in practice. Even if the price level is doubling each month, money is losing value only at a rate of a few percent per day; thus even in this case individuals will not incur extreme costs to reduce their money holdings.

---

[40]The uncertainty about inflation's costs and benefits raises the possibility that the seemingly high average inflation rates in most industrialized countries in recent decades are in fact optimal. If this is correct, there is not in fact any inflationary bias in monetary policy. We will not pursue this possibility.

[41]See, for example, Tolley (1957) and Friedman (1969).

A second readily identifiable cost of inflation is that nominal prices and wages must be changed more often, or indexing schemes must be adopted. Under natural assumptions about the distribution of relative-price shocks, the frequency of price adjustment is minimized with zero inflation. As Chapter 6 describes, however, the costs of price adjustment and indexation are almost certainly small.

The last cost of inflation that can be easily identified is that it distorts the tax system (see, for example, Feldstein, 1983). In most countries, income from capital gains and interest, and deductions for interest expenses and depreciation, are computed in nominal terms. As a result, inflation can have large effects on incentives for investment and saving. In the United States, the net effect of inflation through these various channels is to raise the effective tax rate on capital income substantially. In addition, inflation can significantly alter the relative attractiveness of different kinds of investment. For example, since the services from owner-occupied housing are generally not taxed and the income generated by ordinary business capital is, even without inflation the tax system encourages investment in owner-occupied housing relative to business capital. The fact that nominal interest payments are deductible from income causes inflation to exacerbate this distortion.

In contrast to the shoe-leather and menu costs of inflation, the costs of inflation through tax distortions may be large. Thus it is important for policymakers to account for these effects. At the same time, these distortions are probably not the source of the public's intense dislike of inflation. These costs are quite specific and could be overcome through indexation. Yet the dislike of inflation seems much broader.

Thus it appears that we must look further to understand the popular view of inflation. There are several ways that inflation may have large costs that are more subtle than the costs just described. Some of the potential costs occur when inflation is anticipated and steady; others arise only if inflation is more variable and less predictable when it is higher.

Other Costs of Steady Inflation

There are at least three ways that steady, anticipated inflation may have large costs. First, because individual prices are not adjusted continuously, even steady inflation causes variations in relative prices as different firms adjust their prices at different times. As a result, inflation increases the departures of relative prices from the values they would have under frictionless price adjustment. Okun (1975) and Carlton (1982) argue informally that this inflation-induced relative-price variability disrupts markets where firms and customers form long-term relationships and prices are not adjusted frequently. For example, it can make it harder for potential customers to decide whether to enter a long-term relationship, or for the parties to a long-term relationship to check the fairness of the price they are trading at by comparing it with other prices. Formal models suggest that inflation can have complicated effects on market structure, long-term relationships, and efficiency (for example, Benabou, 1988, 1992; Benabou and Gertner, 1993; Diamond, 1993; Tommasi, 1994; and Ball and D. Romer, 1993). This literature has not reached any consensus about the effects of inflation, but it does suggest some ways that inflation may have substantial costs. This literature also suggests that the immense disruptions associated with hyperinflations may just represent extreme versions of the effects of more moderate rates of inflation.

Second, individuals and firms may have trouble accounting for inflation (Modigliani and Cohn, 1979; Hall, 1984). Ten percent annual inflation causes the price level to rise by a factor of 45 in 40 years; even 3% inflation causes it to triple over that period. As a result, inflation can cause households and firms, which typically do their financial planning in nominal terms, to make large errors in saving for their retirement, in assessing the real burdens of mortgages, or in making long-term investments.

Finally, steady inflation may be costly not because of any real effects, but simply because people dislike it. People relate to their economic environment in terms of dollar values. They may therefore find large changes in dollar prices and wages disturbing even if they have no consequences for their real incomes. In Okun's (1975) analogy, a switch to a policy of reducing the length of the mile by a fixed amount each year might have few effects on real decisions, but might nonetheless cause considerable unhappiness. Since the ultimate goal of policy is presumably the public's well-being, such effects of inflation would represent genuine costs.

Costs of Variable Inflation

Empirically, inflation is more variable and less predictable when it is higher (see, for example, Okun, 1971; Taylor, 1981; and Ball and Cecchetti, 1990). Okun, Ball and Cecchetti, and others argue that the association arises through the effect of inflation on policy. When inflation is low, there is a consensus that it should be kept low, and so inflation is steady and predictable. When inflation is moderate or high, however, there is disagreement about the importance of reducing it; indeed, the costs of slightly more inflation may appear small. As a result, inflation is variable and difficult to predict.

If this argument is correct, the relationship between the mean and the variance of inflation represents a true effect of the mean on the variance. This implies some potentially important additional costs of inflation. First, since many assets are denominated in nominal terms, unanticipated changes in inflation redistribute wealth. Thus greater inflation variability increases uncertainty and lowers welfare. Second, with debts denominated in nominal terms, increased uncertainty about inflation may make firms and individuals reluctant to undertake investment projects, especially long-term ones.[42] And finally, highly variable inflation (or even higher average inflation alone) can also discourage long-term investment because firms and individuals view it as a symptom of a government that is functioning badly, and that may therefore resort to confiscatory taxation or other polices that are highly detrimental to capital-holders.

Empirically, there is a strong negative association between inflation and investment, and between inflation and growth (Fischer, 1991, 1993; Rudebusch and Wilcox, 1994). At this point, however, there is little evidence concerning whether these relationships are causal. It is not difficult to think of reasons that the associations might not represent true effects of inflation. In the short run, negative supply shocks are associated with both higher inflation and lower productivity growth. In the long run, governments that follow policies detrimental to growth—protectionism, large budget deficits, and so on—are likely to also pursue policies that result in inflation (Sala-i-Martin, 1991b).[43]

For high inflation rates, one can argue that the issue of whether the association between inflation and growth represents an effect of inflation on growth is of limited relevance. For a country to reduce inflation from very high levels, it is likely to need to adopt a broad range of budgetary and policy reforms. Thus growth is likely to rise, even though it may be the other reforms and not the reductions in inflation that bring it about.[44] In contrast, inflation can be reduced from moderate to low levels without fundamental policy reforms. Thus for moderate and low inflation, the issue of causation is crucial.

Potential Benefits of Inflation

So far we have considered only costs of inflation. But inflation can have benefits as well. Tobin (1972) observes that if it is particularly difficult for firms to cut nominal wages, real wages can make needed adjustments to sector-specific shocks more rapidly when inflation is higher. Summers (1991) notes that since nominal interest rates cannot be negative, low inflation (by causing usual nominal rates to be low) may limit the Federal Reserve's ability to stimulate aggregate demand in response to contractionary shocks. And just as inflation above some level can disrupt long-term planning and increase uncertainty, so too can inflation below some level. Given that average inflation has been significantly positive over the last several decades, it is not

---

[42]If these costs of inflation variability are large, however, there may be large incentives for individuals and firms to write contracts in real rather than nominal terms, or to create markets that allow them to insure against inflation risk. Thus a complete account of large costs of inflation through these channels must explain the absence of these institutions.

[43]Moreover, the estimates of Fischer and of Rudebusch and Wilcox suggest that at moderate inflation rates, a 1-percentage-point reduction in inflation is associated with roughly a 0.2-percentage-point increase in growth. This association is so large that it is difficult to identify plausible ways that it can represent an effect of inflation on growth.

[44]This argument is due to Allan Meltzer.

clear that zero inflation minimizes uncertainty and is least disruptive. Finally, as described above, inflation is a potential source of revenue for the government; under some conditions it is optimal for the government to use this revenue source in addition to more conventional taxes.

In addition, it is possible that the public's aversion to inflation represents not some deep understanding of the costs of inflation that has eluded economists, but a misapprehension. For example, Katona (1976) argues that the public perceives how inflation affects prices but not wages. Thus when inflation rises, individuals attribute only the faster growth of prices to the increase; they therefore incorrectly conclude that it has reduced their standard of living. Alternatively, individuals may dislike inflation just because times of high inflation are also times of low real growth; but if the high inflation is not in fact the source of the low growth, again inflation does not actually make them worse off.

Concluding Comments

As this discussion shows, research has not yet yielded any firm conclusions about the costs of inflation and the optimal rate of inflation. Thus economists and policymakers must rely on their judgment in weighing the different considerations. Loosely speaking, they fall into two groups. One group views inflation as pernicious, and believes that policy should focus on eliminating inflation and pay virtually no attention to other considerations. Members of this group generally believe that policy should aim for zero inflation or moderate deflation. The other group concludes that extremely low inflation is of little benefit, or perhaps even harmful, and believes that policy should aim to keep average inflation low to moderate but should keep other objectives in mind. The opinions of members of this group about the level of inflation that policy should aim for generally range from a few percent to close to 10 percent.

Problems

9.1. Consider a discrete-time version of the analysis of money growth, inflation, and real balances in Section 9.2. Suppose that money demand is given by $m_t - p_t = c - b(E_t p_{t+1} - p_t)$, where m and p are the logs of the money stock and the price level, and where we are implicitly assuming that output and the real interest rate are constant (see [9.36]).

(a) Solve for p_t in terms of m_t and $E_t p_{t+1}$.

(b) Use the law of iterated projections to express $E_t p_{t+1}$ in terms of $E_t m_{t+1}$ and $E_t p_{t+2}$.

(c) Iterate this process forward to express p_t in terms of m_t, $E_t m_{t+1}$, $E_t m_{t+2}$, ... (Assume that $\lim_{i \to \infty} E_t[\{b/(1 + b)\}^i p_{t+i}] = 0$. This is a no-bubbles condition analogous to the one in Problem 7.7.)

(d) Explain intuitively why an increase in $E_t m_{t+i}$ for any $i > 0$ raises p_t.

(e) Suppose expected money growth is constant, so $E_t m_{t+i} = m_t + gi$. Solve for p_t in terms of m_t and g. How does an increase in g affect p_t?

9.2. Consider a discrete-time model where prices are completely unresponsive to unanticipated monetary shocks for one period and completely flexible thereafter. Suppose the *IS* and *LM* curves are $y = c - ar$ and $m - p = b + hy - ki$, where y, m, and p are the logs of output, the money supply, and the price level; r is the real interest rate; i is the nominal interest rate; and a, h, and k are positive parameters.

Assume that initially m is constant at some level, which we normalize to zero, and that y is constant at its flexible-price level, which we also normalize to zero. Now suppose that in some period—period 1 for simplicity—the monetary authority shifts unexpectedly to a policy of increasing m by some amount $g > 0$ each period.

(a) What are r, π^e, i, and p before the change in policy?

(b) Once prices have fully adjusted, $\pi^e = g$. Use this fact to find r, i, and p in period 2.

(c) In period 1, what are i, r, p, and the expectation of inflation from period 1 to period 2, $E_1[p_2] - p_1$?

(d) What determines whether the short-run effect of the monetary expansion is to raise or lower the nominal interest rate?

9.3. Assume, as in Problem 9.2, that prices are completely unresponsive to unanticipated monetary shocks for one period and completely flexible thereafter. Assume also that $y = c - ar$ and $m - p = b + hy - ki$ hold each period. Suppose, however, that the money supply follows a random walk: $m_t = m_{t-1} + u_t$, where u_t is a mean-zero, serially uncorrelated disturbance.

(a) Let E_t denote expectations as of period t. Explain why, for any t, $E_t[E_{t+1}[p_{t+2}] - p_{t+1}] = 0$, and thus why $E_t m_{t+1} - E_t p_{t+1} = b + h\bar{y} - k\bar{r}$.

(b) Use the result in part (a) to solve for y_t, p_t, i_t, and r_t in terms of m_{t-1} and u_t.

(c) Does the Fisher effect hold in this economy? That is, are changes in expected inflation reflected one-for-one in the nominal interest rate?

9.4. Suppose you want to test the hypothesis that the real interest rate is constant, so that all changes in the nominal interest rate reflect changes in expected inflation. Thus your hypothesis is $i_t = r + E_t \pi_{t+1}$.

(a) Consider a regression of i_t on a constant and π_{t+1}. Does the hypothesis that the real interest rate is constant make a general prediction about the coefficient on π_{t+1}? Explain. (Hint: for a univariate OLS regression, the coefficient on the right-hand-side variable equals the covariance between the right-hand-side and left-hand-side variables divided by the variance of the right-hand-side variable.)

(b) Consider a regression of π_{t+1} on a constant and i_t. Does the hypothesis that the real interest rate is constant make a general prediction about the coefficient on i_t? Explain.

(c) Some argue that the hypothesis that the real interest rate is constant implies that nominal interest rates move one-for-one with actual inflation in the long run—that is, that the hypothesis implies that in a regression of i on a constant and the current and many lagged values of π, the sum of the coefficients on the inflation variables will be 1. Is this claim correct? (Hint: Suppose that the behavior of actual inflation is given by $\pi_t = \rho\pi_{t-1} + e_t$, where e is white noise.)

9.5. Policy rules, rational expectations, and regime changes. (See Lucas, 1976, and Sargent, 1983.) Suppose that aggregate supply is given by the Lucas supply curve, $y_t = \bar{y} + b(\pi_t - \pi_t^e)$, $b > 0$, and suppose that monetary policy is determined by $m_t = m_{t-1} + a + \varepsilon_t$, where ε is a white-noise disturbance. Assume that private agents do not know the current values of m_t or ε_t; thus π_t^e is the expectation of $p_t - p_{t-1}$ given $m_{t-1}, \varepsilon_{t-1}, y_{t-1}$, and p_{t-1}. Finally, assume that aggregate demand is given by $y_t = m_t - p_t$.

(a) Find y_t in terms of m_{t-1}, m_t, and any other variables or parameters that are relevant.

(b) Are m_{t-1} and m_t all one needs to know about monetary policy to find y_t? Explain intuitively.

(c) Suppose that monetary policy is initially determined as above, with $a > 0$, and that the monetary authority then announces that it is switching to a new regime where a is zero. Suppose that private agents believe that the probability that the announcement is true is ρ. What is y_t in terms of m_{t-1}, m_t, ρ, $\bar{y}$, b, and the initial value of a?

(d) Using these results, describe how an examination of the money-output relationship might be used to measure the credibility of announcements of regime changes.

9.6. Regime changes and the term structure of interest rates. (See Blanchard, 1984; Mankiw and Miron, 1986; and Mankiw, Miron, and Weil, 1987.) Consider an economy where money is neutral. Specifically, assume that $\pi_t = \Delta m_t$ and that r is constant at zero. Suppose that the money supply is given by $\Delta m_t = k\Delta m_{t-1} + \varepsilon_t$, where ε is a white-noise disturbance.

(a) Assume that the rational-expectations theory of the term structure of interest rates holds (see [9.6]). Specifically, assume that the two-period interest rate is given by $i_t^2 = (i_t^1 + E_t i_{t+1}^1)/2$. i_t^1 denotes the nominal interest rate from t to $t + 1$; thus, by the Fisher identity, it equals $r_t + E_t[p_{t+1}] - p_t$.

(i) What is i_t^1 as a function of Δm_t and k? (Assume that Δm_t is known at time t.)

(ii) What is $E_t i_{t+1}^1$ as a function of Δm_t and k?

(iii) What is the relation between i_t^2 and i_t^1; that is, what is i_t^2 as a function of i_t^1 and k?

(iv) How would a change in k affect the relation between i_t^2 and i_t^1? Explain intuitively.

(b) Suppose that the two-period rate includes a time-varying term premium: $i_t^2 = (i_t^1 + E_t i_{t+1}^1)/2 + \theta_t$, where θ is a white-noise disturbance that is independent of ε. Consider the OLS regression $i_{t+1}^1 - i_t^1 = a + b(i_t^2 - i_t^1) + e_{t+1}$.

(*i*) Under the rational-expectations theory of the term structure (with $\theta_t = 0$ for all t), what value would one expect for b? (Hint: for a univariate OLS regression, the coefficient on the right-hand-side variable equals the covariance between the right-hand-side and left-hand-side variables divided by the variance of the right-hand-side variable.)

(*ii*) Now suppose that θ has variance σ_θ^2. What value would one expect for b?

(*iii*) How do changes in k affect your answer to part (*ii*)? What happens to b as k approaches 1?

9.7. (Fischer and Summers, 1989.) Suppose inflation is determined as in Section 9.4. Suppose the government is able to reduce the costs of inflation; that is, suppose it reduces the parameter a in equation (9.9). Is society made better or worse off by this change? Explain intuitively.

9.8. Solving the dynamic-inconsistency problem through punishment. (Barro and Gordon, 1983b.) Consider a policymaker whose objection function is $\sum_{t=0}^{\infty} \beta^t (y_t - a\pi_t^2/2)$, where $a > 0$ and $0 < \beta < 1$. y_t is determined by the Lucas supply curve, (9.8), each period. Expected inflation is determined as follows. If π has equaled $\hat{\pi}$ (where $\hat{\pi}$ is a parameter) in all previous periods, then $\pi^e = \hat{\pi}$. If π ever differs from $\hat{\pi}$, then $\pi^e = b/a$ in all subsequent periods.

(*a*) What is the equilibrium of the model in all subsequent periods if π ever differs from $\hat{\pi}$?

(*b*) Suppose π has always been equal to $\hat{\pi}$, so $\pi^e = \hat{\pi}$. If the monetary authority chooses to depart from $\pi = \hat{\pi}$, what value of π does it choose? What level of its lifetime objective function does it attain under this strategy? If the monetary authority continues to choose $\pi = \hat{\pi}$ every period, what level of its lifetime objective function does it attain?

(*c*) For what values of $\hat{\pi}$ does the monetary authority choose $\pi = \hat{\pi}$? Are there values of a, b, and β such that if $\hat{\pi} = 0$, the monetary authority chooses $\pi = 0$?

9.9. Other equilibria in the Barro–Gordon model. Consider the situation described in Problem 9.8. Find the parameter values (if any) for which each of the following is an equilibrium:

(*a*) **One-period punishment.** π_t^e equals $\hat{\pi}$ if $\pi_{t-1} = \pi_{t-1}^e$ and equals b/a otherwise; $\pi = \hat{\pi}$ each period.

(*b*) **Severe punishment.** (Abreu, 1988, and Rogoff, 1987.) π_t^e equals $\hat{\pi}$ if $\pi_{t-1} = \pi_{t-1}^e$, equals $\pi_0 > b/a$ if $\pi_{t-1}^e = \hat{\pi}$ and $\pi_{t-1} \neq \hat{\pi}$, and equals b/a otherwise; $\pi = \hat{\pi}$ each period.

(*c*) **Repeated discretionary equilibrium.** $\pi = \pi^e = b/a$ each period.

9.10. Consider the situation analyzed in Problem 9.8, but assume that there is only some finite number of periods rather than an infinite number. What is the unique equilibrium? (Hint: reason backward from the last period.)

9.11. More on solving the dynamic-inconsistency problem through reputation. (This is based on Cukierman and Meltzer, 1986.) Consider a policymaker who is in office for two periods and whose objective function is $E[\sum_{t=1}^{2} b(\pi_t - \pi_t^e) +$

$c\pi_t - a\pi_t^2/2]$. The policymaker is chosen randomly from a pool of possible policymakers with differing tastes. Specifically, c is distributed normally over possible policymakers with mean $\bar{c}$ and variance $\sigma_c^2 > 0$. a and b are the same for all possible policymakers.

The policymaker cannot control inflation perfectly. Instead, $\pi_t = \hat{\pi}_t + \varepsilon_t$, where $\hat{\pi}_t$ is chosen by the policymaker (taking π_t^e as given) and where ε_t is normal with mean zero and variance $\sigma_\varepsilon^2 > 0$. ε_1, ε_2, and c are independent. The public does not observe $\hat{\pi}_t$ and ε_t separately, but only π_t. Similarly, the public does not observe c.

Finally, assume that π_2^e is a linear function of π_1: $\pi_2^e = \alpha + \beta\pi_1$.

(a) What is the policymaker's choice of $\hat{\pi}_2$? What is the resulting expected value of the policymaker's second-period objective function, $b(\pi_2 - \pi_2^e) + c\pi_2 - a\pi_2^2/2$, as a function of π_2^e?

(b) What is the policymaker's choice of $\hat{\pi}_1$ taking α and β as given and accounting for the impact of π_1 on π_2^e?

(c) Assuming rational expectations, what is β? (Hint: use the signal-extraction procedure described in Section 6.3).

(d) Explain intuitively why the policymaker chooses a lower value of $\hat{\pi}$ in the first period than in the second.

9.12. The tradeoff between low average inflation and flexibility in response to shocks with delegation of control over monetary policy. (Rogoff, 1985.) Suppose that output is given by $y = \bar{y} + b(\pi - \pi^e)$, and that the social welfare function is $\gamma y - a\pi^2/2$, where γ is a random variable with mean $\bar{\gamma}$ and variance σ_γ^2. π^e is determined before γ is observed; the policymaker, however, chooses π after γ is known. Suppose policy is made by someone whose objective function is $c\gamma y - a\pi^2/2$.

(a) What is the policymaker's choice of π given π^e, γ, and c?

(b) What is π^e?

(c) What is the expected value of the true social welfare function, $\gamma y - a\pi^2/2$?

(d) What value of c maximizes expected social welfare? Interpret your result.

9.13. (a) In the model of reputation analyzed in Section 9.5, is social welfare higher when the policymaker turns out to be a Type 1, or when he or she turns out to be a Type 2?

(b) In the model of delegation analyzed in Section 9.5, suppose that the policymaker's preferences are believed to be described by (9.23), with $a' > a$, when π^e is determined. Is social welfare higher if these are actually the policymaker's preferences, or if the policymaker's preferences in fact match the social welfare function, (9.9)?

9.14. Money versus interest-rate targeting. (Poole, 1970.) Suppose the economy is described by linear IS and LM curves that are subject to disturbances: $y = c - ai + \varepsilon_{IS}$, $m - p = hy - ki + \varepsilon_{LM}$, where ε_{IS} and ε_{LM} are independent, mean-zero shocks with variances σ_{IS}^2 and σ_{LM}^2, and where a, h, and k are positive. Policymakers want to stabilize output, but they cannot observe y or the shocks, ε_{IS} and ε_{LM}. Assume for simplicity that p is fixed.

(a) Suppose the policymaker fixes i at some level $\bar{\imath}$. What is the variance of y?

(b) Suppose the policymaker fixes m at some level $\bar{m}$. What is the variance of y?

(c) If there are only LM shocks (so $\sigma_{IS}^2 = 0$), does money targeting or interest-rate targeting lead to a lower variance of y?

(d) If there are only IS shocks (so $\sigma_{LM}^2 = 0$), does money or interest-rate targeting lead to a lower variance of y?

(e) Explain your results in parts (c) and (d) intuitively.

(f) When there are only IS shocks, is there a policy that produces a variance of y that is lower than either money or interest-rate targeting? If so, what policy minimizes the variance of y? If not, why not? (Hint: consider the LM curve, $m - p = hy - ki$.)

9.15. Uncertainty and policy. (Brainard, 1967.) Suppose output is given by $y = x + (k + \varepsilon_k)z + u$, where z is some policy instrument controlled by the government and k is the expected value of the multiplier for that instrument. ε_k and u are independent, mean-zero disturbances that are unknown when the policymaker chooses z, and that have variances σ_k^2 and σ_u^2. Finally, x is a disturbance that is known when z is chosen. The policymaker wants to minimize $E[(y - y^*)^2]$.

(a) Find $E[(y - y^*)^2]$ as a function of x, k,y^*, σ_k^2, and σ_u^2.

(b) Find the first-order condition for z, and solve for z.

(c) How, if at all, does σ_u^2 affect how policy should respond to shocks (that is, to the realized value of x)? Thus, how does uncertainty about the state of the economy affect the case for "fine tuning"?

(d) How, if at all, does σ_k^2 affect how policy should respond to shocks (that is, to the realized value of x)? Thus, how does uncertainty about the effects of policy affect the case for "fine tuning"?

9.16. Growth and seignorage, and an alternative explanation of the inflation-growth relationship. (Friedman, 1971.) Suppose that money demand is given by $\ln(M/P) = a - bi + \ln Y$, and that Y is growing at rate g_Y. What rate of inflation leads to the highest path of seignorage?

9.17. (Cagan, 1956.) Suppose that instead of adjusting their real money holdings gradually toward the desired level, individuals adjust their expectation of inflation gradually toward actual inflation. Thus equations (9.39) and (9.40) are replaced by $m(t) = Ce^{-b\pi^e(t)}$ and $\dot{\pi}^e(t) = \beta[\pi(t) - \pi^e(t)]$, $0 < \beta < 1/b$.

(a) Follow steps analogous to the derivation of (9.45) to find an expression for $\dot{\pi}^e(t)$ as a function of $\pi(t)$.

(b) Sketch the resulting phase diagram for the case of $G > S^*$. What are the dynamics of π^e and m?

(c) Sketch the phase diagram for the case of $G < S^*$.

Chapter **10**
UNEMPLOYMENT

10.1 Introduction: Theories of Unemployment

In almost any economy at almost any time, many individuals appear to be unemployed. That is, there are many people who are not working but who say they want to work in jobs like those held by individuals similar to them, at the wages those individuals are earning.

The possibility of unemployment is a central subject of macroeconomics. There are two basic issues. The first concerns the determinants of average unemployment over extended periods. The central questions here are whether this unemployment represents a genuine failure of markets to clear, and if so, what its causes and consequences are. There is a wide range of possible views. At one extreme is the position that unemployment is largely illusory, or the working out of unimportant frictions in the process of matching up workers and jobs. At the other extreme is the view that unemployment is the result of non-Walrasian features of the economy and that it largely represents a waste of resources.

The second issue concerns the cyclical behavior of the labor market. As described in Chapter 5, the real wage does not appear to be highly procyclical. This is consistent with the view that the labor market is Walrasian only if labor supply is highly elastic or if shifts in labor supply play an important role in employment fluctuations. But as we saw in Section 4.10, there is little support for the hypothesis of highly elastic labor supply. And it seems unlikely that shifts in labor supply are central to fluctuations. The remaining possibility is that the labor market is not Walrasian, and that its non-Walrasian features are central to its cyclical behavior. That possibility is the focus of this chapter.

The issue of why shifts in labor demand appear to lead to large movements in employment and only small movements in the real wage is important to all theories of fluctuations. For example, we saw in Chapter 6 that if the real wage is highly procyclical in response to demand shocks, it is essentially impossible for the small barriers to nominal adjustment to generate substantial nominal rigidity. In the face of a decline in aggregate demand, for example, if prices remain fixed the real wage must fall sharply; as a result, each firm has a huge incentive to cut its price and hire labor to produce additional output. If, however, there is some non-Walrasian feature of the labor market that causes the cost of labor to respond little to the overall level of economic activity, then there is some hope for theories of small frictions in nominal adjustment.

This chapter considers various ways in which the labor market may depart from a competitive, textbook market. We investigate both whether these departures can lead to substantial unemployment and whether they can have important effects on the cyclical behavior of employment and the real wage.

If there is unemployment in a Walrasian labor market, unemployed workers immediately bid the wage down until supply and demand are in balance. Theories of unemployment can therefore be classified according to their view of why this mechanism may fail to operate. Concretely, consider an unemployed worker who offers to work for a firm for slightly less than the firm is currently paying, and who is otherwise identical to the firm's current workers. There are at least four possible responses the firm can make to this offer.

First, the firm can say that it does not want to reduce wages. Theories in which there is a cost as well as a benefit to the firm of paying lower wages are known as *efficiency-wage* theories. (The name comes from the idea that higher wages may raise the productivity, or efficiency, of labor.) These theories are the subject of Sections 10.2 through 10.4. Section 10.2 first discusses the possible ways that paying lower wages can harm a firm; it then analyzes a simple model where wages affect productivity but where the reason for that link is not explicitly specified. Section 10.3 considers an important generalization of that model. Finally, Section 10.4 presents a model formalizing one particular view of why paying higher wages can be beneficial. The central idea is that if firms cannot monitor their workers' effort perfectly, they may pay more than market-clearing wages to induce workers not to shirk.

The second possible response the firm can make is that it wishes to cut wages, but that an explicit or implicit agreement with its workers prevents it from doing so.[1] Theories in which bargaining and contracts affect the macroeconomics of the labor market are known as *contracting models*.

Contracting models are the subject of Sections 10.5 through 10.7. Section 10.5 presents some basic models of contracting. Sections 10.6 and 10.7 then investigate what happens when some workers are represented in the bargaining process and others are not. Section 10.6 explores the implications of this distinction between *insiders* and *outsiders* for the cyclical behavior of labor costs and for average unemployment. Section 10.7 investigates its effects on the behavior of unemployment over time.

---

[1]The firm can also be prevented from cutting wages by minimum-wage laws. In most settings, this is relevant only to low-skill workers; thus it does not appear to be central to the macroeconomics of unemployment.

The third way the firm can respond to the unemployed worker's offer is to say that it does not accept the premise that the unemployed worker is identical to the firm's current employees. That is, heterogeneity among workers and jobs may be an essential feature of the labor market. In this view, to think of the market for labor as a single market, or even as a large number of interconnected markets, is to commit a fundamental error. Instead, according to this view, each worker and each job should be thought of as distinct; as a result, the process of matching up workers and jobs occurs not through markets but through a complex process of search. Models of this type are known as *search models*, or *search and matching models*, or the *flow approach* to labor markets. They are discussed in Section 10.8.

Finally, the firm can accept the worker's offer. That is, it is possible that the market for labor is approximately Walrasian. In this view, measured unemployment consists largely of people who are moving between jobs, or who would like to work at wages higher than those they can in fact obtain. Since the focus of this chapter is on unemployment, we will not develop this idea here. Nonetheless, it is important to keep in mind that this is one view of the labor market.

10.2   A Generic Efficiency-Wage Model

Potential Reasons for Efficiency Wages

The central assumption of efficiency-wage models is that there is a benefit as well as a cost to a firm of paying a higher wage. There are many reasons that this could be the case. Here we describe four of the most important (see Yellen, 1984, and Katz, 1986, for surveys and references).

First, and most simply, a higher wage can increase workers' food consumption, and thereby cause them to be better nourished and more productive. Obviously this possibility is not important in developed economies. Nonetheless, it provides a concrete example of an advantage of paying a higher wage. For that reason, it is often a useful reference point.

Second, a higher wage can increase workers' effort in situations where the firm cannot monitor them perfectly. In a Walrasian labor market, workers are indifferent about losing their jobs, since identical jobs are immediately available. Thus if the only way that firms can punish workers who exert low effort is by firing them, workers in such a labor market have no incentive to exert effort. But if a firm pays more than the market-clearing wage, its jobs are valuable. Thus its workers may choose to exert effort even if there is some chance they will not be caught if they do not. This idea is developed in Section 10.4.

Third, paying a higher wage can improve workers' ability along dimensions the firm cannot observe. Specifically, if higher-ability workers have higher reservation wages, offering a higher wage raises the average quality of the applicant pool, and thus raises the average ability of the workers the firm hires.[2]

Finally, a high wage can build loyalty among workers, and hence induce high effort; conversely, a low wage can cause anger and desire for revenge, and thereby lead to shirking or sabotage. Akerlof and Yellen (1990) present extensive evidence that workers' effort is affected by such forces as anger, jealousy, and gratitude. For example, they describe studies showing that workers who believe they are underpaid sometimes perform their work in ways that are harder for them in order to reduce their employers' profits.[3]

Other Compensation Schemes

This discussion implicitly assumes that a firm's financial arrangements with its workers take the form of some wage per unit of time. An important question is whether there are more complicated ways for the firm to compensate its workers that allow it to obtain the benefits of a higher wage less expensively. The nutritional advantages of a higher wage, for example, can be obtained by compensating workers partly in kind (such as by feeding them at work). To give another example, firms can give workers an incentive to exert effort by requiring them to post a bond that they lose if they are caught shirking.

If there are cheaper ways for firms to obtain the benefits of a higher wage, then these benefits lead not to a higher wage but just to complicated compensation policies. Whether the benefits can be obtained in such ways depends on the specific reason that a higher wage is advantageous. For that reason, we will not attempt a general treatment. The end of Section 10.4 discusses this issue in the context of efficiency-wage theories based on imperfect monitoring of workers' effort. In this section and the next, however, we simply assume that compensation takes the form of a conventional wage, and investigate the effects of efficiency wages under this assumption.

Assumptions

We now turn to a model of efficiency wages. There is a large number, N, of identical competitive firms.[4] The representative firm seeks to maximize its real profits, which are given by

---

[2]When ability is observable, the firm can pay higher wages to more able workers; thus observable ability differences do not lead to any departures from the Walrasian case.

[3]See Problem 10.5 for a formalization of this idea. Three other potential advantages of a higher wage are that it can reduce turnover (and hence recruitment and training costs, if they are borne by the firm); that it can lower the likelihood that the workers will unionize; and that it can raise the utility of managers who have some ability to pursue objectives other than maximizing profits.

[4]We can think of the number of firms as being determined by the amount of capital in the economy, which is fixed in the short run.

$$\pi = Y - wL, \tag{10.1}$$

where Y is the firm's output, w is the real wage that it pays, and L is the amount of labor it hires.

A firm's output depends both on the number of workers it employs and on their effort. For simplicity we neglect other inputs and assume that labor and effort enter the production function multiplicatively. Thus the representative firm's output is

$$Y = F(eL), \qquad F'(\bullet) > 0, \quad F''(\bullet) < 0, \tag{10.2}$$

where e denotes workers' effort. The crucial assumption of efficiency-wage models is that effort depends positively on the wage the firm pays. In this section we consider the simple case (due to Solow, 1979) where the wage is the only determinant of effort. Thus,

$$e = e(w), \qquad e'(\bullet) > 0. \tag{10.3}$$

Finally, there are $\bar{L}$ identical workers, each of whom supplies one unit of labor inelastically.

Analyzing the Model

The problem facing the representative firm is

$$\max_{L,\,w} F(e(w)L) - wL. \tag{10.4}$$

If there are unemployed workers, the firm can choose the wage freely. If unemployment is zero, on the other hand, the firm must pay at least the wage paid by other firms.

When the firm is unconstrained, the first-order conditions for L and w are[5]

$$F'(e(w)L)e(w) - w = 0, \tag{10.5}$$

$$F'(e(w)L)Le'(w) - L = 0. \tag{10.6}$$

We can rewrite (10.5) as

$$F'(e(w)L) = \frac{w}{e(w)}. \tag{10.7}$$

Substituting (10.7) into (10.6) and dividing by L yields

$$\frac{we'(w)}{e(w)} = 1. \tag{10.8}$$

---

[5]We assume that the second-order conditions are satisfied.

Equation (10.8) states that at the optimum, the elasticity of effort with respect to the wage is 1. To understand this condition, note that output is a function of the quantity of effective labor, eL. The firm therefore wants to hire effective labor as cheaply as possible. When the firm hires a worker, it obtains $e(w)$ units of effective labor at a cost of w; thus the cost per unit of effective labor is $w/e(w)$. When the elasticity of e with respect to w is 1, a marginal change in w has no effect on this ratio; thus this is the first-order condition for the problem of choosing w to minimize the cost of effective labor. The wage satisfying (10.8) is known as the *efficiency wage*.

Figure 10.1 depicts the choice of w graphically in (w, e) space. The rays coming out from the origin are lines where the ratio of e to w is constant; the ratio is larger on the higher rays. Thus the firm wants to choose w to attain as high a ray as possible. This occurs where the $e(w)$ function is just tangent to one of the rays—that is, where the elasticity of e with respect to w is 1. Panel (a) shows a case where effort is sufficiently responsive to the wage that over some range the firm prefers a higher wage. Panel (b) shows a case where the firm always prefers a lower wage.

Finally, equation (10.7) states that the firm hires workers until the marginal product of effective labor equals its cost. This is analogous to the condition in a standard labor-demand problem that the firm hires labor up to the point where the marginal product equals the wage.

Equations (10.7) and (10.8) describe the behavior of a single firm. Describing the economy-wide equilibrium is straightforward. Let w^* and L^* denote the values of w and L that satisfy (10.7) and (10.8). Since firms are identical, each firm chooses these same values of w and L. Total labor demand is therefore NL^*. If labor supply, $\bar{L}$, exceeds this amount, firms are unconstrained in their choice of w. In this case the wage is w^*, employment is NL^*, and there is unemployment of amount $\bar{L} - NL^*$. If NL^* exceeds $\bar{L}$, on the other hand, firms are constrained. In this case, the wage is bid up to the point where demand and supply are in balance, and there is no unemployment.

Implications

This model shows how efficiency wages can give rise to unemployment. In addition, the model implies that the real wage is unresponsive to demand shifts. Suppose the demand for labor increases. Since the efficiency wage, w^*, is determined entirely by the properties of the effort function, $e(\cdot)$, there is no reason for firms to adjust their wages. Thus the model provides a candidate explanation of why shifts in labor demand lead to large movements in employment and small changes in the real wage. In addition, the fact that the real wage and effort do not change implies that firms' labor costs do not change. As a result, in a model with price-setting firms, the incentive to adjust prices is small.

(a)

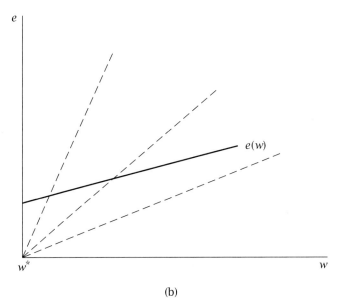

(b)

FIGURE 10.1 The determination of the efficiency wage

Unfortunately, these results are less promising than they may appear. The difficulty is that they apply not just to the short run but to the long run: the model implies that as economic growth shifts out the demand for labor, the real wage remains unchanged and unemployment trends downward. Eventually, unemployment reaches zero, at which point further increases in demand lead to increases in the real wage. In practice, however, we observe no clear trend in unemployment over extended periods. In other words, the basic fact about the labor market that we need to understand is not just that shifts in labor demand appear to have little impact on the real wage and fall almost entirely on employment in the short run; it is also that they fall almost entirely on the real wage in the long run. Our model does not explain this pattern.

10.3   A More General Version

Introduction

With many of the potential sources of efficiency wages, the wage is unlikely to be the only determinant of effort. Suppose, for example, that the wage affects effort because firms cannot monitor workers perfectly and workers are concerned about the possibility of losing their jobs if the firm catches them shirking. In such a situation, the cost to a worker of being fired depends not just on the wage the job pays, but also on how easy it is to obtain other jobs and on the wages those jobs pay. Thus workers are likely to exert more effort at a given wage when unemployment is higher, and to exert less effort when the wage paid by other firms is higher. Similar arguments apply to situations where the wage affects effort because of unobserved ability or feelings of gratitude or anger.

Thus a natural generalization of the effort function, (10.3), is

$$e = e(w, w_a, u), \qquad e_1(\bullet) > 0, \quad e_2(\bullet) < 0, \quad e_3(\bullet) > 0, \qquad (10.9)$$

where w_a is the wage paid by other firms and u is the unemployment rate, and where subscripts denote partial derivatives.

Each firm is small relative to the economy, and therefore takes w_a and u as given. The representative firm's problem is the same as before, except that w_a and u now affect the effort function. The first-order conditions can therefore be rearranged to obtain

$$F'(e(w, w_a, u)L) = \frac{w}{e(w, w_a, u)}, \qquad (10.10)$$

$$\frac{we_1(w, w_a, u)}{e(w, w_a, u)} = 1. \qquad (10.11)$$

These conditions are analogous to (10.7) and (10.8) in the simpler version of the model.

Assume that the $e(\bullet)$ function is sufficiently well behaved that there is a unique optimal w for a given w_a and u. Given this assumption, equilibrium requires $w = w_a$; if not, each firm wants to pay a wage different from the prevailing wage. Let w^* and L^* denote the values of w and L satisfying (10.10)–(10.11) with $w = w_a$. As before, if NL^* is less than $\bar{L}$, the equilibrium wage is w^* and there is unemployment of amount $\bar{L} - NL^*$. And if NL^* exceeds $\bar{L}$, the wage is bid up and the labor market clears.

This extended version of the model has promise for accounting for both the absence of any trend in unemployment over the long run and the fact that shifts in labor demand appear to have large effects on unemployment in the short run. This is most easily seen by means of an example.[6]

Example

Suppose effort is given by

$$
e = \begin{cases} \left(\dfrac{w-x}{x}\right)^{\beta} & \text{if } w > x \\ 0 & \text{otherwise,} \end{cases}
\tag{10.12}
$$

$$
x = (1 - bu)w_a,
\tag{10.13}
$$

where $0 < \beta < 1$ and $b > 0$. x is a measure of labor-market conditions. If b equals 1, x is the wage paid at other firms multiplied by the fraction of workers who are employed. If b is less than 1, workers put less weight on unemployment; this could occur if there are unemployment benefits or if workers value leisure. If b is greater than 1, workers put more weight on unemployment; this might occur because workers who lose their jobs face unusually high chances of continued unemployment, or because of risk aversion. Finally, equation (10.12) states that for $w > x$, effort increases less than proportionately with $w - x$.

Differentiation of (10.12) shows that for this functional form, the condition that the elasticity of effort with respect to the wage equals 1 (equation [10.11]) is

$$
\beta \frac{w}{[(w-x)/x]^{\beta}} \left(\frac{w-x}{x}\right)^{\beta-1} \frac{1}{x} = 1.
\tag{10.14}
$$

Straightforward algebra can be used to simplify (10.14) to

$$
\begin{aligned}
w &= \frac{x}{1 - \beta} \\
&= \frac{(1 - bu)}{1 - \beta} w_a.
\end{aligned}
\tag{10.15}
$$

For small values of β, $1/(1 - \beta) \simeq 1 + \beta$. Thus (10.15) implies that when β is small, the firm offers a premium of approximately fraction β over the index of labor-market opportunities, x.

---

[6]This example is based on Summers (1988).

Equilibrium requires that the representative firm wants to pay the prevailing wage, or that $w = w_a$. Imposing this condition in (10.15) yields

$$(1 - \beta)w_a = (1 - bu)w_a. \tag{10.16}$$

For this condition to be satisfied, the unemployment rate must be given by

$$u = \frac{\beta}{b} \tag{10.17}$$

$$\equiv u_{EQ}.$$

As equation (10.15) shows, each firm wants to pay more than the prevailing wage if unemployment is less than u_{EQ}, and wants to pay less if unemployment is more than u_{EQ}. Thus equilibrium requires that $u = u_{EQ}$.

Substituting (10.17) and $w = w_a$ into the effort function, (10.12), implies that equilibrium effort is given by

$$e_{EQ} = \left[\frac{w_a - (1 - bu_{EQ})w_a}{(1 - bu_{EQ})w_a} \right]^{\beta}$$

$$= \left[\frac{1 - (1 - \beta)}{1 - \beta} \right]^{\beta} \tag{10.18}$$

$$= \left(\frac{\beta}{1 - \beta} \right)^{\beta}.$$

Finally, the equilibrium wage is determined by the condition that the marginal product of effective labor equals its cost (equation [10.10]): $F'(eL) = w/e$. We can rewrite this condition as $w = eF'(eL)$. Since total employment is $(1 - u_{EQ})\bar{L}$ in equilibrium, each firm must hire $(1 - u_{EQ})\bar{L}/N$ workers. Thus the equilibrium wage is given by

$$w_{EQ} = e_{EQ}F'\left(\frac{e_{EQ}(1 - u_{EQ})\bar{L}}{N} \right). \tag{10.19}$$

Implications

This analysis has three important implications. First, (10.17) implies that equilibrium unemployment depends only on the parameters of the effort function; the production function is irrelevant. Thus an upward trend in the production function does not produce a trend in unemployment.

Second, relatively modest values of β—the elasticity of effort with respect to the premium firms pay over the index of labor-market conditions—can lead to nonnegligible unemployment. For example, either $\beta = 0.06$ and $b = 1$ or $\beta = 0.03$ and $b = 0.5$ imply that equilibrium unemployment is 6%.

Third, firms' incentive to adjust wages or prices (or both) in response to changes in aggregate unemployment is likely to be small for reasonable cases. Suppose we embed this model of wages and effort in a model of price-setting firms along the lines of Chapter 6. Consider a situation where the economy is initially in equilibrium, so that $u = u_{EQ}$ and marginal revenue and marginal cost are equal for the representative firm. Now suppose that the money supply falls and firms do not change their nominal wages or prices; as a result, unemployment rises above u_{EQ}. We know from Chapter 6 that small barriers to wage and price adjustment can cause this to be an equilibrium only if the representative firm's incentive to adjust is small.

For concreteness, consider the incentive to adjust wages. Equation (10.15), $w = (1 - bu)w_a/(1 - \beta)$, shows that the cost-minimizing wage is decreasing in the unemployment rate. Thus the firm can reduce its costs, and hence raise its profits, by cutting its wage. The key issue is the size of the gain. Equation (10.12) for effort implies that if the firm leaves its wage equal to the prevailing wage, w_a, its cost per unit of effective labor, w/e, is

$$
\begin{aligned}
C_{FIXED} &= \frac{w_a}{e(w_a, w_a, u)} \\[2mm]
&= \frac{w_a}{\left(\dfrac{w_a - x}{x}\right)^{\beta}} \\[2mm]
&= \frac{w_a}{\left[\dfrac{w_a - (1 - bu)w_a}{(1 - bu)w_a}\right]^{\beta}} \\[2mm]
&= \left[\frac{1 - bu}{bu}\right]^{\beta} w_a.
\end{aligned}
\tag{10.20}
$$

If the firm changes its wage, on the other hand, it sets it according to (10.15), and thus chooses $w = x/(1 - \beta)$. In this case, the firm's cost per unit of effective labor is

$$
\begin{aligned}
C_{ADJ} &= \frac{w}{\left(\dfrac{w - x}{x}\right)^{\beta}} \\[2mm]
&= \frac{x/(1 - \beta)}{\left\{\dfrac{[x/(1 - \beta)] - x}{x}\right\}^{\beta}} \\[2mm]
&= \frac{x/(1 - \beta)}{[\beta/(1 - \beta)]^{\beta}} \\[2mm]
&= \frac{1}{\beta^{\beta}}\frac{1}{(1 - \beta)^{1-\beta}}(1 - bu)w_a.
\end{aligned}
\tag{10.21}
$$

Suppose that $\beta = 0.06$ and $b = 1$, so that $u_{EQ} = 6\%$. Suppose, however, that unemployment rises to 9% and that other firms do not change their wages. Equations (10.20) and (10.21) imply that this rise lowers C_{FIXED} by 2.6% and C_{ADJ} by 3.2%. Thus the firm can save only 0.6% of costs by cutting its wages. For $\beta = 0.03$ and $b = 0.5$, the declines in C_{FIXED} and C_{ADJ} are 1.3% and 1.5%; thus in this case the incentive to cut wages is even smaller.[7]

In a competitive labor market, in contrast, the equilibrium wage falls by the percentage fall in employment divided by the elasticity of labor supply. For a 3% fall in employment and a labor supply elasticity of 0.2, for example, the equilibrium wage falls by 15%. And without endogenous effort, a 15% fall in wages translates directly into a 15% fall in costs. Firms therefore have an overwhelming incentive to cut wages and prices in this case.[8]

Thus efficiency wages have a potentially large impact on the incentive to adjust wages in the face of fluctuations in aggregate output. As a result, they have the potential to explain why shifts in labor demand mainly affect employment in the short run. Intuitively, in a competitive market firms are initially at a corner solution with respect to wages: firms pay the lowest possible wage at which they can hire workers. Thus wage reductions, if possible, are unambiguously beneficial. With efficiency wages, in contrast, firms are initially at an interior optimum where the marginal benefits and costs of wage cuts are equal.

10.4   The Shapiro–Stiglitz Model

The source of efficiency wages that has probably received the most attention is the possibility that firms' limited monitoring abilities force them to provide their workers with an incentive to exert effort. This section presents a specific model, due to Shapiro and Stiglitz (1984), of this possibility.[9]

Presenting a formal model of imperfect monitoring serves three purposes. First, it allows us to investigate whether this idea holds up under

---

[7]One can also show that if firms do not change their wages, for reasonable cases their incentive to adjust their prices is also small. If wages are completely flexible, however, the incentive to adjust prices is not small. With u greater than u_{EQ}, each firm wants to pay less than other firms are paying (see [10.15]). Thus if wages are completely flexible, they must fall to zero—or, if workers have a positive reservation wage, to this reservation wage. As a result, firms' labor costs are extremely low, and thus their incentive to cut prices and increase output is high. Thus in the absence of any barriers to changing wages, small costs to changing prices are not enough to prevent price adjustment in this model.

[8]In fact, in a competitive labor market, an individual firm's incentive to reduce wages if other firms do not is even larger than the fall in the equilibrium wage. If other firms do not cut wages, some workers are unemployed. Thus the firm can hire workers at an arbitrarily small wage (or at workers' reservation wage).

[9]Dickens, Katz, Lang, and Summers (1989) document the importance of worker theft and shirking in the United States and argue that these phenomena are essential to understanding the labor market.

scrutiny. Second, it permits us to analyze additional questions; for example, only with a formal model can we ask whether government policies can improve welfare. Third, the mathematical tools the model employs are useful in other settings.

Assumptions

The economy consists of a large number of workers, $\bar{L}$, and a large number of firms, N. The workers maximize their expected discounted utilities, and firms maximize their expected discounted profits. The model is set in continuous time. For simplicity, the analysis focuses on steady states.

Consider workers first. The representative worker's lifetime utility is

$$U = \int_{t=0}^{\infty} e^{-\rho t} u(t)dt, \qquad \rho > 0. \tag{10.22}$$

$u(t)$ is instantaneous utility at time t, and ρ is the discount rate. Instantaneous utility is

$$u(t) = \begin{cases} w(t) - e(t) & \text{if employed} \\ 0 & \text{if unemployed.} \end{cases} \tag{10.23}$$

w is the wage and e is the worker's effort. There are only two possible effort levels, $e = 0$ and $e = \bar{e}$. Thus at any moment a worker must be in one of three states: employed and exerting effort (denoted "E"), employed and not exerting effort (denoted "S," for shirking), or unemployed (denoted "U").

A key ingredient of the model is its assumptions concerning workers' transitions among the three states. First, there is an exogenous rate at which jobs end. Specifically, if a worker begins working in a job at some time t_0 (and if the worker exerts effort), the probability that the worker is still employed in the job at some later time t is

$$P(t) = e^{-b(t-t_0)}, \qquad b > 0. \tag{10.24}$$

(10.24) implies that $P(t+\tau)/P(t)$ equals $e^{-b\tau}$, and thus that it is independent of t: if a worker is employed at some time, the probability that he or she is still employed time τ later is $e^{-b\tau}$ regardless of how long the worker has already been employed. This lack of *time dependence* simplifies the analysis greatly, because it implies that there is no need to keep track of how long workers have been in their jobs. Processes like (10.24) are known as *Poisson processes.*

An equivalent way to describe the process of job breakup is to say that it occurs with probability b per unit time, or to say that the *hazard rate* for job breakup is b. That is, the probability that an employed worker's job ends in the next dt units of time approaches $b\,dt$ as dt approaches zero. To see that our assumptions imply this, note that (10.24) implies $P'(t) = -bP(t)$.

The second assumption concerning workers' transitions between states is that firms' detection of workers who are shirking is also a Poisson process. Specifically, detection occurs with probability q per unit time. q is exogenous, and detection is independent of job breakups. Workers who are caught shirking are fired. Thus if a worker is employed but shirking, the probability that he or she is still employed time τ later is $e^{-q\tau}$ (the probability that the worker has not been caught and fired) times $e^{-b\tau}$ (the probability that the job has not ended exogenously).

Third, unemployed workers find employment at rate a per unit time. Each worker takes a as given. In the economy as a whole, however, a is determined endogenously. When firms want to hire workers, they choose workers at random out of the pool of unemployed workers. Thus a is determined by the rate at which firms are hiring (which is determined by the number of employed workers and the rate at which jobs end) and the number of unemployed workers. Because workers are identical, the probability of finding a job does not depend on how workers become unemployed or on how long they are unemployed.

Firms' behavior is straightforward. A firm's profits at t are

$$\pi(t) = F(\overline{e}L(t)) - w(t)[L(t) + S(t)], \qquad F'(\bullet) > 0, \quad F''(\bullet) < 0, \qquad (10.25)$$

where L is the number of employees who are exerting effort and S is the number who are shirking. The problem facing the firm is to set w sufficiently high that its workers do not shirk, and to choose L. Because the firm's decisions at any date affect profits only at that date, there is no need to analyze the present value of profits: the firm chooses w and L at each moment to maximize the instantaneous flow of profits.

The final assumption of the model is $\overline{e}F'(\overline{e}\overline{L}/N) > \overline{e}$, or $F'(\overline{e}\overline{L}/N) > 1$. This condition states that if each firm hires $1/N$ of the labor force, the marginal product of labor exceeds the cost of exerting effort. Thus in the absence of imperfect monitoring, there is full employment.

The Values of E, U, and S

Let V_i denote the "value" of being in state i (for $i = E, S$, and U). That is, V_i is the expected value of discounted lifetime utility from the present moment forward of a worker who is in state i. Because transitions among states are Poisson processes, the V_i's do not depend on how long the worker has been in his or her current state or on his or her prior history. And because we are focusing on steady states, the V_i's are constant over time.

To find V_E, V_S, and V_U, it is not necessary to analyze the various paths the worker may follow over the infinite future. Instead we can use *dynamic programming*. The central idea of dynamic programming is to look at only a brief interval of time and use the V_i's themselves to summarize what occurs after the end of the interval.[10] Consider first a worker who is employed and exerting effort at time 0. Suppose temporarily that time is divided into intervals of length Δt, and that a worker who loses his or her job during one interval cannot begin to look for a new job until the beginning of the next interval. Let $V_E(\Delta t)$ and $V_U(\Delta t)$ denote the values of employment and unemployment as of the beginning of an interval under this assumption. In a moment we will let Δt approach zero. When we do this, the constraint that a worker who loses his or her job during an interval cannot find a new job during the remainder of that interval becomes irrelevant. Thus $V_E(\Delta t)$ will approach V_E.

If a worker is employed in a job paying a wage of w, $V_E(\Delta t)$ is given by

$$V_E(\Delta t) = \int_{t=0}^{\Delta t} e^{-bt} e^{-\rho t}(w - \overline{e})dt + e^{-\rho \Delta t}[e^{-b\Delta t} V_E(\Delta t) + (1 - e^{-b\Delta t})V_U(\Delta t)].$$

(10.26)

The first term of (10.26) reflects utility during the interval $(0, \Delta t)$. The probability that the worker is still employed at time t is e^{-bt}. If the worker is employed, flow utility is $w - \overline{e}$. Discounting this back to time 0 yields an expected contribution to lifetime utility of $e^{-(\rho+b)t}(w - \overline{e})$.[11]

The second term of (10.26) reflects utility after Δt. At time Δt, the worker is employed with probability $e^{-b\Delta t}$, and is unemployed with probability $1 - e^{-b\Delta t}$. Combining these probabilities with the V's and discounting yields the second term.

If we compute the integral in (10.26), we can rewrite the equation as

$$V_E(\Delta t) = \frac{1}{\rho + b}[1 - e^{-(\rho+b)\Delta t}](w - \overline{e})$$

(10.27)

$$+ e^{-\rho \Delta t}[e^{-b\Delta t} V_E(\Delta t) + (1 - e^{-b\Delta t})V_U(\Delta t)].$$

Solving this expression for $V_E(\Delta t)$ gives

$$V_E(\Delta t) = \frac{1}{\rho + b}(w - \overline{e}) + \frac{1}{1 - e^{-(\rho+b)\Delta t}} e^{-\rho \Delta t}(1 - e^{-b\Delta t})V_U(\Delta t).$$

(10.28)

As described above, V_E equals the limit of $V_E(\Delta t)$ as Δt approaches zero. (Similarly, V_U equals the limit of $V_U(\Delta t)$ as t approaches zero.) To find this

---

[10]If time is discrete rather than continuous, we look one period ahead. See Sargent (1987b) for an introduction to dynamic programming.

[11]Because of the steady-state assumption, if it is optimal for the worker to exert effort initially, it continues to be optimal. Thus we do not have to allow for the possibility of the worker beginning to shirk.

limit, we apply l'Hôpital's rule to (10.28). This yields

$$V_E = \frac{1}{\rho + b}[(w - \overline{e}) + bV_U]. \tag{10.29}$$

Equation (10.29) can also be derived intuitively. Think of an asset that pays dividends at rate $w - \overline{e}$ per unit time when the worker is employed and no dividends when the worker is unemployed, and assume that the asset is being priced by risk-neutral investors with required rate of return ρ. Since the expected present value of lifetime dividends of this asset is the same as the worker's expected present value of lifetime utility, the asset's price must be V_E when the worker is employed and V_U when the worker is unemployed. For the asset to be held, it must provide an expected rate of return of ρ. That is, its dividends per unit time, plus any expected capital gains or losses per unit time, must equal ρV_E. When the worker is employed, dividends per unit time are $w - \overline{e}$, and there is a probability b per unit time of a capital loss of $V_E - V_U$. Thus,

$$\rho V_E = (w - \overline{e}) - b(V_E - V_U). \tag{10.30}$$

Rearranging this expression yields (10.29).

If the worker is shirking, the "dividend" is w per unit time, and the expected capital loss is $(b + q)(V_S - V_U)$ per unit time. Thus reasoning parallel to that used to derive (10.30) implies

$$\rho V_S = w - (b + q)(V_S - V_U). \tag{10.31}$$

Finally, if the worker is unemployed, the dividend is zero and the expected capital gain (assuming that firms pay sufficiently high wages that employed workers exert effort) is $a(V_E - V_U)$ per unit time.[12] Thus,

$$\rho V_U = a(V_E - V_U). \tag{10.32}$$

The No-Shirking Condition

The firm must pay enough that $V_E \geq V_S$; otherwise its workers exert no effort and produce nothing. At the same time, since effort cannot exceed $\overline{e}$, there is no need to pay any excess over the minimum needed to induce effort. Thus the firm chooses w so that V_E just equals V_S:[13]

$$V_E = V_S. \tag{10.33}$$

---

[12] Equations (10.31) and (10.32) can also be derived by defining $V_U(\Delta t)$ and $V_S(\Delta t)$ and proceeding along the lines used to derive (10.29).

[13] Since all firms are the same, they choose the same wage. Thus V_E and V_S do not depend on what firm a worker is employed by.

Since V_E and V_S must be equal, (10.30) and (10.31) imply

$$(w - \overline{e}) - b(V_E - V_U) = w - (b + q)(V_E - V_U), \tag{10.34}$$

or

$$V_E - V_U = \frac{\overline{e}}{q}. \tag{10.35}$$

Equation (10.35) implies that firms set wages high enough that workers strictly prefer employment to unemployment. Thus workers obtain rents. The size of the premium is increasing in the cost of exerting effort, $\overline{e}$, and decreasing in firms' efficacy in detecting shirkers, q.

The next step is to find what the wage must be for the rent to employment to equal $\overline{e}/q$. Rearranging (10.30) to obtain an expression for w yields

$$w = \overline{e} + \rho V_E + b(V_E - V_U)$$

$$= \overline{e} + \rho V_U + (b + \rho)(V_E - V_U) \tag{10.36}$$

$$= \overline{e} + (a + b + \rho)(V_E - V_U),$$

where the last line uses (10.32) to substitute for ρV_U. Thus for $V_E - V_U$ to equal $\overline{e}/q$, the wage must be

$$w = \overline{e} + (a + b + \rho)\frac{\overline{e}}{q}. \tag{10.37}$$

This condition states that the wage needed to induce effort is increasing in the cost of effort ($\overline{e}$), the ease of finding jobs (a), the rate of job breakup (b), and the discount rate (ρ), and is decreasing in the probability that shirkers are detected (q).

It turns out to be easier to express the wage needed to prevent shirking in terms of employment per firm, L, rather than the rate at which the unemployed find jobs, a. To substitute for a, we use the fact that, since the economy is in steady state, movements into and out of unemployment must balance. The number of workers becoming unemployed per unit time is N (the number of firms) times L (the number of workers per firm) times b (the rate of job breakup).[14] The number of unemployed workers finding jobs is $\overline{L} - NL$ times a. Equating these two quantities yields

$$a = \frac{NLb}{\overline{L} - NL}. \tag{10.38}$$

Equation (10.38) implies $a + b = \overline{L}b/(\overline{L} - NL)$. Substituting this into (10.37) yields

---

[14]We are assuming that the economy is large enough that although the breakup of any individual job is random, aggregate breakups are not.

$$w = \bar{e} + \left(\rho + \frac{\bar{L}}{\bar{L} - NL}b\right)\frac{\bar{e}}{q}. \tag{10.39}$$

Equation (10.39) is the *no-shirking condition*. It shows, as a function of the level of employment, the wage that firms must pay to induce workers to exert effort. The more workers who are employed, the smaller is the pool of unemployed workers and the larger is the number of workers leaving their jobs, and so the easier it is for unemployed workers to find employment. The wage needed to deter shirking is therefore an increasing function of employment. At full employment, unemployed workers find work instantly, and so there is no cost to being fired and thus no wage that can deter shirking. The set of points in (NL, w) space satisfying the no-shirking condition (NSC) is shown in Figure 10.2.

Closing the Model

Firms hire workers up to the point where the marginal product of labor equals the wage. From equation (10.25) for profits, this condition is

$$\bar{e}F'(\bar{e}L) = w. \tag{10.40}$$

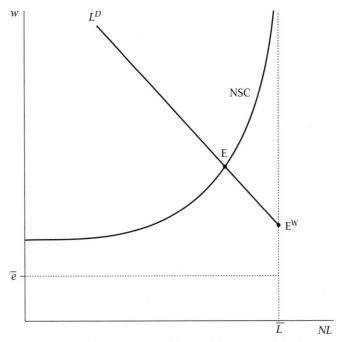

FIGURE 10.2   The Shapiro–Stiglitz model

The set of points satisfying (10.40) (which is simply a conventional labor demand curve) is also shown in Figure 10.2.

Labor supply is horizontal at $\bar{e}$ up to the number of workers, $\bar{L}$, and then vertical. In the absence of imperfect monitoring, equilibrium occurs at the intersection of labor demand and supply. Our assumption that the marginal product of labor at full employment exceeds the disutility of effort $(F'(\bar{e}\bar{L}/N) > 1)$ implies that this intersection occurs in the vertical part of the labor supply curve. The Walrasian equilibrium is shown as Point E^W in the diagram.

With imperfect monitoring, equilibrium occurs at the intersection of the labor demand curve (equation [10.40]) and the no-shirking condition (equation [10.39]). This is shown as Point E in the diagram. At the equilibrium, there is unemployment. Unemployed workers strictly prefer to be employed at the prevailing wage and to exert effort, rather than to remain unemployed. Nonetheless, they cannot bid the wage down: firms know that if they hire additional workers at slightly less than the prevailing wage, the workers will prefer shirking to exerting effort. Thus the wage does not fall, and the unemployment remains.

Two examples may help to clarify the workings of the model. First, a rise in q—an increase in the probability per unit time that a shirker is detected—shifts the no-shirking locus down and does not affect the labor demand curve. This is shown in Figure 10.3. Thus the wage falls and employment

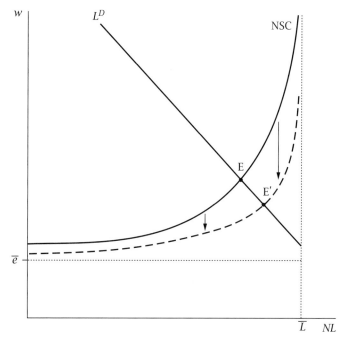

FIGURE 10.3   The effects of a rise in q in the Shapiro–Stiglitz model

rises. As q approaches infinity, the probability that a shirker is detected in any finite length of time approaches 1. As a result, the no-shirking wage approaches $\bar{e}$ for any level of employment less than full employment. Thus the economy approaches the Walrasian equilibrium.

Second, if there is no turnover ($b = 0$), unemployed workers are never hired. As a result, the no-shirking wage is independent of the level of employment. From (10.39), the no-shirking wage in this case is $\bar{e} + \rho\bar{e}/q$. Intuitively, the gain from shirking relative to exerting effort is $\bar{e}$ per unit time. The cost is that there is probability q per unit time of becoming permanently unemployed and thereby losing the discounted surplus from the job, which is $(w - \bar{e})/\rho$. Equating the cost and benefit gives $w = \bar{e} + \rho\bar{e}/q$. This case is shown in Figure 10.4.

Implications

The model implies the existence of equilibrium unemployment, and suggests various factors that are likely to influence it. Thus the model has some promise as a candidate explanation of unemployment. Unfortunately, the model is so stylized that it is difficult to determine what level of unemployment it predicts or to use it to derive specific predictions concerning the behavior of unemployment over time.

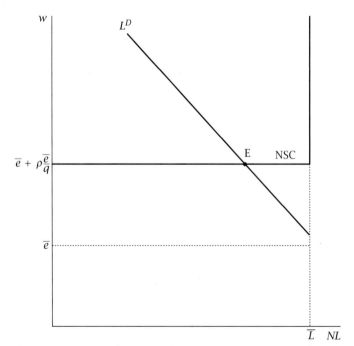

FIGURE 10.4   The Shapiro–Stiglitz model without turnover

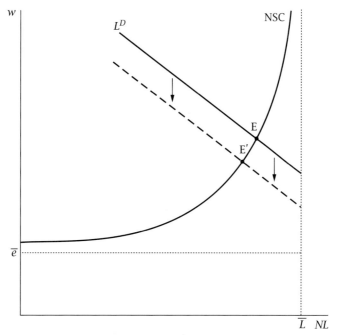

FIGURE 10.5   The effects of a fall in labor demand in the Shapiro–Stiglitz model

With regard to short-run fluctuations, consider the impact of a fall in labor demand, shown in Figure 10.5. w and L move down along the no-shirking locus. Since labor supply is perfectly inelastic, employment necessarily responds more than it would without imperfect monitoring. Thus the model suggests one possible reason that wages may respond less to demand-driven output fluctuations than they would if workers were always on their labor supply curves. Again, however, the model is sufficiently stylized that it is difficult to gauge its quantitative implications.[15]

Finally, the model implies that the decentralized equilibrium is inefficient. To see this, note that since the marginal product of labor at full employment, $\overline{e}F'(\overline{e}\overline{L}/N)$, exceeds the cost to workers of supplying effort, $\overline{e}$, the first-best allocation is for everyone to be employed and exert effort. Of course, the government cannot bring this about simply by dictating that firms move down the labor demand curve until full employment is reached: this policy causes workers to shirk, and thus results in zero output. But Shapiro and Stiglitz note that wage subsidies financed by lump-sum taxes or profits taxes improve welfare. Such a policy shifts the labor demand curve up, and thus increases the wage and employment along the no-shirking locus. Since the value of the additional output exceeds the opportunity cost of

---

[15] This discussion compares steady states with different levels of labor demand rather than analyzing the dynamic effects of a temporary or permanent change in labor demand. See Kimball (1994) for an analysis of the dynamics of the Shapiro–Stiglitz model.

producing it, overall welfare rises. How the gain is divided between workers and firms depends on how the wage subsidies are financed.

Extensions

The basic model can be extended in many ways. Here we discuss three.

First, an important question about the labor market is why, given that unemployment appears so harmful to workers, employers use layoffs rather than work-sharing arrangements when they reduce the amount of labor they use. One might expect workers to place sufficient value on reducing the risk of unemployment that they would accept a lower wage to work at a firm that used work-sharing rather than layoffs. Shapiro and Stiglitz's model (modified so that the number of hours employees work can vary) suggests a possible explanation for the puzzling infrequency of work-sharing. A reduction in hours of work lowers the surplus that employees are getting from their jobs. As a result, the wage that the firm has to pay to prevent shirking rises. If the firm lays off some workers, on the other hand, the remaining workers' surplus is unchanged, and so no increase in the wage is needed. Thus the firm may find layoffs preferable to work-sharing even though it subjects its workers to greater risk.

Second, Bulow and Summers (1986) extend the model to include a second type of job where effort can be monitored perfectly. These jobs could be piece-rate jobs where output is observable, for example. Since there is no asymmetric information in this sector, the jobs provide no surplus and are not rationed. Under plausible assumptions, the absence of surplus results in high turnover. The jobs with imperfect monitoring continue to pay more than the market-clearing wage. Thus marginal products in these jobs are higher, and workers, once they obtain such jobs, are reluctant to leave them. If the model is extended further to include groups of workers with different job attachments (different b's), a higher wage is needed to induce effort from workers with less job attachment. As a result, firms with jobs that require monitoring are reluctant to hire workers with low job attachment, and so these workers are disproportionately employed in the low-wage, high-turnover sector. These predictions concerning wage levels, turnover, and occupational segregation fit the stylized facts about *primary* and *secondary* jobs identified by Doeringer and Piore (1971) in their theory of *dual labor markets*.

The third extension is more problematic for the theory. So far, we have assumed that compensation takes the form of conventional wage payments. But, as suggested in the general discussion of potential sources of efficiency wages, more complicated compensation policies can dramatically change the effects of imperfect monitoring. Two examples of such compensation policies are *bonding* and *job selling*. Bonding occurs when firms require each new worker to post a bond that must be forfeited if he or she is caught shirking. By requiring sufficiently large bonds, the firm can induce workers not to shirk even at the market-clearing wage; that is, they can shift the no-shirking locus down until it coincides with the labor supply curve. If firms are able to require bonds they will do so, and unemployment will be eliminated from the model. Job selling occurs when firms require employees to pay a fee when they are hired. If firms are obtaining payments from new workers, their labor demand is higher for a given wage; thus the wage and employment rise as the economy moves up the no-shirking curve. Again, if firms are able to sell their jobs, they will do so.

Bonding, job selling, and the like may be limited by an absence of perfect capital markets (so that it is difficult for workers to post large bonds, or to pay large fees when they are hired); they may also be limited by workers' fears that the firm may falsely accuse them of shirking and claim the bonds, or dismiss them and keep the job fee. But, as Carmichael (1985) emphasizes, considerations like these will not eliminate these schemes entirely: if workers strictly prefer employment to unemployment, firms can raise their profits by, for example, charging marginally more for jobs. In such situations, jobs are not rationed, but go to those who are willing to pay the most for them; thus even if these schemes are limited by such factors as imperfect capital markets, they still eliminate unemployment. In short, the absence of job fees and performance bonds is a puzzle for the theory.[16]

10.5   Implicit Contracts

The second departure from Walrasian assumptions that we consider in this chapter is the existence of long-term relationships between firms and workers. Firms do not hire workers afresh each period. Instead, many jobs involve long-term attachments and considerable firm-specific skills on the part of workers. Akerlof and Main (1981) and Hall (1982), for example, find that the average worker in the United States is in a job that will last about ten years.

The possibility of long-term relationships implies that the wage does not have to adjust to clear the labor market each period. Workers are content to stay in their current jobs as long as the income streams they expect to obtain are preferable to their outside opportunities; because of their long-term relationships with their employers, their current wages may be relatively unimportant to this comparison. This section and the next two explore the consequences of this observation. This section considers the case where the pool of workers dealing with the firm is fixed; Sections 10.6 and 10.7 investigate the effects of relaxing this assumption.

---

[16]See Shapiro and Stiglitz (1985) and Akerlof and Katz (1989) for further discussion of these issues.

The Model

Consider a firm dealing with a group of workers. The firm's profits are

$$\pi = AF(L) - wL, \qquad F'(\bullet) > 0, \quad F''(\bullet) < 0, \qquad (10.41)$$

where L is the quantity of labor the firm employs and w is the real wage. A is a factor that shifts the profit function. It could reflect technology (so that a higher value means that the firm can produce more output from a given amount of labor), or economy-wide output (so that a higher value means that the firm can obtain a higher relative price for a given amount of output).

Instead of considering multiple periods, it is easier to consider a single period and assume that A is random. Thus, for example, when workers decide whether to work for the firm, they consider the expected utility they obtain in the single period given the randomness in A, rather than the average utility they obtain over many periods as their income and hours vary in response to fluctuations in A.

The distribution of A is discrete. There are K possible values of A, indexed by i; p_i denotes the probability that $A = A_i$. Thus the firm's expected profits are

$$E[\pi] = \sum_{i=1}^{K} p_i [A_i F(L_i) - w_i L_i], \qquad (10.42)$$

where L_i and w_i denote the quantity of labor and the real wage if the realization of A is A_i. The firm maximizes its expected profits; thus it is risk-neutral.

Each worker is assumed to work the same amount. The representative worker's utility is

$$u = U(C) - V(L), \qquad U'(\bullet) > 0, \quad U''(\bullet) < 0, \quad V'(\bullet) > 0, \quad V''(\bullet) > 0,$$
$$(10.43)$$

where $U(\bullet)$ gives the utility from consumption and $V(\bullet)$ the disutility from working. Since $U''(\bullet)$ is negative, workers are risk-averse.[17]

Workers' consumption, C, is assumed to equal their labor income, wL.[18] That is, workers cannot purchase insurance against employment and wage

---

[17]Because the firm's owners can diversify away firm-specific risk by holding a broad portfolio, the assumption that the firm is risk-neutral is reasonable for firm-specific shocks. For aggregate shocks, however, the assumption that the firm is less risk-averse than the workers is harder to justify. Since the main goal of the theory is to explain the effects of aggregate shocks, this is a weak point of the model. One possibility is that the owners are wealthier than the workers and that risk aversion is declining in wealth.

[18]If there are $\bar{L}$ workers, the representative worker's hours and consumption are in fact $L/\bar{L}$ and $wL/\bar{L}$, and so utility takes the form $\tilde{U}(C/\bar{L}) - \tilde{V}(L/\bar{L})$. To eliminate $\bar{L}$, define $U(C) = \tilde{U}(C/\bar{L})$ and $V(L) = \tilde{V}(L/\bar{L})$.

fluctuations. In a more fully developed model, this might arise because workers are heterogeneous and have private information about their labor-market prospects. In the present model, however, the absence of outside insurance is simply assumed.

Equation (10.43) implies that the representative worker's expected utility is

$$E[u] = \sum_{i=1}^{K} p_i [U(C_i) - V(L_i)]. \tag{10.44}$$

There is some reservation level of expected utility, u_0, that workers must attain to be willing to work for the firm. There is no labor mobility once workers agree to a contract; thus the only constraint on the contract involves the average level of utility it offers, not the level in any individual state.

Wage Contracts

One simple type of contract just specifies a wage and then lets the firm choose employment once A is determined; many actual contracts at least appear to take this form. Under such a contract, unemployment and real wage rigidity arise immediately. A fall in labor demand, for example, causes the firm to reduce employment at the fixed real wage while labor supply does not shift, and thus creates unemployment (or, if all workers work the same amount, underemployment). And the cost of labor does not respond because, by assumption, the real wage is fixed.

But this is not a satisfactory explanation of unemployment and real wage rigidity. The difficulty is that this type of a contract is inefficient (Leontief, 1946; Barro, 1977b; Hall, 1980). Since the wage is fixed and the firm chooses employment taking the wage as given, the marginal product of labor is independent of A. But since employment varies with A, the marginal disutility of working depends on A. Thus the marginal product of labor is generally not equal to the marginal disutility of work, and so it is possible to make both parties to the contract better off. And if labor supply is not very elastic, the inefficiency is large. When labor demand is low, for example, the marginal disutility of work is low, and so the firm and the workers could both be made better off if the workers worked slightly more.

Thus we can appeal to fixed-wage contracts with employment determined at the firm's discretion as a potential explanation of unemployment and real wage rigidity only if we can explain why a firm and its workers would agree to such an arrangement. The remainder of this section shows, however, that our assumptions imply that they will in fact agree to a very different contract. Section 10.6 then suggests a variation on our model that could give rise to something much closer to this type of a contract.

Efficient Contracts

To see how it is possible to improve on a wage contract, suppose that the firm offers the workers a contract specifying the wage and hours for each possible realization of A. Since actual contracts do not explicitly specify employment and the wage as functions of the state, such contracts are known as *implicit contracts*.[19]

Recall that the firm must offer the workers at least some minimum level of expected utility, u_0, but is otherwise unconstrained. In addition, since L_i and w_i determine C_i, we can think of the firm's choice variables as L and C in each state rather than as L and w. The Lagrangian for the firm's problem is therefore

$$\mathcal{L} = \sum_{i=1}^{K} p_i [A_i F(L_i) - C_i] + \lambda \left(\left\{ \sum_{i=1}^{K} p_i [U(C_i) - V(L_i)] \right\} - u_0 \right). \quad (10.45)$$

The first-order condition for C_i is

$$-p_i + \lambda p_i U'(C_i) = 0, \quad (10.46)$$

or

$$U'(C_i) = \frac{1}{\lambda}. \quad (10.47)$$

Equation (10.47) implies that the marginal utility of consumption is constant across states, and thus that consumption is constant across states. Thus the risk-neutral firm fully insures the risk-averse workers.

The first-order condition for L_i is

$$p_i A_i F'(L_i) = \lambda p_i V'(L_i). \quad (10.48)$$

Equation (10.47) implies $\lambda = 1/U'(C)$, where C is the constant level of consumption. Substituting this fact into (10.48) and dividing both sides by p_i yields

$$A_i F'(L_i) = \frac{V'(L_i)}{U'(C)}. \quad (10.49)$$

Implications

Under efficient contracts, workers' real incomes are constant. Thus the model appears to imply strong real wage rigidity; in fact, because L is higher when A is higher, the model implies that the wage per hour is coun-

---

[19]The theory of implicit contracts is due to Azariadis (1975); Baily (1974); and Gordon (1974).

tercyclical. Unfortunately, however, this result does not help to account for the puzzle that shifts in labor demand appear to result in large changes in employment. The problem is that with long-term contracts, the wage is no longer playing an allocative role. That is, firms do not choose employment taking the wage as given. Rather, the level of employment as a function of the state is specified in the contract. And, from (10.49), this level is the level that equates the marginal product of labor with the marginal disutility of additional hours of work.

As a result, the model implies that the cost to the firm of varying the amount of labor it uses changes greatly with its level of employment. Suppose the firm wants to increase employment marginally in state i. To do this, it must raise workers' compensation to make them no worse off than before. Since the expected utility cost to workers of the change is $p_i V'(L_i)$, C must rise by $p_i V'(L_i)/U'(C)$. Thus the marginal cost to the firm of increasing employment in a given state is proportional to $V'(L_i)$. If labor supply is relatively inelastic, $V'(L_i)$ is sharply increasing in L_i, and so the cost of labor to the firm is much higher when employment is high than when it is low. Thus, for example, embedding this model of contracts in a model of price determination like that of Section 6.11 would not alter the result that relatively inelastic labor supply creates a strong incentive for firms to cut prices and increase employment in recessions, and to raise prices and reduce employment in booms.

In addition to failing to predict relatively acyclical labor costs, the model fails to predict unemployment: as emphasized above, the implicit contract equates the marginal product of labor and the marginal disutility of work. The model does, however, suggest a possible explanation for apparent unemployment. In the efficient contract, workers are not free to choose their labor supply given the wage; instead the wage and employment are simultaneously specified to yield optimal risk-sharing and allocative efficiency. When employment is low, the marginal disutility of work is low and the hourly wage, C/L_i, is high. Thus workers wish that they could work more at the wage the firm is paying. As a result, even though employment and the wage are chosen optimally, workers appear to be constrained in their labor supply.

10.6 Insider-Outsider Models

The analysis in Section 10.5 assumes that the firm is dealing with a fixed pool of workers. In reality, there are two groups of potential workers. The first group—the insiders—are workers who have some connection with the firm at the time of the bargaining, and whose interests are therefore taken into account in the contract. The second group—the outsiders—are workers who have no initial connection with the firm but who may be hired after the contract is set. This distinction may be important for both fluctuations and unemployment.[20]

Insiders and Outsiders and the Cyclical Behavior of Labor Costs

Consider a firm and a set of insiders. The firm and the insiders bargain over the wage and employment as functions of the state. Hours are fixed, so labor input can vary only through changes in the number of workers. The firm's profits are

$$\pi = AF(L_I + L_O) - w_I L_I - w_O L_O, \tag{10.50}$$

where L_I and L_O are the numbers of insiders and outsiders the firm hires, and w_I and w_O are their wages. As before, A is random, taking on the value A_i with probability p_i. The insiders have priority in hiring; thus L_O can be positive only if L_I equals the number of insiders, $\bar{L}_I$.

Oswald (1987) and Gottfries (1992) argue that labor markets have two features that critically affect the problem facing the firm. The first is that, because of normal employment growth and turnover, most of the time the insiders are fully employed and the only hiring decision concerns how many outsiders to hire. Taking this to the extreme, here we assume that L_I always equals $\bar{L}_I$. Since the insiders are always employed, their utility depends only on their wage:

$$u_I = U(w_I), \qquad U'(\bullet) > 0, \quad U''(\bullet) < 0. \tag{10.51}$$

The second feature of labor markets emphasized by Oswald and Gottfries is that the wages paid to the two types of workers cannot be set independently: in practice, the higher the wage that the firm pays to its existing employees, the more it must pay to its new hires. Again adopting an extreme form for simplicity, we assume that w_O rises one-for-one with w_I:

$$w_O = w_I - c, \qquad c \geq 0. \tag{10.52}$$

Finally, we assume that the insiders have sufficient bargaining power and that the gap between insider and outsider wages (c) is sufficiently small that the firm is always able to hire as many new workers at $w_I - c$ as it wants. Thus the model applies most clearly to a firm that faces a strong union or that must pay a high wage for some other reason.

It is convenient to think of the firm's choice variables as w_I and L_O in each state. w_O is determined by w_I and equation (10.52); L_I is fixed at $\bar{L}_I$.

---

[20]Important contributions to the insider-outsider literature include Shaked and Sutton (1984); Solow (1985); Gregory (1986); Lindbeck and Snower (1988); Blanchard and Summers (1986, 1987); Oswald (1987); and Gottfries (1992).

As in the previous section, the firm must provide the insiders with expected utility of at least u_0. The Lagrangian for the firm's problem is thus

$$\mathcal{L} = \sum_{i=1}^{K} p_i [A_i F(\overline{L}_I + L_{Oi}) - w_{Ii} \overline{L}_I - (w_{Ii} - c)L_{Oi}] + \lambda \left\{ \left[\sum_{i=1}^{K} p_i U(w_{Ii}) \right] - u_0 \right\}.$$

(10.53)

The first-order condition for L_{Oi} is

$$p_i [A_i F'(\overline{L}_I + L_{Oi}) - (w_{Ii} - c)] = 0,$$

(10.54)

or

$$A_i F'(\overline{L}_I + L_{Oi}) = w_{Ii} - c.$$

(10.55)

Equation (10.55) implies that, just as in a conventional labor demand problem, but in sharp contrast to what happens with implicit contracts, employment is chosen to equate the marginal product of labor with the wage. The reason is that outsiders, who are the workers relevant to the marginal employment decision, are not involved in the original bargaining. The insiders and the firm act to maximize their joint surplus. They therefore agree to hire outsiders up to the point where their marginal product equals the wage they must be paid; the outsiders' preferences are irrelevant to this calculation.

The first-order condition for w_{Ii} is

$$-p_i (\overline{L}_I + L_{Oi}) + \lambda p_i U'(w_{Ii}) = 0.$$

(10.56)

This implies

$$U'(w_{Ii}) = \frac{\overline{L}_I + L_{Oi}}{\lambda}.$$

(10.57)

Since L_{Oi} is higher in good states, (10.57) implies that $U'(w_{Ii})$ is higher. This requires that w_{Ii} is lower—that is, that the wage is countercyclical. Intuitively, the firm and the insiders want to keep the expenses of hiring outsiders down; they therefore lower the wage in states where employment is high. In short, this model implies that the real wage is countercyclical and that it represents the true cost of labor to the firm.

It is easy to think of changes that weaken these results. For example, if there are states in which some insiders are laid off, for those states the contract would equate the marginal product of labor with the opportunity cost of insiders' time rather than with the wage. Similarly, if there is not an unlimited supply of outsiders, this would tend to make the wage increasing rather than decreasing in A. Such changes, however, do not entirely undo the result that insider-outsider considerations reduce the cyclical sensitivity of the marginal cost of labor to firms.

The critical assumption of the model is that the outsiders' and insiders' wages are linked. Without this link, the firm can hire outsiders at the prevailing economy-wide wage. With inelastic labor supply, that wage is low in recessions and high in booms, and so the marginal cost of labor to the firm is highly procyclical.

The insider-outsider literature has not made a definitive case that outsiders' and insiders' wages are linked. Gottfries argues that such a link arises from the facts that the firm must be given some freedom to discharge insiders who are incompetent or shirking and that an excessive gap between insiders' and outsiders' wages would give the firm an incentive to take advantage of this freedom. Blanchard and Summers (1986) argue that the insiders are reluctant to allow the hiring of large numbers of outsiders at a low wage because they realize that, over time, such a policy would result in the outsiders controlling the bargaining process. But it is far from clear that tying insiders' and outsiders' wages is the best way of dealing with these problems. If the economy-wide wage is sometimes far below $w_I - c$, tying the insiders' and outsiders' wages is very costly. The firms and the insiders might therefore be better off if they instead agreed to some limitation on the firm's ability to hire outsiders, or if they charged new hires a fee (and let the fee vary with the gap between w_I and the economy-wide wage). Thus we can conclude only that *if* a link between insiders' and outsiders' wages can be established, insider-outsider considerations have potentially important implications.

Unemployment

If the entire labor market is characterized by insider power, greater insider power reduces employment by raising the wage and causing firms to move up their labor demand curves. Thus in this case the insider-outsider distinction provides a candidate explanation of unemployment.

The more realistic case, however, is for there to be insider power only in part of the labor market, with the rest relatively competitive. But even in this case, insider power can increase average unemployment. When some sectors offer higher wages than others, workers have an incentive to try to obtain jobs in those sectors. New entrants to the labor market are therefore slower to accept jobs in the competitive sector, and workers who have been laid off from the high-wage sector accept longer spells of unemployment before they give up hope of returning to their old jobs.[21]

This reasoning suggests that the contracting considerations investigated in Section 10.5 may also increase average unemployment. In the model analyzed there, the employment of the workers represented in the contracts is efficient. But we ignored the issues of whether such arrangements cover

---

[21]See Problems 10.11 through 10.13 for examples of the effects of wage dispersion.

the entire economy, and of how workers come to be represented in such arrangements. If there are two sectors, one with explicit or implicit contracts and one with employment and wages largely determined competitively, and if workers fare better in the contract sector, then again they have an incentive to accept greater unemployment to increase their chances of obtaining these high-quality jobs.

There is relatively little evidence concerning how important these mechanisms are to actual unemployment. Summers (1986b) argues that such *wait unemployment* is central to the determination of average unemployment. He presents evidence both across U.S. states and over time that general measures of wage dispersion and measures of wage differences between "high-quality" and "low-quality" jobs are strongly associated with differences in average unemployment rates. This is precisely what one would expect if workers' efforts to obtain jobs paying more than the market-clearing wage are an important source of unemployment. Thus the limited evidence we have suggests these models may offer a promising route to understanding unemployment.

10.7 Hysteresis

One of the building blocks of the previous model is the assumption that the insiders are always employed. This assumption is likely to fail in some situations, however. Most importantly, if the insiders' bargaining power is sufficiently great, they will set the wage high enough to risk some unemployment: if the insiders are fully employed with certainty, there is a benefit but not a cost to them of raising the wage further. In addition, unusually large negative shocks to labor demand are likely to lead to some unemployment among the insiders.

Variations in employment can give rise to dynamics in the number of insiders. Under many institutional arrangements, workers who become unemployed eventually lose a say in wage-setting; likewise, workers who are hired eventually gain a role in bargaining. Thus a fall in employment caused by a decline in labor demand is likely to reduce the number of insiders, and a rise in employment is likely to increase the number of insiders. These changes in the number of insiders then affect future wage-setting and employment.

These ideas are developed formally by Blanchard and Summers (1986).[22] Blanchard and Summers focus on Europe in the 1980s, where, they argue, the conditions for these effects to be relevant were satisfied: workers had a great deal of power in wage-setting, there were large negative shocks, and the rules and institutions led to some extent to the disenfranchisement from the bargaining process of workers who lost their jobs .

---

[22]See also Gregory (1986) and Blanchard and Summers (1987).

Assumptions

We consider a simplified version of Blanchard and Summers's model. The wage is set unilaterally by the insiders, and employment is chosen by the firm. The number of insiders in one period is determined by the previous period's employment; thus

$$N_{It} = L_{t-1}. \tag{10.58}$$

For simplicity, both the insiders and the firm neglect the impact of their decisions on the future number of insiders; thus they maximize their current-period objective functions each period.

The representative firm's profits are

$$\pi_t = A_t L_t^\alpha - w_t L_t, \qquad 0 < \alpha < 1, \tag{10.59}$$

where we assume for simplicity that all workers are paid the same wage, regardless of whether they are insiders.[23] The first-order condition for the firm's choice of employment is

$$\alpha A_t L_t^{\alpha-1} = w_t. \tag{10.60}$$

Solving (10.60) for L yields the labor demand curve:

$$L_t = \left(\frac{1}{\alpha A_t}\right)^{1/(\alpha-1)} w_t^{1/(\alpha-1)}$$

$$\equiv C_t w_t^{-\beta}. \tag{10.61}$$

Shocks to labor demand are modeled by assuming that A is random, which implies that C is random. Specifically, C_t is assumed to take the form

$$C_t = C_t^0 \varepsilon_t, \tag{10.62}$$

where C_t^0 is a component of C_t that is known when workers set the wage and ε_t is an i.i.d. random shock that is determined after w_t is set.

In setting the wage, the insiders face a tradeoff between the expected fraction of the membership that is employed and the wage conditional on being employed. To see the consequences of endogenous changes in the number of insiders in the strongest possible form, assume that the insiders' period-t objective function is the expected fraction of the insiders who are employed times utility conditional on being employed, and that this utility takes the form w_t^b ($0 < b < 1$). Since the insiders are assumed to be hired first and the number of insiders hired cannot exceed the number available, insider employment is the smaller of total employment and the number of

---

[23] Assuming that insiders' and outsiders' wages differ by a constant, as in Section 10.6, has no important implications for the analysis.

insiders. These assumptions imply that the period-t objective function is

$$u_t = E\left[\min\left\{\frac{L_t}{N_{It}}, 1\right\}\right] w_t^b. \tag{10.63}$$

Note that we are implicitly assuming that the unemployed get no utility; the effects of relaxing this assumption are discussed below.

Implications

To analyze the model, begin by substituting (10.61) for L_t and (10.62) for C_t into (10.63). This yields

$$u_t = E\left[\min\left\{\frac{C_t^0 \varepsilon_t w_t^{-\beta}}{N_{It}}, 1\right\}\right] w_t^b. \tag{10.64}$$

Next, define $x_t = (C_t^0/N_{It}) w_t^{-\beta}$; x_t is the ratio of employment to the number of insiders if $\varepsilon_t = 1$. With this definition, w_t^b equals $x_t^{-b/\beta}(C_t^0/N_{It})^{b/\beta}$. Thus (10.64) becomes

$$u_t = E[\min\{\varepsilon_t x_t, 1\}] x_t^{-b/\beta} \left(\frac{C_t^0}{N_{It}}\right)^{b/\beta}. \tag{10.65}$$

N_{It}, the number of insiders, and C_t^0, the expected position of labor demand, affect the objective function only multiplicatively. Thus they cannot affect the value of x_t that maximizes the objective function. The insiders therefore choose the same value of x each period. If x^* denotes this optimal value, the definition of x implies that the insiders' choice of w_t is

$$w_t = \left(\frac{N_{It} x^*}{C_t^0}\right)^{-1/\beta}, \tag{10.66}$$

The labor-demand equation, (10.61), then implies that employment is

$$L_t = \varepsilon_t N_{It} x^*. \tag{10.67}$$

Equations (10.66) and (10.67) imply that insiders adjust to changes in labor demand and to the number of insiders (that is, to changes in C^0 and N_I) only by adjusting the wage, and not by altering the probability of employment. Concretely, consider the effects of a low realization of ε. The unexpectedly low level of labor demand causes the firm to hire relatively few workers, and so the number of insiders falls. When the remaining insiders decide on the wage for the following period, they can afford to set a higher wage, since there are fewer of them for the firm to employ. Thus the one-time shock to labor demand—the low value of ε—has a long-lasting effect on employment. With workers' objective function and the firm's profit function taking the specific functional forms we have assumed, the effect is permanent: as (10.67) shows, the fall in employment is passed fully into reduced employment in the following period—and hence in all subsequent periods as well.

Since it is the unpredictable movements in demand—the ε's—that have permanent effects, the model implies that employment is a *random walk with drift*. That is, the change in employment equals a constant term (reflecting the fact that expected employment can be either more or less than N_{It}) plus an unpredictable component. If insiders determine wages only in some sectors, only employment in these sectors behaves this way. But if insiders set wages in virtually all of the labor market, then it is aggregate employment that follows a random walk with drift. Blanchard and Summers argue that this latter prediction accords well with Europe's experience in the 1980s, and that the mechanism outlined here provides a likely explanation.

Extensions

Forward-looking behavior by the insiders and the firm does not alter the central result of the model. The knowledge that this period's hiring affects next period's number of insiders increases the firm's hiring for a given wage (so that workers set lower wages in the future), and moderates the insiders' wage-setting for a given labor demand curve (to ensure that they remain insiders). But the changes in the number of insiders, given the functional forms for utility and profits, still cause shocks to have permanent effects.

Similarly, more complicated rules for insider status lead to more interesting dynamics but do not eliminate the permanent component of employment fluctuations. Suppose, for example, that it takes two periods of unemployment to lose one's position as an insider. Then a negative shock to labor demand does not immediately lead to a higher wage. (Indeed, if the insiders are forward-looking, it leads to a fall in the wage as the unemployed insiders try to keep their insider status.) But a second negative shock leads to a fall in the number of insiders, which has a permanent effect on the paths of the wage and employment. Formally, the wage and employment still have a unit root. One implication of this discussion is that a fall in aggregate demand that is only moderately long—such as the one experienced by the United States in the early 1980s—may not have a permanent effect on unemployment, but an extended one— such as those experienced by many European countries in the same period—may.

Other plausible changes in the model, however, eliminate the strong result that one-time shocks have permanent effects on employment. Suppose, for example, we modify the insiders' objective function, (10.63), to include positive utility in the event of unemployment. Then it is less attractive for the insiders to reduce the wage to increase the probability of employment when the number of insiders is large and the wage is low than it is when the number of insiders is small. Similarly, if the firm has some bargaining power or the outsiders have some weight in the insiders' objective function, the wage does not rise to fully offset reductions in the number of insiders.

Under plausible assumptions, introducing considerations like these causes employment to return gradually to its initial level after a one-time demand shock. Without membership dynamics, however, employment returns immediately to its initial level. Thus making the number of insiders endogenous still has important implications for the dynamics of employment.

Situations where one-time disturbances permanently affect the path of the economy are said to exhibit *hysteresis*. In the context of unemployment, two sources of hysteresis other than the insider-outsider considerations we have been examining have received considerable attention. One is deterioration of skills: workers who are unemployed do not acquire additional on-the-job training, and their existing human capital may decay or become obsolete. As a result, workers who lose their jobs when labor demand falls may have difficulty finding work when demand recovers, particularly if the downturn is extended. The second additional source of hysteresis is through labor-force attachment. Workers who are unemployed for extended periods may adjust their standard of living to the lower level provided by income-maintenance programs; in addition, a long period of high unemployment may reduce the social stigma of extended joblessness. Because of these effects, labor supply may be permanently lower when demand returns to normal.

10.8   Search and Matching Models

The final departure of the labor market from Walrasian assumptions that we consider is the simple fact that workers and jobs are heterogeneous. In a frictionless labor market, firms are indifferent about losing their workers, since identical workers are costlessly available at the same wage; likewise, workers are indifferent about losing their jobs. These implications do not appear to be accurate descriptions of actual labor markets.

When workers and jobs are highly heterogeneous, the labor market has little resemblance to a Walrasian market. Rather than meeting in centralized markets where employment and wages are determined by the intersections of supply and demand curves, workers and firms meet in a decentralized, one-on-one fashion, and engage in a costly process of trying to match up idiosyncratic preferences, skills, and needs. Since this process is not instantaneous, it results in some unemployment. In addition, it may have implications for how wages and employment respond to shocks.

This section presents a model of firm and worker heterogeneity and the matching process. Because modeling heterogeneity requires abandoning many of our usual tools, even a basic model is relatively complicated. As a result, the model here only introduces some of the issues involved.[24]

The Model

The economy consists of workers and jobs. Workers can be either employed or unemployed, and jobs can be either filled or vacant. The numbers of employed and unemployed workers are denoted E and U, and the numbers of filled and vacant jobs are denoted F and V. Each job can have at most one worker. Thus F and E must be equal. The labor force is fixed at $\bar{L}$; thus $E + U = \bar{L}$. Throughout, we consider only steady states.

The number of jobs is endogenous. Specifically, vacancies can be created or eliminated freely; there is a fixed cost of C per unit time, however, of maintaining a job (either filled or vacant). C can be thought of as reflecting the cost of capital.

The model is set in continuous time. When a worker is employed, he or she produces output at rate A per unit time and is paid a wage of w per unit time. A is exogenous and is assumed to be greater than C; w is determined endogenously. For simplicity, costs of effort and of job search are ignored. Thus a worker's utility per unit time is w if employed, and zero if unemployed. Similarly profits per unit time from a job are $A - w - C$ if it is filled, and $-C$ if it is vacant.

The key assumptions of the model concern how workers become employed. Positive levels of unemployment and vacancies can coexist without being immediately eliminated by hiring. Instead, unemployment and vacancies are assumed to yield a flow of new jobs at some rate per unit time:

$$M = M(U, V)$$

$$= KU^{\beta}V^{\gamma}, \qquad 0 \le \beta \le 1, \quad 0 \le \gamma \le 1.$$

(10.68)

The *matching function*, (10.68), proxies for the complicated process of employer recruitment, worker search, and mutual evaluation. It is not assumed to exhibit constant returns to scale. When it exhibits increasing returns ($\beta + \gamma > 1$), there are *thick-market effects*: increasing the level of search makes the matching process operate more effectively, in the sense that it yields more output (matches) per unit of input (unemployment and vacancies). When the matching function has decreasing returns ($\beta + \gamma < 1$), there are *crowding effects*.

In addition to the flow of new matches, there is turnover in existing jobs. As in the Shapiro–Stiglitz model, jobs end at an exogenous rate b per unit time. Thus the dynamics of the number of employed workers are given by

---

[24]For examples of search and matching models, see Diamond (1982); Pissarides (1985); Mortenson (1986); Howitt (1988); Blanchard and Diamond (1989); and Hosios (1990). The model in this section is closest to Pissarides's.

$\dot{E} = M(U, V) - bE$. Since we are focusing on steady states, M and E must satisfy

$$M(U, V) = bE. \qquad (10.69)$$

Let a denote the rate per unit time that unemployed workers find jobs, and α the rate per unit time that vacant jobs are filled. a and α are given by

$$a = \frac{M(U, V)}{U}, \qquad (10.70)$$

$$\alpha = \frac{M(U, V)}{V}. \qquad (10.71)$$

As in the Shapiro-Stiglitz model, we use dynamic programming to describe the values of the various states. The "return" on being employed is a "dividend" of w per unit time minus the probability b per unit time of a "capital loss" of $V_E - V_U$. Thus,

$$rV_E = w - b(V_E - V_U), \qquad (10.72)$$

where r is the interest rate (see equation [10.30] for comparison). Similar reasoning implies

$$rV_F = (A - w - C) - b(V_F - V_V), \qquad (10.73)$$

$$rV_U = a(V_E - V_U), \qquad (10.74)$$

$$rV_V = -C + \alpha(V_F - V_V). \qquad (10.75)$$

Two conditions complete the model. First, when an unemployed worker meets a firm with a vacancy, they must choose a wage. It must be high enough that the worker wants to work in the job, and low enough that the employer wants to hire the worker. Because neither party can find a replacement instantaneously, however, these requirements do not uniquely determine the wage; instead, there is a range of wages that makes both parties better off than if they had not met. We assume that the worker and the employer set the wage so that each of them gets the same gain.[25] That is,

$$V_E - V_U = V_F - V_V. \qquad (10.76)$$

Second, as described above, new vacancies can be created and eliminated costlessly. Thus the value of a vacancy must be zero.

Without the frictions, the model is simple. Labor supply is perfectly inelastic at $\bar{L}$, and labor demand is perfectly elastic at $A - C$. Thus, since $A - C > 0$ by assumption, there is full employment at this wage. Shifts in

---

[25]See Problem 10.15 for the implications of alternative assumptions about how the surplus is divided.

labor demand—changes in A—lead to immediate changes in the wage and leave employment unchanged.

Solving the Model

We solve the model by focusing on two variables, employment (E) and the value of a vacancy (V_V). Our procedure will be to find the value of V_V implied by a given level of employment, and then to impose the free-entry condition that V_V must be zero.

We begin by considering the determination of the wage and the value of a vacancy given a and α. Subtracting (10.74) from (10.72) and rearranging yields

$$V_E - V_U = \frac{w}{a + b + r}. \qquad (10.77)$$

Similarly, (10.73) and (10.75) imply

$$V_F - V_V = \frac{A - w}{\alpha + b + r}. \qquad (10.78)$$

Since our splitting-the-surplus assumption (equation [10.76]) implies that $V_E - V_U$ and $V_F - V_V$ are equal, (10.77) and (10.78) imply

$$\frac{w}{a + b + r} = \frac{A - w}{\alpha + b + r}. \qquad (10.79)$$

Solving this condition for w yields

$$w = \frac{(a + b + r)A}{a + \alpha + 2b + 2r}. \qquad (10.80)$$

Equation (10.80) implies that when a and α are equal, the firm and the worker divide the output from the job equally. When a exceeds α, workers can find new jobs more rapidly than firms can find new employees, and so more than half of the output goes to the worker. When α exceeds a, the reverse occurs.

Recall that we want to focus on the value of a vacancy. Equation (10.75) states that rV_V equals $-C + \alpha(V_F - V_V)$, and the splitting-the-surplus assumption implies that $V_F - V_V$ equals $V_E - V_U$. Thus rV_V equals $-C + \alpha(V_E - V_U)$. Substituting expression (10.80) for w into (10.77) for $V_E - V_U$ implies

$$V_E - V_U = \frac{A}{a + \alpha + 2b + 2r}. \qquad (10.81)$$

Thus,

$$rV_V = -C + \frac{\alpha A}{a + \alpha + 2b + 2r}.$$ (10.82)

Equation (10.82) expresses V_V in terms of C, A, r, b, a, and α. a and α, however, are endogenous. Thus the next step is to express them in terms of E. The facts that $a = M(U,V)/U$ (equation [10.70]), that $M = bE$ (equation [10.69]), and that $E + U = \overline{L}$ imply

$$a = \frac{bE}{\overline{L} - E}.$$ (10.83)

Similarly, (10.71) implies

$$\alpha = \frac{M(U,V)}{V}$$

$$= \frac{bE}{\{bE/[K(\overline{L} - E)^\beta]\}^{1/\gamma}}$$ (10.84)

$$= K^{1/\gamma}(bE)^{(\gamma-1)/\gamma}(\overline{L} - E)^{\beta/\gamma},$$

where the second line uses the matching function, (10.68), to substitute for V.

Equations (10.83) and (10.84) imply that a is increasing in E and that α is decreasing. Thus (10.82) implies that V_V is a decreasing function of E. As E approaches $\overline{L}$, a approaches infinity and α approaches zero; hence V_V approaches $-C/r$. Similarly, as E approaches zero, a approaches zero and α approaches infinity. Thus in this case V_V approaches $(A - C)/r$, which we have assumed to be positive. This information is summarized in Figure 10.6.

The equilibrium level of employment is determined by the intersection of the V_V locus with the free-entry condition, $V_V = 0$. Imposing this condition on (10.82) and using (10.83) and (10.84) to substitute for a and α yields

$$\frac{K^{1/\gamma}(bE)^{(\gamma-1)/\gamma}(\overline{L} - E)^{\beta/\gamma}}{[bE/(\overline{L} - E)] + K^{1/\gamma}(bE)^{(\gamma-1)/\gamma}(\overline{L} - E)^{\beta/\gamma} + 2b + 2r} A = C.$$ (10.85)

This expression implicitly defines E, and thus completes the solution of the model.

The Impact of a Shift in Labor Demand

We now want to ask our usual question of whether the imperfection we are considering—in this case, the absence of a centralized market—affects

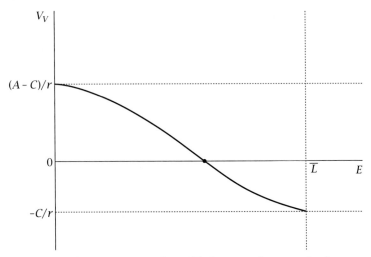

FIGURE 10.6   The determination of equilibrium employment in the search and matching model

the cyclical behavior of the labor market. Specifically, we are interested in whether it causes a shift in labor demand to have a larger impact on employment and a smaller impact on the wage than it does in a Walrasian market.

To address this question, begin by considering the steady-state effects of a fall in A. From (10.82) or (10.85), this shifts the V_V locus down. Thus, as Figure 10.7 shows, employment falls. In a Walrasian market, in contrast, employment is unchanged at $\bar{L}$. Intuitively, in the absence of a frictionless market, workers are not costlessly available at the prevailing wage. The decline in A, with C fixed, raises firms' costs of searching for workers relative to the profits they obtain when they find one. Thus the number of firms—and hence employment—falls.

In addition, the matching function (10.68), together with the fact that $M(U, V)$ equals bE is steady state, implies that steady-state vacancies are $(bE/K)^{1/\gamma}/(\bar{L}-E)^{\beta/\gamma}$. Thus the decline in A and the resulting decrease in the number of firms reduce vacancies. The model therefore implies a negative relation between unemployment and vacancies—a *Beveridge curve*.

The model does not imply substantial wage rigidity, however. From (10.83) and (10.84), the fall in E causes a to fall and α to rise: when unemployment is higher, workers cannot find jobs as easily as before, and firms can fill positions more rapidly. From (10.80), this implies that the wage falls more than proportionately with A.[26]

The dynamics of the transition between the two steady states are also of interest. Since there is no reason for firms whose positions are filled to

---

[26]Since $w = A - C$ in the Walrasian market, the same result holds there. Thus it is not clear which case exhibits greater wage adjustment. Nonetheless, simply adding heterogeneity and matching does not appear to generate strong wage rigidity.

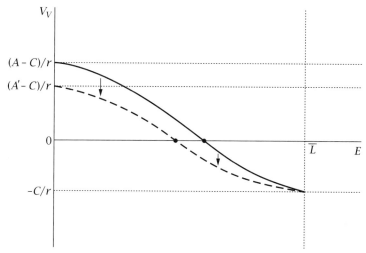

FIGURE 10.7   The effects of a fall in labor demand in the search and matching model

discharge their workers, employment and unemployment do not change discontinuously at the time of the shock. The reduced attractiveness of hiring, in contrast, causes V_V to fall unless some firms exit. Thus there is exit, and hence a discontinuous drop in V. In practice, this could take the form of some firms with openings stopping their attempts to fill them.

With employment and unemployment the same as before but vacancies lower, the flows into employment exceed the outflows, and so unemployment rises. Thus the fall in A leads only to a gradual rise in unemployment. Finally, as unemployment rises, the value of a vacancy would rise if vacancies did not change; thus vacancies must rise as unemployment rises. This implies that the initial drop in V exceeds its steady-state response—that is, that there is overshooting.

A temporary change in A leads to smaller employment responses. The value of a filled job is clearly higher when A is temporarily low than when it is permanently low. Thus there is a smaller fall in the number of vacancies, and hence a smaller rise in unemployment. In the extreme case of an infinitesimally brief decline in A, V_V and V_U are unaffected. In this case, firms and workers simply share the loss equally by reducing the wage by half the amount that A falls, and there is no impact on employment or unemployment.[27]

In short, although search and matching considerations have interesting implications for the functioning of labor markets, this model of them does

---

[27]In addition, as first pointed out by Oi (1962), the fact that a firm cannot costlessly replace its workers makes it more reluctant to discharge workers in response to a temporary downturn if the marginal product of labor falls below the disutility of working. Thus in this case frictions and heterogeneity dampen the response of employment to shocks.

not suggest that they crucially change the cyclical behavior of the wage and employment.

Unemployment

Search and matching models offer a straightforward explanation for average unemployment: it may be the result of continually matching workers and jobs in a complex and changing economy. Thus, much of observed unemployment may reflect what is traditionally known as *frictional* unemployment.

Labor markets are characterized by high rates of turnover. In U.S. manufacturing, for example, over 3% of workers leave their jobs in a typical month. Moreover, many job changes are associated with wage increases, particularly for young workers (Topel and Ward, 1992); thus at least some of the turnover appears to be useful. In addition, there is high turnover of jobs themselves. In U.S. manufacturing, at least 10% of existing jobs disappear each year (Davis and Haltiwanger, 1990, 1992). These statistics suggest that a nonnegligible portion of unemployment is a largely inevitable result of the dynamics of the economy and the complexities of the labor market.[28]

Unfortunately, it is difficult to go much beyond this general statement. Existing theoretical models and empirical evidence do not provide any clear way of discriminating between, for example, the hypothesis that search and matching considerations account for one-quarter of average unemployment and the hypothesis that they account for three-quarters. The importance of long-term unemployment in overall unemployment suggests, however, that at least some significant part of unemployment is not frictional. In the United States, although most workers who become unemployed remain so for less than a month, most of the workers who are unemployed at any time will have spells of unemployment that last more than three months; and nearly half will have spells that last more than six months (Clark and Summers, 1979). And in the European Community in the late 1980s, more than half of unemployed workers had been out of work for more than a year (Bean, 1994). It seems unlikely that search and matching considerations could be the source of most of this long-term unemployment.

Welfare

Because this economy is not Walrasian, firms' decisions concerning whether to enter have externalities both for workers and for other firms. Entry makes it easier for unemployed workers to find jobs, and increases their bargaining power when they do. But it also makes it harder for other firms to find workers, and decreases their bargaining power when they do.

---

[28]See also the literature on sectoral shocks discussed in Section 4.10.

As a result, there is no presumption that equilibrium unemployment in this economy is efficient. In one natural special case, for example, whether equilibrium unemployment is inefficiently high or inefficiently low depends on whether γ, the exponent on vacancies in the matching function (equation [10.68]), is more or less than one-half (see Problem 10.17).

Such ambiguous welfare effects are characteristic of economies where allocations are determined through one-on-one meetings rather than through centralized markets. In our model, there is only one endogenous decision—firms must decide whether to enter—and hence only one dimension along which the equilibrium can be inefficient. But in practice, participants in such markets have many choices. Workers can decide whether to enter the labor force, how intensively to look for jobs when they are unemployed, where to focus their search, whether to invest in job-specific or general skills when they are employed, whether to look for a different job while they are employed, and so on. Firms face a similar array of decisions. There is no guarantee that the decentralized economy produces an efficient outcome along any of these dimensions. Instead, agents' decisions are likely to have externalities either through direct effects on other parties' surplus or through effects on the effectiveness of the matching process, or both (see, for example, Mortenson, 1986).

This analysis implies that there is no reason to suppose that the natural rate of unemployment is optimal. This observation provides no guidance, however, concerning whether observed unemployment is inefficiently high, inefficiently low, or approximately efficient. Determining which of these cases is correct—and whether there are changes in policy that would lead to efficiency-enhancing changes in equilibrium unemployment—is an important open question.

10.9 Empirical Applications

Contracting Effects on Employment

In our analysis of contracts in Section 10.5, we discussed two views of how employment can be determined when the wage is set by bargaining. In the first, a firm and its workers bargain only over the wage, and the firm chooses employment to equate the marginal product of labor with the agreed-upon wage. But, as we saw, this arrangement is inefficient. Thus the second view is that the bargaining determines how both employment and the wage depend on the conditions facing the firm. Since actual contracts do not spell out such arrangements, this view assumes that workers and the firm have some noncontractual understanding that the firm will not treat the cost of labor as being given by the wage. For example, workers are likely to agree to lower wages in future contracts if the firm chooses employment to equate the marginal product of labor with the opportunity cost of workers' time.

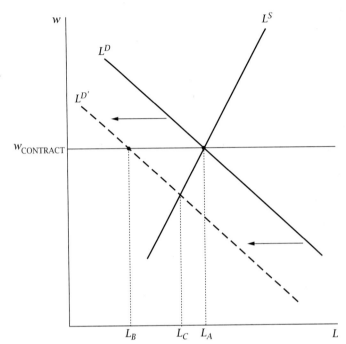

FIGURE 10.8   Employment movements under wage contracts

Which of these views is correct has important implications. If firms choose employment freely taking the wage as given, evidence that nominal wages are fixed for extended periods provides direct evidence that nominal disturbances have real effects. If the wage is unimportant to employment determination, on the other hand, nominal wage rigidity is unimportant to the effects of nominal shocks.

Bils (1991) proposes a way to test between the two views (see also Card, 1990). If employment is determined efficiently, then it equates the marginal product of labor and the marginal disutility of work at each date. Thus its behavior should not have any systematic relation to the times that firms and workers bargain.[29] A finding that movements in employment are related to the dates of contracts—for example, that employment rises unusually rapidly or slowly just after contracts are signed, or that it is more variable over the life of a contract than from one contract to the next—would therefore be evidence that it is not determined efficiently.

In addition, Bils shows that the alternative view that employment equates the marginal product of labor with the wage makes a specific prediction about how employment movements are likely to be related to the times of contracts. Consider Figure 10.8, which shows the marginal product of labor, the marginal disutility of labor, and a contract wage. In

---

[29]This is not precisely correct if there are income effects on the marginal disutility of labor. Bils argues, however, that these effects are unlikely to be important to his test.

response to a negative shock to labor demand, a firm that views the cost of labor as being given by the contract wage reduces employment a great deal; in terms of the figure, it reduces employment from L_A to L_B. The marginal product of labor now exceeds the opportunity cost of workers' time. Thus when the firm and the workers negotiate a new contract, they will make sure that employment is increased; in terms of the diagram, they will act to raise employment from L_B to L_C. Thus if the wage determines employment (and if shocks to labor demand are the main source of employment fluctuations), changes in employment during contracts should be partly reversed when new contracts are signed.

To test between the predictions of these two views, Bils examines employment fluctuations in U.S. manufacturing industries. Specifically, he focuses on twelve industries that are highly unionized and where there are long-term contracts that are signed at virtually the same time for the vast majority of workers in the industry. He estimates a regression of the form

$$\Delta \ln L_{i,t} = \alpha_i - \phi Z_{i,t} - \theta(\ln L_{i,t-1} - \ln L_{i,t-10}) + \Gamma D_{i,t} + \varepsilon_{i,t}. \quad (10.86)$$

Here i indexes industries, L is employment, and $D_{i,t}$ is a dummy variable equal to 1 in quarters when a new contract goes into effect in industry i. The key variable is $Z_{i,t}$. If a new contract goes into effect in industry i in quarter t (that is, if $D_{i,t} = 1$), $Z_{i,t}$ equals the change in log employment in the industry over the life of the previous contract; otherwise, $Z_{i,t}$ is zero. The parameter ϕ therefore measures the extent to which employment changes over the life of a contract are reversed when a new contract is signed. Bils includes $\ln L_{i,t-1} - \ln L_{i,t-10}$ to control for the possibility that employment changes are typically reversed even in the absence of new contracts; he chooses $t - 10$ because the average contract in his sample lasts ten quarters. Finally, $D_{i,t}$ allows for the possibility of unusual employment growth in the first quarter of a new contract.

Bils's estimates are $\phi = 0.198$ (with a standard error of 0.037), $\theta = 0.016$ (0.012), and $\Gamma = -0.0077$ (0.0045). Thus the results suggest highly significant and quantitatively large movements in employment related to the dates of new contracts: when a new contract is signed, on average 20% of the employment changes over the life of the previous contract are immediately reversed.

There is one puzzling feature of Bils's results, however. When a new contract is signed, the most natural way to undo an inefficient employment change during the previous contract is by adjusting the wage. In the case of the fall in labor demand shown in Figure 10.8, for example, the wage should be lowered when the new contract is signed. But Bils finds little relation between how the wage is set in a new contract and the change in employment over the life of the previous contract. In addition, when he looks across industries, he finds essentially no relation between the extent to which employment changes are reversed when a new contract is signed and the extent to which the wage is adjusted.

Bils suggests two possible explanations of this finding. One is that adjustments in compensation mainly take the form of changes to fringe benefits and other factors that are not captured by his wage measure. The second
is that employment determination is more complex than either of the two
views we have been considering.

Interindustry Wage Differences

The basic idea of efficiency-wage models is that firms may pay wages
above market-clearing levels. If there are reasons for firms to do this, those
reasons are unlikely to be equally important everywhere in the economy.
Motivated by this observation, Dickens and Katz (1987a) and Krueger and
Summers (1988) investigate whether some industries pay systematically
higher wages than others.[30]

These authors begin by adding dummy variables for the industries that
workers are employed in to conventional wage regressions. A typical specification is

$$\ln w_i = \alpha + \sum_{j=1}^{M} \beta_j X_{ij} + \sum_{k=1}^{N} \gamma_k D_{ik} + \varepsilon_i, \qquad (10.87)$$

where w_i is worker i's wage, the X_{ij}'s are worker characteristics (such as
age, education, occupation, and so on), and the D_{ik}'s are dummy variables
for employment in different industries. In a competitive, frictionless labor
market, wages depend only on workers' characteristics and not on what
industry they are employed in. Thus if the X's adequately capture workers'
characteristics, the coefficients on the industry dummies will be zero.

Dickens and Katz's and Krueger and Summers's basic finding is that the
estimated γ_k's are large. Katz and Summers (1989), for example, consider
wage differences among U.S. workers in 1984 across *two-digit* industries.[31]
Since Katz and Summers consider a sample of over 100,000 workers, it is
not surprising that they find that most of the γ's are highly significant. But
they also find that they are quantitatively large. For example, the standard
deviation of the estimated γ's (weighted by the sizes of the industries) is
0.15, or 15%. Thus wages appear to differ considerably among industries.

Dickens and Katz and Krueger and Summers show that several possible
explanations of these wage differences are contradicted by the data. The
estimated differences are essentially the same when the sample is restricted

---

[30]See Katz and Summers (1989, pp. 216–247) for a summary of this literature. Groshen
(1991) examines wage differences among firms within industries.

[31]Two-digit industries refers to the Standard Industrial Classification (or SIC). One-digit
industries are very broad industries, such as durable goods manufacturing, communica-
tions, and retail trade. Two- digit industries are narrower classifications within these broad
groups; for example, two-digit industries within durable goods manufacturing include furniture and motor vehicles. Three-, four-, and five-digit industries are even finer distinctions.

to workers not covered by union contracts; thus they do not appear to be the result of union bargaining power. The differences are quite stable over time and across countries; thus they are unlikely to reflect transitory adjustments in the labor market (Krueger and Summers, 1987). When broader measures of compensation are used, the estimated differences typically become larger; thus the results do not appear to arise from differences in the mix of wage and nonwage compensation across industries. Finally, there is no evidence that working conditions are worse in the high-wage industries; thus the differences do not appear to be compensating differentials.

There is also some direct evidence that the differences represent genuine rents. Krueger and Summers (1988) and Akerlof, Rose, and Yellen (1988) find that workers in industries with higher estimated wage premia quit much less often. Krueger and Summers also find that workers who move from one industry to another on average have their wages change by nearly as much as the difference between the estimated wage premia for the two industries. And Gibbons and Katz (1992) consider workers who lose their jobs because the plants they are working at close. They find that the wage cuts the workers take when they accept new jobs are much higher when the jobs they lost were in higher-wage industries.

Two aspects of the results are more problematic for efficiency-wage theory, however. First, although many competitive explanations of the results are not supported at all by the data, there is one that cannot be readily dismissed. No wage equation can control for all relevant worker characteristics. Thus one possible explanation of the finding of apparent interindustry wage differences is that they reflect unmeasured differences in ability across workers in different industries rather than rents.[32]

To understand this idea, imagine an econometrician studying wage differences among baseball leagues. If the econometrician could only control for the kinds of worker characteristics that studies of interindustry wage differences control for—age, experience, and so on—he or she would find that wages are systematically higher in some leagues than in others: major-league teams pay more than AAA minor-league teams, which pay more than AA minor-league teams, and so on. In addition, quit rates are much lower in the higher-wage leagues, and workers who move from lower-wage to higher-wage leagues experience large wage increases. But there is little doubt that large parts of the wage differences among baseball leagues reflect ability differences rather than rents. Just as an econometrician using Dickens and Katz and Krueger and Summers's methods to study interleague wage differences in baseball would be led astray, perhaps econometricians studying interindustry wage differences have also been led astray.

Several pieces of evidence support this view. First, if some firms are paying more than the market-clearing wage, they face an excess supply of workers, and so they have some discretion to hire more able workers. Thus it would be surprising if at least some of the estimated wage differences did

---

[32]See, for example, Murphy and Topel (1987b); Hall (1989); and Topel (1989).

not reflect ability differences. Second, higher-wage industries have higher capital-labor ratios, which suggests that they need more skilled workers. Third, workers in higher-wage industries have higher measured ability (in terms of education, experience, and so on); thus it seems likely that they have higher unmeasured ability. Finally, the same patterns of interindustry earnings differences occur, although less strongly, among self-employed workers.

The hypothesis that estimated interindustry wage differences reflect unmeasured ability cannot easily account for all of the findings about these differences, however. First, quantitative attempts to estimate how much of the differences can plausibly be due to unmeasured ability generally leave a substantial portion of the differences unaccounted for (see, for example, Katz and Summers, 1989). Second, the unmeasured-ability hypothesis cannot readily explain Gibbons and Katz's findings about the wage cuts of displaced workers. Third, the estimated wage premia are higher in industries where profits are higher; this is not what the unmeasured-ability hypothesis naturally predicts. Finally, industries that pay higher wages generally do so in all occupations, from janitors to managers; it is not clear that unmeasured ability differences should be so strongly related across occupations. Thus, although the view that interindustry wage differences reflect unmeasured ability is troubling for rent-based explanations of those differences, it does not definitively refute them.

The second aspect of this literature's findings that is not easily accounted for by efficiency-wage theories concerns the characteristics of industries that pay high wages. As described above, higher-wage industries tend to have higher capital-labor ratios, more educated and experienced workers, and higher profits. In addition, they have larger establishments, and larger fractions of male and of unionized workers (Dickens and Katz, 1987b). No single efficiency-wage theory predicts all of these patterns. As a result, authors who believe that the estimated interindustry wage differences reflect rents tend to resort to complicated explanations of them. Dickens and Katz and Krueger and Summers, for example, appeal to a combination of efficiency-wage theories based on imperfect monitoring, efficiency-wage theories based on workers' perceptions of fairness, and worker power in wage determination.

In sum, the literature on interindustry wage differences has identified an interesting set of regularities that differ greatly from what simple theories of the labor market predict. The reasons for those regularities, however, have not yet been convincingly identified.

Problems

10.1. Union wage premia and efficiency wages. (Summers, 1988.) Consider the efficiency-wage model analyzed in equations (10.12)–(10.19). Suppose, however, that fraction f of workers belong to unions that are able to obtain a wage that exceeds the nonunion wage by proportion μ. Thus, $w_u = (1+\mu)w_n$, where w_u and w_n denote wages in the union and nonunion sectors; and the average wage, w_a, is given by $fw_u + (1 - f)w_n$. Nonunion employers continue to set their wages freely; thus (by the same reasoning used to derive [10.15] in the text), $w_n = (1 - bu)w_a /(1 - \beta)$.

(a) Find the equilibrium unemployment rate in terms of β, b, f, and μ.

(b) Suppose $\mu = f = 0.15$.

   (i) What is the equilibrium unemployment rate if $\beta = 0.06$ and $b = 1$? By what proportion is the cost of effective labor higher in the union sector than in the nonunion sector?

   (ii) Repeat part (i) for the case of $\beta = 0.03$ and $b = 0.5$.

10.2. Efficiency wages and bargaining. Summers (1988, p. 386) states "In an efficiency wage environment, firms that are forced to pay their workers premium wages suffer only second-order losses. In almost any plausible bargaining framework, this makes it easier for workers to extract concessions." This problem asks you to investigate this claim.

Consider a firm with profits given by $\pi = (eL)^\alpha /\alpha - wL, 0 < \alpha < 1$, and a union with objective function $U = w - x$, where x is an index of its workers' outside opportunities. Assume that the firm and the union bargain over the wage, and that the firm then chooses L taking w as given.

(a) Suppose that $e \equiv 1$, so that efficiency-wage considerations are absent.

   (i) What value of L does the firm choose given w? What is the resulting level of profits?

   (ii) Suppose that the firm and the union choose w to maximize $U^\gamma \pi^{1-\gamma}$, where $0 < \gamma < \alpha$ indexes the union's power in the bargaining (this is known as the *Nash bargaining solution*). What level of w do they choose?

   (iii) What is $\partial(\ln w)/\partial\gamma$ at $\gamma = 0$?

(b) Suppose that e is given by equation (10.12) in the text: $e = [(w - x)/x]^\beta$ for $w > x$, where $0 < \beta < 1$.

   (i) What value of L does the firm choose given w? What is the resulting level of profits?

   (ii) Suppose that the firm and the union choose w to maximize $U^\gamma \pi^{1-\gamma}, 0 < \gamma < \alpha$. What level of w do they choose? (Hint: for the case of $\beta = 0$, your answer should simplify to your answer in part [a][ii].)

   (iii) What is $\partial(\ln w)/\partial\gamma$ at $\gamma = 0$? Is this elasticity higher with efficiency wages than without, as Summers argues? Is the impact of bargaining on the wage qualitatively different with efficiency wages, as Summers implies?

10.3 Describe how each of the following affect equilibrium employment and the wage in the Shapiro–Stiglitz model:

(a) An increase in workers' discount rate, ρ.

(*b*) An increase in the job breakup rate, b.

(*c*) A positive multiplicative shock to the production function (that is, suppose the production function is $AF(L)$, and consider an increase in A).

(*d*) An increase in the size of the labor force, $\bar{L}$.

10.4 Suppose that in the Shapiro–Stiglitz model, unemployed workers are hired according to how long they have been unemployed rather than at random; specifically, suppose that workers who have been unemployed the longest are hired first.

(*a*) Consider a steady state where there is no shirking. Derive an expression for how long it takes a worker who becomes unemployed to get a job as a function of b, L, N, and $\bar{L}$.

(*b*) Let V_U be the value of being a worker who is newly unemployed. Derive an expression for V_U as a function of the time it takes to get a job, workers' discount rate (ρ), and the value of being employed (V_E).

(*c*) Using your answers to parts (*a*) and (*b*), find the no-shirking condition for this version of the model.

(*d*) How, if at all, does the assumption that the longer-term unemployed get priority affect the equilibrium unemployment rate?

10.5 The fair wage-effort hypothesis. (Akerlof and Yellen, 1990.) Suppose there is a large number of firms, N, each with profits given by $F(eL) - wL, F'(\cdot) > 0, F''(\cdot) < 0$. L is the number of workers the firm hires, w is the wage it pays, and e is workers' effort. Effort is given by $e = \min[w/w^*, 1]$, where w^* is the "fair wage"; that is, if workers are paid less than the fair wage, they reduce their effort in proportion to the shortfall. Assume that there are $\bar{L}$ workers who are willing to work at any positive wage.

(*a*) If a firm can hire workers at any wage, what value (or range of values) of w yields the highest profits? For the remainder of the problem, assume that if the firm is indifferent over a range of possible wages, it pays the highest value in this range.

(*b*) Suppose w^* is given by $w^* = \bar{w} + a - bu, b > 0$, where u is the unemployment rate and $\bar{w}$ is the average wage paid by the firms in this economy.

 (*i*) Given your answer to part (*a*), what wage does the representative firm pay if it can choose w freely (taking $\bar{w}$ and u as given)?

 (*ii*) Under what conditions does the equilibrium involve positive unemployment and no constraints on firms' choice of w? (Hint: in this case, equilibrium requires that the representative firm, taking $\bar{w}$ as given, wishes to pay $\bar{w}$.) What is the unemployment rate in this case?

 (*iii*) Under what conditions is there full employment?

(*c*) Suppose the representative firm's production function is modified to be $F(AL_1 + L_2), A > 1$, where L_1 and L_2 are the numbers of high-productivity and low-productivity workers the firm hires. Assume that the fair wage for type-i workers is given by $w_i^* = (\overline{w}_1 + \overline{w}_2)/2 - bu_i$, where $\overline{w}_i$ is the average wage paid to workers of type i and u_i is their unemployment rate. Finally, assume there are $\overline{L}$ workers of each type.

(*i*) In equilibrium, is there unemployment among high-productivity workers? Explain. (Hint: if u_1 is positive, firms are unconstrained in their choice of w_1.)

(*ii*) In equilibrium, is there unemployment among low-productivity workers? Explain.

10.6 Implicit contracts without variable hours. Suppose that each worker must either work a fixed number of hours or be unemployed. Let C_i^E denote the consumption of employed workers in state i, and C_i^U the consumption of unemployed workers. The firm's profits in state i are therefore $A_i F(L_i) - [C_i^E L_i + C_i^U(\overline{L} - L_i)]$, where $\overline{L}$ is the number of workers. Similarly, workers' expected utility in state i is $(L_i/\overline{L})[U(C_i^E) - K] + [(\overline{L} - L_i)/\overline{L}]U(C_i^U)$, where $K > 0$ is the disutility of working.

(*a*) Set up the Lagrangian for the firm's problem of choosing the L_i's, C_i^E's, and C_i^U's to maximize expected profits subject to the constraint that the representative worker's expected utility is u_0.[33]

(*b*) Find the first-order conditions for L_i, C_i^E, and C_i^U. How, if at all, do C^E and C^U depend on the state? What is the relation between C_i^E and C_i^U?

(*c*) After A is realized and some workers are chosen to work and others are chosen to be unemployed, which workers are better off?

10.7 Unemployment insurance. (This follows Feldstein, 1976.) Consider a firm with revenues $AF(L)$. A has two possible values, A_B and A_G ($A_B < A_G$), each of which occurs half the time. Workers who are employed when $A = A_G$ and unemployed when $A = A_B$ receive an unemployment insurance benefit of $B > 0$ when $A = A_B$. Workers are risk-neutral; thus the representative worker's expected utility is $U = (w - K)/2 + \{(L_B/L_G)(w - K) + [(L_G - L_B)/L_G]B\}/2$, where w is the wage (which is assumed without loss of generality to be independent of the state), K is the disutility of working, and L_B and L_G are employment in the two states. The firm's expected profits are $[A_G F(L_G) - wL_G]/2 + [A_B F(L_B) - wL_B - fB(L_G - L_B)]/2$, where f is the fraction of unemployment benefits that are paid by the firm. Assume $0 \le f \le 1$.[34]

(*a*) Set up the Lagrangian for the firm's problem of choosing w, L_G, and L_B to maximize expected profits subject to the constraint that workers' expected utility is u_0.

(*b*) Find the first-order conditions for w, L_G, and L_B.

---

[33]For simplicity, neglect the constraint that L cannot exceed $\overline{L}$. Accounting for this constraint, one would find that for A_i above some critical level, L_i would equal $\overline{L}$ rather than being determined by the condition derived in part (*b*), below.

[34]In the United States, a firm's unemployment insurance taxes only partly account for the extent to which the firm's workers obtain unemployment insurance; that is, the taxes are only partially *experience-rated*. Thus f is between zero and one.

(c) Show that a fall in f (or a rise in B if $f < 1$) reduces L_B.

(d) Show that a fall in f (or a rise in B if $f < 1$) raises L_G.

10.8 Implicit contracts under asymmetric information. (Azariadis and Stiglitz, 1983.) Consider the model of Section 10.5. Suppose, however, that only the firm observes A. In addition, suppose there are only two possible values of A, A_B and A_G ($A_B < A_G$), each occurring with probability one- half.

We can think of the contract as specifying w and L as functions of the firm's announcement of the state, and as being subject to the restriction that it is never in the firm's interest to announce a state other than the actual one; formally, the contract must be *incentive-compatible*.

(a) Is the efficient contract under symmetric information derived in Section 10.5 incentive-compatible under asymmetric information? Specifically, if A is A_B, is the firm better off claiming that A is A_G (so that C and L are given by C_G and L_G) rather than that it is A_B? And if A is A_G, is the firm better off claiming it is A_B rather than A_G?

(b) One can show that the constraint that the firm not prefer to claim that the state is bad when it is good is not binding, but that the constraint that it not prefer to claim that the state is good when it is bad is binding. Set up the Lagrangian for the firm's problem of choosing C_G, C_B, L_G, and L_B subject to the constraints that workers' expected utility is u_0 and that the firm is indifferent about which state to announce when A is A_B. Find the first-order conditions for C_G, C_B, L_G, and L_B.

(c) Show that the marginal product and the marginal disutility of labor are equated in the bad state—that is, that $A_B F'(L_B) = V'(L_B)/U'(C_B)$.

(d) Show that there is "overemployment" in the good state—that is, that $A_G F'(L_G) < V'(L_G)/U'(C_G)$.

(e) Is this model helpful in understanding the high level of average unemployment? Is it helpful in understanding the large size of employment fluctuations?

10.9 Does worker influence on the wage after shocks to labor demand are realized affect the cyclical characteristics of the labor market?

(a) (This follows McDonald and Solow, 1981.) Consider a union with the objective function $[U(w) - K]L + U(w_u)(N - L), U'(\cdot) > 0$, where N is the number of union members, L is the number who are employed, $K > 0$ is the disutility of working, w is the wage, and w_u is unemployment compensation. The firm's profits are $AL^\alpha/\alpha - wL, A > 0, 0 < \alpha < 1$. The union sets w after A is known, and the firm then chooses L given w and A. (Assume throughout the problem that the constraint that L cannot exceed N is not binding.)

   (i) What is the firm's choice of L given w and A?

   (ii) Given its knowledge of how the firm will behave, what is the union's choice of w given A? Given this, how does L vary with A?

(b) Given the union's objective function, what is labor supply under spot markets—that is, if the union takes w as given and chooses L to maximize its objective function? How do w and L vary with A under spot markets?

(c) Suppose the union's objective function is $wL - [\sigma/(\sigma + 1)]L^{(\sigma+1)/\sigma}$, $\sigma > 0$, instead of the expression in part (a).

  (i) How do w and L vary with A under spot markets?

  (ii) Redo part (a)(ii) using the modified union objective function. Does assuming that the wage is determined by the union rather than by spot markets affect the elasticities of w and L with respect to A?

10.10 Does worker influence on the wage and employment after shocks to labor demand are realized affect the cyclical characteristics of the labor market?

(a) (This is based on McDonald and Solow, 1981.) Consider a union and a firm with the objective functions assumed in part (a) of Problem 10.9. The union chooses w and L given A, subject to the constraint that the firm's profits must be at least some level, π_0.

  (i) Set up the Lagrangian for the union's maximization problem.

  (ii) Find the first-order conditions for w and L.

  (iii) What role does w play in this model?

  (iv) How does L vary with A? Compare your answer with your finding in part (b) of Problem 10.9 concerning how L varies with A under spot markets.

(b) Suppose the union's objective function is given instead by the expression in part (c) of Problem 10.9. Redo parts (i) and (ii) of part (a) using the modified union objective function. Compare how L varies with A with your finding in part (c)(i) of Problem 10.9 concerning how it varies under spot markets.

10.11 The Harris–Todaro model. (Harris and Todaro, 1970.) Suppose there are two sectors. Jobs in the primary sector pay w_p; jobs in the secondary sector pay w_s. Each worker decides which sector to be in. All workers who choose the secondary sector obtain a job. But there is a fixed number, N_p, of primary-sector jobs. These jobs are allocated at random among workers who choose the primary sector. Primary-sector workers who do not get a job are unemployed, and receive an unemployment benefit of b. Workers are risk-neutral, and there is no disutility of working. Thus the expected utility of a primary-sector worker is $qw_p + (1 - q)b$, where q is the probability of a primary-sector worker getting a job.

(a) What is equilibrium unemployment as a function of w_p, w_s, N_p, b, and the size of the labor force, $\overline{N}$?

(b) How does an increase in N_p affect unemployment? Explain intuitively why, even though unemployment takes the form of workers waiting for primary-sector jobs, increasing the number of these jobs can increase unemployment.

(c) What are the effects of an increase in the level of unemployment benefits?

10.12 Partial-equilibrium search. Consider a worker searching for a job. Wages, w, have a probability density function across jobs $f(w)$ that is known to the worker; let $F(w)$ be the associated cumulative distribution function. Each time the worker samples a job from this distribution, he or she incurs a cost of C, where $0 < C < E[w]$. When the worker samples a job, he or she can either accept it (in which case the process ends) or sample another job. The worker maximizes the expected value of $w - nC$, where w is the wage paid in the job the worker eventually accepts, and n is the number of jobs the worker ends up sampling.

Let V denote the expected value of $w - n'C$ of a worker who has just rejected a job, where n' is the number of jobs the worker will sample from that point on.

(a) Explain why the worker accepts a job offering $\hat{w}$ if $\hat{w} > V$, and rejects it if $\hat{w} < V$. (A search problem where the worker accepts a job if and only if it pays above some cutoff level is said to exhibit the *reservation-wage property*.)

(b) Explain why V satisfies $V = F(V)V + \int_{w=V}^{\infty} wf(w)dw - C$.

(c) Show that an increase in C reduces V.

(d) In this model, does a searcher ever want to accept a job that he or she has previously rejected?

10.13 In the setup described in Problem 10.12, suppose that w is distributed uniformly on $[\mu - a, \mu + a]$, and that $C < \mu$.

(a) Find V in terms of μ, a, and C.

(b) How does an increase in a affect V? Explain intuitively.

10.14 Describe how each of the following affects equilibrium employment in the model of Section 10.8:

(a) An increase in the job breakup rate, b.

(b) An increase in the interest rate, r.

(c) An increase in the effectiveness of matching, K.

10.15 Suppose we replace the assumption in equation (10.76) that the worker and the firm divide the surplus from their relationship equally with the assumption that fraction f of the surplus goes to the worker and fraction $1 - f$ goes to the firm: $(1 - f)(V_E - V_U) = f(V_F - V_V)$.

(a) How does this change in the model affect the equation implicitly defining E, (10.85)?

(b) How does a change in f affect the equilibrium level of E?

10.16 Consider the model of Section 10.8. Suppose the economy is initially in equilibrium, and that A then falls permanently. Suppose, however, that entry and exit are ruled out; thus the total number of jobs, $F + V$, remains constant. How do unemployment and vacancies behave over time in response to the fall in A?

10.17 The efficiency of the decentralized equilibrium in a search economy. Consider the model of Section 10.8. Let the interest rate, r, approach zero, and assume that the firms are owned by the households; thus welfare can be measured as the sum of utility and profits per unit time, which equals $AE - (F + V)C$. Letting N denote the total number of jobs, we can therefore write welfare as $W(N) = AE(N) - NC$, where $E(N)$ gives equilibrium employment as a function of N.

(a) Use the matching function, (10.68), and the steady-state condition, (10.69), to derive an expression for the impact of a change in the number of jobs on employment, $E'(N)$, in terms of $N, \bar{L}, E(N), \gamma,$ and β.

(b) Substitute your result in part (a) into the expression for $W(N)$ to find $W'(N)$ in terms of $N, \bar{L}, E(N), \gamma, \beta,$ and A.

(c) Use (10.82) and the facts that $a = bE/(\bar{L} - E)$ and $\alpha = bE/V$ to find an expression for C in terms of $N_{EQ}, \bar{L}, E(N_{EQ}),$ and A, where N_{EQ} is the number of jobs in the decentralized equilibrium.

(d) Use your results in parts (b) and (c) to show that if $\beta + \gamma = 1$, $W'(N_{EQ}) > 0$ if $\gamma > \frac{1}{2}$ and $W'(N_{EQ}) < 0$ if $\gamma < \frac{1}{2}$.

(e) If γ is $\frac{1}{2}$ but $\beta + \gamma$ is not necessarily 1, what determines the sign of $W'(N_{EQ})$?

REFERENCES

A

Abel, Andrew B. 1982. "Dynamic Effects of Permanent and Temporary Tax Policies in a q Model of Investment." *Journal of Monetary Economics* 9 (May): 353–373.

Abel, Andrew B. 1990. "Asset Prices under Habit Formation and Catching Up with the Joneses." *American Economic Review* 80 (May): 38–42.

Abel, Andrew B., and Bernanke, Ben S. 1992. *Macroeconomics.* Reading, Mass.: Addison-Wesley.

Abel, Andrew B., and Eberly, Janice C. 1994. "A Unified Model of Investment under Uncertainty." *American Economic Review* 84 (December): 1369–1384.

Abel, Andrew B., Mankiw, N. Gregory, Summers, Lawrence H., and Zeckhauser, Richard J. 1989. "Assessing Dynamic Efficiency: Theory and Evidence." *Review of Economic Studies* 56 (January): 1–20.

Abraham, Katharine G., and Katz, Lawrence F. 1986. "Cyclical Unemployment: Sectoral Shifts or Aggregate Disturbances?" *Journal of Political Economy* 94 (June): 507–522.

Abramovitz, Moses. 1956. "Resource and Output Trends in the United States since 1870." *American Economic Review* 46 (May): 5–23.

Abreu, Dilip. 1988. "On the Theory of Infinitely Repeated Games with Discounting." *Econometrica* 56 (March): 383–396.

Aghion, Philippe, and Howitt, Peter. 1992. "A Model of Growth through Creative Destruction." *Econometrica* 60 (March): 323–351.

Aiyagari, S. Rao. 1994. "Uninsured Idiosyncratic Risk and Aggregate Saving." *Quarterly Journal of Economics* 109 (August): 659–684.

Aiyagari, S. Rao, Christiano, Lawrence J., and Eichenbaum, Martin. 1992. "The Output, Employment, and Interest Rate Effects of Government Consumption." *Journal of Monetary Economics* 30 (October): 73–86.

Aiyagari, S. Rao, and Gertler, Mark. 1985. "The Backing of Government Bonds and Monetarism." *Journal of Monetary Economics* 16 (July): 19–44.

Akerlof, George A. 1969. "Relative Wages and the Rate of Inflation." *Quarterly Journal of Economics* 83 (August): 353–374.

Akerlof, George A., and Katz, Lawrence F. 1989. "Workers' Trust Funds and the Logic of Wage Profiles." *Quarterly Journal of Economics* 104 (August): 525–536.

Akerlof, George A., and Main, Brian G. M. 1981. "An Experience-Weighted Measure of Employment and Unemployment Durations." *American Economic Review* 71 (December): 1003–1011.

Akerlof, George A., Rose, Andrew K., and Yellen, Janet L. 1988. "Job Switching and Job Satisfaction in the U.S. Labor Market." *Brookings Papers on Economic Activity*, no. 2, 495–582.

Akerlof, George A., and Yellen, Janet L. 1985. "A Near-Rational Model of the Business Cycle, with Wage and Price Inertia." *Quarterly Journal of Economics* 100 (Supplement): 823–838. Reprinted in Mankiw and Romer (1991).

Akerlof, George A., and Yellen, Janet L. 1990. "The Fair Wage-Effort Hypothesis and Unemployment." *Quarterly Journal of Economics* 105 (May): 255–283.

Alesina, Alberto. 1988. "Macroeconomics and Politics." *NBER Macroeconomics Annual* 3: 13–52.

Alesina, Alberto, and Drazen, Allan. 1991. "Why Are Stabilizations Delayed?" *American Economic Review* 81 (December): 1170–1188.

Alesina, Alberto, and Sachs, Jeffrey. 1988. "Political Parties and the Business Cycle in the United States, 1948–1984." *Journal of Money, Credit, and Banking* 20 (February): 63–82.

Alesina, Alberto, and Summers, Lawrence H. 1993. "Central Bank Independence and Macroeconomic Performance." *Journal of Money, Credit, and Banking* 25 (May): 151–162.

Allais, Maurice. 1947. *Économie et Intérêt.* Paris: Impremerie Nationale.

Altonji, Joseph G. 1986. "Intertemporal Substitution in Labor Supply: Evidence from Micro Data." *Journal of Political Economy* 94 (June, Part 2): S176–S215.

Altonji, Joseph G., Hayashi, Fumio, and Kotlikoff, Laurence J. 1992. "Is the Extended Family Altruistically Linked? Direct Tests Using Micro Data." *American Economic Review* 82 (December): 1177–1198.

Altonji, Joseph G., and Siow, Aloysius. 1987. "Testing the Response of Consumption to Income Changes with (Noisy) Panel Data." *Quarterly Journal of Economics* 102 (May): 293–328.

Altug, Sumru. 1989. "Time-to-Build and Aggregate Fluctuations." *International Economic Review* 30 (November): 889–920.

Andersen, Leonall C., and Jordan, Jerry L. 1968. "Monetary and Fiscal Actions: A Test of Their Relative Importance in Economic Stabilization." Federal Reserve Bank of St. Louis *Review* 50 (November): 11–24.

Arrow, Kenneth J. 1962. "The Economic Implications of Learning by Doing." *Review of Economic Studies* 29 (June): 155–173. Reprinted in Stiglitz and Uzawa (1969).

Atkeson, Andrew, and Phelan, Christopher. 1994. "Reconsidering the Costs of Business Cycles with Incomplete Markets." *NBER Macroeconomics Annual* 9: 187–207.

Auerbach, Alan J., and Kotlikoff, Laurence J. 1987. *Dynamic Fiscal Policy.* Cambridge: Cambridge University Press.

Azariadis, Costas. 1975. "Implicit Contracts and Underemployment Equilibria." *Journal of Political Economy* 83 (December): 1183–1202.

Azariadis, Costas, and Drazen, Allan. 1990. "Threshold Externalities in Economic Development." *Quarterly Journal of Economics* 105 (May): 501–526.

Azariadis, Costas, and Stiglitz, Joseph E. 1983. "Implicit Contracts and Fixed-Price Equilibria," *Quarterly Journal of Economics* 98 (Supplement): 1–22. Reprinted in Mankiw and Romer (1991).

B

Backus, David, and Driffill, John. 1985. "Inflation and Reputation." *American Economic Review* 75 (June): 530-538.

Backus, David, and Kehoe, Patrick J. 1992. "International Evidence on the Historical Properties of Business Cycles." *American Economic Review* 82 (September): 864-888.

Baily, Martin Neil. 1974. "Wages and Employment under Uncertain Demand." *Review of Economic Studies* 41 (January): 37-50.

Baily, Martin Neil, and Gordon, Robert J. 1988. "The Productivity Slowdown, Measurement Issues, and the Explosion of Computer Power." *Brookings Papers on Economic Activity*, no. 2, 347-420.

Balke, Nathan S., and Gordon, Robert J. 1989. "The Estimation of Prewar Gross National Product: Methodology and New Evidence." *Journal of Political Economy* 97 (February): 38-92.

Ball, Laurence. 1988. "Is Equilibrium Indexation Efficient?" *Quarterly Journal of Economics* 103 (May): 299-311.

Ball, Laurence. 1990. "Intertemporal Substitution and Constraints on Labor Supply: Evidence from Panel Data." *Economic Inquiry* 28 (October): 706-724.

Ball, Laurence. 1991. "The Genesis of Inflation and the Costs of Disinflation." *Journal of Money, Credit, and Banking* 23 (August, Part 2): 439-452.

Ball, Laurence. 1993. "The Dynamics of High Inflation." National Bureau of Economic Research Working Paper No. 4578 (December).

Ball, Laurence. 1994a. "Credible Disinflation with Staggered Price-Setting." *American Economic Review* 84 (March): 282-289.

Ball, Laurence. 1994b. "What Determines the Sacrifice Ratio?" In N. Gregory Mankiw, ed., *Monetary Policy*, 155-182. Chicago: University of Chicago Press.

Ball, Laurence, and Cecchetti, Stephen G. 1988. "Imperfect Information and Staggered Price Setting." *American Economic Review* 78 (December): 999-1018. Reprinted in Mankiw and Romer (1991).

Ball, Laurence, and Cecchetti, Stephen G. 1990. "Inflation and Uncertainty at Short and Long Horizons." *Brookings Papers on Economic Activity*, no. 1, 215-254.

Ball, Laurence, and Mankiw, N. Gregory. 1994. "A Sticky-Price Manifesto." *Carnegie-Rochester Conference Series on Public Policy* 41 (December): 127-151.

Ball, Laurence, and Mankiw, N. Gregory. 1995. "Relative-Price Changes as Aggregate Supply Shocks." *Quarterly Journal of Economics* 110 (February): 161-193.

Ball, Laurence, Mankiw, N. Gregory, and Romer, David. 1988. "The New Keynesian Economics and the Output-Inflation Tradeoff." *Brookings Papers on Economic Activity*, no. 1, 1-65. Reprinted in Mankiw and Romer (1991).

Ball, Laurence, and Romer, David. 1989. "The Equilibrium and Optimal Timing of Price Changes." *Review of Economic Studies* 56 (April): 179-198.

Ball, Laurence, and Romer, David. 1990. "Real Rigidities and the Non-Neutrality of Money." *Review of Economic Studies* 57 (April): 183-203. Reprinted in Mankiw and Romer (1991).

Ball, Laurence, and Romer, David. 1991. "Sticky Prices as Coordination Failure." *American Economic Review* 81 (June): 539-552.

Ball, Laurence, and Romer, David. 1993. "Inflation and the Informativeness of Prices." National Bureau of Economic Research Working Paper No. 4267 (January).

Barro, Robert J. 1972. "A Theory of Monopolistic Price Adjustment." *Review of Economic Studies* 34 (January): 17–26.

Barro, Robert J. 1974. "Are Government Bonds Net Wealth?" *Journal of Political Economy* 82 (November/December): 1095–1117.

Barro, Robert J. 1976. "Rational Expectations and the Role of Monetary Policy." *Journal of Monetary Economics* 2 (January): 1–32.

Barro, Robert J. 1977a. "Unanticipated Money Growth and Unemployment in the United States." *American Economic Review* 67 (March): 101–115.

Barro, Robert J. 1977b. "Long-Term Contracting, Sticky Prices, and Monetary Policy." *Journal of Monetary Economics* 3 (July): 305–316.

Barro, Robert J. 1978. "Unanticipated Money, Output, and the Price Level in the United States." *Journal of Political Economy* 86: 549–580.

Barro, Robert J. 1986. "Reputation in a Model of Monetary Policy with Incomplete Information." *Journal of Monetary Economics* 17 (January): 3–20.

Barro, Robert J. 1987. "Government Spending, Interest Rates, Prices, and Budget Deficits in the United Kingdom, 1701–1918." *Journal of Monetary Economics* 20 (September): 221–247.

Barro, Robert J. 1989. "Interest-Rate Targeting." *Journal of Monetary Economics* 23 (January): 3–30.

Barro, Robert J. 1991. "Economic Growth in a Cross Section of Countries." *Quarterly Journal of Economics* 106 (May): 407–443.

Barro, Robert J. 1993. *Macroeconomics.* Fourth edition. New York: John Wiley and Sons.

Barro, Robert J., and Becker, Gary S. 1988. "A Reformulation of the Economic Theory of Fertility." *Quarterly Journal of Economics* 103 (February): 1–25.

Barro, Robert J., and Becker, Gary S. 1989. "Fertility Choice in a Model of Economic Growth." *Econometrica* 57 (March): 481–501.

Barro, Robert J., and Gordon, David B. 1983a. "A Positive Theory of Monetary Policy in a Natural Rate Model." *Journal of Political Economy* 91 (August): 589–610.

Barro, Robert J., and Gordon, David B. 1983b. "Rules, Discretion and Reputation in a Model of Monetary Policy." *Journal of Monetary Economics* 12 (July): 101–121.

Barro, Robert J., and Grossman, Herschel I. 1971. "A General Disequilibrium Model of Income and Employment." *American Economic Review* 61 (March): 82–93.

Barro, Robert J., and King, Robert G. 1984. "Time Separable Preferences and Intertemporal Substitution Models of the Business Cycle." *Quarterly Journal of Economics* 99 (November): 817–840.

Barro, Robert J., Mankiw, N. Gregory, and Sala-i-Martin, Xavier. 1995. "Capital Mobility in Neoclassical Models of Growth." *American Economic Review* 85 (March): 103–115.

Barro, Robert J., and Sala-i-Martin, Xavier. 1991. "Convergence across States and Regions." *Brookings Papers on Economic Activity,* no. 1, 107–182.

Barro, Robert J., and Sala-i-Martin, Xavier. 1992. "Convergence." *Journal of Political Economy* 100 (April): 223–251.

Barsky, Robert B., Mankiw, N. Gregory, and Zeldes, Stephen P. 1986. "Ricardian Consumers with Keynesian Propensities." *American Economic Review* 76 (September): 676–691.

Barsky, Robert B., and Miron, Jeffrey A. 1989. "The Seasonal Cycle and the Business Cycle." *Journal of Political Economy* 97 (June): 503–534.

Basu, Susanto. 1993. "Intermediate Goods and Business Cycles: Implications for Productivity and Welfare." Unpublished paper, University of Michigan (September).

Baumol, William. 1986. "Productivity Growth, Convergence, and Welfare." *American Economic Review* 76 (December): 1072-1085.

Baumol, William. 1990. "Entrepreneurship: Productive, Unproductive, and Destructive." *Journal of Political Economy* 98 (October, Part 1): 893-921.

Baxter, Marianne, and Crucini, Mario J. 1993. "Explaining Saving-Investment Correlations." *American Economic Review* 83 (June): 416-436.

Baxter, Marianne, and King, Robert G. 1993. "Fiscal Policy in General Equilibrium." *American Economic Review* 83 (June): 315-334.

Baxter, Marianne, and Stockman, Alan C. 1989. "Business Cycles and the Exchange-Rate Regime: Some International Evidence." *Journal of Monetary Economics* 23 (May): 377-400.

Bean, Charles R. 1994. "European Unemployment: A Survey." *Journal of Economic Literature* 32 (June): 573-619.

Beaudry, Paul, and DiNardo, John. 1991. "The Effect of Implicit Contracts on the Movement of Wages over the Business Cycle: Evidence from Micro Data." *Journal of Political Economy* 99 (August): 665-688.

Beaudry, Paul, and Koop, Gary. 1993. "Do Recessions Permanently Change Output?" *Journal of Monetary Economics* 31 (April): 149-163.

Becker, Gary S., Murphy, Kevin M., and Tamura, Robert. 1990. "Human Capital, Fertility, and Economic Growth." *Journal of Political Economy* 98 (October, Part 2): S12-S37.

Benabou, Roland. 1988. "Search, Price Setting and Inflation." *Review of Economic Studies* 55 (July): 353-376.

Benabou, Roland. 1992. "Inflation and Efficiency in Search Markets." *Review of Economic Studies* 59 (April): 299-329.

Benabou, Roland, and Gertner, Robert. 1993. "Search with Learning from Prices: Does Increased Inflationary Uncertainty Lead to Higher Markups?" *Review of Economic Studies* 60 (January): 69-94.

Benassy, Jean-Pascal. 1976. "The Disequilibrium Approach to Monopolistic Price Setting and General Monopolistic Equilibrium." *Review of Economic Studies* 43 (January): 69-81.

Benhabib, Jess, Rogerson, Richard, and Wright, Randall. 1991. "Homework in Macroeconomics: Household Production and Aggregate Fluctuations." *Journal of Political Economy* 99 (December): 1166-1187.

Bernanke, Ben S. 1983a. "Irreversibility, Uncertainty, and Cyclical Investment." *Quarterly Journal of Economics* 98 (February): 85-106.

Bernanke, Ben S. 1983b. "Nonmonetary Effects of the Financial Crisis in the Propagation of the Great Depression." *American Economic Review* 73 (June): 257-276. Reprinted in Mankiw and Romer (1991).

Bernanke, Ben S. 1993. "The World on a Cross of Gold: A Review of 'Golden Fetters: The Gold Standard and the Great Depression, 1919-1939.'" *Journal of Monetary Economics* 31 (April): 251-267.

Bernanke, Ben S., and Blinder, Alan S. 1988. "Credit, Money, and Aggregate Demand." *American Economic Review* 78 (May): 435-439. Reprinted in Mankiw and Romer (1991).

Bernanke, Ben S., and Gertler, Mark. 1989. "Agency Costs, Net Worth, and Business Fluctuations." *American Economic Review* 79 (March): 14-31.

Bernanke, Ben S., and Gertler, Mark. **1990.** "Financial Fragility and Economic Performance." *Quarterly Journal of Economics* 105 (February): 87-114.

Bernanke, Ben S., and Lown, Cara S. **1991.** "The Credit Crunch." *Brookings Papers on Economic Activity,* no. 2, 205-247.

Bernanke, Ben S., and Parkinson, Martin L. **1991.** "Procyclical Labor Productivity and Competing Theories of the Business Cycle: Some Evidence from Interwar U.S. Manufacturing Industries." *Journal of Political Economy* 99 (June): 439-459.

Bernheim, B. Douglas. **1987a.** "Ricardian Equivalence: An Evaluation of Theory and Evidence." *NBER Macroeconomics Annual* 2: 263-304.

Bernheim, B. Douglas. **1987b.** "Ricardian Equivalence: An Evaluation of Theory and Evidence." National Bureau of Economic Research Working Paper No. 2330 (July).

Bernheim, B. Douglas. **1991.** "How Strong Are Bequest Motives? Evidence Based on Estimates of the Demand for Life Insurance and Annuities." *Journal of Political Economy* 99 (October): 899-927.

Bernheim, B. Douglas, and Bagwell, Kyle. **1988.** "Is Everything Neutral?" *Journal of Political Economy* 96 (April): 308-338.

Bernheim, B. Douglas, Shleifer, Andrei, and Summers, Lawrence H. **1985.** "The Strategic Bequest Motive." *Journal of Political Economy* 93 (December): 1045-1076.

Bils, Mark J. **1985.** "Real Wages over the Business Cycle: Evidence from Panel Data." *Journal of Political Economy* 93 (August): 666-689.

Bils, Mark J. **1987.** "The Cyclical Behavior of Marginal Cost and Price." *American Economic Review* 77 (December): 838-857.

Bils, Mark J. **1991.** "Testing for Contracting Effects on Employment." *Quarterly Journal of Economics* 106 (November): 1129-1156.

Black, Fischer. **1974.** "Uniqueness of the Price Level in Monetary Growth Models with Rational Expectations." *Journal of Economic Theory* 7 (January): 53-65.

Black, Fischer. **1982.** "General Equilibrium and Business Cycles." National Bureau of Economic Research Working Paper No. 950 (August).

Blanchard, Olivier J. **1979.** "Speculative Bubbles, Crashes and Rational Expectations." *Economics Letters* 3: 387-389.

Blanchard, Olivier J. **1981.** "What Is Left of the Multiplier Accelerator?" *American Economic Review* 71 (May): 150-154.

Blanchard, Olivier J. **1983.** "Price Asynchronization and Price Level Inertia." In Rudiger Dornbusch and Mario Henrique Simonsen, eds., *Inflation, Debt, and Indexation,* 3-24. Cambridge: MIT Press. Reprinted in Mankiw and Romer (1991).

Blanchard, Olivier J. **1984.** "The Lucas Critique and the Volcker Deflation." *American Economic Review* 74 (May): 211-215.

Blanchard, Olivier J. **1985.** "Debts, Deficits, and Finite Horizons." *Journal of Political Economy* 93 (April): 223-247.

Blanchard, Olivier J., and Diamond, Peter A. **1989.** "The Beveridge Curve." *Brookings Papers on Economic Activity,* no. 1, 1-60.

Blanchard, Olivier J., and Fischer, Stanley. **1989.** *Lectures on Macroeconomics.* Cambridge: MIT Press.

Blanchard, Olivier J., and Kiyotaki, Nobuhiro. **1987.** "Monopolistic Competition and the Effects of Aggregate Demand." *American Economic Review* 77 (September): 647-666. Reprinted in Mankiw and Romer (1991).

Blanchard, Olivier J., and Summers, Lawrence, H. **1986.** "Hysteresis and the European Unemployment Problem." *NBER Macroeconomics Annual* 1: 15-78.

Blanchard, Olivier J., and Summers, Lawrence, H. 1987. "Hysteresis in Unemployment." *European Economic Review* 31 (1987): 288–295. Reprinted in Mankiw and Romer (1991).

Blinder, Alan S. 1994. "On Sticky Prices: Academic Theories Meet the Real World." In N. Gregory Mankiw, ed., *Monetary Policy,* 117–150. Chicago: University of Chicago Press.

Blinder, Alan S., and Fischer, Stanley. 1981. "Inventories, Rational Expectations and the Business Cycle." *Journal of Monetary Economics* 8 (November): 277–304.

Blough, Stephen R. 1992a. "The Relationship between Power and Level for Generic Unit Root Tests in Finite Samples." *Applied Econometrics* 7 (July-September): 295–308.

Blough, Stephen R. 1992b. "Near Observational Equivalence of Unit Root and Stationary Processes: Theory and Implications." Unpublished paper, Johns Hopkins University (November).

Bohn, Henning. 1992. "Endogenous Government Spending and Ricardian Equivalence." *Economic Journal* 102 (May): 588–597.

Brainard, S. Lael, and Cutler, David M. 1993. "Sectoral Shifts and Cyclical Unemployment Reconsidered." *Quarterly Journal of Economics* 108 (February): 219–243.

Brainard, William. 1967. "Uncertainty and the Effectiveness of Policy." *American Economic Review* 57 (May): 411–425.

Braun, R. Anton. 1994. "Tax Disturbances and Real Economic Activity in the Postwar United States." *Journal of Monetary Economics* 33 (June): 441–462.

Breeden, Douglas. 1979. "An Intertemporal Asset Pricing Model with Stochastic Consumption and Investment." *Journal of Financial Economics* 7 (September): 265–296.

Bresciani-Turroni, Constantino. 1937. *The Economics of Inflation: A Study of Currency Depreciation in Post-War Germany.* London: Allen and Unwin.

Brock, William. 1975. "A Simple Perfect Foresight Monetary Model." *Journal of Monetary Economics* 1 (April): 133–150.

Bryant, John. 1983. "A Simple Rational Expectations Keynes-Type Model." *Quarterly Journal of Economics* 98 (August): 525–528. Reprinted in Mankiw and Romer (1991).

Buchanan, James M. 1976. "Barro on the Ricardian Equivalence Theorem." *Journal of Political Economy* 84 (April): 337–342.

Bulow, Jeremy, and Summers, Lawrence H. 1986. "A Theory of Dual Labor Markets with Applications to Industrial Policy, Discrimination, and Keynesian Unemployment." *Journal of Labor Economics* 4: 376–414.

Burns, Arthur F., and Mitchell, Wesley C. 1944. *Measuring Business Cycles.* New York: National Bureau of Economic Research.

Burnside, Craig, Eichenbaum, Martin, and Rebelo, Sergio. 1993. "Labor Hoarding and the Business Cycle." *Journal of Political Economy* 101 (April): 245–273.

C

Caballero, Ricardo J. 1990a. "Expenditure on Durable Goods: A Case for Slow Adjustment." *Quarterly Journal of Economics* 105 (August): 727–743.

Caballero, Ricardo J. 1990b. "Consumption Puzzles and Precautionary Savings." *Journal of Monetary Economics* 25 (January): 113–136.

Caballero, Ricardo J. 1991. "Earnings Uncertainty and Aggregate Wealth Accumulation." *American Economic Review* 81 (September): 859-871.

Caballero, Ricardo J. 1993. "Durable Goods: An Explanation for Their Slow Adjustment." *Journal of Political Economy* 101 (April): 351-384.

Caballero, Ricardo J., and Engel, M. R. A. 1991. "Dynamic (S,s) Economies." *Econometrica* 59 (November): 1659-1686.

Caballero, Ricardo J., and Engel, M. R. A. 1993. "Heterogeneity and Output Fluctuations in a Dynamic Menu-Cost Economy." *Review of Economic Studies* 60 (January): 95-119.

Caballero, Ricardo J., and Lyons, Richard K. 1992. "External Effects in U.S. Procyclical Productivity." *Journal of Monetary Economics* 29 (April): 209-225.

Cagan, Philip. 1956. "The Monetary Dynamics of Hyperinflation." In Milton Friedman, ed., *Studies in the Quantity Theory of Money,* 25-117. Chicago: University of Chicago Press.

Calvo, Guillermo. 1978a. "On the Indeterminacy of Interest Rates and Wages with Perfect Foresight." *Journal of Economic Theory* 19 (December): 321-337.

Calvo, Guillermo. 1978b. "On The Time Consistency of Optimal Policy in a Monetary Economy." *Econometrica* 46 (November): 1411-1428.

Campbell, John Y. 1994. "Inspecting the Mechanism: An Analytical Approach to the Stochastic Growth Model." *Journal of Monetary Economics* 33 (June): 463-506.

Campbell, John Y., and Cochrane, John H. 1995. "By Force of Habit: A Consumption-Based Explanation of Aggregate Stock Market Behavior." National Bureau of Economic Research Working Paper No. 4995 (January).

Campbell, John Y., and Deaton, Angus. 1989. "Why Is Consumption So Smooth?" *Review of Economic Studies* 56 (July): 357-374.

Campbell, John Y., and Mankiw, N. Gregory. 1987. "Are Output Fluctuations Transitory?" *Quarterly Journal of Economics* 102 (November): 857-880.

Campbell, John Y., and Mankiw, N. Gregory. 1989a. "Consumption, Income, and Interest Rates: Reinterpreting the Time Series Evidence." *NBER Macroeconomics Annual* 4: 185-216.

Campbell, John Y., and Mankiw, N. Gregory. 1989b. "International Evidence on the Persistence of Economic Fluctuations." *Journal of Monetary Economics* 23 (March): 319-333.

Campbell, John Y., and Perron, Pierre. 1991. "Pitfalls and Opportunities: What Macroeconomists Should Know about Unit Roots." *NBER Macroeconomics Annual* 6: 141-201.

Caplin, Andrew S., and Leahy, John. 1991. "State-Dependent Pricing and the Dynamics of Money and Output." *Quarterly Journal of Economics* 106 (August): 683-708.

Caplin, Andrew S., and Spulber, Daniel F. 1987. "Menu Costs and the Neutrality of Money." *Quarterly Journal of Economics* 102 (November): 703-725. Reprinted in Mankiw and Romer (1991).

Card, David. 1990. "Unexpected Inflation, Real Wages, and Employment Determination in Union Contracts." *American Economic Review* 80 (September): 669-688.

Card, David. 1991. "Intertemporal Labor Supply: An Assessment." National Bureau of Economic Research Working Paper No. 3602 (January).

Cardoso, Eliana. 1991. "From Inertia to Megainflation: Brazil in the 1980s." In Michael Bruno et al., eds., *Lessons of Economic Stabilization and Its Aftermath,* 143-177. Cambridge: MIT Press.

Carlton, Dennis W. 1982. "The Disruptive Effects of Inflation on the Organization of Markets." In Robert E. Hall, ed., *Inflation: Causes and Effects*, 139–152. Chicago: University of Chicago Press.

Carlton, Dennis W. 1986. "The Rigidity of Prices." *American Economic Review* 76 (September): 637–658. Reprinted in Mankiw and Romer (1991).

Carmichael, Lorne. 1985. "Can Unemployment Be Involuntary? Comment." *American Economic Review* 75 (December): 1213–1214.

Carroll, Christopher D. 1992. "The Buffer-Stock Theory of Saving: Some Macroeconomic Evidence." *Brookings Papers on Economic Activity*, no. 2, 61–156.

Carroll, Christopher D. 1994. "How Does Future Income Affect Consumption?" *Quarterly Journal of Economics* 109 (February): 111–147.

Carroll, Christopher D., and Summers, Lawrence H. 1991. "Consumption Growth Parallels Income Growth: Some New Evidence." In B. Douglas Bernheim and John B. Shoven, eds., *National Saving and Economic Performance*, 305–343. Chicago: University of Chicago Press.

Cass, David. 1965. "Optimum Growth in an Aggregative Model of Capital Accumulation." *Review of Economic Studies* 32 (July): 233–240.

Cass, David, and Shell, Karl. 1983. "Do Sunspots Matter?" *Journal of Political Economy* 91 (April): 193–227.

Cecchetti, Stephen G. 1986. "The Frequency of Price Adjustment: A Study of the Newsstand Prices of Magazines." *Journal of Econometrics* 31 (August): 255–274.

Chevalier, Judith A., and Scharfstein, David S. 1994. "Capital Market Imperfections and Countercyclical Markups: Theory and Evidence." National Bureau of Economic Research Working Paper No. 4614 (January).

Chiang, Alpha C. 1984. *Fundamental Methods of Mathematical Economics.* Third edition. New York: McGraw-Hill.

Cho, Jang-Ok, and Cooley, Thomas F. 1990. "The Business Cycle with Nominal Contracts." Unpublished paper, University of Rochester (December). *Economic Theory*, forthcoming.

Christiano, Lawrence J., and Eichenbaum, Martin. 1990. "Unit Roots in Real GNP: Do We Know, and Do We Care?" *Carnegie-Rochester Conference Series on Public Policy* 32 (Spring): 7–61.

Christiano, Lawrence J., and Eichenbaum, Martin. 1992a. "Current Real-Business-Cycle Theories and Aggregate Labor-Market Fluctuations." *American Economic Review* 82 (June): 430–450.

Christiano, Lawrence J., and Eichenbaum, Martin. 1992b. "Liquidity Effects, Monetary Policy and the Business Cycle." National Bureau of Economic Research Working Paper No. 4129 (August).

Clark, Kim B., and Summers, Lawrence H. 1979. "Labor Market Dynamics and Unemployment: A Reconsideration." *Brookings Papers on Economic Activity*, no. 1, 13–60.

Cochrane, John H. 1988. "How Big Is the Random Walk in GNP?" *Journal of Political Economy* 96 (October): 893–920.

Cochrane, John H. 1994. "Permanent and Transitory Components of GNP and Stock Prices." *Quarterly Journal of Economics* 109 (February): 241–265.

Cochrane, John H., and Hansen, Lars Peter. 1992. "Asset Pricing Explorations for Macroeconomics." *NBER Macroeconomics Annual* 7: 115–165.

Cogley, Timothy. 1990. "International Evidence on the Size of the Random Walk in Output." *Journal of Political Economy* 98 (June): 501–518.

Cogley, Timothy, and Nason, James M. 1995. "Effects of the Hodrick-Prescott Filter on Trend and Difference Stationary Time Series: Implications for Business Cycle Research." *Journal of Economic Dynamics and Control* 19 (January/February): 253-278.

Constantinides, George M. 1990. "Habit Formation: A Resolution of the Equity Premium Puzzle." *Journal of Political Economy* 98 (June): 519-543.

Cook, Timothy, and Hahn, Thomas. 1989. "The Effect of Changes in the Federal Funds Rate Target on Market Interest Rates in the 1970s." *Journal of Monetary Economics* 24 (November): 331-351.

Cooley, Thomas F., and Ohanian, Lee E. 1991. "The Cyclical Behavior of Prices." *Journal of Monetary Economics* 28 (August): 25-60.

Cooper, Russell W., DeJong, Douglas V., Forsythe, Robert, and Ross, Thomas W. 1990. "Selection Criteria in Coordination Games: Some Experimental Results." *American Economic Review* 80 (March): 218-234.

Cooper, Russell W., DeJong, Douglas V., Forsythe, Robert, and Ross, Thomas W. 1992. "Communication in Coordination Games." *Quarterly Journal of Economics* 107 (May): 739-771.

Cooper, Russell W., and Haltiwanger, John. 1993. "Evidence on Macroeconomic Complementarities." National Bureau of Economic Research Working Paper No. 4577 (December).

Cooper, Russell W., and John, Andrew. 1988. "Coordinating Coordination Failures in Keynesian Models." *Quarterly Journal of Economics* 103 (August): 441-463. Reprinted in Mankiw and Romer (1991).

Craine, Roger. 1989. "Risky Business: The Allocation of Capital." *Journal of Monetary Economics* 23 (March): 201-218.

Cukierman, Alex, Edwards, Sebastian, and Tabellini, Guido. 1992. "Seignorage and Political Instability." *American Economic Review* 82 (June): 537-555.

Cukierman, Alex, and Meltzer, Allan H. 1986. "A Theory of Ambiguity, Credibility, and Inflation under Discretion and Asymmetric Information." *Econometrica* 54 (September): 1099-1128.

Cukierman, Alex, Webb, Steven B., and Neyapti, Bilin. 1992. "Measuring the Independence of Central Banks and Its Effect on Policy Outcomes." *World Bank Economic Review* 6 (September): 353-398.

D

Davis, Steven J., and Haltiwanger, John. 1990. "Gross Job Creation and Destruction: Microeconomic Evidence and Macroeconomic Implications." *NBER Macroeconomics Annual* 5: 123-168.

Davis, Steven J., and Haltiwanger, John. 1992. "Gross Job Creation, Gross Job Destruction, and Employment Reallocation." *Quarterly Journal of Economics* 107 (August): 819-863.

Deaton, Angus. 1991. "Saving and Liquidity Constraints." *Econometrica* 59 (September): 1221-1248.

Deaton, Angus. 1992. *Understanding Consumption.* Oxford: Oxford University Press.

Debelle, Guy. 1994. "The Ends of Three Small Inflations: Australia, New Zealand, and Canada." Unpublished paper, M.I.T. (March).

De Long, J. Bradford. 1988. "Productivity Growth, Convergence, and Welfare: Comment." *American Economic Review* 78 (December): 1138-1154.

De Long, J. Bradford, and Summers, Lawrence H. 1986a. "Are Business Cycles Symmetrical?" In Robert J. Gordon, ed., *The American Business Cycle: Continuity and Change,* 166–179. Chicago: University of Chicago Press.

De Long, J. Bradford, and Summers, Lawrence H. 1986b. "Is Increased Price Flexibility Stabilizing?" *American Economic Review* 76 (December): 1031–1044.

De Long, J. Bradford, and Summers, Lawrence H. 1988. "How Does Macroeconomic Policy Affect Output?" *Brookings Papers on Economic Activity,* no. 2, 433–480.

De Long, J. Bradford, and Summers, Lawrence H. 1991. "Equipment Investment and Economic Growth." *Quarterly Journal of Economics* 106 (May): 445–502.

De Long, J. Bradford, and Summers, Lawrence H. 1992. "Equipment Investment and Economic Growth: How Strong Is the Nexus?" *Brookings Papers on Economic Activity,* no. 2, 157–211.

Denison, Edward F. 1967. *Why Growth Rates Differ.* Washington, D.C.: The Brookings Institution.

Denison, Edward F. 1985. *Trends in American Economic Growth, 1929–1982.* Washington, D.C.: The Brookings Institution.

Diamond, Douglas W. 1984. "Financial Intermediation and Delegated Monitoring." *Review of Economic Studies* 51 (July): 393–414.

Diamond, Peter A. 1965. "National Debt in a Neoclassical Growth Model." *American Economic Review* 55 (December): 1126–1150.

Diamond, Peter A. 1982. "Aggregate Demand Management in Search Equilibrium." *Journal of Political Economy* 90 (October): 881–894. Reprinted in Mankiw and Romer (1991).

Diamond, Peter A. 1993. "Search, Sticky Prices, and Inflation." *Review of Economic Studies* 60 (January): 53–68.

Dickens, William T., Katz, Lawrence F., Lang, Kevin, and Summers, Lawrence H. 1989. "Employee Crime and the Monitoring Puzzle." *Journal of Labor Economics* 7 (July): 331–348.

Dickens, William T., and Katz, Lawrence F. 1987a. "Inter-Industry Wage Differences and Theories of Wage Determination." National Bureau of Economic Research Working Paper No. 2271 (July).

Dickens, William T., and Katz, Lawrence F. 1987b. "Inter-Industry Wage Differences and Industry Characteristics." In Kevin Lang and Jonathan S. Leonard, eds., *Unemployment and the Structure of Labor Markets,* 48–89. Oxford: Basil Blackwell.

Dickey, David A., and Fuller, Wayne A. 1979. "Distribution of the Estimators for Autoregressive Time Series with a Unit Root." *Journal of the American Statistical Association* 74 (June): 427–431.

Dixit, Avinash. 1990. *Optimization in Economic Theory.* Second edition. Oxford: Oxford University Press.

Dixit, Avinash K., and Pindyck, Robert S. 1994. *Investment under Uncertainty.* Princeton: Princeton University Press.

Dixit, Avinash, and Stiglitz, Joseph E. 1977. "Monopolistic Competition and Optimum Product Diversity." *American Economic Review* 67 (June): 297–308.

Doeringer, Peter B., and Piore, Michael J. 1971. *Internal Labor Markets and Manpower Analysis.* Lexington, Mass.: D.C. Heath.

Dolde, Walter. 1979. "Temporary Taxes as Macro-economic Stabilizers." *American Economic Review* 69 (May): 81–85.

Domar, Evsey D. 1946. "Capital Expansion, Rate of Growth, and Employment." *Econometrica* 14 (April): 137–147. Reprinted in Stiglitz and Uzawa (1969).

Dornbusch, Rudiger. 1976. "Expectations and Exchange Rate Dynamics." *Journal of Political Economy* 84 (December): 1161-1176.

Dornbusch, Rudiger, and Fischer, Stanley. 1986. "Stopping Hyperinflations Past and Present." *Weltwirtschaftliches Archiv* 122: 1-47.

Dornbusch, Rudiger, and Fischer, Stanley. 1994. *Macroeconomics.* Sixth edition. New York: McGraw-Hill.

Dunlop, John T. 1938. "The Movement in Real and Money Wage Rates." *Economic Journal* 48 (September): 413-434.

Durlauf, Steven N. 1993. "Nonergodic Economic Growth." *Review of Economic Studies* 60 (April): 349-366.

Dynan, Karen E. 1993. "How Prudent Are Consumers?" *Journal of Political Economy* 101 (December): 1104-1113.

E

Easterly, William. 1993. "How Much Do Distortions Affect Growth?" *Journal of Monetary Economics* 32 (November): 187-212.

Eberly, Janice C. 1994. "Adjustment of Consumers' Durables Stocks: Evidence from Automobile Purchases." *Journal of Political Economy* 102 (June): 403-436.

Eichengreen, Barry. 1992. *Golden Fetters: The Gold Standard and the Great Depression, 1919-1939.* Oxford: Oxford University Press.

Eisner, Robert, and Strotz, Robert H. 1963. "Determinants of Business Fixed Investment." In Commission on Money and Credit, *Impacts of Monetary Policy*, 59-337. Englewood Cliffs, N.J.: Prentice-Hall.

Engel, Charles, and Frankel, Jeffrey. 1984. "Why Interest Rates React to Money Announcements: An Explanation from the Foreign Exchange Market." *Journal of Monetary Economics* 13 (January): 31-39.

Epstein, Larry G., and Zin, Stanley E. 1989. "Substitution, Risk Aversion, and the Temporal Behavior of Consumption and Asset Returns: A Theoretical Framework." *Econometrica* 46 (July): 937-969.

Epstein, Larry G., and Zin, Stanley E. 1991. "Substitution, Risk Aversion, and the Temporal Behavior of Consumption and Asset Returns: An Empirical Analysis." *Journal of Political Economy* 99 (April): 263-286.

F

Farmer, Roger E. A. 1993. *The Macroeconomics of Self-Fulfilling Prophecies.* Cambridge: MIT Press.

Fazzari, Steven M., Hubbard, R. Glenn, and Petersen, Bruce C. 1988. "Financing Constraints and Corporate Investment." *Brookings Papers on Economic Activity*, no. 1, 141-195.

Feldstein, Martin. 1976. "Temporary Layoffs in the Theory of Unemployment." *Journal of Political Economy* 84 (October): 937-957.

Feldstein, Martin. 1983. *Inflation, Tax Rules, and Capital Formation.* Chicago: University of Chicago Press.

Feldstein, Martin, and Horioka, Charles. 1980. "Domestic Saving and International Capital Flows." *Economic Journal* 90 (June): 314-329.

Fethke, Gary, and Policano, Andrew. 1986. "Will Wage Setters Ever Stagger Decisions?" *Quarterly Journal of Economics* 101 (November): 867-877. Reprinted in Mankiw and Romer (1991).

Fischer, Stanley. 1977a. "Long-Term Contracts, Rational Expectations, and the Optimal Money Supply Rule." *Journal of Political Economy* 85 (February): 191–205. Reprinted in Mankiw and Romer (1991).

Fischer, Stanley. 1977b. "Wage Indexation and Macroeconomic Stability." *Carnegie-Rochester Conference Series on Public Policy* 5: 107–147.

Fischer, Stanley. 1991. "Growth, Macroeconomics, and Development." *NBER Macroeconomics Annual* 6: 329–364.

Fischer, Stanley. 1993. "The Role of Macroeconomic Factors in Growth." *Journal of Monetary Economics* 32 (December): 485–512.

Fischer, Stanley, and Summers, Lawrence H. 1989. "Should Governments Learn to Live with Inflation?" *American Economic Review* 79 (May): 382–387.

Fisher, Irving. 1933. "The Debt-Deflation Theory of Great Depressions." *Econometrica* 1 (October): 337–357.

Flavin, Marjorie A. 1981. "The Adjustment of Consumption to Changing Expectations about Future Income." *Journal of Political Economy* 89 (October): 974–1009.

Flavin, Marjorie A. 1992. "The Joint Consumption/Asset Demand Decision: A Case Study in Robust Estimation." Unpublished paper, University of California, San Diego (June).

Flavin, Marjorie A. 1993. "The Excess Smoothness of Consumption: Identification and Estimation." *Review of Economic Studies* 60 (July): 651–666.

Fleming, J. Marcus. 1962. "Domestic Financial Policies under Fixed and under Floating Exchange Rates." *IMF Staff Papers* 9 (November): 369–379.

Foley, Duncan K., and Sidrauski, Miguel. 1970. "Portfolio Choice, Investment and Growth." *American Economic Review* 60 (March): 44–63.

Frankel, Jeffrey A. 1979. "On the Mark: A Theory of Floating Exchange Rates Based on Real Interest Differentials." *American Economic Review* 69 (September): 610–622.

Freedman, Charles. 1993. "Designing Institutions for Monetary Stability: A Comment." *Carnegie-Rochester Conference Series on Public Policy* 39 (December): 85–94.

Friedman, Milton. 1953. "The Case for Flexible Exchange Rates." In *Essays in Positive Economics,* 153–203. Chicago: University of Chicago Press.

Friedman, Milton. 1957. *A Theory of the Consumption Function.* Princeton: Princeton University Press.

Friedman, Milton. 1960. *A Program for Monetary Stability.* New York: Fordham University Press.

Friedman, Milton. 1968. "The Role of Monetary Policy." *American Economic Review* 58 (March): 1–17.

Friedman, Milton. 1969. "The Optimum Quantity of Money." In *The Optimum Quantity of Money and Other Essays,* 1–50. Chicago: Aldine Publishing.

Friedman, Milton. 1971. "Government Revenue from Inflation." *Journal of Political Economy* 79 (July/August): 846–856.

Friedman, Milton, and Schwartz, Anna J. 1963. *A Monetary History of the United States, 1867–1960.* Princeton: Princeton University Press.

Froot, Kenneth A., and Obstfeld, Maurice. 1991. "Intrinsic Bubbles: The Case of Stock Prices." *American Economic Review* 81 (December): 1189–1214.

Fuerst, Timothy S. 1992. "Liquidity, Loanable Funds, and Real Activity." *Journal of Monetary Economics* 29 (February): 3–24.

G

Gale, Douglas, and Hellwig, Martin. 1985. "Incentive-Compatible Debt Contracts I: The One-Period Problem." *Review of Economic Studies* 52 (October): 647–663.

Galor, Oded, and Ryder, Harl E. 1989. "Existence, Uniqueness, and Stability of Equilibria in an Overlapping-Generations Model with Productive Capital." *Journal of Economic Theory* 49 (December): 360–375.

Geary, Patrick T., and Kennan, John. 1982. "The Employment-Real Wage Relationship: An International Study." *Journal of Political Economy* 90 (August): 854–871.

Genberg, Hans. 1978. "Purchasing Power Parity under Fixed and Flexible Exchange Rates." *Journal of International Economics* 8 (May): 247–276.

Gertler, Mark. 1988. "Financial Structure and Aggregate Economic Activity." *Journal of Money, Credit, and Banking* 20 (August, Part 2): 559–588.

Gertler, Mark, and Gilchrist, Simon. 1994. "Monetary Policy, Business Cycles, and the Behavior of Small Manufacturing Firms." *Quarterly Journal of Economics* 109 (May): 309–340.

Gibbons, Robert, and Katz, Lawrence. 1992. "Does Unmeasured Ability Explain Inter-Industry Wage Differentials?" *Review of Economic Studies* 59 (July): 515–535.

Goldfeld, Stephen M. 1976. "The Case of the Missing Money." *Brookings Papers on Economic Activity,* no. 3, 683–730.

Goldfeld, Stephen M., and Sichel, Daniel E. 1990. "The Demand for Money." In Benjamin M. Friedman and Frank Hahn, eds., *Handbook of Monetary Economics,* vol. 1, 299–356. Amsterdam: North-Holland.

Goolsbee, Austan. 1994. "Investment Tax Incentives and the Price of Capital Goods." Unpublished paper, M.I.T. (November).

Gordon, David. 1974. "A Neoclassical Theory of Underemployment." *Economic Inquiry* 12 (December): 432–459.

Gordon, Robert J. 1990. "What Is New-Keynesian Economics?" *Journal of Economic Literature* 28 (September): 1115–1171.

Gordon, Robert J. 1993. *Macroeconomics.* Sixth edition. New York: HarperCollins.

Gottfries, Nils. 1992. "Insiders, Outsiders, and Nominal Wage Contracts." *Journal of Political Economy* 100 (April): 252–270.

Gould, John P. 1968. "Adjustment Costs in the Theory of Investment of the Firm." *Review of Economic Studies* 35 (January): 47–55.

Gray, Jo Anna. 1976. "Wage Indexation: A Macroeconomic Approach." *Journal of Monetary Economics* 2 (April): 221–235.

Gray, Jo Anna. 1978. "On Indexation and Contract Length." *Journal of Political Economy* 86 (February): 1–18.

Greene, William H. 1993. *Econometric Analysis.* Second edition. New York: Macmillan.

Greenwald, Bruce C., and Stiglitz, Joseph E. 1988. "Examining Alternative Macroeconomic Theories." *Brookings Papers on Economic Activity,* no. 1, 207–260.

Greenwald, Bruce C., Stiglitz, Joseph E., and Weiss, Andrew. 1984. "Informational Imperfections in Capital Markets and Macroeconomic Fluctuations." *American Economic Review* 74 (May): 194–199.

Greenwood, Jeremy, Hercowitz, Zvi, and Huffman, Gregory W. 1988. "Investment, Capacity Utilization, and the Real Business Cycle." *American Economic Review* 78 (June): 402–417.

Greenwood, Jeremy, and Huffman, Gregory W. 1991. "Tax Analysis in a Real-Business-Cycle Model: On Measuring Harberger Triangles and Okun Gaps." *Journal of Monetary Economics* 27 (April): 167-190.

Gregory, R. G. 1986. "Wages Policy and Unemployment in Australia." *Economica* 53 (Supplement): S53-S74.

Griliches, Zvi. 1988. "Productivity Puzzles and R&D: Another Nonexplanation." *Journal of Economic Perspectives* 2 (Fall): 9-21.

Grilli, Vittorio, Masciandaro, Donato, and Tabellini, Guido. 1991. "Political and Monetary Institutions and Public Financial Policies in the Industrial Countries." *Economic Policy,* no. 13 (October): 341-392.

Groshen, Erica L. 1991. "Sources of Intra-Industry Wage Dispersion: How Much Do Employers Matter?" *Quarterly Journal of Economics* 106 (August): 869-884.

Grossman, Gene M., and Helpman, Elhanan. 1991a. *Innovation and Growth in the Global Economy.* Cambridge: MIT Press.

Grossman, Gene M., and Helpman, Elhanan. 1991b. "Endogenous Product Cycles." *Economic Journal* 101 (September): 1214-1229.

Grossman, Sanford, and Weiss, Laurence. 1983. "A Transactions-Based Model of the Monetary Transmission Mechanism." *American Economic Review* 73 (December): 871-880.

H

Haavelmo, Trygve. 1945. "Multiplier Effects of a Balanced Budget." *Econometrica* 13 (October): 311-318.

Hall, Robert E. 1978. "Stochastic Implications of the Life Cycle-Permanent Income Hypothesis: Theory and Evidence." *Journal of Political Economy* 86 (December): 971-987.

Hall, Robert E. 1980. "Employment Fluctuations and Wage Rigidity." *Brookings Papers on Economic Activity,* no. 1, 91-123.

Hall, Robert E. 1982. "The Importance of Lifetime Jobs in the U.S. Economy." *American Economic Review* 72 (September): 716-724.

Hall, Robert E. 1984. "Monetary Strategy with an Elastic Price Standard." In Federal Reserve Bank of Kansas City, *Price Stability and Public Policy,* 137-159.

Hall, Robert E. 1988a. "The Relation between Price and Marginal Cost in U.S. Industry." *Journal of Political Economy* 96 (October): 921-947.

Hall, Robert E. 1988b. "Intertemporal Substitution in Consumption." *Journal of Political Economy* 96 (April): 339-357.

Hall, Robert E. 1989. "Comment." *Brookings Papers on Economic Activity,* Microeconomics, 276-280.

Hall, Robert E. 1991. *Booms and Recessions in a Noisy Economy.* New Haven: Yale University Press.

Hall, Robert E., and Jorgenson, Dale W. 1967. "Tax Policy and Investment Behavior." *American Economic Review* 57 (June): 391-414.

Hall, Robert E., and Mishkin, Frederic S. 1982. "The Sensitivity of Consumption to Transitory Income: Estimates from Panel Data on Households." *Econometrica* 50 (March): 461-481.

Hall, Robert E., and Taylor, John B. 1991. *Macroeconomics.* Third edition. New York: W. W. Norton.

Haltiwanger, John, and Waldman, Michael. 1989. "Limited Rationality and Strategic Complements: The Implications for Macroeconomics." *Quarterly Journal of Economics* 104 (August): 463–483.

Hansen, Gary D. 1985. "Indivisible Labor and the Business Cycle." *Journal of Monetary Economics* 16 (November): 309–327.

Hansen, Gary D., and Wright, Randall. 1992. "The Labor Market in Real Business Cycle Theory." Federal Reserve Bank of Minneapolis *Quarterly Review* 16 (Spring): 2–12.

Hansen, Lars Peter, and Singleton, Kenneth J. 1983. "Stochastic Consumption, Risk Aversion, and the Temporal Behavior of Asset Returns." *Journal of Political Economy* 91 (April): 249–265.

Harrington, Joseph E., Jr. 1993. "Economic Policy, Economic Performance, and Elections." *American Economic Review* 83 (March): 27–42.

Harris, John R., and Todaro, Michael P. 1970. "Migration, Unemployment and Development: A Two-Sector Analysis." *American Economic Review* 60 (March): 126–142.

Harrod, R. F. 1939. "An Essay in Dynamic Theory." *Economic Journal* 49 (March): 14–33. Reprinted in Stiglitz and Uzawa (1969).

Hayashi, Fumio. 1982. "Tobin's Marginal q and Average q: A Neoclassical Interpretation." *Econometrica* 50 (January): 213–224.

Hayashi, Fumio. 1985. "Tests for Liquidity Constraints: A Critical Survey." National Bureau of Economic Research Working Paper No. 1720 (October).

Heller, Walter. 1986. "Coordination Failure with Complete Markets, with Applications to Effective Demand." In Walter Heller, Ross M. Starr, and David Starrett, eds., *Equilibrium Analysis: Essays in Honor of Kenneth J. Arrow,* vol. 2, 155–175. Cambridge: Cambridge University Press.

Hodrick, Robert J., and Prescott, Edward C. "Post-War U.S. Business Cycles: An Empirical Investigation." Unpublished paper, Carnegie-Mellon University, 1980.

Hoshi, Takeo, Kashyap, Anil, and Scharfstein, David. 1991. "Corporate Structure, Liquidity, and Investment: Evidence from Japanese Industrial Groups." *Quarterly Journal of Economics* 106 (February): 33–60.

Hosios, Arthur J. 1990. "On the Efficiency of Matching and Related Models of Search and Unemployment." *Review of Economic Studies* 57 (April): 279–298.

Howitt, Peter. 1988. "Business Cycles with Costly Search and Recruiting." *Quarterly Journal of Economics* 103 (February): 147–165.

Hubbard, R. Glenn, and Judd, Kenneth L. 1986. "Liquidity Constraints, Fiscal Policy, and Consumption." *Brookings Papers on Economic Activity,* no. 1, 1–50.

Hubbard, R. Glenn, Skinner, Jonathan, and Zeldes, Stephen P. 1994a. "Precautionary Saving and Social Insurance." Unpublished paper, Columbia University (August). *Journal of Political Economy,* forthcoming.

Hubbard, R. Glenn, Skinner, Jonathan, and Zeldes, Stephen P. 1994b. "The Importance of Precautionary Motives in Explaining Individual and Aggregate Saving." *Carnegie-Rochester Conference Series on Public Policy* 40 (June): 59–125.

I

Inada, Kenichi. 1964. "Some Structural Characteristics of Turnpike Theorems." *Review of Economic Studies* 31 (January): 43–58.

J

Jappelli, Tullio, and Pagano, Marco. 1994. "Saving, Growth, and Liquidity Constraints." *Quarterly Journal of Economics* 109 (February): 83-109.

Jones, Charles I. 1995. "Time Series Tests of Endogenous Growth Models." *Quarterly Journal of Economics* 110 (May): 495-525.

Jorgenson, Dale W. 1988. "Productivity and Postwar U.S. Economic Growth." *Journal of Economic Perspectives* 2 (Fall): 23-41.

Judge, George G., Griffiths, W. E., Hill, R. Carter, Lütkepohl, Helmut, and Lee, Tsoung-Chao. 1985. *The Theory and Practice of Econometrics.* Second edition. New York: John Wiley and Sons.

K

Kaldor, Nicholas. 1961. "Capital Accumulation and Economic Growth." In F. A. Lutz and D. C. Hague, eds., *The Theory of Capital,* 177-222. New York: St. Martin's Press.

Kalecki, Michael. 1938. "The Determinants of Distribution of National Income." *Econometrica* 6 (April): 97-112.

Kamien, Morton I., and Schwartz, Nancy L. 1991. *Dynamic Optimization: The Calculus of Variations and Optimal Control in Economics and Management.* Second edition. Amsterdam: North-Holland.

Karamouzis, Nicholas, and Lombra, Raymond. 1989. "Federal Reserve Policymaking: An Overview and Analysis of the Policy Process." *Carnegie-Rochester Conference Series on Public Policy* 30 (Spring): 7-62.

Kareken, John H., and Solow, Robert M. 1963. "Lags in Monetary Policy." In Commission on Money and Credit, *Stabilization Policy,* 14-96. Englewood Cliffs, N.J.: Prentice-Hall.

Kashyap, Anil K. 1995. "Sticky Prices: New Evidence from Retail Catalogs." *Quarterly Journal of Economics* 110 (February): 245-274.

Kashyap, Anil K, Lamont, Owen A., and Stein, Jeremy C. 1994. "Credit Conditions and the Cyclical Behavior of Inventories." *Quarterly Journal of Economics* 109 (August): 565-592.

Kashyap, Anil K, and Stein, Jeremy C. 1994. "Monetary Policy and Bank Lending." In N. Gregory Mankiw, ed., *Monetary Policy,* 221-256. Chicago: University of Chicago Press.

Katona, George. 1976. "The Psychology of Inflation." In Richard T. Curtin, ed., *Surveys of Consumers, 1974-75,* 9-19. Ann Arbor: Institute for Social Research, University of Michigan.

Katz, Lawrence F. 1986. "Efficiency Wage Theories: A Partial Evaluation." *NBER Macroeconomics Annual* 1: 235-276.

Katz, Lawrence F., and Summers, Lawrence H. 1989. "Industry Rents: Evidence and Implications." *Brookings Papers on Economic Activity,* Microeconomics, 209-275.

Keane, Michael, Moffitt, Robert, and Runkle, David. 1988. "Real Wages over the Business Cycle: Estimating the Impact of Heterogeneity with Micro Data." *Journal of Political Economy* 96 (December): 1232-1266.

Kendrick, John W. 1976. *The Formation and Stocks of Total Capital.* New York: Columbia University Press.

Keynes, John Maynard. 1936. *The General Theory of Employment, Interest, and Money.* London: Macmillan.

Keynes, John Maynard. 1939. "Relative Movements of Real Wages and Output." *Economic Journal* 49 (March): 34-51.

Kimball, Miles S. 1990. "Precautionary Saving in the Small and the Large." *Econometrica* 58 (January): 53-73.

Kimball, Miles S. 1991. "The Quantitative Analytics of the Basic Real Business Cycle Model." Unpublished paper, University of Michigan (November).

Kimball, Miles S. 1994. "Labor-Market Dynamics When Unemployment Is a Worker Discipline Device." *American Economic Review* 84 (September): 1045-1059.

King, Robert G. 1991. "Money and Business Cycles." Unpublished paper, University of Rochester (June).

King, Robert G., and Levine, Ross. 1993a. "Finance and Growth: Schumpeter Might Be Right." *Quarterly Journal of Economics* 108 (August): 717-737.

King, Robert G., and Levine, Ross. 1993b. "Finance, Entrepreneurship, and Growth: Theory and Evidence." *Journal of Monetary Economics* 32 (December): 513-542.

King, Robert G., and Plosser, Charles I. 1984. "Money, Credit, and Prices in a Real Business Cycle." *American Economic Review* 64 (June): 363-380.

King, Robert G., Plosser, Charles I., and Rebelo, Sergio T. 1988. "Production, Growth and Business Cycles: II. New Directions." *Journal of Monetary Economics* 21 (March/May): 309-341.

King, Robert G., and Rebelo, Sergio T. 1986. "Business Cycles with Endogenous Growth." Unpublished paper, University of Rochester.

Kiyotaki, Nobuhiro. 1988. "Multiple Expectational Equilibria under Monopolistic Competition." *Quarterly Journal of Economics* 102 (November): 695-714.

Kiyotaki, Nobuhiro, and Moore, John. 1995. "Credit Cycles." National Bureau of Economic Research Working Paper No. 5083 (April).

Koopmans, Tjalling C. 1965. "On the Concept of Optimal Economic Growth." In *The Economic Approach to Development Planning.* Amsterdam: North-Holland.

Kremer, Michael. 1993. "Population Growth and Technological Change: One Million B.C. to 1990." *Quarterly Journal of Economics* 108 (August): 681-716.

Kremer, Michael, and Thomson, Jim. 1994. "Young Workers, Old Workers, and Convergence." National Bureau of Economic Research Working Paper No. 4827 (August).

Kreps, David M. 1990. *A Course in Microeconomic Theory.* Princeton: Princeton University Press.

Krueger, Alan B., and Summers, Lawrence H. 1987. "Reflections on the Inter-Industry Wage Structure." In Kevin Lang and Jonathan S. Leonard, eds., *Unemployment and the Structure of Labor Markets,* 17-47. Oxford: Basil Blackwell.

Krueger, Alan B., and Summers, Lawrence H. 1988. "Efficiency Wages and the Interindustry Wage Structure." *Econometrica* 56 (March): 259-293. Reprinted in Mankiw and Romer (1991).

Krugman, Paul R. 1979. "A Model of Innovation, Technology Transfer, and the World Distribution of Income." *Journal of Political Economy* 87 (April): 253-266.

Krugman, Paul R. 1991. "Target Zones and Exchange Rate Dynamics." *Quarterly Journal of Economics* 106 (August): 669-682.

Kydland, Finn E., and Prescott, Edward C. 1977. "Rules Rather Than Discretion: The Inconsistency of Optimal Plans." *Journal of Political Economy* 87 (June): 473-492.

Kydland, Finn E., and Prescott, Edward C. 1982. "Time to Build and Aggregate Fluctuations." *Econometrica* 50 (November): 1345-1370.

Kydland, Finn E., and Prescott, Edward C. 1990. "Business Cycles: Real Facts and a Monetary Myth." Federal Reserve Bank of Minneapolis *Quarterly Review* (Spring): 3-18.

L

Lach, Saul, and Tsiddon, Daniel. 1992. "The Behavior of Prices and Inflation: An Empirical Analysis of Disaggregated Price Data." *Journal of Political Economy* 100 (April): 349-389.

Laibson, David. 1993. "Golden Eggs and Hyperbolic Discounting." Unpublished paper, M.I.T. (November).

Lamont, Owen. 1993. "Cash Flow and Investment: Evidence from Internal Capital Markets." Unpublished paper, M.I.T. (November).

Lamont, Owen. 1994. "Corporate Debt Overhang and Macroeconomic Expectations." Unpublished paper, M.I.T. (June).

Leland, Hayne E. 1968. "Saving and Uncertainty: The Precautionary Demand for Saving." *Quarterly Journal of Economics* 82 (August): 465-473.

Leontief, Wassily. 1946. "The Pure Theory of the Guaranteed Annual Wage Contract." *Journal of Political Economy* 54 (February): 76-79.

Lilien, David M. 1982. "Sectoral Shifts and Cyclical Unemployment." *Journal of Political Economy* 90 (August): 777-793.

Lindbeck, Assar, and Snower, Dennis J. 1988. *The Insider-Outsider Theory of Employment and Unemployment.* Cambridge: MIT Press.

Lintner, John. 1965. "The Valuation of Risky Assets and the Selection of Risky Investments in Stock Portfolios and Capital Budgets." *Review of Economics and Statistics* 47 (February): 13-37.

Lipsey, Richard G. 1960. "The Relation between Unemployment and the Rate of Change of Money Wage Rates in the United Kingdom, 1862-1957: A Further Analysis." *Economica* 27 (February): 1-31.

Loewenstein, George, and Thaler, Richard H. 1989. "Anomalies: Intertemporal Choice." *Journal of Economic Perspectives* 3 (Fall): 181-193.

Long, John B., and Plosser, Charles I. 1983. "Real Business Cycles." *Journal of Political Economy* 91 (February): 39-69.

Lougani, Prakash, Rush, Mark, and Tave, William. 1990. "Stock Market Dispersion and Unemployment." *Journal of Monetary Economics* 25 (June): 367-388.

Lucas, Robert E., Jr. 1967. "Adjustment Costs and the Theory of Supply." *Journal of Political Economy* 75 (August): 321-334.

Lucas, Robert E., Jr. 1972. "Expectations and the Neutrality of Money." *Journal of Economic Theory* 4 (April): 103-124.

Lucas, Robert E., Jr. 1973. "Some International Evidence on Output-Inflation Tradeoffs." *American Economic Review* 63 (June): 326-334.

Lucas, Robert E., Jr. 1975. "An Equilibrium Model of the Business Cycle." *Journal of Political Economy* 83 (December): 1113-1144.

Lucas, Robert E., Jr. 1976. "Econometric Policy Evaluation: A Critique." *Carnegie-Rochester Conference Series on Public Policy* 1: 19-46.

Lucas, Robert E., Jr. 1978. "Asset Prices in an Exchange Economy." *Econometrica* 46 (December): 1429-1445.

Lucas, Robert E., Jr. 1987. *Models of Business Cycles.* Oxford: Basil Blackwell.

Lucas, Robert E., Jr. 1988. "On the Mechanics of Economic Development." *Journal of Monetary Economics* 22 (July): 3-42.

Lucas, Robert E., Jr. 1990a. "Why Doesn't Capital Flow from Rich to Poor Countries?" *American Economic Review* 80 (May): 92-96.

Lucas, Robert E., Jr. 1990b. "Liquidity and Interest Rates." *Journal of Economic Theory* 50 (April): 237-264.

Lucas, Robert E., Jr., and Prescott, Edward C. 1974. "Equilibrium Search and Employment." *Journal of Economic Theory* 7 (February): 188-209.

Lucas, Robert E., Jr., and Rapping, Leonard. 1969. "Real Wages, Employment and Inflation." *Journal of Political Economy* 77 (September/October): 721-754.

M

Maddison, Angus. 1982. *Phases of Capitalist Development.* Oxford: Oxford University Press.

Malinvaud, Edmond. 1977. *The Theory of Unemployment Reconsidered.* Oxford: Basil Blackwell.

Mankiw, N. Gregory. 1981. "The Permanent Income Hypothesis and the Real Interest Rate." *Economics Letters* 7: 307-311.

Mankiw, N. Gregory. 1982. "Hall's Consumption Hypothesis and Durable Goods." *Journal of Monetary Economics* 10 (November): 417-425.

Mankiw, N. Gregory. 1985. "Small Menu Costs and Large Business Cycles: A Macroeconomic Model of Monopoly." *Quarterly Journal of Economics* 100 (May): 529-539. Reprinted in Mankiw and Romer (1991).

Mankiw, N. Gregory. 1986a. "The Allocation of Credit and Financial Collapse." *Quarterly Journal of Economics* 101 (August): 455-470. Reprinted in Mankiw and Romer (1991).

Mankiw, N. Gregory. 1986b. "The Equity Premium and the Concentration of Aggregate Shocks." *Journal of Financial Economics* 17 (September): 211-219.

Mankiw, N. Gregory. 1989. "Real Business Cycles: A New Keynesian Perspective." *Journal of Economic Perspectives* 3 (Summer): 79-90.

Mankiw, N. Gregory. 1994. *Macroeconomics.* Second edition. New York: Worth.

Mankiw, N. Gregory, and Miron, Jeffrey A. 1986. "The Changing Behavior of the Term Structure of Interest Rates." *Quarterly Journal of Economics* 101 (May): 211-228.

Mankiw, N. Gregory, Miron, Jeffrey A., and Weil, David N. 1987. "The Adjustment of Expectations to a Change in Regime: A Study of the Founding of the Federal Reserve." *American Economic Review* 77 (June): 358-374.

Mankiw, N. Gregory, and Romer, David, editors. 1991. *New Keynesian Economics.* 2 volumes. Cambridge: MIT Press.

Mankiw, N. Gregory, Romer, David, and Weil, David N. 1992. "A Contribution to the Empirics of Economic Growth." *Quarterly Journal of Economics* 107 (May): 407-437.

Mankiw, N. Gregory, Rotemberg, Julio J., and Summers, Lawrence H. 1985. "Intertemporal Substitution in Macroeconomics." *Quarterly Journal of Economics* 100 (February): 225-251.

Mankiw, N. Gregory, and Summers, Lawrence H. 1986. "Money Demand and the Effects of Fiscal Policies." *Journal of Money, Credit, and Banking* 18 (November): 415-429.

Mankiw, N. Gregory, and Zeldes, Stephen P. 1991. "The Consumption of Stockholders and Nonstockholders." *Journal of Financial Economics* 29 (March): 97-112.

Maskin, Eric, and Tirole, Jean. 1988. "A Theory of Dynamic Oligopoly, I: Overview and Quantity Competition with Large Fixed Costs." *Econometrica* 56 (May): 549-570.

Mauro, Paolo. 1993. "Corruption, Country Risk and Growth." Unpublished paper, Harvard University (November). *Quarterly Journal of Economics,* forthcoming.

McCallum, Bennett T. 1989. "Real Business Cycle Models." In Robert J. Barro, ed., *Modern Business Cycle Theory,* 16-50. Cambridge: Harvard University Press.

McCulloch, J. Huston. 1975. "The Monte Carlo Cycle in Economic Activity." *Economic Inquiry* 13 (September): 303-321.

McDonald, Ian M., and Solow, Robert M. 1981. "Wage Bargaining and Employment." *American Economic Review* 71 (December): 896-908. Reprinted in Mankiw and Romer (1991).

McGrattan, Ellen R. 1994. "The Macroeconomic Effects of Distortionary Taxation." *Journal of Monetary Economics* 33 (June): 573-601.

McKinnon, Ronald I. 1973. *Money and Capital in Economic Development.* Washington, D.C.: The Brookings Institution.

McQueen, Grant, and Thorley, Steven. 1993. "Asymmetric Business Cycle Turning Points." *Journal of Monetary Economics* 31 (June): 341-362.

Meese, Richard, and Rogoff, Kenneth. 1983. "Empirical Exchange Rate Models of the Seventies: Do They Fit Out of Sample?" *Journal of International Economics* 14 (February): 3-24.

Mehra, Rajnish, and Prescott, Edward C. 1985. "The Equity Premium: A Puzzle." *Journal of Monetary Economics* 15 (March): 145-161.

Meltzer, Allan. 1988. *Keynes's Monetary Theory: A Different Interpretation.* Cambridge: Cambridge University Press.

Merton, Robert C. 1973. "An Intertemporal Capital Asset Pricing Model." *Econometrica* 41 (September): 867-887.

Meulendyke, Ann-Marie. 1990. *U.S. Monetary Policy and Financial Markets.* New York: Federal Reserve Bank of New York.

Mishkin, Frederic S. 1982. "Does Anticipated Monetary Policy Matter? An Econometric Investigation." *Journal of Political Economy* 90 (February): 22-51.

Mishkin, Frederic S. 1983. *A Rational Expectations Approach to Macroeconometrics: Testing Policy Ineffectiveness and Efficient-Markets Models.* Chicago: University of Chicago Press.

Modigliani, Franco, and Brumberg, Richard. 1954. "Utility Analysis and the Consumption Function: An Interpretation of Cross-Section Data." In Kenneth K. Kurihara, ed., *Post-Keynesian Economics,* 388-436. New Brunswick, N.J.: Rutgers University Press.

Modigliani, Franco, and Cohn, Richard A. 1979. "Inflation and the Stock Market." *Financial Analysts Journal* 35 (March/April): 24-44.

Modigliani, Franco, and Miller, Merton H. 1958. "The Cost of Capital, Corporation Finance and the Theory of Investment." *American Economic Review* 48 (June): 261-297.

Mood, Alexander M., Graybill, Franklin A., and Boes, Duane C. 1974. *Introduction to the Theory of Statistics.* Third edition. New York: McGraw-Hill.

Moore, Geoffrey H., and Zarnowitz, Victor. 1986. "The Development and Role of the National Bureau of Economic Research's Business Cycle Chronologies." In Robert J. Gordon, ed., *The American Business Cycle: Continuity and Change,* 735-779. Chicago: University of Chicago Press.

Mortenson, Dale T. 1986. "Job Search and Labor Market Analysis." In Orley Ashenfelter and Richard Layard, eds., *Handbook of Labor Economics,* vol. 2, 849-919. Amsterdam: North-Holland.

Mulligan, Casey B., and Sala-i-Martin, Xavier. 1993. "Transitional Dynamics in Two-Sector Models of Endogenous Growth." *Quarterly Journal of Economics* 108 (August): 739-773.

Mundell, Robert A. 1963. "Inflation and Real Interest." *Journal of Political Economy* 71 (June): 280-283.

Mundell, Robert A. 1968. *International Economics.* New York: Macmillan.

Murphy, Kevin M., Shleifer, Andrei, and Vishny, Robert W. 1989a. "Income Distribution, Market Size, and Industrialization." *Quarterly Journal of Economics* 104 (August): 537-564.

Murphy, Kevin M., Shleifer, Andrei, and Vishny, Robert W. 1989b. "Industrialization and the Big Push." *Journal of Political Economy* 97 (October): 1003-1026.

Murphy, Kevin M., Shleifer, Andrei, and Vishny, Robert W. 1989c. "Building Blocks of Market-Clearing Business Cycle Models." *NBER Macroeconomics Annual* 4: 247-286.

Murphy, Kevin M., Shleifer, Andrei, and Vishny, Robert W. 1991. "The Allocation of Talent: Implications for Growth." *Quarterly Journal of Economics* 106 (May): 503-530.

Murphy, Kevin M., and Topel, Robert H. 1987a. "The Evolution of Unemployment in the United States." *NBER Macroeconomics Annual* 2: 11-58.

Murphy, Kevin M., and Topel, Robert H. 1987b. "Unemployment, Risk, and Earnings: Testing for Equalizing Differences in the Labor Market." In Kevin Lang and Jonathan S. Leonard, eds., *Unemployment and the Structure of Labor Markets,* 103-140. Oxford: Basil Blackwell.

Mussa, Michael L. 1977. "External and Internal Adjustment Costs and the Theory of Aggregate and Firm Investment." *Economica* 44 (May): 163-178.

Mussa, Michael L. 1986. "Nominal Exchange Rate Regimes and the Behavior of Real Exchange Rates." *Carnegie-Rochester Conference Series on Public Policy* 25 (Autumn): 117-213.

Muth, John. 1960. "Optimal Properties of Exponentially Weighted Forecasts." *Journal of the American Statistical Association* 55 (June): 290-306.

Muth, John. 1961. "Rational Expectations and the Theory of Price Movements." *Econometrica* 39 (July): 315-334.

N

Nelson, Charles R., and Plosser, Charles I. 1982. "Trends and Random Walks in Macroeconomic Time Series: Some Evidence and Implications." *Journal of Monetary Economics* 10 (September): 139-162.

Nelson, Charles R., and Startz, Richard. 1990. "Some Further Results on the Exact Small Sample Properties of the Instrumental Variable Estimator." *Econometrica* 58 (July): 967-976.

Nordhaus, William D. 1967. "The Optimal Rate and Direction of Technical Change." In Karl Shell, ed., *Essays on the Theory of Optimal Economic Growth,* 53-66. Cambridge: MIT Press.

Nordhaus, William D. 1975. "The Political Business Cycle." *Review of Economic Studies* 42 (April): 169-190.

O

Obstfeld, Maurice. 1986. "Capital Mobility in the World Economy: Theory and Measurement." *Carnegie-Rochester Conference Series on Public Policy* 24 (Spring): 55-104.

Oi, Walter Y. 1962. "Labor as a Quasi-Fixed Factor." *Journal of Political Economy* 70 (December): 538-555.

Okun, Arthur M. 1962. "Potential GNP: Its Measurement and Significance." In *Proceedings of the Business and Economics Statistics Section, American Statistical Association* (Washington, D.C.: American Statistical Association), 98-103.

Okun, Arthur M. 1971. "The Mirage of Steady Inflation." *Brookings Papers on Economic Activity,* no. 2, 485-498.

Okun, Arthur M. 1975. "Inflation: Its Mechanics and Welfare Costs." *Brookings Papers on Economic Activity,* no. 2, 351-390. Reprinted in Mankiw and Romer (1991).

Oliner, Stephen D., and Rudebusch, Glenn D. 1994. "Is There a Broad Credit Channel for Monetary Policy?" Unpublished paper, Federal Reserve Board (January).

Oswald, Andrew. 1987. "Efficient Contracts Are on the Labour Demand Curve: Theory and Facts." London School of Economics, Centre for Labour Economics Discussion Paper No. 284 (June).

P

Page, John. 1994. "The East Asian Miracle: Four Lessons for Development Policy." *NBER Macroeconomics Annual* 9: 219-269.

Parkin, Michael. 1986. "The Output-Inflation Tradeoff When Prices Are Costly to Change." *Journal of Political Economy* 94 (February): 200-224.

Perron, Pierre. 1989. "The Great Crash, the Oil Shock and the Unit Root Hypothesis." *Econometrica* 57 (November): 1361-1401.

Persson, Torsten, and Tabellini, Guido. 1993. "Designing Institutions for Monetary Stability." *Carnegie-Rochester Conference Series on Public Policy* 39 (December): 53-84.

Phelps, Edmund S. 1966a. *Golden Rules of Economic Growth.* New York: W. W. Norton.

Phelps, Edmund S. 1966b. "Models of Technical Progress and the Golden Rule of Research." *Review of Economic Studies* 33 (April): 133-146.

Phelps, Edmund S. 1968. "Money-Wage Dynamics and Labor Market Equilibrium." *Journal of Political Economy* 76 (July/August, Part 2): 678-711.

Phelps, Edmund S. 1970. "Introduction." In Edmund S. Phelps, et al., *Microeconomic Foundations of Employment and Inflation Theory.* New York: W. W. Norton.

Phelps, Edmund S. 1973. "Inflation in the Theory of Public Finance." *Swedish Journal of Economics* 75 (March): 67-82.

Phelps, Edmund S. 1978. "Disinflation without Recession: Adaptive Guideposts and Monetary Policy." *Weltwertschaftliches Archiv* 114: 783-809.

Phelps, Edmund S., and Taylor, John B. 1977. "Stabilizing Powers of Monetary Policy under Rational Expectations." *Journal of Political Economy* 85 (February): 163-190.

Phillips, A. W. 1958. "The Relationship between Unemployment and the Rate of Change of Money Wages in the United Kingdom, 1861-1957." *Economica* 25 (November): 283-299.

Pigou, A. C. 1943. "The Classical Stationary State." *Economic Journal* 53 (December): 343-351.

Pissarides, Christopher A. 1985. "Short-Run Dynamics of Unemployment, Vacancies, and Real Wages." *American Economic Review* 75 (September): 676-690.

Pollard, Patricia S. 1993. "Central Bank Independence and Economic Performance." Federal Reserve Bank of St. Louis *Review* 75 (July/August): 21-36.

Poole, William. 1970. "Optimal Choice of Monetary Instruments in a Simple Stochastic Macro Model." *Quarterly Journal of Economics* 84 (May): 197-216.

Posen, Adam S. 1993. "Why Central Bank Independence Does Not Cause Low Inflation: The Politics Behind the Institutional Fix." Unpublished paper, Harvard University (November).

Poterba, James M. 1984. "Tax Subsidies to Owner-Occupied Housing: An Asset-Market Approach." *Quarterly Journal of Economics* 99 (November): 729-752.

Poterba, James M., and Summers, Lawrence H. 1987. "Finite Lifetimes and the Effects of Budget Deficits on National Saving." *Journal of Monetary Economics* 20 (September): 369-391.

Prescott, Edward C. 1986. "Theory Ahead of Business-Cycle Measurement." *Carnegie-Rochester Conference Series on Public Policy* 25 (Autumn): 11-44.

R

Ramsey, F. P. 1928. "A Mathematical Theory of Saving." *Economic Journal* 38 (December): 543-559. Reprinted in Stiglitz and Uzawa (1969).

Rebelo, Sergio. 1991. "Long-Run Policy Analysis and Long-Run Growth." *Journal of Political Economy* 99 (June): 500-521.

Reinganum, Jennifer F. 1989. "The Timing of Innovation: Research, Development, and Diffusion." In Richard Schmalensee and Robert D. Willig, eds., *Handbook of Industrial Organization*, vol. 1, 849-908. Amsterdam: North-Holland.

Rogerson, Richard. 1988. "Indivisible Labor, Lotteries and Equilibrium." *Journal of Monetary Economics* 21 (January): 3-16.

Rogerson, Richard, and Wright, Randall. 1988. "Involuntary Unemployment in Economies with Efficient Risk Sharing." *Journal of Monetary Economics* 22 (November): 501-515.

Rogoff, Kenneth. 1985. "The Optimal Degree of Commitment to an Intermediate Monetary Target." *Quarterly Journal of Economics* 100 (November): 1169-1189.

Rogoff, Kenneth. 1987. "Reputational Constraints on Monetary Policy." *Carnegie-Rochester Conference Series on Public Policy* 26 (Spring): 141-182.

Rogoff, Kenneth, and Sibert, Anne. 1988. "Elections and Macroeconomic Policy Cycles." *Review of Economic Studies* 55 (January): 1-16.

Romer, Christina D. 1986a. "Spurious Volatility in Historical Unemployment Data." *Journal of Political Economy* 94 (February): 1-37.

Romer, Christina D. 1986b. "Is the Stabilization of the Postwar Economy a Figment of the Data?" *American Economic Review* 76 (June): 314-334.

Romer, Christina D. 1989. "The Prewar Business Cycle Reconsidered: New Estimates of Gross National Product, 1869-1908. *Journal of Political Economy* 97 (February): 1-37.

Romer, Christina D. 1990. "The Great Crash and the Onset of the Great Depression." *Quarterly Journal of Economics* 105 (August): 597–624.

Romer, Christina D. 1993. "The Nation in Depression." *Journal of Economic Perspectives* 7 (Spring): 19–39.

Romer, Christina D. 1994. "Remeasuring Business Cycles." *Journal of Economic History* 54 (September): 573–609.

Romer, Christina D., and Romer, David H. 1989. "Does Monetary Policy Matter? A New Test in the Spirit of Friedman and Schwartz." *NBER Macroeconomics Annual* 4: 121–170.

Romer, David. 1993a. "The New Keynesian Synthesis." *Journal of Economic Perspectives* 7 (Winter): 5–22.

Romer, David. 1993b. "Openness and Inflation: Theory and Evidence." *Quarterly Journal of Economics* 108 (November): 869–903.

Romer, Paul M. 1986. "Increasing Returns and Long Run Growth." *Journal of Political Economy* 94 (October): 1002–1037.

Romer, Paul M. 1990. "Endogenous Technological Change." *Journal of Political Economy* 98 (October, Part 2): S71–S102.

Rotemberg, Julio J. 1982. "Sticky Prices in the United States." *Journal of Political Economy* 90 (December): 1187–1211.

Rotemberg, Julio J. 1984. "A Monetary Equilibrium Model with Transactions Costs." *Journal of Political Economy* 92 (February): 41–58.

Rotemberg, Julio J. 1987. "The New Keynesian Microfoundations." *NBER Macroeconomics Annual* 2: 69–104.

Rotemberg, Julio J. 1994. "Prices, Output and Hours: An Empirical Analysis Based on a Sticky Price Model." National Bureau of Economic Research Working Paper No. 4948 (December).

Rotemberg, Julio J., and Woodford, Michael. 1991. "Markups and the Business Cycle." *NBER Macroeconomics Annual* 6: 63–129.

Rotemberg, Julio J., and Woodford, Michael. 1992. "Oligopolistic Pricing and the Effects of Aggregate Demand on Economic Activity." *Journal of Political Economy* 100 (December): 1153–1207.

Rotemberg, Julio J., and Woodford, Michael. 1994. "Is the Business Cycle a Necessary Consequence of Stochastic Growth?" National Bureau of Economic Research Working Paper No. 4650 (February).

Rubinstein, Mark. 1976. "The Valuation of Uncertain Income Streams and the Pricing of Options." *Bell Journal of Economics* 7 (Autumn): 407–425.

Rudebusch, Glenn D., and Wilcox, David W. 1994. "Productivity and Inflation: Evidence and Interpretations." Unpublished paper, Federal Reserve Board (May).

Runkle, David E. 1991. "Liquidity Constraints and the Permanent Income Hypothesis: Evidence from Panel Data." *Journal of Monetary Economics* 27 (February): 73–98.

S

Sachs, Jeffrey D., and Larrain, Felipe B. 1993. *Macroeconomics in the Global Economy.* Englewood Cliffs, N.J.: Prentice Hall.

Sala-i-Martin, Xavier. 1991a. "Internal and External Adjustment Costs in the Theory of Fixed Investment." Unpublished paper, Yale University (September).

Sala-i-Martin, Xavier. 1991b. "Comment." *NBER Macroeconomics Annual* 6: 368–378.

Samuelson, Paul A. 1939. "Interaction between the Multiplier Analysis and the Principle of Acceleration." *Review of Economics and Statistics* 21 (May): 75-78.

Samuelson, Paul A. 1958. "An Exact Consumption-Loan Model of Interest with or without the Social Contrivance of Money." *Journal of Political Economy* 66 (December): 467-482. Reprinted in Stiglitz and Uzawa (1969).

Samuelson, Paul A., and Solow, Robert M. 1960. "Analytical Aspects of Anti-Inflation Policy." *American Economic Review* 50 (May): 177-194.

Sargent, Thomas J. 1976. "The Observational Equivalence of Natural and Unnatural Rate Theories of Macroeconomics." *Journal of Political Economy* 84 (June): 631-640.

Sargent, Thomas J. 1982. "The End of Four Big Inflations." In Robert E. Hall, ed., *Inflation,* 41-98. Chicago: University of Chicago Press.

Sargent, Thomas J. 1983. "Stopping Moderate Inflations: The Methods of Poincare and Thatcher." In Rudiger Dornbusch and Mario Henrique Simonsen, eds., *Inflation, Debt, and Indexation,* 54-96. Cambridge: MIT Press.

Sargent, Thomas J. 1987a. *Macroeconomic Theory.* Second edition. Boston: Academic Press.

Sargent, Thomas J. 1987b. *Dynamic Macroeconomic Theory.* Cambridge: Harvard University Press.

Sargent, Thomas J., and Wallace, Neil. 1975. " 'Rational Expectations,' the Optimal Monetary Instrument, and the Optimal Money Supply Rule." *Journal of Political Economy* 83 (April): 241-254.

Sato, K. 1966. "On the Adjustment Time in Neo-Classical Growth Models." *Review of Economic Studies* 33 (July): 263-268.

Shaked, Avner, and Sutton, John. 1984. "Involuntary Unemployment as a Perfect Equilibrium in a Bargaining Model." *Econometrica* 52 (November): 1351-1364.

Shapiro, Carl, and Stiglitz, Joseph E. 1984. "Equilibrium Unemployment as a Worker Discipline Device." *American Economic Review* 74 (June): 433-444. Reprinted in Mankiw and Romer (1991).

Shapiro, Carl, and Stiglitz, Joseph E. 1985. "Can Unemployment Be Involuntary? Reply." *American Economic Review* 75 (December): 1215-1217.

Sharpe, William F. 1964. "Capital Asset Prices: A Theory of Market Equilibrium under Conditions of Risk." *Journal of Finance* 19 (September): 425-442.

Shea, John. 1995. "Union Contracts and the Life-Cycle/Permanent-Income Hypothesis." *American Economic Review* 85 (March): 186-200.

Sheffrin, Steven M. 1988. "Have Economic Fluctuations Been Dampened? A Look at Evidence Outside the United States." *Journal of Monetary Economics* 21 (January): 73-83.

Shefrin, Hersh M., and Thaler, Richard H. 1988. "The Behavioral Life-Cycle Hypothesis." *Economic Inquiry* 26 (October): 609-643.

Shell, Karl. 1966. "Toward a Theory of Inventive Activity and Capital Accumulation." *American Economic Review* 56 (May): 62-68.

Shell, Karl. 1967. "A Model of Inventive Activity and Capital Accumulation." In Karl Shell, ed., *Essays on the Theory of Optimal Economic Growth,* 67-85. Cambridge: MIT Press.

Sheshinski, Eytan, and Weiss, Yoram. 1977. "Inflation and Costs of Price Adjustment." *Review of Economic Studies* 44 (June): 287-303.

Shiller, Robert J. 1990. "The Term Structure of Interest Rates." In Benjamin M. Friedman and Frank Hahn, eds., *Handbook of Monetary Economics,* vol. 1, 627-722. Amsterdam: North-Holland.

Shleifer, Andrei. 1986. "Implementation Cycles." *Journal of Political Economy* 94 (December): 1163-1190. Reprinted in Mankiw and Romer (1991).

Sichel, Daniel E. 1993. "Business Cycle Asymmetry: A Deeper Look." *Economic Inquiry* 31 (April): 224-236.

Simon, Carl P., and Blume, Lawrence. 1994. *Mathematics for Economists.* New York: W. W. Norton.

Skinner, Jonathan. 1988. "Risky Income, Life Cycle Consumption, and Precautionary Savings." *Journal of Monetary Economics* 22 (September): 237-255.

Solon, Gary, Barsky, Robert, and Parker, Jonathan A. 1994. "Measuring the Cyclicality of Real Wages: How Important Is Composition Bias?" *Quarterly Journal of Economics* 109 (February): 1-25.

Solow, Robert M. 1956. "A Contribution to the Theory of Economic Growth." *Quarterly Journal of Economics* 70 (February): 65-94. Reprinted in Stiglitz and Uzawa (1969).

Solow, Robert M. 1957. "Technical Change and the Aggregate Production Function." *Review of Economics and Statistics* 39: 312-320.

Solow, Robert M. 1960. "Investment and Technical Progress." In Kenneth J. Arrow, Samuel Korbin, and Patrick Suppes, eds., *Mathematical Methods in the Social Sciences 1959,* 89-104. Stanford: Stanford University Press. Reprinted in Stiglitz and Uzawa (1969).

Solow, Robert M. 1979. "Another Possible Source of Wage Stickiness." *Journal of Macroeconomics* 1 (Winter): 79-82.

Solow, Robert M. 1985. "Insiders and Outsiders in Wage Determination." *Scandinavian Journal of Economics* 87: 411-428.

Solow, Robert M., and Stiglitz, Joseph E. 1968. "Output, Employment, and Wages in the Short Run." *Quarterly Journal of Economics* 82 (November): 537-560.

Stiglitz, Joseph E. 1979. "Equilibrium in Product Markets with Imperfect Information." *American Economic Review* 69 (May): 339-345.

Stiglitz, Joseph E., and Uzawa, Hirofumi, editors. 1969. *Readings in the Modern Theory of Economic Growth.* Cambridge: MIT Press.

Stock, James H., and Watson, Mark W. 1988. "Variable Trends in Economic Time Series." *Journal of Economic Perspectives* 2 (Summer): 147-174.

Stockman, Alan C. 1983. "Real Exchange Rates under Alternative Nominal Exchange Rate Systems." *Journal of International Money and Finance* 2 (August): 147-166.

Stokey, Nancy L., and Lucas, Robert E., Jr., with Prescott, Edward C. 1989. *Recursive Methods in Economic Dynamics.* Cambridge: Harvard University Press.

Summers, Lawrence H. 1981a. "Capital Taxation and Accumulation in a Life Cycle Growth Model." *American Economic Review* 71 (September): 533-544.

Summers, Lawrence H. 1981b. "Taxation and Corporate Investment: A q-Theory Approach." *Brookings Papers on Economic Activity,* no. 1, 67-127.

Summers, Lawrence H. 1986a. "Some Skeptical Observations on Real Business Cycle Theory." Federal Reserve Bank of Minneapolis *Quarterly Review* 10 (Fall): 23-27.

Summers, Lawrence H. 1986b. "Why Is the Unemployment Rate So Very High Near Full Employment?" *Brookings Papers on Economic Activity,* no. 2, 339-383.

Summers, Lawrence H. 1988. "Relative Wages, Efficiency Wages, and Keynesian Unemployment." *American Economic Review* 78 (May): 383-388.

Summers, Lawrence H. 1991. "How Should Long-Term Monetary Policy Be Determined?" *Journal of Money, Credit, and Banking* 23 (August, Part 2): 625-631.

Summers, Robert, and Heston, Alan. 1988. "A New Set of International Comparisons of Real Product and Price Levels: Estimates for 130 Countries, 1950-85." *Review of Income and Wealth* 34 (March): 1-26.

Summers, Robert, and Heston, Alan. 1991. "The Penn World Table (Mark 5): An Expanded Set of International Comparisons, 1950-1988." *Quarterly Journal of Economics* 106 (May): 327-368.

Swan, T. W. 1956. "Economic Growth and Capital Accumulation." *Economic Record* 32 (November): 334-361. Reprinted in Stiglitz and Uzawa (1969).

T

Tarshis, Lorie. 1939. "Changes in Real and Money Wage Rates." *Economic Journal* 49 (March): 150-154.

Taylor, John B. 1979. "Staggered Wage Setting in a Macro Model." *American Economic Review* 69 (May): 108-113. Reprinted in Mankiw and Romer (1991).

Taylor, John B. 1980. "Aggregate Dynamics and Staggered Contracts." *Journal of Political Economy* 88 (February): 1-23.

Taylor, John B. 1981. "On the Relation between the Variability of Inflation and the Average Inflation Rate." *Carnegie-Rochester Conference Series on Public Policy* 15 (Autumn): 57-86.

Tinbergen, Jan. 1952. *On the Theory of Economic Policy.* Amsterdam: North-Holland.

Tobin, James. 1969. "A General Equilibrium Approach to Monetary Theory." *Journal of Money, Credit, and Banking* 1 (February): 15-29.

Tobin, James. 1972. "Inflation and Unemployment." *American Economic Review* 62 (March): 1-18.

Tobin, James. 1980. *Asset Accumulation and Economic Activity.* Chicago: University of Chicago Press.

Tobin, James, and Brainard, William. 1963. "Financial Intermediaries and the Effectiveness of Monetary Control." *American Economic Review* 53 (May): 383-400.

Tolley, George S. 1957. "Providing for the Growth of the Money Supply." *Journal of Political Economy* 65 (December): 465-485.

Tommasi, Mariano. 1994. "The Consequences of Price Instability on Search Markets: Toward Understanding the Effects of Inflation." *American Economic Review* 84 (December): 1385-1396.

Topel, Robert H. 1989. "Comment." *Brookings Papers on Economic Activity,* Microeconomics, 283-288.

Topel, Robert H., and Ward, Michael P. 1992. "Job Mobility and the Careers of Young Men." *Quarterly Journal of Economics* 107 (May): 439-479.

Townsend, Robert M. 1979. "Optimal Contracts and Competitive Markets with Costly State Verification." *Journal of Economic Theory* 21 (October): 265-293.

Tsiddon, Daniel. "On the Stubbornness of Sticky Prices." *International Economic Review* 32 (February): 69-75.

Tversky, Amos, and Kahneman, Daniel. 1974. "Judgment under Uncertainty: Heuristics and Biases." *Science* 185 (September): 1124-1131.

U

Uzawa, Hirofumi. 1965. "Optimum Technical Change in an Aggregative Model of Economic Growth." *International Economic Review* 6 (January): 12-31.

V

Van Huyck, John B., Battalio, Raymond C., and Beil, Richard O. 1990. "Tacit Co-ordination Games, Strategic Uncertainty, and Coordination Failure." *American Economic Review* 80 (March): 234–248.

Van Huyck, John B., Battalio, Raymond C., and Beil, Richard O. 1991. "Strategic Uncertainty, Equilibrium Selection, and Coordination Failure in Average Opinion Games." *Quarterly Journal of Economics* 106 (August): 885–910.

Vickers, John. 1986. "Signalling in a Model of Monetary Policy with Incomplete Information." *Oxford Economic Papers* 38 (November): 443–455.

W

Walsh, Carl E. 1995. "Optimal Contracts for Central Bankers." *American Economic Review* 85 (March): 150–167.

Warner, Elizabeth J., and Barsky, Robert B. 1995. "The Timing and Magnitude of Retail Store Markdowns: Evidence from Weekends and Holidays." *Quarterly Journal of Economics* 110 (May): 321–352.

Watson, Mark W. 1986. "Univariate Detrending Methods with Stochastic Trends." *Journal of Monetary Economics* 18 (July): 49–75.

Weil, Philippe. 1989a. "Overlapping Families of Infinitely-Lived Agents." *Journal of Public Economics* 38 (March): 183–198.

Weil, Philippe. 1989b. "The Equity Premium Puzzle and the Risk-Free Rate Puzzle." *Journal of Monetary Economics* 24 (November): 401–421.

Weil, Philippe. 1990. "Nonexpected Utility in Macroeconomics." *Quarterly Journal of Economics* 105 (February): 29–42.

West, Kenneth D. 1988. "The Insensitivity of Consumption to News about Income." *Journal of Monetary Economics* 21 (January): 17–33.

Woglom, Geoffrey. 1982. "Underemployment Equilibrium with Rational Expectations." *Quarterly Journal of Economics* 97: 89–107.

Woodford, Michael. 1990. "Learning to Believe in Sunspots." *Econometrica* 58 (March): 277–307.

Woodford, Michael. 1991. "Self-Fulfilling Expectations and Fluctuations in Aggregate Demand." In Mankiw and Romer (1991), vol. 2, 77–110.

Woodford, Michael. 1994. "Price Level Determinacy without Control of a Monetary Aggregate." Unpublished paper, University of Chicago (September). *Carnegie-Rochester Conference Series on Public Policy,* forthcoming.

Working, Holbrook. 1960. "A Note on the Correlation of First Differences of Averages in a Random Chain." *Econometrica* 28 (October): 916–918.

Y

Yellen, Janet L. 1984. "Efficiency Wage Models of Unemployment." *American Economic Review* 74 (May): 200–205. Reprinted in Mankiw and Romer (1991).

Yotsuzuka, Toshiki. 1987. "Ricardian Equivalence in the Presence of Capital Market Imperfections." *Journal of Monetary Economics* 20 (September): 411–436.

Young, Alwyn. 1994. "The Tyranny of Numbers: Confronting the Statistical Reality of the East Asian Growth Experience." National Bureau of Economic Research Working Paper No. 4680 (March). *Quarterly Journal of Economics,* forthcoming.

Z

Zeldes, Stephen P. 1989. "Consumption and Liquidity Constraints: An Empirical Investigation." *Journal of Political Economy* 97 (April): 305–346.

NAME INDEX

SUBJECT INDEX